A STRONG SUPPORTING CAST

Charlotte Bonham Carter photographed in 1964 at her home, Binsted Wyck, Hampshire.

A Strong Supporting Cast

The Shaw Lefevres 1789–1936

F.M.G. WILLSON

THE ATHLONE PRESS
London & Atlantic Highlands, NJ

First published 1993 by
THE ATHLONE PRESS LTD
1 Park Drive, London NW11 7SG
and 165 First Avenue,
Atlantic Highlands, NJ 07716

British Library Cataloguing in Publication Data
*A catalogue record for this book is available
from the British Library*

ISBN 0 485 11435 6

Library of Congress Cataloging-in-Publication Data

Willson, F. M. G. (Francis Michael Glenn), 1924–
    A strong supporting cast : the Shaw Lefevres
1789–1936 / F.M.G. Willson.
        p.   cm.
    Includes index.
    ISBN 0-485-11435-6 : $70.00
    1. Shaw Lefevre family.   2. Politicians--Great
Britain--Biography.   3. Great Britain--Biography.
CT787.S53W55   1993
941.08′0922--dc20
    [B]

Typeset by
Bibloset

Printed and bound in Great Britain by the
University Press, Cambridge

For Jean

Contents

Acknowledgements

It was in the early 1950s that I first came across references to John George Shaw Lefevre. His name appeared frequently in various mid-nineteenth century administrative contexts which I was exploring as a graduate student in Oxford, and he appealed to me as being particularly representative of a group of able men who spent their careers in that grey constitutional stratum through which the later line dividing the politician from the civil servant had not been drawn firmly. But it was not until over thirty years afterwards that I was able to renew my early interest, and then discovered the rest of the Shaw Lefevre family. Compiling their history has been a task spread over the last six years, and has only been possible with the help of a large number of people and institutions.

The research required an extended visit to Haddo House, and considerable travelling to consult other archival material: this was made possible by the award of a grant by the Leverhulme Trust, in 1986. Publication has been assured by the generous and imaginative sponsorship of the Charlotte Bonham Carter Charitable Trust. I wish to express my gratitude to the Trustees of both charities.

The most important primary sources for this study are to be found in a number of collections. I am particularly grateful for the gracious permission of Her Majesty The Queen to make use of material in the Royal Archives at Windsor. For access to and permission to quote from family and other archives, I am indebted to June, Marchioness of Aberdeen; to the Trustees of the Beaverbrook Foundation; to the late Lady Bonham Carter; to the Trustees of the Broadlands Archives; to Lieutenant Colonel C.M.L. Clements; to the Earl of Dalhousie; to Mr and Mrs J.W.O. Elliot; to Sir Matthew Farrer; to the Hon. Mrs Gascoigne; to the Controller of Her Majesty's Stationery Office; to Mr D.C. Holland; to the Earl of Radnor; to Mrs E.L. Rogers; to the Principal and Fellows of Somerville College, Oxford; and to Mr S.C. Whitbread.

For expert advice and guidance on a variety of aspects of the family history I am most fortunate to have had helpful discussions or correspondence with the late Mr Alfred Beacham; with Mr H.E. Paston-Bedingfield, Rouge Croix Pursuivant of Arms; with Dr David Butler; with Mr Albert Cooper; with Mr G. Nigel Capel Cure; with Dr Decie Denholm; with the late Mr H. Foster; with

Mr Negley Harte; with Mr Jack Lavers; with Dr Keith Laybourn; with Dr Maxine Merrington; with Professor David Murray; with Dr Henry Pelling; with Mr William Oxley Parker; with Mr Barry Shurlock; with Lucy, Lady Spencer-Smith; with the late Mr Duncan Stirling; with Arthur Tattersall; with the Countess Waldegrave; with Mr R.J.B. Walker; and with my brother, Burnett Willson.

A long list of record offices, research institutes, university and public libraries, company archives, and other institutions is given in the note on sources at the end of this book. I am grateful for the unfailingly helpful and courteous attention of the officers of all of them, and for the expert advice given me on portraits by members of the staffs of the Courtauld Institute of Art, the National Portrait Gallery, and the Victoria and Albert Museum. My special thanks are due to the Clerk of the Records and his staff at the House of Lords Record Office for their help with the Shaw Lefevre Mss; to Mrs Marita Prendy, sometime Curator of the Whitbread Mss; to Mr Nicholas Redman of Whitbread & Co.; to Ms Pauline Adams, Librarian and Archivist of Somerville College, Oxford; and to Dr C.M. Woolgar of Southampton University. Some of the research and writing was done at the University of California, Santa Cruz: I thank Professor Buchanan Sharp for his helpful comments on an early draft, and I gratefully acknowledge the assistance extended to me there through the extremely useful mechanism of intra-library loans.

I am especially grateful to my wife, who gave me much assistance with the research, and a great deal of constructive criticism of the writing, whilst always providing the encouragement and moral support which is invaluable in any venture of this kind.

Hammersmith
June 1993

List of Family Trees and Illustrations

ILLUSTRATIONS
Frontispiece   Lady Bonham Carter (1893–1989)

Between pages 224 and 225
1. Helena Lefevre, née Selman (1734–1816).
   From a miniature by Henry Edridge
2. Charles Shaw Lefevre (1758–1823).
   From a mezzotint by William Ward after John Jackson.
   It was mistakenly reproduced in A.I. Dasent, *Lives of the Speakers*
   (London, 1911), as a portrait of Shaw Lefevre's eldest son, Charles.
3. Heckfield Place. Photographed in 1987.
4. Charles Shaw Lefevre, Viscount Eversley (1794–1888).
   From the portrait by Hubert von Herkomer.
5. Emma Laura Shaw Lefevre, later Viscountess Eversley (1798–1857).
   Photograph by Mason & Co., from a portrait attributed to
   Samuel William Reynolds, junior.
6. Sir John George Shaw Lefevre (1797–1879).
   From the portrait by Sir John Watson-Gordon.
7. Henry Francis Shaw Lefevre (1802–1880).
   Photograph by Edgar Scamell, from a portrait by an unknown artist.
8. George John Shaw Lefevre, later Baron Eversley (1831–1928).
   Photographer unknown

9. Rachael Emily, later Lady Hamilton Gordon (1828–1889). Photograph by Brady, New York.
10. Madeleine Septimia Shaw Lefevre (1835–1914). From the portrait by R. Jacomb-Hood.
11. Sophia Emma Wickham (1833–1929). Photograph by Lucas & Tuck.

Numbers 1, 5, 7, 9, and 11 are reproduced by kind permission of Mr Nicholas Wickham-Irving; 2 and 8 by courtesy of the National Portrait Gallery. For 2, I am also obliged to the Basingstoke and Deane District Council, in whose offices the original portrait now hangs. Racal Electronics, plc, were good enough to authorise the inclusion of the photograph of Heckfield Place. Number 4 was made available from a Private Collection by the Courtauld Institute of Art. Numbers 6 and 10 are reproduced by courtesy of the Scottish National Portrait Gallery and of the Principal and Fellows of Somerville College, Oxford, respectively.

Foreword

Persecuted refugees finding a secure home in England have added many talents to those of our native stock. The Huguenots just over 300 years ago brought with them a canny ability to thrive and make money. The Lefevre family after leaving Rouen, settled in Spitalfields, worshipping in the church of Christchurch. The first generation married Rouenais, and then moved on to Walthamstow. From then on, until Charlotte Bonham Carter's death in 1989, the descendants of the beneficiaries of Isaac Lefevre's estate increased their inheritance.

Charlotte Bonham Carter was the elder child of Col. Lewis Ogilvy C.B., 60th Rifles, and his wife Lucy Wickham, and the first grandchild of William Wickham and the lively Sophia Emma Shaw Lefevre. She was educated at Miss Potts' school in Eastbourne and in Dresden, but not send to university. Although remarkably clever, a well-off young lady's secure future was predicted for her. The First World War changed this view, and Charlotte joined the staff of the Foreign Office in 1916 as a typist, moving to MI5 to track Lenin's movements from Switzerland to Russia. After the war was over, she returned to the Foreign Office to join the Delegation to the Paris Peace Conference for six months in 1919, where she met Sir Edgar Bonham Carter whom she married in 1926. This happy marriage lasted for thirty years, and the two of them devoted their lives to helping each other's work with numerous good and great causes – archaeology, all the arts, town planning, agriculture, and many others, from their house in Paddington, and from Wyck, the estate in Hampshire which Charlotte and her mother finally inherited in 1929.

During the 1930s, like so many others, Charlotte became aware of the dangers of Nazi Germany and gained her pilot's licence in the hope that she would be called to active service. This was, however, not to be. But she was seconded form the Foreign Office to the R.A.F. to serve with Photographic Intelligence at Medenham. Legends abound as to her resourcefulness in combining meticulous and brilliant attention to her duties with a social life based on her home in Radnor Place and the care of her mother's estate in Hampshire.

After Edgar's death, in 1956, she energetically pursued their combined good causes, entertained her perpetually renewing circle of friends both in

London and Hampshire, gardened energetically on her estate, succeeded her mother as churchwarden in their parish church, travelled extensively, and collected art avidly until her death at the age of 96.

The residue of her estate forms a charity to benefit charities in which she was most interested and her trustees have much pleasure in helping to produce this book which charts the progress and intermarrying of her grandmother's family.

From the Shaws came good health, good humour and good looks. The Speaker, Viscount Eversley, surely the best combination of the two families' gifts, is remembered to this day for his civility, wit and firmness in his years of office.

Charlotte, too, was a deft handler of council and committee affairs. In her later years, after apparently taking a refreshing nap during the discussion of a difficult item on the agenda, she would pounce on an aspect of a problem neglected by other more attentive members and deftly propose a solution.

It is sad that there is no Shaw Lefevre of today to take an active role in business or politics. No matter the heavy-handed, self-opinionated blasts of George Shaw Lefevre, Lord Eversley, in whom no trace of his uncle's wit and charm can be found, he was, as they all were, on the right side of every reforming movement of the Victorian and Edwardian era – education, women's rights, Ireland, pensions, Hampstead Heath and all other commons and footpaths. Without their energy, persistence and determination, these reforms would have waited a further generation to pass on their benefits.

With care and patience, Professor Willson charts the ascent of the two families and takes us through the tributaries of their descendants. He places them with unerring skill in their historical context and brings them to life by means of his shrewd observation of their characters. Thanks to him, warts and all, neither pygmies nor giants, they stand 'immersed in time'.

Nicholas Wickham-Irving

Introduction

After the captains and the kings depart, so long as they really have been supreme political leaders, their lives readily attract attention and appraisal from each succeeding generation. And those much less tangible phenomena, a ruling class – or any other class, the mass, the people, or society, are also subject to continuous, if inevitably more abstract, probing and assessment of their historic functions. What are less usual are records of those who played important but secondary roles at the upper levels of a country's political life. And even rarer is concern shown for the personal and family experience of such people. This relative neglect is understandable: the second rankers never achieved the maximum attainable power to stamp the impress of their ideas, or their genius for manipulating the ideas of others, on one or more generations. Good, even outstanding, initiative, service and loyalty are, more often than not, unexciting. Those of the second rank whose personal histories can easily find a place on the shelves were either properly valued for highly specialized accomplishments, or were possessors of a certain glamour or a certain notoriety often not central to the politics of their day, or not of lasting significance.

But no complex society can be run by a succession of brilliant and persuasive leaders alone. The immediate, essential structural support on which leaders rely comes from a sizeable but relatively small group of people who are part only of the much larger concept of a predominant segment, or an establishment, or a ruling party, congregation or class. Such a group will certainly include some rivals to those who reach the supreme positions, but most others in it will find their satisfactions in contributing at high but ultimately subordinate levels to upholding and consolidating the system of government under which they live. By far the majority of them will be formidably intelligent, self-interested, social and political conformists, and most of them and their families will lead influential but unexceptionable lives. In modern bureaucratic Britain they are probably most nearly defined, with that ironic mockery which helps to blunt the worst features of power, privilege and class-consciousness, as constituting a category known as the great and the good.

This phenomenon could not be traced in a society during periods of intense, revolutionary disruption, simply because any such continuing cadre would not have time to form, let alone to survive. In more stable eras, however, when major social and political change seeped into a nation slowly but profoundly, an understanding of the membership, attitudes, activities, circumstances, evolution, and flavour of this unstructured but nonetheless recognizably cohesive group must surely enhance overall historical judgement. This book is an attempt to help to enrich the texture and colour of that understanding. It tells the story of one family which belonged unequivocally to the ruling class of Britain throughout the nineteenth century. Several of its members would certainly have been on a contemporary list of the great and the good, less ironically fashioned than today's, and would certainly have appeared in the political record just below the uppermost levels of the Whig-Liberal hierarchy.

If one accepts the notion that the nineteenth century filled the interval between the French and Russian Revolutions, then the Shaw Lefevres were practically coterminous with it. The marriage which founded the family took place just a few weeks after the storming of the Bastille; and only three persons who bore the family name at birth survived after 1917, when each of the three was already over 75 years old. There were only twenty-four of them altogether – the founders and twenty-two descendants baptised as Shaw Lefevres – a remarkably small number considering the fecundity of the period through which they spread their potentially reproductive lives. And of the twenty two descendants, six died in infancy or early childhood, while of the remaining sixteen, only four were male. All four men married, one of them twice, but from the five unions a single boy child survived to adulthood, and he died without leaving an heir. Of the twelve daughters who grew to womanhood, only seven married, and one of the seven died childless. But if procreation was hardly a major achievement, longevity was characteristic: those who survived childhood were tenacious of life. No less than eleven of the sixteen mature Shaw Lefevres reached 75 or more, three living to over 80 and three into their mid-90s. The last survivor, a spinster of 94, died in 1936.

From the outset they were well-to-do, and some of them were wealthy. Their forebears had begun in trade and industry and had entered the ranks of professional people, bankers and landowners by the later years of the eighteenth century. On the base provided for them, the new family, while retaining and extending their landed and business interests, turned mainly to public life. Only one of the men followed a financial and commercial path, attracting little or no public attention, suffering some disasters, but eventually amassing a sizeable fortune. The other four all became members of Parliament. One achieved eminence as a long-serving Speaker of the House of Commons, who set standards of parliamentary behaviour still deeply cherished. One served in three cabinets, but will perhaps go down in history as one of the first politicians to arouse our environmental conscience. Both of these were raised to the peerage. Another had only momentary elective experience, but was briefly a junior minister and subsequently one of the outstanding public servants of his time – an important figure in many guises, not least as an original Poor Law commissioner, and for a long spell as Clerk of the Parliaments. Save in the 1820s, for a few months in 1886 and between 1895 and 1906, there was always one and sometimes two Shaw Lefevres working, or eligible to work, in the Palace of Westminster, from 1796 until 1928.

While the interrelatedness of the membership of the upper class of British society in the nineteenth century is well documented, the extent of family connections and the incidence of shared school and college experience which followed and eased the careers of the Shaw Lefevres is still one of the striking features of their history. Sojourn at Eton and Trinity College, Cambridge, and marriages to the Whitbreads, the Curries, the Mildmays, the Le Marchants, the Hamilton-Gordons, the Ducies, the Elliotts and the Wickhams, marked their firm entrenchment in the financial, political and social establishments of their times. And theirs is a history which underlines the contribution Huguenot refugees have made to their adopted country.

Their range was wider than the narrowly political or social. While never part of the recognized intellectual and artistic coteries, various of them had significant intellectual powers and developed serious academic responsibilities – they boasted two wranglers: one of them was a remarkable linguist and for twenty years the vice-chancellor of the University of London; they played a part in pioneering higher education for women by providing Somerville Hall, Oxford, with its first principal. Among their daughters' consorts were one of the three great colonial proconsuls of the third British Empire, a comptroller and auditor-general, a leading London solicitor, and a Conservative MP. Through the female line a fourth-generation son was to be a long-serving Liberal peer, and a fourth-generation daughter married a Liberal MP who turned Liberal Unionist, served as Financial Secretary to the Treasury, edited the *Edinburgh Review*, and was known as 'The Last of the Whigs.'

Even so compact a family group embraces a wide divergence of personality, temperament and experience. And the material available about the members varies enormously in quantity and interest. It is impossible to claim authoritative coverage of the whole clan, and it would be tendentious in the extreme to impose universal themes on so many separate, personal histories. Those who achieved most prominence, and those who left most written evidence of their lives, doubtless receive in these pages a disproportionate amount of attention: a family biography must suffer from such an imbalance, and can only attempt to take careful account of the extent of influence exercised by the men and women most of whose actions went unrecorded and most or all of whose private jottings have not survived. Such influence might be insignificant in a family which was fragmented and far-flung, but the Shaw Lefevres, though not claustrophobic, suffered no breakaways and included only one member who lived for a long period abroad – all the others were to be found in London or in country houses within 50 miles of the capital and usually less than that distance from each other. Physical proximity was another dimension of their familial and class solidarity.

There is clear evidence of a great deal of mutual respect and affection between the component elements of the family, and the longevity of many of its members may well have enhanced a sense of closeness and continuity. There were some domestic unhappinesses and some internal disharmonies, but they were rarely dramatic and never melodramatic or scandalous. Indeed, it is the lack of the untoward which constitutes a strong reason for examining their experience. Several of them were unusually able and successful people, but their abilities, their successes and their luck did not ensure them inclusion on the tablets of the unarguably great, of the arguably famous or notorious, or of the beguilingly eccentric. They were, essentially, extremely capable doers, rather than thinkers. Their ideas were orthodox and their social behaviour unremarkable. They were thus almost certainly very representative, both in their individual capacities and in their family and domestic lives, of the supportive element which lived close to and underpinned the ruling few. They were the kind of people who, over three generations, brought persistent ambition, high competence and solid endeavour to the tasks which came their way, and demonstrated those qualities unquestioningly, and in the main unreflectively, within the prejudices of the social milieu in which they moved and had their being. Their story must surely illustrate something of the origins, the character, attitudes and conduct, the strengths and weaknesses, and the relevance of that thin stratum of society from which, for better or worse, some leadership was drawn and on which all leadership depended, during a great age of national achievement.

CHAPTER I

Shaws

On 3 September 1789 a marriage was celebrated at the parish church of St Mary the Virgin in the Northamptonshire village of Tichmarsh, some 70 miles north-west of London. The bridegroom was a tall, well-set-up young man, just three weeks short of his thirtieth birthday, who had been known to himself and the world until recently as Charles Shaw, Barrister, of Lincoln's Inn. But in accordance with the wishes of his future father-in-law, he had applied, successfully, for a Royal Licence which permitted him to add the family name of his fiancée to his own. Thus when the bride, Helena Lefevre, then 22 years of age, was joined in matrimony with Charles, they began the family of Shaw Lefevre. And it is as well at the outset to declare that the name was never hyphenated.

The couple had journeyed from London to be married by the bridegroom's brother-in-law, Revd Littleton Powys, who had become the husband of Charles's only sister – and only surviving sibling – eleven years previously. Helena had no connection with Northamptonshire, and was herself an only surviving child. The new Mr and Mrs Shaw Lefevre were each to inherit family estates: but whereas Charles's expectations were modestly comfortable, Helena's prospective wealth was to endow her and her partner with what those who chronicled the affairs of the privileged described as an ample fortune. Each had reached this promising material situation from very different backgrounds, and at least some of their and their successors' temperaments and attitudes must have been influenced by the natures and experiences of their predecessors. It is worth looking briefly, therefore, at what can be known of the earlier history of the two strands which came together at Tichmarsh.

Shaw is a common enough name in Yorkshire and Lancashire. There is no sign, in Shaw Lefevre history, of any great eagerness within the family to hunt backwards into the origins of *their* Shaws, and the trail to-day suffers from that lukewarm attitude. To be fair, it is probably true that those origins would not have been much easier to trace a century or more ago than they are today, because seemingly almost no Shaw family documents survived or were preserved by the Shaw Lefevres. For the eighteenth-century Shaws the evidence is, simply, very limited, and the known facts have to be supplemented by some mildly speculative narrative.

Lancashire was the earliest home of the Shaws, but the branch which produced our dramatis personae had moved into the West Riding of Yorkshire and settled, probably not later than the middle of the seventeenth century, in the village of Notton, near Royston, between the towns of Wakefield, to the north, and Barnsley to the south. One of them, Thomas Shaw, lived in Wakefield where, on 3 November 1680, his son William was baptized. William was one of eleven children, and must have been among the longest lived, for he reached the age of 87. Of his ten brothers and sisters, only one married, or widowed, sister, Sarah Broughton, is mentioned in his will, by which she was favoured with an annuity of two guineas. William was a grocer who prospered in the trade, and allied himself in marriage to Mary Ambler, daughter of a successful saddler of York. Mary's father, John Ambler, married to the daughter of a Lord Mayor of the city, was himself influential in civic affairs, being appointed Chamberlain (a financial officer) in 1705, and serving as Sheriff in 1727–8; he set William an example by living to the age of 81.

William Shaw and Mary Ambler were married in York Minster on 28 February 1719. William's business concerns were centred on Wakefield. Some branch of the Amblers appears to have moved there and also became involved in grocery, though whether there was any commercial connection between the two families is unknown. It is clear that the Shaws were upwardly mobile: when William died in 1768, he was listed in official documents as William Shaw, Gentleman, and his will refers to his 'estate and estates . . . both real and personal . . . and . . . securities for money due . . . whether on Mortgage in Fee/Terms of Years yet to come, unexpired Bonds notes [and] arrears of rents.' William had established himself as a landowner: how extensive his holdings were is not known, but they were no doubt sufficient to justify the claim made by the early Shaw Lefevres that the Shaw side of the family had inherited patrimonial estates. Whatever the size and value of William's property, the most significant aspect of it was that it descended, relatively unencumbered, to only one of his children.

Different sources, taken together, suggest that William and Mary Shaw had six children, but the hardest records point to only three who survived childhood. Of these, the eldest son, John, born in 1720, did not marry until he was 44 years old, and left no offspring. A daughter, Priscilla, died unmarried in 1748. The key figure in our tale was the third survivor, George, baptized on 17 August 1723. He was the first of his family to become a professional man. As a boy, he was sent to the Free Grammar School at Wakefield and from there, in 1741, was awarded a Storie Exhibition and was enrolled at Trinity College, Cambridge. Neither the 'Free' Grammar School nor the Storie Exhibition should be allowed to give an impression of the relative poverty of George, for the Free Grammar School was so described more because of its academic breadth than because of the impecuniosity of its clients, and the exhibition, similarly, was not on offer to the really poor.[1] On the other hand, George was admitted to Trinity as one of the sizars – the least-well-off and least-privileged group in the rigidly stratified undergraduate body of the university. Sizars were then only rising above the practice whereby they had been required to serve their richer brethren at mealtimes. But the sizars and their immediate superiors in the student scale, the pensioners, constituted the solid, if socially inferior, majority of Cambridge undergraduates, who had won their way in and were determined to qualify themselves to enter professional life, most of them as clergymen of the Church of England.[2] George was no exception: he took his Bachelor's degree in 1744, and four years later was ordained at York. That was in June 1748. Almost immediately he was appointed by the Vicar, Revd Timothy Lee, to be Curate of Felkirk, a village only a few miles south-east of Wakefield, and began his clerical career with a yearly stipend of four guineas.

Given the modest material success which his father seems to have achieved, it is perhaps doubtful whether George ever had to make do with only four guineas a year. In any event, the small income from the curacy did not deter him from marrying very soon after he settled into Felkirk. His bride was a Felkirk woman, Mary Green, just a month older than himself. Mary's mother had been a Shipley, one of whose brothers – another grocer – had become successful in business in London and was to present a gift of plate to Felkirk Church in 1758. This was the first link to London in the Shaw history, and it was to be very significant in the evolution of the Shaw Lefevres. Though the genealogical evidence is not quite compelling, one of Mary Green's brothers, Joseph, has been claimed as the probable founder, through two sons, of two landed families.[3] Even if this is not fully proven, it is clear enough that the Greens, perhaps more than the Shaws, were fairly prosperous. The newly-wed George and Mary Shaw, therefore, in all likelihood began their life together among families enjoying increasing wealth, and would have had reasonable prospects of being financially comfortable.

Not much progress could be expected in the Church, however, without the backing and sympathy of patrons. Among the local aristocracy was the family of Monckton, whose head was Viscount Galway. Many of them were buried in the family vault in Felkirk Church. The living of Felkirk was in the gift of the Archbishop of York. There had been exchanges of land between the Moncktons and the Church at Felkirk in 1702, and John Monckton, the first Viscount Galway, was buried there, along with two of his daughters, in 1751. It is very likely that George Shaw helped to officiate at that funeral and he must have been known to the family. Galway's second wife was Jane Westerna, an Irishwoman whose family were of Dutch origin, and, of

THE SHAWS AND THE GREENS

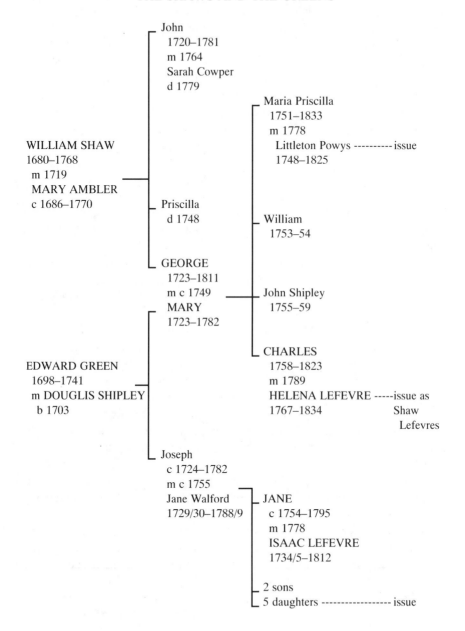

John
1720–1781
m 1764
Sarah Cowper
d 1779

WILLIAM SHAW
1680–1768
 m 1719
MARY AMBLER
c 1686–1770

Priscilla
 d 1748

GEORGE
1723–1811
m c 1749
MARY
1723–1782

Maria Priscilla
1751–1833
m 1778
  Littleton Powys ---------- issue
1748–1825

William
1753–54

John Shipley
1755–59

CHARLES
1758–1823
m 1789
HELENA LEFEVRE -----issue as
1767–1834   Shaw
                    Lefevres

EDWARD GREEN
1698–1741
 m DOUGLIS SHIPLEY
 b 1703

Joseph
c 1724–1782
m c 1755
Jane Walford
1729/30–1788/9

JANE
c 1754–1795
m 1778
ISAAC LEFEVRE
1734/5–1812

2 sons
5 daughters ----------------- issue

their four surviving children, John Monckton, born in 1739 and therefore 9 years old when George Shaw moved to Felkirk, was to be important to the new curate almost forty years later. But this early contact with a Whig landed family may well have led to the first preferment which George Shaw received.

Ten years after beginning his career, in September 1759, George was installed as Rector of Kirk Smeaton, only ten miles to the east; but he continued to be Curate of Felkirk as well. Kirk Smeaton was in the gift of that arch-Whig, Charles Watson-Wentworth, second Marquis of Rockingham. The double arrangement lasted for nearly ten years, and there is nothing to show how George shared his time between the two parishes, though he officiated at practically every marriage service held at Felkirk until 1767–8. But, on 2 December 1768, he became Vicar of Womersley, a neighbouring parish to Kirk Smeaton, on the presentation of Stanhope Harvey, its patron and another Whig, though a much lesser one than Rockingham. Whether as the result of legal necessity or of negotiations between patrons, or both, George Shaw relinquished his tenure of Kirk Smeaton simultaneously, but only for a brief spell. Soon afterwards, on 28 March 1769, he was reinstated to it by Rockingham and from then on had two livings, very close together, instead of one living and a curacy, ten miles apart. But after less than two years, in September 1770, he obtained the Archbishop's permission to appoint a curate at Kirk Smeaton and allowed him an annual payment of £26.5s.[4]

Three sons and a daughter were born to George and Mary, but only the first and the last lived beyond their early childhood. There was, therefore, a gap of seven years between the two who reached adulthood: Maria Priscilla was baptized on 15 April 1751 and Charles on 17 October 1758. We know nothing of Maria's childhood, but perhaps the move from Felkirk to Kirk Smeaton and Womersley weakened the family's connection with Wakefield, for when Charles was ready he was sent to the Free Grammar School at Leeds, a little further north. The first historian of that school wrote, plaintively, in 1822, that 'no registers of the scholars have been kept, or at least preserved', and Charles is not included in the surviving short list of those who went up to Cambridge after 1765.[5] But as the Headmaster was a Trinity College man, and as George no doubt wanted Charles to follow in his footsteps, Charles duly entered Trinity in October 1775 – as a pensioner, signalling his family's improved position in the world since his father's student days.

That improvement may well have reflected the fact that George seems to have been peculiarly favoured by his father, and by the late, childless marriage of his elder brother, John, to Sarah Cowper in 1764 – by which time George had been married for eighteen years. William Shaw died only four years later, and by his will left everything to George, save for modest annuities for his widow, and for John. He also provided that George should be the recipient of the remaining household property after the deaths of his mother and brother. William may have been convinced that John and Sarah would never have children, or he may have known that John had other resources to fall back on, or he may have written John off as an unworthy son. Whatever was the truth of that matter, George inherited most of the estate, and could well have received a little more when his mother died at the end of 1770. Any remaining doubts that George would have a clear field disappeared with his sister-in-law's death in 1779 and with the burial of his brother John on 15 January 1781.

We have no figures for George's income, but in 1775, when he was 52 years old, he held the two livings of Kirk Smeaton and Womersley, and he had practically the whole of the earnings of his parents' estates. At about the same time as his son Charles matriculated at Trinity, George made two major moves – he decided that he had sufficient means to give up the living at Womersley, and to live in London. He continued to be Rector of Kirk Smeaton, but as we have seen, he had installed a curate there since 1770. He became, in fact, a largely, if not a completely, absentee incumbent, a not unusual phenomenon in the Anglican Church of the period. We do not know exactly when George's move south began, but when Charles, at the beginning of his second year at Cambridge, was admitted to Lincoln's Inn, he was recorded as being the son of Revd George Shaw of Wimpole Street, Cavendish Square. Exactly two years later, in 1778, Charles' sister, Maria Priscilla, was married at St Mary le Bon to Revd Littleton Powys, from the same address. When George Shaw's wife, Mary, died, in June 1782, she was buried at St Mary le Bon, and a few months later George conducted a marriage service in that church. From 1788 onwards the local records show Shaw as the ratepayer in respect of 21, Queen Anne Street West, and from 1792 to 1812 he was listed under that address in *Boyle's Court Directory*. Number twenty one – since renumbered – was one door from the junction with Wimpole Street. Thus it is reasonable to conclude that from the mid-1770s until his death in 1811, George Shaw spent much if not all of his time in a modest London house in the developing district north of Oxford Street – 'quite a genteel neighbourhood', whose residents in that era included Edmund Burke, the dramatist Richard Cumberland, William Windham, James Boswell, J.M.W. Turner and the fashionable portrait painter Henry Edridge, who was to put images of Shaw Lefevres on to canvas.[6]

In the light of what happened in the dozen following years, it may be correct to suggest that the Shaws came to London because of the influence of the thriving Joseph Green, Mary Shaw's brother. And it may be that, apart from the lure of the capital city, they came because they thought that by doing so they would have a better base from which they could enhance their children's chances in life. Whether or not they deserve credit for special foresight, their two children certainly made successful marriages in the metropolitan environment. We shall come to Charles very soon, but his sister was to wed eleven years before he did. Unfortunately, there is nothing to show how Maria Priscilla's meeting and subsequent marriage with Littleton Powys came about, though initial contact through the social network of the clergy may be the most likely explanation. It was a liaison which almost certainly benefited both George and his son. Littleton Powys was the brother of the Member of Parliament for Northamptonshire, who was to be raised to the peerage in 1797 as Baron Lilford. Littleton himself held livings in Northants all his life. He and Maria Priscilla had seven children, and though only once or twice is there any more mention of the Powys family in this chronicle, it is interesting to note that Littleton and Maria Priscilla were the great-grandparents of the novelist John Cowper Powys, who shared with the Shaws and Shaw Lefevres the tendency to long life – he died in 1963 at the age of 91. As we shall see, Charles Shaw may have been helped by Littleton's brother when he entered politics; but, long before that, it seems highly probable that the connection of Powys and Shaw may have been a factor in the engineering of Revd George Shaw's final ecclesiastical preferment.

In the last two months of 1788, when George Shaw was 65 years old, he relinquished the rectorship of Kirk Smeaton and was installed as Rector of Seaton in Rutland. He was to hold his new position until his death, in London, in August 1811, at the age of 88. During the nearly twenty-three years of his incumbency of Seaton his signature does not appear in any of the parish registers and his place was clearly filled by curates and neighbouring clergy.[7] The living was worth £649 a year in 1849, and its equivalent half a century before may have been quite sufficient by itself, let alone when added to private means, to enable its holder to employ a curate and to enjoy a leisurely life elsewhere. But the intriguing aspect of Shaw's occupancy of the rectorship is the strong likelihood that he obtained it by a combination of influences arising from his daughter's marriage and from his early connections with the Moncktons in Felkirk. Seaton fell vacant through the death of Revd Peter Westerna, a relative – probably a brother – of the Jane Westerna who had married the first Viscount Galway. Jane's son, John Monckton, after a brilliant military career, had partly inherited and partly purchased the extensive estate of Fineshade Abbey, which straddled the borders of Northants and Rutland. One result of this was that he had become the patron of the nearby parish church – at Seaton. Close by were the lands of the Powys family. It is hard to resist the notion that the vacancy at Seaton was known to Littleton and Maria Priscilla Powys, that George Shaw was able to appeal to Colonel John Monckton on the grounds of affectionate memory, and that the Powys interest was willing to support his appointment.[8]

Whether or not this is somewhere near the true nature of the process by which George Shaw became Rector of Seaton, the background of steadily if modestly increasing material well-being, of a family climbing up the social ladder and establishing intimate and confident contact with powerful and influential people, is important as a backdrop to the life of Charles Shaw, the future Charles Shaw Lefevre. Charles would only have known his entrepreneurial grandfather, William, for a few of his childhood years, but may well have inherited from him strong commercial instincts. From his father – no laggard as an entrepreneur, though in the context of the church rather than the market place – he had the advantage of the guidance of an educated man who had both professional and social ambition and who must have developed some capacity for diplomatic negotiation.

There are only one or two brief descriptions of George Shaw and his wife Mary and they are those of a grandchild. George was 'a tall, big man. He wore a wig and black silk stockings and knee breeches. He was a great Greek scholar. He always gave me a handsome tip whenever I went to see him before going to school.' And there was a memory of Mary, who 'used in her younger days to give dinner parties every Sunday followed by whist but she lived long enough to abuse violently those who did so' – perhaps a reflection of a strong response to evangelical enthusiasm late in life. There is nothing more about them, except that for at least forty years Revd George Shaw was the Chaplain to the 61st Regiment of Foot, a regiment constituted in 1758, when it is probable that George was commissioned. Apart from an initial encampment at Chatham, and short periods in 1782–3 and 1796–7, the regiment was continuously abroad, serving in the West Indies, Ireland, Minorca, Gibraltar, Guernsey, the Cape of Good Hope, Egypt, Malta, Naples and Sicily. It is highly unlikely that the Chaplain accompanied them to or visited them at any of those stations; but George was listed each year until 1797, after which the regimental rolls of officers did not include their spiritual colleagues.[9] Awareness of his father's military duty may not have been lost on Charles, however, for he was to become an enthusiastic leader of yeomanry.

It is time to return to Charles at Cambridge in the mid-1770s. If the father was 'a great Greek scholar' the son must have set out to enhance the academic reputation of the family. Charles took five years over his first degree, but then turned up as tenth wrangler in 1780, and was elected a Fellow of Trinity in 1782. The only record which remains of the seven years during which he held the Fellowship shows his income from the College, which ranged from just over £40 to a maximum of £84 annually.[10] There is nothing to indicate his intellectual interests, and no sign of how much time he spent in residence. The Fellowship was only given up when he married, and long before that he had turned away from Cambridge in order to qualify himself in law and then to practise it. But there was no apparent pressure for him to do so, and though he had been admitted to Lincoln's Inn in 1776, he was not called to the Bar until February 1787. He then chose to work the Midland Circuit, and one wonders whether he shared any of the attitudes to it expressed by the cynically ambitious and supremely self-confident Samuel Romilly, who had joined it from Gray's Inn in 1784:

> All circuits were indifferent to me, for I had no friends or connexions on any one of them; and my choice fell upon the Midland, because there appeared to be fewer men of considerable talents or of high character as advocates upon it than upon any other, and consequently a greater opening for me than elsewhere. It was, besides, shorter than some other circuits, and would, therefore, take me for a less time from the Court of Chancery; and, what was no unimportant consideration, my travelling expenses upon it would be less.

Romilly denounced the incompetence and indolence of Midland Circuit members old and young, but was kinder about his colleagues in 1786, taking the view that by then the 'society . . . had much improved . . . by the addition of several men for whom I entertained a very great regard.' We must each draw our own conclusions from the fact that Charles Shaw is not listed among either Romilly's angels or devils; a strong possibility is that Charles was not present enough to be taken seriously by so perfervid and dedicated a practitioner.[11]

It has to be suggested that Charles, from his student days until his marriage, did not respond enthusiastically to his prospects either as a churchman, as an academic or as a lawyer, and it is clear from family reminiscences and the contemporary, potted biographies that, having become a barrister, he treated his practice in a desultory fashion. At the same time there is nothing to show that he was a mere, frivolous man-about-town, and his subsequent life does not encourage any attempt to portray him in his twenties as either a fool or a knave. He probably had sufficient means to lead a comfortably genteel existence, and drifted along for some years without any definite sense of vocation. When he made a lukewarm choice to practise law, he may have picked the Midland circuit for no more blameworthy reason than that it would bring him from time to time within easy reach of his sister and the Powys family; the possibilities are numerous and there is no way of proving which, if any of them, might have been the reality. But the most likely clue to his activities and his attitudes is the family connection which, as we shall see, almost certainly led to his marriage.

For it is worth considering that Charles may have been convinced, or may have been persuaded, that the only way in which a young man of moderate means could establish a formidable base from which he might pursue his ambitions and talents, was to find a wife whose fortune was a great deal larger than his own. Whether a deliberate search for such a wife was the most serious call on his time, and for how long, we know not: indeed, as it happened, he might very well not have had to search at all. But once he began at the Bar, Charles had to wait only two-and-a-half years before he was united with a woman whose material wealth was indeed sufficient to lift him into a stratum of society well above that from which he sprang. And in that new stratum he soon saw what he wanted to achieve.

CHAPTER II

Lefevres into Shaw Lefevres

Helena Lefevre came from very different stock. On her father's side she was a Huguenot, descendant of a family who almost certainly came to England from France as refugees in the late seventeenth century. One has to qualify that possibility because of an absence of absolutely unequivocal evidence and the existence of several confused family traditions. The family name had numerous variants – Fever, Le Fever, Lefebure, Le Fevre among them – and there were several families bearing one or other of them, even in the areas where Helena's grandparents' generation began to make themselves prosperous. Some of those families had come to England long before the end of the seventeenth century, and there are suggestions, equally equivocal, in some of the local histories, that at least part of Helena's family may have been among them. On the weight of the evidence, it is most probable that her great-grandfather did escape from France to avoid the persecutions which followed the revocation of the Edict of Nantes, but exactly when and how he did so is unclear. In the lore of at least one set of relatives over two centuries later, the refugees escaped from the French coast in an open boat covered with straw, before crossing the English Channel. More sober accounts merely claim that they reached Southampton safely.

Whether Peter Lefevre, Helena's great-grandfather, made an escape full of drama and danger, or whether it was quietly efficient and uneventful, he did not arrive in England without some capital, however, in whatever form he managed to bring it with him. He had been born near Rouen, in Normandy, about 1650, had married Ann Le Mercier or Le Marcis of Balbec, and had inherited land only a short time before he and his wife, with their two children, fled at an indeterminate date in the mid-1680s.

The estate they left behind apparently became reclaimable decades later, after the persecution of the Huguenots stopped, but – so family legend has it – the lawyer entrusted with negotiating its return was drowned during the Revolution, and with him died all hopes of recovery.[1] The age of the elder Lefevre child, Magdalen, is uncertain, but the younger, Isaac, was born only a few weeks before he was taken to England. The exiled family settled first on Blean Common in Kent, not far from Canterbury, in which city Peter 'embarked in trade.' Though they had found a new land for themselves and their successors, neither Peter nor Ann lived long to enjoy their freedom from religious persecution. A second son, Peter, was born to them, but Ann died in Canterbury in 1694, reputedly after giving birth to twin girls who did not survive. It is claimed in the family record that Peter remarried, that there was no issue from the new partnership, and that his second wife died before Peter himself went to his grave when he was about 47. However, there seems to be no documentary proof of these developments, though a marriage between a Peter Le Fevre and a Madeleine de Mecon is listed in the register of a Canterbury church only four months after the death of Peter's first wife. The three Lefevre children – Magdalen, Isaac and Peter – were taken in by their mother's niece, Mme Madeleine Grandville, who lived in the strongly Huguenot district of Spitalfields on the fringe of the City of London. Thus were they introduced into that remarkable colony of diligent and entrepreneurial immigrants, just before the beginning of the eighteenth century.

Family memory has it that Magdalen married twice but either had no children or none who survived infancy. She has no further place in this story, unlike her two brothers; but there was for a long time a tradition that in addition to them, there was a third brother, John. That belief was only undermined by genealogical searches in the late nineteenth and early twentieth centuries. Apparently there had been a dual approach to the compilation of the family tree from old records and memories which had credited 'John' with an adventurous life as a Lieutenant Colonel in Marlborough's armies, and as having married a lady with the same family name as the wife of his brother, Peter. 'John', who was certainly not mentioned at all in any of the wills of the Lefevres of the same generation, was correctly demolished. On the other hand, the legend of the army connection was so strong within the family that, though there seem to be no surviving contemporary documents to prove it, some warlike experience may well have been an early episode in the young Peter's life before he began his aggressive and successful business career.[2]

All but minor genealogical doubts can be put aside when we reach Isaac (c. 1685–1746) and Peter Lefevre (c. 1690–1751), the male children of their exiled parents. Both became successful: Isaac as a scarlet dyer and Peter as a distiller of malt, though both had additional and some overlapping business interests. Peter especially became known in his mature years as a thrusting industrialist and an acquirer of land in the developing areas east and north-east of the City of London, in the marshy lower reaches of the River Lea. His early years remain mysterious, but if he was the adventurous and swashbuckling soldier of family belief, he must have been extremely young to have achieved any high rank. He must certainly have abandoned any military life by the time of his wedding, in his mid-20s, and thereafter concentrated on his several commercial enterprises. He and his bride, Elizabeth Debonnaire, were married at St Olave's, Southwark, in 1716. The partnership seems to have been felicitous, but childless. Prosperity, though, was apparently always a goal and an achievement. They lived for some time in West Ham, but made their main home in Walthamstow, where in Peter's last years they occupied a mansion then called, among other names, Winns, which now houses the William Morris Museum.

Peter achieved local prominence in 1727, when he bought the Three Mills at Bromley-by-Bow from Lord Bathurst. Up to then the Three Mills produced only flour, but Peter was to be among the leaders of those who were keen to take advantage of the increasing demand for distilling, which had been helped by a prohibition on importing spirits from abroad. In 1730 he and his partner, John Grace of St Leonards, a mealman, leased St Thomas Mills at Stratford, and four years later they joined with John Debonnaire, a relative of Peter's wife, and two other distillers, Daniel Bisson and Christopher Barton, all three of West Ham, to trade and deal jointly together 'in the several arts trades or mysteries of mealmen cornfactors millers and distillers in buying selling and grinding corn and grain and malt spirits.' Peter invested £9,000 of the £31,000 capital and leased the mills to the partnership for £602 a year. Spirit distilling began on a large scale and was to be carried on at Three Mills until 1941. The Lefevre interest did not extend long beyond Peter's death, however. Indeed, although his brother Isaac became an additional partner in 1740–1, there was a split in the partnership four years later when Christopher Barton left, taking control of some of the operations. The Three Mills, however, continued to be the major concern of Peter and his other colleagues.[3]

Peter Lefevre, as well as being a formidable entrepreneur, was able to put energies elsewhere than into his business. Consciously or not, he moved steadily into the accepted pattern of well-to-do English society. He embraced the Church of England, serving as churchwarden and overseer in the West Ham Vestry in 1729–32, and as churchwarden of St Mary's, Walthamstow in the 1740s. By the middle of the century he was a sufficiently prestigious public figure to be appointed High Sheriff of the County of Essex for the year 1751, but died during his term of office.[4] What became of his fortune thereafter is better postponed until we have looked at the life of his elder brother.

Isaac Lefevre had a less colourful career, but in terms of family a much more fruitful one. He became a moderately prosperous scarlet dyer and silk weaver, but the proceeds of his efforts had to meet the needs of a sizeable brood of young Lefevres. Isaac went through what may well have been a typical crisis for young, second generation Huguenot immigrants to England. When he was about 20, at a time when conditions for those of his faith were much easier than when his father was forced to flee, Isaac was drawn back to France and pressed by his mother's family to stay. He did pass some time in Paris, but finally decided to return and settle permanently in England. He married within months of his brother and, like Peter, chose a wife from the Huguenot community – Judith Séné, whose family hailed from Picardy. Their wedding was at St Michael's, Cornhill, and their union produced four sons and two daughters who survived infancy, and more than three – possibly six – other offspring who did not.

Isaac seems to have followed a doggedly straightforward course in the silk trade, but towards the latter part of his life, doubtless influenced by his more flamboyant brother, he became a minor partner in the Three Mills and also operated a brewhouse in Poplar. He died in 1746, at the age of about 60, and left his real estate to his wife for her life and then to his eldest son, John, distributed the rest of his fortune in trust equally to all his children for their lives, and afterwards to whoever was then his heir-at-law. Thus, save in the matter of real estate, he made no special provision for John, who was to be the crucial figure in the growing fortunes of the Lefevres and the father of Helena, who was to marry Charles Shaw.

Isaac did this because his brother, Peter, without children of his own, had stood as godfather for John and had made it clear that he wished to 'adopt' and 'provide for' him. On the strength of that apparent promise, Isaac did not differentiate between John and his other children. But, for reasons seemingly now unknowable, when Peter died, five years later, he made John one of his executors but left him only £100, though the will can be read as implying a desire that on his wife's death John should benefit equally along with his brothers and sisters. This came about after Peter's widow, Elizabeth, died in 1756, when the real estate had to be sold and the proceeds divided. John received about £5,000, as did each of his brothers and sisters, so that Isaac's expectation of special treatment for John was disappointed.

However, the sale of Peter's assets was conducted by the executors, of whom John was one, and half of them were bought bv John's widowed mother, Judith – a transaction which surely represented some attempt to compensate for Peter's neglect. Judith, who lived until 1780, put the share purchased from the trustees of Peter's will in trust for all her children for life, and thereafter for whoever would then be regarded as her late husband's heir-at-law. Though John received far less than he had hoped in the 1750s, and had to wait until after his mother's death to inherit his father's property and a somewhat larger share of Peter's money, those delays and the rather complex legalities were to be of particular benefit to his only daughter, the future Helena Shaw Lefevre.

The apparently deprived John Lefevre (1721/2–1790) was sent in his early childhood to attend school in France, at Balbec, and spent his holidays with his mother's relatives at Rouen. Perhaps this was a reflection of his father's ambivalent feelings about having decided to remain in England. Indeed, such ambivalence was probably shared with the Le Marcis family, several of whose members in addition to Peter Lefevre's wife and her sister,

THE LEFEVRES

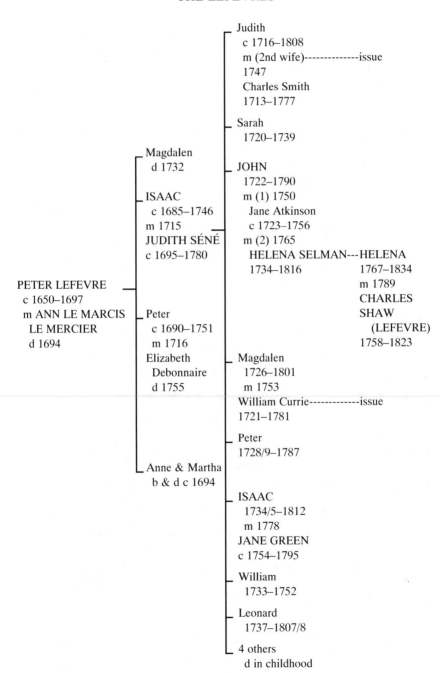

Madame Grandville, had come to England in the late seventeenth century. One subsequent reflection of this Anglo-French experience was that by the 1740s at least one branch of the Le Marcis clan was carrying on a textile printing business on both sides of the Channel and employing John Lefevre as their English agent.[5] That must have been some ten years after John was brought back to London, in 1730, when he would have been about nine, and enrolled at Merchant Taylors' School, where he was a pupil until 1734. It is hinted in family papers that he was intended to go on from there to St John's College, Oxford, but it may well have been during those London school years that Peter Lefevre, his uncle, proposed to adopt and provide for him. There was probably a condition attached to the offer which led John to abandon the prospect of going to university. Instead, he became a distiller, the protégé of his uncle, and in due course a very successful one.

Despite his early sojourn in France, John himself, like one of his brothers and both his sisters, followed the rough rule of immigrant groups – that it is the third generation which is fully assimilated into the receiving society – and married outside the Huguenot community. John and his first wife, Jane Atkinson of Walthamstow, were the 'favoured inmates' of his uncle Peter's house – the 'resort of the fashionable and gay', which makes the later failure of Peter Lefevre to 'provide' all the more puzzling. But that disappointment, which was indeed a severe blow to John and Jane, seemed only to have added greater drive to John's very considerable ability and energy, and his financial affairs quickly recovered from the setback. They were enhanced by partnership and good relations with his younger brother, Peter.

This Peter Lefevre (1728–1787), the second son of Isaac, had been sent as a young man to work in a commercial house in Lisbon; he stayed for some years, acquired a love of Iberia, its literature and ambience, and developed there what his niece was to describe as a 'dignified politeness of manner which distinguished him through life' – though she admitted that 'he was more formed for the pursuits of literature than for active business.' Nonetheless, Peter had more than a negligible share of the family's commercial spirit, and after their father's death he and John were partners in the Poplar brewhouse. When he died, unmarried, he left John the greater part of his fortune, amounting to some £40,000. At that time John Lefevre had less than three years to live, but by then his only child, so long as she was able to survive, was clearly destined to inherit most of the accumulating assets of three generations of the family. John's other two brothers, Isaac (1734/5–1812) and Leonard (1737–1808), were to live for many years beyond John, but neither fathered any child. Leonard frittered away his share, but Isaac was worth over £100,000, and left several thousands to each of his remaining kin.[6] His special contribution to our history, though, was, as we shall see, that in providing a link through his marriage, he helped to bring about the Shaw Lefevre connection.

In the middle years of the eighteenth century the Lefevres were over-whelmingly committed to distilling, and were thriving. It was in this period that distillers, like brewers and other successful industrialists, were beginning to be attracted to banking, at least as a sideline.[7] And it was through the younger daughter of Isaac Lefevre, John's sister, Magdalen (1726–1801), that the family were to become involved in the world of finance. Magdalen had married, in 1753, William Currie, a young man from an old Scottish family who lived near Duns in Berwickshire. He had probably moved to London on the suggestion of Luke Currie, a relative who was an attorney in Cheapside, among whose clients was Isaac Lefevre. William probably helped his father-in-law and in 1767, or perhaps a little earlier, he and a partner set up in business as malt distillers at Limehouse. Currie may also have had some business connection in the distilling context with Isaac Lefevre, John's brother. In any event, in 1773 he took the risk of moving into banking with some of the previous associates of one Fordyce, whose house had 'crashed' the year before.

The new firm, called Mason, Currie, James and Yellowly, went into business initially for a period of eleven years, at 29 Cornhill. Currie, while retaining his distilling interests, put in £10,000 of the £30,000 nominal capital, and the venture prospered, though it never, in his time, produced the kind of profits which came from his established concerns as a distiller. When, in 1780, his partner Mason pulled out, Currie, as senior partner, persuaded John Lefevre, his brother-in-law, to come into the banking partnership, which henceforward operated under the style of Currie, Lefevre, James, Yellowly & Co. John Lefevre put in £10,000 and the Lefevre family interest thus established was to last until 1811, though only John was an active partner until his death in 1790. Thereafter his brother Isaac took his place but without any share in the capital, and was paid £500 a year for the use of his name, an arrangement which ended on his death, when the name Lefevre disappeared from the bank's title.[8]

Like William Currie's, John Lefevre's foray into banking was only a small part of his successful business career. Profits from distilling were far larger, but the fledgling bank – destined to become part of Glyn Mills and now the Royal Bank of Scotland – did well enough. In our context, more significant than the extent of the gains was the fact that the banking exercise almost certainly extended the network of family and subsequent political connections. One of the bank's partners, Jacob Yellowly, may have been the same man who was an employee of Whitbread's Brewery, and later became a partner there; the bank certainly numbered the Whitbreads among its clients; a granddaughter of the first Samuel Whitbread and the younger daughter of the second Samuel Whitbread were to marry Shaw Lefevres, one of whom was himself to enter the banking world in the 1820s. In 1780, John Lefevre bought shares in the Sun Fire Office, another of the bank's clients.

and began a connection which led to his son-in-law becoming a director, and his grandson the chairman, of that pioneering insurance company.[9]

William Currie died prematurely in 1781 when, accidentally, he caused an explosion by unwisely holding a lighted candle too close to a fermenting vat which he was trying to inspect. Shortly after this some or all of the remaining Lefevre distilling businesses were combined with those of Currie and, according to a distinguished banking descendant of William, the profits of the distillery were 'not less' than £30,000 per annum. William left Magdalen with ten children: one of the younger sons, another Isaac, had been firmly directed towards banking by his father, who 'placed him in the counting house' at a very early age, 'with a threat . . . that he would brain him if he were caught outside it.'[10] This parental firmness did no apparent material harm, for Isaac became a very successful banker, was 'highly respected in the City, and was consulted by Mr. Pitt with regard to the loans raised during his administration to prosecute the war with France.' He married Mary Anne Raikes, thus bringing the Lefevres close to a family which paid respect to both God and Mammon by producing two Governors of the Bank of England and the founder of the Sunday School Movement. And in a later generation, Isaac and Mary Anne's second son, Raikes Currie, who became the virtual head of the bank, also had a long career as an MP for Northamptonshire beginning in 1837, and kept up the connection with the Shaw Lefevres.

John Lefevre's other sister, Judith (1716–1808), who was older than Magdalen, became the second wife of Charles Smith (1713–1777), who inherited several flour mills from his father at Barking. The original Smith money came through marriage into the Marriner family who 'acquired notice and opulence in the service of the East India Company.' Charles Smith was sufficiently rich to be able to leave the mills to be managed by his partner, while he settled at Stratford Langthorne to become an authority on the Corn Laws, publishing tracts which were quoted approvingly by Adam Smith and influenced some parliamentary decisions.[11] He and Judith produced children who were to retain contact with the Shaw Lefevres in their widened political and social catchment area during the nineteenth century.

But our spotlight must be focused predominantly on John Lefevre, for the fortune which he made, despite disappointments on the way, was to provide most of the strong financial base from which his daughter and Charles Shaw were in due course to launch themselves on to the social and political scene. It is clear that John was a tough character. In his business dealings there was evidence of a combative and unsqueamish nature, and as a banker who played 'an important part' in the growth of Curries & Co., he did not mince his words. He had

his own theory of banking. A particular customer's account was nearly always overdrawn and . . . catching him one day at the counter, [Lefevre] said, 'Mr . . . you and I must understand one another something better than we seem to do. I'm afraid you don't know what Banking is; give me leave to tell you. It's my business to take care of *your* money, but I find you are always taking care of *mine*! Now that is not Banking Mr . . . ; it must be the other way. I'm the Banker, not you. You understand me now Mr . . .? I'm sure you do!'

Nor was John inhibited by any code of over-courteous social forbearance. At his dinner table, when suffering from an extremely boring and long-winded guest, John seized on a small break in the flow of the monologue to remark, 'You need not talk any more, Mr . . . ., *if you don't like it.*'[12]

Despite his industrial and financial success, it was John's increasing interest in real property which was particularly crucial to his descendants. No doubt through his uncle Peter's connections he was involved in property in Walthamstow in the late 1740s and, over and above his distilling concerns, he acquired during the rest of his life, particularly after and as a result of his second marriage, a range of land and houses in the still largely rural east London areas of Bow, Old Ford, Bromley, Wapping and Edmonton, as well as in Buckinghamshire and Essex. And as his landed interests increased, so his commitment to distilling was reduced. He took over from Peter Lefevre as a leading partner in the Three Mills, the other major participant being Daniel Bisson, but that arrangement came to an end in 1759, and with it the Lefevre part-ownership of the mills. John certainly continued to be deeply concerned with distilling, as the owner of property and water rights in the Lea Valley, which were of crucial importance to that industry, but from practical distilling he was steadily disengaging, and seems to have let go his final shares in 1787 to two Smith nephews.[13]

There is nothing in the Lefevre papers to suggest that the family retained any active, or indeed inactive, concern with distilling after John's death, though the likelihood that sizeable investment remained cannot be discounted. Nor does John seem to have taken over anything of his father's business as a dyer, or carried on the dyehouse which came to him after the death of his second wife's father. But from both he inherited real property, all of which perhaps fuelled further his ambition to become a substantial landowner. What was to be the main home of the Shaw Lefevres, however, was to be established by John 40 miles west of London, on the site of an old farmhouse at Heckfield, not far south of Reading, near the old Roman Road, or 'Devil's Highway', which forms the boundary between the county of Berkshire, to the north, and what we know as Hampshire, but was then the County of Southampton. Almost a century later, Anthony Trollope was to claim that

in England there is no prettier district, no country in which moorland and woodland and pasture are more daintily thrown together to please the eye, in which there is a sweeter air, or a more thorough seeming of English wealth and English beauty and English comfort. Those who know Eversley and Bramshill and Heckfield and Strathfieldsaye will acknowledge that it is so.[14]

John had begun to look for a country place for his daughter in 1775, and bought several adjoining properties in and around Heckfield – a 'small Jacobean mansion' called The Grove, a farmhouse known as Bakers, Coppid Hall, School Farm, and others. On this initial estate, after living briefly in Bakers, he recognized the possibilities for rebuilding and extending the house so that it would have fine views to the north-east. 'How the old farm pond could eventually become terraced lakes, and the heather slopes flanking them become stands for fine trees of every description, was his inspiration.' For a start, he knocked down parts of Bakers and added to what remained, to produce 'a small box-like manor or hunting lodge with four major rooms on the ground floor and two upstairs floors,' and renamed the property Heckfield Place. Its development into a much bigger, and grander, house was still to come when John died.[15]

The wedding of John Lefevre and Jane Atkinson was held at Walthamstow on New Year's Day 1750. Jane died six-and-a-half years later, aged 29, soon after a child had been born who did not survive infancy. There had been no other children. Jane was buried at West Ham. We have only one vignette of her, contained in a brief memoir of a few pages which gives an outline history of the Lefevres and was probably written by John's niece, Judith Smith, not many years before she died in 1832. Though the whole memoir has about it more than a note of dutiful hagiography, and is not without some internal inconsistencies, it none the less offers an interesting glance into a very different family from what might be imagined from scrutiny only of their commercial ventures:

Jane Atkinson was a woman of much personal attraction, and of enlightened understanding, improved by every species of cultivation. She was well skilled in the dead and living languages, and her knowledge of Greek and Hebrew was subservient to the constant study of the Holy Scriptures. In her latter years the loss of an only child, ill health, and pecuniary disappointments contributed to wean her from this world. Her chief associates were the celebrated Divines of her day; among them Wesley, Venn, Dodderidge, Whitfield may be mentioned. She cared not for minor differences of opinion, it was enough that they were in heart and life sincere Christians. The ascetic habits which she gradually acquired sometimes cast a gloom over her husband's house, but he admired and respected her motives even when he suffered by their effects.

Jane died in 1756, and John did not remarry until nine years later, when he was 42. His new wife, Helena Selman, was twelve years his junior, and was destined not only to be with John for his remaining twenty-five years, but to live another quarter century as a widow and to die in 1816 at the age of 81. The only child of the marriage was a daughter, Helena, born on 23 February 1767 at Bromley in Middlesex, and destined to become Helena Shaw Lefevre.

We can trace Helena Selman's ancestry better on her maternal than on her paternal side. Four generations and a hundred-and-fifty-seven years before her birth, William Lyster (Lister) of Thornton in Yorkshire, offspring of an old and well-documented family, married, on 17 February 1610, Mary Bellasys, daughter of Sir Henry Bellasys, Bt. Lyster was then 19, but only five years later he was knighted. He became MP for East Retford, fought on the Parliament side in the Civil War, was at Marston Moor and commanded troops in Yorkshire in 1645. Thereafter he was MP for the West Riding and for the City of York. He and Mary had eight sons and three daughters. The sixth son, Matthew, was born about 1626 and spent over ten years from the age of 30 as Consul at Cyprus, appointed by the Levant Company. Matthew returned to England in 1667 and lived at Old Ford. Civil War enmities did not prevent him from marrying the daughter of a royalist in the following year. His bride, Sarah Sparke, was the daughter of Revd Edward Sparke DD, a theologian of some note, who has a place in history as a victim of persecution during the Commonwealth, and who subsequently became Vicar of Walthamstow and Chaplain to Charles II.

Matthew and Sarah Lister had four daughters, and one of them – another Sarah – married, in 1703, Daniel Selman, a well-established scarlet dyer who may also have had trading interests with Turkey.[16] Although the name, Selman, appears in several of the parish registers of east London, it has not been possible to trace Daniel's origins. From his union with Sarah came at least one son and a daughter. The son, Lister Selman, born in 1708, was always described as a dyer, though clearly one rich enough to enjoy substantial leisure to pursue literary concerns. He, too, had a home at Old Ford, but acquired in addition the substantial property of Chalfont House in Buckinghamshire. At the age of 22 Lister married yet another Sarah – Sarah Mitford, whose father, Samuel, was the second son of a substantial merchant trading with Sweden and perhaps with Turkey, and a member of the well-known family whose roots lay in Northumberland. Samuel lived for most of his adult life in Ireland, where Sarah was born in the same year as her future husband. Her mother's family name, and the date of her marriage to Samuel, have not proved traceable either in London or Dublin. Her given name was either Helen or Helena. She and her husband died in Dublin in 1721/2, and it is probable that their daughter was then brought to London and raised there. Sarah's aunt, Philadelphia, had married a goldsmith, George

Merttins, who became Lord Mayor of London, and there can be little doubt that Sarah herself lived in affluent circumstances.

There were only two daughters from the partnership of Lister and Sarah Selman. The elder, Sarah again, was the bride of Revd Robert Hare of Hurstmonceaux, godson of Sir Robert Walpole, whose family owned 'the Vache' at Chalfont; and through this union came the much later connection of the Shaw Lefevres with the writer and traveller, Augustus Hare.[17] The younger daughter, Helena, was born on 18 January 1734. Her mother died in 1738, when she and her sister were small children, and the two girls grew up under their father's careful guidance.

Judith Smith, our only witness, becomes pious and adulatory in the extreme about Lister Selman and his daughter Helena. Lister Selman, she wrote, was 'distinguished by his gentlemanlike manners and by the kindness and benevolence of his character, and his good qualities flowed from the pure source of religious principle.' He died in his younger daughter's arms in 1779, and was buried at West Ham. Helena, according to Judith Smith, was

> in every quality of the head and heart . . . a pattern of female excellence. So spontaneously did the fulfilment of each duty flow from her, that she seemed to need no principle to guide her, and yet so steadfast, so *erect* were her principles that they would have bent the most stubborn spirit to virtue. In short in all eyes but *her own*, her life was as bright an example of sinless obedience to the precepts of the Gospel as human frailty would allow, and the humility and charity which shone conspicuously in every action completed the catalogue of Christian graces which adorned her.

A much later comment, by her eldest grandson, was to the effect that she had a most beautiful complexion, but was so afraid of damaging it that she dared not either laugh or smile.[18]

The only child of John and Helena Lefevre was thus the offspring of a mother who is portrayed as a formidably and perhaps overbearingly moral and religious woman, and of a father who suffered from both the extreme devoutness and tragic early death of his first wife, and from disappointment at his uncle's inexplicable failure to support him as much as he had expected. Perhaps not surprisingly, in the eyes of his business colleagues, John Lefevre was 'a silent and reserved character',[19] but in private life he appears as a normally equable and not uncultured man. His niece thought of him as:

> a man of quick parts and of a very sensitive mind; the little leisure he had for reading, be employed chiefly in the study of French literature, and he had an intimate acquaintance with the best authors of the best period. He spoke the French language with the correctness of a native. In all the relations of social life he was friendly and affectionate; he never remembered an injury and never forgot a kindness.

It is not easy, though, to see this hard-driving, successful and wealthy entrepreneur, steadily buying his way into the upper reaches of business and into the social stratum of the landed gentry, as having, in Judith Smith's words, 'no desire to raise his family above the middle rank to which they were born; that rank which comprehends within it, most of virtue and of happiness.'

But whatever their separate natures, and whatever the full character of their union, John and Helena Lefevre must surely have given their child an upbringing marked by piety, seriousness and some gentility, within an ever increasing material prosperity. And without doubt, whatever her personal appearance and demeanour may have been, to a gentleman in search of a wife, the younger Helena must have seemed an extremely desirable heiress.

Charles Shaw and Helena Lefevre were both products of almost a century of social and economic advance by each of their families. The successful Yorkshire grocery business of William Shaw, combined with his inheritance or acquisition of land, laid the base for the long career of his son as a comfortably endowed, university educated, Anglican parson. The Revd George, in turn, was able to see his son through an academically outstanding but leisurely and extended spell at Cambridge, and then launched at the Bar, though apparently without any great need to earn his own living. Meanwhile the refugee Peter Lefevre's sons, probably with less, initially, than William Shaw's capital available between them, made a great deal of money as distillers, dyers, traders and bankers.

By the 1770s it could well have been the case that the Shaw fortunes were more or less static, while the Lefevres' were still forging dynamically upwards. Charles's inheritance must have been somewhat reduced by whatever dowry his father had to provide for Maria Priscilla, his only sister – but the connection with the Powys family would certainly have compensated him for that in social terms. Helena Lefevre was even more the beneficiary of the failure of her parents' brothers and sisters either to marry or to have the good fortune to see their offspring survive to maturity. Here, then, were two young people from the relatively new but solidly established mercantile and professional class, each well prepared and confident of being able to move easily within and above the social strata in which they had been raised; each free to inherit comprehensively from their fathers.

While there is very little documentary evidence, there is, fortunately, strong genealogical data to support the straightforward claim that Charles and Helena met, and that their relationship developed, through a family connection. It will be remembered that Mary Shaw, wife of Revd George Shaw, had a brother, Joseph Green. Joseph, who was very close to Mary in age, must have decided to migrate southwards, perhaps encouraged to do so by his mother's family, the Shipleys, at least one branch of whom had done well in business in London. Joseph followed suit, and by the 1750s was settled at Stratford, Essex, where he married Jane Walford, daughter of William Walford of Bocking, a village near Braintree in the same county. Jane Walford's mother was Oliver Cromwell's niece (Jane Cromwell, sister of Oliver, had married General Desborough); and the Walfords, who were clothiers, 'had obtained by interest with the Protector, a contract for supplying baize for the private soldiers in the Parliamentary army.' Joseph and Jane Green had at least nine children, and as was mentioned earlier, it is probable that their fortune was sufficient to help two of their sons to establish landed families in the early nineteenth century. The eldest daughter of this prosperous couple, Jane, married in 1778 Isaac Lefevre, the younger brother of John. Thus Jane Lefevre (nee Green), who was cousin to Charles Shaw, became also aunt to the young Helena Lefevre. Jane herself died, childless, in 1795.[20]

1778 was an important year for both Shaws and Lefevres. On 24 March Jane Green and Isaac Lefevre were married at West Ham; the ceremony was witnessed by Maria Shaw, who could have been either Charles's mother or his sister, and Judith Smith, who could have been either Isaac Lefevre's elder sister or his spinster niece, whose memories of her relatives we have been quoting. On 21 November, at St Mary le Bon, Maria Priscilla Shaw was married to Littleton Powys. In that year, Charles Shaw was a Cambridge undergraduate aged 19, and Helena Lefevre was a girl of eleven. During the following nine years there is little doubt of the closeness of the Shaws, the Greens and at least the Isaac Lefevres, because we have records of baptisms in the Green family in which, among the godparents, are listed 'Uncle' and 'Aunt Shaw', 'Charles Shaw', 'Isaac Lefevre', 'Mr. Lefevre' and 'Sister Lefevre'.[21] It is reasonable to suppose that Charles and Helena must have met on many family occasions, and that John Lefevre had plenty of opportunities to notice and assess Charles Shaw. It is also reasonable to suggest that Charles may have found himself interested and involved to some extent in the commercial and financial world of the Lefevres and the Greens. Such an involvement, and the possibility that he might look forward to marrying Helena, could explain both his apparent uncertainty and indifference over choosing a career, and the modest enthusiasm he brought to his legal work.

The details must be left to the imagination. A marriage settlement there must have been, but it does not appear to have survived. Nor has any document which would give an idea of what resources George Shaw may have passed to his son. There is nothing on paper to challenge Judith Smith's assertion that the marriage of Charles and Helena was a love match. John must have insisted on Charles taking the Lefevre name and arms. One can understand the ambitious Charles acquiescing happily enough.

John Lefevre deserves to have the last word, as it were, on the creation of the Shaw Lefevres, because his was the greatest contribution to the new family's future well-being. Only three months after Charles and Helena came out of the parish church at Tichmarsh, man and wife, John brought about his own death in a sadly ludicrous fashion. He cut a finger nail 'too close, which produced mortification in the area', and after a short illness he died at Old Ford, on 16 January 1790. Judith Smith's eulogy of him ends with this comment on the marriage he had so recently attended:

No alloy of vanity debased the purity of his views for his daughter's establishment in life. He sanctioned a choice which was founded on mutual love, but whose fortunate results he lived not long enough to witness; yet he felt the value of the son whom he had obtained, and he was disturbed by no forebodings as to his daughter's fate; with his dying breath he blessed her . . . 'and she was blessed.'

CHAPTER III

Into Politics

In five months, from the date of his adoption of a new family name, through his marriage, to the death so soon afterwards of his father-in-law, Charles Shaw Lefevre passed from the modest comfort of parsonage, university and law chambers, to the status of landed gentleman, endowed with what all the potted biographies describe as an ample fortune. Doubtless he was already equipped with the degree of education and gentility essential for recognition within the squirearchy, and his great height and good bearing gave him a formidable presence. But it is impossible to believe that John Lefevre, who had only recently bought his way into the landed class, would have accepted as husband for his only child a man who, however handsome and polished, did not strike him as being financially capable and with strong entrepreneurial ambition. By John's early demise Charles was quickly put to the test, and there can be no question that he came through with achievements with which his wife's father would have been well content. For the new Shaw Lefevres, combining Helena's wealth and Charles' enterprise, launched themselves confidently into the society of rural gentry – that independently-minded segment of the small, ruling elite. They were late arrivals and were never totally dependent on the agricultural economy, but they enjoyed during their lifetimes the last era of the landed classes' real hegemony and embraced their habits and values. Their children would struggle with the slippage of their class down the economic and political slopes, and their grandchildren would witness its near emasculation. But the personal futures of Charles and Helena in 1790, despite the shadow cast by the French Revolution, by an unsuspected, forthcoming quarter of a century involving war and a subsequent period of depression and agitation, were bright: opportunities were there to be seized, and seized they were.

Charles made no pretence of continuing what had been only a perfunctory practice at the Bar. He set about the task, beloved of the land-owning fraternity, of extending and consolidating the main family base, Heckfield Place. That effort was to be continued by his eldest son, and it is as well to describe its overall character and outcome at this point in the family's history. It is a tale of cool, aggressive and persistent land dealing and enclosure, stretching over seventy years. A modern local historian records with some asperity how the Shaw Lefevres, 'from 1790 until 1860, bought every field, cottage and manor that they could lay hands on, and negotiated exchanges with their neighbouring landlords . . . until there was a consolidated estate of over 4000 acres.'

Apart from the economic advantages sought by this process of acquisition and rearrangement, the Heckfield estate was planned to allow the owners seclusion, beauty, and the opportunity to preserve game and organize shooting. So father and son used their powers as lords of two local manors, and their legal knowledge:

> to exterminate many copyholds, leaseholds and lifeholds, so that event-
> ually all cottage property came under their control as freehold – [and most
> of those cottages were] razed so that the . . . pleasure grounds, park and
> . . . drive could be enclosed in a park fence.

While the tone of this comment is hostile, its hostility is not backed up by any evidence of harshness or viciousness on the part of the Shaw Lefevres. Their acquisition and treatment of property, with the certainty that it entailed displacement of humbler folk, was unquestionably part of a well-documented pattern. And the agricultural labourers of Hampshire were amongst the worst sufferers from economic and social deprivation during the period – they played a major role in the Captain Swing disturbances of 1830. But there is nothing which reveals either Charles or his eldest son as particularly unkind or uncaring landlords, and their own property was not attacked. At the same time, there is no evidence that they left behind a reputation for unusual gentleness or outstanding charity.[1]

The elder Charles certainly added to Heckfield Place and its grounds during his occupancy, but his son made considerable additions. By the middle of the 1850s both ends of the original 'plain, boxlike house' had been extended to provide more accommodation for guests and servants, and much money – though apparently not always quite enough – had been spent on more elaborate decoration. The 'new reception rooms' were equipped with 'marble chimney pieces from France, and the new drawing room with a fine plaster-work ceiling.' The brickwork was 'decorated with quoin stones, window dressings and balustrades, but these were not of brown stone which they imitated, but some stucco composition which has ill withstood the weather.' A terrace was 'laid out on the North-East side enclosed by a pretty stone balustrade and furnished with elegant stone flower baskets, probably of Italian make and design.'[1] The result of all this development was – and is – a pleasant, strong, sturdy and beautifully-sited mansion, but not one which is distinguished architecturally. It was, though, for a hundred-and-five years the focal point of the Shaw Lefevre clan, and the home of the families of the founder, Charles, and of his eldest son, Charles.

Heckfield was by no means the only Lefevre estate, and Heckfield was not, in 1790, the immediate property of Charles and Helena. John Lefevre's will, dated only a month before he died, provided that his holdings in or near Hackney, Old Ford, Bow, Bromley St Leonard, St John Wapping, Edmonton and Stepney in the County of Middlesex, and his lands in Heckfield and neighbouring Eversley, should pass to his widow for life and then to Charles and Helena. In fact, the newly-married couple shared Heckfield with Mrs Helena Lefevre until she died in 1816. During the 1790s the young Charles himself acquired many 'Freehold Messuages, Farms, Lands, Tenements, and Hereditaments . . . contiguous to and intermixed with' the Heckfield estate. In 1802 Mrs Lefevre, Charles and Helena agreed to an exchange whereby the Middlesex holdings would be vested in Charles and the newly acquired lands around Heckfield would be consolidated with the original estate there which would remain, as required by John Lefevre's will, for his widow's use for the rest of her life. This major rearrangement could only be implemented by an act of Parliament. At the time, the annual income from each of the two parcels of land was roughly £500 to £600. The gross value of the Middlesex estate alone was estimated to be over £12,000 and was expected to rise to £15,000.[2]

A further major addition to the family's possessions was Burley Manor, on the edge of the New Forest near Ringwood, and its acquisition reflects the good fortune which Charles Shaw Lefevre experienced and the diplomacy which he combined with his business acumen. Burley Manor, dating back to the reign of Henry VII, had come into the possession of one James Mowbray in 1780. When Mowbray died in 1801, the Manor passed to his elderly sisters, Hannah and Sarah, and Charles Shaw Lefevre was appointed one of the Trustees. There is evidence of Charles' concern for them as a legal and financial adviser, and his letters to them were couched in warm, personal terms. Six years later, both sisters died and left him the whole estate. It was to give a good deal of trouble and anxiety to the family over the next forty years, but it was not an asset to be despised, having rental income which reached a peak of over £650 in 1813.[3]

Yet other lands and houses crop up in the scattered records of the family – in Buckinghamshire, for instance, probably part of the estate of John Lefevre's father-in-law, Lister Selman; and several in Essex, including property at Walthamstow, thought to have been the first piece of land acquired by a Lefevre – almost certainly Peter, son of his refugee father.[4] And there was always a London residence, though whether it was owned or rented is unclear. For at least the first few years of their married life, Charles and Helena lived when in town among the legal fraternity at 10 Bedford Square, then on the edge of open fields; but by 1801, in keeping with Charles' firm establishment in political life, they had moved to 4 New Street, Spring Gardens, and over twenty years later went to nearby 9

Whitehall Place, both houses being in a residential area fashionable amongst peers, parliamentarians and public servants until the middle of the nineteenth century.[5]

It is not possible to give exact figures of the Shaw Lefevres' assets and income: but the extent of the lands they held; the apparent success they enjoyed in manipulating and extending their holdings; their retention of investment in brewing, insurance, banking and in the East India Company; and the style in which they lived, all combine to buttress a claim that they would be found comfortably within that group of about one thousand families – the wealthy gentry – who each commanded annual incomes of over £3,000 and who owned between them 15 per cent of English land.[6] And it is worth pointing out that the pound sterling, which was worth, in 1800, almost twenty times its value in the late 1980s, subsequently increased in value to a peak of practically forty times its value today, by 1880. The relevant arithmetical adjustments, if made throughout the text hereafter, make it clear that in late twentieth century terms it would be appropriate to describe the Shaw Lefevres, collectively, as being worth millions, and some members of the clan as enjoying annual incomes ranging from a quarter to three quarters of a million pounds. And it is worth stressing that those incomes were enjoyed when the weekly wages of the unskilled labourer were counted in shillings, not pounds – in present day terms, very roughly, less than fifteen hundred pounds a year.

It was from an initially assured and potentially improving financial position, therefore, that Charles Shaw Lefevre was able to command local attention and then to launch himself into national politics. He pursued a traditional local route, first becoming an active magistrate for Hampshire, then Chairman of Quarter Sessions, and subsequently, in 1800, Recorder of Basingstoke, his nearest Hampshire town. His other striking concern with local affairs was his raising and commanding a troop of yeomanry to meet the threat of invasion by the French. In fact he adopted his new county role enthusiastically; but like many of the new landed gentry, he needed – and succeeded within seven years of coming to Heckfield – to complete the transition and seal his status by finding a seat in the House of Commons.

The political stage on to which Charles stepped, in the last years of the eighteenth century, was far removed from the rigidly structured, party-aligned theatre which was to become the accepted setting for the power struggles of most of the nineteenth and twentieth centuries. Deeper research and conflicting theories have not yet produced or yielded to any overwhelming consensus about the nature of political loyalties while George III was on the throne and while his son acted as Regent in the years of his father's incapacity. The uncertainties are particularly strong in the period of Shaw Lefevre's membership, from 1796 to 1820. The early eighteenth century ascendancy of the Whigs had long been shattered, and the loss of the American colonies, the impact of the French Revolution, and the outbreak of war with France, had severely weakened what, with all the dangers of using a more modern concept, might be described as liberal or reformist attitudes, while strengthening the hands of those who were unhappy at the prospect of any further reduction of the royal prerogative. Moreover, Parliament was under the spell of William Pitt the Younger, who had, by 1796, been Prime Minister – since the age of 24 – for an unbroken twelve years and who was, by then, too, the leader of a nation at war. War tends to strengthen any government capable of rising to emergencies, and to make opposition suspect as at worst unpatriotic and at best unnecessarily factious.

Such concerted opposition as had existed in the recent past was greatly diluted when Lord Portland fell out with Charles James Fox after war began in 1793; thereafter the opposition politicians were divided into several factions whose interests and alliances were so diverse and so transitory as to be largely ineffectual. But nor was there any solid phalanx of government supporters which constituted a clear, tightly-organized majority. All governments had their own severe problems in attaching to a core of placemen a sufficient number of independent members. Each of the major issues of the period cut across such party lines as there were. The monarch guarded his prerogatives jealously, held on some important topics highly prejudiced opinions, and had sufficient power and support in the system to be a formidable ally or a stubbornly effective opponent. This diffusion or even non-existence of well-organized, majority-supported central power, and an equally weak cadre of opposition, left those numerous MPs who were neither placemen nor totally under the control of sponsors, very free to manoeuvre among the cliques which represented special interests or which grew up around leading personalities. It also meant that the politics of their constituencies were often, for the individual member or candidate, far more compelling than those of Westminster. This was so particularly for the large group of country gentlemen in the House of Commons who were especially independent, if not necessarily especially vocal, though never slow to defend their economic and social privileges.

Charles Shaw Lefevre was one of the country gentlemen, but hardly a traditional one. In contrast to most of them, his social origins were relatively humble, his experience more urban, and his interests and financial resources more diverse. As a late entrant to the class, in a fluid political era, his independence and his sense of direction were sometimes uncertain. His name does not appear more than a few times in the literature of early nineteenth century politics. The researchers who have counted division lists and made exhaustive surveys of constituencies must certainly have him in their files, but have never found him sufficiently unique to warrant special notice. He never held office, he made no famous speeches, he had commonplace ideas;

and while clearly an active Member, he was rather pompous and uninspiring as a contributor to debate, though his height made him an impressive figure – Canning is reputed to have remarked, mischievously, that 'There are only two great men in the world – Shah Abbas and Shaw Lefevre.'[7]

Most of the biographical dictionaries of the nineteenth and early twentieth centuries defined Charles Shaw Lefevre, rather brusquely, as an Independent Whig. Late twentieth-century scholars would be happier to stress the adjective and almost dismiss the noun, at least for all but Charles' later years. Nonetheless, Charles' career was marked by a progression – uneven, but understandably so, in the contemporary confusion of loyalties – from pro- to anti-Government and, less easily proven, from both independence and a largely conservative stance, to greater sympathy with more liberally-inclined partisanship on some but not all major issues. Moreover, he was a doughty constituency member, and a devotee of the details of House of Commons' practice, the latter enthusiasm surely influencing particularly his eldest son who, as we shall see, was to preside over the House for eighteen years in a very different political era, but also his second son, who was to be for an even longer spell the chief official of the House of Lords.

In the English political culture of 1796, if a gentleman had money, a country estate, the right connections, and the will to acquire a seat in the House of Commons, he could buy one. Charles Shaw Lefevre bought one of the two seats assigned to the borough of Newtown, on the Isle of Wight. The Isle had long been a place whose parliamentary seats had been available, at a cost in jobs and influence, to those prepared to support the Government, and a few leading landed families dominated the scene and the bargaining. Newtown was a classic rotten borough, with only thirty-nine voters whose eligibility turned on their being burgage tenement holders. The thirty-three burgages – some being split – were usually held on life grants by non-resident friends of the owners: effectively two men had the disposal of the seats – Sir Richard Worsley and Sir John Barrington, both of whom had chosen to sit in them.

Barrington had been in the Commons since 1780, and after 1790 was an 'unobtrusive' supporter of Pitt, but his health began to fail and in 1796 he simply sold the seat to Charles Shaw Lefevre. The price is not known, but Worsley could have sold his place for £4,500 five years before, and a later member for Newtown reckoned his seat cost him £1,200 a year. Nor is it known how Barrington and Shaw Lefevre came to make the deal, or even who approached who. Charles, however, must have been regarded as a desirable candidate: he was wealthy, he lived near the Isle of Wight and within the same county, and had already given good service to that county. There might have been introductions through London business and legal contacts, and Charles' connection with Thomas Powys, his brother-in-law, might have helped. Powys, MP for Northamptonshire, was a typical, independent country gentleman but, unusually, a 'forceful and passionate speaker,' who had been prominently opposed to Pitt in 1784 over a constitutional issue: like so many others, however, he had rallied to the government after the revolution in France. None of these factors challenged in significance the two fundamental requirements – money and support of Pitt's administration. With those needs met, Charles Shaw Lefevre, in his 38th year, was returned, unopposed, for Newtown, Isle of Wight, 'in the Barrington interest.'[8]

For four years Charles was an apparently able and diligent new backbench member, supporting Pitt and showing enough orthodoxy to be trusted, in 1799, to move the House's thanks for the Address from the Throne. His assumed character as a country gentleman protective of country pursuits could scarcely have been given a better boost than by his successful introduction and pilotage of a bill, in the same session, which restored the opening of the season for shooting partridges to 1 September each year! That bill was, in fact, the only piece of public legislation which he introduced during his parliamentary career. But he did develop a particular enthusiasm for procedure and for committee work, and ultimately became so knowledgeable that he was spoken of later in his Commons' years as a possible Speaker – which indicates that he must have attracted considerable respect and been regarded with some cordiality by large numbers of his fellow members.[9] His concern with procedural techniques may have been a reflection of one of the most significant friendships of his life, that with Henry Addington, who had been occupying the Speaker's chair for six years before Shaw Lefevre was elected to Parliament. Whether their friendship was established before 1796 or only through contact first made after Charles reached Westminster, is unknown. Again, Thomas Powys could have been a link, inasmuch as he seconded the motion which extended Addington's tenure of the Speakership in September 1796.[10] Though not many letters between them survive, the early friendship between Addington and Shaw Lefevre was close. Charles and Helena lent the whole Addington family their London house on occasion, while Helena seems to have enjoyed a companionship at Heckfield with both the first and second wives of Henry Addington. It was, for Charles, a politically fateful relationship.[11]

Early in 1801 Pitt lost the premiership because of his failure to persuade George III and many of his own supporters to accept a degree of emancipation for Roman Catholics from their political disabilities, as part of the new union of the Dublin and London Parliaments. Shaw Lefevre then and for the rest of his career was opposed to Catholic emancipation, and that may have been the main or even the only initial cause of a personal distrust of Pitt which set in and remained strong throughout the last five years of the great man's life. Pitt was replaced as Prime Minister by Henry Addington, and for a decade Charles was regarded as an Addingtonian, though on several occasions a wobbly one, during which time his leader, ennobled as Viscount Sidmouth in

1805, moved in and out of office. Eventually Shaw Lefevre broke politically with Sidmouth in 1810-12, and thereafter was a steadily anti-Government man, until ill-health forced him into virtual retirement from the House in 1819, and to relinquish his seat in 1820. This somewhat tortuous political odyssey was not by any means confined to the environs of the Palace of Westminster. It was at least as much, or more, influenced by a change in its local starting point, which involved abandoning the privileged and tranquil jobbery of the Isle of Wight for the vigorous corruption and the brawling electioneering of the Borough of Reading.

While Charles remained a supporter of the Government interest by backing Addington, he was either unwanted at Newtown after 1801, or was unwilling to stay. It is unclear whether Sir John Barrington was not attracted to Henry Addington, or whether he and Shaw Lefevre had other policy differences, or whether he wanted more money than Charles was willing to pay. In any event, Barrington sold the seat to Charles Chapman, an East India merchant who was said to be worth £70,000 – most of which he lost, later, through gambling.[12] Whatever the circumstances, for the election of 1802 Charles had to find another seat, and he played a canny double hand. He successfully manoeuvred himself into an uncontested seat for the Cornish borough of Bodmin, and simultaneously was nominated for and won one of two bitterly contested seats at Reading. Having won the latter, he decided to stay in it. The circumstances of both Bodmin and Reading in 1802 illustrate the complexity of the political structure, as well as demonstrating the flexible independence of Shaw Lefevre.

The 'negotiation' about Bodmin preceded the Reading election.[13] The Cornish borough was in the gift of Francis Basset, whose family fortunes came from Cornish mining. Basset had been MP for Penryn since 1780, and like Thomas Powys had transferred his allegiance to Pitt in 1793. He was rewarded three years later by being raised to the peerage as Lord de Dunstanville, but deserted Pitt for Addington in 1801. Dunstanville was happy, therefore, to sponsor Shaw Lefevre as a friend of Government in the following year, and when Charles decided to stay at Reading, the resulting Bodmin vacancy was made available for another Addingtonian nominee.[14] Bodmin, though, like Newtown, was a matter of discreet bargaining with only derisory reference to an electorate. The atmosphere of Reading, the county town of Berkshire, only forty miles west of London, was redolent of more overt political and social conflict.

Reading was an ancient 'scot and lot' borough. In such a borough, those male citizens whose incomes were assessed as large enough to make them liable to pay any local charges – only, seemingly, the Poor Rate in Reading – were entitled to vote. This arrangement produced a list of roughly 8–900 voters in the early nineteenth century, or 6 per cent of the population of the town. With such a number, and because Reading had for a long time experienced 'a singularly noticeable absence of any great and predominating interest', was 'never under the influence of a great territorial family' and never 'a Treasury borough', the electors had an unusual degree of independence.[15] But, given the conditions of contemporary politics, that independence was qualified by such unpleasant realities as threats of eviction, open bribery, physical intimidation and massive drunkenness at the polls. The borough had an unenviable reputation as one of the most corrupt in the country.[16] It has been asserted in a careful study that in the second half of the eighteenth century the sentiments of the electors were 'predominantly' Whiggish, and that in the following fifty years Reading was the headquarters of dissent in Berkshire.[17] Even so, party divisions seem often to have been blurred or deliberately concealed to such an extent that before 1800 'the party hue of the majority of the candidates' cannot be discerned.

However true that may have been of the past, the Reading electors after the turn of the century, despite the several shifting groups of politicians in Parliament, seem to have had no difficulty or compunction about thinking of their local contests in two-party terms: 'After 1800 every contest was fought on a party programme, with the old, corrupt Reading Corporation a firm supporter of the Tory Party and the middle class townsmen and traders supporters of the Whigs.'[18] And, it is claimed, the harbinger of this change was none other than Charles Shaw Lefevre, defined with emphasis, because of his long membership of the Addington connection, as 'a party man.'[19]

Whether or not, in fact, Shaw Lefevre's two opponents in 1802 were any more or less partisan in simple, national terms, they certainly put up a bitter fight against the intruder. It was a three-sided contest for the two borough seats, and the two sitting members have been labelled 'Independent Tories': one was the veteran Francis Annesley, sometime Master of Downing College, Cambridge, and the other was John Simeon, Recorder of Reading. Both were members of the Reading Corporation, and the main proponents of ousting at least one of them from the House of Commons were those people hotly opposed to the long-established custom whereby the Corporation nominated the MPs. They wanted a restoration of popular election – they wanted the borough 'opened':

> the inhabitants of Reading, conceiving that the old interests which had long preponderated there, might be overturned, looked out for a man of character and opulence, that would come forward as their champion and assert their independence.[20]

Charles was to be their champion. He fought an epic battle, and came second to Annesley, defeating Simeon by 110 votes. It was by far the hardest of the three elections in which he was opposed; it must have cost him a good deal of money – the tale was told that he opened the borough with a golden key, at a cost of £20,000 – and he must have known that by his decision to take Reading rather than Bodmin, he was exposing himself, very probably, to more electoral anxiety and more expense, in the future.[21] Why did he fight Reading at all?

There is no convincing written evidence on which to base an answer to that question, save a hint in a biographical index of 1808, that Charles 'preferred a seat for a borough in the neighbourhood of his country residence to one in a distant county'[22] – not by any means a frivolous suggestion, for travel was slow and difficult, and Reading was a mere forty miles from Westminster as against Bodmin's two-hundred-and-forty-five: the ambitious like to be near the centre of power. But there is nothing to tell us to what extent, if any, Charles' decision to fight Reading was urged on him by Addington and his colleagues as a deliberate attempt to deseat obvious opponents in open conflict; or how much it was a personal venture intended by Shaw Lefevre to draw attention to himself, to prove himself an aggressive politician on the national scene, and at the same time to strengthen his position as a local leader. These two possibilities are not at all mutually exclusive. There is little reason to doubt that Addington and friends would have blessed the idea, especially as Charles would be installed safely at Bodmin if he failed; but it is more likely that their moral support would have followed, rather than preceded or instigated, Charles' response to a Reading invitation. And it is probably fair to exonerate Charles from any suggestion that he was seeking notoriety in order to gain ministerial office, of any desire for which there is not the slightest sign throughout his career.

Certainly there was a local initiative: after the people opposed to the sitting members decided that 'their neighbour, Mr. Lefevre', was 'the fittest person' to represent them, 'a few friends accordingly waited on him, with a tender of their services, and he answered nobly to their call.'[23] But perhaps, aside from all the substantive political reasons, Charles Shaw Lefevre answered the call because he enjoyed the prospect of a real scrap. There was in him much of the extrovert, and he had a streak of combative, Yorkshire aggressiveness: one can imagine that he itched to take on an awkward group of voters and a couple of worthy antagonists. It would be a fresh experience; he had enough money, and a safe seat elsewhere if he did not win. And, maybe, he was a little resentful at being, as he had been at Newtown and would have been at Bodmin, essentially at the mercy of individual or governmental patronage for his political future. For it is worth bearing in mind that he was, by profession, a lawyer – to a degree representative of the rising cadre of such men in political life – and doubtless had his share of professional independence, which was combined with and perhaps underpinned the vaunted, traditional independence of the country gentlemen whose ranks he had joined as a result of his advantageous marriage.

Reading received Charles' assiduous attention for seventeen years. He was returned unopposed in 1806 and 1807, and fought two further elections, in 1812 and 1818. His success in 1802 was due in part to 'the new vigour which he infused into the Reading Whig Party', but he had, throughout, 'a slight edge with the professional men', while 75 per cent of his vote came from 'retailers, craftsmen, artisans and labourers.'[24] But at least until after 1812 he showed no reluctance to buy his votes: his reputation was long-lived, for when, fifty years later, his grandson was returned for the same seat, the conservative *Berkshire Chronicle* commented that:

> A fond remembrance of the older Lefevre dwells in the breasts of less opulent possessors of the franchise; for did he not open the whole of the public houses throughout the borough for the dispensation of gratuitous beer; and was he not endowed with the *soubriquet* of 'The Fox' from his adroitness in conduct of electoral matters?

He consolidated his position by giving an annual dinner to his supporters; and he met the expense of his elections from his own resources, which probably meant spending a lot more than £4,000 each time.[25] He learned quickly not to offend municipal pride – for his simultaneous election for Bodmin in 1802 was denounced heartily by his opponents as unforgiveable double dealing – no previous candidate for Reading, and no later one, ever so insured himself against possible defeat.

Once he had taken the plunge, Shaw Lefevre fulfilled the general expectation that Reading should be represented by a local man. He never again jeopardized his reputation for local patriotism by repeating the Cornish episode in any form. And at Westminster he seems to have taken his full and proper part in handling locally inspired legislation and in presenting local petitions to Parliament. He was, in short, a self-interestedly generous representative who was well able to meet demands on his purse, and he was a sound man of business. Reading saw no need to have contests in the elections of 1806 and 1807. In 1812 and 1818, Shaw Lefevre was comfortably in first place in two three-cornered fights. His victory in 1802, and his skill and sufficient responsiveness to local needs, had made him practically unassailable. Here are two small recollected scenes of Charles at the height of his local successes:

> opposite the Crown, at the time of an election at which Charles Shaw Lefevre . . . was returned, I was placed in a window where I could with safety see the procession. I think this was in 1812. At length the honourable Member arrived with his friends, accompanied by a lot of garland women and a band of music. As was the custom with successful candidates, he threw silver money to the people who followed him, and they scrambled and fought for it. Here Mr. Lefevre delivered his final throw of cash, and

a three shilling piece came through the window of the room in which I was standing.[26]

On 3 June 1818:

> Mr Lefevre made his public entry into town to begin canvassing for the approaching general election. On his arrival at Whitley turnpike, the horses were taken from his carriage and he was drawn round the town by men, accompanied by a great concourse of people.

And on 19 June, after his place at the top of the poll was announced, 'Mr. Lefevre was carried to the Crown Inn amidst the greeting of the populace.'[27]

The influence of even so relatively free and lively an electorate as Reading's was not strong enough to enable it to dictate policy to a well-established, wealthy and stubbornly independent MP, but nor could the member ignore altogether its overall enthusiasms, anxieties and tendencies. From the election of 1807 onwards Shaw Lefevre embraced a diplomatic combination of support for 'the just prerogative of the Crown' with the promotion of 'the civil and religious liberties of the people', alongside a careful watch on increased expenditure and the investigation of abuses.[28] It was a nicely calculated package, presented to an argumentative Reading audience in May 1807 and it is very likely that it reflected his awarenesss of the kind of local criticism which was made privately, to her spendthrift father, by the writer Mary Russell Mitford, a near but hostile neighbour, a month earlier. Miss Mitford, who had taken great offence because Shaw Lefevre, wittingly or unwittingly, had muddled an offer of help from her father during the previous election late in 1806, wrote, on 10 April 1807:

> You wish to know what I thought of the Lefevres' visit; and I assure you . . . that I think just the same of them now as I did before. They were . . . tolerably civil; and Mr. Lefevre sported some intolerably bad puns, which were, I suppose, intended for our entertainment; but they did not discompose my gravity. In short, I believe that he has no inclination to meet you, and was glad to find you were in Town. Little minds always wish to avoid those to whom they are under obligations; and his present 'trimming' in politics must conspire to render him still more desirous not to meet you, till he has found which party is *strongest*. That will, I am of opinion, decide which he will espouse.

And five days later, after reading a report of Charles' speech on a proposal by Samuel Whitbread for a reform of the Poor Law, she complained that it was 'incomprehensible':

In fact, I would defy the most expert solver of enigmas to resolve the question of which side he meant to support. Do you remember the definition of 'modern candour' in Mr. Canning's 'New Morality'? The member for Reading seems to have laid claim to this virtue in its highest perfection. According to him, 'Black's not so black, nor white so very white.' In short, the more I know of this gentleman the more I am convinced that, under a roughness of manner, he conceals a very extraordinary pliancy of principle and a very accommodating conscience. He holds in contempt the old fashioned manly virtues of firmness and consistency, and is truly 'a vane changed by every wind.'[29]

Charles cannot have been the only MP groping for a sustainable role in 1807, and Miss Mitford's vitriolic attack is doubtless too strong.[30] The confusion of power at Westminster since Addington's replacement by Pitt in 1804 was at a high level and was to continue for many years. Shaw Lefevre wanted to be a supporter of Government, but his distrust of Pitt was deep, and even the Sidmouth link began to weaken. At the beginning of 1806, one of Sidmouth's colleagues reported to Vansittart that Charles, while still 'firm to us', was 'inclined in the next instance to Foxes party, however he highly approves of your preserving your consequence by keeping aloof from too close a connexion with any other Persons.'[31] In fact, from the fall of the Talents Ministry, early in 1807, which meant that Sidmouth was out of office, Charles 'gradually drifted into regular, but essentially independent opposition.'[32] And independent or not, much of it might well be attributed (on one occasion it was so, angrily, by Sidmouth himself) to Charles' willingness to go along with his Reading supporters so far as to vote for parliamentary reform, to petition for the release of the radical Sir Francis Burdett, and to oppose the reappointment of the Duke of York as Commander-in-Chief, all burning issues of the period. After Sidmouth rejoined Government as Liverpool's Home Secretary in 1812, Charles' political break with him was complete, and it is probable that personal relations between the families lapsed after Sidmouth's first wife died in 1811. Sidmouth did not marry again until shortly after Shaw Lefevre's death in 1823, but the political differences which had separated the two men did not prevent the second Lady Sidmouth from being a close friend of Charles' widow.[33]

Near the end of his parliamentary career, Charles could fairly boast that he had stuck to his 1807 pledges, even if one has to acknowledge that his deft and careful draftsmanship had given him wide margins within which to operate. He maintained his course in opposition to the end, though he continued to demand economy and refuse new taxes, to denounce any emancipation of Roman Catholics, and to avoid any formal or even symbolic attachment to the re-emergent Whig Party.[34] Reading's 'Whiggish' voters had given Charles loyal backing: he in turn devoted much of his parliamentary time to the town's interests and to related matters such as the Poor Law; but he also held the majority's loyalty by meeting, to no small extent, their reformist ambitions.

One cause of Henry Addington's popularity with the country gentlemen was his addiction to relaxed, friendly conversation with them, accompanied by the consumption of port. Addington himself 'greatly enjoyed . . . the drinking of large quantities . . . in 1803 . . . over twenty glasses a day.'[35] There is no suggestion that Charles Shaw Lefevre imbibed more than his share, but he did become a chronic sufferer from gout, which seems to have forced his virtual retirement from the House of Commons in 1819 and the relinquishing of his seat in the following year. He was then sixty two – young for a Shaw, a Lefevre, or a Shaw Lefevre – but he was to live for only three more years.

The exiguous record leaves an impression that Charles may well have worn himself out. Certainly his restless land dealings, his full-blooded and none too scrupulous electioneering, his procedural expertise and his diligence in the debates, committees and divisions of the House of Commons, and his lively participation in the yeomanry, were wearing enough. But he also had his commercial interests and legal duties – he was for twenty-three years a Director and for the last two, Treasurer, of the Sun Fire Office, and he retained his Recordership of Basingstoke until his death. He had been elected a Fellow of the Royal Society in 1797, when that institution was as much or more a gentlemen's club than a community of eminent scientists, and he was a member of its Council in 1806–7, though he attended only his inaugural meeting.[36] Perhaps, though, he was influenced there during that year to dispute the motion in the Commons that Dr Jenner should be rewarded with £10,000 for his vaccine innoculation. Shaw Lefevre argued that the system was not infallible and, in any case, that it had been invented in Dorset a generation earlier.[37]

Overall, despite the dutiful, posthumous praise of 'his popular manners and deportment', there is about Charles' public life little light-heartedness, little evidence that he was able to take things easily, in his stride. Rather, there is some hint of the shrewdness of a man who, having had one supreme piece of good fortune, strained every nerve to make the most of it. In the midst of the effusiveness of one obituary there slips a reference which illuminates Charles Shaw Lefevre's hard sense of public competition, and perhaps more than a trace of a watchful and tiring anxiety – he had, it was written, a 'quick perception of every man's character.'[38] If this tough, successful, social and political climber had a warmer, less combative side to his character, it would most likely be displayed within his home and family circle.

CHAPTER IV

Enter Three Sons

Though Helena Lefevre survived her husband, John, for twenty-six years, there is practically nothing available which would add to or modify her niece's description of her severely virtuous nature. In 1806, when she was 71, her portrait was painted by Edridge, showing her holding a magnifying glass while teaching her youngest grandson to read. The *Reading Mercury* in its obituary of Charles, could only recall, courteously, his 'venerable mother-in-law.'[1] Nor is it clear whether she lived always with Helena and Charles, after her husband died at Old Ford, or whether she for some of the time kept an establishment of her own. A document referring to her will, dated June 1816, defines her as 'formerly of Old Ford in the County of Middlesex but late of Heckfield Place in the county of Southampton.'[2] She died in the family's house at 9 Whitehall Place, and was buried, from St Martin-in-the-Fields, near her husband in the churchyard at West Ham. One might well imagine her exercising a rather stern, grandmotherly influence over her daughter's children, who were respectively 21, 19 and 15, when she died; but none of their surviving papers mentions her.

Of her daughter, Helena Shaw Lefevre, we have greater, though still modest, knowledge, and what we have suggests that she was a much more worldly woman. John Hodgkin, a prominent Quaker who was a contemporary legal colleague and close friend of Helena's son John, remembered her in her early fifties as:

> a very superior woman. She was a good linguist, a great reader, and took a lively interest in political and general affairs. She was a capital illustration of the saying that women make men. The success in life both of Charles and John [her sons] was pre-eminently due to the qualities both inherited from their mother; and to her skill in grouping around her the first characters of the time, both the aristocracy of talent and the talent of the aristocracy.[3]

And this view of her is not incompatible with the recollection, in 1881, of her then elderly daughter-in-law, Lady Emily Shaw Lefevre. Emily and her husband, John, lived with Helena for a short while after their marriage in 1824, and Emily remembered her as 'a very stately, very clever old lady – very literary. I was greatly alarmed at her but later on learnt to know what a kind and good heart she had.'[4] Charles Shaw Lefevre obviously had married not only a wealthy heiress but an intelligent, educated woman and a very capable hostess, whose social polish must have been a major asset. Not that Charles was lacking in grace: his geniality may have been calculated, but his surviving letters are not inelegant, he owned and played two valuable violins, and he was confidently at ease in society.[5] Mary Russell Mitford's attribution of 'roughness of manner' on Charles' part has to be read with due scepticism – though one can well believe that he retained a native Yorkshire directness.

It is from Mary Russell Mitford's mother that we have kinder, if mildly amused reports of Charles and Helena entertaining friends in the country. Charles' height – and perhaps Helena's – was no doubt responsible for the Mitford family's playful reference to them as Gog and Magog. In a letter to her daughter in 1802 Mrs Mitford describes how, after a concert in Reading, she and her husband were invited to Heckfield Place:

> The night was dry, though cold, and, being moonlight, our drive was a very pleasant one; and we reached their truly hospitable mansion before twelve. Sandwiches, negus, etc., was immediately brought in, and after half an hour's pleasant chat, we separated for the night. I cannot attempt to detail what an agreeable day we had on Friday. The gentlemen dedicated the morning to field sports: the ladies accompanied me round the grounds, and afterwards we took a ride round Lord Rivers' park before we dressed for dinner, when there was an addition to our members of a Mr. Milton, his wife and two daughters; the youngest of whom, Miss Fanny Milton, is a very lively, pleasant young woman.[6]

Four years later, and only a few weeks before the unfortunate incident which so incensed Mary Russell Mitford, her mother gave another view of two Helenas and a convalescent Charles at home:

> I . . . did but just get in time to Heckfield Place. The two ladies received me in great spirits. Mr. Lefevre got down to his own room the day before, and Mrs. S.L. had been out a short airing with him in the carriage. We were soon informed dinner was upon the Table . . . in the dining room. We had some delightful eels at the top, soup in the middle, and a haunch of Lord Stowell's venison at the bottom, a boiled chicken on my side, and what was on the other I do not recollect. Some venison was sent in to Gog, but he thought it very bad, and sent for some chicken. We had after, a brace of partridge at top, a very fine rabbit at the bottom, a dish of pease in the middle, tipsey-cake on one side, and grape tart on the other.

Except some pease, I dined on the fish and venison, and tasted nothing else. Their greenhouse grapes . . . are admirable, and we had some very good peaches, a pine, pears and walnuts. The pine, not being tasted, Mrs. Lefevre ordered it to be put in my carriage, with many apologies for its not being so large as she could have wished . . . Magog, who had gone to visit her good man, returned to say that Mr. L hoped I would excuse his deshabille, and begged we would take tea and coffee in his room, and on the old lady ringing again for the butler to tell him to take it thither at the hour she had ordered, he told her his master had directed him to bring it in immediately, so we repaired thither without delay. I am happy to say our good friend looks better than I expected, and was in excellent spirits.[7]

With such a diet and even a moderate liking for port, it is hardly surprising that Charles suffered from gout. But the richness of their table was only one instance of the lifestyle that the family could afford. They kept a yacht of some forty or fifty tons at Cowes, and in the summer months 'entertained a great many people on board and constantly took people out for the day'. That was in the years from about 1810 to 1816, and was a risky business, first because there were privateers in the area, which made it unsafe to go out of sight of the coast; and second because the crew took to making secret trading expeditions on their own account, which led Charles to dismiss the captain and sell the yacht.

Little is known about the Shaw Lefevres' social life in London, but at Heckfield there seems to have been a constant flow of guests. This continued after Charles' death, partly because his eldest son was equally hospitable and partly because Helena maintained many friendships, including a particularly intimate one with her neighbour in Whitehall Place, the rich, widowed Mrs Braithwaite, who in the early 1820s spent several months at a time at Heckfield. The two ladies each had 'a pair of handsome black horses, and they used to drive the four together' – but this memory of Emily Shaw Lefevre's led her to recall the quarrel which had ruined the friendship and which was attributed to mischief made by Helena's senior daughter-in-law, Emma Laura Shaw Lefevre, née Whitbread.[8] By then, the second generation of Shaw Lefevres was in vigorous young manhood.

Charles and Helena had four sons, of whom the third died in infancy. It was a small number of children by the standards of the period, and the boys came into the world at moderate intervals – in July 1794, January 1797, August 1800, and July 1802. The two eldest were born in Bedford Square, the two youngest at Heckfield, the third was christened Henry Francis, and lived only for six months; the same names were given to the fourth child. As much of the rest of this book tries to show, the three who reached maturity were a remarkable trio, not only in their careers but even in their life spans, which together totalled over 254 years. Charles Shaw Lefevre, later Viscount

THE SHAW LEFEVRES

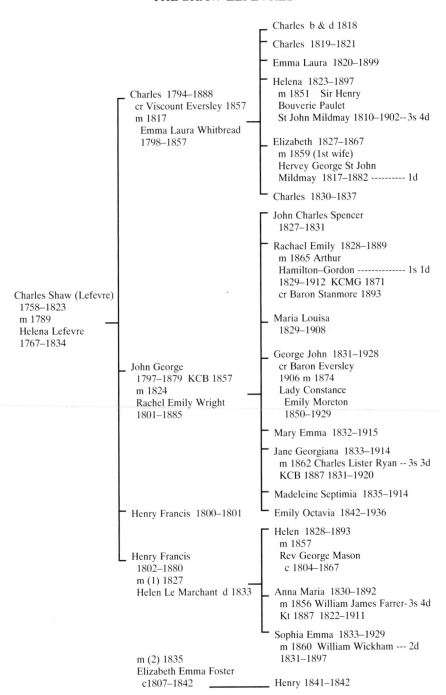

Charles b & d 1818

Charles 1819–1821

Emma Laura 1820–1899

Helena 1823–1897
  m 1851   Sir Henry
  Bouverie Paulet
  St John Mildmay 1810–1902-- 3s 4d

Elizabeth 1827–1867
  m 1859 (1st wife)
  Hervey George St John
  Mildmay 1817–1882 ---------- 1d

Charles 1830–1837

Charles 1794–1888
  cr Viscount Eversley 1857
  m 1817
  Emma Laura Whitbread
  1798–1857

John Charles Spencer
  1827–1831

Rachael Emily 1828–1889
  m 1865 Arthur
  Hamilton–Gordon -------------- 1s 1d
  1829–1912 KCMG 1871
  cr Baron Stanmore 1893

Maria Louisa
  1829–1908

George John 1831–1928
  cr Baron Eversley
  1906 m 1874
  Lady Constance
  Emily Moreton
  1850–1929

Mary Emma 1832–1915

Jane Georgiana 1833–1914
  m 1862 Charles Lister Ryan -- 3s 3d
  KCB 1887 1831–1920

Madeleine Septimia 1835–1914

Emily Octavia 1842–1936

Charles Shaw (Lefevre)
1758–1823
m 1789
Helena Lefevre
1767–1834

John George
  1797–1879 KCB 1857
  m 1824
  Rachel Emily Wright
  1801–1885

Henry Francis 1800–1801

Helen 1828–1893
  m 1857
  Rev George Mason
  c 1804–1867

Anna Maria 1830–1892
  m 1856 William James Farrer- 3s 4d
  Kt 1887 1822–1911

Sophia Emma 1833–1929
  m 1860 William Wickham --- 2d
  1831–1897

Henry Francis
  1802–1880
  m (1) 1827
  Helen Le Marchant d 1833

m (2) 1835
Elizabeth Emma Foster
c1807–1842

Henry 1841–1842

Eversley, lived to be 94; the middle brother, John George, reached 82; and the youngest, Henry Francis, died at 78.

There are only a couple of stories of their early childhood. One is about Charles, who must have been no more than ten when – on his way to visit the circus – he was taken briefly into the House of Commons, where he heard Fox speak and, apparently much impressed, asked his father, 'Why that gentleman was in such a passion?' The other story tells how, when George III came to see his former aide-de-camp, Sir William Pitt, and Lady Pitt, at Highfield, near Heckfield Place, and visited an inn at Hartford Bridge on his way to Weymouth, a Shaw Lefevre child was once 'found sitting on the lap of one of the Princesses, who was stuffing him with sweetmeats', and how Charles was kissed by the monarch himself and John taken 'a great deal of notice of' by the Royal Family.[9] These were early introductions to politics and pomp.

Unlike the Shaws, the Shaw Lefevres were not destined for the middle class modesties of a Wakefield or Leeds Grammar School. Charles went to Winchester; but John, after beginning at Dr Faithfull's establishment at Warfield, was enrolled in Dr Keate's house at Eton, 'on account of his health', Keate apparently offering a gentler environment than was provided for the Wykehamists![10] Charles and Henry seem to have been robust boys, but John was sickly from the outset, and was always delicate. But however delicate he was, Charles and Helena never went to see him. He was packed off to school on the coach and once, when he was 12 and Eton was suddenly closed because of an outbreak of scarlet fever, he got as far as:

Bagshot on my way to Heckfield and then heard that my father and mother were at Burley Manor near Ringwood. I had no money – I did not know how to go on, but the landlord at Bagshot who was in my father's yeomanry took me under his protection and furnished me with an open letter to all the inns on the road and I reached Burley safely to the great surprise of my parents.[11]

Henry was also entrusted to the care of Dr Keate. School years passed, seemingly without undue incident, and in due course each of the three sons entered Trinity College, Cambridge, in the wake of their father and grandfather.

Charles, whose headmaster, Mr Goddard, claimed as a boy of 'very high stamp' – though he regretted that he was a Whig[12] – matriculated in 1811 and graduated in 1815, being admitted to Lincoln's Inn in the same year. He took his MA and was called to the Bar in 1819 but, like his father, the law was not for long to be his calling. Charles was not by nature scholarly, and while being a thoroughly competent student, he did not leave any particular reputation behind him at Trinity. His enthusiasms were those of a well-to-do countryman; he had the country in his bones in a way which, one senses, his father never did. The younger Charles, to his far distant dying day, simply loved the life of Heckfield and its rural setting. He hunted – on occasion, through the family connection with the Powys, with the Pytchley – and he became, and remained, one of the best shots in his county. So keen a sportsman was he

> that his serious mother, slow to discern the greater qualities of her first born son, sorrowfully observed, 'As for Charles, he is only fit to be a gamekeeper.' But whatever her estimate of his intellect, she was assuredly proud of his person, as he grew to be one of the tallest and handsomest men of his generation.[13]

So handsome and so well-placed a young man must have been kept prominently in the sights of many mothers anxiously seeking husbands for their daughters, and was doubtless attractive to many of the eligible young ladies themselves. It is not surprising that he married at a relatively early age, just before he reached 23. We do not know what degree of parental manoeuvring was involved, but neither Charles nor his parents could have made, in worldly terms, a shrewder choice of partner than Emma Laura Whitbread. Emma was the youngest child of Samuel Whitbread II, that reluctant brewer whose radical politics and extensive charitable concerns were backed by his enormous wealth. Emma was 17 when her remarkable father committed suicide, in 1815, and it may be that his death influenced her family and herself in favour of an early marriage. There had been business connections between Samuel Whitbread's father and John Lefevre through Currie's bank, and Charles Shaw Lefevre, senior, must have maintained contact with Samuel II, in the City as well as at Westminster, where they were contemporaries. Shaw Lefevre was clearly to the political right of Whitbread during the former's Addingtonian years, but Charles' leftward move would have drawn them somewhat closer together.

Whatever the extent of the two families' relationship, it was far more than a nodding acquaintanceship. Just before their father's death, the two Whitbread sons, William Henry and Samuel III, who were only a year or two younger than Charles, had gone with him to Scotland on a walking tour of the Highlands and to call on Sir Walter Scott, with whom they talked for three hours in Edinburgh.[14] And it is very likely that Emma was intimate with the Shaw Lefevres well before her marriage. She was a great friend of Henry, Charles' younger brother, who was just four years younger than herself: they 'used to have races as to which could eat their apple charlotte the faster' – surely a competition more likely in earlier years than in the later teens.[15] From the young Charles Shaw Lefevre's point of view, his future mother-in-law was at least as significant a symbol of his own political prospects as the example and fame of his bride's late father, for Lady Elizabeth Whitbread was the sister of the second Earl Grey, who was to resist the lure of his remote Northumbrian fiefdom sufficiently to become the Prime Minister whose ultra-aristocratic Whig administration would carry through Parliament and Palace the Great Reform Bill of 1832. Just for good measure, Charles' walking companions, who were to become his brothers-in-law, were soon to be members of Parliament, while Emma's elder sister had married a future Earl Waldegrave, though she herself did not live to become his countess.

Charles and Emma were married at St Margaret's, Westminster, on 24 June 1817, by the Hon. and Revd Edward Grey, Emma's uncle. The marriage settlement provided annuities of £1,250 for the couple, drawn from trust funds totalling £25,000 set up by their families earlier. £10,000 of that capital remained intact and was the subject of legal moves to safeguard it in 1829.[16] There may well have been a further dowry, but whatever the material advantages of the union, the couple's youth and the few relics of their early years together give some support to the notion that this was also a genuine love match. The handful of poems and letters which Charles wrote to Emma before and after their marriage are florid and immature, but nonetheless touchingly tender and sincere.[17] Regrettably, the initial happiness of the union was to be marred by the death of children, and in later years the couple's marital relationship deteriorated. They presented Charles and Helena with their first grandson in May 1818, but the baby lived for less than two months. A second son was born in September 1819, but he, too, died, in July 1821. Both boys had been christened Charles. Two daughters, the first named Emma Laura after her mother and the second called Helena after her grandmother, were born in 1820 and 1823 respectively, and they were the only grandchildren living when Charles, senior, died.

During these years the young Charles practised a little law, but discovered an inherited political interest. From the beginning he threw off some – but by no means all – of his father's independent stance, became more of a thoroughgoing Whig, and expended a lot of effort on the successful campaign of his brother-in-law, Samuel Whitbread III, to win an election for the county of Middlesex in 1820. But he resisted an invitation to take over his father's seat for Reading when Charles, senior, gave it up in that year. Since 1815 he had been a shareholder and director of the Sun Fire Office, alongside his father, and would continue in that role until 1841.[18]

Charles and Helena, having seen their eldest son married in 1817, were to experience another kind of family triumph in the following year. John, their second son, was quite a different character from his elder brother. Despite Hodgkin's opinion that both Charles' and John's success reflected the special virtues of their mother, Charles, in longer perspective, was seemingly an almost undiluted Shaw. He was tough but less combative than his father, perhaps because he had not had to fight his way up. He had a serene confidence, showing itself to the world as warm geniality, combined with acute judgement of men and events, and an uncomplicated but never simplistic authority and power of decision.

John was far more his mother's son. He was a gentle, earnest intellectual; sensitive, timorous and anxious – the last two qualities deriving most probably from poor health – but fiercely ambitious. He was a classic middle child, always a little uncertain of himself and so self-driven that we would apply to him now the inelegant title of workaholic. He was to become a polymath, but wanted to move in the world of affairs, so that his remarkable career straddles the law, the hustings, the bureaucracy, the academy and the library, in a fascinating but not wholly successful search for self-fulfilment. At Eton his tutor, Revd William Brodrick, felt that he 'was marked by great religious tenderness and susceptibility.'[19] As a boy he must have shown his promise, just as clearly as his health gave cause for concern: his father would not allow him to take music lessons because he thought they would overtax him and interfere with his more academic work.

At Cambridge, where he inherited Charles' rooms in Mutton Court Corner at Trinity (since given the more salubrious name of Angel Court) John was, despite being limited to a maximum of six hours' work a day, a brilliant student. We have vivid, inside views of his early *annus mirabilis*, 1818, which reveal not only the personal and collegiate competitiveness of a university much more rigorous than in his father's day – and half a world away from the Cambridge of George Shaw – but also John's own acute apprehensions of failure. The climactic, gladiatorial examination scene is described in a letter written by John's close friend and future brother-in-law, Denis le Marchant, in January 1818:

The examination on Monday was equal – the candidates for Senior Wrangler were Hinde of St. John's, Malkin, Lefevre, Pope of Emanuel, Greenwell Bennet and Hutchins of Pembroke all good men and true. Hinde was considered certain by everyone – bets were even in his favour – he had read his Newton four years ago and had been employed here in getting up his subjects – after him the others were considered nearly equal – Lefevre was put down for 4 and if very lucky third – on Monday evening Lefevre Hinde and Malkin were considered the favourites – Tuesday, things continued on the same equality with the exception of Hinde who very decidedly excelled the others – Greenwood and Pope vanished but on the Evening papers Lefevre totally failed and a man named Hawkes of Trinity a follower of Mr. Simeon particularly distinguished himself in the Evening Problems – on Wednesday Morning Lefevre still continued to descend doing only 2 Problems his Antagonists proportionably rising – he was then put down by all the sect of Malkin as 8 or 9 Wrangler & indeed we were all very melancholy about him – his own state of mind it is impossible to describe – his health was considerably impaired and his failure seemed inevitable but on Wednesday Evening he again rose and excelled every one – on Thursday the day of rest he was excused the Senate house on account of his ill health – Rose and I drank tea with him and did all we could to console him – he said he only cared for his father's disappointment – *he knew* he had done badly and had sent up less papers than the others – his modesty and timidity are so great that we hoped he was deceived particularly as the Moderators declared that all the men had done remarkably well and it was one of the best years they had ever known – on Friday morning to our utter astonishment Hinde Malkin and Lefevre were bracketed for Senior Wranglership everyone looked aghast – all feared – the friends of Malkin were confident of his success – Lefevre was more delighted than any man I ever saw – Third was more than he ever expected and the examination had been throughout particularly unfavourable to him from the little book work set. Problems having been chiefly in the papers – he cared little for the result – the examination on Friday was very high – the three competitors each wrote out every question but Lefevre's papers were so elegant and superior to the rest that at ½ past 10 he was declared *Senior Wrangler*.[20]

That was on 24 January 1818, John's 21st birthday. His own reactions to the drama are best given in his own words. Two days before, he had written:

My dear Father & Mother,
I do not like to send you unwelcome news but I would advise you to prepare for the worst. You cannot conceive my present state of mind. I am and have been so miserable that I should consider myself very lucky if I escape without a serious illness.
I did very ill on Tuesday in the daytime and became so exhausted and unwell in the evening that I could hardly do anything. In short what will become of me I know not. I have been treated with great kindness by everybody – Peacock one of the examiners who is a fellow of Trinity Coll – seeing that I looked ill – got me out from attendance without application to-day – All the other men were forced to go four times and have their names called; the Paley in which they are said to be examined, is a matter of form, as they are only kept in the Senate house 1 or 3 minutes.
I do not wish to make you needlessly anxious but I assure you that I know I shall fall, but how far, nobody can tell.

On the following day he felt better:

I cannot be lower than third. I do not look for more as I have been ill and unlucky all the time. I must now stay for Smith's prize & I would be obliged to you not to wait for me at Heckfield as my stay is very uncertain. Malkin Hinde and myself have been at work 7 hours to-day, there is great interest excited as there has not been an instance of 3 contending for Senior Wrangler for 4 or 5 years.

Half an hour after noon on Friday, 24 January, John wrote to his elder brother a single line, almost defiantly triumphant:

> Dear Charles
> I am Senior Wrangler
> John Lefevre

Four days later he wrote again to his father, using the same formula of expected failure and poor health in the context of the examination for the Smith's Prize, and complaining that he was 'tired as a dog . . . we have had 8 hours every day.'[21]

But, of course, he won the prize. It was a marvellous double victory in what all the dons agreed was an exceptionally strong field. An Eton contemporary, quoted in a congratulatory letter to John's mother, recalled how at school, 'When I used to attack [John] he would always say: "But for all that, I should like to be Senior Wrangler at Cambridge."'[22] He was, in fact, the first Etonian to achieve that status, and was celebrated by a fellow Cambridge student as being 'the *superlatively* great man of his year.'[23] Within his family, his academic success was credited with having cured his father of a fit of gout.

There is a danger that the clear streak of invalidism, the strong hint of hypochondria, in John Shaw Lefevre, could be seen as implying that he had an irritable, heavily self-pitying disposition. But the evidence of many is quite to the contrary. One of his most insightful friends, John Hodgkin, whom he met first shortly after leaving Cambridge, described him as indeed suffering feeble health and being, in appearance, 'thin and sallow', but 'gentle, playful, almost ladylike in his manner', and likely to have been taken superficially for 'a person of light accomplishments.' He had, however, 'the eye of pure intellect' his style was 'sprightly' and 'his wisdom had more of the flame of wit and somewhat of the peculiar neatness which marks the best specimens of French literature and science.'[24] Nor was John an impractical swot, incapable or unreliable in any real emergency. In the late summer of 1817 he had spent some weeks studying with a mathematics coach, Mr Jacob, and a group of fellow students, at Ilfracombe on the North Devon coast. One of those students was Alexander D'Arblay, son of Fanny Burney, whose mother came down to be with him. One day Madame D'Arblay and her dog were cut off by the tide at Wildersmouth, and were rescued as a result of John Shaw Lefevre's active and very competent response to a call for help from Alexander. Nearly thirty years later Madame D'Arblay's *Life and Letters* were published: some time afterwards, John was at a breakfast party at Macaulay's when, to his great embarrassment, his host (who was his contemporary at Trinity) read to his guests Madame D'Arblay's highly dramatized account of the incident, with her closing assertion that, 'To Mr. Le Fevre . . . I probably owe my life.'[25]

In 1819 John was elected to a fellowship of Trinity, and like his father before him, retained it until his marriage. Fellows' incomes had increased quite considerably since the 1780s, and John received about £170 during each year of his tenure. But he went out of residence on 2 October 1919, and it is unlikely that he spent any considerable spells in Cambridge over the next five years.[26] He lived for several months after leaving Trinity with his parents at Marseilles, whence his father had gone in search of health, and passed the time studying Italian and Modern Greek, and in taking lessons in drawing. He was to master many other languages during the rest of his life. But as the second son, without the assured future of his elder brother and needing to earn his living, he entered the Inner Temple, and was taken into George Harrison's chambers in 1821–2. It was there that he fell in with John Hodgkin, who observed him closely and thought of him, in retrospect, as:

> a man who sees a deep truth by intuition, who looks through an entire process to the end, and reaches the result at a glance, yet without anything approaching to a guess . . . this was . . . mainly the result of an intense concentration of his whole mental power upon the one object before him, than of any really distinct quality of mind – and yet it did at times appear . . . almost like a sixth sense.[27]

Before these valuable mental capacities were to be employed in public settings, John was to use them over ten hard years in learning and practising the trade of conveyancing; but he also took time and opportunity to establish his own family. In 1822 he accompanied his father to Buxton, where Charles took the waters. Among other visitors was a Nottingham banker, Ichabod Wright of Mapperley Hall, with his wife and at least one of their family of thirteen surviving children – a fourteenth had died in infancy. The unmarried daughter who accompanied them was Rachel Emily, who was to remember that month in Buxton as being

> most eventful for me for it was there that I first met Mr. Lefevre. He was there with his father at the same time that we were and we sat opposite at the Table d'hote. He was alone with his father who was very gouty. He was introduced to me by a Mr. Lamb at a little dance in the Hotel. He had taken his degree and was a Fellow of Trinity. I said of him 'That gentleman must have been in the West Indies he looks so ill.'[28]

It was the unplanned beginning of the longest and probably the happiest of the Shaw Lefevre partnerships.

In the years around 1820, while Charles and John were branching out towards family life, politics and law, their younger brother, Henry Francis was, in turn, at Cambridge. Henry is the most elusive, the least documented, of all the male Shaw Lefevres, and because of his eventual great financial success, the lack of evidence is particularly tantalizing. As a child he had spent a good deal of time at Burley, of which he was particularly fond, and where he rode the half-wild New Forest ponies in the intervals of being tutored by his father's steward, a dissenting minister called Thomas Eyre, before he was sent to Eton. He was admitted to Trinity in 1819 and matriculated in the following year; but, like Charles, he left no special reputation behind him. He was 'a gay young man who used to enjoy life'[29]: his brother John, preparing his fiancée to meet his brothers, wrote of 'my Charles' vanity of which he has a little, being very handsome and *comme il faut* – and Henry's cassowary form and laughing visage, for he has been continuously laughing since he heard of *our* intentions.'[30] Poor Henry, he would need his resolute cheerfulness, for much of his life was to be no laughing matter.

Thus were placed the three young men as they grew to a first maturity in the fifteen years after Waterloo. They were very privileged people, but the economic and social conditions in which the great majority of their fellow citizens lived were harsh, and the public tensions which arose under an unsympathetic government were all too often released violently. These were the years from Peterloo to Captain Swing, when in quiet, rural England the burning ricks lit up the skies at night, and when a very rough justice filled the ships with wretched human cargoes bound for Australia. Charles Shaw Lefevre, senior, was among those who saw and accepted – if largely out of self-interest – the need for constitutional reform; but substantial landowners like himself, who were also the people responsible for local administration and enforcement of law, could not have been unaffected by the fears and real physical dangers of living through those bad years in the exposed, unhappy countryside.

Though there is no tangible evidence to quote, one wonders whether some part of Charles' increasing debility may have been due as much to the stresses of Heckfield and Basingstoke as to any major worries at Westminster and Reading. Certainly he had health and strength enough to fight and win convincingly the election of 1818, but thereafter he began to fail rapidly. He cast his last vote in the Commons on 18 May 1819 and later in the year, as we have seen, he travelled to France with Helena and John. Helena kept a journal which is careful and precise about the sightseeing, but says nothing of their personal life. For a while Charles, junior, was able to reassure his father's constituents that their Member of Parliament was regaining his health, but in the winter of 1819-20 it had become clear that he could not continue. In a letter from his eldest son to the *Reading Mercury*, published on 28 February 1820, it was announced that he would not stand again.

From then onwards there is a peculiar lacunae in the records, and the circumstances of Charles' last days are unknown save in bare outline. Whatever the exact sequence of events, Charles Shaw Lefevre died at his house in Whitehall Place on 26 April 1823, in his 65th year. His granddaughter, Sophia Wickham, was to tell her daughter, a century later, that he died as a result of being given an overdose of colchicum by a well-known physician who introduced the drug as a remedy for gout. Only a few published obituaries are available, and there is so complete an absence of personal reminiscence or condolence that we must assume that family reticence led to destruction of all private expressions of grief and sympathy.

There is a claim in the family papers that Charles Shaw Lefevre was offered a baronetcy by the Prince Regent, and that he refused it on the grounds that he had done nothing to deserve such an honour.[31] Whether it is strictly true or not, it is a good story with which to take leave of this strong but enigmatic character. For Charles's refusal could be interpreted as illustrating several sides of his personality. Did he refuse because the offer was part of a political strategy to which he was honestly resistant? Or did he refuse because he thought a baronetcy was too modest, and preferred to wait in hopes of a peerage? Or was his refusal, as it would be more charitable to suppose, a reflection of some genuine humility, an expression of his professional self-respect and his streak of Yorkshire independence, stiffened, perhaps, by Helena's inherited regard for the severe traditions of Huguenot thrift, rectitude and discipline? No doubt, as would fit the image of a competent politician, the reality was more ambiguous, and not the less reputable because of its ambiguity. The politics of Charles' time were more complex and difficult than at many periods of British history. He showed in his career a lively capacity for seizing opportunities when they came along, for consolidating his winnings, and for balancing – quite impressively – his vision of self-interested independence with a shrewd appreciation of the need to respond to contemporary social pressures. Of his class and his era he may well have been of above average stature; as private persons, he and Helena could legitimately take pride in the three sons for whose futures they had provided such sound foundations.

CHAPTER V

Families, 1823–1834

The matriarch, Helena Shaw Lefevre, lived for eleven years after losing her husband. When she died, in August 1834, her three sons were all family men – though the youngest, Henry, had by then been a widower for eighteen months – and were all settled into the ways in which they would go for the rest of their working lives. While the three brothers and their households lived in apparent harmony and had some shared concerns, only Charles, the new head of the family, remained a genuine devotee of country life. His two younger brothers showed no real liking for, and no professional interest in, agriculture or rural pursuits. They were urban men who had to establish themselves and earn a good deal more than what their relatively small shares of the parental capital would provide if, as was obvious, they wanted to be sufficiently well-to-do to live and have influence in the privileged strata of power and wealth. Charles, despite a long and prestigious career at Westminster, was happiest at Heckfield; John almost always had some place outside London, but he lacked the will and the interest to focus attention on being other than a metropolitan person; while Henry seems to have been totally absorbed in the City, and lived for most of his adult life in Belgravia and Mayfair.

These years of their early married lives, of the rearing of children, and of their initial political, professional and business endeavours, were years when the country was rapidly developing an industrial economy and when the population was growing at a very high rate. Both factors produced major social and political pressures which erupted into occasional violence, seen by some as approaching revolution, though in retrospect it is argued that such fears were much exaggerated. The climax of the period was the Reform Bill of 1832 – that strategic constitutional retreat which a dramatically bare majority in the House of Commons and a determined Whig government imposed on a reluctant ruling class, thereby saving the bulk of that class's collective power for at least another generation. Charles and John, while following their own lines of development, were to be enmeshed in the politics of reform. Both were strong supporters of the Whig governments of 1830 onwards. Charles entered Parliament in 1830, John in 1832; but whereas that was the beginning of an unbroken term of twenty-seven years for Charles, John was quickly unseated because of irregularities in his election. John, however, was much involved in the progress of the reform legislation as a backroom boy. Henry kept away from politics, but through a banking connection may have affected, just marginally, his brothers' adventures. All that was to come several years after their father died. Much of their futures and of their characters were shaped in the 1820s.

The young master of Heckfield took his new responsibilities quietly. Though he had enjoyed wealth and status since birth, Charles nonetheless followed his father's example of abandoning the law and spending several years entrenching himself locally. We have seen already that he was keen and able to extend his land holdings and to enlarge his home. He also took his place as a magistrate and was elected by the corporation of Basingstoke to succeed his father as Recorder, though that office was abolished by the Municipal Act of 1835. He picked up his father's enthusiasm for leading the North Hampshire Yeomanry. In these legal, military and other local contexts Charles was to come into business and neighbourly contact with the Duke of Wellington, to whom a grateful nation had, in 1817, awarded the estate of Strathfield Saye, a mile or two from Heckfield, and who was Lord Lieutenant of Hampshire from 1820 until his death in 1852.

The Duke kept his eye on the county's affairs as best he could, given his national activities, and not surprisingly he was less in touch than he would have wished with local politics during the turbulent years of reform and particularly during his two spells at 10 Downing Street. He found it convenient and pleasant to spend the winter months, from November to January, at Strathfield Saye, not least because he liked fox hunting and was the major financial supporter of the local hunt.[1] He and Charles were far apart, politically, but in the local administration of justice they had limited, polite dealings, especially about the filling of places in the magistracy. On Yeomanry affairs there was a good deal of co-operation – the North Hants troops declined, were disbanded and then re-established during the Duke's lieutenancy, and Shaw Lefevre was prominent and persistent as their colonel. He and the Duke exchanged a lot of formal correspondence, and were often in touch with the Home Secretary of the day.[2]

Privately, there were a few adjustments of land holdings between Heckfield and Strathfield Saye, and the families met socially, at least in the normal routine of genteel country life. Charles' sister-in-law Emily remembered visiting Wellington's home with Helena, to call on the Duchess, in or about the year 1826:

> We found her standing before a large Bible on an easel. She said it was always ready on the easel whenever she had a spare moment. She took us round the grounds to a field where she shewed us the celebrated chestnut horse (Marengo) I think ridden in Spain – I am not sure but I think also at Waterloo. The horse looked old and infirm – she said it would remain there

as long as it lived. . . . I did not know then what an unhappy [sic] that poor woman was, or how badly the Duke treated her.[3]

Charles and Emma had lived briefly after their marriage at Burley, which was made available to them by John, to whom the manor had been transferred as part of his inheritance;[4] but they returned to Heckfield, long before Helena was widowed. In London, Charles occupied 99 Great Russell Street for a few years, but in due course took over 9 Whitehall Place, which was to be his and Emma's home in town until the early 1830s.

Their comfortable prosperity cannot have reconciled them to their greatest shared tragedies – the loss of three sons. Charles and Emma had six children, three boys and three girls, but only the girls survived childhood. As we have seen, the first two boys, both christened Charles, had lived but briefly and died before the end of 1821. The three girls – Emma Laura, Helena and Elizabeth – arrived in 1820, 1823 and 1827 respectively. Two years later, Charles suffered so serious a bout of bilious fever as to endanger his life, but he recovered, and in 1830 his third and last son was born. This was just as his father was about to begin his parliamentary career, and must have seemed a particularly happy omen. But, to take our story a little way ahead, the young Charles lived only until 1837. He died after a long struggle with measles. There was to be no male heir. Sophia Wickham, Charles Shaw Lefevre's niece, was of the opinion that the three boys had 'died of the doctor – drugs and starvation being very much the fashion of the day.'[5] Be that as it may, the loss of them clouded Charles's and Emma's lives, and must have contributed in some measure towards what was seen later by several observers as an unsatisfactory partnership.

We left John Shaw Lefevre at Buxton in 1822, just meeting Emily Wright. There is in later papers a slight, if ambiguous, hint of some immediate mutual attraction, but there is no sign of any attempts on either side to ensure any further meetings. No doubt the illness and death of the elder Charles Shaw Lefevre would in any case have interrupted the smooth process of a growing intimacy. But it is almost certain that mere chance brought John and Emily together again. In 1824 the Wright family took 75 Harley Street for the London season, and throughout May and June of that year life for the still spinster daughters was a succession of social events, successful for Emily's sister Henrietta, who enjoyed and accepted a proposal of marriage from Henry Edward John Howard, a future bishop, while riding in the dicky of an open carriage on an expedition to Dulwich. Emily's most persistent host was a Mr Plumer, at whose house one evening she found John Shaw Lefevre as a fellow dinner guest. John was also present at 'the last agreeable party' of the season, after having dined at home with the Wrights on 9 July. The next we hear of them was early in November, when John arrived to be the guest of the Wrights at Mapperley Hall, a few miles from Nottingham.[6] Mapperley had been built by Mr Wright in the last years of the eighteenth century, in part of Sherwood Forest, when a historian of the county thought it 'a good house, which . . . promises, in a few years, to be a pleasing embellishment to the Mansfield and Southwell road.'[7] It was a good house for John on this occasion: he had come, clearly, to win Emily, and the progress of the campaign has been recorded with endearing simplicity.

A day or so after he had settled in, John appeared in the room where Emily was teaching a younger sister. 'He came and shoved a little piece of paper before me, on which was written "I love you"', Emily recalled. This had the predictable effect of making Emily rush upstairs to an elder sister for advice. All she received, however, was the question, 'Do you think you would be happy?' and had to consider the problem overnight. The next day, when a family group went riding, John declared himself to Emily: 'He believed he had been a very good son and brother and he was quite sure he should make a good husband [and] he asked me if I would be his wife.' There are two versions of what happened next. According to one of the Wright sisters, 'Emily was so frightened that she galloped off home – he tried to follow but not being a rider, could not keep up.' The less amusing reality is probably that given by Emily herself, who claimed that she rode on to tell her father, who then sent her home with a sister while he interrogated her suitor. When Emily reached the house, she told her mother the news and then went to lie down, in which recumbent and apprehensive posture she was found by her father. Ichabod had no doubts: he had 'seen enough' of John to know that his daughter 'should be very happy'. And so the engagement was sealed. A few days later John returned to London, while at Mapperley great preparations were begun for a wedding at the end of the year.

Negotiations about a marriage settlement were friendly and straight-forward. John told Ichabod of his financial prospects, which clearly were dominated by the resources and attitudes of Helena Shaw Lefevre. John would be given '£15,000 in 3%s now', and his mother would leave him property worth '£1600 a year perfectly unfettered'. And John had no worries about everyday living: 'As to our present income that will be a matter between my mother and myself – for at present I cannot make any estimate of the expense we are likely to be at – but I feel confident that Emily will have everything that can contribute to her personal comfort and happiness.' Ichabod Wright, with so many daughters, was understandably modest about the dowry: 'I wish I could give her a Fortune adequate to your expenses – I cannot – You understand it is 2500 and the same sum I shall leave her at my death. She may have more from her Mother if she survives me.' And he added, with typical sincerity and a serene confidence in his child's humility: 'I have no doubt your Profession will produce a sufficient income if you have health to pursue it and if it fails Emily will most contentedly share with you whatever you may possess. The Man and not the fortune is her object as it is mine.'

Her father was almost certainly correct in being sure of Emily's willingness to accept what life brought her with philosophic calm. She had been raised in a happy home, almost at the mid-point of a very large family, but in childhood and adolescence there had been few indulgences. Late in life she told one of her daughters of how she remembered the death of the Princess Charlotte in 1817:

> I was a girl of fifteen and I was standing in the stocks in the school room at Mapperley with an iron back board strapped . . . when my mother came into the room crying and told us of the sad event. The backboards I speak of were covered with red leather and worn for an hour or two every day by all girls at that time. We were made to kneel and curtsey in the stocks nearly every day, the feet being placed in position to turn them out. My recollections of the Stone parlour (our school-room) were not agreeable. We had buttermilk and brown bread only for supper.

This dutiful girl was not cowed, however, and in the years after she was 18 she seems to have led a pleasant social life, visiting friends and her several married brothers and sisters, going to balls and festivals, and observing the worldly scene with sensitivity and an eye for detail. Listening to Henry Brougham in court at York, she thought him, 'a most extraordinary looking man, tho' very intelligent, the muscles of his face and especially his very long turned up nose are in continual agitation twitching up and down till it is almost frightful to look at – and this increases from earnestness when he is speaking.' Nor was Emily averse to complaining on occasion that some of her male acquaintances were 'not agreeable'. And in a letter to her sister Henrietta Howard, just after her engagement to John Shaw Lefevre, she speaks with delicacy and fondness, but at the same time with a fair measure of calculated contentment:

> You will be no less surprised than we all are at the very unexpected tidings this letter will carry: so sudden a change has taken place in my thoughts and prospects that I cannot yet compose myself to say more than these few lines to you dear Henrietta who I know will participate in the feelings my other sisters and my dear father and mother have for me, and which almost overcome me. Yesterday I can hardly believe it, decided my future fate in life. God grant it may be as happy a one as my four married sisters are blessed with and I can wish no more. I feel confidence in the hope and quite happy in the prospect before me – I cannot say quite happy, so many feelings of a mixed nature seem to rush upon me – the idea so painful of parting with all I have hitherto held dearest *will* intrude. I am rejoiced that

you met your future brother-in-law before you left us. I feel certain you will find in him a kind and excellent one; my knowledge of the high esteem in which he is held by many whose opinion I value weighed much in my decision and I have the great happiness of witnessing the satisfaction and pleasure it appears to give to all around me.

But of all the documents which have survived from those last months of 1824, none is more interesting than a long letter which John wrote to Emily, describing his working life hitherto and laying bare his worldly ambitions while denying that he has any, thus unconsciously revealing a good deal of his character:

Be under no uneasiness about me – my situation and prospects are fortunately just such as to enable me to use exactly that quantity of exertion that is desirable for my health, and to render it unnecessary to do more than is prudent. I am not at all an ambitious person for I have already in a small way tasted the gratifications arising from that profession and I find that altho' the fruit is fair to look at it is dust and ashes within. My object in life is to be the centre of a circle of happiness, and to be liked not for my situation in life but for myself. I certainly was born a selfish person but by setting up the motive I have mentioned I have very much diminished this defect, for of course selfishness is quite incompatible with the attainment of these ends. I had originally intended to practise at the Chancery Bar but in the course of my education for that it was necessary for me to pass a year with a Conveyancer and I liked his employment so well that I determined to follow it. I was however prevailed upon by him to give up this determination as he was *unwise* enough to think that my prospects of distinction were greater than to make it proper for me to adopt the quieter line of the profession. In an evil hour I acceded to his 'advice' and went for a year nominally to a Chancery Barrister (Duckworth). This year I entirely wasted partly from extreme dislike to this type of practice. . . . It was not till I saw you again in London this year that I conceived it possible to recover my happiness. . . . My wish at present is to undertake what I before desired namely Conveyancing both from my inclination to that particular mode of employment and from its being less laborious and less harassing to the nerves. My legal friends still entertaining abroad notions about me desire to dissuade me from leaving the paths of ambition and I am obliged to develop my plans gradually to them – but my resolution is settled and I think I have considered the matter with far greater interest and attention than they have – so that for some years at least I shall employ myself in this way and if I find that they have not overrated me I shall use my means of exertion not to obtain distinction as a lawyer but in some other way (in Parliament for instance). Should I be right in my own estimate of myself I shall have no occasion to consider this matter but shall continue as a Conveyancer till we think we have acquired sufficient property to be thoroughly comfortable.

As to my sheet anchor being the law – as far as *worldly* prospects are concerned it is to a certain extent true for I certainly if anything happened to Maman could not maintain you in such luxury as she lives in but we should be quite sufficiently well off and I have little doubt but that if Henry continues as affectionate a brother as he is now we might keep up both Burley and Whitehall Place jointly with perfect ease or in case he should not like to be with us we might by ourselves keep up either of them without difficulty.

Five weeks after John had thus unburdened himself, he and Emily were married in the parish church of St Leodegarius at Basford, near Mapperley. Emily's sister, Nevil, had married, a few months before, a wealthy hunting parson, John Webb Edge, who conducted the wedding service on a day when the sun shone but when, after weeks of almost constant rain, the road was so bad that the party had to drive through turnip fields to the church. John's two brothers had arrived a couple of days before – John had looked forward with wry pleasure to the prospect of the thirty-four handshakes which the two would have to make between them in being introduced to the Wright family. He had also warned Emily of Charles' vanity and of Henry's pleased amusement at the idea of John and Emily marrying. As it happened, Charles was particularly well received. Nevil Webb Edge thought him 'charming, very handsome, a very fine figure, and the most good-tempered amiable, sweet countenance I ever saw – his manner so remarkably kind and pleasing to his new sister'. Henry, in her view, was not blessed with 'this prepossessing appearance and . . . is much younger', but Nevil doubted not that Emily 'will also much like him.'

John and Emily took three days to reach Burley Manor from Mapperley, stopping at Welford, Oxford and Winchester on the way. Two weeks later they went to Heckfield, and shortly afterwards to London, to take up residence in the family house, 9 Whitehall Place. A few days afterwards they were the guests of the second Earl Spencer at dinner – an event reflecting a connection which John had already made, and which was to be increasingly important not only to him, but also to his elder brother.

John had met George Spencer, third son of the second Earl, while studying in Northamptonshire with a tutor, Mr Faithful, and through George had been introduced to the Spencer family. In 1822, the two young men had travelled on the continent together, the only recorded memory of their trip being of an occasion when they fell in with a shooting party led by the King of Bavaria, and were invited to share the royal dinner under the trees. By the time of his marriage, John was on terms of easy intimacy with the Spencers; the value of this connection was proved in 1826, when the Earl proposed that John should become a confidential legal and financial auditor and adviser for the extensive Spencer estates. This was a big boost for the young conveyancer, who had been called to the Bar shortly after his wedding and only set up his own chambers at 7 Fleet Street after he took on the Spencer work.

For the next eight years – and for much longer at a reduced level of involvement – John handled the land dealings and the finances of the second and third Earls. He worked closely with them, but also through the small group of solicitors, land agents and stewards who exercised detailed control over the family properties, which were concentrated particularly in Northamptonshire and in the Wandsworth, Battersea and Wimbledon areas south-west of London. There survive hundreds of relevant letters, memoranda, accounts and the like. At times the exchanges between John and his masters were daily, even hourly – concerned with sales, leases, loans, investments, and the higher strategies of major land ownership.[8] And as the relationship grew closer, so did the intimacy of the advice sought and given on the family's affairs. For all of this work, John received a fee of £500 annually, which does not seem over generous when compared with the overall income from the estates and the size of many of the transactions. There were, however, additional compensations.

John and Emily spent the first year of their life together at 9 Whitehall Place, with Helena. Emily had to adjust to a very new environment. 'I often long for a walk in the country and to see something fresh like spring flowers: the view from my window is upon a blank wall with Northumberland House peeping above.' Helena read to her while she drew, and her mother-in-law also gave her lessons in Italian. 'John returns about 4 when we take a walk,' and then the ladies retired to a tiny sitting room on the ground floor for their 'evening hour', from which seclusion they were drawn when John 'sent down and knock[ed] at the door', no doubt to remind them of his existence. The many calls and visits which followed their marriage seem to have been succeeded by a much quieter spell. They went out 'very little' during the season, though Emily remembered one of her first big parties, at Lansdowne House, when 'my dress was pink satin and I wore beautiful diamond earrings given me as a wedding present . . . these were afterwards stolen.'

There rises from Emily's few, scattered memories, the shade of a gentle, unsophisticated young woman, not quite at ease in her strange metropolitan surroundings. She was probably rather relieved when Charles and Emma decided to move into 9 Whitehall Place, and she and John took 'a very nice comfortable house at Balham', where she had some kind friends upon whom she called frequently, 'riding on my donkey'. And though apparently much better at handling a horse than was her husband, who alarmed his family and friends with the number of riding accidents he suffered, Emily might have been happy enough with a humble donkey, for she, too, had several unpleasant misadventures with over-lively steeds.

On 27 June 1827, at Balham, a son was born and christened John Charles Spencer. He was the first of their eight children, and the only one they lost during the long span – almost fifty-five years – of their married life. Ichabod Wright, seeing his grandson at the age of 15 months, wrote in his diary that the baby was engaging, beautiful and intelligent, and it is interesting that, half a century later, both John and Emily, in their last years, recalled the little boy in similar terms: John told Augustus Hare that he was 'the dearest, most engaging child'; and Emily, when blind and within a year of her death, spoke of her first born as having been 'beautiful and engaging'.[9] They were to enjoy him for less than four years.

It was while they were at Balham, that Earl Spencer invited John to act for him, and suggested, also, that John might like to lease Terrace House, Battersea, a handsome, small seventeenth century mansion on the banks of the Thames. John, keen 'to settle at Battersea believing that I should be more useful by residing there in reference to the duties I had undertaken', bought a forty-five year lease for £3,150, and moved his family to their new home in 1828. Terrace House, still standing but now called Old Battersea House, was to be John and Emily's home for several years, and the birthplace of all but two of their children.[10] The first two daughters, Rachael Emily and Maria Louisa, were born there in 1828 and 1829.

Emily was again pregnant at the end of 1830, and John persuaded her to go with him to spend Christmas at Heckfield, leaving all three children in good health and in the care of a nurse. John was to blame himself bitterly for persuading Emily to leave them. The nurse went one day to visit her brother, who was suffering from scarlet fever, and brought the infection back to Battersea. The eldest child, John, became very ill, but only when the fever had taken a fatal hold were the parents told. They rushed back from Heckfield, but the boy died on 11 January 1831. Rachael had also been infected and was so dangerously ill that the doctor 'could only pronounce her to be living by holding a feather to her mouth.' The household was plunged into crisis and panic, the parents' concern for Rachael helping only to divert their thoughts from the loss of John. 'Maria, one year old, was removed to the Dining Room and completely shut up for a month', and Emily 'only once saw her when hearing her screams in the night from cutting teeth, I went down and lanced her gums with a penknife.' Rachael lived, but was 'a most wretched little sorrowful child . . . for some years.'[11] Fortunately, Emily survived these shocks without suffering any immediate major physical problems, though later poor health may well have been triggered by the emotional stress of those months. Her second son, George John, was safely delivered on 12 June 1831. The next two children, Mary Emma and Jane Georgiana, followed in 1832 and 1833.

The major advantages of the Spencer connection for the Shaw Lefevres were social prestige and an inevitable involvement in the political network of which the family was so important a part. The eldest son and heir to the earldom was Viscount Althorp, the formidably able though reluctant Whig politician who was to manage the Reform Bill in the House of Commons. John was not only privy to the expenditure of Spencer funds on elections, but was also to be entrusted by Althorp with the analysis of his electoral chances at Northampton, and once Reform was well and truly launched, as we shall see, he was given responsibility for a major exercise in the redrawing of constituency boundaries. Nor was John slow to respond eagerly to these challenges. As he had promised Emily, he was by no means averse to thinking of the possibility of a political career. He worked hard for the Spencers, and clearly made a good impression. By the end of 1830 Lavinia, Countess Spencer, was writing to Brougham, shortly after his appointment as Lord Chancellor, on John's behalf. She spoke in terms calculated to appeal to the new Baron's considerable ego, though not without conveying some slight note of old aristocratic mockery:

> Amongst a very few Sweets, great patronage involves a terrible dispro-
> portion of bitters, and, in confirmation of this Agro Dolce mixture, here
> I come to plague you with a petition. But it is your lot – and worried
> you must be by friend and foe, so without further preface, I will come
> to the point and leave my apology to your beautiful and encouraging
> good nature.

> Amongst your extensive and wide spreading fields of patronage allow me
> to hope that an honest and clever law friend of ours may at a proper
> opportunity find a respectable situation allotted to him by you. He is
> Lord Spencer's law agent. He is the only instance of an Etonian being a
> Senior Wrangler as I believe – and in every way he is fitted to do credit
> to any protection that you may be inclined to shew him. His character,
> attainments, and industry, will bear the strictest scrutiny, and Mr. John
> Lefevre after such investigation will be found worthy of the favour of
> Him who will be the greatest Chancellor that ever filled that high station.

> Althorp will supply to you every other detail you may require to know,
> relative to our friend, and to him I refer you, rather than annoy you with
> them in writing.[12]

As John Shaw Lefevre's old fellow student and now his brother-in-law, Denis Le Marchant, had recently become Private Secretary to Brougham, John was by no means without friends in the new Whig hierarchy. It is impossible to ignore the probability that through these new relationships, he was able to help his brother Charles's entry into politics, though Charles was launched at Westminster primarily by a much more radical aristocrat.

The youngest of the Shaw Lefevre brothers made his own contribution to the network of useful acquaintances which was to help the others in their political and governmental ventures. Henry Francis had finished at Cambridge in 1824, and at roughly the same time was admitted to Lincoln's Inn. Like his brothers, he was not attracted to the law as a lifetime occupation, but unlike them he did not even bother to qualify, and was never called to the Bar. His real interest lay in surgery, and he made a habit of attending hospitals to watch operations. However, 'surgery was not considered a profession for a gentleman', and Henry turned to banking, joining the firm of Bouverie and Antrobus. Not long afterwards, in March 1827, he married Helen Le Marchant, daughter of a famous general and brother of Denis Le Marchant who, as we have seen, was an admiring fellow student of John Shaw Lefevre, and whose sojourn at Cambridge overlapped Henry's. Almost simultaneously, Henry displaced Antrobus and was the junior partner from then on in the bank of Bouverie and Lefevre.[13]

It is reasonable to suppose that there may well have been longer connections than those of 1827 between several of the parties involved, all of whom were descendants of French, Huguenot or Channel Islands' families. Philip Pleydell-Bouverie, the fifth son of the second Earl Radnor, had begun his banking practice at the age of 25, in 1813. He had been trained by Messrs Bosanquet & Co., and operated his business from 33 Craven Street, off the Strand.[14] The second Earl Radnor and Charles Shaw Lefevre, senior, were more than nodding acquaintances at Westminster in the early years of the century,[15] while the third Earl, then Viscount Folkestone, was a fellow MP with Charles from 1801 to 1820. One might well speculate on the possibility that some of their predecessors were known to each other in the close world of the London merchants. Moreover, the two families lived in neighbouring counties – the Radnors in Wiltshire – and though the Shaw Lefevres were relative newcomers and much less extensively endowed, they would be known to each other through shared interests as landowners, agriculturalists and local administrators of justice, law and order. Moreover, in 1814, Viscount Folkestone had married, as his second wife, a daughter of the Mildmays of Dogmersfield Park, close neighbours of the Shaw Lefevres, with whom there would be future marital links. All that be as it may, Henry's first marriage, while it did not make him an active political figure, established or consolidated connections which, in the case of the Bouveries, were to be crucial for his brother Charles in 1830, and which, in the case of the Le Marchants, brought him business partners and his brother John a colleague for life – and on occasion a rival – in governmental affairs.

Unfortunately, there is less material available to chronicle Henry Francis's life than is the case for his brothers, and particularly little relating to his sadly brief first marriage. A couple of surviving appointment books of Helen's bear witness to a busy social life in 1827 and 1828, and to frequent contact with other members of their families.[16] She gave birth to three daughters – Helen in February 1828, Anna Maria almost exactly two years later, and Sophia Emma on 13 February 1833. But seven days after Sophia was born her mother died, leaving Henry Francis a widower at 30, with three small children. A family document records the affecting story of how the dying Helen called for her brother, Denis, in order to tell him how happy a life she had enjoyed, but how before Denis arrived she had lapsed into unconsciousness and never rallied. Henry was distraught; he thought seriously of giving up his business and entering the Church, but heeded his brother Charles's strong plea not to abandon a financial career for which he had shown himself well suited. There are no details of the arrangements Henry Francis made for the care of his children in the two years after Helen's death, but Emma Laura offered advice on their education, while Denis Le Marchant and his wife, Eliza, made great efforts to look after them.[17] Eliza was the granddaughter of that Charles Smith of Stratford Langthorne, who had written so learnedly on the Corn Laws and who had married Judith Lefevre, brother of John Lefevre. She was, therefore, second cousin to each of the three Shaw Lefevre brothers.

This bitter personal loss came only three years after Henry Francis had apparently found himself at odds with Philip Pleydell-Bouverie and had pulled out of the banking partnership which he had entered in 1827. The details of the affair, which came to a head in the latter part of 1829, are unknown, but Pleydell-Bouverie took exception to Henry's proposal to break their connection. Henry asked for advice from Denis Le Marchant and from his elder brother, Charles. In turn those two consulted Francis Baring of the famous banking family. None could see any valid grounds for Bouverie's objections, and the partnership was dissolved on 23 June 1830.[18] Henry, whose inheritance had not been substantial and whose income was only moderate, was then steered by his brother-in-law, Denis Le Marchant, into a new partnership with an elderly, distant, relative of the Le Marchants, a Mr John Thomas, who had begun life as a draper with a firm called Bowerbank Monkhouse, in 1790, and had later developed his own considerable trading business with the Channel Islands, with Manchester, and with Russia.[19] Late in 1830, Thomas and his son went into partnership with Henry under the title, Thomas, Son and Lefevre, with offices at 21 Austin Friars.

In the next chapter we shall see that the minor fracas between Henry and Philip Pleydell-Bouverie came at a particularly embarrassing time for – and could have had some bearing on – the political prospects of Charles Shaw Lefevre. Fortunately, no damage seems to have resulted, but it is highly likely that the affair was known throughout the Bouverie and Shaw Lefevre clans.

Since 1826, when John and Emily had gone to live in Balham, Helena Shaw Lefevre had shared the London house and Heckfield Place with Charles and Emma. She celebrated her 67th birthday in February 1834. There is nothing to indicate that she suffered poor health, and much to justify a claim that the opposite was the case. She enjoyed a comfortable – indeed, as John had implied to Emily, a luxurious style of living – and had been the guest of the Spencers on more than one occasion in the early 1830s. She had always been fond of France, and in June 1834 she began a two months holiday there, accompanied by two of her unmarried nieces, Harriet and Eleanor Powys, both women in their forties. She wrote cheerfully to Charles on her arrival, 'I feel myself as much at home in France, and as much disposed to like it as ever', and from Harfleur, a fortnight later, she told her daughter-in-law, Emma, how relieved she was to have received a first batch of mail and to know that the delay had 'arisen from accidental causes, and not by the illness of any of those whom I so dearly love.'[20] She kept abreast of the political life in which two of her children were by then much embroiled. John was at that time Under Secretary of State for the Colonies, and when his chief, Lord Stanley, resigned, Helena wrote on 17 July expressing her opinion of the significance of the change, but showing no anxiety about her second son: 'With regard to John's individual interests, I feel assured that conducting himself as he ever will, with unsullied integrity he must prosper in the end.'[21]

The holiday and the letters went on pleasantly until almost the middle of August, when Helena was struck down by an attack of what a Scottish doctor who attended her described as 'bilious Termittent fever, with severe diarrhoea'. Dr Douglas gave this message to be sent with a letter by one of the Powys ladies, but he also wrote privately and directly to John Shaw Lefevre, explaining that he could not 'for obvious reasons' include in that open letter his opinion that 'the state of Mrs Lefevre is of a graver character'.[22]

All three Shaw Lefevre brothers were alarmed but a little incredulous about the news from Le Havre. 'I cannot persuade myself that our poor mother's case is so bad as the Scotsman makes it out,' wrote Henry to Charles. But they acted quickly to agree that one of them should go to France, and discussed whether it would be advisable to take a doctor along. John, however, was of the opinion that Helena's 'constitution is so peculiar that we doubt whether a physician who did not know her would be of any service.' It was suggested to Charles that he was in the best position to go, as Henry had acute business problems, and John, in a precarious and uncertain political situation, told his elder brother that 'you know precisely how I am situated'.[23] All these exchanges took place within a day or two, but it is unclear how and in what order the three men went to Le Havre. Eventually they all went, but all arrived too late: their mother had died of an illness which 'seemed to end in something blood poisoning' [sic] on 17 August.[24] It was a sudden, totally unexpected loss. Helena had lived to be 67 – only three years older than her husband had been at the time of his death. She had welcomed fifteen of their eighteen grandchildren into the world, and had wept for the loss of four of them. Of all the Shaw Lefevre women, she leaves an impression of having been the most elegant, the most cultivated, and the most shrewd.

CHAPTER VI

Brothers for Reform

For Charles and John Shaw Lefevre the four years from the summer of 1830 were among the most exciting of their lives. From being well-to-do, fairly young, private citizens at the beginning of the new decade, they were translated into public men during the triumphant return of the Whigs, the great struggle to pass the Reform Bill, and the change of leadership from Grey to Melbourne. Both brothers reached the Palace of Westminster. Charles began an unbroken career of twenty-seven years in the House of Commons. John's election was successfully challenged and he was turned away, but was recruited almost immediately into governmental administration. Both would spend most of the rest of their working days in Westminster and Whitehall.

If John had made the most promising political contact through his legal work for the Spencers, and if Henry Francis had made and unmade a business relationship with Philip Pleydell-Bouverie, youngest brother of the third Earl Radnor, it was their eldest brother who was first called to Parliament – by none other than that same third Earl Radnor! The young Charles Shaw Lefevre seems to have avoided any interventions in parliamentary contests after his energetic and enthusiastic role in the election of his brother-in-law, Samuel Whitbread, for Middlesex in 1820. He had turned away from the chance of succeeding his father as MP for Reading. Nor does he appear to have been prominent in Southampton county politics in the 1820s, though his contacts through the bench of magistrates and the yeomanry must have made him very well aware of the members and the leanings of the dominant families in a county overwhelmingly concerned with matters agricultural, save for the naval dockyards at Portsmouth. By 1830 he must have known the ground thoroughly, and he had apparently built some reputation as a holder of distinctly reformist views. He was on friendly terms with John Cam Hobhouse, and in 1830 was again active in the election for the Middlesex seat, which Whitbread was giving up. He hoped that Hobhouse would stand, though in the end the seat was filled by Joseph Hume, despite Charles's doubt that Hume had sufficient financial support.[1] In that same year, 1830, however, Charles was himself to enter the House of Commons. Like his father before him, he owed his seat to a patron, but more fortunately than his father, the exercise was inexpensive.

Although thirty-four years elapsed between the first and second Charles Shaw Lefevres' initial elections to the Commons, the circumstances of the younger man's candidature were still deeply coloured by the character of the unreformed House, then in its final two years of existence. He was to become, briefly, one of the two Members for Downton, in Wiltshire, which was, like Newtown in the Isle of Wight, a burgage borough. The seat was in the gift of Earl Radnor, who owned ninety-nine out of the one hundred burgage tenures and admitted that 'one of the properties that gave a vote was in the middle of a watercourse.'[2] The big difference between Sir John Barrington in the Isle of Wight in 1796, and Lord Radnor a generation later in Wiltshire, was that whereas the former had no problems of conscience about either the unreformed system or about the sale of the seat at Newtown, the latter was a keen reformer who for twenty-seven years as an MP before he succeeded his father and moved to the House of Lords, had built a personal reputation as the friend of William Cobbett and the holder of advanced liberal views. In this he was very much the opposite of his father, the second Earl, who had as much prejudice in favour of the existing order as his son had against it.

When a seat at Downton had fallen vacant in 1826, the second Earl had only recently read and was full of admiration for a defence of the Church of England by Robert Southey, the Poet Laureate. Radnor, assuming that Southey would always uphold the constitutional *status quo*, simply nominated him for the seat at Downton, whereupon the obedient voters of the borough duly elected Southey to Parliament. The poet only heard about this some weeks later, in Amsterdam, and no doubt to Radnor's chagrin, escaped as quickly as possible from the House of Commons by proving that he was disqualified by his lack of a necessary minimum estate.[3] The third Earl Radnor was as headstrong as his father, and as soon as he succeeded to the title, in 1828, he set about looking for men to fill the seats at Downton who would be willing to pledge themselves to help bring about the disenfranchisement of the borough. He took care, though, not to follow the bizarre example of his parent and nominate fancied candidates without consulting them. At the same time, he had no compunction about exercising his power over the hapless voters of Downton – he told a somewhat anxious Brougham, in 1831, that 'Of the Burgages at Downton I have no more doubt than I have of my footman's answering the bell when I ring.'[4]

Radnor's power to fill the Downton seats was not lost on his youngest brother, Philip Pleydell-Bouverie, who wanted to be an MP and was seeking fraternal support. As we have seen, his disagreement with Henry Francis Shaw Lefevre had been simmering for some months, and it is difficult to believe that Radnor was unaware of it and of the forthcoming dissolution of the banking partnership on 30 June. But the Earl was either ignorant of the affair, or indifferent to it, or felt that it cast no doubt on the integrity or suitability of Charles Shaw Lefevre. For on 11 June he wrote forthrightly to Charles:

> Would a seat in the House of Commons be agreeable to you? If it could, I should be happy to direct that you be returned for Downton at the next election.
>
> My opinions are, I believe, not unknown to you: but I do not wish you to consider yourself as at hand to answer for them, though I will candidly state to you that my first reason for making to you this proposal is that I believe you to be ultra liberal (the more ultra the better) not likely to vacate your seat by taking place, or to misuse it for promoting any personal interest, and resolve to do all you can to destroy the patronage of your patron.

However much the ground had been prepared for this approach, one might well ask what manner of politically-inclined young man, generally sympathetic to reform, could have resisted such an invitation? Certainly not Charles Shaw Lefevre. His response was couched in terms of conventional respect, but was not without a touch both of that cautious awareness of the dangers of excessive enthusiasm, and of the psychological necessity of claiming to be non-partisan, which he had inherited from his father and his class. He did not delay in accepting Radnor's offer:

> Your kindness has placed within my reach what has always been the highest object of my ambition, and I know not how sufficiently to thank your Lordship for this great mark of your Confidence.
>
> My political opinions are decidedly liberal, I might almost call them ultra-liberal – I am not a party man, nor do I wish to be considered as one – since I should always feel disposed to watch with great jealousy the proceedings of those in power whether Whigs or Tories.
>
> I am a decided friend to Parliamentary Reform to its fullest extent short of annual Parliaments and Universal Suffrage. I wish to see the expense of elections reduced as low as possible and to allow every person the privilege of voting who is capable of using it independently. I am an advocate for Election by Ballot and the extinction of all Parliamentary Patronage without making any exception in favour of the Borough of Downton.
>
> Should this brief statement of my opinions prove satisfactory to your Lordship I shall be most proud to accept the honour you propose to confer

upon me, pledging myself at the same time never to use any parliamentary influence I may obtain as a stepping stone to the promotion of my own interests.

Radnor replied in a kind letter which shows something of the good opinion Charles must already have attracted from shrewd observers of people:

You have written much more in explanation of your opinions than there was any occasion for: I had a sufficient pledge in your personal character that you will do what you think right and in your good sense and understanding that you are able to form a right judgement. This is quite sufficient for me; and whether we differ about universal suffrage and annual Parliaments or not I shall, I am quite assured, be perfectly satisfied with my representative.[5]

Radnor's timing was impressive. King George IV died on 26 June 1830, and as was the established constitutional practice, Parliament was dissolved and a general election followed in July and August. Meanwhile, the Government, headed for the last two and a half years by the Duke of Wellington, continued in office. But the cosy arrangement about Downton was not to be implemented without an intervening crisis. Philip Pleydell-Bouverie, in his search for a parliamentary seat, had been negotiating with Henry and James Brougham and the Lowther interest, immensely strong in the northern counties of Cumberland and Westmorland. The mercurial Henry Brougham, then at the height of his fame and notoriety, was long established in the Commons, though soon to be removed to 'another place'. His brother James had sat for the Cornish Borough of Tregony since 1826, but wanted to find another constituency. These two potential candidates threatened the Downton scenario already set up by Radnor, and for Charles Shaw Lefevre what followed cannot have been entirely without worry, because of the possibility of repercussions of his advisory role to his brother Henry in the break up of the Bouverie-Lefevre banking partnership.

On 8 July, Philip Pleydell-Bouverie came to see Radnor and told him that Henry Brougham had reached a compromise with the Lowthers, whereby he – Brougham – would not stand for Westmorland, but was to have at his disposal another Lowther seat – Cockermouth. Neither of the two Brougham brothers, however, would be very acceptable to Cockermouth, and, in any case, they themselves preferred to be free of the influence of the Lowthers. Henry Brougham wanted Radnor to put James in for Downton; in return, Henry Brougham would ensure that Radnor could nominate anyone he wished for Cockermouth. Radnor was taken by surprise and did not like the plan; he would be 'very sorry' to have to lose Lefevre and, if he had to, would prefer Henry Brougham to James Brougham as a nominee for Downton. Radnor did express willingness to bring in whosoever his brother Philip wanted for the second Downton seat.

There the matter rested between them, but later in the evening Philip sought out Charles Shaw Lefevre, and if there had been any strain between them it was apparently removed. The next day Bouverie talked to Henry Brougham and the result of those conversations, duly reported to Radnor, was a proposed agreement – James Brougham would take Henry's previous seat at Winchelsea, Henry and Philip Pleydell-Bouverie would fill the two Downton places, and Charles Shaw Lefevre would have Cockermouth, but the latter guaranteed only for the coming Parliament. Under pressure, Radnor, as he wrote afterwards, agreed reluctantly, but 'very soon after PPB had gone, I bethought myself again of pressing that the arrangement should be as my first impression was, that Shaw Lefevre should be left alone, and that the other seat I should give to PPB, returning him or his nominee, as he should choose'. Moved strongly by these second thoughts, Radnor sent notes to Henry Brougham and Philip Pleydell-Bouverie, and failing to contact them, went to see Shaw Lefevre, whom he found 'most ready to adopt any plan I wish', but sharing Radnor's own 'distrust of the Lowthers'.[6]

By this time Radnor was thoroughly unhappy about the situation, and expressed himself uninhibitedly in an aide memoire:

I dislike the plan in every way.

1st because an arrangement of this [kind] is disagreeable to me – that I am patron of Downton, proceeding in a straightforward way, interfering with no other, and do not like to be interfered with.

2nd because the Lowthers are the most jobbing, tricky, pushing people possible.

3rd because the probability is, that Lord Lonsdale [the head of the Lowthers] would not bring in a Member quite free of [?] and trouble, as I should do at Downton, so that my nomination for Cockermouth would be a very different thing from my nomination to Downton.

4th because in case of deaths of the parties it is most probable that there will be some dispute. If PPB's nominee dies I should of course feel free to bring in another – will the other party in case of PPB's death bring in my nominee? – and if they hesitate, how can I refuse the arrangement?

I very much regret that the idea has been mooted, for I fear my limitations and dislikes annoy PPB: but I confess the more I think of it, the more difficulties and subjects of annoyance I discover – PPB is of course anxious to accommodate his friend Brougham. I am anxious to accommodate both; but Brougham is uncertain and unsteady – and the Lowthers are tricky and pressing – nor can we secure ourselves. How strange, that people cannot proceed on a direct straightforward course, doing their able purpose quite openly, neither more nor less.

Radnor held the most powerful cards, and he had his way. He saw Henry Brougham the following day and settled the matter. Shaw Lefevre would have one of the Downton seats and the other would go to Philip Pleydell-Bouverie's nominee, who was expected to be James Brougham. And so it happened. Charles Shaw Lefevre and James Brougham were returned for Downton on 2 August. Philip Pleydell-Bouverie took Cockermouth, and Henry Brougham was returned for the County of York. Charles never met his constituents, and declared years afterwards that the seat did not cost him a penny.[7] He sealed the bargain with Radnor, a shade unctiously, when thanking the Earl:

> it adds not a little to the satisfaction which I feel on the present occasion to know that it was your wish (which I can assure your Lordship was reciprocal on my part) that I should not ever nominally represent the Borough of another person – I set too high a confidence so honourably reposed in me ever to abuse it.[8]

But the experience of being a mere pawn in the hands of powerful *prima donnas*, and of having been just saved from the possibility of being driven to choose between Cockermouth, two-hundred-and-fifty miles north in unknown territory, or no seat, must have underlined for Charles the fragility of his newly acquired status. As a result of the general election, he was in a House of Commons far more likely than any recent predecessor to push through a reform bill which would abolish the representation of the Borough of Downton, and he was committed to such abolition. In fact the speed of progress towards reform was perhaps faster than he might have expected. The new Parliament met in mid-September 1830, and the Duke of Wellington's ministry resigned within a few weeks. The second Earl Grey took office in November, with Henry Brougham as Lord Chancellor and Viscount Althorp as Chancellor of the Exchequer. A reform bill was introduced on 1 March 1831, and in a night of tremendous drama three weeks later, the second reading was agreed to in the Commons by a vote of 302 to 301. When the opposing forces rallied and inflicted defeats on the Government at committee stage, Grey persuaded the new King, William IV, to dissolve Parliament, in April. Once more, the old representative system was put to work, with another general election in May.

While Charles had been establishing himself, somewhat precariously, in the House of Commons, his brother John had advanced far in the confidence of Earl Spencer and Viscount Althorp. He handled financial aspects of several constituencies of concern to them, and was particularly involved in the by-election to which Althorp had to submit himself as a result of his taking office under the Crown in Grey's administration.[9] John's closeness to Althorp while the first Reform Bill was being framed and introduced may well have been very useful to Charles when the latter had to consider carefully his medium term parliamentary future, knowing that the days of Downton were numbered. Whether by instinct, or as a result of information coming discreetly to him, or through both, Charles kept his eye on his own county, Southampton, while knowing that he could almost certainly retain his Downton seat until reform was achieved. The dissolution of April 1831 forced him to make a very late shift of constituency.

The full details of what happened in April 1831 are not available, but enough is known to suggest the likely course of events. One can assume that Charles would not have allowed the six months since his election for Downton to go by without seeking ways of ensuring his tenure of a place at Westminster in a reformed Parliament. The appearance of the following statement, undated but almost certainly circulated in April 1831, was probably due, to some extent at least, to his own and his partner's efforts and to their ready willingness to be drafted:

We the undersigned Freeholders of the County of Southampton considering that in the present eventful Crisis we ought to have as our representatives in Parliament Men of known attachment to the principles of Reform and being fully satisfied that the essential qualification is possessed in an eminent degree by Sir James Macdonald of Woolmer Lodge Baronet and Charles Shaw Lefevre of Heckfield Esq. are of opinion that they ought to be requested to become Candidates for the representation of the County whenever an election may take place and believing that for many years past fit and proper Men have been deterred from coming forward on account of the very heavy Expense incidental to a County Election we each of us pledge ourselves to vote for them and support their Interest at such Election without putting them to any Expense.[10]

The nine signatories were headed by Thomas Baring of Stratton Park, John Bonham Carter of Petersfield, and William Seymour of Odiham, the first and last being bankers, and the other the locally powerful Member for Portsmouth.

Charles and James Macdonald were indeed nominated for the County of Southampton and returned unopposed on 6 May, the tide of enthusiasm for reform having run so high as to have destroyed the confidence of the potential Tory opposition. But the decisive moves over who should stand for Downton cannot have taken place until very close to the election. Thomas Creevey, who was fishing for a nomination, knew from Radnor on 21 April that Shaw Lefevre was to stand for Hants. But in a letter to Radnor dated 24 April, his agent, Boucher, wrote that he would 'pay particular attention to your Lordship's instructions in respect of . . . Downton', that the necessary action would be 'deferred to the last day allowed for it', and that he would then propose to the electors the Hon. Philip Pleydell-Bouverie and Charles Shaw Lefevre Esq'. Radnor must have been kept hanging till near the deadline, but on 28 April he had made his new dispositions: Thomas Creevey was to replace Shaw Lefevre. A week later his agent reported that at the poll, 'Mr. Creevey and Mr. Brougham were unanimously elected.'[11] Charles Shaw Lefevre had made a crucial strategic decision, and never had cause to regret it.

The Parliament elected in May 1831 met soon afterward and the battle for the Reform Bill began again, with the country tense and riotously inclined, a majority of the Commons still in support, the Lords and the monarch still reluctant. Over the following months of struggle compromises were patched up and more advanced plans produced. The most obvious target of the reformers had always been the pocket boroughs, and the main beneficiaries of their abolition were to be the hitherto scandalously underrepresented large towns. But the political price of that redistribution was a substantial increase in the county seats to mollify the powerful and intransigent landed interests. One of the tasks to be undertaken on behalf of the Government was, therefore, a redrawing of the boundaries of the county constituencies. That job was entrusted, no doubt on Althorp's recommendation, to John Shaw Lefevre. It was the first of a long list of official commissions which came John's way, and like most of them, was a labour of love for which he received no fee. There are clear signs that his devotion to the electoral and political cause of reform was, in the short run, harmful to his attempt to build up a solid professional practice, and reflected his underlying desire to make a career in the world of public affairs. But he did not have sufficient income to make his way easy: financial troubles, family illness and overwork combined to make these two or three years particularly wearing.[12]

Redrawing the counties began in November 1831 and John grumbled to Earl Spencer that it was a more difficult exercise than he had anticipated; but by the end of January he had finished it and reported that 'The County members have in general approved of my Carving.'[13] In due course his work was incorporated in the rearrangements brought about by the Reform Bill, after it had passed through all its late, stormy stages. A final crisis forced the King to agree to create enough new peers to override opposition in the Lords, if necessary. This left the die-hard peers without a veto, and the Bill received the royal assent on 7 June. By then, with yet another general election bound to come soon, primed as he was by so intimate a connection with Spencer and Althorp, and almost certainly encouraged by his brother's occupation of a Hampshire county seat, John Shaw Lefevre went in search of a constituency for himself.

Early in June he wrote to Spencer 'I am going . . . to-morrow as far as Petersfield with the idea of introducing myself there or rather of being

introduced by some influential individuals . . . to the . . . future electors.'
It is unclear exactly who all these influential individuals were, but they
certainly included John Bonham Carter, who was to throw his considerable
local political weight into the contest, being keen to see a Whig triumph over
the old-established Tory family, the Jolliffes, who regarded the constituency
as their fiefdom.[14] John felt that he was well received at Petersfield, and
had 'a fair prospect of success'; he must have felt that the birth of his third
daughter, a few days later, was a favourable omen. Mary Emma 'came into
the world last night whilst I was most comfortably asleep – my wife went
thro' it so favourably that she determined that she would give me the pleasure
of a surprise in the morning.'[15]

John was duly adopted as a candidate for Petersfield, so that in the first
post-Reform election, held in December 1832, two Shaw Lefevres were
standing for Southampton county seats. Though by then he had eighteen
months experience behind him, Charles had in fact made a quiet entry to
the House of Commons; he had taken only a minimal part in the debate
on the Reform Bill in 1831, and spoke not at all on the floor of the House
during 1832. But he had been on hand for all the vital divisions, and he
had proclaimed his special care for local government, and for the domestic
arrangements of the chamber, by serving in his first two sessions on select
committees dealing with such down-to-earth topics as 'the possibility of
making the House of Commons more commodious, and less unwholesome',
the civil list, steam carriages, Westminster improvement, sheriffs' expenses,
sewers, highways, and Regents Park. The only exotic exercise he was lured
into – and never repeated – was to consider in committee a bill concerned
with the affairs of the Zemindar of Nozeed.

Like most of his contemporaries, he must have been continuously
pre-occupied with what was likely to be the impact on him, personally,
of the Reform Act. Charles may well have had a peculiarly valuable source
of inside information about future county constituencies in his brother John,
and may have had an early hint that Southampton was to be divided into two
constituencies – North and South Hants – each with two members. As he had
apparently served conscientiously and given solid support to Reform and as
he was so unequivocally resident in North Hants, it is not surprising that he
became one of the candidates for that division. In December 1832 he and
his Whig partner, James Winter Scott, were to be pitted against the eldest
son of the Duke of Wellington, the Marquis of Douro, and Walter Long, in
a decisive contest.

The local Tories were not very sanguine about their chances in Hampshire,
and Wellington was not inclined to put up a fight without some reasonable
chance of success. He was pressed hard by John Fleming, who had held one
of the county seats before 1831, but as late as 7 September 1832, he was
cautious and reluctant. In a somewhat repetitive letter to Fleming, he wrote:

I shall be very sorry indeed if you should not be returned as Member for one or other of the Divisions of the County of Hants. I have considered the Govt. as too strong for us in the S. Division, considering that the Dissenters and the Radicals will act with the Whigs; and the whole supported by the Influence of the Govt. Still however you and the country gentlemen could I conceive carry one Member for the S. Division.

We are stronger in the N. Division if our force was to act as one united Body. But the Barings are against us – Sir Thomas will carry with him the Whigs, Dissenters and Radicals and will be supported by the Govt. as well as by Alexander Baring. But I think that we might throw out Mr Lefevre. People look to me for this operation, which I confess will be very disagreeable to me, by means of my own son. First I don't know that he wishes it himself, or would undertake it, particularly against Mr Lefevre; secondly, I don't know that he is likely to succeed. Thirdly, although the subject has been mentioned to me by some [?] I don't know that it is desired by the County that my son should represent it. Fourthly and principally – Mr. Lefevre and I live in the same Parish, we are the best of Neighbours and Friends. The County deserves all the advantage of the absence of political dispute; and I think [would] be very sorry to see a contest established in my own Parish between my Son and my Neighbour.

I would support any body else, but I confess that I would prefer to support any other rather than my son against Mr Lefevre and I am anxious to avoid a personal contest with a neighbour in my own Parish. This is my feeling upon this subject. I think that [if] you or Sir W. Heathcote or Mr. John Pollen or Lord Porchester would stand for the Northern Division we should throw out Mr Lefevre. We might have the same chance with Lord Douro, but for the reasons which I have stated I should prefer that it was any other individual.[16]

But Fleming and his friends were not to be deterred, and were helped by a tactical error when Shaw Lefevre advertised his specific commitment to shorter parliaments, the abolition of slavery, the commutation of tithes, the revision of the poor and corn laws, and the removal of 'all useless monopolies'. Some of this aroused the suspicion of his less enthusiastic supporters as well as spurring on his potential opponents. The experience taught Charles that 'it was far more convenient to make do with generalisations.'[17] The Duke's doubts and scruples were swept aside: Douro accepted the invitation to stand, was an active candidate and was willing to make a personal canvass which, it was reported to Wellington, produced a list of supporters representing a hundred thousand acres of land in the northern division. The

Tories played on the fact that Charles' running mate, James Winter Scott –
Sir Thomas Baring having retired from public life – had expressed himself to
the electors more moderately and was more likely to be the successful Whig
candidate. They implied, privately, that Shaw Lefevre particularly, though
Scott too, was unwilling to incur much expense.[18]

In the event, all of this was Tory whistling in the wind. When the votes
were counted, the two Whigs were comfortable victors: Charles received
1,111 votes and his partner 1,082, against the Marquis of Douro's 723 and
Walter Long's 701. It was the only contest Charles Shaw Lefevre ever fought
for in the five succeeding general elections he was returned unopposed.

At Petersfield, brother John had a much more difficult election. It was
traditionally a Tory seat being defended by a traditional family candidate;
but the tide of reform was flowing strongly. It was as well that it was doing so,
because the few documents available show that John Shaw Lefevre tackled
the election with the same meticulous care for detail, the same intellectual
grasp and integrity, and the same lack of passion and distaste for the rough
and tumble, which he brought to all his other manifold tasks. The Whig
managers were, quite rightly, 'very nervous about Petersfield', and Dennis
Le Marchant may have been as surprised as he was gleeful when he reported
that, 'the contest between Joliffe and Lefevre was neck and neck – 89 each
upon the 1st day, and a majority of one to Lefevre upon the 2d. The rejoicing
at Brooks's was . . . great . . .'[19] The taste of success in so unlikely a
constituency was sweet, though John must have recognized immediately
that a victory by one vote would not go unchallenged. But at Christmas
of the year 1832, on the eve of a new era in British politics, there were two
victories to celebrate in the Shaw Lefevre family. It must have been a happy
festival: Charles and John had not only won elections; both had male heirs,
and between them six daughters; Henry had two daughters and a third child
was expected soon. All the family must have looked to the future with some
degree of complacency.

The new Parliament met on 29 January 1833 and within a week the
Petersfield Tories petitioned for a rejection of John's election. The petition
was referred to a committee on 26 February and on 5 March was upheld: the
committee had concluded that ten electors who had cast votes for John were
not properly qualified.[20] He was out. But for Charles, the future seemed set
fair, and he settled into his by now familiar roles as landed gentleman, county
dignitary and MP. Neither in this, his third parliamentary session, nor in the
succeeding ones, did he ever develop into a regular or a powerful debater on
the floor of the House of Commons. He followed his instincts, concentrating
his efforts in those areas in which he was closely interested and in which
he could claim first hand knowledge and experience. But, far more than his
younger brother, he had a natural understanding of and sympathy with the

surface manifestations and the nuances of parliamentary politics. He had a thick skin, a serene confidence, more than a touch of personal authority, and an easy going geniality – all of which made him well liked, but which never weakened his patient thrustfulness, persistence and independence: he was always his own man. In 1833 and 1834 he developed what he had displayed in the first two sessions – a devotion to the committee work involved in enquiring into and monitoring the legislation influencing local government, the militia, agriculture – particularly the corn laws, the organization of the House of Commons, and the increasing difficulty of handling fairly and satisfactorily the growing number of private bills being floated in Parliament.

That he impressed the Government of the day as an efficient and dependable member can be deduced from the fact that he was entrusted with moving the address at the beginning of the 1834 session. It was a nice gesture to invite him to repeat what his father had done thirty-five years before and though the majority of the House was in a mood to see the world through strongly rose-tinted spectacles on that occasion, Charles' speech was highly praised by many who heard it, including Lord Stanley, who 'could not have wished a word altered', and Le Marchant, who recorded that it was 'excellent, quite in character, simple and yet sufficiently spirited.'[21] Le Marchant often reported Charles's views on policy and on back-bench attitudes to Brougham.[22] Though he seemed to have no appetite for ministerial office, Shaw Lefevre was regarded as a rising man.

In contrast, by the middle of March 1833 John, after rather more than two years of exciting political involvement, was apparently back to where he had started from as a young conveyancer with a promising major client in the person of the Earl Spencer. And he had been aware for some months that he had been losing hold of his own affairs. He had unburdened himself to Spencer in September 1832:

> I am going into the New Forest for a few days to make some arrangements respecting my unfortunate property there. I feel a good deal out of spirits about it. In fact it has so happened that my life has been so full of labour for the last four years that I have been unable to bestow the necessary attention to my own affairs and am now suffering from the consequences of this inevitable neglect.
>
> Your Lordship will have a better idea of the nature of my life when I tell you that in the course of that period I have not had altogether more than three months with my family undisturbed by business and that short time has been broken into innumerable fragments. With all this and without any expensive habit of any kind, to find that I cannot by my own exertions earn enough to support myself and family without breaking in upon my own resources, is a mortifying

and painful circumstance and necessarily is a source of much anxiety to me.[23]

This is not an untypical example of the anxiety and self doubt about his financial and professional status in which John indulged frequently. One senses that his family and friends accepted it as an inescapable result of his mild, nervous temperament and did not take it too seriously. Certainly there was never any sign of serious deprivation in the material circumstances of any of the Shaw Lefevres! But John worried a great deal, and nothing gave him more concern than his 'unfortunate property', Burley Manor. The estate never seemed to produce as much income as John hoped, and as early as November 1831 he thought of selling all or part of it. By March 1832 he had given his solicitor instructions to sell, and was willing to take a 'very moderate price'. He spoke only the truth three months later, when he told a correspondent that 'I cannot find time to live there'. In July, he thought he had a buyer, and the price was haggled down to £17,000, but the deal fell through. By November, John had to be content with letting the Manor House for six years and the adjoining park on a year to year basis.[24] With this and his loss of the Petersfield seat behind him, it is reasonable to believe that he would be depressed and uncertain where he was going. Fortunately, briefs began to flow into his chambers, perhaps reflecting the fact that, however unlucky he had been electorally, his name had become known more widely. But the next development took him completely by surprise.

At the end of March 1833 there occurred one of those reshuffles which enliven the course of cabinet government from time to time by providing endless opportunity for gossip and assessment of who is on the way up or down. This one included the removal of the existing ministers at the Colonial Office – Lord Goderich, the Secretary of State, and Lord Howick, the 'arrogant and waspish' son of the Prime Minister, who had been under-secretary and an MP.[25] Goderich was replaced by Lord Stanley, who was to cross the floor in a few years' time and to become, as the 14th Earl of Derby, thrice Prime Minister in minority Tory administrations. On 29 March, John Shaw Lefevre '. . . was at dinner when a note arrived. He thought it some formal notification connected with Lord Spencer . . . and was reading it carelessly out to his wife when he perceived its purport.'[26] Stanley had written:

Though I have not the pleasure of being personally known to you, I am induced by the high character which you have for ability and attention to business, to make you a proposal which I trust will not be disagreeable to you, and which should you accede to it, will, I am satisfied, be for the advantage of His Majesty's service. You are probably aware that Lord Goderich's resignation of the Seals of the Colonial Office will be accompanied by the retirement of Lord Howick from the Office of Under Secretary; and in succeeding Lord Goderich in a position, at the present moment, of peculiar difficulty, it will give me great satisfaction to secure the benefit of your services as Under Secretary of State. The arrangements of the Government will not admit of the Colonial Under Secretary holding a seat in Parliament, and the public service, should you accept my offer, will thus derive some advantage from the otherwise unfortunate decision upon the Petersfield petition.[27]

Stanley had first offered the under-secretaryship to John Bonham Carter, that same MP for Portsmouth who had backed Charles Shaw Lefevre for the Hampshire county seat. But Bonham Carter was always more interested in local affairs, and is reputed to have turned down the chance of office under the Whigs no less than four times during his career.[28] This was one of those times, but had he accepted, one wonders how the problem of too many ministers in the Commons would have been solved – presumably by a move of Bonham Carter or someone else to the Lords. Once Bonham Carter's refusal became known within the magic circle of power and influence, the serendipity which results from the happy conjunction of people and places came into play.

Henry Lewis Wickham was principal private secretary to Viscount Althorp. He was the son of William Wickham, the distinguished diplomat and politician who had been a friend of Abbot and Grenville – and of the first Charles Shaw Lefevre. The Wickhams were yet another Hampshire family, and lived at Binsted Wyck, close to both Portsmouth and to Petersfield. Henry Lewis Wickham was roughly contemporary with the second Charles Shaw Lefevre, would have been much aware of the Petersfield election, and as a fellow private secretary, was in regular contact with Denis Le Marchant. Out of this nest of Hampshire Whigs came the suggestion, from Wickham to his master, Althorp, that John would be a good substitute for Bonham Carter.[29] Althorp was enthusiastic and recommended John to Stanley so strongly that Stanley looked no further. Althorp wrote about this to his father, in terms which are not only interesting for his view of John Shaw Lefevre, but also for his attitude towards how much junior ministers could legitimately pursue other than their official business while in office:

You will be very angry with me for what I have been doing. Stanley wanted an Under Secretary of State and it was necessary that he should not be in Parliament. He asked me if I knew any one fit for it and I recommended to him the man I thought best qualified of any man in the country John Lefevre, he took my recommendation and Lefevre has accepted the Office. I am confident that he can do all you require from him quite consistently with his official duties. I have just seen him and he is of the same opinion. I should be very sorry if my recommendation of him should deprive you of his assistance but as most of the business he has to do for you has been done in London I do not see that his having this office should produce this effect at all, and I thought it a duty I owed to the public to get the use of his great abilities for the public service and a duty to him to give him the opportunity which this situation will give him of rising to the degree of eminence which his capacities will now certainly lead him. For a man of Lefevre's abilities and character attached to Stanley must rise to the top of everything in the country.[30]

Stanley's proposal was not one which John felt he could accept without very careful thought. After he and Emily had prayed for divine guidance, he told her that 'he felt fully equal to undertake the situation,'[31] but he then went to consult his mother, and no doubt took his elder brother at least into his confidence, as well as some of his trusted friends. The risk was considerable: the post he was offered was political and could come to an end without much notice and without any guarantee of another appointment. One of the main reasons why he was in the running for it was the accident of the Government having filled all the ministerial places available in the House of Commons: normally – and in any future reshuffle of the Whig administration – it would be expected that, as had been the case with Howick, the under-secretary would be either an MP or a peer. And even though he felt able to continue to help Spencer as an adviser on financial matters, he could not seriously attempt to maintain a full conveyancing practice simultaneously with being the junior minister at the Colonial Office. Once he gave up the practice it would not be easy to begin another.

But John wanted to take the job: the gamble at Petersfield had not come off, but the ambition to be a man of affairs was not diluted. It is difficult to withstand enthusiasm, and his family and friends, if they did have any doubts as to the wisdom of the move, did nothing to dissuade him. Moreover, despite his worrying nature, he was aware that he would have means of maintaining himself and his family far in excess of most of his fellow creatures, even if he had a setback. He took the post. Denis Le Marchant was delighted and claimed that John 'had always hated the law, of which his department was the driest branch' – a rather surprising statement, given John's keenness about conveyancing eight years before. But even if he overstated John's lack of devotion to a legal career, Le Marchant confided to his diary a view of John's qualities, on the eve of his becoming under-secretary of State for the Colonies, which is consistent with much of what was to be said about John in later years and after his death:

He is a man of very clear head and of indefatigable industry and most courteous deportment. He dreads responsibility but there is none in his present post, so that I trust he will do for it. He has been for fifteen years one of my most intimate friends. I rendered him some little services at Cambridge that took his heart, and he certainly has lost no opportunity of returning them with interest. He is one of the best specimens of Cambridge scholarship – a scientific mathematician, a respectable classic, an accomplished linguist, being not only familiar with French, Spanish and Italian, but well acquainted with German, Dutch and Danish, and besides this, no mean political economist. He has not much taste or he would make more of his acquirements.[32]

John was a junior minister for almost a year and a half. The Colonial Office, when he entered it, was dominated by the controversy over how to bring slavery to an end, and was heavily involved in trying to produce a viable and acceptable compromise between the demands of the abolitionists on the one hand and of the West Indian slave owners, on the other hand. But that problem was not one faced with a united team of ministers and advisers. Goderich and Howick had not always seen eye to eye; Howick was the more aggressive, but they both relied heavily on two senior permanent officials, Henry Taylor and James Stephen. Indeed, the office had been for some years developing towards the more modern pattern in which the senior civil servants were to become prominent as advisers on policy and takers of many major decision within their interpretation of the Minister's views. Stanley, however, would have none of this, and insisted that the formulation of policy and the making of all important decisions should be shared by himself and his Under-Secretary of State. But he did not care for Howick, who had to make way for John Shaw Lefevre. Stephen, the legal expert, was confined closely to technical legal matters and Taylor, to his chagrin, was 'reduced to the level virtually of copying clerk. "My work at the Office," he wrote, "is mere amusement."'[33] It was not a happy ship: Stanley distrusted both the senior officers, Taylor particularly felt bitter towards Stanley, and Stephen distrusted Shaw Lefevre. John complained to some friends that he was not getting appropriate help from Stephen and Stephen heard of the grumble. An extremely cool exchange of letters followed, and official face-to-face contacts between the two men must have been acutely embarrassing for some time thereafter.[34]

There is little doubt that the two ministers were, as Le Marchant admitted, perfect novices in the business; but, whereas Stanley was politically responsible and, as might be expected of the heir to a great aristocratic title, totally self-confident, John was clever and industrious but in no way combative. They worked together harmoniously enough, but were overburdened by the very system which they had set up, and it is understandable that their pragmatic approaches produced responses to problems which 'were frequently contradictory'. Taylor readily admitted that John 'is as patient, assiduous and laborious as it is possible for any man to be and has a fair share of passive understanding' but 'everyday . . . has not a chance of getting through his business.'[35] These, however, were the strictures of a not unreasonably discontented civil servant: they were not immediately influential in the upper reaches of the government.

The Slave Emancipation Act was put on the statute book in August 1833 and a scheme of compensation for slave owners was introduced. John was made one of the commissioners entrusted with the distribution of £20 million of compensatory funds, though he admitted many years later that he had not given that task as much of his time and energy as he put into most of his other work.[36] When John and Emily returned from a trip late in November 1833 Emily remembered how:

> before I had time to unpack or provide a nurse or doctor Jane [Georgiana] was unexpectedly born. A dinner party was to have taken place a day or two after. A fortnight after I had a severe attack of illness from the nurse having opened the window. I was so ill that the Doctor was sent for in the middle of the night without my husband knowing. I passed a most dreadful night – hundreds of slaves' heads staring at me from all round the walls of the room. It was the time of the emancipation of the slaves, in which John was engaged. The Doctor bled me, which was certainly a strong remedy and left me very weak for some time after our return to Battersea.[37]

Emily appears to have been almost incredibly protective of her husband's rest!

Whatever might be the judgement on the performance of the Colonial Office ministers, retrospectively, John was certainly in no danger so long as Stanley was his chief. Stanley, however, was becoming increasingly unhappy with the Whigs, and when it was suggested in Cabinet that Irish church revenues should be diverted to secular purposes, he scribbled to a colleague that 'Johnny Russell has upset the coach', resigned, and left the party for ever in June 1834. John was left undisturbed in his post under a new Secretary of State, Thomas Spring Rice. But not for long. He became something of a political embarrassment in the summer of 1834. This was in part due to Stanley's resignation, but the situation was made more difficult by the resignation of Grey as Prime Minister only a month later, and his replacement by Melbourne. There seems to have been no connection, or any particular sympathy, between Melbourne and the Shaw Lefevres. John did not have a seat in either House, and Melbourne was doubtless keen to have at his disposal as much patronage as possible to meet the demands of parliamentarians. But Melbourne was particularly dependent on Althorp's leadership in the Commons, and John Shaw Lefevre was Althorp's protégé.

A solution was found in the area of one of the Whig Government's most controversial initiatives. A bill had been introduced to make radical changes in the administration of the Poor Law. The proposal included the establishment of a highly-centralized system headed by a three-man Poor Law Commission. The sad and bitter condition of agricultural labour, and the arguments over how it should be improved, is one of the great themes of the social and economic history of the century of industrialization from 1750 onwards – and beyond – and cannot be encapsulated without severe danger of serious distortion. Whether or not it was recognized at the time that the work – indeed, the very existence – of the new commission, was to be so full of sound and fury, and a sound and fury so long extended, it was recognized that the membership of the commission was a matter of extreme political delicacy. The Government appointed two commissioners whose political complexions were not excessively Whiggish: Frankland Lewis had held junior office under Canning and Wellington, while Captain Nicholls was an experienced Poor Law administrator and an acknowledged expert on its problems. The Government also appointed the brilliant but persistent administrative reformer, Edwin Chadwick, who had expected to be a commissioner, to be Secretary. On 4 August the Cabinet named John Shaw Lefevre as the third commissioner, with a salary of £2,000 a year.

The availability of the third Poor Law commissionership had come up at a very convenient time to ease the situation at the Colonial Office and still make good use of John. There cannot be much doubt that Althorp was instrumental in the matter, and there is documentary proof that he was well pleased by the Cabinet's agreement.[38] Some who have written authoritatively on the Poor Law have dismissed John's appointment as a mere piece of Whig patronage – a 'job' of the worst kind, and have pointed to his close personal relations with Althorp and Spencer, and their presumed sense of obligation to him, as the only reason for his nomination. But the idea that the whole episode was simply a gross settlement of debt, a thoughtless 'jobs for the unqualified boys' exercise, must surely be questioned. The Government cannot have been unaware of the political storms ahead in the implementation of their new Poor Law, even if they underestimated their intensity; and why should they be expected not to want a trusted man of their own way of thinking intimately involved in the new operation, able to exercise an influence in line with their ideas, and to keep them discreetly in touch with problems and possibilities as they arose? And while John had no experience of Poor Law administration, and may have been dragged along in an overburdened routine at the Colonial Office, he was a practising lawyer who had shown that he had a first class mind and was industrious and meticulous in handling detail: detail would come aplenty at the Poor Law Commission.

Sidney and Beatrice Webb believed that it was John's tact and discretion in the handling of the boundaries of the county constituencies in 1832 which recommended him to the Government for the Poor Law exercise; but they were also of the opinion that among the young men of Whig connections, he was 'perhaps, the most talented.'[39] From a longer perspective, it might have been suggested that John was insufficiently combative for a seat in which he would have to face the anger and unhappiness of so many of the clientele, and the unrestrained, abusive criticism of much of the press, as well as to have to work alongside so abrasive a person as Edwin Chadwick. Even in that context, though, there would be those who would argue that to have so moderate a person on the board would help to produce harmony. Whatever the considerations which were debated round the Cabinet table, John Shaw Lefevre was soon to join his two new colleagues to form a triumvirate fated to be known to history as the Three Kings (or Bashaws) of Somerset House.

CHAPTER VII

To the Speaker's Chair

Only a few weeks after Helena Shaw Lefevre's death in August 1834 the reform Government of Grey and Melbourne came to an abrupt end. Melbourne had agreed to take over from Grey in part on the condition that Althorp remained Leader in the Commons. But when Althorp's father – and John Shaw Lefevre's patron – the second Earl Spencer died in November 1834 Althorp was removed to the Lords. Melbourne and William IV then demonstrated their failure to appreciate the fundamental shift in the balance of constitutional power which had been effected by the 1832 Reform Act. The Prime Minister, unsure of his party's ability to control a House of Commons in which Irish and Radical members were increasingly restless, offered his resignation. Not only did the King accept it, but proceeded to invite the Tories to form an administration. Wellington was entrusted with the premiership until Sir Robert Peel could be called home from Italy, and the Duke probably enjoyed a memorable administrative interlude during which, single-handed, he kept the government of the country going by driving from one Whitehall department to another each morning of the next few weeks, doing the necessary minimum of business.

For the last time, a reigning monarch (admittedly given the chance by a minister who lacked confidence in his own immediate political situation) had tried to replace an administration which had the support of a majority of the House of Commons by one which did not. Peel, understanding better the embarrassing constitutional position he had inherited, made the best of a bad job. He went to the country, produced that famous prototype of modern political party propaganda, the Tamworth Manifesto, and won a lot more seats for the Tories (or Conservatives, as they were beginning to be called) – though nothing like a working majority. Even so, he struggled for three months to hold on to power, but could not swing enough support in the new Commons, and after a string of defeats he gave up in April 1835. Melbourne returned and the Whigs began a second term in office which would see Queen Victoria on to the throne and which, despite alarms and excursions, would continue until the autumn of 1841.

In these seven years Charles Shaw Lefevre reached and, after surviving an anxious run up to his first re-election, established himself in the Chair of the House of Commons for a long and distinguished spell. Neither he nor his brother John were threatened or disturbed by the short period of Conservative rule in 1834–5. Wellington, Carnarvon and others agreed that there was no point in opposing Charles, who had established himself firmly in North Hants.[1]

By the time the reinstated Whig administration settled into office in the late spring of 1835, he was an experienced parliamentary politician. In less than five years he had sat for three constituencies and had gone through the negotiations involved in four elections, even though he had only had to appeal once to the electors in a contest; while in the House of Commons he had made a quiet mark as a dependable party supporter and a capable committee man. In the next four years he became a leading figure in the House, though he continued to operate mainly through committee work and rarely spoke on the floor. Nor did he widen the range of his interests, which remained those most natural to a country based member – agriculture, local government and the militia – together with that inherited passion for the esoteric intricacies of the procedure and working of Parliament which is rarely shared, in any one generation, by more than a small minority of the elected representatives of the people.

In that special context, Charles spent no small amount of time and effort, both before and after he became Speaker, and even later, in the unspectacular world of private legislation, bringing about changes to rationalize and facilitate the handling of a mass of business which, nowadays, only very occasionally attracts any wide public notice.[2] That work brought him into close contact with a sizeable proportion of his fellow members, whose respect and liking for him must have been significantly helpful for his future status. Moreover, as we shall see, his expertness in this context gave him a remarkable opportunity to display his talents at a particularly appropriate time for his career in the House of Commons. But in the more general, public realm Charles also achieved some political prominence in the years 1836-9, first in the long-running controversy about the price of corn; second by being entrusted with the headship of a commission to look into the problems of providing more effective policing in the counties of England and Wales; and third by his involvement in controversial legislation about tithes.

On 8 February 1836, in response to the long continued discontent of much of the landed interest, the House of Commons appointed a select committee, 'to inquire into the state of Agriculture and into the causes and extent of the Distress which still presses upon some important Branches thereof.'[3] There were thirty-six members, and they included Lord John Russell, Sir Robert Peel, Sir James Graham and the Lords Chandos, Howick and Stanley. Nor was the membership of these luminaries merely nominal: the committee took evidence on thirty-eight days; Peel and Graham attended most of the sessions, and Russell, despite his heavy governmental duties, turned up for about a third of them. It is a measure of Charles Shaw Lefevre's standing that Russell proposed him as chairman, that he was elected unanimously, and that his performance in the chair won him high praise. But the committee, while hearing much expert opinion and giving it careful attention, was hopelessly divided. Charles presented a draft report for the consideration of the committee on 9 July and insisted later that he had drawn it up 'without consulting any member of the Government, or any of those gentlemen with whom I had the honour of being associated in this protracted negotiation'. Five days afterwards the committee abandoned the attempt to develop any compromise statement, and agreed only 'to report their evidence, without observations, to the House'. The most crucial arguments had centred on the effects of the duty on imported corn, and the committee's inability to find common ground was only one more episode in a disagreement which had lasted for decades, and which was to be broken dramatically by Peel ten years later, when he carried the repeal of the corn laws but at the cost of losing office and splitting the Tory Party.

Not surprisingly, there were 'unfounded statements . . . circulated in some of the public journals' about the committee's failure to produce a report, and Charles, probably nettled both by such comment and by the rejection of his draft, decided to publish his views in the form of a letter to his constituents in August. His thirty-nine page pamphlet argued for a reduction in the present rate of duty on corn and in favour of a lower but fixed duty. Rather trenchantly, he told his constituents that 'if you have felt the least disappointment at the result of our labours, you must not consider me individually responsible for it', and he attributed the absence of any recommendations 'not to any want of consideration on the part of the Committee for the interests of the farmer, but entirely to the impossibility of advancing any proposition which would meet with the concurrence of a majority of its members.'[4]

Perhaps inevitably, this forthright tactic did not go unanswered. One of the witnesses who had appeared before the committee, annoyed both by the 'fruitless result' of the committee's work and by the 'unprecedented circulation to which the pamphlet published by Mr. Shaw Lefevre . . . has attained', put out an even longer review, rebutting Charles' thesis; and another weighty contribution to the debate was made by a fellow member of the committee.[5] Even as late as February 1839, there appeared in print a letter pleading for a four month 'compromise standstill', to give experience and to allow time for everyone to calm down in the unrelenting controversy about the corn laws. This last letter was from that Henry Wickham who, when Althorp's private secretary, had helped to manoeuvre Charles' brother John into the under-secretaryship at the Colonial Office, and who, in 1839, was just beginning a spell as Chairman of the Board of Stamps and Taxes. By that time Charles' reputation was such that Wickham felt able to write, about his own proposal, that 'should you agree with me as to its merits, it cannot be in better hands, as the weight which you possess in the House, and to which you are so justly entitled, will enable you to give it due effect.'[6]

Just as this difficult exercise came to a close, Russell asked Charles to be the chairman of a three-man Royal Commission which would usually be known as the Rural Police Commission, but whose duties were described officially as being 'to inquire as to the best means of establishing an efficient Constabulary Force in the counties of England and Wales.'[7] At first Charles refused, pleading pressure of work in Parliament and at Heckfield,[8] but Russell was insistent: he had decided on Edwin Chadwick and Colonel Rowan, chief of the Metropolitan Police, as the other commissioners. Almost certainly, Russell told Chadwick of Charles' reluctance, whereupon the touchy Chadwick wrote to Charles and in due course received the following reply:

It did not require a perusal of the able article in the *Edinburgh Review* which you have had the kindness to send me, to convince me of your qualification for the Commission which the Government are about to appoint. Nor had I the least doubt of our acting together with the greatest cordiality. But I declined the honour of being your colleague because I felt that I had not that time to bestow upon it which favour the importance of the subject required and I did not consider myself justified in allowing Colonel Rowan and yourself to take the labouring day whilst I remained the nominal Head of the Commission.

Lord John Russell has written to me to say that *three* days of my time will be sufficient. If that is so I cannot rightly understand the nature of the duties which he wishes me to undertake. Unfortunately I cannot leave home just at present or I would go to London for the purpose of having some conversation with you upon the subject – but if you can be spared from Somerset House I shall be most happy to see you at Heckfield on any day this week after to-morrow – and my brother will tell you of the various conveyances by which you can find your way to us. It will give you an opportunity of convincing me that I am wrong in declining Lord John Russell's proposal and in that case I will most willingly retreat. If you are not successful in prevailing upon me to alter my determination I shall at all counts profit by the pleasure of your society and I shall be most happy to communicate all the information I possess in connexion with the object of your Commission.[9]

This smoothly diplomatic response brought Chadwick to Heckfield, where he may indeed have been wholly responsible for persuading Charles to take on the chairmanship. It is quite likely, though, that Charles himself had come to think warmly of the idea, as the inquiry was to deal with matters much in the forefront of his mind as a result of his experience as a landowner and a magistrate. What must be regarded as highly likely is that Charles was not taken in by Russell's sly, or naive, notion that the chairman would not need to put in more than three days' work! That was not Charles' style, and though the obsessive and energetic Chadwick was the 'ideas man' and took much of the strain and most of the drafting, subsequent correspondence over the two-and-a-half years of the commission's existence shows that Shaw Lefevre's contribution was real and his control quite definite.

Chairman and secretary seem to have worked fairly amicably together, but what was impressive about Charles, over and above his strong Whig propensities, was his instinctive political sense and his innate moderation. After his initial talk with Chadwick he tried hard to have the membership of the commission widened, telling Russell:

> We both . . . think it *very desirable* that other persons whose opinions on these matters are new to the public, should be associated with us in this Commission. Col. Rowan will naturally be considered too much prejudiced in favour of a police similar to that under his command. Mr. Chadwick will be suspected of being too well inclined to connect the New Constabulary with the Poor Law Guardians, and I am already to a certain extent committed in the Co[unty] Rate Report. The person who above all others I should prefer seeing at the head of the Commission is the Duke of Richmond – and if Lord Langdale could also be prevailed upon to join it, I feel confident that any Report proceeding from a Board so constituted would meet with that Respect which is so essential to the success of any plan we may think it right to propose.[10]

But as so frequently in such affairs, the choice of membership was ideologically crucial. Chadwick's Benthamite enthusiasm led him to push Langdale and to be hostile to Richmond. Russell had no intention of going Chadwick's way – he wanted a country gentleman in the chair, and as Richmond could not find the time, Russell kept to the original three. In fact, Richmond was much consulted and supported Shaw Lefevre's moderate Whig line of approach. Moreover, Chadwick also failed to get a young protégé appointed as secretary to the commission, Russell insisting on a Home Office man, Redgrave. Charles may have been happy not to have a Chadwick nominee, but he did remark, tartly, that, 'The Home Office is certainly not the best School in the world for an active man of business.'[11]

Shaw Lefevre, Rowan and Chadwick were appointed on 20 October 1836 and thereafter the enquiry took its course – a much longer one than was originally hoped. Inevitably Chadwick did most of the work, but Charles kept his political ear close to the ground, and passed his intelligence on to the secretary:

I dined yesterday in company with divers Squires of strong Tory politics and led them to the discussion of the advantages of an improved local constabulary in which they all agreed, and I suspect we shall have more opposition from the out and out radicals than from any other quarter.[12]

I fear some of the Queries you have sent me will *bother* the Country Squires – we shall not obtain satisfactory answers from them.

The Tories are making a vast struggle against us, as I dare say you have found out long before this from the answers to our Queries which have been already sent out.[13]

Drafting was not far advanced by the beginning of 1838, when Charles wrote cheerfully but urgently to Chadwick:

I am happy to be able to add . . . that the Village Dogberries are gradually declining in the Estimation even of the great unpaid. Crime is making very rapid strides in the rural districts and Gentlemen begin to feel their pockets and possessions exceedingly insecure. Pray work at the Report, because I verily believe something might be done during the present Session if it could be brought out in time.[14]

But that was too optimistic a prospect: final drafting was not complete a year later, and many points had to be argued about before Chadwick sent what he hoped was the final proof to Charles on 2 March 1839 and proposed to send it simultaneously to Russell. His draft was not well received by Shaw Lefevre and Rowan, however. Charles insisted on delay, and he and Rowan demanded a major last minute change of emphasis in order to ensure that their recommendations reflected their support of local control through the landed establishment – much to Chadwick's chagrin.[15] The report was signed on 27 March 1839. Its recommendations were not popular and even its modest centralizing principles were much watered down in subsequent legislation. But while there was some public abuse of Chadwick, Charles does not seem to have lost any face.

Shaw Lefevre had been enthusiastic about the commutation of tithes, one of the many reforms introduced by the Whig Government, and had congratulated Russell on the appointments of the tithe commissioners, in 1836.[16] In March 1837 he became chairman of a select committee to examine problems which would be involved in making parochial assessments of tithes in the context of the Poor Rate, and heard evidence from some of the tithe commissioners. A year later he and a colleague introduced a bill to regulate parochial assessments on the lines of the proposals contained in the select committee report, but the bill ran into serious opposition: one of the tithe commissioners published a hostile pamphlet of over sixty pages, and the bill was eventually lost on its way to committee.[17]

While these mixed legislative fortunes may have hurt Charles' standing in some eyes, they did not tarnish his generally high reputation. He was 'a very popular person in private society'[18] and was safe in his North Hampshire seat, being liked and respected by Tories as well as Whigs. At the general election of 1837 he was returned unopposed, but significantly for the future of Hampshire politics and for him personally, the second seat for the northern division of the county was filled by a Tory, Sir William Heathcote, Bt., who was also unopposed. That outcome, in a situation of declining rural support for the Whigs, smacks of a tacit and informal agreement to divide the spoils and to avoid the expense of contests. It was a factor in the small drama which was to affect Charles's future four years afterwards.

It was about this time that an observer of political life at Westminster published a volume of sketches of contemporary MPs, including one of Charles Shaw Lefevre. The Member for North Hampshire was described as:

> a man of great urbanity of manner . . . a man of extensive information on most of the topics which occupy the attention of the legislature . . . he is always listened to by the House. His matter, if deficient in depth, has usually the attribute of good sense to recommend it. His speeches are always short. He seems to be in a hurry to get through what he means to say; hence he gives a great deal of matter in a small compass. His style is smooth and easy, without exhibiting any appearance of that polish which is the effect of study. His delivery is rapid, but always fluent. He is scarcely ever at a loss for the proper phraseology; nor does he, except in rare cases, and then but slightly, falter in his utterance. His enunciation is distinct, and he has a clear and agreeable voice of considerable compass. He is moderate in his action. When he rises, he usually puts his hat under his left arm, and makes a gentle movement with his right hand. He generally fixes his eye as exclusively on some particular member, as if that member were the only individual in the house . . . He is a good looking man, with a very intellectual expression of countenance. His complexion is clear, and symptomatic of good health.[19]

In 1837 Charles's good standing in the Commons and with the Government was enhanced by his being chosen, prophetically as it might seem in retrospect, to move the re-election of Abercromby as Speaker. The graceful speech with which Charles did so was an unintended rehearsal for a more difficult speech he was to make in 1839. Abercromby had been in the chair since 1835. He had succeeded the Tory, Manners Sutton, who had been Speaker since 1817, and who had been ousted by the Whigs in a contest which had aroused and left much bitterness. Abercromby had not been a great success, and since the end of 1836 he had been particularly keen to be out of a position which had become increasingly difficult for him. He agreed, only very reluctantly, to continue after the beginning of 1838, on condition that there should be a thorough review of his proposals for changes in legislative procedures. This gave Shaw Lefevre a splendid chance to demonstrate his special capacities: clearly with the approval of the Government, he moved the appointment of a select committee on which 'some of the most experienced and influential members on either side consented to serve'. He was then chosen to take the chair:

> and owing in great measure to the sedulous pains taken by him to make clear by anticipation what the working of the reformed system would be, and the exercise of his powers of individual suasion, he succeeded in carrying a report almost unanimously in the committee, and which embodied well-nigh all the recommendations of the Speaker.[20]

But while this exercise further enhanced Shaw Lefevre's reputation, the outcome did not mollify the unhappy Abercromby who, after confidential discussions with Russell and Peel, announced his departure early in May 1839 on the very same evening when the Melbourne Government, having a day or two before suffered a moral defeat on a matter of colonial policy, decided to resign. Thus the chair fell vacant just as there began that tangled and ludicrous crisis of the Bedchamber, whose outcome was the failure of Peel to form a Government and the continuance of the Whigs for the last two of their troubled, tempestuous but only once interrupted spell of nearly eleven years in power. While Abercromby took his reward and moved to the Upper House as Lord Dunfermline, the Whig hierarchy recognized that their senior candidate for the Speakership, and a man who had wanted the place for a long time, was the then Chancellor of the Exchequer, Spring Rice. But to add to the Whig leaders' troubles, Russell received 'from all quarters information . . . that the Radicals would not support Mr. Rice, and that the only candidate whom the Whigs could carry was Mr. Lefevre.'[21]

Responsible parliamentary opinion was favourable to Charles. Many 'men of judgement and weight' tendered their support, spontaneously, 'to the member for Hampshire, if he would allow himself to be put in nomination'.[22] Given his extrovert confidence, his enthusiastic work on procedural matters and his obvious high competence and popularity, it is unlikely that Charles hesitated. He used to tell friends, in later life, how the first unofficial approach was made:

> while standing behind the Chair surrounded by a group of county members, among whom were Mr. Ashford-Sandford, and his old friend Mr.

Robert Palmer, one of the party said, 'Now, Lefevre, we mean to have you as our Speaker,' and this friendly joke was soon found to express the general sentiment of the country gentlemen and the Ministerial party. The Ministers who had favoured the claims of Mr. Spring Rice were soon forced to defer to the unmistakeable choice of their followers.[23]

Clearly, Charles was unusually able to charm both those perched on the solid trees of conventional Whig rural society, and those who sang from the more storm tossed branches of contemporary radicalism; and yet attract the respect of those who possessed that sense of 'gravitas' peculiarly beloved of the British establishment. But he could not, in 1839, charm many of the more severely partisan Tories: they had unforgiving memories of the ousting of Manners Sutton in 1835, and their prospects of an immediate re-entry to office were feverishly high. Peel, in his initial, difficult audience with the young and hostile Queen Victoria on 8 May, mentioned that Henry Goulburn was keen to stand for the Speakership, and that a contest for the chair might provide an indication of the power of a new Government to control the House of Commons.[24] The Conservatives really wanted their own man in the chair, and in Henry Goulburn they had a formidable candidate, a very experienced parliamentarian and minister, an 'excellent man of business, of unblemished character, and many high qualities', though 'in form and features . . . an infelicitous contrast to . . . his rival'.[25]

One can only speculate on whether, if the election for Speaker had been held with a new Government in office, or after a dissolution of Parliament, there would ever have been a Speaker Shaw Lefevre. But within two days of first meeting the Queen, Peel and his colleagues refused to try to form an administration, and Melbourne was back as Premier. This must have strengthened the determination of the Tories to run Goulburn for the Speakership. The lines of battle were drawn: the two contenders had to go through the embarrassing business of self-advertisement in speeches to the House on 27 May 1839 and each tried hard to combine a decent modesty with a sufficiency of partisanship; readers of the Hansard version might find Shaw Lefevre the winner on points – he had a lighter touch than his opponent, who was inclined to self-righteousness. But the words, spoken in the midst of so turbulent and high-spirited a clash of party interests, were mere polite preliminaries to the vote. Shaw Lefevre scraped home by only 18 votes – 317 to 299. It is a mark of the closeness of the struggle in the House of Commons of the 1830s that Abercromby's majority had been even smaller, 316 votes to 306. This time, however, so small a majority produced a great Speaker: Melbourne was well pleased, telling the young Queen how much he admired Charles's 'stature', and dismissing poor Abercromby as 'a crusty fellow'.[26]

The Whigs hung on for two more uninspiring and rather tired years, during which the opposition gained internal strength in the country but could not quite shift enough support in the Commons to bring the Government down until June 1841, when a 'no confidence' motion was carried by one vote, forcing Melbourne to ask for a dissolution. At the subsequent election Sir Robert Peel led his Conservatives to a substantial victory: when the new parliament met, the debate on the address ended in a win for Peel and his followers by 91 votes. Melbourne resigned, and by the end of August, Peel was Prime Minister. Had the feelings of 1835 or 1839 still prevailed, there is little doubt that the clear-cut majority for the Conservatives would have led to Charles Shaw Lefevre being replaced as Speaker. Indeed, down in Hampshire, once the election results were known, the ever watchful and hopeful John Fleming wrote to the Duke of Wellington that Charles' re-election to the chair was most likely to be opposed, and that 'the consequence of his defeat, I presume would be, his elevation to the Peerage. In that case our Party ought to be prepared with a successor to represent them in North Hants.'[27]

But it is likely that Fleming was appealing, too late, to the one man who may have ensured that Charles still had the most essential, the most basic, qualification for the Speakership – a seat in the House of Commons. At the general election of 1841, Shaw Lefevre and Heathcote had again been returned unopposed for the northern division of Hampshire. But Charles Greville, after telling Henry Reeve about the 'grand difference in the Conservative body . . . a large part of the Tories are eager to turn out Lefevre, while the more moderate and prudent wish not to disturb him,' went on to argue that the Tories would have done 'much better to have turned [Lefevre] out of Parliament, which they could have done. But this the Duke of Wellington would not permit, and I thought [Lefevre] was allowed to retain his seat expressly that he might retain the Chair.'[28] Whether such had been the Duke's intention, or whether he had simply considered the Conservative strength in North Hants insufficient to carry both seats, and preferred a comfortable sharing of places between the parties, or even whether he simply liked and respected his neighbour too much, must remain matter for conjecture. But certainly Wellington's forbearance was one of a number of fortunate circumstances which worked to Charles Shaw Lefevre's advantage.

Greville's and Fleming's comments reflected the real hostility to continuing Shaw Lefevre in the chair which developed quickly among a small group of the more extreme members of the new majority party as soon as the extent of the Conservative victory at the polls was clear. The Whigs would still be in office when Parliament reassembled – it not yet being the convention that a Government resigns immediately, without meeting Parliament, if the decision of the voters is definitely unsympathetic - and the election for the Speakership would take place as soon as the new Parliament met. In the last two weeks of July the fate of Shaw Lefevre was effectively decided within the Conservative ranks.

The first rumblings of danger reached Peel from his political managers, Bonham and Fremantle, on 20 and 22 July.[29] They reported that some country back-benchers, of whom Sir John Tyrell was one of the ringleaders, together with Lord Lowther and the Duke of Buckingham, were intent on removing Shaw Lefevre, who they accused of being partisan in his composition of the committees which the House set up to handle election petitions – a charge never taken seriously. The initiative was quickly seized upon by 'the hotheads of the Carlton'[30] and strong criticism of the party leadership's alleged weakness over the whole business was voiced by Sir Richard Vyvyan and Benjamin Disraeli. The most direct public display of opposition to the continuance of Shaw Lefevre appeared in a leader – probably the work of Horace Twiss,[31] – and a letter to *The Times*, on 2 August, from 'Pittacus', which was attributed by several of Peel's colleagues to Disraeli, though the latter denied it in a letter to Peel.[32] This demonstration of distrust for Peel has been seen as 'only a passing cloud, and a very small one at that, at the most not bigger than a man's hand', but significant in terms of the cataclysmic internal party division which was to come five years further on.[33]

In part, the hostility to Charles was a personal one, for no prominent and generally popular politician is without some who dislike him; in part it was an expression of extreme political bitterness against the Whigs, aimed at an obvious and vulnerable target; in part it was a reflection of the still widely accepted notion that the chair belonged to the majority force in the House; and it was in part an expression of anxiety among those strong Tories who felt that while the election had shown the new-found power of the party, the leadership had not yet given any unequivocal indication as to the manner and the timing of an all out attack on the Whig Government. Only the last of these constituted a major threat, and for a few days the party managers were worried. They pressed Peel to take a firm stand one way or the other at once, and warned him that 'Concurring in Shaw Lefevre's election will be attributed to weakness and dissensions among ourselves unless we move an amendment to the Address, be the speech from the Throne what it may'.[34] They tacitly agreed with Lowther's shrewd assessment: 'The Speakership will soon be forgotten if they throw plenty of Cayenne into the Amendment, but milk and water will not *now* suit Tory stomachs.'[35]

Lord John Russell advised Melbourne to resign if the Whigs were defeated on the Speakership, because that would deny the Tories the moral advantage of putting the Whigs out as a result of a vote on the Queen's Speech; and Russell even suggested that Peel would support Shaw Lefevre simply in order to postpone the Whigs' departure until the manner of that departure would bring the new Government maximum advantage.[36] But this was an excessively Machiavellian interpretation of Peel's motives. Sir Robert had no doubt that Shaw Lefevre should be re-elected without opposition, but he believed so because Charles had done an excellent job as Speaker, and because the continuance of a Speaker who had shown such competence and neutrality made the best constitutional sense. He felt, too, that the Conservatives should rise above petty recrimination.[37]

Peel had little respect for some of the wild men in his own party who were keenest to challenge Shaw Lefevre, and described two of them to Graham as 'blockheads'.[38] But, wisely, he consulted several of his senior colleagues and found most of them shared his own view. Wellington, who was reported by Lady Holland as preferring to maintain Lefevre,[39] told Peel – as did one or two others – that 'if there had been any one of our own Party pre-eminently fitted for the situation, it would have been good policy to have proposed him'. But the obvious person, Goulburn, had lost interest and 'strange to say he is not so popular as he ought to be in the House of Commons'.[40] Bonham and Fremantle were quite sure that the Conservative Party could not find anyone who would 'discharge the duties of the office so efficiently and give the new administration so much support and assistance in carrying on the business of the House, as the present Speaker'.[41] And more than one correspondent implied, admiringly, that Charles could keep the hooligans in order! On the strength of all this, Peel set about pacifying the leading opponents of continuing Charles in the chair, through diplomatic letters and by supporting Bonham's persistent lobbying. The strength of Peel's conviction can be judged from a note he sent to Stanley:

> If it is really intended to try the strength of parties let that Question be manfully brought to issue upon an address for the Removal of the present ministry from office. I say, however, do not injure and damage the character of an individual. Do not commit such an act of injustice as to remove a Speaker against whom you have not only admitted that there is no personal charge but whom you have admitted to be pre-eminently qualified for the station.[42]

Peel did not wait for the absolute assurance he knew he could not get, but wrote directly to Shaw Lefevre on 1 August:

> It may be convenient to you to receive an intimation, previously to the meeting of Parliament, of the course which will probably be pursued in regard to the election for the Chair by those Members . . . who are opponents of Her Majesty's Government. I can answer for myself, that my own vote will be given with great satisfaction in favour of your Re-election as Speaker. I shall give that vote as much from sincere respect for yourself and confidence in your qualifications for the Office as from a strong impression that it is not for the public's advantage that the election

for the Chair should be selected, under circumstances like the present, as new ground for a party contest.

I cannot give you an assurance that the course which I intend to pursue will be universally acquiesced in by the party with which I am connected, because I have not had, and cannot hope to have the opportunity of communication with the greater number of them. But I have consulted those who take an active part in debate and in the general business of the House of Commons, and I am confident that of them a decided majority will take the course which I propose to take, and that they cordially concur in the feelings which induce me to adopt it.[43]

This handsome and considerate gesture elicited from Charles a warm letter of thanks, in which he spoke of 'the generous and cordial support which I have invariably received from you and which has tended materially to lessen the difficulties which must always attach to the Office of Speaker'. Le Marchant, when he heard of Peel's civilized attitude, wrote to Melbourne about it and Melbourne, who was 'quite touched' by his rival's courtesy, reported it to an approving Queen Victoria.[44] At the same time, Charles lost no time in discussing the next move with Russell and suggesting to him who might propose and second his re-election. He remembered, when writing to Russell, that 'when I proposed Abercromby . . . I received my instructions from yourself'.[45]

By the early days of August, the insurrection within the Conservative ranks was over. All but a few 'avowed malcontents' had come round to accepting Peel's view, and those malcontents were 'not worth consideration for *they* will never be pleased'.[46] On 13 August Bonham claimed that the feud over the Speakership was 'entirely over', and that some of those who had been making the most trouble were 'endeavouring to turn all that has occurred into a sort of "lark" on the part of the Anti-Lefevres generally. It is perhaps as well to accept this excuse, *if* they really do mean to keep quiet.'[47] He need not have worried. When the House met on 19 August Charles Shaw Lefevre was the only nominee for the Speakership.

Charles was not to suffer again the trauma of uncertainty about his acceptability for re-election. He had laid the foundations for his continuance as Speaker by his fine performance from 1839 to 1841. Nonetheless, in 1841 it was the absence of any strong, alternative candidate, the forbearance of the Duke of Wellington, and above all, the enlightened attitude of Sir Robert Peel, which saw Shaw Lefevre back in the chair. He had that share of good luck which is almost always needed to ensure a great career. He would give the House of Commons splendid service for another sixteen years, and would establish a powerful tradition of political neutrality for its future presiding officers to follow.

CHAPTER VIII

From Poor Law to Free Trade

The introduction of the new Poor Law created enormous bitterness among the poverty stricken, a bitterness doubtless exacerbated by the wide welcome and acceptance of its harsh discipline by most of the well-to-do, whether Whigs or Tories – though it had its persistent critics within the establishment, of whom *The Times* was the strongest. But its political abrasiveness should not be allowed to overshadow the magnitude of its administrative implications, which in turn had their own political and constitutional effects. The apparently centralizing apparatus of the Poor Law Commission certainly reduced the complexity of the existing situation by creating less than 700 local units out of over 15,000 parishes. But these new units, made the responsibility of local Boards of Guardians, in practice became the core of the modern system of local government, and immediately showed their unwillingness to accept, blindly, central direction. Their independence, and the continuous unpopularity and criticism of the commission, eventually led to a major constitutional shift, whereby the statutory three-man commission set up in 1834 was abolished, and the central functions of supervision of the local operations were made the direct responsibilty of a minister.

But for the first dozen years, the three statutory commissioners struggled with the duty to enforce a policy whereby the practice of giving outdoor relief to the poor should be replaced to the maximum possible extent by providing residential accommodation in workhouses. What was to be offered in the workhouses was to be so minimal that the poor would make every effort to avoid becoming residents of them. Thus would social and economic discipline be reasserted, and the cost to the local tax payer be reduced. In *Oliver Twist*, Charles Dickens has left us an immortal vision of some of the worst features of the new system, and the evidence of some well-documented episodes gives full credence to his imaginative denunciation. But the new system was only brought into being over several years; its character and experience were complex and regionally variable; its severity was unceasingly attacked, and its originally clear-cut formulas were never fully implemented. The extent of the success and failure of the New Poor Law, as an instrument of social policy during a period when the economic conditions of society were undergoing rapid and constant change, is likely to be controversially re-interpreted by each succeeding wave of historians.

John Shaw Lefevre looked back on his seven years as a Poor Law Commissioner as the hardest of his life. But it was not just because of the political uproar that he found it hard, though he disliked any public exposure and the criticism of the press. The kind of vituperation directed against him and his partners is well represented by a splendidly abusive anonymous letter, carefully preserved among his papers, from a citizen outraged by what he had heard of the:

> diet and incarceration of the Poor, confined in your Bastile in the Isle of Thanat. . . . I should not have conceived that such monsters as you and your colleagues and underlings could be found in Briton. But you are a tool to that detested faction the Whigs, and for Two Thousand a year, you would murder by starvation and other Cruelties the Aged and infirm, and bring up the young as a curse to the Country for weakness and debility – when I compare your diet for the Poor (numbers of whom have lived in respectability) and the list of dainties which your Lady sends in writing into your kitchen (many of whom I have by me) wherein Half the Globe is ransacked to furnish your Table, when you invite the Gourmands of your cursed faction to dinner. I shall get my friend Cleave to give us a drawing in his Paper of a Union Bastile with its Bread and Scaldmilk Cheese and water, and a Battersea Table, as set out, with all the French Dishes, and Sin no more Denman saying Grace, and your other Irish Co-ercion Bill friends, eager for the Gorge – But beware the Ides of March, there are a few Trechia, and Alibands yet, who will take vengeance for your Cruelty to their Parents and relatives on your unfeeling Head.[1]

What took a greater toll on John was the grinding administrative toil involved in the negotiation of the changes, and the establishment of the regulations demanded by the new scheme, with the hundreds of parishes and the new Boards of Guardians. Most of that negotiation was done by the assistant commissioners, who had regional responsibilities and travelled extensively; the commissioners, however, not only had to cope with the problems as seen by their own officers, but with the constant pressure exerted by the local churchmen and dignitaries who operated the system, and by the landed proprietors who resisted any proposal which weakened their local influence or outraged their own sense of how to deal with the impoverished. All of these had political sensibilities and many of them had access to channels of influence at Westminster, which meant that they could not, with safety, be ignored.[2] In addition, the assistant commissioners were, on the whole, an intelligent, capable and persistent team who did not always agree with each other and needed diplomatic handling at the centre, while relationships within the board, especially with Chadwick, were anything but easy.

That John almost certainly played a wearing role as peacemaker can be implied from a letter sent to him by his previous ministerial chief, Stanley, when he left the commission. Stanley sympathized with him for holding an 'Office which from its very nature must be a very thankless one, and must expose its occupant to incessant attack both in and out of Parliament', but none the less regretted his departure 'because I own that I have looked upon you as a check upon the more theoretical views of one of your Colleagues and your Secretary – and I fear that without you the Board will stand even more in need of ballast than it does at present.'[3]

There is, however, little to show how much and how distinctively John Shaw Lefevre pursued fundamental argument within the organization, because for all his obvious yearning for the political life, he kept his views on policy so much to himself (or, at any rate, so rarely expressed them on paper) that one can be forgiven for wondering how strongly he felt about the directions in which the institutions he served were going, and whether he was not much more interested in the process of simply keeping them working, and improving their functioning, to fulfil policies laid down by more committed colleagues. At the same time, he was not merely the nominee of the Whig hierarchy but was himself fully attuned to the thinking and the basic assumptions of the ruling landed class in which he had been raised, and the political reactions of whose members he understood instinctively. He would not be comfortable with or sympathetic to any more strictly rational and utilitarian tendencies of colleagues or subordinates. He had, as it were, the sharp mind and the patrician attitude of a senior civil servant of a later generation, but at the same time thought of himself as a Whig politician. As with his brother Charles, for all the latter's political acuteness, and like Charles who, too, to the end of his life was loyal to his party, he had a strong leaning towards cross-bench moderation or even neutrality.

Despite the undoubted strain of being a Poor Law Commissioner, it is difficult not to suspect that had John been content to limit his professional energies to coping with that major task, he might well have been able to continue without damaging his health. But John had been busy with voluntary activities ever since he came down from Cambridge, partly because he was genuinely enthusiastic about a whole range of concerns, and partly because of a persistent ambition for worldly success and recognition. He was, at one and the same time, a social improver and a climber up the political and social hierarchies. By 1830, when he was 33 years old, his traits as a compulsive worker with poor health, a mild and worrying nature, and a sensitive conscience, were becoming clear. What is not clear to the late-twentieth-century enquirer is how John did as much as he seems to have done! For in addition to his professional work and all the voluntary activities in which he must have invested quite a percentage of his available energy, he 'relaxed' by learning several new languages. And there is no doubt that his health was shaky and quite often put him out of action for days at a time. Even allowing for the fact that servants freed him from all humble, time-taking domestic tasks, one is driven to ask whether he can really have had many free hours to spend with his family, what constituted the normally expected load a senior participant in public life should carry, and whether the pace and character of living has changed so fundamentally that we distort and exaggerate the intensity with which our predecessors applied themselves to work and play. But however multifarious his concerns, John apparently needed wifely support to boost his confidence: his father-in-law, usually given to rather bland comment on his family, remarked wryly, in 1829, that Emily 'appears in excellent spirits, except about her husband who will not allow her to think he can be happy in her absence.'[4]

His father had seen to it that John was elected to a Fellowship of the Royal Society as early as 1820, and though he does not appear to have been active in its scientific work, he did retain a lively interest in mathematics throughout his life, and expressed it and a concern for other subjects through membership of the Society for the Diffusion of Useful Knowledge. He was proposed as a member of that Society by Brougham and Tooke, and served from 1828 until 1846. John was among the first ten elected members of the Political Economy Club: he was invited to attend the inaugural meeting and was elected at the subsequent session, when Ricardo was in the chair and James Mill was vice-chairman.[5] He attended regularly until 1831, when the meetings began to clash with those of the conveyancing community. John was also among the early members of the London Library and of the Athenaeum – in the latter case he followed his brother Charles, who had been a founding member and served on the club's committee in the 1830s. His stint at the Colonial Office had brought John new imperial connections. He was offered by Lord Glenelg, the President of the Board of Control for India, the headship of the Indian Law Commission, but turned it down because of 'the number and age of my young family'.[6] One may wonder how Indian development could have differed if Lefevre and not Macaulay had designed the legal system. The temptation of India was resisted, but almost immediately afterwards John was invited into the London organization which was planning the colonization of South Australia.

This was not fresh territory. The idea of a new colony in South Australia, inspired by the theories of Gibbon Wakefield, survived the abandonment of a short-lived Emigration Commission which lasted from June 1831 to August 1832. Subsequently, a South Australian Association had been set up in 1833 by a group of enthusiasts led by Robert Gouger, with strong financial backing from George Fife Angus. That group sought the encouragement of the Government and lobbied the Colonial Office, where most of their business was handled, sympathetically, by John Shaw Lefevre. John softened the suspicions Stanley had of the proposers, who were mostly Radicals. Bargaining over the necessary new legislation was delicate and intense. A breakthrough was achieved in March 1834, in a pleasantly informal situation. Robert Gouger had come to present a new plan just as 'his [Lefevre's] luncheon came in, and I told him that if he would allow me to read to him the heads of the plan more in detail, while he ate his lunch, I should be glad.' John ate, listened and was favourably impressed, and the consequent bill, which was introduced in July 1834 and attracted the support of the Duke of Wellington, became law on 15 August.[7] The Colony of South Australia was not to be officially proclaimed until the end of 1836, but under the act of 1834 a Colonization Commission for South Australia was appointed in May 1835 to act 'as an intermediary board between the colony and the Colonial Office'. John Shaw Lefevre was one of the ten commissioners: Robert Torrens, a fellow member of the Political Economy Club, was chairman, and the secretary was a friend destined for fame as a public servant – Rowland Hill.

One of the immediate concerns of Government and the commissioners was to find the first governor of the new colony. While John was still at the Colonial Office he had thought Torrens a good candidate, but Stanley would have none of him, and it was not until the following May that a naval officer, Captain Hindmarsh, a 'jovial hearty and energetic man', recommended by Lords Auckland, Palmerston and Howick, came on the scene and was subsequently appointed. Hindmarsh did not have a successful career as governor and was soon repatriated, but he took with him to Australia an intriguing contribution from the Shaw Lefevre household. Immediately before he embarked, Hindmarsh was invited to stay a night with the Shaw Lefevres at Battersea. Emily remembered that:

> I had sown in my garden a little patch of Indian corn and in the unusually hot sun of that summer it had fully ripened and was very fine. He was delighted with the large handsome ears. I got up early and gathered a bag full for Captain Hindmarsh to take with him. From that small bag, he afterward wrote and told me, Australia was covered with Indian corn, which was not known there before. The town of Adelaide was then building, and I gave the first Bell to the first Church. We often heard from Captain and Mrs Hindmarsh. How odd I thought it when she wrote to me for patterns of the most fashionable sleeves![8]

John Shaw Lefevre was probably put on the South Australia Commission in something of the same spirit that he was put on the Poor Law Commission

– as an able man who enjoyed the confidence of the Whig hierarchy by having been a parliamentary candidate, a junior minister, the protégé of Spencer, and as one who could be trusted to act as a continuous link with government. But he was to be continued in that capacity after the Whigs went out of office. The original South Australian Commission was revoked in January 1840, the ten commissioners being reduced to only three, who were to be paid and were to form at the same time a new body, the Colonial Land and Emigration Commission, with much wider responsibilities than South Australia. John was not one of the three, but a few weeks after Torrens resigned, in April 1841, John was made an unpaid Land and Emigration commissioner, a post which he held for five years.

The full amalgamation of the South Australian Commission's affairs with those of the Land and Emigration Commission was not completed until early in 1843, but thereafter John served on a South Australian committee of the commission until he resigned in May 1846. Admittedly, after 1843 he 'appeared at but rare intervals'[9] but by 1846 he could add to his record a spell of over twelve years of intimate concern for the establishment and early development of South Australia. His colonial responsibilities had begun with the emancipation of West Indian slaves; it continued with the creation of an antipodean colony without convicts. Those remedial, imaginative and humanitarian concerns might be seen by liberal critics of his administrative career as some compensation for his part in the rigorous domestic application of the new Poor Law.

During what must have been the exceptionally heavy work of the first months of 1835, when the whole superstructure of the Poor Law Commission was being created, John was simultaneously producing numerous reports for his patron, the third Earl Spencer, on a strategy which would guarantee the viability of the Spencer estates.[10] A clue as to his allocation of the working day is given in a letter from one of his juniors to a man concerned with Spencer affairs, pointing out that 'in general after 2 o'clock [Mr. Lefevre] is exclusively engaged on Public Business.'[11]

The Spencer concern was much reduced after 1835, but John's advice was sought quite often over the next decade. And there was no lack of competition for any time he may have gained through such reduction. His restless curiosity found another outlet in the creation of what we might now describe as a rather leisurely 'think tank' to consider, 'in the first instance . . . matters of scientific amusement rather than of importance.' He wrote to Rowland Hill:

> It has frequently occurred to me that if eight or ten individuals of average intellect were to direct their attention simultaneously and in concert on any specific object which it might be desirable to invent, or any particular

subject which it might be useful to explain, their joint efforts might produce a more satisfactory result than the unaided powers of a single person, although such person might be considerably superior to any one of the parties to the combination. I am anxious to try this experiment, and it would give me great pleasure if you would join me in it.

With the help of Hill and one of the assistant Poor Law commissioners, Coode, John gathered together a group of men, most of whom were already prominent or who were to become prominent in the coming years, including Dr Arnott, Lyon Playfair, Edwin Chadwick, Henry Cole, Arthur Symonds, Frederic Hill – Rowland's brother, Wentworth Dilke – father of Charles Dilke, and Professor Wheatstone, inventor of the electric telegraph. There do not seem to be any surviving records, but Rowland Hill recalled that among the first subjects discussed were Wheatstone's telegraph and his own notion for a printing machine.[12]

The intellectual and educational enthusiasms which John Shaw Lefevre had demonstrated at Cambridge, in the Political Economy Club, through his part in the Society for the Diffusion of Useful Knowledge, by his passion for learning new languages, by his Fellowship of the Royal Society (however slight his participation in the scientific work of that body), and by his continuing interest in mathematics, came to a special fruition in the context of the new University of London. That institution's early history is quite complex.[13] It opened first in 1828, as the result of Henry Brougham's persistence, in the form of a college free of religious influence, financed by private subscription, and called the University of London. The reaction against its godless character was strong enough to encourage the setting up of the Anglican sponsored King's College, which opened in 1831.

During the subsequent five years the future development of the two institutions was the subject of continuous lobbying and growing government involvement. Brougham, Russell and Melbourne were all caught up in the search for a sound basis from which progress could be made, but the main credit for shaping an acceptable compromise plan belongs to the Chancellor of the Exchequer, Spring Rice – the same man whose ambition to be Speaker was to be thwarted by the greater parliamentary appeal of Charles Shaw Lefevre. In 1835 the Cabinet decided that the original University should henceforward be known as University College, and that it and King's College and any subsequently approved bodies of the same character, should prepare their pupils for examinations which would be conducted by a new University of London, which would have the power to award degrees. Thus began, in 1836, the second University of London, as an examining and degree awarding, but not a teaching or research institution.

There is no evidence that John Shaw Lefevre was involved in any of the negotiations which led to the settlement of 1836, though the official

Historical Review of the University, first published in 1912, records politely that he had 'interested himself in [its] formation'. When the membership of the governing body of the new university, the Senate, was announced, John's name was one of the thirty-eight listed. He fitted the situation very conveniently from various standpoints: his personal qualities were admirably suited to an academic enterprise; he was a Government man on a senate wholly appointed by Government; and he was a lawyer – one of several representatives of that profession, although they were greatly outnumbered by medical men and scientists. But it may well be that he owed his appointment in large part not only to his political contacts, but to the fortunate experience of having been at Trinity College, Cambridge – as had Spring Rice and both the chosen first chancellor and first vice-chancellor of the university – the Earl of Burlington and John William Lubbock, respectively. More than a quarter of the whole senate were Trinity College men, and it is significant that the Cabinet plan for the new university stated that it would 'act as a Board of Examiners, and . . . perform all the functions of the Examiners in the Senate House of Cambridge'.

The new Senate did not meet until 1837, and after the first three meetings, the minutes of which give no record of attendance, practice soon showed the extent to which the big membership was largely window-dressing. The average number of senators who turned up at meetings settled down at about ten or a dozen, the hard core comprising the chancellor and vice-chancellor and a group most of whom were professionally engaged in academic work, especially medicine. John was not among this small group; indeed, between April 1837 and mid-June 1842 he was present at only 26 of the 145 meetings. He was a member of the Committee of the Faculty of Laws, and was elected as one of the two auditors of the university in 1841.[14] But there is little to show what manner of experience his senatorial status brought to John. His papers include a handful of letters, in 1838, from candidates, or their sponsors, for the registrarship of the university, seeking his support.[15] There is no pattern discernible from his attendance at meetings, and it is reasonable to assume that he came when he could, or perhaps turned out on some special appeal for support on particular questions. The first two or three years were dominated by the formal, structural matters peculiar to the situation of a brand new institution, but there were some important academic arguments, as well as administrative and financial problems, which had to be faced in seeing the new university properly established. Indeed, discussions may have been far more theoretical, because of the absence of any direct responsibility for teaching and research, than would be the case in a more orthodox educational institution.

John must have found it all an intriguing contrast to another, slighter, duty which he had acquired, namely the auditorship of Trinity College, Cambridge, for which he had been urged to stand by friends and had been elected in 1837-8: one of his supporters had remarked that 'Your connection with the London university will be no prejudice to you'.[16] That duty entailed only two visits to Cambridge each year, but he did receive, annually, for undertaking it, as we saw earlier, 'twenty guineas and a barrel of audit ale'. The parsimony of Government allowed of no such frivolous generosity in its metropolitan seat of learning! But John's standing in the London senate must have risen steadily, despite his relatively infrequent attendance. He was much more likely to turn up for meetings of the committee of the Faculty of Laws than for meetings of the senate; but that committee only met ten times between May 1837 and March 1842.[17] It may be, though, that at the six he attended and in other ways, John was particularly impressive. He may, of course, have been consulted informally on senate business: and he may have been recognized as a person particularly useful in dealing discreetly with ministers and with the Treasury. Alas, these speculations cannot be proven: but the Chancellor of the University, the Earl of Burlington, obviously thought him a very worthwhile – or at least a potentially very worthwhile – lay member, for on 7 June 1842 he addressed him thus:

> You will have seen by the notice sent to the Members of the Senate that Sir John Lubbock does not wish to be re-elected to the office of Vice-Chancellor for next year. On looking through the list of our members it appears to me that we could not choose a fitter successor to him than yourself, and I am anxious to know whether if elected you would object to fill the office for the ensuing year. The choice of course rests with the members of the Senate generally, but I am unwilling to allow the day of Election to arrive without taking any preliminary steps on the subject. The number of our meetings has latterly diminished very considerably, and unless anything unexpected should occur, there is no reason to suppose there will be any increase of business during next year. Though it cannot be said that the presence of the Vice Chancellor is absolutely necessary, yet it is certainly desirable he should usually be able to attend. The members of the Medical Profession are so liable to be unexpectedly called off, that I think it would be desirable not to select one of them to fill the Office if any other member of the Senate is willing to serve, and so large a number of Fellows belong to that profession the number from whom we can choose is rather limited.[18]

John did not take any offence at the notion of being the best of a limited field, and in due course he became vice-chancellor for the following year – but in all probability he never envisaged that the formality of re-electing him would be repeated nineteen times. He was not, by virtue of his new post, the chief academic and executive officer of a full university, but the vice-chairman of an increasingly complex and influential examining body.

He shared the chair with the chancellor, though as the years passed John presided more often than his formal superior, and neither of them was able to attend every meeting. But, as Burlington had indicated in 1842, the senate was meeting less frequently as the organization became more established, and after John became vice-chancellor they usually came together only at roughly monthly intervals during the academic year.

In 1841 John was in his seventh year as a Poor Law commissioner; he had only recently finished nearly five years as a commissioner for South Australia, and was just beginning as a Land and Emigration commissioner; he was, clearly, an important senator of the new University of London. Somerset House, which was the headquarters of the Poor Law Commission, also accommodated the university, and the Land and Emigration Commission's office was only a few blocks away in Adelphi Terrace, so John had no great physical problems in keeping in close touch with all his responsibilities. But he was increasingly tired of the strain of his life, and of being separated too much from his family. His Poor Law work had entailed some travelling, and one senses from the occasional letter to Emily a mix of weariness and ingenuous obsession with his own interests: 'I trust that after one more Sunday we shall pass many Sundays uninterruptedly together. I want to resume my usual ways – for it is a great trial to me to be thus unsettled . . . I have had no time to read anything for the last three weeks and it has been with great difficulty that I have been able to keep up my Hebrew'.[19] So far as his situation at the Poor Law Commission is concerned, John has been described as being, in 1838, 'near the end of his tether', though the evidence for this assertion is not clear.[20] Three years later, however, John decided he was not well enough to continue.

There is no good reason to question the decline in John Shaw Lefevre's health, whether it was due entirely to the physical and mental strain of holding so unpopular and contentious a position, or whether it was due in part to his own injudicious acceptance of tasks additional to his Poor Law duties. But in dealing with political natures, one must always probe a little into the timing of decisions which affect personal futures. For John was a political animal, even though he was never a successful politician. 'I dine at Holland House on Tuesday. I did not like to refuse. It does not answer to make myself too scarce amongst my political patrons and friends', he had written to his wife in 1836.[21] It is particularly unfortunate, therefore, that the record of what exactly transpired in the summer of 1841 is so exiguous. For John must have been well aware of the shakiness of the Whig Government, and it would be naive to believe that he had no anxieties as to what his future might hold if he were in so exposed a position as Poor Law commissioner with an unfamiliar administration in office. Even the Whig Government had only extended the Commission's life by a one and then a two year spell since 1839.

John Shaw Lefevre could hardly be blamed for seeking pastures new. And it is surely not too fanciful to think of him watching for possible fresh directions among his network of family and friends. Which brings us back to Denis Le Marchant. It will be remembered that Le Marchant, a friend of John's at Cambridge, and the brother-in-law of Henry Shaw Lefevre, had been private secretary to Brougham during the exciting years of the early 1830s, and had been a very successful propagandist in the cause of reform. His reward, in 1834, was appointment as Clerk of the Crown in Chancery. The death of his sister, Helen, in 1833, had left him uncle to three Shaw Lefevre nieces; and as we have seen, his own marriage, to Sarah Eliza Smith, had brought him another, though rather distant, link with the Shaw Lefevres.

Like John, Denis Le Marchant was politically and governmentally ambitious, and felt himself to be well placed within the party. He was certainly listed by Melbourne as a possible junior minister for the Colonial Office when the Whigs came back into office, and later in 1835 he was exploring the possibility of being given a very senior appointment in the Post Office.[22] But it was not until 1836 that he was able to leave the Court of Chancery for one of the joint assistant secretaryships at the Board of Trade, a post regarded as part of the civil service establishment, and newly subject to the requirement that it be held by a person legally qualified.[23] But he ached to enter the political ranks, and the possibility that he should become vice-president of the Board of Trade was mooted, though not followed through, in 1839.[24] One wonders whether he and John Shaw Lefevre, perhaps through family acquaintance, then discovered each others concerns and were able together to persuade ministers to agree to some official changes.

On 19 June 1841, a fortnight after the defeat of the Melbourne Government in the House of Commons, and just four days before parliament was dissolved, Le Marchant was appointed joint secretary to the Treasury: simultaneously John Shaw Lefevre, who had resigned from the Poor Law Commission, was appointed to the post which Le Marchant had just vacated at the Board of Trade, now retitled joint secretary. So unclear were the announcements about the new Treasury nominations – if indeed any announcements were made – that the most careful record has to admit the uncertainty as to the distribution of responsibilities between the two new secretaries.[25] But Le Marchant's earlier reputation as a publicist for the party's policies, and his correspondence with Russell during the subsequent general election, imply that he in fact inherited the traditional patronage secretaryship, with its special concern for electoral strategy and organization.[26] Le Marchant also stood as a candidate for Harwich, but was defeated, so that he had sacrificed a safe post at the Board of Trade fruitlessly, and by August 1841 was in the wilderness. The consolation prize – surely a reflection of a heavy sense of obligation on the part of the outgoing Government – was a baronetcy, gazetted in their last days in office. Russell had written somewhat plaintively to Melbourne that 'In former days Le Marchant would have got a pension. But it cannot be thought of now'.[27]

While Lord Stanley regretted Shaw Lefevre's departure from the Poor Law Commission, he thought John had made a more prudent move than had Le Marchant, and his electoral scepticism was well founded: he wrote to John:

> I conclude that your new Office is one of those which are considered as independent of political changes, though if it is so I do not understand its late possessor vacating it for one avowedly political: for I do not find that the supporters of the Government look with any confidence to the result of the approaching Elections.[28]

Illness, or tiredness, or an anxiety to find a quieter and more secure position, or some combination of such motives, must have driven John to negotiate a co-ordinated move from the Poor Law Commmission to the Board of Trade. Wittingly or unwittingly, Denis Le Marchant was involved in that move and suffered as a result, though he would appear again, almost uncannily, in Shaw Lefevre governmental and parliamentary territory a few years later. John Shaw Lefevre came through the 1841 transition more satisfactorily, though not without some bruising. The financial penalty was that he lost a quarter of his salary, the gain was a permanent position. In 1842, at the age of 45, he was a senior civil servant – a joint secretary to the Board of Trade; he was a Land and Emigration commissioner; and he was the vice-chancellor of the University of London. But he had not abandoned his political aspirations, and was by no means settled into an orthodox bureaucratic mould.

CHAPTER IX

'La Reyne le Veult'

If Charles Shaw Lefevre had been fortunate in the political circumstances of his re-election to the Speakership in 1841, his good fortune in that aspect of his tenure was to continue throughout the next sixteen years. In the northern division of Hampshire he was never opposed, even though sympathy for the Whigs was weakening steadily among the rural landowning gentry. No doubt his neutrality in the House of Commons and his local prestige protected him. At Westminster he had the support of Sir Robert Peel, and when in 1846 that reserved and awkward statesman split the Tory Party over the repeal of the Corn Laws, Charles went on presiding over a House in which, until long after he had retired from it, political loyalties were fluid and governmental majorities often uncertain. There was, therefore, an absence of that extreme, clear-cut partisanship which had attended his first election as Speaker in 1839, and the only likelihood of his removal came from a tentative manoeuvre by Derby and Disraeli in August 1852, when they were intrigued by the possibility of attracting Palmerston to join their first, short-lived, minority administration as Home Secretary. Spencer Walpole was very willing to give up the Home Office for the Speakership, Palmerston was mildly interested, and thus the plot hinged on the prospect that Shaw Lefevre 'might be willing to retire and take his peerage.' Charles, however, apparently showed no such willingness; the plan was abandoned and the incumbent of the chair was left to decide his own time for taking his peerage – which he did, interestingly enough, when Lord Palmerston was Prime Minister.[1]

The fact that political conditions helped to keep Charles in the chair for so long a period does not detract from his great success as Speaker. Even the argument that he never had to cope with the procedural guerilla warfare waged later in the century by the Irish members can be met to a great extent by recalling the atmosphere of the House when he first presided over it:

> Party spirit was inflamed by many burning questions; the rude spirits of a Reformed Parliament had not yet been broken to the rules and traditions of order. Ministers had been weakened by successive defeats and failures; their party was disunited; and the Radicals and O'Connell's tail were uneasy allies on their right flank. The Opposition, supported by the House of Lords in every assault upon the Ministerial policy, were hostile,

aggressive, and confident. There were fierce passages of arms between Lord Stanley and O'Connell; Ministers were hotly pressed, alike by friends and foes; and the excitement of the strife too often found expression in unaccustomed clamour and disorders.[2]

Discipline, in short, was 'relaxed', and it was not uncommon to hear 'braying, baa-ing, crowing, mewing of animals' and 'other disorderly interruptions'.[3] And a few years later there came Peel's traumatic repeal of the Corn Laws, which

aroused the bitterest animosities and passions. The scathing sarcasms of Mr. Disraeli, the fierce denunciations of Lord George Bentinck, and the wild clamour of enraged protectionists assailed the falling statesman; and rarely have the walls of the House of Commons witnessed more exciting scenes than during the closing months of his last painful struggles. These stormy contests were a severe ordeal to the Speaker.[4]

Shaw Lefevre's first claim to fame rests on his ability to restore order, to re-establish the dignity and authority of the chair, and to set a standard of behaviour in an arena of legitimate, fierce conflict which, save in a few bad years, has been an acceptable goal of the House ever since. Part of this achievement reflected his practical espousal of the political neutrality of his office. He does not seem to have spoken or written about the desirability of that neutrality – he simply donned it like a familiar coat. It might be argued that he was helped by never having been an intense partisan, and that he realized that it paid him to be even less partisan in an era of confused and unclear political alliances, though the latter suggestion is a little shabby. From the outset, he abandoned the practice of his predecessors of speaking and voting in committee on highly controversial issues. Only once, in the penultimate year of his tenure, did he speak in committee, and then only on the non-controversial matter of the management of the British Museum.[5] But his success in insisting on an orderly House was due to the strength of a personality which embraced political neutrality along with other qualities probably more readily recognized and respected by members, not least among them being a geniality which ensured his popularity. He was, of course, among a great majority of men of his own class and background, for this was still the period in which more than three quarters of the MPs, irrespective of party allegiance, were themselves of, or were closely connected with, the landed elite. Even so, they were an assembly of over 650 individualists, unlikely to heed a presiding officer unless he had a natural aptitude for presiding. Charles was, quite simply, in modern terms, 'a natural' for the job he found himself doing.

The Speaker's physical appearance and his voice, combined with his sense

of theatre, remained indelibly in the minds of those who knew him and
saw him in action. He had an imposing presence: a handsome man, tall
and dark, he processed into the chamber with a conscious but nonetheless
natural and easy dignity, and it was said of him that 'the mere rustle of
his robes was sufficient to restore order.'[6] An eyewitness of the funeral of
the Duke of Wellington at St Paul's in 1852 told how, when the Speaker
entered the cathedral, 'such was the effect of his commanding presence and
stately dignity' that, led by the Members of Parliament, every one in the
vast congregation rose simultaneously.[7] His voice was, to use the words
of several commentators, clear, manly, rich and sonorous, and Montagu
Butler remembered 'the grand leonine roar of his "Order, Order!"' as 'quite
irresistible' fifty years after hearing it.[8]

Shaw Lefevre's manner was invariably fair, courteous, tactful and conciliatory, and his temper was never ruffled: but he was unyieldingly, though
good-naturedly, firm and his rulings were scarcely ever challenged. He had
the sportsman's sharp reactions to support his political intuition, and when
twenty members leapt up to speak, simultaneously, he picked on one
unhesitatingly, explaining afterwards that 'I have been shooting rabbits
all my life, and have learnt to mark the right one.'[9] But, above all, he
was insistent that the dignity of the chair be respected, and brought to the
position the glamour which was inherent in it as a unique national institution.
For instance, at the official Speaker's dinners, when fifty members were his
guests, he reintroduced an old rule by which they had to appear in full dress.[10]
In all its outward manifestations, his regime was indeed a splendid one.

In his old age, Charles was asked by a niece how he accounted for his success in keeping order, and his answer illuminates something of his assessment
of his fellows and his down-to-earth technique for dealing with them:

> He said he thought it was due to certain principles which he always acted
> upon. One of these was, that at the beginning of a new parliament, he
> was most particular that every form of the House should be observed.
> He would not allow anything to be passed over; so that the new Members
> were trained into good ways from the beginning and the smallest signs of
> disorder were checked at once.
> He said: 'I always tried to foresee difficulties and to avert them. Many
> people will tell you that it is better to wait till a crisis arises and then
> to deal with it at the moment; but I never thought that a wise plan. My
> idea was, never to let a Member make a fool of himself if I could help it,
> and the course I adopted was this: If I saw in the orders for the day that a
> Member had given notice of anything irregular, I would send for him and
> talk it over with him and explain to him that such and such things could
> not be.' He added that at last, he had but to lean forward in the Chair and
> they minded him.

Then he said, 'So much depended on studying the characteristics of the Members. During those long sittings and adjourned debates, when I was supposed to be asleep, I used to watch them and learn from their expressions and even from their gestures what they were like and what sort of tempers they had and how best they could be managed. Then when the occasion arose one knew how to deal with them. They could not all be treated alike. The hot-tempered could always be managed by gentleness. This study was much more interesting to me than the actual debate, and it kept up my attention. Dan O'Connell had the Irish Members entirely under his control and could lead them by a sign or a nod. I once had to call him to order for using improper language, but after that he always helped me.'[11]

The outward gloss was no false front, for it was merely the suave reflection of a total grasp of the rules and procedures, an ability to apply and to extend them with despatch, and an enthusiasm to see them improved. So complete and assured was his control of the House, as a result of the combination of his expert knowledge and his commanding manner, that if 'a situation arose for which there was no precedent he would calmly make one, forestalling any possible objections by observing blandly that it was the well known practice of the House.' As a student of the Speakership has asked, 'Who would presume to argue with such a procedural oracle?'[12] Only in his keenness to facilitate the business of the House did he fail to achieve all that he thought necessary.

Charles had been a leader in improving the handling of private bills in the 1830s, and when faced as Speaker with the growing pressures of both public and private legislative proposals on the time of the House, he put forward to select committees in 1848 and 1854 extensive plans for clearing away many of the ancient practices.[13] In that exercise he had the advantage of having at his right hand Thomas Erskine May, who in his junior years as an examiner of petitions for private bills, had published, in 1844, the first edition of his now monumental and authoritative treatise on the procedure of the Commons.[14] The two men were agreed on what needed to be done, but though most of their recommendations were accepted, the more radical ideas which threatened to involve some limitation of debate were turned down.[15] Perhaps Charles was ahead of his time, given the later traumas of the House, but his thrustful wish to remove obstacles may reflect some authoritarian tendency lurking beneath all the *bonhomie* – it had shown itself earlier in his partial endorsement of Chadwick's centralizing passion in the proposed organization of the rural police – also unacceptable to the establishment of the day.

Shaw Lefevre did not have a free hand to deal with the complicated staffing arrangements of the House of Commons, however strong his influence. He had to negotiate with those members who were themselves procedurally expert and specially interested, on the one hand, and with the Government, usually through the Prime Minister or the Chancellor of the Exchequer as regards money and patronage, on the other hand. Even on details of accommodation he was limited: when he was asked to help with the visit of a French Vicomte, he replied with a touch of asperity that 'My own authority does not extend to the Ladies Gallery (if such a miserable hole as they occupy is worthy of such a designation) over which Lord Charles Russell [the Serjeant-at-Arms] exercises an absolute control.'[16] But he was not greedy for staff, and was obviously keen to rationalize the availability of expert knowledge for the ultimate benefit of both members and Government.[17]

There is only a small amount of correspondence extant between Charles and the leading statesmen of his time in the chair, among them Peel, Russell, Palmerston and Gladstone. Much of it is about technical questions concerning the business of the House of Commons, and in it, as in those men's public statements about Charles' quality as Speaker, there is every sign of genuinely high respect for him. But one senses that between him and Sir Robert Peel there was a personal warmth which came from their mutual interest in agriculture, and perhaps from the attraction to each other of two men who, despite their public status, were essentially loners. On one occasion when Peel invited Charles to Drayton Manor, he warned him that Prince George of Cambridge would be there, but went on, with far more relish, to say that he wanted to show Charles 'the draining which I have in contemplation under the superintendence of Mr. Josiah Parkes.' And in the year of Peel's fall from power, he and the Speaker were exchanging letters and data about a new method of box-feeding bullocks.

Only months before Peel's fatal accident, Charles regretted that because of a shooting trip he would not be able to visit Drayton, but told Peel how he had 'enjoyed enough fresh air and exercise to do away with the ill effects of the last session.'[18] It was the cry of the outdoorsman, recognized very early in his Speakership by a journalist who noticed that 'he seizes every opportunity to indulge in the healthful exercise of riding on horseback.'[19] He rode every day on Rotten Row, mixing business with pleasure, for his companions were sometimes members who would settle matters with him and then ride straight down to the House, leaving their grooms to lead the horses home. He often had one or more of his daughters, nieces and other young ladies on each side of him as well, and he taught them all how to wheel round in the right curve so that they rode back in the same straight line – a manoeuvre he called 'The Parliamentary Slow Train.' His horsemanship and his work for and pride in the Hampshire Yeomanry always earned him a military salute from the Queen when he bowed to her as she passed.[20]

There can be few other men who achieved any office as high as the Speakership of the House of Commons who attracted so much praise and so little criticism, either when he held the position or afterwards, as Charles Shaw Lefevre. It is inconceivable that there were no members dissatisfied with his rulings, resentful of his popularity or just unhappy with his personality; but no contemporary murmurings against him seem to have survived. There were those who implied, after his retirement, that he was 'only' a great Speaker. When there was a possibility that he might be appointed Lord Lieutenant of Ireland, in 1864, the rather cruel comment was made, privately, by the then Editor of *The Times*, John Delane, that he would 'look the part well enough, and as looks are most part of the duties there would be no occasion to complain.' And he was given only modified praise by the Earl of Selborne, who felt that he had nothing like the 'natural ability' of his brother John.[21] But such snipings, which could certainly be challenged, cannot dim the brightness of those eighteen years in the chair. It was the good fortune of Parliament that so strong a man, with so clear a notion of what the Speaker's role should be, was enabled, by his own ability and by the political accidents of the era, to have the chance to consolidate so admirable a regime.

Long after Charles Shaw Lefevre had become Viscount Eversley, he dined one evening in 1875 with the Prince of Wales, at Strathfield Saye. Charles never smoked, and when the Prince commented on that abstemiousness, the retired Speaker explained, 'You see, Sir, *I* belong to the last century.'[22] Whether or not that was a totally adequate reason for being a non-smoker, the idea that Charles was an eighteenth rather than a nineteenth century character is certainly a fair claim in a political context. He had grown up in an eighteenth-century constitutional tradition, had been given a seat in the House of Commons in accordance with the eighteenth-century practice of aristocratic patronage, and showed throughout his life no enthusiasm for any advance on the Whig Reform Act of 1832, under which he conducted himself so notably as Speaker. He took no significant part in national politics after his retirement in 1857, and without undue exaggeration or inaccuracy his parliamentary career could be said to have been conceived and conducted in eighteenth-century terms: the prospect of popular democracy was not to be accepted, let alone to be regarded as inevitable, until ten years after Charles moved out of the chair. However much he helped to control a volatile House and modernize its procedure, his was a detached eminence which protected him against electoral challenge and from changes which were beginning to affect the lives of ordinary members, of ministers, and of public servants.

It is as well not to break into the record of Charles's long spell in the chair. We must postpone consideration of John Shaw Lefevre's sojourn at the Board of Trade, therefore, and follow, first, the course of events in the late 1840s which brought Charles and John, together with Denis Le Marchant, into a remarkable parliamentary proximity, and which provided the two younger men with solid bases for the rest of their careers.

Among the host of sinecure offices which were increasingly attacked and reduced in number by the reformers of the late eighteenth and early nineteenth centuries, one of the 'most notorious' was the post of Clerk of the Parliaments, whose somewhat equivocal title meant then, as it means today, that its holder acted mainly as the clerk of the House of Lords. But he also carried on some of the duties of the original clerkship of what was then a unicameral legislature, and continued – again, as today – to preside as clerk when the two Houses, or a representative combination of their members, met together on such occasions as the state opening of Parliament, or to give the royal assent to legislation. Like so many offices, this one had become virtually a piece of private property, and was 'owned' by persons who collected the considerable stipend but rarely or never performed any of the duties.

In 1788 the office had come into the hands of George Rose, MP for Lymington until his death in 1818, who handed it on to his son Sir G.H. Rose, who sat in the Commons for Southampton and then for Christchurch from 1818 until 1844, with only one short break. A few years earlier a probing select committee had discovered that the clerk was receiving fees amounting to £5,000 a year, and an official house, but that no clerk had done any duty for nearly a century! Reform, however, was not to be achieved in a hurry, and not by any sudden, drastic diminution of the income of the Rose family. In 1824 an act provided that when the post next fell vacant, it should thereafter be filled in person and that the clerk assistant at such time should automatically succeed to it. Sir G.H. Rose, apparently unmoved by this development, continued to hold on to the office and was still absentee Clerk of the Parliaments in 1848, when the then clerk assistant had to be replaced. Rose was then 77 years old, and it was widely assumed that the new clerk assistant would almost certainly succeed to the clerkship a few years hence. Thus, even though the fees had been abolished and a salary of £4,000 in 1824 was reduced to £2,500 in 1848, the prospects of whoever became clerk assistant in the latter year were attractive, for the clerk, under the new arrangements, would only be removable by the sovereign on an address from the House of Lords, there was no statutory retiring age, the duties were regarded as not very onerous, and the status of the post as an ancient office of state, despite all its recent murky, sinecure past, was very high.[23]

How many other contenders there may have been for this desirable official position is unclear, but there were at least three – Sir David Dundas, Denis Le Marchant and John Shaw Lefevre. Although the Prime Minister, Lord John Russell, was the crucial dispenser of this piece of patronage, the person most concerned with whoever was to have it was the Lord Chancellor, to whom the clerk assistant would be most directly responsible. The Chancellor was Lord Cottenham, then near the end of the second of two terms on the Woolsack. He was a cold, reserved man, overwhelmingly interested in professional legal matters, who rarely spoke in Cabinet unless he was asked, directly, for his legal opinion.[24] Indeed, as William Brougham (a younger brother of Lord Brougham, who would succeed to the Barony in 1868), since 1835 a Master in Chancery, told John Shaw Lefevre, 'You will not find him [Cottenham] very communicative.'

Cottenham's first choice was Dundas, who was MP for Sutherland and had been Solicitor General since July 1846, but who was in poor health and about to resign his office.[25] The clerkship was offered to him, only to be refused after much discussion, some of it with William Brougham, who seems to have been something of a broker in the whole affair and who had John in mind as the next most desirable candidate. Cottenham at first brushed John aside because he 'knew nothing of appeal business and would have to learn altogether the art of drawing Decrees', but Brougham assured him that John could make himself thorough master of anything in three months and would work like a horse – arguments which helped to convince the Lord Chancellor, after Dundas withdrew, that John would be the best alternative.[26]

Denis Le Marchant had been out of office for five years after 1841, during which time he edited Horace Walpole's *Memoirs of George III*. When the Whigs came to power again in 1846 he was returned unopposed to fill a seat for Worcester, but did not contest it at the general election of 1847. Lord John Russell then did for Le Marchant what Lord Grey had done for John Shaw Lefevre fourteen years before – appointed him to be an under-secretary of State despite his not having a seat in the House of Commons. This post was at the Home Office, where Le Marchant helped in the struggle to contain the Chartist agitation which was sweeping the country.

When he was made aware of the clerk assistant vacancy, Le Marchant 'was cockered up to ask Lord John [Russell] "to put my name on the list of candidates."' But he did not take his chances very seriously. Russell, however, must have been anxious to pursue Le Marchant's interests and had put his and John's names before Cottenham and Lord Lansdowne, the Lord President of the Council. Both peers were 'decidedly of the opinion that Lefevre's would be the more acceptable appointment to the Lords.' The Prime Minister told Le Marchant that he 'could not on such a matter overrule their decision', but suggested that Le Marchant might, if he wished, have John Shaw Lefevre's joint secretaryship at the Board of Trade. Le Marchant was much put out:

> I did not attempt to disguise from Lord John that I thought this not very handsome treatment, but in the uncertain state of politics and seeing that the Home Office was not the road to preferment I determined to return to the Board of Trade, truly sorry that I ever left it.

Le Marchant reckoned that what he called his 'escapade' of having taken a seat for Worcester and then the under-secretaryship at the Home Office had cost him 'very nearly £10,000'.[27] He returned to the Board of Trade, taking over from John just seven years after he had made way for him in order to try, unsuccessfully, to be returned for Harwich in 1841. As he could not have the House of Lords' post, he remained on Lord John Russell's conscience, with an interesting result for our chronicle.

There is nothing to indicate whether or not Charles Shaw Lefevre was in any way influential in the matter of his brother's appointment as clerk assistant, but it would be surprising if he was unable, or too scrupulous, to put in a word on John's behalf. There was a Littleton Powys and a young Waldegrave on the staff of the House in 1848, and it would be naive to think that Charles had been totally averse to using his position in traditional fashion to meet the demands of his relatives.[28] But however gratified he may have been about John's new job, he was not to be at all enthusiastic about the last episode in the mid-century re-arrangements of the lives of John and of Denis Le Marchant. That occurred two years afterwards, when the clerkship of the House of Commons fell vacant, through the death of the incumbent, John Henry Ley.[29]

Russell took advantage of this new vacancy to pay his debt to Le Marchant. He proposed to Labouchere, the President of the Board of Trade, that Le Marchant should be replaced at the Board by James Booth, and that Le Marchant should become Clerk of the House. Labouchere was content, and Le Marchant swallowed his real ambition:

> Political employment would have suited me better, and would have been more to my taste, but a combination of obstacles having dashed my hopes in that direction, there was no office that I coveted so much as either of the Parliamentary Clerkships.[30]

Charles Shaw Lefevre was not pleased. He wanted his protégé, Erskine May, to have the clerkship. The fact that another member of his family had landed a safe and prestigious post was no compensation for Le Marchant's inexperience. Many years later Charles felt that 'Russell's conduct in giving [Le Marchant] that appointment (merely as a provision for a friend and an old supporter of the government) [was] quite unjustifiable.' At the time he wrote rather coolly to Russell, saying that 'Le Marchant is an old friend of mine, and if you determine to appoint him, I will do my best to *train* him and make him a good Clerk.'[31]

Thus by the spring of 1848, and for nine years thereafter, the organization and smooth running of the two Houses of Parliament were, to a very considerable degree, the responsibility of two brothers, who were joined in that enterprise for the last seven of those years by a brother-in-law. Charles and John were to leave behind them notable reputations for their achievements in office, but no more theatrical expression of their partnership exists than

Denis Le Marchant. *Illustrated London News*, 22 Feb 1851.

the memory of the two brothers performing the ancient ceremony of giving the royal assent to legislation. The Clerk of the Parliaments, 'standing with his back to Mr. Speaker, and turning his head with the condescension of reflected royalty, announces the Queen's assent in the time-honoured words, "La Reyne le veult."' And John was, apparently, no less able than his brother to look the part, for he was reported as possessing:

> a bearing and presence most appropriate to the traditions that are embodied in these forms, and his appearance . . . is always calculated to remind the members that they are living under a system which may seem to the vain to be laughable, but which from its antiquity and success must always be respectable.[32]

One could imagine the brothers – or certainly the robust Charles – claiming with some justice that the bills of the 1850s became acts only with the blessing of the Shaw Lefevres!

Although nothing came of the suggestion that Speaker Shaw Lefevre might be willing to make way for someone else in 1852, he had by then been in office since 1839, and many people must have begun to wonder whether he might not soon decide to retire. His acceptability and his authority were so well established, however, that he had sailed confidently through the turmoil of the post Corn Law years and the Chartist uproar, had seen Peel and Wellington go to their graves in elaborate rituals over which he helped to preside, had rejoiced with the nation in its enthusiastic reception of the Great Exhibition of 1851, and after the fall of the first Conservative administration of Lord Derby, took the Coalition Government of Lord Aberdeen, the Crimean War, and the accession of the irrepressible Palmerston to the Prime Ministership in February 1855, in his stride. But six months later several papers, led by the *Morning Chronicle*, reported that rumours of Charles's impending retirement had 'assumed a more tangible shape, probably on account of the Rt. Hon. Gentleman's health having apparently been affected by his arduous and responsible duties.' The *Chronicle* even had a title – Baron Heckfield – ready for Charles, and thought his probable successor would be either Sir George Grey or Mr Baines.[33]

Whether this suggestion was part of a serious political manoeuvre, or whether it was just a journalistic blunder, it had no backing from Charles. His reaction was swift and politically defensive, and interesting in its forecast of uncertainties to come. He wrote to Erskine May:

> I cannot imagine by whom that paragraph was inserted . . . my attention was not drawn to it for at least a week after its appearance, when I saw it for the first time in a County paper – and then I had to answer letters of congratulation etc as well as to contradict it in all the County journals to prevent the commencement of a canvass in North Hampshire – all of which excited my wrath exceedingly. . . . I do not anticipate a meeting of Parliament in November, but if Ministers receive any factious opposition in the Spring I fear there will be a Dissolution – and then I feel the difficulties of my position will commence.[34]

The dissolution did not happen until more than a year later, in the early spring of 1857, but its inevitability then triggered Charles' resignation, which he announced on 9 March of that year. It is clear that he calculated the advantages of going very shrewdly. Erskine May claimed that he was the first to know of the Speaker's intention after Charles' family, and 'felt that for his own interests a more favourable opportunity for his retirement could not have arisen.'[35] Charles may well have believed – correctly – that local patience with a non-partisan, but nonetheless a Whig, member was waning. Certainly, at the subsequent election, two Conservatives were returned for North Hampshire, which thereafter remained a safe Conservative constituency. But he may well also have considered that his prospects of continuing in the chair, if party strengths after an election were nicely balanced, and if there was a real chance of the Conservatives taking over, might be weak. And not only would he not relish a challenge and a loss of place; he also faced the possibility that he might lose the chance of negotiating an honourable and generous retirement with Lord Palmerston as Prime Minister.

As it turned out, Palmerston survived the general election and did not lose office until early in 1858. It is by no means unlikely, however, that quite apart from the political calculations which Charles made in the previous year, he had begun to feel that he had been in the chair long enough. When he did retire, one mathematically inclined reporter pointed to the length of Charles's service – of sixty-two Speakers, his tenure was the longest but one – and concluded that he had 'sat for above 18,000 hours in the chair itself, without reckoning the laborious attendance in his official room' during hours when the House was not actually sitting.[36] He could, with reason, have begun to find the strain too wearing. He confessed to his family that 'he found his best ear did not reach as far as it had done and from time to time was required to do, down the House.' And the Queen recorded him as saying that he 'felt himself getting very deaf and therefore feared he could no longer be of any use.'[37] Nobody who has suffered the embarrassment involved in missing what a chairman should have heard, will fail to understand Charles' worry. And lastly, there loomed a domestic upset because the Speaker's quarters in the new Houses of Parliament were almost ready, and the lease of the official house in Eaton Square, where the Shaw Lefevres had lived for many years, would soon come to an end. It made sense to leave job and house together.[38]

Charles was not to get all that he wanted on giving up without something of a tussle. At first he was offered a barony, together with a pension of £2,000 for two lives. For the sake of the office of Speaker and because of his own assessment of his personal worth, Charles pushed for more. Precedents were examined and then his willing accomplice, Erskine May,

> prepared a memorandum of his eminent services and of the signal improvements he had effected in the proceedings of the House. This [wrote May] he forwarded to Lord Palmerston in a letter stating that it had been written by me and acknowledging in a very handsome manner the assistance he had received from me in carrying into effect all the improvements referred to in the Memorandum. The next day he was informed that he would be created a Viscount.[39]

Charles refused the initial pension because 'he could not bear the thought of being a burden to posterity',[40] but was happy to take £4,000 a year for the rest of his own life. Palmerston accepted this and the claim for a notch up in the peerage without delay. That claim was based largely on the award of a viscountcy to Manners Sutton in 1835, despite the fact that the two Speakers prior to Manners Sutton, and Abercromby, who had come between him and Shaw Lefevre, were only awarded baronies. The Prime Minister's justification of the amended proposal was put to Queen Victoria on 18 March:

> The present Speaker is very anxious that his services, which, in fact, have been more meritorious and useful than those of Mr Manners Sutton, should not appear to be considered by your Majesty as less deserving of your Majesty's Royal favour, and as the present Speaker may justly be said to have been the best who ever filled the chair, Viscount Palmerston would beg to submit for your Majesty's gracious approval that he may be created Viscount Eversley. It will be well at the same time if your Majesty should sanction this arrangement that a Record should be entered at the Home Office stating that this act of grace and favour of your Majesty being founded on the peculiar circumstances of the case, is not to [be] deemed a precedent for the cases of future Speakers.
>
> Lord Canterbury [Manners Sutton] was also made a Grand Cross of the Civil Order of the Bath; it will be for your Majesty to consider whether it might not be gracious to follow in all respects on the present occasion the course which was pursued in the case of Mr Manners Sutton.[41]

On the day following Palmerston wrote to say that all was well.[42] Charles Shaw Lefevre was to become Viscount Eversley, he was to have his GCB, and Parliament would vote him a pension of £4,000 a year. He had chosen the title from a village close to Heckfield, a small part of which he owned; he liked the sound of it, and with his instinct for public relations he was fully aware that the place was widely known, being the home of his neighbour, that zealous and energetic Christian preacher and writer, Charles Kingsley.[43] But Charles had not merely gained personal benefit by his persistence, for despite Palmerston's diplomatic reservation, the Shaw Lefevre precedent established a convention – from his time onward a viscountcy was offered automatically to every retiring Speaker until the award of Life Peerages largely replaced hereditary ennoblements in the 1960s.

The leading men of the House of Commons all paid their tributes to Charles a week before the details of the retirement were settled, and while their speeches underlined the genuine admiration which was showered on him publicly, their fulsome praise, couched in the rolling phrases of House of Commons rhetoric, is perhaps less worth quoting than a more private expression of respect found among family papers. It came from a contemporary, Sir Henry George Ward, a fellow MP with Charles from 1832 until 1849, who in 1857 was Governor of Ceylon and who was to die from cholera while Governor of Madras, only three years later. Ward had little or nothing to gain from paying court to Charles, and his letter is that of a rather lonely man writing from far away without any selfish material motive. His words express what was surely the quality which made Shaw Lefevre so fine a Speaker:

> You were certainly born for the place which you so long and nobly filled, for you assumed the whole authority from the moment that you took the Chair; and, if your sway were willingly submitted to it was because every man felt in his heart that power could never be placed in abler or more impartial hands.[44]

CHAPTER X

Omnibus Commissioner

John Shaw Lefevre, raised in the same era and sharing the same basic political ambition as his elder brother, was far more vulnerable to the pressures of nineteenth-century constitutional development. He had begun his political life in the eighteenth-century aura of aristocratic hegemony, but his first, unsuccessful attempt to enter the House of Commons was made under the new arrangements consequent on the Reform Bill he had played a part in shaping. He had been privileged, briefly, to fill a ministerial post without a seat in Parliament – one of the later, though by no means the last, examples of a possibility which was to become normally unacceptable. And his place on the statutory Poor Law Commission exposed him, as neither an elected politician nor a tenured civil servant, to much public obloquy. When, in 1841, he moved fully into the civil service, it was to a service still organized on eighteenth-century lines – he was appointed through political patronage to a post which gave him virtually safe tenure until retirement. In fact, he and his brother-in-law, Denis Le Marchant, had already established themselves in that peculiar and quite short-lived mid-nineteenth-century category of constitutional hybrids, half politicians, half civil servants – and both were to compound that status still further.[1]

The Board of Trade which John served was, like all the great Departments of State, a very small show by twentieth-century standards. It had an establishment of less than fifty when he joined it, and it grew only slightly during his tenure of nearly seven years. The Board, like many of its fellow organizations, had become a mere phantom: the membership included the highest dignitaries of Church and State, but while the 'Board' still met formally for part of John's time and its decisions were minuted throughout his spell, in effect this meant regular meetings of only the two ministers, the President and Vice-President, who were responsible to Parliament, with the two joint assistant secretaries in attendance. Of one of its earlier manifestations – for the organization had first appeared on the scene as long ago as 1694 – a wit had proclaimed that:

These high officials, all agree,
Are grossly overpaid.
There never was a Board, and now
There isn't any Trade.

John Shaw Lefevre would no doubt have objected strongly to being considered overpaid, having just lost a quarter of the salary he had received at the Poor Law Commission. But he would have been on indisputably stronger ground in arguing that there was, in the 1840s, plenty of trade, and, what is more, free trade. For during the previous decade or more, the Board had been a base from which the free trade doctrine had been sedulously propagated. Even so, its executive work hitherto had been quite limited, and it was only during the 1840s that new functions arising out of the developing economy and technology were increasingly entrusted to it.[2]

What was the single most senior permanent post at the Board of Trade, and what came to be known in terms still used – the permanent secretary – had been divided between two assistant secretaries in 1829; and as we have seen, since 1836, when Denis Le Marchant was appointed to be one of them, it had been made obligatory that whoever filled that particular job should be a person with legal qualifications. The other assistant secretaryship was focused primarily on the economic and statistical aspects of the Board's work, though in so small a unit there was a good deal of overlapping of effort and interest. John's partner, for all but the last few months of his term of office, was John McGregor, another constitutional hybrid, who left to become MP for Glasgow, when he was succeeded by George Richardson Porter. Both are remembered chiefly as statisticians who shared with John Whiggish and utilitarian sentiments. More important for John were his ministerial chiefs, particularly Gladstone and the Earl of Dalhousie.

There was no time for John to settle into any routine during the last six weeks of Melbourne's administration, in the summer of 1841, when Labouchere was president and Fox Maule (later Lord Panmure) vice-president of the Board. They were replaced when the Conservatives took office by Lord Ripon and the young Gladstone, and in May 1843 Gladstone became president and had the Earl of Dalhousie as his junior. John had been in contact with Gladstone at least once before, when in 1835 the latter had sent him a long paper on West Indian educational problems. The older man had not agreed with all of Gladstone's views, but respected 'the spirit of candour and fairness' which he felt pervaded the whole document.[3] Their new conjunction developed into a friendly, if sometimes rather delicate, lifelong relationship.

At the Board, Gladstone quickly assumed a major role. He remembered finding himself without guidance from the 'good natured but timid' Ripon, who seemed happy to let his energetic vice-president take 'the ordinary business of the department' into his hands 'to transact with the Secretaries, one of them Macgregor, a loose-minded Free Trader, the other Lefevre, a clear and scientific one.'[4] And John must have been brought some way into the president's domestic circle, for when the crisis over Maynooth led to Gladstone's resignation in 1845, Mrs Gladstone wrote 'That kind, hearty Mr Lefevre . . . was turned quite sick.'[5] Dalhousie took over from Gladstone, and after Peel's fall, John served under the Earl of Clarendon for a year, until, in the last of these short-lived ministerial tenures, reminiscent of the game of musical chairs, Labouchere returned to the presidency. John had five changes of political chief in seven years as joint secretary.

The rapid turnover of leadership did not prevent a steady progress of innovation and inquiry in the Board of Trade's widening area of responsibility. The reduction and rationalization of tariffs was the subject of much external negotiation, for which John's earlier experience with the colonies and with the compensation of the slave owners was very relevant. The supervision of the new railways and the concern to apply more stringent controls to the operating conditions of merchant ships and seamen both came increasingly within the Board's range as the decade passed. The latter doubtless owed some of its origins to, and had much of its impact on the departure of thousands of hopeful citizens overseas, with which John was still concerned as an emigration commissioner. And as a one-time Director of the London and South Western Railway he could contribute practical business knowledge to the problems of the booming 'iron roads'.

The registration of joint-stock companies, beginning in 1844, was started under his overall supervision. The first registrar found John 'exceedingly civil, not at all of a *don*' and was told very frankly by him that 'with moderate industry I may in a month or two know more about the matter than anyone else and be a person to be referred to by the Board of Trade on matters "which we know nothing about."' He came to regard John as:

> the most amiable of men, also clear headed, most industrious, of great literary accomplishments, a man of the world, and a thorough man of business. He was always cordial and friendly, though he could pull me up when I was careless, in a way of his own.[6]

There is no good reason to doubt that John Shaw Lefevre was a perfectly sound administrator; but whether it was because of his own curious, probing mind, or because of his acute political consciousness and ambition, or simply because he had proved already that he was an able analyst and investigator, with some flair as a conciliator, he found himself, at the Board of Trade, further enhancing a reputation as a trustworthy but unaggressive adjudicator. In 1841 he was still a member of a commission which had been set up in 1838 to consider how to replace the standards of weights and measures which had disappeared when the great fire of 1834 destroyed the Houses of Parliament.

That was largely a scientific enquiry for which his mathematical training was relevant. It is intriguing, at the same time, to find that most of his colleagues, headed by the Astronomer Royal, were Trinity College, Cambridge, men and that several of them were also on the strength of the University of London. Their highly technical report was signed on 21 December 1841 and eighteen months later the same group with a few additions were constituted a commission to superintend the construction of new standards of length and weight – a task which took ten years.[7] It is amazing to think of so leisurely an approach to such matters in an era of tremendous growth of industry and commerce. John might well have regarded it as a pleasant, unstressed background activity to his many more politically controversial experiences over that period.

Within six months of joining the Board of Trade he was a member of a four-man team appointed by the Treasury to examine, at some speed, how exchequer bills were made out and issued. This was the forerunner of a much more sensational investigation into fraud, conducted by a different group. The first enquiry was held in January 1842, during which fifteen witnesses were heard, their evidence sifted and a report prepared.[8] If that called for use of his legal expertise, another early concern must have stretched his patience and his diplomatic flexibility to the limit. He was caught for several years in the tortuous and frequently vicious struggles which arose out of the experience of the government sponsored schools of design, set up originally as a single London institution to improve British design in the new world of industrial production. John represented the Board on the council of the schools, and found the bitter quarrels between the dogmatic proponents of different views of what should be taught so unpleasant that at one point he asked Dalhousie to let him continue to give advice as to the nature of the Board of Trade's directives to the school, but to remove him from the council. Dalhousie felt that John's formal departure would give offence, and instead suggested that he simply abstain from attending the meetings:

> If any authority is wanting to sanction your doing this, you have mine. You will thus get rid of the anxiety and annoyance, and may aid them with advice and guide me with counsel as effectively as if you were entirely freed from the Council.[9]

This simple solution relieved John but did not appear to have improved the affairs of the quarrelsome artists and designers. Just before and for some time after John left the Board of Trade he was much engaged, in 1848 and 1849, in the replacement of the council by a committee of management of the school. His concern for design brought him into contact with Henry Cole, that bustling administrator of education and the arts – 'the incarnation of "Father Christmas" or of "Old King Cole",' as Augustus Hare was to describe him – whom he first met quite by accident on a Chelsea steamer in 1847.[10] This and the publicity which the controversy over the school of design received may well have helped to draw John into dealings with the artistic community in Scotland who, as we shall see, involved him in their affairs. John was not without feeling for or knowledge of painting: at the very least, as Quentin Bell has remarked, he 'knew enough about art to buy a Titian for £60.'[11] But by 1849 he was so heavily involved in other work that it is neither surprising nor unfair that a professional journal should complain, while commending his 'good-natured tact', that he had become so much 'a sort of omnibus . . . Commissioner for everything which needs to be coerced into quietude', that 'If he has any leisure, he must want it for sleep, and cannot afford to give it to the School of Design.'[12]

That John was overextended first became apparent in 1845, when he asked Gladstone to remove him from the Emigration Commission. The Minister agreed, with that elaborate courtesy which in all probability should not make us unduly suspicious of the accuracy and sincerity of his message:

> I could scarcely tell how you could have been able to discharge any of the duties of the Emigration Board at periods when to my knowledge you have been worked at the Board of Trade beyond the ordinary measure of human endurance, if I did not well know that you are one of those who do not admit the word impossible into their vocabulary with respect to the discharge of duty, and in whose own eyes their services appear to be of small account in the same proportion as others perceive them to be great and signal.[13]

When the Whigs returned to power in July 1846 the post of Secretary of State for War and Colonies went to the third Earl Grey, who had succeeded his father in 1845, and who, as Viscount Howick, had been John Shaw Lefevre's predecessor as under-secretary of State for the Colonies in 1833. Grey was only in office for a few months before it became necessary to find a new Governor for Ceylon, and he offered the place to John. It was not a particularly surprising choice, politically or administratively, given John's experience at the Colonial Office, the fact that he had been offered a place on the Indian Law Commission, and his work for South Australia and for emigration, quite apart from his tenure at the Poor Law Commission and the Board of Trade. Whether John was gubernatorial metal is more open to doubt: his strengths were those of the constructive conciliator and the backroom analyst and planner, rather than of the chief executive and the decision maker of last resort.

But John wanted the job, and insisted later in life that he wanted it more than anything else which had come his way. He turned it down, in January 1847, 'because an instant answer was demanded, and he could not at once find any means of providing for the children he could not take with him', but he was 'very miserable', severely disappointed, and obviously put off his bureaucratic stroke.[14] Political ambition, never really subdued, had come to the surface again, and had quite likely been reinforced by the fact of Denis Le Marchant's return to the House of Commons in 1846. John only recovered his zest for life when, with a general election due in the summer of 1847, he was invited, soon after refusing Ceylon, to contest a seat for Cambridge University. But while that prospect was developing, another possibility was floated in his direction by the new Prime Minister, Lord John Russell, using the Speaker as his intermediary.

So intense had become the criticism of the administration of the Poor Law by the mid 1840s that the Whigs decided to replace the non-parliamentary three-man Commission with a Poor Law Board, headed by a President responsible to Parliament – in other words, to accept the notion of direct ministerial responsibility for the administration of the Poor Law. Russell, in May 1847, was in search of a President, and probably had in mind Lord Chichester.[15] He put to the Speaker the idea that John might be one of the secretaries of the new Board (presumably, though it is not absolutely clear, the parliamentary secretary) while the President sat in the Lords. The brothers conferred, and John was not favourably impressed. As Charles reported to Russell:

> He does not appear to have any objection to serve under a Peer at the new Poor Law Board, provided the said Peer is not *merely ornamental*. But considering that he began life twelve years ago as Under Secretary of State, he seems to feel that it would be rather a retrograde movement to end by being one of the Secretaries of a Board of which he was once at the head. In addition to this, his best chance of coming into Parliament is for the University of Cambridge, where many persons are very anxious to have him, and he is afraid that a subordinate office of that kind would not be acceptable there. Had it been equivalent in position to a Vice Presidency the same objection would not apply.[16]

No more was heard of the suggestion, and Russell was still looking for appointees in September.[17]

John Shaw Lefevre was well known within the Whig hierarchy and within the liberal intelligentsia, and the absence of exact knowledge of who took the first steps in organizing his candidature for Cambridge University is not particularly important. What is significant is that an attempt was to be made to storm such a bastion of Toryism: there had been no opposition candidates since 1832, no liberal member since 1830; after 1847 there were only a couple of contested elections during the rest of the century, and another liberal was not returned until 1922. In 1847 the outcome was bound to turn on the attitudes of the great preponderance of Anglican clergy in the electorate. The absence of any great, clear-cut schism between the major political groups simply increased the significance of ecclesiastical response.

The sitting members were Charles Ewan Law, the Recorder of London, and Henry Goulburn, Charles Shaw Lefevre's old opponent for the Speakership in 1839, who had been Peel's Chancellor of the Exchequer and had followed Peel into political uncertainty after the Corn Law crisis. Goulburn had gravely offended some churchmen by voting to transfer the national grant to the Roman Catholic Maynooth College, in Ireland, from the annual votes to the Consolidated Fund, 'thus getting rid of a constantly recurring source of discord and animosity' in the House of Commons – the same matter which had caused Gladstone so much mental agony and his resignation and short-lived absence from Peel's Government in 1845. Goulburn was also in danger 'as being obnoxious to the Tractarian party, which at the time was beginning to raise its head.' Law was joined as a fellow candidate by the 24-year old Viscount Fielding (the Earl of Denbigh) in a strong Tory, protectionist and no-popery platform. Goulburn, though a Peelite, had great status and respect. The main struggle was bound to be between these three men of differing conservative persuasions.

John Shaw Lefevre, as the standard-bearer of the more liberal elements, was regarded as having 'very little chance of success with a constituency containing so large a clerical element.' Those, like the conservative lawyer Frederick Pollock, a manipulative operator in the election, who wanted to ensure that there was at least one moderate returned, knew that Goulburn had the best chance and that 'any official coalition with Lefevre' during the canvass would weaken that chance. Moreover, collegiate jealousy threatened the more liberally inclined candidates, for not only were both of them Trinity men, but so was Fielding. It is not surprising, therefore, that this unique four-sided contest was regarded by one of the older dons as 'the most important election that ever took place for the Representation of this University.'[18]

John, for the second – and last – time, had chosen to fight a constituency where the scales were heavily loaded against him; but whereas in 1832 the great surge of feeling for reform gave him hope of being able to capture Petersfield, in 1847 it was the lack of national political fervour which encouraged him to think of succeeding at Cambridge. He counted on a mood which, at least one newspaper implied, would favour a moderate, secular approach:

At a time when the great commercial centres and communities of the kingdom are displaying in general an absence of extreme political feeling, and substituting for such a close attention to the especial interests and development of commercial enterprise, the universities should come to consider academical interests apart from the old fanatical speculations about church and state. To members of the universities so disposed, Mr Lefevre will be a welcome candidate.[19]

Those 'so disposed' were respectably numerous. The committee which sponsored John was headed by Sir Edward Ryan, a judge recently returned from India who was a near contemporary of John's: he was another Trinity man, active on the Judicial Committee of the Privy Council, and recently brought into contact with John through having been made a railway commissioner in 1846. He was to be a close colleague and friend, and his son, some fifteen years later, was to marry one of John's daughters. Among those who either joined the committee or pledged themselves to John were Macaulay, Charles Babbage, William Brougham, Edward Pleydell Bouverie, Edward Ellice, Samuel Jones Loyd (the future Lord Overstone) a brother-in-law, John Romilly, and Sir John Lubbock, John's predecessor as vice-chancellor of London University, to name only a handful. The campaign was organized in Cambridge by James Cartmell of Christ's College, and in London by John E. Blunt, and with so scattered an electorate a major effort had to be made through correspondence, not only to win support but also to persuade many of the voters to make their way to Cambridge in order to cast their votes.

John did his share of letter writing – including an early, diplomatic missive to the Master of Trinity – but his essential written contributions were his election address and one or two published responses to particular challenges.[20] In them he underlined the low-key, fence-sitting position he had adopted on matters other than his general support of the university and of the government of the day. When pushed to declare himself on the issue exercising so many fierce Cantabrigian ecclesiastical minds and souls – the future status of the Irish Roman Catholic establishment – he wrote:

I respect, but I do not share in, the conscientious scruples of those persons who deem the Endowment of the Roman Catholic Clergy in Ireland to be a national sin. At the same time I think that such a measure is open to various and grave objections, of which I do not see the solution, and which render it very improbable that any proposition of this nature will come before the ensuing Parliament.

I know not how the requisite funds can be provided without injustice to persons holding other religious opinions; and I recognize the difficulty of adjusting the relations between an endowed Roman Catholic Church and the State, without danger to the Constitution.

I believe, moreover, that the measure would be obnoxious to the majority of the community in England and Scotland; and that, if not repudiated, it is at all events not desired by the Roman Catholic Clergy or Laity in Ireland.

Upon these grounds, were I called upon now to decide upon such a proposition, I should certainly oppose it. Nevertheless, I do not feel myself justified in giving any pledge or promise with respect to the course which I may feel it my duty to adopt in reference to this question, in case it should be necessary for me to decide upon it as your Representative.

It may be that those who give positive pledges of opposition to all Roman Catholic Endowment, have discernment enough to see that the present difficulties in which Ireland is involved can be solved, and the anomalies of its social condition remedied, without entering upon that important question. I cannot myself lay claim to such foresight, and I will not, therefore, make any declaration which will prevent me from applying to that question, if it should arise in Parliament, my unbiassed consideration and unfettered judgement.

Whilst reserving to myself this right of consideration and judgement, I can give you the earnest assurance, an assurance which, coming from one whose forefathers at no distant period suffered persecution and exile for their Protestant opinions, is entitled to confidence, that I will do everything in my power to promote, and nothing to impair, the safety and welfare of our Protestant Established Church.[21]

Such a typical, cool, cautious, reserved statement is unlikely to have mollified, let alone converted, many who held strong anti-catholic views, and would certainly not have given comfort to those who were desperate to ensure that the moderate Goulburn did not go down before the high churchmen. The tacticians, Pollock, who was on Goulburn's London committee, and Thomas Flower Ellis, an active Trinity canvasser for John, spent the railway journey to Cambridge on the first of five polling days – 30 July – planning the vote. Pollock and Ellis, as the former relates:

arranged . . . that as many of Lefevre's supporters should vote for Goulburn as could be induced to do so, in order to save his seat, and in return Goulburn's people should give their second vote to Lefevre in order to give him a respectable place at the Poll. So on arrival at Cambridge I went straight to our Committee and got the approval of Phelps (Master of Sydney [Sussex College]) the Chairman. Ellis went to Lefevre's Committee and afterwards, I think, we went together to both Committees to complete the arrangement and in the result Goulburn's seat was secured.[22]

What the numbers would have been had this tactic not been followed cannot be estimated, but when the votes were counted, the two sitting members were returned, Law with a comfortable 1,486, but Goulburn only beating Fielding by 42 votes – 1,189 to 1,147. John received 860, and felt that Ryan's decision to accept the advice of Ellis and Pollock had been prudent and had prevented an 'ignominious and blameable' defeat: Goulburn – as indeed he should have done – much appreciated the 'honourable and generous' conduct of John's supporters towards him: no less than 689 of the 860 who voted for John also voted for Goulburn.[23] John and his party were well pleased at having made as much impact as they had, but John admitted some squeamishness about having to ask people to split their votes – he was really not suited to the hustings, even of so intellectual a constituency as that of Cambridge University.[24]

The Earl of Clarendon had succeeded Dalhousie as President of the Board of Trade on the change of Government, and obviously did not see John as committed permanently to his joint secretaryship. He sympathized with John's defeat at Cambridge, though he had expected it, but felt that 'the glory of having attempted the thing and of having fought a good battle and laid the foundation I hope for better things another time must be your consolation.'[25] As a senior party figure Clarendon was probably well aware of at least some of the political hopes, expectations and manoeuvres which at this period, as we have seen, were affecting both John Shaw Lefevre and Denis Le Marchant, reflecting the stimulus given to their ambitions by the return of the Whigs to office and the success of the party in holding on to power after the general election held in the summer of 1847. Among his many concerns, the Prime Minister had on his hands these two extremely able 50-year-old supporters, deserving of reward and avid for advancement. Neither of them, however, had shown himself to be a natural parliamentary politician, and neither had found himself a safe seat.

In the autumn of 1847, John went back to his heavy Board of Trade work. He was about to be engulfed for several years in extraordinary activity in many directions, and would only stay for a matter of months on the Board's payroll. But before he left to take up his new post as clerk assistant and heir to the Clerkship of the Parliaments, John was asked by Russell, in November 1847, to take an unpaid vacancy on the Ecclesiastical Commission, a body which had been set up in 1836 to reform and handle the complex problems of the lands and properties of the Established Church. He was to put in a long stint, dealing with those problems, and brother Charles would, in time, join him in coping with them.[26] In mid-1848, though, John must have congratulated himself in having at last found a safe position of high status: henceforward he could look to a secure future.

There can hardly ever have been another post, apart from the outright sinecures, which seems to have been regarded as quite so honourable, interesting, opulent, and undemanding of more than gentle effort, as that of the officer who was seemingly certain to inherit the Clerkship of the Parliaments when he was appointed clerk assistant, just as the century was coming up to its half way mark. For Ichabod Wright, John Shaw Lefevre's new situation combined 'Dignity, Ease, Emolument and Permanency', as compared with his Board of Trade secretaryship, which was 'harassing to his mind and fatiguing to his body, with emolument unequal to his talents and services.'[27] Lady Cottenham congratulated Emily on the 'increased leisure and consequent comfort and enjoyment' which would come John's way.[28] Gladstone thought the clerkship 'a post of so much comfort, dignity and freedom.'[29] John himself was without doubt delighted to have his income improved by a thousand pounds a year, but at the age of 51 his reply to Gladstone's congratulations must surely be among his most sepulchral efforts: the reader must wonder – without too much conviction – whether there was some hint of a slightly amused self-mockery in it. 'I hope and pray', wrote John, 'that the leisure I shall derive from these arrangements will be spent worthily and with due regard to the gradual approach of the termination not only of my official career but of my earthly pilgrimage.'[30]

There was little likelihood that John's conscience would allow him to take life easily because the House of Lords' schedule was not too demanding, and, in any event, his availability, his high competence and his known willingness to accept additional tasks at no cost to the Treasury, ensured that he was kept busy. In the future immediately after he took up his new position there was unfinished business to clear up, north of the border. That business had begun almost as soon as he was relieved of responsibility for emigration to far distant parts of the world, in 1846. John was in demand in Edinburgh, where a row of rather similar dimensions to that which had afflicted the London School of Design had blown up between the Scottish Royal Academy, the Royal Institution and the Board of Manufactures, all of which had overlapping concerns for the support and encouragement of art and for the training of artists and designers in the northern kingdom. Some weeks in Edinburgh not long after the Cambridge election enabled him to put forward a report to the Treasury containing compromises acceptable to all the Edinburgh parties. However, financial restraints were not overcome until John wrote again to the Treasury, suggesting ways forward, in May 1849. That brought a breakthrough, marked by a Treasury minute approving a new scheme, six months later. The most dramatic part of the solution was John's firm recommendation that Scotland should have a National Gallery. That recommendation was duly sponsored, and in gratitude the Royal Academy of Scotland commissioned its President, Sir John Watson-Gordon, to paint John's portrait, which still finds a home in the gallery.[31]

Having got John to Edinburgh, the Government decided to make more use of him there. The Home Secretary, Sir George Grey, then responsible for Scottish affairs, asked for an enquiry to be made into the working of the annuity tax in the Scottish capital. The proceeds of that local tax were used to meet part of the cost of the stipends of the clergy of the Scottish Church in the city, and controversy had broken out over its allocation, as well as over its fundamental justification. Scots churchmen and the citizens of Edinburgh were very capable of being intensely disputatious, and John may well have had some sleepless nights before submitting a 27-page report, with 80 pages of appendices, at the end of April 1849.

He had found the job 'very troublesome', and told Gladstone that he had 'the dissatisfaction of knowing beforehand that nobody will concur in it.'[32] That was a correct estimation of the report's reception; but as in the case of the artists, John kept in close touch with the problem and came up exactly a year later with a new scheme for the clergy. However, the matter had become increasingly political; John's efforts were soon of only historical concern, and he was not called to give evidence to a select committee which considered the matter and whose proceedings covered 700 printed pages, in 1851.[33] The annuity tax was eventually abolished in 1860, but the whole subject of the ministers' stipends and who should pay them remained on the political agenda well into the next decade.[34]

Yet a third task, of a very different nature, was entrusted to John in Scotland at this time. In October 1848 he undertook for the Treasury a review of the expenditure of the Scotch Fishery Board, reported on 24 January 1849, and was involved in the reactions to his report in July of that year. This, too, was a subject which continued to exercise the Board and the Treasury for several years, though John does not seem to have been further involved.[35] His three single-handed enquiries in Scotland show the extent to which he was by then respected, and used, by the inner circles of Westminster and Whitehall. But they were by no means the only instances of the pressure to which John, willingly or not, submitted himself in addition to his main duties at the Board of Trade or the House of Lords.

He had been involved during his last year or two at the Board of Trade with some aspects of the affairs of the chartered New Zealand Company. That company's tangled experience with land dealings led to its decision to relinquish the charter. The subsequent financial negotiations with H.M. Government became so complicated that, in August 1850, the Colonial Secretary, Earl Grey, persuaded the Treasury to allow the appointment of John to report on certain questions whose resolution would influence a potential settlement between the company and the Government. This had to be done quickly, and the report was duly finished and presented to Grey on 16 November. Like his report on the Annuities Tax, John's adjudication of the New Zealand company's affairs did not meet with the full agreement of the Treasury, and negotiations were to drag on for several years, with John retaining an active interest.[36]

The incredible list of engagements is not finished. No doubt because of his established reputation as a mathematician and his vice-chancellorship of the young University of London, John was made, in May 1848, an additional member of a Royal Commission to inquire into the Constitution and Government of the British Museum, which had begun its labours in June 1847, and which reported in 1850. John's Scottish enquiries were given priority, however, and he was able, after he joined it, to attend only five of the fifty-six sessions which the commission held to take evidence. Nonetheless, he was a signatory to the report and may well have been free to take part in the long period of drafting the final version.[37] And, on top of all these responsibilities, and arising out of his membership of the Ecclesiastical Commission, John was put on a Royal Commission on Episcopal and Capitular Estates whose work began in January 1849, and ended with two reports, the first in January and the second in July of the following year.[38]

Thus in the four years from the beginning of 1847 until the end of 1850 John had been offered a colonial governorship, had fought a parliamentary election, and had enquired into and in some cases had been arbitrator or conciliator in the affairs of artists and designers in two countries. In addition, he was involved in the construction of new national standards for measures of length and weight, the financial difficulties of adventures in New Zealand, the future of the British Museum, the earthbound concerns of the Established Church in England and of the clergy of the Scottish Church in Edinburgh, and the financial arrangements of the Scottish fisheries. Alongside all these, he had switched his main, continuing employment from the Board of Trade to the House of Lords, and throughout had continued to be the vice-chancellor of the University of London, attending three quarters of the ten or so meetings each year and presiding at about half of them.

The flow of new work was not to recede in the 1850s, or even in the 1860s, but the intensity of the years between 1847 and 1850 was unique and must have imposed a considerable strain on a physical constitution which, even allowing for a touch of hypochondria, was not strong. Given the fact that his wife was certainly not robust, and that they had seven children who, in 1850, ranged from 22 down to 8 years of age, it speaks well for his character and his self control that, despite the pressures of his manifold professional activities, there is no hint of neurotic bad temper and a good deal of casual evidence to show that he was much loved within his family circle and was well liked by colleagues for his mild and friendly disposition. The mildness of his temperament is reflected in the measured judgements of his findings, expressed after meticulous enquiry in fastidious though unexciting prose.

What is surprising is that a man blessed with so much intellectual capacity, so personally ambitious, so closely involved in political affairs, and so committed a Whig, wrote nothing – or nothing that has survived –

which shows the slightest passion about public questions, or the slightest originality. He took it for granted that 'reform', as it had been accepted and understood within his family throughout his lifetime, was a process of rational rearrangement of institutions and practices to meet broadly utilitarian notions – though under aristocratic guidance – in the context of the changes which were being forced on to an increasingly industrial society. He was the instrument, not the initiator, of such rearrangement. No doubt his legal training and his addiction to conveyancing foreshadowed a somewhat arid, procedural approach. His reports are careful, comprehensive as to background and delineation of the problems he is facing, cautious, sympathetic to a degree more often than not unwelcomed by more stringent authority, but overall somewhat bloodless.

But at the same time this is a man who mastered numerous languages, translated novels from Spanish and Dutch and fables from the Russian, was interested in technical inventions, enjoyed the company of Babbage, Sidney Smith and Macaulay, corresponded with Gladstone about the readability of Homer, discussed religious belief and emotion with unusually little establishment reserve, and exchanged long distance arguments with Brougham over geometric theorems.[39] Despite his political ambition and his hybrid constitutional status, there is much about John Shaw Lefevre's character and attitude which fits the popular stereotype of the fully-developed senior civil servant of the late-Victorian years and the twentieth century – the clever, wise, experienced, cultivated, balanced, non-partisan adviser – quite as much as his elder brother's conduct in the chair made *him* the classic model of the strong but scrupulously impartial Speaker of the House of Commons.

There is surprisingly little written material about John's work as Clerk of the Parliaments, and none to suggest whether and, if so, how much he and his brother may have consulted each other on the technical problems of procedure. Such consultation is highly likely, though, for John is credited with having brought about 'a vital re-organization of the Standing Orders' of the House of Lords, and must have wanted to draw on Charles' experience. But the post itself was by no means the slight, mechanical affair which might be inferred from the numerous intimations that John had landed himself a 'soft' job. Undoubtedly, the pace of life, in a House which, though over 450 peers were eligible to attend, attracted on average less than 100 daily, was much quieter than Charles had to keep up in the Commons. The Lords' sessions were never unduly long and the rules of debate were quite relaxed.

John would have found it all infinitely less taxing than being a full-time administrator at the Board of Trade, but he did not spare himself in the service of the peers of the realm. He was, of course, always present at the Table when the House was sitting, and must have spent a good deal of time and effort in discussions with the Lord Chancellor about the order and arrangement of business, as well as being an authoritative source of information and advice for all the noble Lords who attended and spoke. This politically-oriented legislative work gave John a wonderful range of intimate contact with many of the most powerful men in the country, and underlines the remarkable extent of the knowledge and insight which the two Shaw Lefevre brothers must have shared about the parliamentary manoeuvrings of their era. But the Clerk of the Parliaments was also the Registrar of the House of Lords in its capacity as the court of final appeal, and was responsible for ensuring the proper care of records – legislative and judicial – a duty which was to be of increasing concern for John as his term of office lengthened. Indeed, it was that special concern, together with his attention to all aspects of the clerk's responsibilities which, in the words of one of his successors, 'established the post in public estimation as . . . one of the great offices of the state, one well worthy to rank with Civil Service heads of government departments.'[40]

By 1853 John had been lured into more new professional fields. The proposals of the Royal Commission on Episcopal and Capitular Estates, of which he had been a member, did not receive the blessing of the Government, but it was accepted that the machinery of the Ecclesiastical Commission needed to be strengthened. In August 1850 a three-man Church Estates Commission was established; it was to work as part of the whole Ecclesiastical Commission operation, and in particularly close relationship with the Estates Committee of that commission, but with certain executive powers. The chairman of the new Church Estates Commission, Lord Chichester, was paid and, like the second commissioner – John Shaw Lefevre (who was not paid) – was an appointee of the Crown. The third estates commissioner, who was appointed by the Archbishop of Canterbury, was paid, and the post went to Charles Shaw Lefevre's old antagonist, Henry Goulburn.

The three estates commissioners were all simultaneously members of the Ecclesiastical Commission and of its Estates Committee, and from the moment of their appointment were to be a dominant force. Indeed, for all practical purposes they, together with only one or two other commissioners, *were* the Ecclesiastical Commission for the next decade or more; and with the exception of John, the whole group were members of one or other House of Parliament. Not that they were necessarily always in agreement with each other. They attended the bulk of the meetings of all three entities, which meant, for John, anything from thirty-five to forty-seven meetings each year. As a conveyancer, he probably found much of the subject matter professionally familiar and straightforward, but his main role was that of watchdog for the tenants of Church land. The Home Secretary, Grey, explained to Russell in 1856, that:

In dealing with Church property, which they have done very extensively, Goulburn was looked upon as taking care of the interests of the Church, while Lefevre's presence was considered a security to the lessees against any harsh proceeding with regard to them, Chichester holding the balance between them.[41]

In this, at any rate, of John's many roles, the political side of the hybrid, and the inherited possessiveness of the landed class, were uppermost.

Just as his mathematics, his linguistic ability and his vice-chancellorship no doubt went a good way to justifying his involvement in the British Museum enquiry, so John's legal standing and university connection must have made him a natural choice for a royal commission to inquire into legal education, which had a life of fifteen months and reported in August 1855.[42] But more significant for John's future was an exercise of a supremely practical kind – how to implement the intention enshrined in an act of 1853, to introduce a system of competitive entry to the Civil Service of the East India Company.[43] Macaulay chaired a group of five, John sharing the labour with the Principal of Haileybury, Lord Ashburton (William Bingham Baring), and Benjamin Jowett.[44] Their work naturally brought them to the attention of the Governor General of India, Lord Dalhousie, who had remained on very friendly terms with John since their time together at the Board of Trade. Indeed, Dalhousie wrote of John a year or two later, 'I love the old boy with all my heart and owe much to him. He is one of the best of human beings and there are not many abler, though diffident to a fault.'[45] Dalhousie's reaction to the new order makes interesting reading, as part of that interminable argument as to what is the best method of recruiting and training public servants:

It is quite superfluous to say that I admire Mr Macaulay's Report as a piece of writing. And if the whole of the Civil Service of India is to be appointed by the operation of competition, I do not know that any better scheme could be devised than that which you have submitted. But I have grave doubts whether the men whom this system of competition will raise up will prove to be better administrators in practice than the 'Twice born' have been before them. A first class man or a Wrangler coming out to India at 24 after such tests successfully passed, will hardly be so ductile as he must be, if he is soon to learn the perfectly novel and multifarious duties of an assistant in the mofussil. Time alone can solve this doubt. I wish only that you had added to your probationers' curriculum (as they call it in Scotland) the peremptory requirement of *practical Civil Engineering*. Were young officers to start out with a knowledge of how to build a bridge, form an embankment, and survey and construct a road, an immense material benefit would be gained, and its effects would be felt at once throughout every District in India.[46]

John, as the vice-chancellor of a university which was confined to being an examining body; and John as the recent member of a committee to create an examining body for the Indian Civil Service, was an obvious person to involve in the establishment of competitive entry for the home Civil Service. In May 1855 he joined Sir Edward Ryan, who had headed his Cambridge candidacy committee, as one of the original Civil Service commissioners. Once again, this was an unpaid position, but its duties were to take a sizeable proportion of John's efforts for the next seven years.

In 1856 John was 59. He had by then much more reason than in 1848 to believe that the end of his official career was in sight. He was also well aware that his elder brother would not remain for much longer Speaker, and that on relinquishing the chair, Charles would be raised to the peerage. The two brothers seem, always, to have been good friends, and just at this time Charles was making sure, in his most effective, diplomatic fashion that John would soon be elected to membership of the exclusive Grillions Club.[47] But despite his being in such demand, John's basic political ambitions had never been satisfied, and he may well have watched with some envy the apparently effortless progress of Charles' rise over the years. In short, John had reached the point at which he felt he was owed some demonstration of gratitude, some recognition of the value of his services to the state – and to the Whig Party. Whether he secretly hoped to join his brother and be created, almost simultaneously, a peer of the realm, is uncertain, but that he wanted a title, that he wanted it soon, and was persistent in his search, is quite clear. He had always cultivated the powerful and, even allowing for the sycophantic practices of Bagehot's deferential society, John's letters frequently mixed excellent, independent opinions and straightforward good sense with a smattering of elaborate servility which might well have irritated some of his influential correspondents.

John prepared and had printed a memorandum detailing all he had done since the early 1830s, and that memorandum, in various forms, was used by him at several points during the rest of his working life. He proclaimed at the outset that:

> Various circumstances have led me to the conviction that it is necessary for me to take a proper opportunity of briefly placing on record some of the various honorary, although laborious, duties which I have performed in addition to my official functions since I first entered the public service.

Then came a detailed listing of all but a very few of his activities, followed by three paragraphs which are worth quoting in full, to give the flavour of his approach and attitude:

In making this enumeration of the proceedings in which I have been engaged, I have advisedly omitted to mention other honorary public employments which I have undertaken at the wish of Her Majesty's Government, but in which, owing to my conflicting engagements in other contemporaneous Commissions, I have been unable to take any important part; but upon this point I may observe that, when such conflicts of duty have occurred my course has invariably been to address myself to that business which I have deemed most urgent, and in which I have expected to be most useful, and, I may add, that with regard to my principal and primary duties in the House of Lords, I have never permitted any other duties whatsoever to conflict with them.

On the contrary, I have been studiously careful not at any time to lose sight of my position and obligations as an officer of the House of Lords, and I have watched with considerable vigilance my own proceedings, lest I should be accidentally betrayed into any neglect of duty towards their Lordships by reason of my other voluntary public avocations; and although of course I cannot judge of the efficiency of my services as Clerk Assistant, I can speak confidently as to the spirit in which they have been rendered, and as to my anxiety to give to the service of the House whatever time and personal attendance its affairs might require.

The only mode in which I have found it practicable to accomplish the extra objects of my official life, which I have above described, has been by making diligent use of the vacations and recesses of Parliament, and of those portions of the ordinarily vacant days during the session which I did not require for the conduct of my incidental business connected with the House of Lords; by throwing aside, with regret, almost all my intellectual pursuits; by encroaching on the time justly applicable to my personal affairs and to my duties to my family; and by venturing to the extreme margin of my health and strength, and not unfrequently beyond it.[48]

It is not at all unlikely that this document, in one version or another, was distributed to quite a number of people at the top level of Government, but the main target was the Prime Minister, Lord Palmerston. John must have lobbied the Lord Chancellor, his immediate chief, and he certainly sent a copy to Sir George Grey, the Home Secretary; but he had for a long time enjoyed close relations with Russell and Gladstone, and was about to be brought into more intimate contact with Granville, who was to succeed Lord Burlington as the Chancellor of London University. The discussion of what to do for John was going on in the early spring of 1856, and whatever previous decision had been reached, Granville called on Palmerston at the end of April and 'asked him to give a step to John Le Fevre in the Bath.'[49] John's persistence and his apparently rather querulous stance must have been picked up and found somewhat tiresome by those working near him, for a letter between two unidentifiable officials refers to the memorandum as 'this beautifully drawn statement. . . . It *breathes his spirit* which is saying a great deal. I hope *for the sake of us all* that some public recognition is awaiting him.'[50]

Palmerston put to the Queen a request that John be given a Commandership of the Civil Order of the Bath in July 1856, but he had to give more details, to get Granville to make a special explanation of the case, and even to remind Her Majesty about it six months later, before John's knighthood was safely conferred late in January 1857.[51] During the last months of the previous year John was much concerned, as vice-chancellor, to find a new Chancellor of the University of London, and tried to assure Brougham that the duties of the post were anything but onerous.[52] In the end neither Russell, Brougham nor the Duke of Somerset would agree to serve, and on Christmas Eve, Granville wrote 'I have made Chancellor of the University of London, after a great fight on my part, and some delay. John Lefevre was the guilty party. He persuaded George Grey that I should be the best.'[53] This may not have done John's case for recognition any harm at all. He got his title three months before his brother's transition from the House of Commons to 'another place', where they would be together, one serving the other, until 1875.

CHAPTER XI

Families, 1835–1860

The death of Helena Shaw Lefevre did not weaken the links between her three sons and their families. In part this was because of the genuine affection which they felt towards each other, a claim which has to be modified only mildly to take proper account of differences in the temperaments and interests of individuals and couples. The loss of Helen, Henry's wife, and the resulting motherless state of three young girls, was a concern which no doubt brought them all closer in the middle 1830s. Charles was accepted happily as the head of the family, and Heckfield Place was a symbol of continuity and stability as well as a regular gathering place. But alongside the ties of sentiment was a web of financial arrangements and interactions. Unfortunately, there is insufficient data available on which any detailed schema could be based, but the tone and the content of the fragmentary papers still extant imply occasional renegotiation of rights to property inherited from their parents, the making of loans to one another, the frequent discussion of investments, and a sharing of advice on all matters financial. In this context, the characteristic situations and reactions of the brothers fell into a pattern which remained easily recognizable for the rest of their lives.

Charles' ownership and extension of the Heckfield and other estates, together with his additional commercial interests, made him the dependable rich man of the family. But status and prosperity were not accompanied by a very satisfactory marriage. We have touched, briefly, on the tragic deaths of Charles' and Emma's three sons. It would be very understandable if that loss explained altogether the sad severity which appears to have marked Emma's demeanour; but that severity had older origins. As yet we have no comprehensive history of the Whitbread family; Samuel Whitbread II's suicide is still a mystery, and documentary evidence about his children is patchy.[1] We do, however, have rather more than a hint of the atmosphere in which Emma Laura had been raised.

Samuel Whitbread II had himself been

> the object of much parental solicitude, but of no indulgence. The strictness of life that usually prevailed among Dissenters extended to the bringing up of their children, who were systematically guarded against all evil

influences by early religious instruction, enforced by almost Spartan discipline.

Samuel I brought to his role as a parent not only that dissenting background, but the strong influence of John Howard, the great penal reformer, who regarded:

> children as creatures possessed of strong passions and desires, without reason or experience to control them . . . [whom] nature seemed to mark out as subjects of absolute authority . . . the first and fundamental principle to be inculcated upon them was implicit and unlimited obedience. And as this cannot be effected by any reasoning process, before reason has its commencement, it must be done by co-ercion . . . but the co-ercion [to be] practised [should be] the most calm and gentle, while at the sametime . . . steady and resolute. This also was the opinion of Mr. Whitbread, and he acted up to it in the education of his son.[2]

Samuel II may not have been quite so severe in his parental views, but it is not hard to believe that some shades of grandparental rigour recurred in the upbringing of his four children. Certainly his youngest daughter may well have been shaped by, and in some respects have suffered from, the application of the Howard doctrine. It may be of some significance that one of the few papers in the Whitbread archives concerning Emma is a report by her governess to her father when she was 11, which makes rather curious reading: 'I have no objection to Emma', wrote the governess, 'tho I know her temper is faulty and her mind apathetic. . . . I am sure I can never make her mind simple, honest, ingenuous, and what is knowledge, what are accomplishments compared to a good heart and a pure mind?' And she goes on to suggest that 'With *consistency*, judgement, tenderness blended with severity if *absolutely* necessary something might be done, sensibility awakened, emulation aroused, activity of mind excited, but I doubt that being performed under the paternal roof, for reasons which I need not point out.' This rather cryptic statement precedes an expression of concern for Samuel Whitbread, who the governess knows is 'horrified by the difficulties you witness' with Emma. Too much weight should not be given to this isolated letter. The governess was about to leave, and offered to take Emma into her own charge, which may suggest that she had a selfish interest to pursue; and there is only the slightest reference to Emma's mother, which might indicate some estrangement on the latter's part from the governess.[3] But the notion that Emma was difficult and probably unhappy as an 11-year-old is not insignificant in the light of evidence about her later development.

It is unlikely that the late-twentieth-century mind can penetrate, let alone sympathize with the apparently harsh, joyless attitude to life on earth which appeared to dominate the thinking of many conscientiously Christian people in England two hundred years ago. The evangelical movement produced perhaps more than its share of charismatic flagellants of human weaknesses in others as well as themselves, and the appeal of their message may well have been compelling to many who were by nature or conditioning unhappy, uncertain or even unstable. One powerful evangelical priest was the Welshman, William Howels, who in 1817 became the lessee of the Episcopal Chapel in Long Acre, and attracted a dedicated congregation until his death in 1832. It seems that Emma Laura Shaw Lefevre was one of that congregation, and that Howels' teachings encouraged her to exercise a 'gloomy religious influence' on her family.

How much Emma's apparently grim philosophy can be attributed to evangelical fervour, how much to some basic defect of character or unfortunate childhood treatment, how much to the distorting bitterness of losing all three male children, cannot be calculated. But her niece, Henry Shaw Lefevre's youngest daughter, Sophia Wickham, recalling 'so many Christmasses of our lives at Heckfield' thought:

> Aunt Emma clever but her temper not good and such a love of tyrannising. . . . My aunt had a most strong sense of the importance of seniority, so she made a great deal of my sister Helen who was never afraid of her so got on famously. Annie who was most timid she did not care for – and I as the youngest was treated almost like a criminal, hardly allowed to speak! I used to hate her so and think of her in connection with the words 'if I give my body to be burned and have not charity it profiteth me nothing.'

This is, again, evidence to be used with care. Sophia, in old age, admitted that she was 'a very upstart, forward sort of child.' But we must remember the family tradition that Emma was the cause of a falling out between her mother-in-law and her close friend, Mrs Braithwaite; and in other contexts Sophia's views are supported by more detached commentators. Even her brother-in-law, Henry, with whom she was close, recorded in his diary that in the week of his father's death and burial, in 1823, Emma was 'particularly impracticable'.[4]

Sophia felt that Emma had given her three daughters 'such an inferior education', and the eldest of them, also Emma, confessed to John Martineau in later life that 'her mother disliked her as a girl, and used to make her clean the grates, and gave her gloves with holes in them, and even used to send her to the butcher's to fetch the meat, lest she should be proud.'[5] And if one accepts the sharpness of childrens' perceptions of adult relationships, one cannot ignore Sophia's comment that while Charles's wife 'adored him she could not refrain from snubbing and scolding him, particularly before us girls at meals – we could not help noticing it and we all took his part.'

Charles's reactions seem to have been not unlike his attitude to recalcitrant parliamentarians – 'He never lost his temper, never answered back, but somehow treated it as chaff, turned it off with a joke or with a pun – for he was very fond of punning.' William Wickham, Sophia's husband, who was close to and exceedingly fond of Charles in his later years, was unforgiving about Emma Laura, describing her in his journal as:

> an odious woman, clever, grasping and overbearing, her pleasure seemed to be to make everyone she had to do with, miserable; this is what I have learned from relations, not from one or two, but from all who have talked to me of her; not from one of them did I hear otherwise. I think his [Charles's] easiness of disposition made him give way to her too much, but I am not blaming him, the difficulties were so great and a quiet life so desirable, but I have heard that she became at last so intolerable that he contemplated a separation, when her sudden death solved the difficulty.

However grey and abrasive was Emma's view of human, earthbound existence, it did not seem to have interfered with her acceptance of a high standard of material comfort, which her husband had little difficulty in providing. They lived at 35 Eaton Place until Charles became Speaker, but because much of the Houses of Parliament, including the Speaker's apartments, had been destroyed by fire in 1834, the Shaw Lefevres' official residence was 71 Eaton Square throughout his eighteen-year tenure of the chair. His promotion brought Charles considerable additional resources: a salary of £5,000 a year, an initial outfit allowance of £1,000, and a payment towards the cost of running his official residence of over £2,500 for the first two years, and about £1,600 annually thereafter. In addition, he was the last Speaker to receive, as a personal gift on taking office, £6,000 towards the cost of a service of plate.[6] Nor did his new commitment restrict his business interests. In 1840 he became one of the eight partners in Whitbreads' brewery, and remained a partner for the rest of his life. He put in £18,750, then 5 per cent of the capital, and had no managerial responsibilities; but he increased his investment steadily, and when he died he owned 16 per cent of the shares and his executors received nearly £120,000 from the business.[7]

One result of this connection was the arrangement whereby Whitbreads began and have continued to provide the dray-horses which pull the enormously heavy, splendidly decorated but rather primitively engineered Speaker's coach on great State occasions, and the coachmen and footmen who tend it. Charles may well have initiated this tradition by requesting the coach to drive him from Eaton Square to Parliament for major ceremonies.[8] The expenses of the Speaker were doubtless considerable, but from 1839 Charles had his income from estates, his profits from Whitbreads – averaging £3,000 to £4,000 in each of the early years of his partnership, but rising thereafter - and his parliamentary salary, as well as some other investment earnings. He was, indeed, beginning to enjoy the high summer of his financial fortunes, and he and Emma Laura, between them, cannot have been worth less than £15,000 to £20,000 a year.

Despite some tensions, there was no sign of serious disruption during the early and middle years of a long partnership. For a quarter of a century Charles and his family had moved between Heckfield and Westminster, without hint of any major irregularity or trauma, save for the loss of his mother and of his third and only surviving son, both twenty or more years before his retirement in 1857. Domestic life, his career, his expansion and consolidation of the Heckfield estate and of his interest in the Whitbreads' business, all contributed to a smooth, financially secure rhythm. Emma continued in her clever and 'rather masterful' way, but she lost both her elder sister, Elizabeth Waldegrave, in 1843, and her mother, Lady Elizabeth Whitbread, three years later. Her mother, having already disposed of a sizeable share of her fortune to her Waldegrave grandchildren, left everything else to Emma, who gained considerably in monetary terms but also became possessed of furnishings which could only be accommodated at Heckfield by rearranging some of the interior.

If, at Heckfield, Emma sometimes played the domestic tyrant, she was well able to fill the role of gracious hostess in Westminster. Sophia remembered her aunt insisting that the children ' had to eat whatever was given us to the last crumb,' and how Emma's

> keen eyes saw round the whole table as if by magic. If there was a thing I detested it was Muttonbroth and we always began the early dinner with that – the next item, or what always fell to my share, was the drumstick of a turkey which I loathed, and was in daily terror that I should be made to keep my plate and go over it again – the dreadful sinews fairly beat me.

But on the nights of the Speaker's dinners in Eaton Square, Emma provided richer fare and employed a chef. She and her daughters, while excluded from the dinners, always appeared in high gowns to receive friends afterwards, and they were regaled with 'an immense number of sweets, Genoa pastry with cream, Baba au rhum and quantities of things in moulds.' The remnants were sometimes brought for the delectation of the nieces – Henry's motherless daughters - on the following day, a practice rather grudgingly recognized as 'one of her few, though original, kindnesses.'[9] But if Emma was a stern mother and aunt, she and Charles still maintained Heckfield as a strong family centre, and their kindnesses included one worth particular notice.

Emma's only sister, Elizabeth, had married William Waldegrave in 1812, and by him had three sons and five daughters. Her husband was a successful naval officer who also served as MP for Bedford (Whitbread territory) from 1815 to 1818, between two spells of active service. He became overbearingly conscious of the duties of an evangelical Christian, and imposed that consciousness on his wife and children. His was a gloomy faith, and it may be that his sister-in-law, Emma, was influenced by him as well as by the Revd William Howels. But however much Emma may have seemed religiously inclined to her young niece, she seemed much less so to her elder sister, who regretted Emma's lack of fervency! Lady Elizabeth Whitbread, their mother, was not deeply affected by evangelical enthusiasm. It is hardly surprising that there was one Waldegrave child, at least, who rebelled against the parental pressure. That child was their eldest son, born in 1816, and though he did not become Viscount Chewton until his father succeeded as eighth Earl Waldegrave in 1846, he is best called by that title for the sake of clarity.

The Whitbreads, the Waldegraves and the Shaw Lefevres were fairly close during Chewton's childhood; Charles Shaw Lefevre and Samuel Whitbread III were colleagues as well as brothers-in-law, and Charles took some interest in the career of George Waldegrave, one of Chewton's younger brothers, who helped in a small way to build Charles' case for a viscountcy in 1857.[10] Chewton was taken off to sea by his father into South American waters, as a midshipman, and at the early age of 13 he survived a shipwreck of which he later wrote a long account for his Aunt Emma.[11] Then he spent two unproductive years at Trinity College, Cambridge, and in a thoroughly unsettled state of mind was sent to Canada with the idea of trying his hand at farming. But only months after arrival in North America he joined the volunteers who were organized to fight an uprising of French Canadians, and thereafter became a professional soldier, serving in Canada, at home, in India, and finally in the Crimea, where he was killed at the Battle of Alma when he was 38-years-old, in 1854.

While dutiful Victorian memoirs treat him as a young military hero, Chewton, while clearly something of a charmer, had extravagant tastes and turned to his grandmother, Lady Elizabeth Whitbread, to his aunt and uncle at Heckfield, and to the famous Whig hostess Frances, Countess Waldegrave, widow of the seventh Earl, for support, sympathy and defence in his stormy dealings with his disapproving parents. His mother died in 1843, and when his father inherited the earldom three years later he did so without any increase of income, because all the estate had been left, unencumbered, to Frances. Although the eighth Earl married, as his second wife, in the same year as he inherited the title, a moderately wealthy woman, he did not become much more generous to his eldest son, even though the new countess 'had money enough to besprinkle the south coast with strictly Evangelical churches.'[12] Chewton, in turn, did not make matters easier by marrying the penniless sister of a brother naval officer. That was in July 1850; almost exactly four years later he was killed, leaving a widow with one son and expecting a second child – born four months afterwards – another son.

For at least the last few years of Chewton's life, Charles and Emma came to look upon him almost as their own child, seeing him, no doubt, as a substitute for the three sons they had lost by 1837. Chewton spent a good deal of time at Heckfield, enjoying the shooting with his uncle. Charles and Emma approved of his marriage in the teeth of his father's opposition; the young couple must have spent most of Chewton's last year together at a house quite near Heckfield, possibly owned by the Shaw Lefevres; and after Chewton was killed, Charles and Emma were very kind to his widow, who remained a friend of theirs and of their daughter Emma for the rest of their lives. But the price paid for this intimacy was deteriorating and quite bitter relations between Charles and Chewton's father. The Shaw Lefevres felt that Waldegrave could have been and should have been more generous to Chewton, and Charles, in his strong and direct manner, did not hesitate to say so in terms to which Waldegrave took grave offence. After Chewton's death there was little contact, but when Charles retired from the chair, Waldegrave wrote a letter which exemplified his sad, religious character and offered some sort of olive branch, though in the context of his own quite accurate estimation that he would not be long of this world – in fact he died in 1859.

> I rejoice that you have given notice of retirement – as I cannot live long it is a pleasure to me that you will be in the House of Peers. If you live to see one of my successors enter the Lords pray as you have steered your own course well teach him to imitate your example. I trust God of his infinite mercy will endow him with sense and prudence. Lady Chewton possesses sense and as her boy will be very poor he has perhaps more prospect of doing well than most. I trust in God's promise to my children in the 2nd Commandment, and their mother's blessing will rest upon the grandchildren. Thank you for your kind word for Samuel and for your kindness to George. He is his Mother's child full of Talent and Singleheartedness.[13]

It is unlikely that the death of Lord Chewton made any significant impact on the tensions within the Shaw Lefevre marriage. But whatever vision the retired Speaker and his wife may have had of whether they should spend their remaining years together or apart, the shattering reality can hardly have occurred to them unless there was some unspoken premonition of which we shall never know. They moved in the late spring of 1857 from the Speaker's official residence to a house in nearby Eaton Place, but the sanitary arrangements of the new home depended in part on an open drain, which was blamed, subsequently, for Emma's being quickly struck down by what was assumed to have been diptheria. During her illness, on 20 June, six months after her 59th birthday, the new Viscount Eversley was to attend a Queen's Ball, and his full dress suit was sent to the House of Lords so that he could go directly from there. Emma's condition worsened drastically that evening, and a messenger arrived at the House of Lords in time to prevent Charles from leaving for the ball. But Emma had lost consciousness before he reached home, and she died soon afterwards.[14] She and Charles had been married for almost exactly four decades; he was nearly 63, and would live for a further thirty-one years.

If there was some doubt about the viability of Charles's and Emma's marriage, there was none about that of John and Emily Shaw Lefevre. They suffered no problems of incompatibility, and their difficulties were the normal ones of a large family with less money than they would like to have had, compounded by several changes of professional roles for John, and the lack of a fixed home base. Their income, in the twenty years after Helena's death, ranged from about £3,000 to £5,000 a year, a little more than half from salary and the rest from the rental of the Burley estate and other investments – all sources producing quite variable sums. John was neither an entrepreneur nor a good financial manager, despite his remarkable intellectual range and his cool grasp of administrative complexities. He was frequently months or even years behind in meeting minor debts, and he made various decisions about property which never produced the kind of easy success which followed his elder brother's more extensive dealings. Indeed, he owed a good deal of the capacity to cope with the style of living he wanted for his large family to the patient concern of his brothers and the generosity of a particular Cambridge friend, Samuel Jones Loyd, who became his brother-in-law.

Loyd was almost an exact contemporary of John Shaw Lefevre, a fellow schoolboy at Eton and a fellow undergraduate at Trinity College. In 1829 he married Harriet, the third of the ten daughters of Ichabod Wright and a sister of Emily, to whom she was very close. Their first child, a son, died in infancy, and their only other child was a daughter, Harriet, who grew up in intimate friendship with John Shaw Lefevre's girls. Loyd's father, Lewis, a dissenting clergyman who married the daughter of a Mancunian banker, and forsook his spiritual calling for a partnership in the bank, was a major figure in the financial world. Samuel Jones Loyd was to take his father's fortunes to enormous heights; to exercise great influence on financial policy; to become if not the richest, certainly one of the richest men in the kingdom; to be raised to the peerage as Lord Overstone; and to be worth, when he died in 1883, over two million pounds in addition to owning 30,000 acres worth £60,000 a year. The relationship of the Loyds and the Shaw Lefevres was the source of great benefit and great disappointment to the less affluent family. One of the first benefits came in 1847, when Loyd made a donation of £500 towards John's expenses at the Cambridge University election.[15] Other contributions were to follow. This generosity helped to compensate for the reduced income which John suffered through his willingness to devote a lot of time to unremunerated work.

In large part John's private financial difficulties – which were certainly less severe than he believed them to be – reflected a very different family situation from those of his brothers. To the son and four daughters already with them by the end of 1833, John and Emily were to add two more girls – Madeleine Septimia in 1835, and nearly seven years later, Emily Octavia, the last of the third generation and the last of all those born Shaw Lefevres to die – she lived until 1936. This sizeable brood no doubt made severe demands on John's purse, but the major domestic anxiety was caused less by financial than by all kinds of health problems, which increasingly plagued Emily and the children. No doubt correctly, to some extent, the blame for illness was placed on the riverside setting of Terrace House. Emily had lost her first child there, six other children were born to her, and the eldest of them had nearly died, in that house, in only eight years. But even if such a rate of reproduction may have seemed normal to contemporaries, it would hardly be surprising if one or more of those pregnancies had left Emily with some deeply established weaknesses which would not have been the fault of the River Thames.

To concern about health and money was added John's discovery, in the early 1830s, that Battersea was not, after all, a very convenient place for him to live. A year or two after his appointment as a Poor Law commissioner he decided to make a move, and in 1836–7 he invested part of his marriage settlement money and some other capital in a new house to be built in Hyde Park Gardens. It cost him £5,500,[16] and the family took possession of it in 1839. While the house was being planned and built, John was offered the stewardship of the Spencers' Surrey Manors, in 1837, presumably for some specified reward, but he refused: the third Earl, to whom he had frequently poured out his financial woes, and would do so again, remarked with a trace of understandable irritation, that 'you are sometimes a little too much inclined to the self denying system.'[17] But despite his lack of means, John was adamant about his voluntary work. Even when he was trying to cope with a cut in salary after he left the Poor Law Commission in 1841, and could see 'no means of increasing his income' by 'labour or exertion', he argued that:

> altho I conceive myself to have a perfect right to employ my leisure as I think fit in doing anything I may deem useful I do not think it is proper whilst my time is paid for by the public to receive any money or advantage equivalent to money for anything else that I do. I trust that this will not be deemed an exaggerated scruple. I have acted on it always – with the single exception of an annual fee of £20 and a butt of ale from Trinity College which I consider to be an honorarium.[18]

He never abandoned this position.

On top of all his metropolitan worries, Burley Manor was not proving to be a viable investment, and in 1840 John sold the manor house and some of the acreage, though other parts of the estate remained in Charles Shaw Lefevre's hands until the early 1850s. John leased Terrace House to Kay-Shuttleworth for use as a training college for teachers, and for four years the family had only the one home, in Hyde Park Gardens. These rearrangements, alas, did not help Emily, whose health was so delicate that she was unable to leave the new house 'except occasionally to ride on her pony for a short time.'[19] Nonetheless, she gave birth safely to her last daughter, Emily Octavia, at Hyde Park Gardens in 1842. But a few months later, when some of the children and the servants contracted scarlatina – which had carried off their first child and nearly killed their second, years before – John told Gladstone that his cares had 'been augmented by the circumstance that my wife is obliged to remain on one floor in consequence of debility.'[20] Even three years on, Ichabod Wright, reviewing the condition of his thirteen surviving children, wrote, 'All . . . well except Emily and Septimia.'[21] It is not surprising that the move to Hyde Park Gardens was short-lived.

In addition to her physical difficulties, Emily had a rather timid and anxious temperament. She was a countrywoman who did not seem to fit confidently into urban society and found it hard to cope with the sophisticated and assertive political community in which John moved. Ties with her own family were very strong, and there may well have been some element of escape from London behind the fact that she and the children spent a good proportion of the time away from home, either at Mapperley Hall, or at Brighton in lodgings, or at the houses of friends and married sisters. John, too, had his share of absences on official visits, and when the family were away he often lived at his club. The whole family made at least one extended trip to the Continent, in 1846, when their return was delayed by the illness of their eldest daughter, Rachael, and in 1849 they took a house in the Border country at Jedburgh for a spell of some months when John was working in Edinburgh. There is no suggestion of any strain about the frequent separations, but there was a real difficulty in accommodating John's need to live within easy reach of Westminster, and the need and desire of Emily to have the space and quiet of a country house.

In 1843, Hyde Park Gardens was let, and the Shaw Lefevres leased West Side House, on the edge of Wimbledon Common, a small eighteenth-century building of similar dimensions to Terrace House, though architecturally inferior. Wimbledon was still quite rural. Among their neighbours there were their distant banking relative, Raikes Currie and, perhaps a little embarrassingly for John, James Stephen, his old adversary at the Colonial Office.[22] They lived at Wimbledon for only five years, but fortunately for the English countryside, long enough for their son, the young George Shaw

Lefevre, then in his early teens, to fall in love with the common, the protection of which was to be his first major victory in environmental politics, twenty years later.

John may not have found it very convenient living so far from his work, but it was the change of role from assistant secretary at the Board of Trade to Clerk of the Parliaments which forced yet another domestic move. The new job carried with it an official residence, 6 Old Palace Yard, a solid home of which a neighbouring house still stands, now in somewhat eccentric isolation, opposite the House of Lords' tower. Ichabod Wright, then 82, confided to his diary that John and Emily's new home 'possessed many comforts, its thick stone walls excluding the heat, it has a fine view of the magnificent Houses of Parliament.'[23] But Emily, once again, had lost her rural home.

Some four years after John had settled into his new office, and perhaps had discovered the financial benefits of a larger salary and of living in an official house, rent-free, he and Emily decided once more to find another place in the country.[24] In 1853 they rented the Tudor manor, Sutton Place, near Woking – rather more than a century before it was converted into a luxurious residence for Paul Getty. It is possible that the house – owned by Thomas Mornington Webbe-Weston – came to their notice through the family connections with the Waldegraves, for Sutton Place had been occupied, until her death in August 1852, by Mrs Anne Hicks, previously the widow of the sixth Earl. Be that as it may, John paid an annual rent of only £345 for Sutton Place. At the same time he was receiving £650 for Hyde Park Gardens, £350 for Whitehall Place, and an unknown rental for Terrace House, Battersea. His income from salary and these three properties was about £4,000 a year, and there must have been a good deal more from inherited interests. He was not in the same league as Charles, but perhaps, at a low point in Henry's life, he was more comfortably placed than his younger brother.

If the 1830s and 1840s were years of high success for Charles and of substantial progress for John, they were years of grief and disaster for Henry. In the business context his troubles reflected the experience of the firm of which he had become a partner in 1830 – Thomas, Son & Lefevre. Five years before that, John Thomas had helped finance the operations of a Manchester businessman, C.B. De Jersey who, in combination with J.A. Frericks of Hamburg, was exporting cotton twist and was later to export textile machinery to Russia. Indeed, De Jerseys became, in the early 1840s, the largest concern in that trade, and in the half century following, they built and equipped over a hundred and twenty cotton mills in Russia. The whole enterpise was spearheaded by a remarkable entrepreneur, Ludwig Knoop of Bremen. Knoop, who was originally one of De Jersey's clerks, in effect took control of the business in later years, though retaining the name of De Jersey for some of his operations.

We can assume that reasonable prosperity was enjoyed by Thomas, Son & Lefevre in the 1830s, but by the mid-1840s there were signs that their Russian enterprise was becoming potentially dangerous. They had established an affiliated company in St Petersburg called John Thomas & Co., to whom De Jerseys shipped cotton twist for sale in Russia. There was a feeling in the City of London that Thomas, Son & Lefevre were over-extended as a result of this venture, which was regarded as untypical speculation on their part. In 1846 the Bank of England considered that while the firm was:

> A1 in the eyes of the world . . . a degree of caution should be exercised, there is too much pig upon bacon as they generally pay by 3 mo. dfts. of their own house in Russia on their own House here.[25]

In the following year the warning was proved to have been fully justified. A sudden inability to sell cotton twist in Russia meant that expected remittances exceeding £400,000 from St Petersburg, failed to appear in London. Thomas, Son & Lefevre could not meet the bills drawn on them by De Jerseys, who had to pay the bills themselves, and Henry's house suspended business on 4 October. Altogether, their liability amounted to more than £600,000.

Where personal responsibility for this debacle might fairly be concentrated is unknown. It is clear, however, that before the crisis of 1847, Henry Shaw Lefevre not only enjoyed good standing in financial circles, but also that he – rather than the Thomases – was regarded as the major figure in the firm. *The Times* reported, sympathetically, when business was suspended, that any problem which had 'originated in some merely temporary circumstances' would have caused no fundamental anxiety because:

> from the feeling entertained for Mr. Lefevre, any reasonable assistance would have been at his command if the difficulties of his house could have been clearly shown to be such as by time and good management might have been overcome.

Since 1841 Henry had been a director of the Sun Fire Office, succeeding his brother Charles. And he had also been treasurer of St Luke's Hospital since 1843. He offered to resign the latter post when the 1847 crash occurred, but was re-elected with the full confidence of the governors of the Hospital. There is no record of any concern on the part of the Sun Fire Office. Nonetheless, in view of the serious nature of his company's collapse, it was as well that Henry had established good standing previously – and that he had impeccable connections.[26]

In the three weeks subsequent to the suspension, Henry was able to rely on family, friends and reputation for substantial moral support. His brother-in-law, the ubiquitous Denis Le Marchant, brought in Thomas Baring and others, and Henry was given a considerable boost by another relative, Samuel Jones Loyd, the future Lord Overstone. At a creditors' meeting held on 19 October, while not a creditor himself, Loyd arrived and stated that he came merely 'out of personal respect to Mr. Lefevre.' His presence, together with the favourable and confident analysis given to the creditors by the chairman of the meeting, Bonamy Dobree, and perhaps the knowledge of the extent of reserves which might be available to Henry through his family, enabled a postponement to be agreed in order to allow more information and, hopefully, more remittances, to reach London from St Petersburg, whence Henry's partner, Thomas, had repaired at high speed. Henry told John that while the meeting had 'passed off very satisfactorily. . . . I am somewhat in the situation of a prisoner at the Old Bailey, who gets his trial postponed until next session.'[27] The fraternal worry which this affair must have produced is reflected in a comment of John Shaw Lefevre in a letter to Gladstone, to the effect that 'the last few weeks have produced various trials domestic and otherwise to myself.'[28]

The postponement of a decision as to the future of the firm was to be an extended one, however, and negotiations stretched over a whole year. Fortunately, remittances were made from St Petersburg which helped to pay off the debts, but it was not until 30 December 1848 that it was announced that Thomas, Son & Lefevre had that day paid their last dividend, had thus met all their obligations in full, and had resumed trading. *The Times* felt that 'the manner in which they have liquidated all their engagements is highly to their honour.'[29] But the long term cost was heavy. Before they could resume their operations in Russia, Thomas, Son & Lefevre had to place a large sum in the hands of De Jerseys as security against any repetition of the misadventure of 1847. That sum was to be retained by De Jerseys, as a loan, until after Henry's death. But in addition, Henry was to lose both his partners very quickly. The younger Thomas retired from the firm soon after the bankruptcy and in 1850 John Thomas died. His capital was then withdrawn and Henry was left on his own, with only just enough resources to keep the business going. He renamed the firm H.S. Lefevre & Co., and had to face the long haul of rebuilding capital from savings. He was to show an enormous capacity for financial recovery, but it demanded 'a continuous course of self denial.' That would have been hard enough in happy personal circumstances, but Henry's private life had been doubly tragic.

We have seen how Henry was a good friend of Emma Whitbread when they were both no more than adolescent, and it was almost certainly through Emma, now Henry's sister-in-law, that he was remarried less than two years after the death of his first wife, Helen. His new partner was a great-granddaughter of Samuel Whitbread I, from the latter's first marriage to Harriet Hayton. The second daughter of that marriage was christened Emma Maria Elizabeth and she married, in 1780, the twelfth Baron St John of Bletso, taking to him a dowry of £30,000.[30] The eldest of the four daughters of the St Johns was, in turn, called Emma, and her husband, whom she married in 1806, was a clergyman, the Revd John Foster, son of Thomas Foster of Erringdon Park, Yorkshire. Like George Shaw and the first Charles Shaw Lefevre, John Foster was the product of local education, in his case at Halifax School, who went on to graduate from Trinity College, Cambridge. He and the Hon. Emma had a son and a daughter, and since 1815 John had been rector of Sarratt in Hertfordshire. The daughter, Elizabeth Emma (Bessy) Foster, was a close friend of Emma Shaw Lefevre, though a few years younger.

There is no doubt that Henry and Bessy Foster had known each other for some time, because of the latter's friendship with Emma Shaw Lefevre. But there is some disagreement over what part the now undisputed mistress of Heckfield played in the making of the match. According to Henry's granddaughter, Lucy Ogilvy, recording the version given by her mother, Sophia Wickham, Emma promoted the marriage and persuaded Henry to propose, in writing. Henry, on the other hand, asserted emphatically, in a letter to the sister of his first wife, that not only had Emma refrained from intervening, but had persuaded Henry's mother against encouraging the suit.[31] Perhaps one might read this as Henry protesting too much. But whatever the influence and involvement of others, his proposal was accepted. The wedding of Henry, now 33 and the father of three small girls, and Bessy Foster, aged 28, took place at Sarratt on 2 December 1835.

There are a few available details of the lives of Henry's three daughters during the years of his second marriage, and they will be given a little later. But the lives of Henry and his second wife cannot be properly reconstructed. Stepchildrens' recollections of Bessy portray her as 'a very nice person' who 'did not in the least understand children.' Stepmother Emma was overshadowed in those recollections by Aunt Emma and her severities, but it is not really clear which of the two women was the more responsible for the heavy, religious aura, and the sense of guilt, which seems to have permeated the family. Bessy Foster Shaw Lefevre was the only daughter of a divine – but a divine who was remembered by his step-grandchild, Sophia, as being particularly kind. Emma Whitbread Shaw Lefevre's adoption of extreme evangelical zeal has already been mentioned. The one piece of hard evidence we have – from Bessy's deathbed, to be quoted shortly – reveals her as perhaps more relentless in her spiritual masochism than her sister-in-law.

Henry and Bessy lived in Belgravia – seemingly in more than one house. There was no country home, but Sarratt was visited regularly until Bessy's father died in 1838 and Heckfield drew them and their children into the community of all the Shaw Lefevres, especially at Christmas each year. But neither in the domestic nor the professional contexts is there any record of significant events. Henry worked throughout from his office in Austin Friars and in 1841 was a keen supporter of Lord John Russell's election for the

THE WHITBREADS AND THE SHAW LEFEVRES

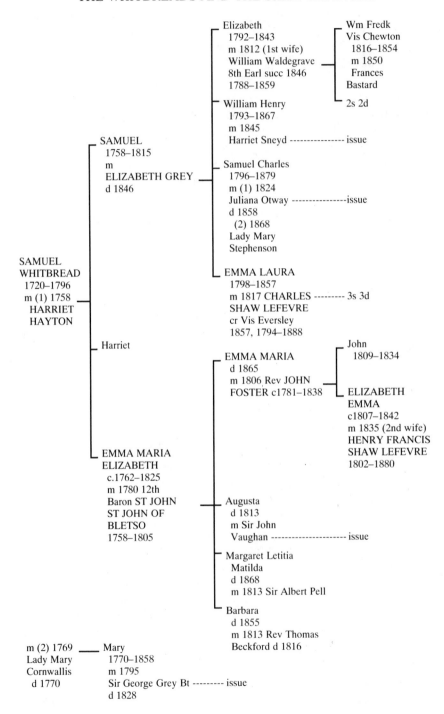

SAMUEL
WHITBREAD
1720–1796
m (1) 1758
HARRIET
HAYTON

SAMUEL
1758–1815
m
ELIZABETH GREY
d 1846

Harriet

EMMA MARIA
ELIZABETH
c.1762–1825
m 1780 12th
Baron ST JOHN
ST JOHN OF
BLETSO
1758–1805

m (2) 1769 ____ Mary
Lady Mary   1770–1858
Cornwallis   m 1795
 d 1770   Sir George Grey Bt --------- issue
                 d 1828

Elizabeth
1792–1843
m 1812 (1st wife)
William Waldegrave
8th Earl succ 1846
1788–1859

Wm Fredk
Vis Chewton
1816–1854
m 1850
Frances
Bastard

2s 2d

William Henry
1793–1867
m 1845
Harriet Sneyd --------------- issue

Samuel Charles
1796–1879
m (1) 1824
Juliana Otway ----------------issue
d 1858
  (2) 1868
Lady Mary
Stephenson

EMMA LAURA
1798–1857
m 1817 CHARLES --------- 3s 3d
SHAW LEFEVRE
cr Vis Eversley
1857, 1794–1888

EMMA MARIA
d 1865
m 1806 Rev JOHN
FOSTER c1781–1838

John
1809–1834

ELIZABETH
EMMA
c1807–1842
m 1835 (2nd wife)
HENRY FRANCIS
SHAW LEFEVRE
1802–1880

Augusta
d 1813
m Sir John
Vaughan --------------------- issue

Margaret Letitia
Matilda
d 1868
m 1813 Sir Albert Pell

Barbara
d 1855
m 1813 Rev Thomas
Beckford d 1816

City of London, joining with his distant relative and fellow banker, Raikes Currie, and others, in publishing an address to voters.[32] By then, however, the personal tragedy of Henry and Bessy was well advanced. On 4 May 1841 Bessy had given birth to a son, who was christened Henry. Subsequently she became seriously ill – there are several references to an abscess, to a bilious fever, and to a deep decline. There are critical comments on her medical treatment – she 'suffered many things of many physicians'; 'the poor thing had no anaesthetics whatever, and the brutes of surgeons loved the knife'; her head was shaved, and altogether 'her case greatly mismanaged and misunderstood.'

Bessy died in April 1842; the baby died four months later. One poignant document has survived. It is a careful copy, in an unformed hand, of the recollection of the 'Last words of my dear Mamma' by Bessy's eldest stepdaughter, Helen, who was then a girl of 13:

> dear Mamma, weak as she was proceeded thus solemnly to address me:
> . . . store up Scripture in your mind; for though, in my youth, I did not learn nearly so much Scripture, as you have, yet during my sufferings, when I could neither read, nor bear to be read to, texts of Scripture have recurred to my mind and afforded me great comfort. I am particularly fond of the LI Psalm, and of all the Penitential Psalms, try to learn as much of the Psalms as you can, and to remember the instruction given you . . . .you will have a great deal to answer for, in another world, for the advantages you have received while on earth. . . . There is salvation in none but Christ, think of your own soul, Helen. . . . I find that a sick bed is no place for repentance. I have deserved every stroke of my suffering: it is very dark at present, but I am told that that is my disease; I feel that Satan is very busy about my sick bed, and the remedies which I have to take prevent my praying as often as I should wish. I feel that I shall never recover and that I am speaking to you for the last time. Pray for me that I may have peace and consolation, peace at the last. . . . When I die I have a sort of presentiment that Baby will soon follow me, if he lives, be kind to him; if you find him and his Papa disagreeing, for he is of a very passionate disposition, urge him to send him to school, and when he comes home for holidays be kind to him, and teach him Psalms and hymns. If I die, comfort your Papa, and do not let him get into the comfortless state in which he was when you poor Mamma died, and be kind to Baby . . . so God bless you, dear Helen, pray for a converted heart.[33]

What sort of impact the loss of two wives and one child within ten years had on Henry, can only be imagined. He was not quite 40 in April, 1842. Bessy's 'prolonged illness upset him . . . most thoroughly' and 'he was never the same again.' It is understandable that he came to accept, increasingly, at least outwardly, the stern religious and moral convictions of his sister-in-law. Inwardly, however, they did little to assuage his sense of bitterness over how life had treated him,[34] and he cannot have been in any buoyant state of mind when the financial crash of his firm occurred only five years after the death of Bessy and the baby son. His two elder daughters were full of anxiety about whether his health was sufficiently good to allow him to run his business alone, after his partners had gone, and the youngest recalled how 'the failure . . . in 1847 and subsequent struggles to repay the money he had borrowed . . . further embittered him.'[35] In 1850 Henry moved to 29 Green Street, close to Grosvenor Square and to Hyde Park, and settled into a grim and cheerless, though remarkably successful endeavour to rebuild his material fortunes. But the early verve and cheerfulness had been destroyed. He would live in Green Street, a widower, for his last thirty years.

One's early years may indeed hold the clue to adult character and experience, and a biographer can only take a very melancholy view, therefore, of that period in the lives of most of the third generation of Shaw Lefevres. For there are few clues to how and to what extent the three daughters of Charles, and the six of John were educated, save for Sophia Wickham's caustic suggestion that Charles' girls were not educated at all! And almost all we know of the childhood of the one boy, John's son George, is that he followed his father to Eton. Surviving family letters have remarkably few references to governesses, but the safest assumption must be that instruction was indeed entrusted to them. There is nowhere the slightest hint that any of Charles's or John's girls ever attended school.

Charles and Emma brought up their daughters in the confident belief that they should become the wives of sound country gentlemen and would need no particular intellectual equipment. Music, though, was certainly on their agenda, and among John Martineau's recollections of dining at Heckfield in 1850, when Emma Laura, Helena and Elizabeth were grown women, was that they entertained him and Charles Kingsley by playing trios for piano, harp and concertina.[36] Charles was as consistent in his ambitions for his daughters as he was consistent about living the life of the country gentleman in which he had been raised and which seemed to give him immense stability and satisfaction – the family motto, it is worth recording, was 'Sans changer'. His two younger daughters were steered firmly into the arms of the landed gentry. The happiest family event of the years which Charles spent as Speaker was the marriage, in 1851, of his and Emma's second daughter, Helena – or Nina as she was always known – to their neighbour, Sir Henry Bouverie Paulet St John Mildmay, fifth Baronet, of Dogmersfield Park, representative of an ancient family with great estates in Essex and Hampshire, one of whose predecessors – 'a downright country squire' – is reputed to have been the model for the rumbustious Western of Fielding's *Tom Jones*.[37] The fifth

Baronet was not made in that mould, and was described by a family member as having been brought up abroad and as being a shy young man who was 'a beautiful linguist and musician'.

Nina was a beautiful woman, and the first of the third generation of Shaw Lefevres to marry. Her marriage established a link between her parents and the family of that Lord Radnor who had married into the Mildmays in 1814, and who, in 1830, had launched her father on his parliamentary career. The Radnor/Bouverie-Mildmay alliances were quite complex, and Helena's younger sister, Elizabeth, was to join her, eight years later, in extending the Shaw Lefevre connection with them.[38] Elizabeth married Hervey George St John Mildmay, a cousin of Sir Henry, who had been a naval captain until he succeeded, unexpectedly, to the country estate of an elder brother in Somerset. Elizabeth went to live there in 1859. Each sister led the confined, comfortable life of the country lady, and neither seemed to have anything of the literary capacity of their cousins to illuminate any of their experience. Such scraps of correspondence as remain reveal nothing but decent commonplace sentiments and a complete absence of interest in the outside world.

The eldest of the three daughters, Emma, the most senior of the third generation, did not marry. In her early and middle life she was no more liked by her cousins, and was less respected, than her mother. The severity of her mother's attitude towards her may have contributed to the development of an unpleasing personality. She was not so physically attractive as her sisters, and perhaps some envy of their married state, and the prospect of a long spinsterhood devoted to the care of an only parent, made her somewhat sour and abrasive. She was 37 when her mother died and she became, in effect, the mistress of Heckfield. This alarmed some of her cousins. One of them remarked that though Emma 'must have looked very nice' at the wedding of Elizabeth, two years later, the idea of Viscount Eversley being left only with his eldest daughter was so disturbing that 'I have now come round to the idea that Uncle Charles *must* marry, in self defence.'[39] And when Elizabeth died, eight years later, apparently in circumstances which implied the possibility of neglect, another cousin wrote that Elizabeth 'was, at heart, the best of the three sisters', and expressed the hope, rather dubiously, that Emma 'had been kind to Bess at that time.'[40] Throughout her middle years she was not regarded with any sympathy in the family, and was variously accused of being extravagant, a poor manager, and very much open to flattery. Sophia Wickham was not her only critic, and felt that Emma was always kind to her, but nonetheless maintained that 'Her tyranny was even narrower and harder than her mother's because her mind was exactly that of a servant and her delight was to surround [her father] with inferior people – TOADIES!' But as we shall see, age was to mellow Emma and the opinions people were to have of her.

It is, perhaps, a reflection of the unhappy and disturbed life of Henry Shaw Lefevre that we know more about the raising of his three daughters than we do about their more fortunately placed cousins. When his first wife died, the eldest daughter, Helen, was five; Anna Maria (Annie) was three; and Sophia only an infant. When Henry remarried, it would seem that almost immediately Helen was sent away to school and that Anna Maria followed quite soon afterwards. The school was chosen by Aunt Emma and clearly appealed to her sense of the need for strict discipline and severe religious instruction. Extracts from the girls' diaries, and the commentary of Sophia's daughter, combine to give a harrowing picture of the three children's experience. Helen and Annie went to Miss Fryers, who presided over a school at The Cedars, Hammersmith – close to where the Olympia exhibition halls now stand. It was 'fearfully expensive and devoid of comfort, the food scanty and of the plainest, but education excellent.' But Miss Fryers had 'a dreadful system of considering every trifle a sin, and therefore every trifle was visited with punishment.' Much worse, Miss Fryers had 'some magnetic influence' which made girls devoted to her as long as they were in her charge, and that influence was particularly exerted over Annie, who was 'trained in morbid habits of self-examination, continually bewailing her sins, especially of pride.'

Helen was clearly a less sensitive child than Annie and survived Miss Fryers better. Both girls were at The Cedars for about nine years, but their younger sister did not join them there. Sophia was entrusted, at the age of 7, to the care of a Miss Ridout, in Brighton. Sophia was certainly the most spirited, critical and astringent observer of the whole of her generation of the Shaw Lefevres, and her spirit was not to be broken. While she remembered Miss Ridout as an admirable teacher, she also recalled her uncontrolled temper. Sophia must have tried that temper, for she recognized that 'when I thought her scoldings unjust, I made her feel I thought so.' Even so, her sojourn with Miss Ridout lasted until her 16th year and then, after a particularly bad quarrel, she was moved to the school of a Mrs Langtry, also in Brighton. But Mrs Langtry's regime was regarded by Henry and his two elder daughters as far too relaxed and Sophia was brought home to be with her sisters. That was in 1849, shortly after Henry had extricated himself from the crash of two years before. It was not a happy household. The three sisters shared one bedroom in a very small house, and Henry's financial weakness was such that he could not afford to keep a carriage. He did employ a companion governess, but the sisters looked back to those years as a period when they had 'not much in the way of amusement or society.'

Given this relatively cheerless childhood – interspersed by some happy interludes and warmed by close and affectionate relationships with some of their cousins, and by the geniality of Uncle Charles – it was natural that Henry's daughters would look for an early escape from their restricted home life through the only route open to them – marriage. They took that route, but only when in their mid- or late-20s, and all between 1856 and 1860. Moreover, they all married into more than comfortably circumstanced families – a tribute either to their own or their father's good matrimonial strategy. The first to wed was the middle daughter, Anna Maria, who in 1856 married William James Farrer, a member of a successful firm of London solicitors which still operates, in a Lutyens building, in Lincoln's Inn Fields.

Helen married a clergyman nearly twenty-five years older than herself, and an invalid. He was George Mason of Copt Howick Hall in Yorkshire, and there is no explanation available of how and where they met. Henry's solid London base, city interests and fraternal political connections might well account for an attachment between Anna and a prominent solicitor, and between his youngest daughter, Sophia, and a politically-minded landowner, but do not seem to fit a distant ecclesiastical acquaintance. Henry must have been quite unaware of any matchmaking, for he was approached suddenly by the Dean of Salisbury, Henry Parr Hamilton, a Trinity College man who may well have been known there to John Shaw Lefevre. Hamilton wrote to Henry to congratulate him on Helen's engagement, which 'we confidently hope and trust . . . will meet your approval . . . greatly as it must surprise you', and went on to explain that, on financial grounds, there needed to be no anxiety:

> [Mason] is Mrs. Hamilton's only Brother. . . . He is Rector of Scruton, near Bedale, [in Yorkshire] a Parish with a population of 410 persons. The living is worth about £600 a year – but this is a secondary consideration, as he will inherit a very large fortune. Meanwhile, his Father who is in his 81st year, will I have no doubt make the young couple perfectly comfortable and independent.[41]

In material terms the Dean was correct, but Helen was not to enjoy her comfort and independence together with her husband for long. George Mason was a sick man, and he and Helen spent most of the nine years remaining to him, after their wedding in October 1857, in the warmer climate of southern Europe. For the first two years they travelled extensively in Italy, France and Spain, and from there Helen wrote those long, carefully composed, highly-descriptive letters so typical of the nineteenth-century well-to-do English abroad. Only here and there in them does one catch the flavour of personal attitudes and concerns – naturally, anxiety about her husband's health, and normal curiosity and comment on the news which reached her about relatives and friends, but equally frequently and at tiresome length the tribulations of dependency on servants.[42]

Several of Sophia's pungent comments on her elders have already been quoted, and they are in no way untypical of this sharp-witted and formidably plain-spoken lady. She married in 1860. Her husband belonged to the political and governmental world of the elder Shaw Lefevres. His grandfather was a famous diplomat, contemporary with the first Charles Shaw Lefevre, and we have come across his father as a fellow member of the Hampshire Whig fraternity with Viscount Eversley and John Shaw Lefevre. The young William Wickham (1831–1897) lived on his estate at Binsted Wyck near Alton, was already active in county affairs, and would graduate to Westminster late in life.

The smallness of Charles' and Henry's families, the early deaths of Henry's two wives, the rather premature death of Lady Eversley, the fact that five of the daughters married and quickly established quite separate homes – all these happenings no doubt ensured that relationships between their members were very normal, usually genial and warm, only rarely involving any major stress. But John and Emily's six girls grew into womanhood in less generous financial circumstances than their cousins, at least before Henry's disaster in 1847. However, as might be expected in the light of John's intellectual interests, he and Emily obviously took their educational duties seriously. Their daughters' letters during their later lives show a sharp and mature awareness of the world around them, a very adequate grasp of current literature, and some elegance of expression. Several of the daughters were quite accomplished amateur artists. There is not a word in the family papers, alas, to suggest who, if anyone other than their parents, was responsible for teaching them, or whether they ever received instruction outside their home.

If a consciousness of their only moderate wealth made John's daughters somewhat defensive towards the better endowed, upper-class social world, an influence much more likely to have kept them particularly close to each other and to their parents was their mother's frailty and apparent possessiveness – she was acutely conscious of the intense, emotional, bonds of family. Her only son, George, and her husband, seem to have been viewed almost as remote beings, quite separate from the reality of the feminine enclave. There was no sign of any unhappiness, or resentment, between the two males and the seven females, but Emily's dependence on the young women verged on being enduringly passionate and not a little morbid. This is revealed in an almost confessional document she wrote in 1860, when she still had twenty-five years to live and when her daughters, all unmarried, ranged from 32 to 18 years of age:

I desire to delineate the characters of my six dear daughters, who still bless and cheer, and make the happiness of our home. I desire to place on record in these few lines, which may meet their eyes after I am taken from them my estimation of their characters individually – tho' if I said generally, I should be quite correct – for in depicting to myself one I find all would deserve the same encomiums. The lights and shades of disposition and of character vary both in each and in all. There is the same high principle, the same excellent warm heart, the same correct judgement, the same refinement and delicacy of mind – and in each I thank God for their firm religious belief which, whatever may be their lot in life, will never fail to support them, to secure their happiness in another world.

From each I have received unceasing affection – each has been to me the truest friend, and in the judgement of each I have found support, dependence and help. No mother was ever more grateful to her children than I am for the happiness they have given, amply rewarding me for the anxiety of their early days. I have a peculiar feeling of gratitude to each – how shall I describe my sense of their forbearance, their consideration for me – thru' the nervousness, the consequence of my very weak health, they have sustained me – thru' duties, the efforts which it was necessary I and P[apa] make for them.[*sic*]

Dear beloved daughters, receive your Mother's tender blessing and your Mother's thanks for all your goodness and watchfulness. May these lines of appreciation of all give pleasure to your hearts and comfort you in the hour of mourning for her, believe that you have been her pride, her delight, her comfort and into God's hands she commends you, trusting all the future will be decided for you.[43]

By the time that was penned, two of the Eversley daughters and all of Henry's were married, and it is hardly surprising that there was speculation amongst them as to why the 'Johns cousins' had been so unsuccessful in the search for husbands. Helen Mason and her sister Sophia chronicled their cousins' misfortunes, perhaps with a little self-satisfaction. 'I quite feel for the poor Johns – all their Sparks seem "to give them the slip."' As a result of the evasiveness of the 'Sparks', the Johns' house 'was again going to be in "a state of rout."' 'Everyone who knows them seems equally surprised at such nice girls all remaining single – George [Mason] thinks . . . that their manner is a little against them – and their numbers.'[44] Certainly 'the Johns women', collectively, seem to have presented a rather formidable front to the masculine world.

The whole of John's family benefitted from the generosity of Lord Overstone, who gave them more than £10,000 during his lifetime, some of it to meet the expense of quite extensive travel, and most in the form of an allocation of £1,000 Consol Stock to each of the six girls. This was a Christmas present in 1858, not long after the only child of the Overstones, Harriet, cousin to the Johns children, had married a hero of the Crimean War, Robert James Lindsay. Lindsay, like Charles Shaw in 1789, took his wife's family name and became Loyd-Lindsay. Subsequently he was to be raised to the peerage as Baron Wantage. Despite the basic kindness of Overstone's giving, there was a shade of emotional blackmail and a degree of patronage about it which caused the 'poor relations' some pain, and must have added to the embarrassments which set in later when the families drifted apart politically. In 1858, Overstone explained to Emily that:

> We have always felt a very sincere interest in the happiness and well being of your family. They have been the chosen and peculiar friends of our dear Harriet; and now that she is in a great degree lost to us, we must hope that they will allow us to associate with them upon terms and in a relationship even more close than that of Uncle and Aunt. This little nest egg will afford to each of our nieces a small income of thirty pounds a year which may be a useful addition to their little resources.[45]

Returning thanks for a subsidy provided in this spirit was not always easy for the younger Shaw Lefevres, but it did not seem to strain the warmth of the feeling which always prevailed between some of them and Harriet.[46]

It is time, at the end of the 1850s, to turn away, for a while, from the dozen female members of the third generation – from Emma Laura, rising 40 and presiding in spinsterly eminence over Heckfield Place; from her two sisters, married into the conformity of the country gentry; from the three married daughters of Henry Francis, allocated neatly to husbands in the law, the church and the landed fraternity; and from the six unmarried offspring of John and Emily, whose current spinsterhood may have been as much or more a reflection of the smaller dowries their father was able to offer, than of any other factors which made them either uninterested, unlucky, unable to attract potential husbands, or unwilling to accept any proposals which came their way. It is time to look at the one male of the generation, poised to begin a political career which would stretch until after the First World War.

CHAPTER XII

Young Radical George

George John Shaw Lefevre was brought up as the only boy in a family of seven. The experience may very well have endowed him with some interesting psychological characteristics. Whether or not they were so deeply ingrained as to be important in explaining his adult personality and behaviour can only be matter for dangerously loose speculation. Certainly, it is impossible to examine his childhood and youth closely – we know as little about his early years as we do of those of his sisters. But it is tempting to brood over the notion that this longest lived of all the Shaw Lefevres – he survived to within a couple of months of his 97th birthday – owed something of his rather brash confidence, and his relatively few but major, petulant lapses of judgement, to over indulgence in the nursery and too much deference within the family to his unique masculinity. Not that he lacked notable ability and strength: he was loyal, combative, tireless, and persistent, and inherited an interesting combination of some of the qualities of his father, uncles and grandfather. His was an industrious, honourable life, but the early, high promise was never quite fulfilled. He reached with ease a plateau near the top of the mountain, and occupied it for a long spell, with some distinction. But he lacked the strong decisiveness and, perhaps, the ultimately necessary hardness, without which he could not find the way to the summit.

George was born to John and Emily Shaw Lefevre in June 1831, five months after the death of his 4-year-old brother. He was between two elder sisters, Rachael and Maria, and four younger ones, Mary, Jane, Madeleine and Emily. In later life there are sisterly references to his kindnesses, and there is certainly nothing in the surviving papers to suggest that he was anything but a normal, affectionate son and brother in a rather unusual family situation. A portrait of him at the age of about 10 or 12 shows him as pleasant and open-faced. When he was 17, a girlfriend of one of his cousins thought him '*such* a nice looking boy . . . he will be very handsome.' But there is no panegyric of George similar to that which his mother poured out about her six daughters, and the letters which he sent her from his various trips abroad are dutiful while being without any signs of particular warmth. There is no surviving – or at least no available – correspondence between George and his wife – and only a scrap or two of what must have passed between him and his father and sisters. There were no children of his marriage, and thus no parental or filial archive. It would be all too easy, therefore, to misrepresent very seriously the quality of his personal relationships. Nonetheless, a reading of all of what there is about George suggests strongly that he was not a man whose very great energies and passionate interests were ever more than slightly engaged by intimate personal and family affairs or, indeed, by any concerns outside his obsessional preoccupations with politics and government and his career within them.

John Shaw Lefevre sent his only son through the same educational route as he had travelled – to Eton in 1843, and then to Trinity College, Cambridge, where the young man took his BA in 1853. George did not emulate his father's brilliant academic performance. He was a respectable *junior optime* and went on in his father's legal footsteps to the Bar, via the Inner Temple, two years later. Like his father, his uncle Charles and his grandfather, he practised law for only a short spell of years. Almost instinctively, it might seem, he was drawn to the more hazardous career of politics. Given his family background and the fact that he grew up in a home environment permeated by political and governmental concerns, it is easily understandable that his ambition was clearly channelled and uncomplicated from the outset.

Despite the demands of a large family, and perhaps with the help of Lord Overstone, money was found to prepare George for a public career by ensuring that he knew something of the wider world. Between Cambridge and the Bar he and two friends, one of them a Whitbread, visited the eastern parts of the United States and Canada, and went as far south as Richmond, Virginia, where they saw the slave market in operation. From America George sent almost a dozen long, well-written accounts of his travels to his parents. In each of the three years beginning 1855 George spent some autumn weeks in south eastern Europe, the Near East, and North Africa. He cruised on Sir Edward Colebrooke's yacht in the Black Sea, and exercised an early enthusiasm for photography by taking pictures – some of them published after his return – of what the Russians left behind after their retreat from Sebastopol. In 1856 he visited three cities of Algeria, then less than twenty years under French rule. A year later he rode from Vienna to Constantinople and went on to Athens and Corfu. He revisited North Africa in 1859, but never evinced any special interest in that part of the world thereafter. His early experience of America, however, almost certainly helped move him to launch his parliamentary career by tackling the diplomatic problems raised in the Civil War era; and for the rest of his life he developed, both as politician and as writer, a deep concern for the fortunes of the declining Ottoman Empire and its European provinces.[1]

It was at the general election of 1859 that George, then 27, made his first attempt to enter the House of Commons. He was approached by the Liberals of the city of Cambridge, but no doubt with his family connections very much in mind, and the practical advantage of having Viscount Eversley's prestige and local influence with the Whig network at his back, he preferred the role of second Liberal candidate for Winchester.[2] One of that city's two seats had been held by a Tory, Sir J.B. East, and the other by a Liberal – John Bonham Carter, son of the Bonham Carter who had been prominent when George's father had stood for Petersfield only months after George's birth. These two were again standing, and George's candidacy was a Liberal response to the Conservatives' decision to run Thomas Fleming of Stoneham Park – second son of the John Fleming who had so strongly urged the Duke of Wellington to have the young Charles Shaw Lefevre opposed in the 1830s. Thus was the 1859 election, in some personal respects, almost a rerun of the internal Hampshire struggle within a narrow social stratum a generation earlier.

But this time, in Winchester, there was to be no Whiggish landslide. George argued in his address that 'the real question to be decided . . . is whether the framing and management of a Reform Bill shall be confided to the Liberal or to the Conservative party.' The electors preferred to see Winchester equally divided on that and other issues, and returned their previous representatives. George's appearance on the scene, however, may well have helped to produce a contest which was reported as 'unprecedentedly severe.' He came at the bottom of the poll, but with sufficient votes to establish him as a worthwhile contender. The figures were East 403, Bonham Carter 348, Fleming 342 and Shaw Lefevre 230.[3] It was a result which was characteristic of George's whole electoral history. He was a candidate for election fourteen times and was opposed on ten occasions, including Winchester in 1859. He lost only three contests, but those three, and at least four others, were hard fought. He never had the financial resources to make his way easy. He earned his victories by hard campaigning, and proved himself to be a bonny fighter.

After Winchester it was only a few months before one of the two Reading seats fell vacant through the appointment of the sitting member, the Solicitor General, to a judgeship. The ensuing contest was notable because the Liberals adopted as their candidate Sir Francis Henry Goldsmid, Baronet, and he was elected in January 1860, becoming the first Jewish member of the House of Commons. George Shaw Lefevre had made a bid for the candidacy, and according to a later, hostile Conservative account, his bid was known to and 'understood' by many influential local Liberals, including the party's agent, Thomas Rogers, before Goldsmid had shown interest. Conservatives – probably not confined to supporters of the Conservative Party – were distinctly hostile to the idea of a non-Christian MP, though not disparaging Goldsmid personally. Their supporting paper, the *Berkshire Chronicle*, asserted bluntly that the Liberals simply 'ditched' Shaw Lefevre because he 'was not a millionaire, though he had 'far stronger claims politically'. Certainly, George withdrew, not wishing 'to divide the Liberal interest', because the poll would have been affected adversely 'even by an appearance of disunion in the Liberal party.'[4]

Whatever currents of controversy over political and constitutional principle and constituency finance were at work among the Reading Liberals, there can be no doubt that George had hoped to be a candidate, that he did not succeed, and that he made the most politic use he could of his disappointment. It was said, publicly, by a leading local Liberal, that George retired from the field 'remembering there were constant changes . . . that they might require another Liberal candidate on some future occasion . . . [and that he was] willing and anxious to make the acquaintance of the constituency.' More importantly, according to the Conservative press, he went away with an implied, if not expressly stated promise, from the Liberal agent and from influential members of the party, that 'on the next vacancy his claims would have the prior consideration.'[5] It was not long before there was an opportunity for the implied promise to be put to the test. Only nine months after Goldsmid's election, Francis Pigott, the long-established holder of the other Reading seat, who was also a Liberal, resigned on becoming Governor of the Isle of Man. His replacement caused the Liberals a good deal of embarrassment, in which George Shaw Lefevre was heavily involved. The plot of this little drama hinged on Pigott family interest and on the role of the Liberal agent, Thomas Rogers.

George may well have had a hint of Francis Pigott's likely resignation, but unfortunately for him, he was 'far away' when the news broke officially. By the time he returned, a meeting of local Liberal notables had adopted Serjeant Gillery Pigott, brother of the retiring member, as a candidate. Viscount Eversley, clearly well-informed of what was going on, considered that the agent Rogers who, Eversley implied, must have known of George's interest in the seat, had 'behaved very ill to George' and played 'a game of his own to give Serjeant Pigott all the advantage of a good start.'[6] But George was not alone in coveting the Liberal candidacy. Within a week of Serjeant Pigott being approved, both George and a Captain Walter, brother of John Walter, MP for Berkshire and main owner of *The Times*, had announced their interest. George issued an address emphasizing the old standing connection of his family with Reading, and criticizing as 'hasty . . . the proceedings of some of the constituency in holding a meeting and selecting a candidate' – a complaint made equally strongly by Walter a little later.[7]

The Reading Liberals thus had three candidates, even before the Conservatives had decided whether or not to contest the seat. It is highly probable that George kept in close touch with his uncle, and Eversley wrote to John, on 10 October, approving of George's electoral strategy:

George appears to be playing his game very cleverly at Reading and I have urged him not to resign just yet, as he does not incur expense by remaining a candidate. . . . I think there is a remote chance for George if Captain Walter resigns, as I expect he will, and if the Tories do not start a candidate of their own, in which case George would be obliged to withdraw and he would do so gracefully to save a Liberal candidate – but in the event of Captain Walter's resigning and no Tory candidate appearing, I think the Tories would support George for this election – to damage Rogers whom they hate – and so long as George maintains his own opinion, and does not truckle to them – I see no objection to his accepting the support of the Tories – after the conduct of Rogers and his friends – and a very reasonable amount of caution on George's part will enable him to steer clear of giving offence to them.[8]

But the situation did not work out as Eversley had hoped. George was clearly losing confidence almost as soon as he had issued his address, and saw that 'there is little or no chance of my getting together a party among the Liberals – and without it I cannot accept support from Conservatives . . . but after all no one can tell what a day or two may produce.'[9] Alas for George, a day or two produced a Tory candidate, and George immediately withdrew. He showed sound political sense, removing any possibility of being blamed for splitting the party's vote, but not missing the opportunity of reminding the Liberals that he had refrained from pressing his case earlier in the year and protesting that, on this second occasion, 'an opportunity should have been afforded me of submitting myself to [the party's] choice on equal terms with any other Liberal candidate.'[10]

The three-way contest within the Liberal ranks had been grist to the mill of the Conservative press, which characterized the whole affair as The Great Pigott Job, and castigated Rogers as the villain of the piece who was attempting, through chicanery and dishonesty, to convert Reading into a nomination borough. But while sympathizing with Shaw Lefevre for the shabby treatment meted out to him in both this and the previous election, the paper also sneered at him for refusing conservative support and abandoning the fight.[11] Ironically, the Conservative candidate, who issued an aggressive address on 19 October, apparently decided a week afterwards that even if there were two Liberal candidates his chances were poor, and also withdrew from the scene.[12] Captain Walter, confounding Eversley's forecast, not only refused to withdraw, but also openly invited 'Independent' support, perhaps counting on the disillusionment of many Liberals with the Pigott-Rogers faction. There was, therefore, a contest, which Pigott won by 586 votes to 435.[13]

After these three attempts in eighteen months, George had to wait almost three years before he achieved his aim. He had behaved with circumspection in Reading in 1860 and had thereby imposed some obligation on the local Liberals. Thereafter he waited for the expected promotion of Serjeant Pigott to be a judge, but confessed to a sister in the summer of 1862 that he did not think that would happen 'yet', and indeed hoped it would not, 'as it would hardly be worth while to be elected for this Parliament.' But most importantly in this waiting period, he made his peace with 'my quondam enemy Mr Rogers who asked me to forget the past and to let him act for me if occasion required.' Rogers, who certainly seems to have had shifting loyalties – he had been a Tory canvasser in 1841 – 'intimated that the Reading people don't like Pigott and will get rid of him at next election.'[14] George was fully cognisant of Rogers' usefulness: he claimed, twenty years afterwards, that Rogers in the earlier period had been 'really alone the organization of the party', and was trusted by it when it existed 'simply and solely for the purpose of selecting a candidate' for an election – at other times the party was 'dormant and almost non-existent.' One may smile at the small hypocrises of politics when reading Rogers' assertion to a celebratory gathering on George's long tenure of the Reading seat, that 'from the time when [Shaw Lefevre] was first introduced to this constituency . . . it has been my pleasure to stand by his side in every battle, and to enjoy the pleasures and excitements of it, and to share with him the gladness of our victories.'[15]

It was perhaps only fair, in view of those earlier unsuccessful forays and the many fierce battles of later years, that George Shaw Lefevre's first entry to the House of Commons was unopposed. In September 1863 Serjeant Pigott was placed on the judicial bench, and was thus relieved of any need to put his popularity to the test at an election. His seat at Reading was declared vacant and George was first in the field. He stated his claim boldly and 'with confidence, recollecting the numerous promises of support which he received on a former occasion, and that he retired from the contest in accordance with the wish expressed rather than endanger the unity of the Liberal party.'[16] In his old age George attributed his easy acceptance to the great respect in which Reading Liberals held the memory of his grandfather, and to the good impression he himself had made at Winchester in 1859.[17] To those factors must be added the good ground work of Rogers, the known strength of local Liberal sentiment, and the age of the Parliament, all of which no doubt contributed to deter anyone from entering the lists against him. He was returned, unopposed, on 17 October 1863, and took his seat when the House of Commons reassembled on 4 February 1864. Except for five crucial months from November 1885 until April 1886, he was to serve continuously as an MP for nearly thirty-two years.

The first Charles Shaw Lefevre had been an independent Whig who became in his later career anti-governmental rather than clearly and outstandingly reformist. The second Charles, George's uncle, began with the strong Whig reformist sentiments of the 1820s and 1830s, but as Speaker put aside his more partisan attitudes though, in his long retirement, he showed clear signs of disquiet over further moves towards democracy. George's father, the most intellectual of the family, pursued the liberal and progressive policies of the mainstream reformers of his time, apparently without questioning them or adding to them any ideas of his own. George, in the same tradition, was to be an active, assiduous advocate of the liberal aims of the second half of the nineteenth century, mainly as those aims were formulated by William Ewart Gladstone, though spiced with a personal radicalism which made a somewhat erratic impact. He was no more an original thinker than other members of his family. He was a sincere but pedestrian orator, and his prose style, while workmanlike, was undistinguished. But he was a genuine, if moderate, radical; and he took a major part in pioneering one great new cause – the preservation of commons, which was the forerunner of what we now call the care of the physical environment. And for his sheer energy and persistence as speaker, administrator, and producer of articles, pamphlets and books, he ought to be credited with having added a dimension of practicability and persuasive publicity to some of the main themes of Gladstonian liberalism, and to some of the pressures to extend its scope.

George assured the electors of Reading in 1863 that he was a fervent supporter of Lord Palmerston's foreign policy. He blamed the 'postponement of many necessary measures' of domestic reform on the preoccupations of foreign affairs and on the 'evenly-balanced state of two great parties in the House of Commons,' and pledged himself to work for 'the abolition of Church-rates, the reform of the Irish Church, [and] the extension of the suffrage,' and to address himself to 'many other questions, in which the old battle of civil and religious liberty of action and thought has yet to be fought.'[18] His keenness to see progress made on the domestic front led him into the first of several unfortunate incidents in his career which resulted from a rather loose tongue and a lack of political tact. In the only major speech of his campaign he tried to take playful exception to a statement of Lord Russell, then Foreign Secretary, who had implied that the Liberals had perhaps reached a stage, after the long period of reform since 1832, when they might 'rest and be thankful'. George had taken insufficient care to phrase his speech in such a way that any report of it would not give offence. But his criticism of Russell, when read in cold print, greatly annoyed the elder statesman. Interestingly, Russell did not write and upbraid George, but sent a letter to John Shaw Lefevre, expressing his pleasure at seeing the son of an old friend in the House, but regretting that George had 'commenced his political career by a bitter attack upon himself.' Hasty apologies soothed the Earl's irritation, but it was six months before Viscount Eversley considered that George's 'imprudent speech' had been forgiven.[19]

Though, in the later years of the long span of his own lifetime, George's claim to be remembered as particularly radical wore thin as new political doctrines emerged, he has been regarded as one of the 'few men of intellect and advanced opinion' who were appearing in Parliament as harbingers of 'a decisive shift in political power to the post-1832 generation.' His name was linked with those of Goschen, Grant Duff, Wilfrid Lawson, George Trevelyan and Arthur Peel, and he was described as 'a somewhat lively and frisky Radical below the gangway, giving an occasional spur to the sluggish administration of Lord Palmerston.'[20] He soon showed his courage, by making clear his repugnance to any recognition by Britain of what he called the 'slave power' of the Confederates of the Southern States of America. This was then a minority position among the English 'classes', and George was very much influenced by Cobden's views, which would not have endeared him to the Prime Minister.

With Cobden's backing he made his maiden speech, on 4 March 1864, on the *Alabama* incident, and nearly came to grief by allowing his indignation to triumph over his sense of what was politically acceptable. After deciding not to use the word, he was carried away and called the seamen of the *Alabama* and her sister ships 'pirates'. Despite protests in the House and a friendly private admonition from the Speaker, the speech was well received. It brought George's name clearly before his contemporaries and, more importantly, his seniors, as that of someone worth watching.[21] One observer wrote that:

> there is no promise that Mr Lefevre will ever be an orator; but he has a good voice, a prepossessing personal appearance, self-possession, an easy flow of language, and the power of arrangement and of keeping his subject . . . well in hand.[22]

The veteran Eversley thought well of the speech, but advised George, through his father, that:

> his future success in Parliament depends very much upon his not speaking too often at first. Lawyers are never very popular with the House, and if they talk too much they are always considered bores – whereas if they speak but rarely and not too long, the House always listens to them with attention.[23]

George Shaw Lefevre had genuinely passionate feelings about political questions, but he had perhaps more intensely passionate ambitions to hold ministerial office. It was this which marked him as his father's son, rather than his uncle's nephew or his grandfather's grandson. And it also reflected and repeated his father's anxieties about money, for there was no obvious large pool of capital from which George could draw an income sufficient to make an official salary a matter of indifference. George Trevelyan recalled Shaw Lefevre's assertion, on achieving his first post, in May 1866, of a 'theory that an official career was as much of a regular calling as the bar, or any other' – a rather odd theory for one who understood full well the shifting sands of parliamentary politics.[24] But however much he may have realized that he could not always be in office, George yearned for an administrative career, and confessed when in his 80s that he had:

> always felt that no occupation in life affords a fuller measure of satisfaction than that of Minister at the head of a great Department of State. This is specially the case when Parliament is not sitting and there is full time for the Minister to devote himself to the administration of the Department and to the development of his policy.[25]

The first step which George was able to take towards official employment came only a few weeks before his election to Parliament, when he was substituted for Lord Hobart as legal member of a three-man royal commission on sea fisheries. The chairman was James Caird MP, a specialist on agriculture, and Professor Huxley was the scientific member. One could well imagine that John Shaw Lefevre's influence helped to place him on the commission, which lasted two years and took him on constant visits to fishing ports. The task was to find out if there were any problems of supply of fish, and whether any modes of fishing or legislative restrictions in being, 'injuriously affected' fisheries. George was an orthodox free-market Liberal; his more expert colleagues were quite unconvinced of there being any scientific or technical need to conserve fish stocks. All three were agreed that there should be no restrictions imposed on fishing, and that existing legislation should be repealed.[26] No doubt the exercise gave George an entrée into the world of governmental administration. The enquiry gave him a knowledge of the subject which was well regarded, and led the Conservative Government to invite him to help in diplomatic discussions with the French on fisheries questions, early in 1867.

From this early stage, George was on the look out for ways of increasing his income. He had been active for some time in arranging investments in railways for himself and his sisters; he had become a director of the Guardian Insurance Company, and was very willing to consider offers of other connections with the business world.[27] His father, however, urged caution when another involvement was broached:

> I am decidedly of opinion . . . that you had better do nothing in the – way of Companies at this moment until you see a little further into your Parliamentary career. If you succeed in your second speech as well as in your first, you will be thought of *at once* for office – for you must not forget that very few aspirants could venture to risk their seat – and that diminishes the number of your competitors.
>
> Moreover, if owing to a change of ministry or from other causes you do

not obtain office your increasing reputation will enable you to get a better position in some company such as Chairman instead of being merely a director. I am very apprehensive too lest by 'going in' for Directorships now you may lose some of the consideration you have gained and that may have a bad effect both in respect of obtaining office and your re-election at . . . dissolution.[28]

It is unclear whether or not George heeded his father's warning. In any event, in retrospect, his business concerns were less memorable, in the first years of his parliamentary career, than the part he played in creating a body to protect what remained of the ancient English commons after centuries of encroachment and enclosure. That process of enclosure had only become a matter for modern concern in the 1860s, as the pressures of a rapidly growing urban population threatened any open space on which it would be possible and profitable to build. Although Shaw Lefevre wrote a standard history of the struggle which he and his colleagues carried on intensively for a generation, and which in different forms has gone on ever since, it is difficult to assess whether and in what proportions his motives were those of a radical social thinker, or those of an ambitious politician who saw a new area in which to make his name, or those of a barrister intrigued by the complex legal issues raised. He was first moved to involve himself by happy memories of living on the edge of Wimbledon Common during his adolescence. He may very well have been helped by knowledge of his father's long experience in handling the Spencers' landed properties, and he cannot have been unaware – perhaps a little mischievously – that his family's fortunes were symbolized by the Heckfield estate, put together through the enclosing enthusiasm of his grandfather and his uncle.[29]

The Earl Spencer was still the Lord of the Manor of Wimbledon, and in the autumn of 1864 he put forward a bill to authorize a well-meaning scheme to create a public park on most of the common, but at the cost of removing the ancient rights of the commoners. The commoners, however, were much opposed, and the initiative to contest the scheme seems to have been taken by Philip Henry Lawrence, an eminent London solicitor and resident of Wimbledon. This opposition merged with a wider argument about the future of all the London commons, and early in 1865 the Member for Lambeth, a Mr Doulton, moved for a select committee which would enquire into the whole subject and include examination of the Wimbledon Common bill. George took part in the debate, became a member of the committee, and worked with Lawrence on drafting the report, which was carried by a majority of two to one. It condemned the notion of purchase and sale of parts of commons in order to secure the residue, and called for preservation of existing rights and improvement of the condition of the commons.[30]

The report was greeted with great hostility by the lords of the manors, who claimed that the commoners' rights had lapsed through non-use, and that they, the lords, were practically the owners of the commons. They began immediately a new series of attempts to enforce enclosures. A long and bitter legal struggle was in prospect, and it was to organize the defence of the commoners' rights that Lawrence suggested the establishment of a society which was initially restricted in its concerns to the London area, though later its coverage was extended to the whole country. Its full modern title is The Commons, Open Spaces and Footpaths Preservation Society, but it was usually thought of in its abbreviated form as the Commons Preservation Society (CPS). Shaw Lefevre always gave great credit to Lawrence as the originator of the idea, but was himself clearly a prime mover in getting the society off the ground. The first meeting was held in his chambers in the Inner Temple on 19 July 1865 and he brought together, among other, mainly legal luminaries, John Stuart Mill – a prominent member until his death – Professor Huxley, Sir T. Fowell Buxton, Thomas Hughes, Cowell Temple (later Lord Mount Temple) and Charles Pollock (later Lord Pollock).

George extracted £1,400 from his friends on the spot, and they elected him chairman. Except for the years when he was in office, he retained the chairmanship for the rest of his life, and devoted enormous effort to helping to fight the court cases which, along with relevant parliamentary action, secured the preservation of the great open spaces of London – the commons of Barnes, Hampstead, Wandsworth, Wimbledon, Tooting and Epping Forest – as well as others within the metropolis and across England and Wales. It was work which was closely related to his wider interest in land questions, and complemented his ministerial enthusiasms, as First Commissioner of Works, for public access to the royal parks and the improvement of some of central London's major roads. He used his parliamentary position and his persuasive powers to involve powerful people in the affairs of the CPS, the list including Dilke, Bryce, Fawcett, Octavia Hill (with whom he worked on the creation of the National Trust), Sir William Harcourt, Fitzmaurice, Granville, the Duke of Westminster, his kinsman Lord Farrer, Dean Stanley and Samuel Morley, to name some of the most prominent.[31] It was an activity which would appear to have been an unsullied success. If its details are rather tedious and if their impact on his life are not much more mentioned in these pages, that should not weaken the claim that what was achieved by his persistent, unspectacular effort, was probably what will be most warmly and gratefully remembered about him.

Another strong manifestation of his radicalism, reflecting especially the influence of Mill, was his championing of the attempt to liberalize the law controlling the property of married women. In the spring of 1868 he joined Mill and Russell Gurney in introducing a bill and took the chair of the select committee to which the bill was referred. Argument continued throughout two sessions and well into the period of the new Liberal Government. George took a leading part throughout, and the proposed legislation was at last passed in 1870. But probably the strongest, most lasting influence on him in this formative period had been that of Cobden, who died in 1865. George was an original member of the Cobden Club; he wrote much for it, and was to be a steadfast protagonist of Free Trade for the rest of his life.[32]

George was easily re-elected for Reading at the general election of July 1865 – he and Goldsmid were opposed only by a mysterious, last-minute Conservative candidate who was totally unknown both before and after the election.[33] His activities and demonstrated abilities in 1864 and 1865, and the apparent safeness of his seat led, as his father and uncle had prophesied, to his being offered a junior ministerial post by the now forgiving Lord Russell. He was made Civil Lord of the Admiralty late in April 1866, and though anxious about the possibility of being opposed when, as was necessary, he had to resubmit himself to the Reading electorate, was relieved of a contest by the absence of any opponent.[34] His chief at the Admiralty was the Duke of Somerset, and he shared the representation of the department in the Commons with the Secretary, T.G. Baring, and another member of the Board, Captain Lord John Hay. He had only a few weeks to savour his new status, and he did not take any part in discussions or questions on the floor of the Commons. In June the Cabinet resigned over franchise questions, and for the next two-and-a-half years George was to be in opposition. But however short his first spell at the Admiralty, it gave him an insight into and a concern for naval affairs which lasted throughout his life. During the immediate future, in February 1867, he was closeted with Childers, Stansfeld and Lord John Hay in discussions of tactics about the Navy estimates, and he took several opportunities in that and the next session to defend the work of the Admiralty under the previous administration.[35]

The second Reform Act, passed in 1867 with the Conservatives in power, was the occasion for what was probably Shaw Lefevre's first entry into political pamphleteering. It was a reaction to the complaints of some of his constituents and of 'the labouring classes in London', about certain results that followed from the 'annexing' of the rating of property for local government purposes to the franchise. He published a closely-argued examination of the history and legal implications of that connection, in which he admitted that he found the 1867 Act 'as wide in theory' as he had wished and indeed 'far more so than I expected.' This was not a particularly radical position, and the whole essay comprised thirty-seven pages of rather arid and uninspiring discussion, but it was characteristic of the solid, careful, coverage and analysis and the persistent seriousness which he brought to all his writing.[36]

But it was in the context of American relations that George added most to his promising parliamentary reputation. He pursued his concern for the interests of the Northern States from the time of the Alabama incident for the next six or seven years. In the autumn of 1866, he had gone to Washington to sample the mood of the United States in the wake of the Civil War, and to relate that mood to the still delicate state of Anglo-American affairs. He travelled widely in America, was well received on account of his known protestations about the predatory Confederate ships, and because of his enthusiasm for improved Anglo-American relations. He developed a close acquaintance with the Secretary of State, William Seward, who introduced him to President Johnson. At home again, he made a strong speech, on 6 March 1868, in favour of submitting the Alabama claim to arbitration, which brought him the plaudits of *The Times* and the hearty congratulations of his uncle, who told John Shaw Lefevre that George had:

> placed his case before the House in a manner which has done him the greatest credit . . . the whole tone of the debate was satisfactory and likely to make a most favourable impression in America. I am satisfied, if George does not speak too often, and treats any question he wishes to take up with as much care and moderation as he has shown in this American debate, he will become a favourite with the House – and must succeed, in the event of any change of Administration, in obtaining a good appointment in a Liberal Government.[37]

George's arguments played no small part in bringing about the changes in British Government attitudes which led to the Treaty of Washington in 1871 and an end to a troublesome dispute.[38] Despite this creditable venture, however, George never became so active again in foreign affairs, though as will be seen, he took no small interest in Greece and the waning Turkish Empire later in his career.

Viscount Eversley's forecast of George's ministerial future brings up the question of how much his interests were forwarded, during the next ten years, by his father; and how much George and his father operated singly or together in that context. The political Shaw Lefevres had never hidden their lights under bushels, or been slow to demand what they thought they were worth, or what they hoped to have awarded to them. It is not surprising, therefore, that after the great Liberal victory of 1868, when there was gossip as to the likelihood of 'something' for George, we should find John Shaw Lefevre writing to the new Prime Minister, expressing concern about a report that 'something' would, in fact, be a return to the civil lordship at the Admiralty. It is clear that father and son discussed the gossip and that George made his own inquiries. Whether he persuaded his father to take any action, and whether John needed any persuasion or even told his son what he was going to do, remains unclear. At any rate, in the context of the civil lordship, John wrote to Gladstone:

The main advantage of places of this kind is the opening they may give for Parliamentary utility and distinction. When my son accepted the place under the late Government he was the second member in the House of Commons representing that department. He would now only be the third Mr Childers First Lord being in the Commons – and he understands from Mr Childers that the more important [part] of the Civil Lord's duties is to be transferred to the Secretary of the Admiralty. Under these circumstances the importance of the place is much lowered. During the past two years he has undoubtedly made much advance in the House. I fear that the contemplated post would tend to extinguish him.[39]

Gladstone, implying his awareness of dealing with a family team, denied the rumour directly. He then went on that 'as I write to remove your apprehensions, perhaps I had better add that what I should propose to your son – through this letter and through you if you will convey with your accustomed kindness the offer – is that he would allow me to name him to Her Majesty for the office of Secretary of the Board of Trade under Mr Bright.' The gratification of father and son can be imagined. John declared, accurately, that the job would suit George, and added diplomatically to the Prime Minister that George's being at the Board would 'remind me of that which I have not forgotten your kindness to myself a quarter of a century ago in that department.'[40]

Viscount Eversley's judgement as to George's chances was thus proved sound. But George's challenge to the rights of large landowners and his general enthusiasm for radical causes were not happily received at Heckfield. Eversley was caught between avuncular approval of his nephew's parliamentary promise, and downright disappointment at his un-Whiggish attitudes. While the viscount made no sign of active disapproval, he offered no helping hand to his nephew. His coolness indicated a distaste, not only for George's particular domestic hobbyhorses, but for the widened franchise and the overall tendencies of the Liberals under Gladstone's influence. William Wickham recorded that Eversley 'never trusted Mr Gladstone and used to say he was a Radical grafted on a Tory and bitterly he abhorred his policy.' The relations between uncle and nephew were no doubt quite strained, for George, being a talkative man, would hardly have hidden his fulsome admiration of Gladstone. As he readily admitted after the Grand Old Man's death:

From my first entrance to the House of Commons in 1863 – and, in fact, for some years before, when I was a constant visitor to the Strangers Gallery and heard all the principal debates – I was completely under the spell, not merely of his eloquence, but of his generous sympathy for everything affecting the better interests of humanity, and of his intense devotion to the public service.[41]

George was well aware of his uncle's apparent neglect of him, and his resentment came to the boil over the election of 1868. He had received a contribution towards the cost of the election from his uncle Henry, who also offered him a loan, should he need it. George was properly grateful, especially as he felt disadvantaged at Reading by Goldsmid, to whom expense was, apparently, a matter of indifference. But, George went on:

> From Lord Eversley I have . . . practically received no aid in the past. He has not even done what lay in his power to do, without expense, namely shewing interest in Reading and paying a little attention to some of the leading people there. Only a week before the late contest he refused the High Stewardship of the Borough and his agent Collins voted against me. Some weeks ago also he told my Father he should give me £100 towards the expenses in the event of a contest; I certainly did not think this was what might be expected from him as the head of our Family and as one who had during a long life received the support of the Liberal Party and in consequence still enjoys a very large pension. I have accordingly written him a letter of which I send you a copy – I do not wish it to be considered as a demand on my part, but rather as a statement of my position with reference to his proposed assistance.[42]

Unfortunately, George's letter to his uncle does not seem to have survived. Henry's response was sympathetic but unhopeful: 'I fear that you will not get more than £100 from the Viscount – he will plead poverty on account of his new house.'[43] Nor do we have Eversley's response, but doubtless the ex-Speaker's diplomatic skills had not deserted him. There was no break in civilized relations, and from time to time the old man gave George sage political advice. He was delighted when George married the only daughter of a wealthy earl, and in the more distant future he would write on occasion to his sister-in-law, complimenting her on George's achievements. But no money ever seems to have come George's way from Heckfield, and he was totally ignored in Eversley's will.

In an era when the idea of paying MPs was unacceptable, George's situation must have been very typical of the young politician of limited means. As his father wrote to Henry Francis:

> Rightly or wrongly (I think the former) George has committed himself to the career of public life as a poor man. The present Election is in fact the turning point. Had he been ousted it would not have been impossible for him to try some other line – but now he must continue on the course he has chosen. In this he will have need of the sympathy and encouragement of his relations in the various periods of political adversity which inevitably take place in the chequered life of a political man.[44]

Thus by the end of 1868, although George had won a relatively easy victory at Reading, and was regarded as an up and coming young man with his foot firmly on the lower rungs of the ministerial ladder, he was conscious of potential financial difficulties. But while he was aware of a problem at Heckfield Place, he cannot have been more than vaguely disturbed by another family development over the last decade which, though it had made no immediate material impact, was to have a very unfortunate significance several years ahead. It will be recalled that, in 1858, George's cousin, Harriet Loyd, the only daughter of Lord Overstone, had married the Crimean War hero Robert Lindsay, a son of the Earl of Crawford, who subsequently took the name of Loyd-Lindsay. The closeness of the Overstones and the John Shaw Lefevres can be gauged from the fact that after the newly-married couple had returned from their honeymoon, Harriet stayed with her aunt and uncle at Sutton Place throughout her husband's spell as a courtier at Windsor. Harriet's mother – Emily Shaw Lefevre's sister – died suddenly in 1864, and thereafter Lord Overstone made his home with his son-in-law and his only daughter, on whom he became increasingly dependent emotionally.

In 1865, Loyd-Lindsay was elected as a Conservative to one of the three seats for the county of Berkshire. Thus he and George were both on the hustings in Reading, the county town of Berkshire, but on opposite sides. Harriet Loyd-Lindsay's warm relations with some of her Shaw Lefevre cousins continued to be close, but as her father moved away from Liberal sentiments and her husband espoused the Conservative cause, some distance was bound to be put between the families. Within a couple of weeks of his election at Reading in 1863, George had an uncomfortable visit with the Overstones and the Loyd-Lindsays. He found them 'very reserved with regard to my election, as I expected. I confess I never stay there with any pleasure or satisfaction as they are so cautious in saying what they think and so very contrary to what I like in friends.'[45] By the end of 1868 George had no illusions – 'Lord Overstone is not likely after his recently published opinions to wish otherwise than unfavourably to my cause. I have received no aid from him in the past and do not look for it in the future.'[46]

Even more ominous, in the longer financial term, was a quarrel between Overstone and John Shaw Lefevre. Their close friendship from Cambridge days, and their family intimacy as brothers-in-law, was broken by politics. John, who moved to Ascot in 1865–6, came on to the list of electors for Berkshire. At the 1868 election he felt in honour bound to support the Liberal candidates, and so cast his vote against Robert Loyd-Lindsay. For this he was not forgiven by Overstone, and for at least three years the two families were 'entirely separated'. Relations were re-established, at least in the context of family business, before John's death in 1879; but as will be seen, Overstone himself was never to relax his resentment and disapproval of George's politics.[47]

As the first, great Liberal administration of Gladstone was launched, George Shaw Lefevre looked back a little self-pityingly on his recent financial experience – 'Circumstances have during the past three or four years been rather unfavourable to me.' But even before he was invited to be John Bright's lieutenant, the politician in him was optimistic. The future circumstances 'will be better. The thrashing we have given the Tories at Reading will I hope be a lesson to them and I may look forward to some years of an undisturbed seat.'[48] The hope was justified: George held on at Reading until 1885.

CHAPTER XIII

Jane and Rachael

While George Shaw Lefevre was establishing himself as a politician, his parents at last found a settled home, and two of his sisters married. John and Emily had never been content with long-continued residence in any one place. After a struggle in which John turned to his most eminent friends for support but eventually lost, he had to give up 6 Old Palace Yard and move into another official house in Spring Gardens in 1860. Even there, their restless spirits shadowed them, for the new residence was renumbered during their stay, from being Number 8 to being Number 18.[1] More significant for their personal interests, they found Sutton Place too much for them, financially, and moved out in 1862.[2] Viscount Eversley, with a practical eye on the poor land drainage of the area, was glad to see them out of a house which, in the late autumn, he 'had no doubt . . . is surrounded by an inland sea.'[3] For three years there was no country retreat, but in 1865 John found – perhaps by the sale of other properties – the capital needed to build a large, rambling, rather undistinguished house on thirty-five acres thickly covered with fir trees, just across the road from Ascot Race Course. John was then 68, and Overstone remarked, with ponderous foreboding, that 'Surely this is a bold step for a man of his age – We build up houses, and cannot tell who shall live in them.'[4]

Ascot Wood House was the family base for some fourteen years. It was built at almost exactly the same time as the red-brick church of All Saints, only a few hundred yards away, and the new churchyard was to be the burial place of several members of the family. Both John and Emily's married daughters were to choose to live practically as close to Ascot Wood House as the church, and the first to be married, Jane Georgiana, with happy memories of Burley, called her home Burley Bushes. Her sister, Rachael Hamilton Gordon, lived in the Red House, equally nearby. Among their neighbours, in this new family complex, was John Delane, editor of *The Times*.

Jane, who until her marriage was invariably called Georgiana within the family, became the wife of Charles Lister Ryan, son of Sir Edward Ryan, John Shaw Lefevre's senior colleague on the Civil Service Commission. Sir Edward had explored with John the possibility of placing Charles Lister in one of the Parliamentary posts in 1850, but without success.[5] However, the younger Ryan no doubt had plenty of opportunity to get to know the Shaw Lefevres, as the two fathers had been friends at least since the Cambridge election of 1847. He entered the Treasury and was to serve as private secretary to three eminent politicians, Gladstone, Stafford Northcote, and Disraeli. He was knighted in 1887. Looking back, he felt that Gladstone had treated him as an employee, Stafford Northcote as a friend, and Disraeli 'with the affection of an older brother.'[6] Gladstone came to the wedding breakfast when Charles and Jane were married in 1862, but the fact that Charles had been his private secretary made him suspect to strong Conservatives in the late 1880s, and threatened to deny him the post of Comptroller and Auditor General, to which he was appointed, however, when Salisbury overrode the objections in 1888.[7]

Apart from her letters to her sister, Rachael, who spent practically all her married life abroad, apparently the only scrap of Jane's writing which still exists is a short account of her memory of being a guest of Nassau Senior at a party in the mid-1850s, when she would be about 21 or 22. Thackeray took her into dinner. His other neighbour at table was Jenny Lind, who did not know who he was, and in some pique he devoted himself to Jane. When Jane remarked on the beauty of Ristori, who was sitting opposite, Thackeray answered, 'Yes, but you think so much of her because she is a great actress. You women are such lion-hunters.' He asked Jane's advice on how much he should give his daughters for dress allowances, discussed the progress of *The Newcombes* which was then being serialized, and performed his party piece for Jane by inscribing the Lord's Prayer on paper the size of a threepenny piece, leaving room for the crown and the 3. Jane was pleased and happy, but very level headed about that little experience, and the same calm, quiet judgement and competence infuses her letters as a mature woman.[8]

The Ryans' marriage was an apparently warm and affectionate partnership which was racked by tragedy. Jane had to deal not only, as the one married daughter in continuous, close proximity to her aging parents, with their and her sisters' traumas, but also with terrible losses within her own family. Of her six children, born between 1863 and 1873, twin boys died from scarlet fever when they were only fourteen months old; her other son did not survive an operation for varicose veins which led to blood poisoning, when he was twenty-two; and her eldest daughter, whose marriage we shall hear about later, succumbed to typhoid at the age of forty-three. Nor was this all. Jane's life was very private, and its very privacy may well have been a source of great strength and solace. She had to bear, in addition to the loss of her own children and her parents, the death of the married sister with whom she had, perhaps, the most intimate understanding, despite their long period of separation.

The stories of that sister – Rachael – and of her younger sister, Madeleine, to whom both Jane and Rachael were close, deserve separate treatment. Of Maria, Mary and Emily, the second, third and sixth of John and Emily's daughters, there is less to be said. They fall into that category of well-to-do Victorian spinsters who have rarely received more than a faintly sympathetic indifference in the memoirs and commentaries of those who survived into or have only lived in the less protected and less claustrophobic society of the twentieth century. There is simply not enough evidence to support any unequivocal judgement that these three ladies were classic examples of a stratum of wasted feminine talent, at one extreme, or were willing hostages to narrowly domestic duty, at another extreme. What can be gleaned is that as young women they were certainly concerned about their own and their sisters' marital prospects; that they moved about the country, visiting family connections and quite consciously seeking invitations to the homes of families equally or more prosperous than their own; and that after 1864, when their distant cousin Augustus Hare first made contact with the Shaw Lefevres, they accompanied him to the continent on occasion and sketched and painted under his guidance.

These three ladies, though they developed an intense, partisan interest in politics, were the less adventurous of the six sisters and, perhaps inevitably, they were the closest to and, willingly or not, the most immediately involved in the care of their parents. In a letter which Arthur Hamilton Gordon wrote to Mrs Gladstone after the death of Lady Emily Shaw Lefevre, there is a striking comment on the status and assumed preoccupation of unmarried daughters. According to Arthur, his wife Rachael's 'loss is as nothing to that of her poor sisters . . . the chief object and interest of whose lives is gone.'[9] Whether or not this accurately described the then states of mind of Maria, Mary and Emily, they may well have become, in their later years, increasingly conscious of their social status. Jack Hamilton Gordon, their nephew, stayed with Maria for awhile when he was in his teens and grumbled to his father that 'I have to sit still and do nothing, as Aunt Maria's conversation is neither lively, clever, or amusing; her chief topic being the Peerage.' When their parents' deaths forced a reduction in their standard of living, they reacted with an understandable outburst of short-lived anxiety and slightly hysterical self-pity. But their father had provided for them better than they had expected, and they were able to settle into comfortable, dignified and relatively anonymous elderly spinsterhood.[10]

Whatever the breadth of their experience and the extent of their achievements, all but one of the Shaw Lefevres led well-travelled but solidly English-based lives. The one exception was John's eldest daughter, Rachael, who became the partner of one of the more aristocratic and remarkable figures in the high-Victorian era of British colonialism. Theirs is a story which demands some introduction to the background and character of Arthur Hamilton

Gordon, son of the Earl of Aberdeen, who would become, after his wife's death, the first Baron Stanmore.

When the Hon. Arthur Hamilton Gordon sailed from England on 5 October 1861, to take up the lieutenant governorship of New Brunswick, he was beginning a new professional career and nursing a great personal hope. Though he was not quite 32-years-old, he had behind him an experience of public life which reflected a privileged, aristocratic background and the good fortune to have been young and very close to his father, the fourth Earl of Aberdeen, when that statesman was Prime Minister from 1852 until 1855. Arthur was the fourth and youngest son. His mother died when he was 5-years-old, and he was educated at home until he entered Trinity College, Cambridge. He was President of the Union at Cambridge, but his enthusiasms were less political than religious. He espoused high church Anglicanism and would have entered the ministry had not his father vetoed the notion on the grounds that there was already one clergyman in the family. But Aberdeen, who had watched anxiously over Arthur's rather delicate health, no doubt also appreciated that this was the most intelligent of his offspring, and launched him into the political world by making him his private secretary. From his early 20s, therefore, Arthur was intimately involved in the exercise of high politics and was on familiar terms with all the notable politicians of the time.[11]

In 1854 Arthur was found a seat in Parliament for Beverly, in Yorkshire, but lost it in 1857. By that time, his father was in poor health and Arthur spent much energy during the following years in caring for him. But first, in 1858, he went at his own expense to be secretary to Gladstone who, being out of office, was entrusted with the task of diplomatic enquiry into the position of the Ionian Islands, then under British rule. This was a mission which produced some profound influences on Arthur's future. It sealed an important intimacy between him and Gladstone, who was twenty years his senior – an intimacy which was to last practically through all but the last years of Gladstone's long life. But that intimacy was made strangely uncomfortable and difficult because of some never explained incident during the mission. That incident left Arthur with the tortured conviction that he had been disloyal to Gladstone, and left both men with some suspicion of each other's political judgement. The acquaintance with the problems of the Ionian Islands, however, moved Arthur to become interested in colonial administration, and in 1859 he approached the Duke of Newcastle, then Colonial Secretary, with the request that he be considered for a governorship.

But it was Arthur's heart, as much as his head, which had been affected in the Ionian Islands. Among the party was Gladstone's eldest daughter, Agnes, and over time, Arthur fell in love with her. Despite his aristocratic demeanour, his intelligence and his knowledge of the great world, he was shy and intensely introspective, and could not bring himself to declare his affection and to ask Agnes to marry him. On returning to England he was preoccupied with his father's illness, and was deeply shocked when Aberdeen died, in December 1860. Since his father's fall from power, and now since his father's death, Arthur had not enjoyed any major sponsorship in politics and had made no great impression as an MP. Gladstone, though now back at the Treasury, may well have been a little cool towards him after the Ionian Islands' incident, and it is unlikely that the ebullient Palmerston, again Prime Minister, would have found Arthur an attractive candidate for office.

Arthur's eldest brother had been a Liberal member for Aberdeenshire until he succeeded to the earldom. When the vacant seat came up for election early in 1861, the Liberal candidate withdrew unexpectedly and a strong attempt was made, locally, to persuade Arthur to take his place. Arthur, conscious that his candidacy would offend some of his family and friends, would not accept, but his supporters insisted on placing his name on the ballot. On polling day, however, the Conservative was a clear victor.[12] Thereafter there must have seemed nothing for Arthur to look forward to in the near future in home politics, and while he had an assured income of £2,000 a year, he had no taste for idleness. So when Newcastle offered him the lieutenant governorship of New Brunswick, in July 1861, with a week to make up his mind, he chose to go. But shortly before he was to sail, this man, who was to become one of the great colonial proconsuls of his time, could not find the courage to ask Agnes Gladstone to be his wife, and begged Mrs Gladstone to put his offer to her. He wrote from the ship to his older, intimate friend, Samuel Wilberforce, Bishop of Oxford, bewailing his own timidity and dilatoriness: 'How could I ever be so blind as not to see in her all that I now see – all that any man should desire in a life's companion! – That she has a kindly feeling for me I feel sure – probably no more.'[13] It was an accurate perception.

By an odd coincidence, at almost the same time as Arthur Hamilton Gordon was setting foot in North America for the first time, Rachael Shaw Lefevre was leaving there for home after some months' stay as the guest of Sir Edmund and Lady Head and companion of their daughter Caroline. Sir Edmund, since his days as one of John Lefevre's assistant Poor Law commissioners and then his successor as a commissioner, had been Governor of New Brunswick and subsequently, from 1854, Governor of Canada, which then comprised only what we now know as Quebec and Ontario. He was, in the autumn of 1861, about to relinquish his post. Although Head had no responsibility for New Brunswick, it is reasonable to assume that Rachael would have heard of a new lieutenant governor of the smaller colony being appointed, and of his expected arrival. It is equally reasonable to assume that Arthur Hamilton Gordon had no knowledge of Rachael's existence, let alone her presence in Canada. The dates of Arthur's arrival and Rachael's departure were within a week or so of each other, but the chance that they may have met is almost nil. What is quite certain is that neither could have had any idea that they would be living in New Brunswick as a newly-wedded couple, a little less than four years later.

In the interim, Arthur was to suffer a deal of frustration, beginning with a letter from Catherine Gladstone which must have arrived very soon after he reached New Brunswick:

> As you desired I told Agnes. She was greatly touched on being told of the high compliment you have paid her – she feels it all very much and is very grateful to you for your good opinion of her. I find she looks upon you as a friend and wishes this to go on. I mean as a *real* friend in whose happiness she takes a great interest and whose progress she will watch with anxiety – but in saying this do not let me mislead you: it would be very wrong in me dear Arthur to hold out the slightest hope of any deeper feeling or to say anything which might lead you to hope.[14]

Hamilton Gordon was an obsessionally hard-working colonial adminis-trator, and in this, his first experience of high, personal responsibility, the demands of his job no doubt helped, greatly, to keep in check the darker influence of a pervasive sense of loneliness and a strong tendency to indulge in self-pity. Agnes' refusal brought him much pain and for several years a degree of embarrassed awkwardness to his relations with the Gladstones.[15] In many respects he was a solitary, unreachable person. He had mixed so closely with his father and his father's colleagues that he had few friends of his own generation, and confessed in his diary that 'much of my life passes in dreaming of the past in which I live more than in the present – so many are gone, none will care for my work as they did.' And to a fellow high Anglican he wrote:

> That craving for love and sympathy, that desire to feel a rest for the heart will probably exist so long as that heart beats – I know what you will say – I know that there is but one perfect love and perfect sympathy and that that is, or ought to be, all sufficient. But I say, too, and *you* I think will not deny it that earthly sympathy and affection are the highest of earthly pleasures.[16]

But Arthur, being capable of having other than spiritual desires, was not unaware of the opposite sex. Unfortunately, as he confided to his diary some six months after arriving in New Brunswick, 'None of the St John ladies are worth looking at. Miss . . . is ladylike and Miss . . . is pleasing, but all are ugly.'[17] By the beginning of 1863, when he wrote a long letter to Wilberforce, he declared himself satisfied with what he considered he was achieving, politically, but admitted that:

Socially I don't suppose I succeed so well. There is too much that is awkward and odd and dismal about me to be ever much liked in society. I am probably supposed to be – and to most persons should (& do) say that I am – perfectly happy. I am surrounded by every comfort, my staff consists of agreeable and well conducted young men – my servants are orderly and active – yet to *you* I may confess that there is an *amari aliquid* which poisons my enjoyment except when I am very busy. I like playing at King – being 'Regulus Quidem' – but the isolation is terrible . . . I have really no home society. I daresay most people would think me silly, but *you* I am sure will fully understand the pain caused by want of sympathy. You will say Why don't you marry? Why because one can't marry in the abstract, but must marry Miss AB or CD and I won't marry unless I fall in love and fancy that love returned. Now I fear that is not a very probable contingency.[18]

Wilberforce, despite his reputation – he was known as 'Soapy Sam' by those who found his unctuous blandiloquence offensive – cut through all this maudlin self-denigration with some smoothly given hard advice:

I cannot tell you how greatly your letter touched me from its being so perfect an exhibition of your own soul. I seemed to see every pulsation of that loving heart, longing for some One on whom to expend the great gift of love which God has committed to you to administer for Him. I see your real interest in your work and yet the great difficulty of your post being King but having no Queen. No Princes: no chosen friend to stand within the circle. . . . My dear Friend I do fully trust that God will give you such an one. Why do you not come home and try. You must not of course marry without affection: but without the Romance of being in love you may: and I believe you ought. Indeed with your sensitive shrinking nature, such a mixture of extreme natural Pride, refinement and warm affection, it is very difficult for you to let yourself sufficiently out to win love; though as you know you *can* keep it when won. There seems to me no other remedy than this for your case; and so I should say come and fall in love.[19]

Arthur took no obvious offence at this acute description of his 'up-tightness', agreed with the desirability of marriage, hoped his forthcoming home visit later in the year would produce a wife, but feared that 'my jealous and exacting disposition will never be satisfied to believe that I am loved and to be the husband of a woman who I did not suppose to love me.'[20] There the matter rested, but the projected visit to England was apparently postponed. Arthur does not seem to have hidden his desire to marry, because another of his older and regular correspondents, Roundell Palmer, the future Earl of Selborne, wrote at this time that, 'if I rightly divine the principal object, which you . . . have in view (others divine it in the same way, so I suppose I cannot be wrong) I trust nothing may happen to prevent, or to defer, what is so important to your happiness.'[21]

Towards the end of November, when Arthur complained again, to Wilberforce, that his isolation could 'never be wholly removed but by an English wife', the Bishop responded that he had 'expected you back to look for her' and warned him 'Do not put it off too long.'[22] The delay was to continue, however, until a family tragedy – the death of his eldest brother, the fifth Earl of Aberdeen – brought Arthur home in April 1864. That visit was extended until late July, and by the time he left for Paris and then to return to Canada, Arthur had apparently found his future partner, though the engagement was not to be announced for almost another year.

When a young man of impeccable aristocratic background is set on finding himself a wife who would have to be from an acceptable – and therefore very narrow – social stratum; and when he is clearly intense, earnest, intellectual and introverted, and unlikely to be attracted by the young, beautiful but light-minded, he is not, perhaps, the easiest of people to accommodate. The fact that Arthur Hamilton Gordon had made his keenness to marry known to Wilberforce, Roundell Palmer and, apparently, 'others', provokes the temptation to look for conspiracy, successful or unsuccessful, behind what transpired. But such temptation has to be balanced against the likelihood of sheer accident as an explanation of how Arthur and Rachael Shaw Lefevre came together.

The bare narrative available does not resolve the matter. Apparently they met at a dinner party early in June 1864, given by the Roundell Palmers, with whom Arthur was spending a few days.[23] Roundell Palmer, who was to be the draftsman of a major reform of the judiciary a decade later, was then Attorney General. He was another of Hamilton Gordon's older friends who shared his strong support of high-church Anglicanism, and he had married a daughter of the eighth Earl Waldegrave – a sister of that Lord Chewton who had been befriended by Charles and Emma Shaw Lefevre – thereby being a nephew of Viscount Eversley by marriage, while Rachael was a niece by blood. Among the other guests were Arthur's sister-in-law, Caroline, wife of his brother, General Alexander Hamilton Gordon, and Edward Cardwell, who had just become Arthur's chief as Secretary of State for the Colonies.

Who can tell whether Rachael was brought in as a reliable female relative to make up a table to balance an unexpected guest from the colonies, or whether she was invited as a carefully calculated move to provide Arthur with the chance of meeting a mature and eligible single lady? One possibility that cannot be ignored is the favourable influence on Rachael's behalf of the Heads. Arthur saw a good deal of Sir Edmund, doubtless taking the opportunity to discuss with a previous governor the contemporary problems he was facing in New Brunswick, and the prospects for the federation of the British North American colonies which were at that very time matter for crucial negotiation. He may very well have heard praise of Rachael's demonstrated aptitude for the colonial situation, as well as respect and approval of her family. Be that as it may, we do have Rachael's reaction to the dinner party, in a letter to her sister, Mary:

> Friday and Saturday I dined out alone, first at the Roundell Palmers, where I met Mrs Gordon and also Mr Arthur Gordon her brother-in-law (Governor of New Brunswick) Cardwells, Robert Cecils, Waldegraves etc – very pleasant . . . Sunday Mrs Gordon came to lunch and brought Mr Gordon she really is nice and more lovely than ever I never admired anyone so much in my life. Next week she goes back to Ireland and we shan't see her again for I don't know when! . . . To-morrow we shall have a garden party and on Thursday a little dinner – viz the J Denmans, Adams (American minister) Lady Kingsdown, Mr Sutton Wester, and Mr A. Gordon. We think our cook will be able to do it. . . . The [Queen's] ball is on 10th perhaps we may fall in with Caroline Gordon there.[24]

The Gordons had registered with Rachael, and though she had a 'very bad headache' on the 'perfect day' of the garden party, she was 'just able to appear.'[25] Rachael had also registered with Arthur; his rather scrappy diary of the London season, in full swing, recorded for that day, 'Stayed at home and wrote. Bathed. Dined at Palmers. RL there, also Caroline.' Subsequently, 'Tea at Lefevres' on 7th and, two days afterwards, 'Wrote. Breakfast at Gladstones. Wrote. Jenny Lind. Dine with Lefevres.' Finally, another meeting with the Lefevres, before the opera, on 14 June. More than this had been going on, surely, for when Rachael's sister Mary wrote to her on ll June about what should be given to a mutual friend as an engagement present, she asked, 'Did you give Arthur anything?'[26]

Whatever had passed, however, Arthur sailed away and a discreet silence followed. If there were letters, they have not survived. But that a proposal may well have been made, and that an acceptance was being negotiated, is clear from Arthur's prevarications over the opportunity to exchange New Brunswick for Hong Kong, which came his way in the following spring. He had been sufficiently intrigued by the idea to ask the Foreign Office whether, if appointed, he would have official access to the King of Siam, but he told Wilberforce, late in May, that in respect of Hong Kong:

> the consideration that it would be almost impossible to marry deters me. I could not think of exposing anyone I loved to such risks, nor should I feel that I had then the same right to put my own health in peril. I should not wish my wife to be reduced to the position of nurse to an invalid of shattered constitution.

And in the same letter he explained that he would not put himself forward as a candidate for election in Aberdeenshire, in the event of an early dissolution of Parliament, as it would cause an inevitable family quarrel.[27]

Shortly afterwards, Rachael must have said 'Yes'. Some less than public declaration must have been made early in June, for Cardwell wrote privately to Arthur congratulating him.[28] Arthur only told Caroline Hamilton Gordon a month later, whereupon she immediately sent a letter of congratulation to Rachael, on 19 July.[29] But there can have been no open announcement. One has to wonder a little about just what shifts of feeling and considerations of other interests may have assailed Arthur, or Rachael, during the previous months, because he wrote with some abruptness to Wilberforce, as late as 31 July:

> I am just about to return to England to be married to Miss Shaw Lefevre. This may rather astonish you after our conversations last year but when I see you I shall have no difficulty in satisfying you on this point. I have in consequence declined Hong Kong.[30]

And the wonderment is increased by Roundell Palmer's undated letter, probably sent in the first half of 1865, in which he told Arthur 'how cordially your offer has been accepted by Miss Lefevre', and how, while he (Palmer), 'did most heartily wish for what is now to be', he had 'felt disappointment at your hesitation to embrace at once so *certain* a prospect of happiness.'[31]

Having made up his mind, however, Arthur did not wait for an official granting of leave, but sailed in mid-August. Under the headline, 'Marriage in High Life', it was reported that Arthur and Rachael were married, by Wilberforce, assisted by Arthur's brother, Revd Douglas Hamilton Gordon, Canon of Salisbury, at St Martin's-in-the-Fields on Wednesday 20 September 1865, 'in the presence of a highly fashionable circle.' Among the hundred guests was Gladstone's son Stephen, acting as his father's representative – a device fully appreciated by Arthur! The presents included a dressing case made to Rachael's own design, and jewellery 'of a magnificent character'.[32] There was a brief honeymoon at Lockinge, lent to them by Robert and Harriet Lindsay, and in Paris and Val Richer; but soon they sailed westwards, to make their first home together at Fredericton, New Brunswick.

We can never know whether this was the love-match laid up in heaven of which Arthur Hamilton Gordon had dreamed, or even how near it became such a union either for him or for Rachael. But it was certainly a marriage of affection and loyalty – and sadness. 'I suppose', Caroline Gordon had written to Rachael, 'the best wish I can make for your future life is that your *Governor* will not call upon you to follow him into too outlandish places.'[33] It was a *cri de coeur* from a soldier's wife, well used to the rule of 'pack and follow'. But it was a hope in vain. Rachael was to have more than her fair share of outlandish places, more than her fair share of the agonies and discomforts of exile. She was the only Shaw Lefevre not fated to end her days at home.

Rachael was 37 when she married – eighteen months older than her husband. But the detail available of her early life is exiguous. She had only just survived the scarlet fever which carried off her elder brother in the winter of 1831–2, and she was so ill on one occasion when on holiday on the continent, in her teens, that the family had to delay their return home to give her time to recover. Presumably she was educated at home by a governess and by her parents, and as the eldest child she was no doubt expected to take a leading part in supervising the other children and in helping a mother whose own health was none too robust. There is no evidence of her having applied herself to the kind of charitable work which apparently occupied her younger sister, Madeleine, nor any sign that she emulated at least three of her sisters' enthusiasm and capacity as amateur artists. And the only comment on her appearance and personality is contained in the gushing letter of a friend of one of Rachael's cousins: in a series of frankly admiring comments on all of John and Emily's brood, Rachael, then 21, is described as 'very handsome . . . very warm hearted and affectionate very amiable and merry, full of fun and clever too.'[34]

It is not until 1861 that we have some chance of judging what she was like. In that year, Rachael spent some seven months in the household of the Governor of Canada, mostly in Quebec, apparently as the companion of Caroline Head, who was at least eleven or more years younger than herself. John Shaw Lefevre and Edmund Head were old friends and colleagues, the daughters knew each other well, and it may be that Rachael's presence was seen particularly as helpful in softening the dreadful blow the Heads had suffered less than two years earlier, when their only son, then aged 19, had been drowned. The expense of Rachael's trip was in all probability met by Lord Overstone. The party travelled by way of Cork, New York and Boston, and arrived in Quebec in late February, so that Rachael experienced the final rigours of a Canadian winter. She returned home with the Heads, sailing from Boston at the end of October.

Rachael's letters from Canada, where she had her 33rd birthday, were essentially in the same mould as those she was to write from so many 'outlandish places' in the future. They are the letters of one with a sound grasp of the language but without any elegance of expression. Her descriptions are very readable, her comments are often sharp though never witty, her emotional sincerity is unquestionable. As was inevitable, she wrote most of the letters over days or even weeks, while waiting for the usually unknowable dates when the mail ships would arrive, and as a result the topics and the moods change drastically from page to page. But even allowing for the circumstances under which she wrote, it is clear that though she was an intelligent and sensitive woman, her mind was not highly disciplined, and she switched suddenly from subject to subject, from high seriousness to sheer triviality, without notice. Sometimes it is almost as though (which was very likely the case) she was sitting with pen in hand trying to ignore her consciousness of an empty vista of time and space, and allowing her mind to turn away from her main theme to take refuge in unexpected flurries of personal or domestic detail. The Canadian letters are light-hearted, interesting commentaries. In those of her later years there comes through a careful generosity and kindness, but besprinkled, nonetheless, with a rather resigned indignation, some querulousness and understandable layers of anxiety and regret. Given her circumstances, they were the letters of a person of courage whose dignity and self-respect allowed her less than what she might well have claimed, of the indulgence of self-pity.

Any woman raised in the higher reaches of London society was likely to be taken aback by the limited facilities and provincial outlook of colonial settings. 'The shops in Quebec are *abominable*. It will be quite impossible for me to get a dress or anything', she reported in her first week there; and perhaps a little piqued by her consciousness of advancing spinster status, she found that 'the general impression is that I am Lady Head's sister! How people do talk in a place like this.'[35] But she quickly and easily settled into the routine of the Governor's household, and while apparently having little to say about the Canadians with whom she came in touch, she was spikily critical of a species which she would meet everywhere she went as a 'Governor's lady' – the visiting British who appeared regularly at government houses in search of contacts and hospitality. The younger ones attracted her particular scorn:

> found Lord— calling, he is a miserable little specimen of the 'Snobility,' something between a little used up Yew tree and a Mossboy . . . his one idea is Buffalo hunting. He is 22 but looks 16 . . . (I have a strong suspicion that he drinks!)
>
> the other two were Lord— and his brother Mr— ages about 22 and 17. They are two of the most singular looking beings you ever saw. They have very handsome faces – but their hair had evidently been shaved and had grown all the same length like a brush. They have the most old fasioned prim manners. They came into the room each with one hand on their heart and made a very low bow![36]

The social highlight of her visit was the arrival, for a short tour, of the Queen's second son, Prince Alfred, in June, and her experiences in accompanying him to Niagara, Hamilton and Toronto, parts of the journey being by river-boat. The Prince was then 16, and seems to have demonstrated all the normal adolescent tendencies, perhaps enhanced by the unnatural strain of being continuously 'on show'. Rachael thought the Prince's tutor and guardian very severe with him, and she good-naturedly put up with the young royal's juvenile antics, including smoking whenever he could avoid his mentor, and regaling the ladies with slightly *risque* stories. Rachael found him 'a nice little fellow very brown and sailor-like and boyish, with a rather shy manner and very pretty voice and evidently full of fun.' Among less exalted visitors she did not find it fun to be pursued by a young man who seems to have been recommended to the Heads by her parents; and she was very unimpressed by Mr and Mrs Anthony Trollope who were among those passing through: 'We didn't much fancy them. He is rather vulgar looking and coarse, but good natured – intensely conceited and she ugly, self-important and commonplace and we had quite enough of them.'[37]

In view of her future life in New Brunswick, however, it is intriguing that one of Rachael's last impressions of Quebec was of the dinner given by Sir Edmund Head to the Executive Council of Canada before he relinquished his office:

On Monday the Executive Council came for a farewell dinner – ten of them, and no ladies but ourselves. The Attorney General, Mr Macdonald, who is the cleverest man of the lot distinguished himself by getting completely drunk, he was decidedly screwed when he arrived, and the first glass of wine finished him off – he attempted to make a speech after dinner, but failed, and was obliged at last to retire – and came back in such a maudlin state that we didn't know what he would do next! Mr Rose's successor Mon Cauchon who is a *most vulgar* pig after upsetting a decanter and eating the paper of his fondue cut his finger badly, and wiped it on the table cloth! Mon Cartier (Prime Minister) is about the best, and is very lively and amusing, he came after dinner and sat himself between Capt. Rettelach and me and sang some French Canadian boat songs (for which he is famous) in a low voice and made us two join in the chorus. We were very glad when they all departed.[38]

After returning home, Rachael's life resumed its apparently normal social pattern. In August 1862 she and her youngest sister, Emily, then 20, had a small adventure – a sea voyage from London to Grantown as the prelude to visiting various Scottish friends. The two sisters wrote a joint account of it, but Rachael's contribution seems to have been dominant, and the little piece, which is printed as Appendix I, throws some light on her attitudes as well as being illustrative of the hazards of mid-Victorian travel. Her recent Canadian experience had doubtless enhanced her ability to take the unusual and the difficult in her stride.

Rachael's spell in Quebec was her introduction to colonial life; in that respect parallel to Arthur's sojourn in the Ionian Islands. But her apparently happy and good-humoured experience of what she saw of the emergent rough, self-governing democracy of Canada, from the privileged perspective of the Governor's residence in Quebec, was in sharp contrast to her husband's increasing hostility to his official situation in the capital of New Brunswick. There, as years later in New Zealand, Rachael's presence kept his impatience in check, but the plain fact was that while Arthur had grown up among the cultivated, aristocratic segment of the British governing class, and had been particularly influenced by the attitudes of Peel towards probity and efficiency in public life, he had also inherited his elders' elitist and paternalistic bias and was never to attempt, let alone to succeed, to divest himself of it. He was shocked by 'the venality rampant in the government and politics of New Brunswick',[39] and had no diplomatic deftness or informal friendliness which would have eased his relations, as an appointed governor, with the fiercely competitive and touchy elected representatives either of that territory or, twenty years later, of New Zealand. 'All my "gifts" such as they are', he once told Gladstone, 'are those of a despotic, and not of a constitutional ruler',[40] and Rachael came to admit to Madeleine 'how utterly unfit he is to be the Governor of a Constitutional Colony. . . . He *cannot* sit down and lead an easy life and submit to be dictated to . . . and know that measures that he disapproves of are being passed, in which he is not allowed a voice.'[41] When Arthur left Fredericton on 1 October 1866, he noted in his journal, 'At 8 a.m. I left New Brunswick for ever . . . for five years a home and on the whole a happy one. . . . But the escape from the thraldom of such a set as my Ministers is welcome.'[42]

The one year which Arthur and Rachael spent together in North America cannot have been easy, given the lieutenant governor's apparent political unpopularity and his official difficulties, which included notable differences with his ministers and with the Colonial Office over the negotiations for Canadian federation, and also having to deal with a futile but worrying outbreak of Fenian violence. More intimately, the normal human experience of getting used to each other must have been made a little harder, though interesting, by having to learn, simultaneously, to work as a team in that extremely isolated and vulnerable stratum of political and social life in which both surrogate constitutional monarchs and, in a more extreme form, 'despotic' colonial governors and their consorts, moved and had their being. Rachael, though she obviously had the bearing and confidence of an upper-class London lady to carry her through her official duties, was used to the close home life of mother and sisters, and easy access to a wide circle of friends and acquaintances with whom she was on level terms. In Fredericton in 1865–6, as would be the case for most of the rest of her life, that 'support system' was practically non-existent. She came up against the brutal loneliness of the highly-placed, the absence of anyone save her husband to whom she could talk without the consciousness of being watched, listened to and assessed for diplomatic error, or for any lack of personal neutrality, or simply being judged on her physical appearance and demeanour. And here, as elsewhere, Rachael and Arthur were rarely able to meet and mix with people of their own social class. Neither was desirous or capable of finding acceptable or even interesting, save in a strictly professional context, the officials whom they led or the senior members of the local communities, native, emigrant or expatriate, whom they were duty-bound to cultivate and entertain. Arthur could never find enough intellectual stimulation among them. For Rachael, they were, quite simply, not her kind of people.

All these realities of the gubernatorial existence were no doubt sufficiently novel in this first, short phase of their married lives as not to weigh too heavily on them, and they were, despite the New Brunswick winter, still living in climatic conditions more or less familiar to them. But Rachael admitted that 'it was *months* before I got really to like New Brunswick – in fact it was only just before I went away that I began to feel really at home, and to take an interest in it.'[43] While this was a typical reaction to every new place they went, there was a more significant cause of Rachael's lack of enthusiasm during her first married years. Between 1865 and the birth of her first child in 1869, when she was 41, she suffered numerous miscarriages, three of them in one early spell of only eight months; and though the letters do not make it entirely clear, it is almost certain that she was plagued with one or more of these misfortunes before leaving New Brunswick. This may explain the arrangement made after Arthur accepted appointment as Governor of Trinidad, whereby Rachael's sister Madeleine came out to join her for the last weeks in Fredericton, to accompany her on the voyage to the West Indies, and to stay with her there for several months.

None of Hamilton Gordon's posts was arranged without much negotiation and manoeuvring, for Arthur was ambitious, petulant and prickly. His father-in-law, in his usual mild way, helped in this first transfer by talking with the Secretary of State, Cardwell, and by giving polite but firm advice to Arthur. He insisted that Trinidad would be real promotion, which Arthur had contested, because:

> The power of the Governor and his consequent responsibilities and means of usefulness and fame are . . . considerably greater [than those of the Lieutenant Governor of New Brunswick] altho' not so great . . . as to afford due scope to your many valuable qualities.

And he reported the opinion of a 'hale' jurist who had spent thirty-seven years in Trinidad, that the climate was not injurious to ladies who followed a prudent diet and took regular exercise. But John Shaw Lefevre was quite clear that Arthur, if he took Trinidad, should not regard it as a stopgap, warned him that the prospect of another appointment was neither immediate nor too bright, especially if there was a change of minister at the Colonial Office, and ended, quite sharply, 'One word more – Cardwell was exceedingly kind and friendly. If you do or do not accept, do not forget this.'[44]

Arthur took the hint, and the Hamilton Gordons and Madeleine left New Brunswick in October 1866. They spent a little time at Niagara and about a week in New York, not too happily, because they knew nobody and because Rachael had bad trouble with her teeth. On the morning of the day they left, she 'spent three hours with a Dentist . . . and endured greater agony the whole time than I ever felt in my life – he stopped eight teeth and his charge was $38!' But she was happy to have had a brief meeting with her brother George, who had come out with Madeleine and was beginning a second, short visit to the USA. George was by then not only an MP of three years' standing, but had just recently been appointed to his first governmental office – a lordship of the Admiralty. He saw them off from New York, not envying them their prospects for the voyage, 'as the steamer looked very uncomfortable and was crowded with second rate people.' He probably was witness to a final crisis, in which the Hamilton Gordons' house steward and maid walked off the ship and were only persuaded to return at the very last moment.

Rachael, again in a 'delicate state of health', cannot have been too pleased with life, and the voyage, which eventually brought them to Trinidad early in November, was reported as particularly miserable.[45] But they had arrived, safely, in the world of the tropical colonies where, with one short exception, Arthur was to make the rest of his official career and to make his greatest mark; and in which Rachael, apart from some stays in England, was to spend most of the rest of her life, struggling gamely with a degree of remoteness, uncertainty and heartache which it is hard to imagine and recreate in an era of geographical precision, jet aircraft, incredibly rapid electronic communications, antibiotics and air-conditioning. It was the real beginning of the dominant pattern of their lives together.

CHAPTER XIV

Journeyman Years

If ever a young junior minister with a liking for administration was given a marvellous opportunity to indulge his enthusiasm and ambition, it was George Shaw Lefevre as secretary to the Board of Trade in 1869 and 1870. He owed that opportunity, at the moment of choice, to Gladstone, but in practice it was the gift of his President, John Bright. For Bright, one of the most influential propagandists and orators of his time, was not only supremely unconcerned about administration, and temperamentally totally unsuited to handling the details of departmental responsibility, but in addition, his health was suspect. Indeed, in the autumn of 1869 his health failed so badly that he had to give up all real work, though he remained nominally head of the Board until he resigned in December 1870. From the outset of his term, therefore, Shaw Lefevre had an unusually important role to play, and for almost eighteen months was virtually head of the department.

George discovered quickly that while Bright was no administrator, he also 'had a positive aversion to legislation, or to Government interference of any kind, and . . . carried the policy of *laissez-faire* to the extreme.' This meant that while the President was still active, practically nothing was done to promote legislation, and he 'devoted himself mainly to work in the Cabinet.' As for running the office, George was told, 'You must do most of the work' and only worry him with important questions. Bright

> had a great distaste, and almost an incapacity, for wading through a bundle of official papers. It was said . . . that he did not know how to untie the tape which held them together. I don't think he often did this. I don't recollect his ever writing a minute on them. He liked me to state the case to him, and he would then discuss it fully and with practical common sense. What he said was always of the greatest value, and his conclusions were sound and wise. Sometimes, however, before deciding, he would go down to the House of Commons and discuss the matter with some friend in the smoking room there, and it was difficult then to meet the arguments or objections of this unknown person.[1]

The Gladstonian passion for free trade and for minimal governmental expenditure had no more loyal interpreter than Shaw Lefevre, but he was by no means averse to legislation to encourage enterprise and to regulate it in the public interest. Bright on one occasion told a delegation that George was 'a Radical Chap' who was prepared to go much further than he – Bright – felt it wise to do. As George recalled, 'It was somewhat a novel sensation to be publicly called a Radical Chap by Mr Bright.'[2] Once Bright was removed by illness, George was freer to push forward into new fields. But first he channelled his energies into saving money, and manipulated the Treasury into setting up an enquiry by himself and the Permanent Secretary of the Board, Sir Thomas (later Lord) Farrer, into the statistical work of the Board and the Customs authority. (Farrer and George were related by marriage, Farrer's brother being the husband of Anna Maria, second daughter of Henry Francis Shaw Lefevre and cousin to George.) This enquiry took up most of 1869. It led to a considerable administrative reform and a substantial saving. George also attacked what he believed to be unnecessary and unwise expenditure on certain harbours, and in 1870 he bore the brunt of an attack by a minority of protectionists on the newly-negotiated Commercial Treaty with France.[3]

Having thus safeguarded and consolidated his position as one of economic orthodoxy, he was able to chance his arm in other directions. In the winter of 1869 he talked with de Lesseps, who had come to England in search of funds to complete the Suez Canal and was willing to give Britain a 'commanding interest' in the company. George tried, unsuccessfully, to persuade Gladstone to seize the chance offered, and believed that had he been in the Cabinet 'the result might have been different.'[4] Another potentially embarrassing incident on the high seas – a collision between an American warship and a British merchant steamer – led to an appeal to the Board of Trade which George had to handle and which forced him to defend himself against an accusation that he was giving way to American pressure. This coincided with much work on the amendment of legislation relating to merchant shipping. On the home front, he piloted measures regulating insurance companies and, perhaps most notably, introduced a general tramways bill.

Those influential people who owned private carriages were hostile to tramways being laid down in streets, and George believed that his proposals appeared to be so stringent that the House of Lords only passed them because they were confident that, under them, no tramways would be built. He also included a provision whereby local authorities could only concede to private companies the right to lay down tramways for twenty-one years, after which the local authorities themselves could take them over, if they so desired, on payment of compensation. The legislation, which introduced procedures to replace the use of numerous private bills, was hard fought but survived intact, and led in time to a great participation by local authorities in providing public transport. Perhaps, if Bright had not been ill, the legislation would have been at least delayed for some years. Uncle Eversley must have been reminded of his own efforts to improve private bill procedure during the railway mania of the 1840s. It is interesting, too, in a family context, that the Viscount chaired a joint committee of Lords and Commons on a bill to facilitate the provision of tramways in London, in 1872.[5]

Given his buoyant temperament and the hard work he had put in at the Board of Trade, it was reasonable for George to have had expectations of substantial promotion. But, when Bright eventually had to resign, George was to be disappointed. He had not impressed everybody favourably: in an article mourning the temporary loss of Bright, the *Daily News* was plainly hostile:

> It involves no disparagement to the Parliamentary Secretary of the Board of Trade to say, that having been chosen in virtue of sufficient qualifications for a secondary and subordinate post, he did not exhibit capacity for a position for which he had not been, and never would have been, thought of. Mr Lefevre is a man of excellent intentions and of respectable talents; but the accidental prominence given him by Mr Bright's unfortunate illness proved amply that he has a much longer apprenticeship to serve than that which he has already passed through, in order to qualify him for the headship of an important department of State.[6]

Bright offered comfort:

> I see some miserable fellow seeks to depreciate you in *The Daily News*, and goes out of his way to do it. Dont be annoyed at this – the newspapers cannot destroy a man. I am a living proof of that. It is however disgraceful that a Paper, wishing to be 'the Liberal organ' should do what it can to damage consistent members of its own party.[7]

If George had entertained any hope of becoming the head of the department, it was immediately dashed. Gladstone took the opportunity to move Chichester Fortescue from the Irish Secretaryship to the Presidency of the Board of Trade. Shaw Lefevre accepted that Fortescue, who had been embroiled in the great controversies over the disestablishment of the Irish Church and the attempts to introduce some reforms into Irish land holding, was better entitled to promotion and a seat in the Cabinet.[8] But he was not pleased when Gladstone offered him the under-secretaryship of State at the Home Office, under H.A. Bruce (later Lord Aberdare).

George sent a somewhat petulant reply to the Prime Minister, claiming that there was very little difference between the status of the secretary of the Board of Trade and the under-secretary at the Home Office, especially when the heads of both departments would be in the House of Commons. He went further and declared, rashly, that until his appointment to the Board of Trade, that post had been considered the more important of the two and had carried with it the rank of Privy Councillor. And after pressing on Gladstone details of how much he had carried in the absence of Bright, and how much was in train at the Board of Trade as a result, he went on:

> I think it may be a question whether it is for the public interest that I should leave this Department at the present time, even though so competent a man as Mr Fortescue is to be at the head of it. Although therefore I have felt at first somewhat disinclined to remain as Junior when I have so long fortuitously acted as Chief and with the authority which such a position gave me, yet I am not sure that I should not be acting wisely in doing so. It may be however that the work of the Home Office will be more important. I will therefore leave it in your hands to decide whether I shall do most service to your Government and the country by remaining at the Board of Trade or by going to the Home Office.[9]

Having sent this graceless missive to Downing Street, he also wrote and told Fortescue about the position he had taken. The more mature and experienced politician replied that he had 'little doubt that Mr G will choose the H.O. for you, if you have left it to him', though adding, tactfully, 'because your services would be very valuable there.'[10] And so it turned out. Gladstone gave no ground:

> I think that your estimate of the Office you hold in relation to the old V.Prship of the B. of Trade, and also in relation to an Under Secretaryship of State is too high: and on this subject I have no doubt whatever. What I took into view was your just claim to a step, and also the fact that Mr Fortescue will doubtless wish to transact the business of his own Department, which you might not unjustly look upon as entailing upon you an internal retrocession. At the same time, while I thus place the matter before you in this double light I do not feel that I ought to press you to do anything except what may be most agreeable to yourself in the matter.[11]

George decided that discretion was the better part of valour, and took the Home Office job.[12] But he was very discontented, and sent his father an extremely long letter in which he laid out in great detail his labours and achievements at the Board of Trade and in the House of Commons, and argued his case for preferment over several contemporaries whom he considered to have been more generously treated.[13] Whether this letter was compiled on his father's suggestion, and whether John Shaw Lefevre tried to ensure that Gladstone knew of George's discomfiture, is matter only for speculation, but certainly the Home Office appointment was short-lived. After only two months, when he had scarcely come to grips with work which he did not like, Gladstone one day 'beckoned to him in the House of Commons, to come and sit beside him, and said, "You may have the

Admiralty if you like."' George, who always had trouble in controlling himself, blurted out, 'I am so glad I do so hate the Licensing Bill.' In fact he had found himself disapproving of all Bruce's measures, and thought the work of the Home Office very flat after his experience at the Board of Trade.[14]

It is just possible that Gladstone had come to know George more closely, and to appreciate his potentialities, because of the fact that George and Arthur Hamilton Gordon were brothers-in-law. Arthur and Gladstone had been negotiating over the proposed publication of Lord Aberdeen's correspondence, and since George had taken the Home Office post the Prime Minister had asked and received aid from him in trying to establish Arthur's exact intentions.[15] But whether or not this helped to bring George to mind when it was necessary to find a new secretary to the Admiralty, that was the office to which George happily succeeded in March 1871. He had enjoyed his earlier spell as Civil Lord under the Duke of Somerset; he was to be well pleased with his greater responsibilities under G.J. Goschen; and he was to stay at the Admiralty until the Government went out of office in February 1874.

By the time George moved from Home Office to Admiralty the initial surge of the reforming zeal of the first Gladstone administration had ended. Irish disestablishment, Irish land, and national education had been enormously controversial and exhausting, as had basic reforms of the army and navy, spearheaded by Cardwell and Childers. Indeed, Childers had worn himself out by his exertions, and had pressed ahead so fast at the Admiralty that he had aroused strong professional opposition which resulted in a serious loss of morale in the service. From the time when Goschen replaced Childers, shortly before George's appointment as secretary, the second half of the Government's term became less productive overall, and was marked by signs of an increasing loss of public confidence. At the Admiralty, George recorded how Goschen had a difficult job to win back naval support, and how he tackled it:

> He brought to the task a mind of exceptional subtlety and penetration. He was not a reformer of the type of Mr. Childers. I cannot recall to mind that he effected any reform of importance during his three years of office at the Admiralty. His was essentially a conservative type of mind. He was cautious, conciliatory, and rather timid as to new adventures.[16]

Though the Admiralty ministers thus had a relatively quiet time, Shaw Lefevre, who was always a diligently busy departmental administrator, was almost always concerned in the House of Commons, as he had been while at the Board of Trade, with departmental business, that at the Admiralty being mainly of a routine, if quite extensive, nature. Almost his only major intervention in other matters was his continued participation in the debates on the Married Women's Property Bill. In fact, throughout this famous administration, George learned his trade as a minister, concentrating on his own responsibilities and laying firm foundations for the rest of his career. Meanwhile, the traditional family search for recognition was not neglected. He and his father did their best for each other. In 1873 George asked Gladstone to propose John for membership of the Privy Council, and John did the same for his son just as Gladstone was going out of office a year later, using the material of George's long letter of 1871 in his argument while denying that his son was aware of his intentions. Neither attempt was successful, though Gladstone expressed himself very satisfied with George's performance.[17]

The general election at the beginning of 1874 was called very suddenly, and only eleven days separated the announcement of dissolution from the casting of votes at Reading. For the first time, election was by secret ballot. George Shaw Lefevre had his closest fight since he first ventured into politics at Winchester fifteen years before. This time he topped the poll, though he was only three votes in front of Goldsmid; but the gap between them and the two Conservative candidates was less than 150 votes. The figures were: Shaw Lefevre 1794, Goldsmid 1791, Attenborough 1652 and Mackenzie 1631. The major focus of the contest was the religious aspect of Forster's Education Act of 1870, which had roused the wrath of Nonconformists. The two Reading Liberals found it essential to declare their support for amendment, and this ensured sufficient Nonconformist votes to take them back to Westminster. But while they survived the national swing which saw Disraeli displace Gladstone, the Reading election was particularly significant for George, in the light of what was to happen in 1880 and 1885. He came under direct criticism from the religiously inclined press, which claimed that he 'undoubtedly made a mistake when he yielded to pressure, and threw in his lot with the Secular Educationists.'[18] But on the larger question of the future of the Established Church, the two Liberal candidates differed. Goldsmid was in favour of disestablishment, George was not: his position on this matter lost him Nonconformist votes while mollifying Anglican loyalists.

The controversy over religious allegiance would not go away in the next decade, and the strength of feeling about the Established Church in Reading was eventually to be disastrous for Shaw Lefevre. But for the moment he was secure enough, and for six years was to be free of the shackles of office. He celebrated a few weeks after the election by getting married. He was nearly 43, and had almost certainly been seeking a wife for some time. It is, perhaps, unlikely that the prospect of marriage had been considered by him with even the modest degree of romanticism and precipitousness that had attended his father's wooing of Emily Wright, on the edge of Sherwood Forest, exactly half a century earlier.

George gave the impression, publicly at least, of being rather a cold man, and one suspects that the desirability of marriage was for him more closely allied to the advantages of orthodox status and material well-being than to more intimate aspects of pleasure and comfort. His brother-in-law, Arthur Hamilton Gordon, whose own agonies about what constituted an appropriate state of mind, in this context, will be remembered, had apparently come round to accepting very earthbound attitudes. On hearing that George's eventual choice of a partner would make him independent, Arthur confirmed a long-standing Shaw Lefevre approval of prudent financial arrangements: the bride would be 'a much better match than Miss—' and the engagement meant that 'Lord— cannot sneer at [George] as a mere political adventurer.' In fairness to George, he must have been regarded as a desirable husband, simply on account of his apparent political promise. There was a tradition in the family of G.W.E. Russell that on one occasion in these early years, a young lady was told by her host for dinner that 'You will sit between two young men, one of whom will certainly be Prime Minister, but I can't tell you which it will be.' The two were George Shaw Lefevre and George Trevelyan.[19]

Lady Constance Moreton, who became Lady Constance Shaw Lefevre on 24 March 1874, when she was nearly 24, was the only daughter of the third Earl Ducie, a Liberal peer who owned extensive estates in Gloucestershire and Oxfordshire. There is nothing to tell us, unequivocally, how she and George became acquainted, though the slight possibility that they may have met through a connection in charity work between Constance's mother and George's sister Madeleine, is considered in another chapter. From a Shaw Lefevre standpoint, however, how the marriage came about was unimportant by comparison with its social and financial advantages. Rachael Hamilton Gordon enthused in a series of letters from the time when the news broke in December 1873:

> It is a most satisfactory marriage in every way, and we are all delighted, and rejoiced that he has found a wife at last. She is said to be charming. She is rather shy and reserved, very nice-looking, without being actually handsome, and tall. . . . She has *some* money, which of course is a very good thing. . . . Lady Ducie was a great heiress, and there is only one son. . . . Lord Eversley is delighted about it. Lady Constance has enough money to make them very comfortable, though not rich. . . . *She* will have at present about £2000 a year.'[20]

The wedding took place at St Mary's, Bryanston Square. The bride wore 'a dress of rich white satin duchesse, tastefully trimmed with rose points.' There were eight bridesmaids from the two families, with George's side represented by his sisters Madeleine and Emily, joined by the young Florence Mildmay and Madeleine Ryan. The guest list was heavily weighted with the Liberal hierarchy. They all breakfasted at the Ducies' house in Portman Square before the couple left for Paris.[21] George and Constance settled briefly on their return in Charles Street, off Lowndes Square, but were soon to make their London home in Bryanston Square, close to 41 Seymour Street, where George's parents would live after his father's retirement. 18 Bryanston Square was to be the London base of George and Constance for over forty of the fifty-four years they were together.

There were no children of the marriage and there is no evidence that Constance suffered the kind of difficulties which came the way of Rachael Hamilton Gordon. Her childlessness, though, may have made Constance seem rather remote from her husband's family. She may also have felt a little awkward with them because she was so much younger, and like others she may have found the Shaw Lefevre ladies too aggressive, or insufficiently high in the social order, for her taste. The impression from the scattered references is that she seems to have wanted to keep George and herself at some distance, not only from his family, but possibly a little from her own, as well. Her father provided them with Oldbury Place, a country house at Ightham, near Sevenoaks in Kent. There they lived for over twenty years.

What comes out of the exiguous references to Constance is a shadowy sketch of a very private woman, used to a high and unquestioned standard of living, and without ambition to make any big public impact. She was the child of very religious parents and of a mother who was prominent in charitable causes. We know that she liked gardening and disliked music and yachting; that in her late 30s she put on a lot of weight; that she suffered from rheumatism, was in poor health for many years, and eventually had to use a wheelchair. We can discern that George was very devoted to her, and in personal matters deferred to her, perhaps partly because of her independent wealth, but partly because, despite her low public profile, she was in the last resort probably the stronger-willed of the two.

To her sisters-in-law, however, Constance was something of a disappointment. Jane Ryan confided her concern to Rachael Hamilton Gordon seven years after George's marriage, and Rachael replied, from New Zealand:

I am afraid that selfishness is growing upon her – I felt it myself before I left. She did not do the smallest thing to help me when I was going away and George is so particularly *un*selfish. It is certainly not a failing in our family. I don't see how it is to be cured. She gets more rich and prosperous, and doesn't feel the want of anything herself. I think she is much more absorbed in to her own family. Now she has no spare room in London there is so little she can do, for she makes Oldbury so dull that no one will care to go there. I believe it is mostly the result of having no children.

And a few years later, when George's mother died, Rachael complained that 'Constance has not written. I wonder if she has been nice – she is rarely mentioned.' Two years afterwards, when George was showing interest in making a trip to India, Rachael reported that 'George has, I fear, given up his plan of coming. . . . Constance, I believe, won't allow it!' Arthur Hamilton Gordon, on the other hand, wrote after a visit to Oldbury, where he had found George and his sisters argumentative and tiresomely political, that 'Constance was, as usual, very quiet, ladylike, and sensible.'[22]

This lack of total family harmony was slow in developing and was never productive of more than mild, internal, grumbling and gossip. There is nothing to cast doubt on the basic happiness of George and Constance's marriage, and for George it must have brought not merely a conventional sense of enhanced well-being, but a great sense of freedom from some of the financial anxieties which were obstacles to his political ambition. He had established himself as a promising contender for senior rank in the Liberal Party, he had been in the Commons for ten years and in office for five, and now, in opposition, he had time and opportunity to spread his wings. He widened his range of interests, he spoke and wrote with tremendous energy, and as a result certainly became better known. But perhaps because he had never taken his uncle's advice not to speak too frequently, he did not become, as Eversley had thought possible, one of the House's favourites. He was a combative partisan who attracted strong opposition: he seemed to relish the rough and tumble of political in-fighting but had not the natural charm and grace which might have evoked popularity and even a tolerant affection among those who differed from him.

In the same year as he married, he published a long essay on the game laws – in part a by-product of his concern for all matters to do with land use. He dwelt much on history and legality and his conclusions cannot have pleased his uncle, for they called for restraints on existing privileges and embodied his opinion that the present laws 'do grave injustice to a great body of tenant farmers.'[23] In 1877 George read a paper to the Social Science Association and published an article in the *Fortnightly Review* on entails and English landowners respectively, and in the autumn of that year, on the suggestion of Joseph Chamberlain, and with an eye on the next general election, he compiled a critical 'popular treatise' on the development of land holding.[24] This was splendid preparation for a parliamentary enquiry, of which George was a prominent member, into land titles and transfer, aimed at simplifying procedures and preventing frauds. The enquiry stretched over the sessions of 1878 and 1879, and George put up a rival draft report which, while it was not accepted in its entirety, certainly helped to shape the final document.[25]

Shaw Lefevre was elected a Fellow of the Royal Statistical Society in April 1877, and almost immediately became its president for the next two years. His presidential addresses were in the nature of general surveys of the national economy, and George admitted to finding the subject 'rather dry and hackneyed.'[26] Despite his spell at the Board of Trade, his continuous interest in land use and agriculture and, much later, his close involvement in local government finance, he never showed much interest in macro economic matters. He never held a Treasury post and gave no indication in any of his letters that he ever coveted one. In the 1874–80 Parliament, in addition to his major interests, his speeches and questions touched on a wide variety of social matters – endowed schools, liquor, housing, employers' liability, married women, and charities – as well as the army and navy and foreign and colonial affairs.

George's early acquaintance with Greece and the Turkish empire came to the fore as the eastern question began to dominate public concern. In January 1878 Sir Charles Dilke, the prime mover, involved George in the setting up of a Greek Committee, which existed as a secret group for a year but 'went public' in April, 1879, with the declared objective of 'promoting the interests of Greece in the East'. George became honorary treasurer and persuaded Lord Rosebery to be president after Lansdowne refused. Chamberlain and James Bryce were fellow members of the executive committee, as was F.W. Chesson, a journalist with strong colonial interests who had been trying, unsuccessfully, to involve George in the affairs of Afghanistan. George restricted himself to the Near East, however; one of his speeches was published as a pamphlet for the Greek Committee, of which he remained treasurer until at least the end of the century.[27]

All this activity was to an increasing extent to become secondary to George Shaw Lefevre's passionate concern for Irish affairs. He had taken no part in the debates on Gladstone's Irish measures in the 1868-74 Parliament, and it is unclear whether he was encouraged by others to develop a special grasp of Irish problems, or whether he came to them as part of his general interest in land questions, or even whether the traumas of that unhappy country simply began to intrigue him as a politician and as a lawyer. For whatever reasons, George paid two visits to Ireland early in 1877,[28] and soon after his return he moved for the appointment of a select committee to discover why the scheme of land purchase by tenants, which had been made possible by the so-called Bright clauses of the Land Act of 1870, had been very largely ineffective. The committee, of which he became chairman, sat for two sessions. George's draft report was turned down in favour of one by Horace Plunket, but the compromise document which emerged from the committee and which became law in 1881 included much of what George had suggested.[29]

It was the beginning, for George, of eighteen years during which his Irish interest was the most intense and most problematic aspect of his political career, despite his many other achievements and disappointments. And until old age, he argued and wrote about it, producing in addition to numerous pamphlets two readable and informative accounts of the tangled relationships between Britain and Ireland, at least one of which was still regarded as an essential contribution by the editor of a standard bibliography of British history as late as 1976.[30]

The division of opinion between Goldsmid and Shaw Lefevre about the possibility of disestablishing the Church of England, which was commented on in the context of the 1874 election, is a good introduction to the delicacy of the situation within the Liberal Party for people like George, after Gladstone stood down as leader. In the context of his time, George was indisputably a politician of radical tendencies. But radicals are never easy to categorize exactly, and Shaw Lefevre was no exception to that rule. Though neither very rich nor of ancient family, he was by birth, upbringing and marriage inevitably influenced by Whig traditions. In addition, his admiration for Gladstone was unbounded, and he had no nonconformist enthusiasms. Above all, he was particularly eager for office. Thus, with Granville and Hartington as leaders, and the likelihood of strong Whig influence in any future Liberal administration, the careerist in George ensured that he tried to keep on good terms with the party establishment while accepting a degree of radicalism which did not commit him easily to the views of the more extreme and outspoken Chamberlain and Dilke. Indeed, he and Chamberlain exchanged very hostile letters in 1876, when George objected strongly to Joe's attack on the attitude of Liberal MPs during the debates on the Artisans' Dwellings Bill in the previous session.[31] Even early in 1880, when the likelihood of Gladstone reassuming the leadership was growing ever stronger, George was carefully nurturing his relations with Hartington.[32] No doubt a simple-minded case could be made to characterize him as a trimmer; more accurately, a modern examination of the political *avant garde* of that period puts George on their right wing and describes him as 'a stubbornly independent man who did not pursue the cause of Nonconformity as enthusiastically as did most Radicals.'[33]

In any event, Shaw Lefevre must have been a difficult man for his contemporaries and particularly his senior colleagues to place, precisely, and he may well have been somewhat suspect on account of his apparent brash over-confidence. As early as 1876 he had brought down upon himself the sharp irony of that cynically critical observer of the House of Commons, H.W. Lucy:

It is a peculiarity specially felt in the case of Shaw Lefevre that he has in his time filled several offices. He has been Secretary to the Board of Trade, Under Secretary for the Home Department, and Secretary to the Admiralty; and so sure as any debate springs up on the affairs of any one of these great departments, so certain is Shaw Lefevre to jump up, and in many words rapidly intoned to show how the proposal now before the House is identical with 'a Bill I had the honour to introduce when I filled the office of my hon. friend,' or 'with a scheme I had commenced to work out when I was at the Home Office,' or 'with proposals I had matured during my term of office at the Admiralty.' The coincidences are remarkable, but towards the middle of May their recurrence grows monotonous.[34]

Thus when the Liberals were victorious in April 1880, largely because of Gladstone's crusade in Midlothian, and when that remarkable man refused any office but the Prime Ministership, it is not really surprising that George Shaw Lefevre's many years in Parliament and his experience of office did not produce for him a top job. In large part this was due to Gladstone's decision to depend heavily on the Whig element to fill the senior places, and to keep all the radicals except Chamberlain in relatively junior positions. George was a moderate radical, and not yet a big enough fish to be given a full ministerial post. Moreover, his advancement may well have been delayed by his previous ebullient behaviour, and by his perhaps too obvious tendency to want to run with the hare and hunt with the hounds simultaneously. But his performance as an administrator in 1868-74 ensured his inclusion in the new administration. On 26 April the Prime Minister wrote 'under great pressure' to George, 'to say I hope you will consent as Secretary to the Admiralty to represent the Department in the House of Commons under the new administration.'[35] The only promotion involved was that the First Lord, Northbrook, was in the Upper House; otherwise George could have been excused for thinking that time, for him, in official terms, had stood still for six years.

He had retained his seat at Reading clearly, but in second place to his new Liberal partner George Palmer, a wealthy biscuit manufacturer, powerful local employer and leading Nonconformist, who had taken Goldsmid's place in 1878. In retrospect, this was another augury of an uncomfortable future: in 1880 no less than 246 voters preferred to support Palmer and the only Conservative candidate, Sandeman, rather than Palmer and Shaw Lefevre, so that George's margin of victory over the Tory was only fractionally greater than that between him and Palmer. It was a slippage of confidence from which he was not to recover.[36] His election address was a bland statement, mainly building on the Gladstonian rhetoric about the evils of the foreign and colonial policy of the Disraeli Government: there was nothing definitive about future domestic attitudes, and in general the address foreshadowed the muddled and internally conflicting approaches which dogged the whole of the second Gladstone ministry.[37]

The last term of George's journeyman service was to last seven months. He quickly got back into his stride at the Admiralty, and earned high praise from

Northbrook for his handling of departmental business in the Commons.[38] But he did not allow the Prime Minister to forget his claims. In September he took up his previous request to be made a Privy Councillor. He argued that Granville had recommended it after the present Government was formed, that it had been refused in 1873 because Gladstone could not also give it to Grant Duff, but that Duff was now a PC, leaving George as the only original member of the previous Gladstone administration not so honoured. He stressed his work on Irish land and on 'the Land Question generally'; he claimed that his late father was ignored by Lord Beaconsfield because of the 'strong Liberal opinion' of the Shaw Lefevres, and would certainly have received a peerage from a Liberal Government; he bemoaned the disadvantage to his future career of not being of the Privy Council; and he did not fail to mention his eighteen years in Parliament and his five expensively contested elections.[39] It was a typically persistent recital of Shaw Lefevre qualities and claims. But it was less George's past services than his expert knowledge of the Irish land situation and the help he could give Gladstone in preparing new legislation to deal with it which was the main cause of his reaching ministerial status.

Gladstone tactfully agreed that something should be done for George, but thought any immediate move impracticable.[40] Two months later he found an opportunity:

> I propose to you that you should succeed Adam as First Commissioner of Works. The only objection I can anticipate . . . is that the office will not find employment sufficient for the energies which you have at all times shown in the discharge of public duties. This objection, with your concurrence, I should wish to meet from time to time as occasion may occur by asking you to undertake either the care of some important Bill, or some other definite piece of business.[41]

Even though George was to be a Privy Councillor and to have a full department to look after, his response was as awkward as he had been about exchanging the Board of Trade for the Home Office a decade earlier:

> Though I had no wish to leave the Admiralty I cannot but accept the post of Chief Commissioner of Works under the condition which you so kindly impose of other important work in the House of Commons. It is right that I should inform you that I think a contest at Reading may be anticipated. My majority at the General Election was a sufficient one – viz 220 – but not so large as to deter the Tories. . . . If this, in your view, should make it undesirable to challenge a contest at the present time I shall willingly bow to your decision, but I am prepared myself to meet the occasion.[42]

But of course he took the new post and George Trevelyan took over from him at the Admiralty. The news was leaked to the press, to Gladstone's annoyance.[43]

The Tories of Reading decided not to oppose George, greatly to his relief, but as his sister Rachael told her husband, 'I do not think he need be so afraid. . . . Lord Ducie at once sent him £500!' A comment more significant about the electoral outlook for Reading came to George from Viscount Eversley, still alert, at 86, to the political milieu. He had heard, with pleasure, through his local contacts,

> that the Conservatives were behaving so well to you on this occasion – and I hope it will be some time before they will be able to make use of the increased number of votes which they appear to have acquired since your last election – and if you are in any way interested in restoring peace to Ireland, and in placing the land laws of that wretched country on a more satisfactory footing, you will have a still stronger claim upon their forbearance at a future election.[44]

The new Minister, however, was not very sanguine. Rachael reported that 'It is a *rise* for George, and he will be a Privy Councillor, but I don't think he likes it much. He is not in the Cabinet, and he is rather afraid of its being a shelf.' Arthur Hamilton Gordon was glad to see George promoted, 'but sorry he has got a place for which he is so extremely ill fitted. Secretary for Ireland would have suited him well.'[45] It was a reaction quite wrong in one respect, but almost prophetic in another.

CHAPTER XV

Last Acts of Three Brothers

The widowed Lady Wantage wrote a memoir of her husband in the early 1900s, when she was nearly 70. She looked back to the generation of her father, Lord Overstone, and listing John Shaw Lefevre among his friends, thought they were all men

> of a lofty, somewhat austere type – the keen air of the mountain top, rather than the baking breezes of southern shores; their outlook on life was uncompromising; their sense of duty admitted of no qualifying evasions; their mode of life was simpler than that of to-day.[1]

Perhaps this implies a greater degree of assertiveness than would have been true of John, but it was correct enough about an uncompromising sense of duty on his part, however much he hoped and expected that his devotion would be given proper recognition. He never found it easy to disengage himself from official tasks, but never stopped pursuing his private literary and linguistic interests alongside them. What he does seem to have relinquished increasingly as he grew older was what he had never showed much keenness about or overmuch competence in handling – his family's domestic business. William Wickham, husband of John's niece, Sophia, became very intimate with John and confided to his diary that John handed over the management of all his private affairs

> to his active daughters, who ordered him about as they liked – on one occasion he said to me 'I have in my life coined several words that have obtained currency and now I may say I am *chicken picked.*' But he submitted all the same.[2]

That was certainly true of his last years, but we must pick up John's career from shortly after the time when, by the death of Sir G.H. Rose in 1855, he became *de jure* as well as *de facto* Clerk of the Parliaments.

At an age when today's civil servants take their pensions, John had no thought of retiring and was to stay at the House of Lords until he was 78. But in the later 1850s he was almost as heavily loaded as he had been ten years earlier, and his health gave him and his family some anxiety. Of his work additional to that in the House of Lords, what was causing him most trouble was his combined role of Ecclesiastical and Church Estates commissioner, and his Civil Service commissionership. Before the end of 1855 John had told the Home Secretary, Grey, that he must soon give up the Church Estates post, and only agreed to stay on because of the uncertainty about the possibility of change in the constitution of the commission, and because Henry Goulburn, the Archbishop's appointee, had died. In Grey's view, the extensive labour involved in rearranging the property of the Established Church made it 'difficult if not impossible' to obtain the services of a competent unpaid substitute for John.[3]

Though this problem was recognized, nothing was to be done to solve it quickly. The Archbishop appointed Spencer Walpole in place of Goulburn, which relieved the burden, but Charles Shaw Lefevre hoped John would soon give up the Second Estates commissionership, which he felt should be a paid office.[4] Meanwhile John's involvement in the progress towards open competition for recruitment to the Civil Service was growing heavier. He was a wholehearted believer in the desirability and practicability of devising and organizing an examination system though, in typically cautious fashion, he had told Sir Charles Trevelyan at the outset that his only fear was that the introduction of competition 'will be too stimulating'.[5] But so controversial an innovation brought inevitable discontents from those resentful of the loss of channels of patronage, and from those who were unsuccessful examinees. Both commissioners – Ryan and Shaw Lefevre – were unpaid and had other official posts, and the burden of coping with complaints cannot have made their lives easy. John was uncompromisingly defensive, and on one occasion, when the Prime Minister forwarded to him a bunch of appeals from disappointed candidates, he replied in considerable detail only after expostulating about the constitutional principle involved:

> I cannot repeat in too strong terms the expression of our conviction of the essential importance of maintaining the independence of the authority of this Commission. We believe that its efficiency would be totally destroyed, and that whatever confidence the public may place in its examinations would be entirely lost, if any interference on the part of the Government were to take place with respect to our judgements in individual cases; and we think that any such interference would be inconsistent with the authority under which we act – i.e. the Order of Her Majesty in Council.[6]

John had to be particularly diplomatic with the aged Lord Brougham, who was anxious to manoeuvre his nephew into a parliamentary post and was also critical of some of the examination papers. It may have been with some sense of exasperation that, when Brougham enquired about who might fill a short-lived third Civil Service commissionership which had been vacated by

Edward Romilly, John responded with unusual directness that 'The longer I live the more I am inclined to think that *single seated* functionaries are better than boards and that one is better than two and two than three.'[7] Romilly was not replaced, and however keen John was to see a concentration of power, he suffered from the amount of work to be shared by Ryan and himself. By the late summer of 1857, when he was still as much or more occupied with the Lords, the Church and the Civil Service as he had been for some years, his state of health drove his wife into action. Emily wrote to Sir Edward Ryan, begging him not to reveal to her husband that she had done so, but insisting that if John 'were to attempt to go on with both Commissions he must breakdown – it is quite evident that the work of his three offices has been too much for him', and trusting that Ryan would not allow John to give way to any pressure to go on.[8]

This brought to a climax what was, in effect, a struggle between the Home Office and the Treasury, each wanting to retain John on its commission – Church Estates and Civil Service, respectively. Ryan's reaction to Emily's plea was to explain to Granville that:

I have told the Chancellor of the Exchequer that the position of the Civil Service Commission is such that I must beg to retire if Lefevre withdraws from it at this time. I know of no one who could supply Lefevre's place, and the time is critical for competition is about to be established in most of the public offices.[9]

But the Home Office was firmly of the opinion that it had already been formally decided that John should give up the Civil Service Commission. The Home Secretary, Grey, however, agreed that the matter must be re-opened, and whatever his departmental anxieties, was sympathetic to John:

No one could behave more handsomely than he did. He placed himself in the hands of the Government offering to continue upon whichever the Government thought most important, but objecting most reasonably to continuing on both. . . . I am most anxious that no misconception should exist in Lefevre's mind as to our opinion that we are bound by every consideration of good faith and regard to his wishes to release him from one or the other.[10]

Here the documentary trail fades, but the outcome is clear even if the intermediate negotiations are not. At this point Viscount Eversley was persuaded to lend a hand and from February 1858 took over from John as Second Church Estates commissioner. He did not become an Ecclesiastical commissioner until July 1859, but was *ex officio* a member of the Estates Committee of the commission, on which John continued to serve. Thus John was relieved of much work and both Shaw Lefevres sat on the Estates Committee from February 1858 until November 1859, when Charles gave up the Second Church Estates commissionership. However, both thereafter remained Ecclesiastical commissioners for the rest of their lives, and Eversley served on the Estates Committee until 1872. Thus for forty years one or both brothers acted as influential guardians of the interests of the lessees of Church lands.

Through all these busy years, John had continued as Vice-Chancellor of London University, and it is likely that with Granville's acceptance of the chancellorship, John's share of responsibility may have increased. Granville was a senior minister and not, like his predecessor, Burlington, a man with professional academic interests; and though he was as assiduous in his attendance at the Senate as Burlington had been, the relationship between him and John may well have had more of the flavour of minister and civil servant. But probably more important, by far, than any change of personalities, was the growth of new forces inside the young university. There was still no suggestion that it should be more than an examining and degree awarding body, but as its graduates became more numerous they began to exert pressure to be represented in the hierarchy, to play a part in the formation of policy, and to look forward to the university having its own Member of Parliament. This agitation, which was aimed at Government as much as at the Senate, produced in 1858 a new Charter for the university which, while meeting only the minimum demands of graduates, established Convocation and made room on the Senate for its direct representation there. It was the culmination of a campaign which had begun ten years before.[11]

There is a depressing lack of archives of the early period of the history of the University of London, and there is little to be added from the existing Shaw Lefevre papers. But from the account of the attitudes of early graduates and from the few scraps of evidence available it is clear enough that the Senate was a very conservative body, that the Treasury held the financial reins very tightly, and that John was no enthusiast for overmuch internal democracy. In the negotiation of a new Charter he was unhappy about any remuneration for the Chairman of Convocation and hostile to the proposed existence and proceedings of committees of Convocation. In fact he resisted any idea of Convocation as a continuously acting body and regretted 'a tendency to usurp and encroach on the functions of the Senate.'[12]

Whether this conservative concern was typical of John's view of university affairs in general is a question which cannot be answered with any certainty. One might suspect, however, that it was his sheer caution which was more significant than any doubts about the desirability of new moves. The Senate had refused to sanction the first attempt to allow women to be candidates for degrees, in 1856, and upheld their earlier decision by one vote only in May 1862, only a few months after John had resigned. Granville, obviously still valuing his opinion, had asked John for his views, and it is interesting, in view of the fact that John's daughter Madeleine was to become the first head of an Oxford College for women sixteen years later, to read his reply to the Chancellor:

> I think that the present mode of educating women is objectionable and that it would conduce to their own welfare and that of their husbands and families if their minds were to be trained in the subjects which we have considered requisite for the due general education of young men. I think too that the examination of female candidates for matriculation and degrees might be conducted without serious difficulty or expense and in a manner which would not infringe any feeling of decorum or delicacy, care being taken that they should be examined apart from male candidates and that they should only compete with each other.
>
> Nevertheless I conceive that there is no public opinion favourable to this novel measure and that on the contrary it would create surprise and excite ridicule and perhaps obloquoy (whether just or not is not the question). These latter consequences I should not mind as regards myself but I should be sorry if they attacked either the University or the graduates and I believe that the graduates would complain and very justly if contrary to their opinions, or to the opinions of a considerable part of them we were to go beyond our province and to recommend the Government to make the desired important modification in our Charter.[13]

Whether this was a justifiable political application of Cornford's Theory of Unripe Time, and whether Granville accepted it or not, was irrelevant to what happened at the Senate. The vote on the issue resulted in a tie and the Chancellor's casting vote, by convention, upheld the *status quo*.[14] John, however, on this showing, might just scrape into the company of the angels.

Both the university and the Civil Service Commission lost John in the first two months of 1862, when his health was so threatened that he refused all blandishments to go on serving. Gladstone tried to persuade him to remain on the commission with a different arrangement of work, but John resisted and his firmness and his strongly expressed concern for his colleague, Sir Edward Ryan, was probably responsible for the Treasury's doubtless reluctant decision to make Ryan a full-time, paid commissioner and give him another unpaid partner in place of John. In the close circle of Government, it is not surprising that the newcomer was Sir Edmund Head, John's protégé and successor at the Poor Law Commission and subsequently Governor General of Canada, from where he had just returned. He and John were good friends and, as we know, John's eldest daughter, Rachael, had been a member of Head's Canadian household for the last few months of his tenure of office, in 1861.[15]

As for the University of London – to whose Senate, incidentally, Sir Edward Ryan had been appointed in 1856 – John handed over the vice-chancellorship to George Grote. It was an interesting transition and change of emphasis – from a cultivated, political administrator to a scholarly historian who was also a banker and an MP. John left a unique university which by then had matriculated nearly five thousand students; had moved from accepting degree candidates only from certified teaching institutions, to open entry; had established significant links, nonetheless, with several score colleges, institutes and medical schools across the country; had early extended its singular examination scheme to colonial territories; and had settled firmly into headquarters at Burlington House after a move from Somerset House in 1853. More ancient academic foundations recognized John's worth: Oxford conferred a DCL upon him in 1858 and Dublin gave him an LLD in 1861.

The prestige which John possessed and the respect in which he was held by this period of his life were probably due mostly to his willingness and his undoubted capacity to take on a variety of tasks at relatively short notice and to make a thorough, if not always an acceptable, job of producing new solutions to intractable problems. We might think of him as a kind of Victorian trouble-shooter, were it not that the vision of so potentially assertive and even violent a functionary is risible in the context of John's distaste for the rough-and-tumble. But his numerous, short-term excursions seem to have squeezed out of the record most of what he achieved in the long spell of twenty-seven years during which he was, effectively, whatever his title, Clerk of the Parliaments. The claim that he greatly improved the standing of the office has already been made, but we must take it on trust, so far as the routine work of the clerkship is concerned. If he was at all influential in such highly political matters as the controversy about life peerages, or in the long negotiations of reforms in the structure of the courts, there is no evidence to show it. But what has attracted attention and praise is his labour in the cause of the parliamentary archives and his part in supporting the orderly publication of the statutes. He was a member of the Royal Commission on a Digest of Laws, 1867–70,[16] and out of that came the Statute Law Committee of which John was the first chairman, sharing the unglamorous but invaluable task with such legislative luminaries as Erskine May and Henry Thring. But the more glamorous achievement was:

the installation of the records of the House in the new Victoria Tower in 1864 and the encouragement he gave to the Historical Manuscripts Commission in their listing and calendering. Thanks to his initiative, the vast archives of the House became fully accessible for the first time to the general public, and, for the first time, to two of the clerks in the Parliament Office were assigned in 1871 'the duties of examining such of the muniments of the House of Lords as have not yet been examined, as well as the sorting and arrangement of such historical documents as may be found.'[17]

It was, perhaps, because John could undertake these quiet, scholarly matters within the frontiers of his duties as Clerk of the Parliaments, that his health was less threatened than it had been by his previous, more multifarious activities. He recovered well during the 1860s and was to be involved in two further official enquiries before his retirement. One was really a continuation of that concern for new standards of weights and measures which had come to the fore thirty years earlier and to which he had made his contribution over a period stretching into the 1850s. He was appointed to yet one more probing commission on the subject, which sat for more than a year, in 1867–8.[18] And only six months after his signature was appended to that report, he was invited by the second Derby/Disraeli Government to be one of the special commissioners to undertake the redrafting of the instruments governing the great public schools.[19] He was then in his 72nd year, and put up his typically self-denigrating and melancholy protective screen. He wrote to the Home Secretary, Walpole, suggesting that:

> Mr D'Israeli might wish to insert one or more persons . . . who are more up to the present mark than such an old gentleman as myself so old indeed as hardly likely to remain available till the end of the Commission . . . he need not out of any delicacy towards me hesitate to substitute for me any more serviceable person. As he has very little knowledge of me I do not like to trouble him with a formal communication on the subject.[20]

As always, John accepted the job, and the work involved stretched over several years.

A last major service to the Lords was the compilation of an analysis and arrangement of their standing orders. One suspects that this was perhaps a brotherly labour of love, with assistance from Erskine May. But there is no reason to question John's 'knowledge and mastery of the traditions and precedents', or his technical expertise in 'settling and drawing up decrees and orders on appeals, often long and complicated', from the judicial side of the House, to which the Lord Chancellor referred on the occasion of John's retirement in 1875.[21] For John did, eventually, give up his office as his frailness grew upon him – but not until he was over 78-years-old. When he did so, no further honours came his way, for his Liberal sponsors were out of office, but he received a pension at the same rate as his salary – £2,500 a year.

For the last twenty years of his life John was deeply devoted to watching and promoting wherever possible the political career of his son, George. William Wickham considered that John came to defer almost entirely to

1. Helena Lefevre c. 1807

2. Charles Shaw Lefevre c. 1815

3. Heckfield Place

4. Charles Shaw Lefevre,
   Viscount Eversley, 1883

5. Emma Shaw Lefevre, c. 1840

6. Sir John George Shaw Lefevre, 1861

7. Henry Francis Shaw Lefevre, c. 1830

8. George John Shaw Lefevre c. 1865

9. Rachael Hamilton Gordon, 1866

10. Madeline Shaw Lefevre, 1890

11. Sophia Wickham, c. 1871

George's judgements on public affairs in his later years, but certainly John's written advice to his son-in-law, Arthur Hamilton Gordon, was wise when he was well into his 70s, and one doubts that he was incapable of helping George by exercising a calming and perhaps a restraining influence on the energetic and rather brash younger man.

During these last years his distant relative, Augustus Hare, though very much younger, became something of an habitual figure in John's family, a close friend of the daughters and a sympathetic companion to John himself. There is a glimpse of that family life in the memoirs of a lady who was a guest at one of their parties, in 1874:

> Sir John and Lady Lefevre both aged about 75 sat on two chairs at the door like two old birds on one perch. A select band consisting of Emily Lefevre, Lady Gordon, Tora and her two sisters and some 8 others performed the Toy Symphony. Mr Ward and Mrs Fitzgerald sang.[22]

The artistic enthusiasm of Augustus Hare may well have given stimulus to John's amazing linguistic capacity and to his literary application of it. John translated poetry and other writings from Danish, Swedish, Spanish, Portuguese and Russian. He only began to learn Russian after he was 65, and then collected a large library of Russian works. Though his family was unaware of it, he even learned Basque. Most of his translations remained only in manuscript form, but the exception was a Dutch novel by Van Walree which Longmans published in 1873 as *The Burgomaster's Family* by Christine Muller.

After retiring, John acquired 41 Seymour Street, not far from Marble Arch, to replace his official house. He had previously provided a home for George and his wife, who married in 1874, at 18 Bryanston Square close by, and of course John and Emily retained Ascot Wood House, already the focal point of a Shaw Lefevre community. Emily's ancient father, Ichabod Wright, had died in 1862 at the age of 94, and had left to each of his daughters some £6,000. John sold the house he had built in Hyde Park Gardens about this time, and with his pension and his inherited income from his mother, the family were very comfortably off, if by no means so affluent as Viscount Eversley – or, as we shall see, though they were unaware of it, as his younger brother Henry. It was five years since Jane Ryan had lost her twins, but all her other four children were there to delight the grandparents, while Rachael and her husband, with their girl and boy, made their home at Ascot when on leave from their colonial outposts.

So full and long a professional life was not to be followed by a retirement comparable to that of his elder brother. John's temperament was unsuited to idleness, however comfortable, but he was a tired man. 'And now at eighty', he confessed, 'all is blessing – *all* . . . but it is difficult to remember how old one is. The chief sign of age I feel is the inability to apply regularly to work, the having no desire to begin anything new.'[23] His health, always likely to let him down, eventually gave way in August 1879, and he died rather suddenly but peacefully at Margate on the Kent coast, in his 83rd year.

The tributes to him ranged across the numerous areas of his proven interests and experience; it is clear that his abilities, his conscientiousness and his versatility were enormously admired. 'He was one of the best linguists in England. . . . His powers of acquiring and assimilating knowledge were astonishing and the whole of his life he worked with the utmost assiduity.' What is not clear and perhaps can never be properly assessed is the extent to which he exercised an influence, philosophical, intellectual or political, on the course of the great events in which he was so often involved. He was a 'back-room-boy' who wanted, badly, to have more of the limelight, but did not have the necessary physical strength and insensitivity of mind. 'The defect of his character was timidity. He could not bear the criticism of the press and this would have been a barrier to his ever taking high office – he never overcame this weakness.' Those closest to him echoed the appreciation widely felt of his personal bearing as a gentle, unfailingly courteous and helpful man, full – perhaps too full – of humility.[24]

The Times summed up John's contribution in passages which, a century later, may strike us as a little heavy and fulsome, and indisputably partisan in their historical judgement. But which of today's civil servants would cavil at the prospect of receiving such an accolade?

There are some whose names are ever in men's mouths because their station and calling bring them daily before the notice of their countrymen. There are others to whose labours their generation is not less indebted, but who are easily ignored or forgotten because the work they have to do is withdrawn from the noisy turmoil of current politics. Sir John Shaw Lefevre belonged to this latter class. To some hasty observers it might seem that a man who had never been more than an Under-Secretary of State had played a very insignificant part in the political history of his country. But there are varieties of politicians, and a great philosopher long ago pointed out that the truest politician of all is often one whose labours the people disregard, though his counsel inspires the noisier voice of the practical statesman. Sir John Shaw Lefevre was, in fact, one of those real statesmen, men of native force and acquired culture, of untiring energy and trained conversance with affairs, without whose effective but unobtrusive assistance, Ministers would often be at fault and Parliaments helpless.

Sir John Shaw Lefevre had too much of the statesman in him to become a mere routine administrator. He belonged to a generation of sturdy reformers which knew what it had to do and did it with all its might. The mere enumeration of the measures with which his name is associated suffices to show that he carried into the public service and never relinquished throughout his career that generous enthusiasm for progress, that steady determination to alleviate the lot of his countrymen as far as beneficent and rational legislation could do it, that fundamental moderation and good sense – in a word, that rare assemblage of qualities which marked the generation of legislators to which he belonged.[25]

In the first thirty years of its existence H.S. Lefevre & Co achieved for its founder a sizeable fortune. That success was due, in the main, to the continued association of Lefevres with Ludwig Knoop, who controlled De Jerseys and added further capital from a firm called William Beckfeld & Co. Henry's bankruptcy of 1847 proved to be 'little more than a setback' and by 1875 the three firms were 'so closely allied . . . that it is impossible to say which is the most responsible of the three.' By then, De Jerseys' capital was probably about three quarters of a million pounds, and their reputation among bankers was that of a '"speculative" . . . pushing firm.'[26] Henry obviously did well, but his obligations were great, and while he was in a speculative business, he must have disciplined himself rigidly to meet debts and to accumulate what he regarded as essential reserve capital. Unsurprisingly, some of his relatives did not consider him generous. He admitted two Le Marchant nephews as partners – Henry Denis in 1869 and Francis Charles in 1878. The firm moved from Austin Friars to Warneford Court and eventually, in 1877, to Copthall Buildings, all within the tiny area of the City of London. His steadily-rising status in the financial world may be judged by his long connection with the Sun Fire Office as a director and, from 1867 to his death in 1880, as treasurer and chairman.[27]

The fact that Henry was able to repair his material fortunes did not compensate for the loss of much of his personal happiness. Though he had the satisfaction of grandchildren – seven Farrers and two Wickhams – the death of his sister-in-law, Lady Eversley, in 1857, ended an intimate and affectionate relationship and may well have intensified the dark view of life to which Emma had converted him years before. Ten years later his son-in-law, the invalid George Mason, died, leaving Helen a childless widow at 39. Helen had been very well provided for, and set up home in Brighton, but was frequently resident with her father in Green Street. So, too, were Sophia and her husband, William Wickham, who moved regularly between Green Street and Binsted Wyck. The Farrers were less in evidence, perhaps mainly because Anna Maria had a large family of her own; but there was for some period a 'sad estrangement' between them and the Masons which was 'happily ended through the means of Sir John Lefevre only just in time.'[28] Later, the Farrers seem to have been legal advisers to H.S. Lefevre & Co, and doubtless Henry was gratified when his Farrer son-in-law was knighted.

But the atmosphere in Henry's home was not cheerful; his mood was sombre, and as he grew older he suffered from some undefined wasting disease which attacked and disfigured his face. Nor could he have been unaware of the tensions which had always existed between his eldest and youngest daughters. Helen had a formidably serious, insensitive and overbearing personality; Sophia had a spiky, mischievous, irreverent sense of the ridiculous – she was a very unstuffy Victorian, married to a worldly country gentleman with historical as well as political tastes, who edited his grandfather's diplomatic letters and dedicated the work to Viscount Eversley as the correspondence of the latter's 'own and his father's friend.'[29] Helen and Sophia found it difficult to tolerate each other. Sophia implied that Helen – and some of her unmarried cousins – were 'difficult' because they had no children of their own. Madeleine, John's daughter, whose temperament and judgement were greatly respected in the family, was on occasion instrumental in preventing the explosively indignant Sophia from declaring outright war on her sister. These antagonisms were not even softened after Henry's death.

Henry died in December 1880 aged 78. It is clear that he had been something of an enigma, even to his own family. The following extracts from letters written by his niece, Rachael Hamilton Gordon, to her husband, reveal him as an obsessed and lonely man, wrapped up in his City affairs, and in the grip of some dreadful, progressive, physical malady.

> my Father's younger brother, Henry . . . died three days ago, of bronchitis – *not* of the disease which had been increasingly upon him for some years, and which must have killed him before long. It was something of the nature of cancer (but *not* cancer) quite painless – eating away his face, till for the last year his life has been a kind of living death. It was a most extraordinary case. He went on going to his work in the City (wearing a kind of mask over his face) up to a month before his death. He insisted on going alone in a hansom day after day, long after he could even stand without help, and always collapsing into a sort of unconscious state on his return – passing most of the rest of his time in sleep.
>
> He was always very mysterious about his affairs, no one – not even my Father – had the slightest idea what his income was, or what his business was. It appears now, that he must for some years have had an income of £20,000 a year, and he lived up to about £2000 a year.[30]

When the will was read, it was revealed, 'to the amazement of all his family . . . to the unbounded astonishment of all his friends', that Henry had left to his three daughters nearly £350,000, a figure which may have been less than his real worth, for half a century later a great-nephew claimed that he had left well on 'towards half-a-million of money, at that time an enormous fortune.'[31] In any event, Henry bequeathed something roughly equivalent, in the currency of the late nineteenth century, to at least fourteen million pounds, a hundred and ten years later.

In August 1857, just two months after death had come so unexpectedly to Lady Eversley, Gladstone lost his sister-in-law, wife of Lord Lyttelton and mother of twelve still young children. Towards the end of October, John Shaw Lefevre wrote to Gladstone: 'I can report favourably of my brother. I spent three or four nights with him and found him cheerful. His misfortune is far different from Lord Lyttelton's for his wife's task was done – his daughters grown up.'[32] Like Arthur Hamilton Gordon's notion of the position of spinster daughters, twenty years later, here was another chilly, masculine view – this time of the role of wives. But John's comment on Charles's ability to adjust quickly to widowerhood is in line with other recollections. His niece, Sophia, remembered how 'People were surprised that my Uncle recovered his spirits so rapidly' after Emma's death – a reaction which indicates that the serious incompatibility between them had been discreetly hidden. Indeed, Sophia was probably being unusually discreet herself when she partly credited his recovery from grief to 'his elastic nature.'[33] It fits with the general impression of Charles as a strong, genial, pragmatic, hearty but not over-sensitive patrician who, though always courteous, did not care to be crossed.

There is no good reason to doubt, however, the sincerity of Charles's sorrow at further losses he was to suffer. Two of his daughter Nina's children were to die when they were only 12 and 9, one from typhus in 1867. In that same year, after less than nine years of married life, his youngest daughter, Elizabeth Mildmay, succumbed at the age of 40. These were severe blows to Eversley, by then in his 70s. It was perhaps natural enough that he turned increasingly to the Dogmersfield connection. He tried hard but unsuccessfully to convince Gladstone that Nina's husband was worthy of a peerage[34] and he struck up a special relationship with her second son, Gerald, to whom he was to leave the bulk of his estate. But the death of Elizabeth made even more pronounced the dependence of Charles for companionship, in addition to his by then long-established dependence for household management, on his unmarried eldest daughter, Emma Laura.

We have read the fears and accusations aroused by Emma's apparent domestic tyranny. But as she became elderly, and as Eversley moved into a serene old age, it would seem that Emma changed. From being regarded as a bitter, unmarried, eldest daughter, she achieved a reputation as a distinctly interesting, eccentric and even lovable character. For over thirty years she looked after the aged pensioners who occupied almshouses built by her mother; she provided a building for a Sunday school in one of the more remote villages on the estate; she helped to entertain distinguished guests, but had a disconcerting habit of falling fast asleep over the dinner table, waking during dessert with a cry of 'Crown Derby!' at which the guests turned over their plates to examine the trademarks. She entertained friends to tea, served in zinc mugs, on the uneasily accessible roof of Heckfield Place; she had all the prayer books in the parish church taken out between services to be aired; and she so disliked railway carriages that she had her brougham lifted on to a wagon and sat in it, in splendid isolation from the multitude, for those train journeys she could not avoid making. She was always dressed in black silk; unlike her sisters she was fat and plain and 'curiously without taste'. On occasion she could be jolly, but there were periods when she was recognized as being a sad and lonely woman. After her father died she moved into Kensington, but returned to spend a few weeks each year near Heckfield Place in a rented house, a poor, spiritless, lost soul, sustained to some extent, one hopes, by the recollection of her long companionship with her powerful, self-reliant but probably equally lonely father.[35]

His retirement from the House of Commons freed Charles to do, mostly, what he enjoyed to the full – being a country gentleman with a driving ambition to indulge in land acquisition, farming and field sports, while at the same time pulling his weight as a leader of the rural society and as a prominent magistrate. He continued to be Chairman of Quarter Sessions for the county until well into his 80s, and was a stern disciplinarian, insistent about upholding the status and dignity of court proceedings.[36] He became High Steward of the City of Winchester.

In his own immediate neighbourhood, Charles and the second Duke of Wellington combined to complete the enclosure of Heckfield Common, and when a lady who lived nearby produced a clever caricature of all the animals which used to feed there, protesting at the change, 'Lord Eversley was not best pleased.' In a very rare criticism of the squire of Heckfield, it was claimed that as a result of the enclosure 'the poor people suffered greatly, and the common also was deprived of much of its beauty.'[37] It was no doubt some compensation that the gardens at Heckfield Place were developed into a showplace, under the expert guidance of William Wildsmith (c1838–1890) an horticultural journalist as well as head gardener; that, on occasion, the grounds were thrown open to the public – for instance, over two thousand people visited them in five days in September 1880; and that almost thirty gardeners were employed.[38]

Charles was a regular churchgoer who contributed much to the renovation of his parish church and supported a school for the village children. In his last years he became a conscientious reader of the Bible, but there is no sign of his being more than a very conventional participant in religious rituals. One feels that the Church, for him, was a part of that tight structure of clearly-stratified English society which was owed support far more for secular and constitutional than for spiritual reasons. At Heckfield he had an unfortunate experience with one local vicar, who lost his mind, believed that

Charles and a neighbour were threatening his life, and used to 'take pistols into church under his surplice', before he was placed under restraint. Charles never seems to have numbered divines among his close friends, though he was clearly on good neighbourly terms with Kingsley, the Rector of Eversley. But the latter obviously enjoyed his evenings with Charles as opportunities for 'politicking' rather than for discussion of doctrinal topics. There were, in any event, material advantages in being friendly with Charles; when the exotic Queen Emma of the Sandwich Islands made a formal visit to Eversley vicarage, Kingsley appealed for fruit and was provided from Charles's greenhouses with grapes and melon which 'were magnificent'. And it was at Heckfield that Kingsley met Charles's niece Rachael and her husband Arthur Hamilton Gordon and achieved an invitation to visit them in Trinidad. Near the end of his life, when he was in Denver, Colorado, and in poor health, Kingsley was trying, rather desperately, to make a collection of plants and seeds for Charles.[39]

In the nostalgic vision which haunts the consciousness of those who remembered or were influenced to imagine, as some kind of idyll, the privileged life of the well-to-do in the rural areas of Victorian England, the elderly Viscount Eversley takes his place as almost a pasteboard figure. Heckfield churchyard on Sunday mornings in the 1880s 'was a pleasant meeting-place. . . . Lord Eversley punctiliously raising his high hat and removing his glove; Miss Lefevre solemn and twinkling in her crinoline and sables . . . all cordial and friendly.'[40] One eulogy proclaimed that 'in the more private and domestic walk of family and country life', he was 'a typical Englishman; a man of whom we may say without suspicion of flattery, that he was ever conspicuous for honour and dignity.'[41] Both those who observed him as a social figure in his Hampshire setting, and those who watched him as a tough and experienced Westminster politician, came close to idealizing him in terms which are, perhaps, now regarded, in a much less deferential era, as describing a member of a slightly unbelievable, long-departed species – 'a fine old English Gentleman.'

Such sincere but bland expressions need not be disbelieved, inasmuch as Eversley obviously had the appearance and the manner to justify them, but they soften, far too much, the sharp edges of a personality which remained vigorous to an extraordinary age. John Bright, himself 72, dined with Emily Shaw Lefevre in 1883 and recorded afterwards, 'Lord Eversley there, in his 90th year. A very remarkable man, tall, handsome, in good health, cheerful and active in mind.'[42] If his mind was active, so was his body: he retained his keenness for the outdoors and his acute eyesight till just before his death, and bought himself a new pair of guns every season.[43] But certainly to his intimates he was a man of plain tastes, he was apt to call a spade a spade, and was far more of an outspoken social elitist than might have been regarded as wise or polite by many of those who lauded his public persona.

On returning to Heckfield one day in 1856, he stopped in Reading, where 'all the world were assembled to hear Madame Goldschmidt [Jenny Lind] - her singing was perfectly marvellous – but she is so frightfully plain and makes such ugly faces that one cannot look at her.' Six years later he wrote enthusiastically about Paris and the new boulevards laid out by Haussmann for Napoleon III, concluding that 'We sadly need an arbitrary dictator in matters of taste in England.' On more directly political matters, he was no friend to the extension of the franchise, and told Walpole, Home Secretary in Derby's Government in 1867, that he was 'very anxious to see a copy of your new Reform Bill . . . from what I have read in the newspapers I am very much afraid of it.'[44] When the bill had passed, he unburdened himself to Erskine May in no uncertain terms about its effects:

> People in the country are occupied in preparing for the Election under the new *and especially radical* Reform Act – I am very much afraid the House of Commons will suffer owing to the introduction of many Members of a lower class than we were accustomed to see there. Our old Member Sclater Booth, a quiet well disposed Tory, will be opposed by a low class attorney at Aldershot who, if elected, will be a disgrace to our county. I trust this will not be the case in many counties, but I fear you *will miss the old fashioned County Members* in the House of Commons.[45]

Nor was Charles unwilling to speak his partisan, political mind in the most exalted circles. He dined with the Queen shortly after he had resigned and after Palmerston had survived the recent consultation of the voters:

> Lord Eversley, who is such an agreeable, gentlemanlike man, sat next to me. He is delighted at the result of the elections and at so many mischievous men being turned out – much shocked at the factious proceedings of the Opposition and the combination entered into.[46]

And two years later he was to show that same disapproval of Lord John Russell which we saw earlier in the matter of Denis Le Marchant's appointment as Clerk of the House of Commons. In April 1859, a week after the defeat of the Derby/Disraeli administration in the Commons over the 'fancy franchises' proposal, and with another general election due, he dined with the Queen, who asked him about 'the state of affairs'. Her Journal recorded that:

> He regrets unfortunate personalities and says there is no one to lead the House of Commons since Sir R. Peel's death, and without a good Leader nothing can be done. Lord J. Russell was as bad as any, from his great uncertainty.[47]

The election increased the Conservative strength but did not produce a majority. On 10 June the Government was defeated on a vote of confidence, and the Queen, trying to avoid both Palmerston and Russell, invited Lord Granville to try to form a Government. Eversley, puzzled about what was going on, asked General Grey, private secretary to Prince Albert, whether he knew

> what has passed between Lord Granville and Lord John Russell – I trust the latter has not again stood in the way of the public interest. I think the Queen was quite justified in sending for Lord Granville. We want a new combination, and fresh blood, or the new Government will very shortly share the fate of the old one – and it would be far less invidious for Lord Granville to select a Cabinet than for those who must necessarily be hampered by former alliances.[48]

As it happened, Granville was unacceptable, and Palmerston returned for his last, long spell as Prime Minister. The ex-Speaker may indeed have wished to give most of his attention to his country affairs, but his reputation and Palmerston's high opinion of him ensured that he would be in some demand in London. Almost as soon as he was out of the chair he was approached to be a member of a group of three commissioners to make certain enquiries into the Hanover Crown Jewels, but Emma's death caused him to withdraw.[49] Only weeks afterwards, however, Palmerston came up with the first of several honorary appointments, proposing to the Queen that Eversley should become the Governor of the Isle of Wight. It was an unsalaried job with 'not much duty', which Palmerston would have liked to have merged into the Lord Lieutenancy of Hampshire, but could not bring himself to go to the trouble of introducing a bill to make the change. The main responsibilities of the governor were to appoint a deputy to act as coroner, to be Governor of Carisbrooke Castle, and to appoint the officers of the Isle of Wight militia. The last was, no doubt, the most attractive duty for Charles, who was to be Colonel of the Hampshire Yeomanry for the rest of his life, and who was appointed Yeomanry ADC to the Queen in 1859 on the advice of Sidney Herbert, Secretary for War. Herbert felt that Eversley 'indisputably holds the first place among Yeomanry Officers [so] that it appears to me difficult to pass him over.'[50]

Charles was considered for much more important posts. In 1861 he was offered but declined the governor-generalship of Canada. In 1864 Palmerston thought of him as a possible Lord Lieutenant of Ireland, but took heed of Sir George Grey's doubts and did not make an offer. The Queen, however, felt that Eversley, 'whom Lord Palmerston [had] named, would have done much better' than the eventual nominee, Lord Wodehouse.[51] It seems clear, though, that Charles preferred Hampshire to the rest of the world, and he would only take on relatively minor official tasks outside it.

We have seen how Charles was involved in the affairs of the Ecclesiastical Commission for the last thirty years of his life; but that was only one of several appointments. He was elected a trustee of the British Museum in 1858, and was a trustee of Princess Helena's settlement on her marriage to Prince Christian of Schleswig-Holstein.[52] He had been a member of the Commission on Fine Arts since its first establishment in 1841, and continued until the commission completed its work in 1861. He chaired a royal commission on the volunteer force, in 1862, and served on another, on recruiting for the army, five years later. Disraeli appointed him chairman of the Boundary Commission to define the constituencies under the Reform Act of 1867, announcing him as a person whose name 'would inspire general confidence and prove to the world that no mere party interests will be considered.' But in fact Disraeli was building on the dislike which he and Derby had recognized Eversley felt for the Liberal Reform Bill of 1866, and saw him as remaining biased towards 'the traditional interest' of the country gentlemen.[53]

No more in the Lords than in the Commons did Charles become either a frequent or a notable contributor to debate, though he attended regularly until very late in life, took a share in committee work, and was regarded as an authority on constitutional matters. His deafness must have been something of a hindrance, but in truth, he was out of his natural element:

> In his heart . . . he was still faithful to his early friends, the Commons. The upper Chamber was too cold and listless for one who had spent the best days of his life in the exciting atmosphere of a popular assembly. Nor was he content with its lax observances of those rules of debate which he had been so long in the habit of enforcing, and, being appealed to by Lord Granville, in a Committee, upon a question of procedure, he replied, 'I know the rules of the House of Commons, but I have not yet been able to learn by what particular rules your lordships are supposed to be governed.'[54]

In 1870 Charles was 76, and inevitably he began to slip out of the consciousness of the busy, younger world of national politics and to retire more and more into his county's affairs (in which he remained a powerful force), his beloved Heckfield and his family concerns. He kept a shrewd eye on and offered advice to his nephew George Shaw Lefevre, though George's radical tendencies caused him grave disquiet. Long before he left the Commons he had also cast an avuncular eye over Samuel Whitbread IV, the son of his brother-in-law, Samuel Charles, to whom he had always been close, and to whom he wrote, 'You will be glad to know that young Sam made a very good start in the House yesterday – very good voice and manner – and very well received – the only fault in his speech was that it was a little too short.'[55] Charles's major share in the Whitbreads' enterprise produced a high proportion of his income in these later years. His business letters about it, written even in his 91st year, in a firm, clear hand, show him to be thoroughly in control of his financial affairs. They also indicate a lack of enthusiasm for being involved in any limited liability company, refusing an offer of shares in a proposed take over of Watneys.[56] His reluctance must have been something of an obstacle to his Whitbread partners, who quickly turned their own business into a limited company after his death.

At 85, in 1879, Charles resigned his chairmanship of Quarter Sessions, bringing to an end all but a formal occupancy of a few official positions. Within three years he lost both his brothers and his brother-in-law, Samuel Charles Whitbread. Only his sister-in-law, Emily, remained of his own family generation. Whatever sense of solitude he may have had, he faced the world with tough equanimity and amazingly sound health. In the January of 1885 his murderous devotion to the animal kingdom was quite unabated. By then his daughter Emma:

> is become a very strict Home Ruler and will not let me shoot in cold or doubtful weather and I have not therefore done much in the shooting line this year. We had two very tolerable days in the coverts last week when we had some friends at Heckfield, and they killed 515 pheasants, 15 partridges, 3 woodcocks, 31 hares and 50 rabbits. I am sorry to say that one of my tenants has taken advantage of that abominable Hares and Rabbits Bill and very much reduced the ground game thereby.[57]

In 1885, too, came the last bestowal of honours, when Gladstone proposed to recommend him for the Grand Cross of the Order of the Bath. In his response one may perhaps read just a trace of cynical weariness of the vanities of this world, even though he had never been averse to seeking them. He wrote to Gladstone:

> I heartily thank you for your very kind letter, and if in your opinion my humble services during the eighteen years in which I occupied the Chair of the House of Commons deserve any further recognition, I shall gratefully accept your offer.[58]

Charles's last appearance in public was at one of the ceremonies for the Golden Jubilee of Queen Victoria, in 1887, when he attended a service at St Margaret's, Westminster, with the assembled Commons, and sat between the present and a former Speaker. Then there was a last, quiet, failing year, and on 28 December 1888, he died at Heckfield Place. The obituaries were extensive and did him full honour, but for the vast majority of even the well-informed world, his was the death of a legend rather than of a man they would have recognized as part of their everyday lives. 'The oldest of all Parliamentary Hands has dropped off at last, and Lord Eversley is dead at ninety four', wrote Henry Lucy;[59] and another commentator with a feeling for the past pointed out that Charles had been:

> born in the year in which Robespierre was executed, took his degree in the year of the Battle of Waterloo, entered the House two years before the Great Reform Bill, became Speaker a year before the penny post was instituted, and retired from the Chair in the year of the Indian Mutiny.[60]

Charles was buried at Kensal Green beside his wife and his brother Henry. Many regretted that he did not rest in his beloved Heckfield, among his own parish people, but Emma was insistent on his remains being buried with those of her mother. The Wickhams were particularly upset, and the rebellious Sophia was determined to attend despite Eversley's known dislike of 'ladies at funerals', and of her sister Helen's objections. Sophia took Jeannie Mildmay, Charles's favourite grandchild, and they 'walked together in the long procession, but the last, behind Tate the steward and one or two more of that sort. But we took our places in the pew in the chapel all right.' And while they defied convention, William Wickham:

> was quite sickened at the number of idle gaping people who came to the cemetery to see the sight, crowding in upon the funeral party and thrusting their children forward, others snatching at bits of fern and flowers that fell from the wreaths in moving.

The press, however, gave a noncommital view. The funeral procession from Eaton Square was of twenty carriages, and 'there was at the graveside not only a large and representative gathering of the friends and relatives of the deceased, but also a considerable attendance of the general public.' Nonetheless, there is a note of reproach in the flat reporting prose of *The Times*. The parliamentarians of 2 January 1889 were poorly represented. It was a bitterly cold day, and 'Parliament had just closed its doors after a protracted session. . . . There were but few members present to pay a last tribute to the speaker who had been elected four times in succession to preside over their deliberations.'[61]

One might well feel that the Oldest of Parliamentary Hands would have taken the family differences, the crowd's unruly behaviour, and the apparent indifference of the politicians, in his stride. After all, he had been nothing if not a supreme realist. But Sophia Wickham, late in her own life, must surely have spoken for all the remaining Shaw Lefevres when she recorded that, for the family, after Charles had gone, 'Life was never quite the same again.'

CHAPTER XVI

The First Man after Adam

"THE STORY OF LEFEVRE,"
THE FIRST MAN AFTER ADAM AS COMMISSIONER OF WORKS.

'The First Man After Adam.' *Punch*, 29 Jan 1881.

'What does Sir Henry know of Mr Lefevre?' asked Queen Victoria of her private secretary, at the end of November 1880, when the Prime Minister had told her that George was 'best qualified' to be First Commissioner of Works, and that his 'mode of transacting business would be agreeable to Your Majesty.' Sir Henry Ponsonby replied:

Mr Lefevre (who lives near Windsor) has been a strong Liberal but when in office has been quiet. In the last Liberal Government he was attacked for the shortcomings of the Navy but he made a good defence and proved that he had done his best, but was checked by the Treasury. He would probably do well for the Office of Works.

And in a later memorandum he commented that George 'is *a Gentleman* – related to Lord Eversley – and he believes through his wife to Lord Ducie.'[1] Thus shrewdly reassured, the Queen made no objection. Shaw Lefevre had reached the ministerial plateau.

From the end of 1880 until the middle of 1895 George was a political personage big enough not to be ignored, but not big enough to command entry, save on a few occasions, to the highest and smallest circles of power. For eight of those years he was a minister, and for four of them a cabinet minister, but only as the holder of posts which, though they demanded – and received from him – good administrative leadership, were of relatively marginal political importance. He held the Office of Works for two spells, from November 1880 until November 1884 and from August 1892 until March 1894. He was Postmaster General in 1884–5, and President of the Local Government Board in 1894–5. That he never managed to fill one of the higher positions, or to push himself into the crucial group of half a dozen men who mattered most in the power struggles of the period, was certainly not due to any absence of basic ability or of effort – for his sheer application and the energy which he devoted to causes was phenomenal. His failure to reach the very top was due to a combination of his lack of what we now call charisma, some genuine bad luck in both personal and public affairs, and no small amount of self-inflicted damage.

The social and political stratum in which Shaw Lefevre had been raised, and in which he operated, demanded the kind of sound financial base from which he could provide a relatively opulent material setting for his family, friends and professional activity. It is as well, therefore, to consider the difficulties which came George's way in this context during the years of his greatest political importance. He had never been rich and his elections, as we have seen, always made him very anxious about his financial support. His marriage must have helped enormously. When his father died, in 1879, he inherited the property at Ascot and was doubtless much relieved to find that his unmarried sisters had been better provided for than they had expected. But his mother was still alive, and for six more years George was not in direct possession of a considerable part of his father's assets. His mother and sisters did not leave Ascot Wood House immediately; thoughts of selling it were abandoned in favour of renting, and they retreated to 41 Seymour Street. (Sir Henry Ponsonby, perhaps intentionally, had been rather inaccurate in claiming that George lived near Windsor at the end of 1880!) George was a director of at least one insurance company, and may have had some other sources of City income. He had his ministerial salary, and he must have earned useful additional fees from his writings, which were to become more numerous as the years passed. But beyond these unexceptional gleanings was the firm expectation, by the whole family of John and Emily Shaw Lefevre, that they would benefit significantly on the death of Lord Overstone.

The row between Overstone and John Shaw Lefevre over the latter's failure to desert his Liberalism and vote for Overstone's Tory son-in-law, Loyd Lindsay, had simmered down after the early 1870s. Indeed, relations improved so far that Overstone considered appointing George as his executor, though this never happened. Overstone was nearly 83 when John Shaw Lefevre died, and was one of the country's richest men. Apart from his daughter and son-in-law, he had no closer relatives than his sister-in-law, Emily Shaw Lefevre, and her son and daughters. Despite the fact that the quarrel with John and the radical attitudes of George had left the relationship imperfectly patched-up, it was a most terrible shock, when Overstone died in November 1883, to find that the Shaw Lefevres had been entirely ignored in his will.

So great was the blow that George felt it necessary to ask Gladstone to support an application for a pension under the Political Offices Pensions Act, 1869, to become effective when he was not in receipt of a ministerial salary. The drama of this episode was well caught by the ever-curious and watchful Edward Hamilton, then Gladstone's private secretary. On 3 December 1883, he recorded:

Lefevre came by appointment this morning. I could not make out on going upstairs after his visit what could have passed between him and Mr. G. to have produced so much disturbance of mind. 'I never felt more sick in my life', said Mr.G.; and on my inquiring the cause of his feelings of nausea, I discovered it was the announcement to him by Lefevre that he (Lefevre) and his sisters had been wholly excluded from Lord Overstone's will – (he was their uncle by marriage). . . . 'I have', said Mr. G., 'more sympathy with the commonest thief in the Strand than that old miser and robber'. A man who had died worth some £2,000,000 in the funds and £80,000 a year in land, besides having made over much in his lifetime to his daughter (Lady Lindsay) and son-in-law – a huge fortune but one falling short of general expectation – might have remembered his nephew and nieces-in-law considering how few were his kith and kin.[2]

Gladstone may have been personally indignant not only because of George's plight, but because George's sister, Jane Ryan, was the wife of one of his previous private secretaries. He was sufficiently disturbed by Overstone's neglect of family obligation that when he wrote to the Queen, formally recommending George's pension, he explained that he had satisfied himself that the case was 'within the letter and the spirit of the Act . . . surprising as this must seem when it is considered that Mr Lefevre is the nephew in blood of Lord Overstone recently deceased.'[3]

The disappointment over the will, and the award of the pension, was by no means the end of the story. George was awarded the pension, worth

Lord Overstone. *ILN*, 1 Dec 1883.

£1,200 per annum, on 1 April 1884, but would not have received any money until he left office in June 1885. It may have helped George to avoid some immediate financial embarrassment, but it became an albatross around his neck. It was public knowledge that he drew the pension, and he ran into difficulties because of it almost immediately. At the election of 1885, Gladstone was told of objections taken, and George, hard-pressed at Reading, appealed for help:

> I have not found that my political Pension has created much difficulty here among my friends, though at one time it was commented on in an unfriendly manner by the Tory press. No one of my friends has said anything personally to me about it. It may be, however, as Mr Ashdowne says that a certain number of Liberals are dissatisfied with me on this point and as I cannot afford to lose many votes, I shall esteem it a kindness if you will write a few lines to Mr Ashdowne stating that you thought I was fully justified in applying for the pension which my political services entitled me to, and that I had made considerable sacrifices to a political career. . . . This will be my sixth contest for the Party. I have already spent on these contests more than I have ever received in official income from the various posts I have filled.[4]

Gladstone patiently came to George's aid, but expressed anxieties which must have rung in the younger man's ears many times in the next three years:

> I have replied to my correspondent about your pension in, I hope, prudent terms. It would of course have been of some advantage to say that in the event of an important change in your pecuniary circumstances you would cease to receive it. But this seemed to me to be a matter rather for you than for anyone else to refer to publicly. I do not feel sure that the Pensions List will last very long. It is certainly one of the difficulties of the future.[5]

It is fair to argue that some at least of the loss of votes in George's defeat at Reading in 1885 may have been due to resentment of his pension. And after moving north, to Bradford Central, where he had to fight a by-election and a general election within four months, in 1886, his opponents were not slow to exploit the possibilities of his position. A poster proclaimed George to be 'a servile follower of Mr Gladstone, and a mere place-hunter, with a pension of £1200 a year.' Even his strongly supportive Liberal press went on the defensive, declaring, on polling day, that 'It is not even known that Mr Shaw Lefevre has ever drawn the sum to which his past services to the country have entitled him, it being an honourable custom on the part of gentlemen of position and wealth who have held office under the Crown not to draw their pensions.'[6] George, who must have regretted it in the not too distant future, was not one of those who felt able to so deny themselves.

Contrary to Arthur Hamilton Gordon's opinion, George Shaw Lefevre proved to be a very effective first commissioner at the Office of Works. In fact, he was a good departmental minister there, at the Post Office and at the Local Government Board, and among the knowledgeable his considerable administrative abilities were recognized. Gladstone 'always thought highly (and rightly so) of Lefevre as an administrator', wrote Hamilton in 1885; and the Grand Old Man was reported during his last administration as having 'greatly underestimated' George, who he thought would have made a good colonial governor and even hinted that he was 'just the man to be Viceroy of India.' That opinion lends weight to the validity of Labouchere's proposal in 1882 that there was no better man to be sent as high commissioner to Egypt than George, who was 'able . . . a skilled and successful administrator . . . untainted with the creed that all Orientals are made to be bondsmen for Europeans, and [whose] political principles are exceptionally sound.' Sir William Harcourt felt that there were few men more useful than George – that he 'did not get his desserts', that he had 'indefatigable industry', and that he would not have done badly as First Lord of the Admiralty. Even Rosebery admitted that George was 'sensible-minded, and quite "brushed-up" at the

Local Government Board.' Hamilton, himself to end his career as head of the Treasury, judged that Shaw Lefevre was 'a most handy man in any administrative post.'[7] Clearly, George had administrative virtue; his weaknesses lay elsewhere.

Londoners, particularly, are still living with the outcome of projects which came to fruition under George Shaw Lefevre's leadership during his two spells at the Office of Works. He brought about major alterations to street layouts at Hyde Park Corner and in Westminster, sometimes against Gladstone's personal preference for the retention of ancient thoroughfares. He fought and won several tussles with the royal household over public access to parks; and he was involved in the successful final negotiations with the donor which resulted in the establishment of the Tate Gallery. He fought and lost, after a protracted struggle with Harcourt and the Treasury, a proposal to put the Admiralty and War Office into a single, large, new building in Whitehall. Despite this failure, however, he was regarded as having:

> the knack of bringing great influence to bear upon the Chancellor of the Exchequer, and was thus able to push through more than one useful scheme, some of which had been periodically shelved. . . . He had a great power of mastering detail and was a most valuable exponent in Parliament of the very complicated Estimates of his department.[8]

One incident in his 'public works' period, which George Shaw Lefevre could not have remembered with any pleasure, however, concerned his ambition to see built an annex to Westminster Abbey in which the future famous could be buried when the Abbey itself became too congested. He wanted to have this annex erected on the site of at least one of the houses remaining in Old Palace Yard – where he himself had lived as a young man. In order to ensure that the anti-Establishment Labouchere would not raise objections, he consulted him and asked his advice. 'Labby' thought it an excellent idea – and immediately proceeded to buy the house for himself, blandly stating to the angry George that 'as the place was so close to the Houses of Parliament, it was better to have a live MP in it than a dead statesman or poet.'[9]

At the Post Office, which he had to take under his wing as an additional duty when Fawcett was ill, before succeeding him as Postmaster General, George was long remembered as the minister who introduced the sixpenny telegram. And at the Local Government Board in 1894–5 he was much concerned with the complicated affairs of the young London County Council and its controversial relationship with the City. That was an exercise closely related to his concern for charitable trusts and the influence of the City companies, which occupied some of his time while both in office and in opposition.[10] Indeed, in retrospect, George's experience as a departmental minister was so much centred on metropolitan matters that when he made the transition from Parliament to the LCC after 1895, it can be seen as almost a natural progression.

But while a close study and assessment of Shaw Lefevre's tenure at the Office of Works would be a worthwhile exercise in administrative history, it was his participation in the tortuous politics of the Irish question which was dominant in its effects on his career. Gladstone's elaborately polite and cautious invitation to him to become First Commissioner of Works, with the possibility that he might be invited to help with other duties, was recognized immediately as involving a specific subject matter. In a report of a speech by George only a few days after his appointment as first commissioner, that post was described as having been selected for him by Gladstone 'with a view to his giving the Government more assistance in legislating for Ireland than he was able to do as Secretary to the Admiralty.'[11] By then, George was hard at work on proposals for land reforms which were circulated to the Cabinet at the beginning of January 1881.[12]

It was the first of many private and official memoranda and letters, innumerable speeches and several pamphlets on Irish affairs, which were to come from George over the next many years. He was a recognized authority on the complex problems of the systems of landownership which prevailed and which proved to be, in the short term, politically impossible to reform successfully. It is not intended to rehearse, here, the detail of those problems or to attempt one more blow-by-blow chronology of a conflict which was to be immensely widened by the outright acceptance of the desirability of Home Rule by the Gladstonian Liberals. What follows, therefore, is a consideration only of where George Shaw Lefevre fitted into the story and how he fared. While his specific advice was sometimes thought to be unacceptable, and while he himself on occasion could not bring himself to do Gladstone's bidding, he was in general terms one of Gladstone's most loyal lieutenants, and in his own right an important figure who, had the fates decreed only a little differently in the period from 1882 to 1886, might have provided historians with a significantly changed version of what actually happened.

George could take credit for the fact that the recommendations of the select committee over which he had presided in 1877 and 1878, on the purchase clauses of the Land Act of 1870, were incorporated almost unchanged into the major Irish Land Act of 1881, without opposition. But the reception of the new legislation was compromised by the unrest in Ireland associated with the Land League and the emergence of Parnell as a powerful and dominant leader of Irish nationalism. Though Gladstone did not like it, he was forced by his colleagues to introduce a Coercion Bill before the Land Bill was debated. It was fiercely disputed, but passed. In the meanwhile George had submitted, at the Prime Minister's request, his view of what was needed in the way of land reform, and came up with a combination known as the three Fs – fair rents, fixity of tenure and free sale of the tenant's interest. This went beyond what Gladstone had in mind, but in the subsequent manoeuvres the Land Bill, as it emerged from a tremendous debate in both Houses, incorporated many of the ideas which Shaw Lefevre approved and propounded. But it antagonized the landlords of England and Ireland, and did not satisfy the Irish Party, who had not been consulted about it. Protest continued, and Parnell was arrested and imprisoned. The situation deteriorated, the pressure on the Chief Secretary for Ireland, W.E. Forster, became acute, and by the beginning of 1882 he was contemplating resignation.

It is a measure of George's standing in the context of Ireland in January 1882, that Forster thought it possible that he would succeed him as chief secretary. On the strength of that possibility, he invited Shaw Lefevre to make a visit to Ireland, to see for himself how the Coercion Act was working. George went, and toured several parts of the country. What he saw convinced him that the policy being followed was wrong, and he adopted views which he held sincerely and consistently thereafter: 'I came to the strongest conclusion adverse to coercion, and I determined that I would never myself be responsible, in the future, in any position connected with the government of Ireland, for renewing or administering a Coercion Act.'[13] But George could not move Forster in his direction. He returned to London, and did not report his views to Gladstone. It is a little difficult to believe that so talkative a man would not have confided some at least of his concern to his closest political friends. Whether or not his views, if they became known, were influential, opinion in the Cabinet shifted against Forster as the weeks went by, and eventually, in May, he resigned when it was decided to release Parnell and two compatriots from prison and to try new approaches to solving the Irish problems.

Though Chamberlain, who had played a leading part in pressing for the release of Parnell, proposed to Gladstone that the chief secretaryship should go to William Shaw, the leader of the minority of Irish members who did not support Parnell, and though Shaw Lefevre was regarded by *The Times* as a possibility, it was expected most strongly that Chamberlain would be offered the job. Both Chamberlain and Dilke felt sure that one of them would be appointed.[14] But the Prime Minister thought otherwise. His Chief Whip, Lord Richard Grosvenor, wanted Hartington, but Hartington refused. Grosvenor's second choice was Trevelyan, but that was ruled out because of 'Goschen's feelings.' Grosvenor was least enthusiastic about Chamberlain, but also dismissed Shaw Lefevre with the comment that he 'has not one grain of human sympathy in his composition.'[15] Whether or not Gladstone shared this view, he ignored the claims of the radicals and turned to another Whig – Hartington's brother, Lord Frederick Cavendish. Here is Shaw Lefevre's narrative of subsequent events:

The appointment was made on May 4th, and was announced in the House of Commons that night. On that morning, when crossing the Horse Guards Parade on the way to my office in Whitehall, I met Lord Frederick Cavendish, and had some conversation with him. He told me that he was going to Downing Street, where he expected Mr. Gladstone to offer him the Irish Secretaryship. He was very unwilling, he said, to accept it, as he preferred his then post of Secretary to the Treasury; but he thought that he should have to take the post, as a matter of duty, if pressed upon him. Turning to me, he said, 'Would you like to go to Ireland in place of Forster? If so, I will refuse the post, and I think it will probably be offered to you.' I replied that I could not answer the question, without knowing what was to be the new policy, as I was strongly opposed to renewing coercion. With that our conversation ended, and I never saw Lord Frederick Cavendish again. Two days later he met his end gallantly defending Mr. Burke, the Permanent Secretary for Ireland, from the band of assassins, who murdered both of them.[16]

Thus did George miss his first opportunity to be chief secretary, and possibly a chance of being assassinated. But he was not to be the replacement for Cavendish. The job was offered to Sir Charles Dilke, who indignantly refused it. What deterred him was a change which had been made in the relative positions of the two most senior Irish offices. It was traditional for only one of them to have cabinet status. Forster, as chief secretary, had been a member of the Cabinet; the retiring Lord Lieutenant, Lord Cowper, had not. Now Lord Spencer, already in the Cabinet as Lord President of the Council, was Lord Lieutenant, resident in Dublin and still retaining his cabinet rank. Cavendish had accepted the chief secretaryship without being in the Cabinet, and Dilke was expected to accept the same situation. He was unwilling to be 'a mere mouthpiece'. George Trevelyan, another radical, was less worried, and took the job without the Cabinet.[17]

As Gladstone was now willing to see the post filled by a radical, it was not George Shaw Lefevre's general radicalism which kept him out of the running. George had, in fact, ruled himself out by some untimely criticism of the very people he was generally wishing to help. When, seventeen months later, Spencer was trying to persuade Gladstone that Trevelyan should be promoted to the Cabinet, the Prime Minister told Granville:

It would entail . . . probable jealousies. Take Lefevre for instance. He is a very able man, six years *older* than Trevelyan, and distinctly *ahead* of him in Parliamentary, or at least official, service until Trevelyan's last move; and at that time Lefevre would certainly have had the first turn but for the mere accident that he had just before used one or two very rough expressions about the Irish party.[18]

But though Gladstone retained his good opinion of George, the latter's tendency to say the wrong things at inconvenient times was almost certainly only another aspect of the wider problem posed by his presentation of himself, at least to his colleagues. He was looked at askance, not only by Grosvenor, but also by one much nearer his own political position – John Morley – who remarked, in the early summer of 1882, that 'Lefevre would always be unpopular.'[19] Some years afterwards Harcourt, while giving George much praise and sympathy in other respects, described him as 'not prepossessing' – perhaps as succinct and accurate a summation of his outward demeanour as could be found.[20] Without doubt, Shaw Lefevre's reputation in parliamentary and governmental circles suffered from that characteristic. Nonetheless, he was to have a second chance to be Chief Secretary for Ireland.

For almost two-and-a-half years Trevelyan struggled with the tragic and unrelenting traumas of Ireland, while George Shaw Lefevre soldiered on at the Office of Works and, when Fawcett was ill, at the Post Office. Trevelyan was gradually worn down by the strain of having to keep the disruptive Irish contingent at bay in the Commons, and by the summer of 1884 Spencer was suggesting to Gladstone that the chief secretary would have to be moved. Shaw Lefevre, meanwhile, had been as busy and energetic as ever – with his departmental work; with papers private and public on Irish affairs; with being in the chair for some of the all-night sessions of debate on the Crimes Bill in 1882; with celebrating his twenty years as Member for Reading; with helping to negotiate the reform of the franchise and the redistribution of seats; with being the assiduous chairman of an inquiry into the working of the Charitable Trusts and Allotments Extensions Acts; and with being involved in litigation and legislation dealing with his beloved commons.[21] As we have just seen, by the end of 1883 Gladstone was fully aware of George's high place in the queue for promotion, and it was inevitable that when Trevelyan's fatigue grew dangerous, Shaw Lefevre was again a strong candidate for the Irish secretaryship. In the autumn of 1884 that candidacy was put to the test, and George found himself having to make a decision seen later as the crucial turning point in his political life.

When Spencer concluded, in July 1884, that his colleague had to be relieved, he suggested to Gladstone that Trevelyan should go to the Office of Works and be promoted to the Cabinet, while George Shaw Lefevre should become Chief Secretary for Ireland without a cabinet place.[22] But 'all those concerned' agreed that George would not accept the job if his successor was to be in the Cabinet while he was excluded, and that it was no use hoping to put Shaw Lefevre as well as Trevelyan into the Cabinet, because the Prime Minister was strongly opposed to increasing the membership. There was stalemate, but not for long.

The concern about Trevelyan was only one of several pressing problems of cabinet membership, and it became part, inescapably, of a more complex manoeuvre. Granville, the Foreign Secretary, floated his own scheme to Spencer, who quickly seized on it and returned to his theme towards the end of September. Following Granville, he argued that Dodson, then Chancellor of the Duchy of Lancaster, 'should soon or before the New Year leave office and take a peerage', that Trevelyan should take his place, with the cabinet seat, and that because he, Spencer, was so much away from London, Gladstone should be prepared to increase the Cabinet in size and make way for Lord Rosebery. As for the chief secretaryship, Spencer told the Prime Minister:

> You seemed to think that you could not offer the place to Shaw Lefevre without the Cabinet. I should have thought that to relieve Trevelyan and oblige you he might have done this; it would not be on the ground that the Irish Secretary ought to be left out of the Cabinet but that there was no room in it just now. If this fails you could take Campbell-Bannerman without the Cabinet.[23]

At the beginning of October the Chief Whip came up with a rather similar proposal – Trevelyan and Rosebery to take the places in Cabinet of Dodson and Carlingford (the latter was to be sent 'to Constantinople or anywhere'), while the chief secretary, without mention of the Cabinet, was to be either Shaw Lefevre or Campbell-Bannerman.[24] A meeting of senior ministers – Gladstone, Granville, Harcourt, Childers and Spencer – three days afterwards produced agreement on the Trevelyan/Dodson switch and on the desirability of bringing Rosebery into the Cabinet. However, the latter possibility depended on persuading Carlingford to go. In any case, it was felt that Shaw Lefevre would take the Irish post, but outside the Cabinet.[25] Spencer had agreed earlier that promoting Trevelyan to the Cabinet as chief secretary would not solve the problem of Trevelyan's exhaustion, but he argued that it would be desirable to put the new chief secretary into the Cabinet. Grosvenor resisted this, however, no doubt with the delicate internal balance of the Cabinet in mind, at a meeting on 9 October.[26]

On the same day Gladstone and Childers discussed the Irish appointment, and Gladstone wrote, hopefully, to Spencer:

> Childers and I have both seen Lefevre. Nothing can be better than his behaviour. He is willing to take the Office of Irish Secretary, with no condition whatever as to the Cabinet. But he frankly states his strong present impression as to the Co-ercion Act. It is that there ought to be a change; and he would have to reserve to himself an entire liberty on the question of its renewal.[27]

George had almost certainly considered not only his political conscience, but also his ministerial self-interest. He sincerely disapproved of the policy of coercion; he was genuinely interested in trying to solve the Irish *impasse*; and he probably calculated that he would damage his long-term prospects by trying to insist on immediate membership of the Cabinet. But his willingness to become chief secretary was suddenly and very quickly withdrawn, and the full reasons for that withdrawal will probably never be known.

Spencer and Shaw Lefevre met twice on 10 October 1884, and after the second meeting the incompatibility of their positions seemed very clear. Twenty-eight years afterwards, George published this summary of their discussions:

> I asked Lord Spencer as to his intended policy. The question of the renewal of the Coercion Act, which was to expire in September of 1885, was already looming in the near future. I had a great aversion to Coercion, and was determined that I would never undertake the defence of such a measure as a Minister. . . . I learned from Lord Spencer that he was then determined to renew the Coercion Act. As eleven months remained before the expiration of the existing Act, I suggested that he should at once announce that he would cease to make any use of the powers of the existing Coercion Act, and would revert to the ordinary law. This would afford an experience of some months. If the effect of such a course should prove to be bad, and if there should be a renewal of disturbance, it would always be possible to revert to coercion, and the renewal of the Act would then become defensible. Lord Spencer was not disposed to adopt this suggestion. On this I declined to accept the post.[28]

At the time, he declined it in the following letter to Gladstone:

> I feel compelled to say that I do not think my views as to the enforcement of the Co-ercion Act either at present or in the future are sufficiently in harmony with those of Lord Spencer to enable me to hold the post with advantage to the Government or satisfaction to myself. I can only add that I much regret that I am unable to render assistance in this direction to Lord Spencer and yourself.[29]

Gladstone, having seen a solution to his immediate problem in sight, was unwilling to give up. He was, himself, troubled by the whole issue of coercion; he was not unduly worried by the fact that Spencer and Shaw Lefevre were not in full agreement; and there is no reason to doubt that he wished to make good use of and to forward George's own career. But, above all, he wanted his own way, and he set about composing a formidable letter, which was sent to Spencer for his observations, and then despatched to George:

> I learn by a succinct telegram (of course duly veiled), to my great disappointment and concern, that difficulties have occurred about the execution of the plan which yesterday appeared to be on the point of accomplishment: and that these difficulties, as I gather, are on your side and not on the side of the Lord Lieutenant. If this is a simple retractation of the answer, which yesterday you appeared inclined to give, I have nothing to say.
>
> But if it is not a change of mind as to the office, and means that you are repelled by fears of difference of opinion, I wish, before the door is finally closed, to beg you that you will consider the matter a little further.
>
> I have little doubt that if to-morrow the members of the Cabinet were to write in letters of iron their present views as to the renewal of the Co-ercion or Crimes Bill, and to act upon those views, the Cabinet would go to pieces. I have as little doubt that if they wait until the proper time for action comes, with the evidence ripe and full, and results in clear view, union is likely to prevail.
>
> I do venture to assure you, at the end of a long life, that even decision too late is not in politics a more subtle or dangerous mischief than decision too soon. . . .
>
> Had the Viceroy made the difficulty I should perhaps have thought him fastidious; but your position is far clearer, you are covered more than amply, and I cannot but say to you, if experience teaches me anything that *your* holding back under the circumstances would be an error in judgement, and would be the refusal of a real public service.[30]

Hamilton, in sending the draft to Spencer, thought that 'The advising and warning tone of a letter coming from Mr G in his position and with his vast experience may possibly have its weight.' But by the time he sent this – presumably the afternoon or evening of 10 October – Hamilton must have had some inkling that there was more to George's refusal than the matters of policy, for he added that whether or not George would be swayed by Gladstone's long letter would depend 'on the reason which lies behind Lefevre's decision.'[31]

It is unlikely that we can ever know the detailed truth about George's refusal of the chief secretaryship, but we have two firm indications of the general character of his problem. On the evening of 9 October, after Spencer had finished his discussions with Gladstone and George, he wrote to Trevelyan fairly confidently about the proposed new arrangement, but added that George 'is to come to me in the morning after having seen his wife who is opposed to going to Ireland.'[32] The only hint of what might have been the cause of that opposition comes from the record of a conversation between John Morley and Lord Rendel at Cannes, in 1894. Morley respected Shaw Lefevre for being the first to appreciate correctly the Irish situation, to see that Irish Disestablishment was not enough, and to recognize the special character of the agrarian question. But Morley felt that George had taken a 'fatal step' in not accepting the Irish secretaryship after Trevelyan, for 'a comical reason . . . that Lady Constance (his wife) did not approve of the Land Act', though Morley also believed that Shaw Lefevre would not have liked 'serving under Spencer plus coercion.'[33]

This raises interesting questions about the marital relations of George and Constance, and about what developments in their domestic life were envisaged had George insisted on taking the Irish post. The whole affair may have turned on intimate though essentially petty matters on which it would be idle to speculate, but the possibility that political differences in the family were acute, cannot be dismissed out of hand. The Earl of Ducie, like the great majority of the Whig landowners, became a Liberal Unionist in 1886. And there is near disbelief in an undated letter of 1887 from Rachael Hamilton Gordon to one of her sisters, where she wrote 'I *am* surprised to hear that Constance has become a Liberal, I *wouldn't* have believed it. I am very glad, as now she will be the same as George!'[34] One has to imagine a possible situation, therefore, in October 1884 in which wife and father-in-law, who provided much, if not most, of the material well-being of George Shaw Lefevre, together or separately created an obstacle to George's acceptance of the Irish secretaryship which he could not overcome. But because, as will be seen, George covered his tracks fairly thoroughly, and the surviving evidence is therefore slender, it is impossible to come to any definite conclusion beyond confirming that an objection was successfully sustained by Constance against George becoming chief secretary.

Let us go back to Gladstone's persuasive letter which, apparently unchanged from the original draft, must have crossed with one from George sent from Oldbury Place the next day. George explained to the Prime Minister that:

> In the interval between my conversation with you and my letter of yesterday, domestic difficulties of a serious character arose to my going to Ireland, which Lord Spencer will be able to explain to you quite confidentially, and which though not absolutely fatal to my accepting a post of danger, if duty compelled me to do so, yet were such as to make me consider and weigh much more carefully my position.

Although the letter goes on to refine some of the arguments and differences on policy between Spencer and himself, it was all secondary to the major message. That George felt deeply and seriously about his private dilemma, and was not a little shamefaced at having to disappoint Gladstone, is evident from his final lines – 'If the disposal of my present office elsewhere should in any way facilitate your course I hope you will not allow any consideration for myself to stand in your way.'[35]

George was particularly concerned that his private reasons were kept private. A short note from George to Spencer confirms this. 'I must ask you on no account to say anything of my domestic difficulty to anyone', he wrote, and Spencer honourably destroyed part of a letter from Trevelyan which was obviously commenting with some indignation on the nature of Shaw Lefevre's decision. George also asked Trevelyan to keep the fact that he had been offered the chief secretaryship secret.[36]

What is not clear is whether, had the private reasons not been present, George would have succumbed to Gladstone's arguments. In the future, he was to maintain that his refusal of the chief secretaryship was entirely the result of his distaste for anything to do with a policy of coercion in Ireland. The private reasons were never mentioned, either in his speeches or in the history of the Gladstone era which he published in 1912. His account in that work, however, does include an interesting admission: 'If I had been offered the post immediately after the Phoenix Park murders, I could not have refused it; for it was then a post of great danger. The danger had now passed.'[37] This is in clear conflict with the implication, in his letter of refusal to Gladstone, that the job was potentially dangerous.

Perhaps by the time he wrote in such terms, George had forgotten or had blotted out the memory of whatever domestic trauma had loomed so large in October 1884. But whatever were the proportionate influences of his political and his personal feelings on his decision, he came to take the same view of it as Morley did in 1894, and regretted his refusal of Gladstone's invitation. When the long-widowed Lady Frederick Cavendish sent him a sympathetic and congratulatory letter about his book, *Gladstone and Ireland*, in 1912, he replied:

I thought you would be interested in my little story of Lord Frederick offering to decline the post of Irish Secretary if I was willing to accept it. I don't think Mr Gladstone would have agreed to the substitution. He rightly thought that your husband was the man for the occasion. Later I made the supreme mistake of my career in refusing the post when Trevelyan gave it up. I did not understand how much Mr Gladstone agreed with me as to Coercion in Ireland. He suggested that I should take the post and give it up later when Spencer introduced his Bill. I thought however that this would not be fair to Spencer. As it was Campbell Bannerman took the post. The Government went out of office before the introduction of a Coercion measure and the Tories came into office secretly pledged not to renew coercion. Campbell Bannerman cheerfully took the lead over me and rose to be Premier.[38]

Whether the course of events would have been substantially different had Shaw Lefevre taken the Irish secretaryship either in 1882 or in 1884, must remain no more than an interesting subject for historical reflection. But without doubt George would have become a more important man in the upper reaches of the Liberal Party had he accepted the job when it was firmly offered to him. Though he went on quite quickly to apparent promotion, and though he subsequently lost his way through an electoral disaster, he was almost certainly correct to see, in retrospect, that his decision on 10 October 1884, whatever it achieved for him in his private life, was a political blunder from which he never really recovered. His behaviour shocked Trevelyan, who communicated his shock to Spencer. Even if they kept very quiet, the story must have had some circulation, and it is not unlikely that George lost face, at least among the handful of people who were his main colleagues and rivals. Trevelyan commented:

> The more I think about Lefevre the more sorry I am that he should have taken this line. I regard it as an absolute duty for a public man not to refuse Ireland, except on high public grounds; and the idea that Ireland can be governed on the old jury law is a mere excuse. It may be said that no public man should resign Ireland, and that I fully allow; and unless he can be moved, and have a reasonably good substitute, he should stay till he sank at the post, even though he might grumble and complain. And he is not a better man for complaining, as I confess humbly enough. Lefevre is an extraordinary mixture of public spirit, selfishness, good nature, and a quality difficult to distinguish from want of scruple.[39]

But whatever explanation Shaw Lefevre gave in confidence to Spencer and Gladstone was apparently treated, at least by the Prime Minister, as something far more serious, and worthy of far more respect and sympathy, than is implied by Morley's suggestion that it was 'comical'. And the manner in which he turned down the Prime Minister's offer ensured that George retained goodwill in Downing Street. Hamilton felt that 'Nothing could have been nicer or more loyal in tone' than George's letter of final refusal.[40] Gladstone assured Granville that 'Lefevre has behaved very well'[41] and he wrote to George in quite fulsome terms:

> I thank you for your frank and manly explanation. . . . In all I have ever known you say or do you have been guided exclusively by your convictions of honour and duty: and I am certain that in the present very difficult conjunction, and in all others you may have to meet, you will take no other guide. I greatly rejoice to pay to the son that warm respect and regard which I always felt for the excellent and distinguished father.[42]

The long-term damage which George had done to his own prospects was not apparent in the near future. If the Irish offices were settled, the problems of cabinet membership and balance were not. There was still an urgent need to find a place for Rosebery, and George's entry to the supreme council was more part of a manoeuvre to bring Rosebery in than it was a simple recognition of his own political importance. The opportunity arose when Henry Fawcett, the Postmaster General, whose duties George had been carrying, and who had not been in the Cabinet, died early in November 1884. Gladstone seized his chance. At a meeting with his senior colleagues it was agreed that Shaw Lefevre should move to the Post Office, and that Rosebery should be offered the Office of Works; both were to be taken into the Cabinet, Gladstone abandoning his long-held aversion to increasing the membership by declaring that it was necessary to maintain the existing balance between peers and commoners.[43]

George was delighted, but immediately revealed his capacity for indiscretion by telling friends that he was to succeed Fawcett, with the result that the announcement appeared in the *Daily News* before Gladstone had made his proposal known to the Queen. The Prime Minister was furious. He assured the Queen that he was surprised and mortified, that he had 'at once addressed Mr Lefevre in decided language', and hoped that Her Majesty would 'authorize him to say something to Mr Lefevre' on her behalf.[44] George ate humble pie.[45] But Gladstone had to cope with a much worse development – Rosebery's refusal of office on account of his dislike of the Government's Egyptian policy. The matter was not resolved until February 1885, and until then Shaw Lefevre continued to hold office without being in the Cabinet. Rosebery decided to accept membership of the Government only after the news of the fall of Khartoum and the death of General Gordon. Gladstone adhered to the earlier arrangement: Rosebery and Shaw Lefevre attended their first cabinet meeting on 16 February 1885. They had joined a Government which was in sad disarray and was to fall within a few months. Their entry symbolized the Cabinet's fractured condition. As John Morley remarked to his sister, 'The two new appointments are curiously balanced, as usual. Rosebery is a Jingo, Lefevre is of my persuasion and yours.'[46] It was not an auspicious time for George to reach the top. And it was painful for him, in personal terms, that his aged mother was dying just when he learned of his promotion, and that she never knew of it.[47]

CHAPTER XVII

Frustration and Recovery, 1885–1886

The three Liberal cabinets in which George Shaw Lefevre served, and the years of opposition between, have been subjected by now to intense scrutiny, particularly the months of his first short tenure of cabinet office from February to June 1885.[1] It is very unlikely that more than a few small details of the course of events can be added from a minute examination of George's participation. What follows, therefore, in this and a later chapter, is not a reconstructed version of the period, but only some consideration of George's role, and of what kind of person he proved to be in the top layer of contemporary politicians.

The years 1885 to 1895 witnessed acute internal divisions within the Liberal Party, and remarkably complex manoeuvres across the board of Westminster politics. In such stressful circumstances, the recorded remarks and opinions of those closely involved about each others' virtues or shortcomings have to be viewed with judicious scepticism. They were, after all, occasional snapshots, taken often at widely different times and reflecting particular moments of triumph, worry, impatience or irritation. And as only a few participants kept detailed diaries of events, the contributions of those whom the diarists found less attractive or more awkward may well be underrepresented in the record. There is little doubt, however, that Shaw Lefevre, along with two or three colleagues, was among the less important members of the three cabinets in which he served, and within the party's leadership group. Nonetheless, in such divided councils nobody's vote was without significance.

Despite a cautious appraisal of the evidence, it is undeniable that acute observers had serious reservations about George's demonstrated weaknesses, and those observers included four men who were or were to become Prime Minister. Gladstone was on several occasions very annoyed at Shaw Lefevre's lack of discretion, did not think he made as much of his cases as he could have done, and was reported, late in 1885, as not being keen to have him back in another cabinet – though he took him in again seven years later.[2] Rosebery, who entered the Cabinet with George, has been rightly described as making Shaw Lefevre (and Trevelyan) seem 'colourless and insignificant': he linked George with Childers as the weakest members of the cabinets in which he had served but, as we have already seen, came to have more respect for George as President of the Local Government Board.[3] Asquith thought George a 'weak vessel', with insufficient weight, strength or popularity, 'who always managed to tread on everyone's toes in the House of Commons.'[4] And Arthur Balfour, from the opposing benches, simply could not stand him. The two were in bitter conflict over Ireland, and H.W. Lucy recalled how the 'mere sight' of Shaw Lefevre 'by some subtle, irresistible influence, instantly changed the aspect of Mr Balfour's usually smiling countenance.'[5]

Other Ministers, politicians and civil servants echoed these criticisms. Morley and Hamilton underlined George's unpopularity in the Commons. Augustine Birrell thought him one of the most useful MPs of his time, but could not deny that he was 'one of the dreariest of all parliamentary speakers.' T.P. O'Connor honoured him as 'a man of iron tenacity of purpose and conviction', but felt that 'he always seemed obscure, and his personality also. There was something so quiet, so prosaic, about everything he did, and yet he went on doing it.' *Punch* took George to task more than once for being long-winded, self-important and boring. In a bitingly satirical article on a visit which George paid to the Sultan of Turkey in 1891, he was lampooned in a cruel but clever adaptation, by Lucy ('Toby MP'), of a line from Tennyson's poem, *Locksley Hall*:

Oh the dreary, drear Lefevre! Oh the barren, barren Shaw![6]

Hamilton felt, when George lost his seat at Reading, that he rather deserved his fate because he had been 'far too "cocky" and self-asserting.'[7] Lord Acton, who appreciated George's 'eye for facts', was sure that he would 'not know how to employ them to advantage himself.'[8] Griffith-Boscawen, admittedly a political opponent, thought Shaw Lefevre 'a very dull professor of philosophic Radicalism.'[9] Harcourt, not the politest or gentlest of public men, thought George's manners were atrocious, and on one occasion was so 'angry and disgusted' by Shaw Lefevre's insensitivity that he would have liked to box his ears.[10] Even the strongly supportive *Bradford Observer* implied that George did not conceal his sense of his own superiority:

Mr Shaw Lefevre is not a man who makes the least pretence to the artifices of a demagogue or even to the legitimate art of a rhetorician. He is *par excellence* a logician – and one of rather a severe type – and if he could not carry conviction by dint of bare argument he would probably scorn to persuade at all.[11]

If George had problems in communicating with his parliamentary and ministerial colleagues, there are signs that his behaviour among leading constituents was also, on occasion, abrasive. He does not seem to have had any large, recognizable, personal following, though he was respected for his sheer competence, energy and courage, both by individual politicians and supporters in his constituencies. Even socially, though, he seems to have been something of a liability, for one uninhibited female diarist recorded the 'extreme boredom of having to sit next to George Lefevre' and regarded him as 'the dryest of men.'[12] He suffered, too, from having been in politics for a very long time, and of having been associated with causes which, by the last years of the century, were beginning to be regarded with less reverence than previously. In the 1890s, people as far removed politically as Algernon West and Beatrice Webb regarded him as part of an 'old gang' whom they did not wish to see in places of power.[13]

It may well be that George's reputation was harmed by the sheer length of his own life. He outlived almost everybody who worked closely with him, politically, and his being still alive may have inhibited some of those, younger than himself, who left memoirs, from expressing any views about him, favourable or otherwise. The weight of the available evidence supports the sense that in his public roles he was, above all, without charm – not a very attractive or likeable man. As a private person there are a few signs that he was, in all probability, much warmer and more genial – even, as one of his critics admitted, on occasion quite endearing.[14] He did have a sense of humour, though it operated infrequently and was of a very dry character. And he possessed a great fund of anecdotes which, one fears, were very likely aired rather too often.

Insofar as the scattered but not inconsistent criticisms of Shaw Lefevre can safely be brought together, they seem to reveal a tendency on the part of those apparently close to him politically to write him down as not particularly able, or as without strength. But in the context of his radicalism, this was often at least as much a reflection of George's failure to agree with those who recorded their criticisms of him, as of any personal lack of ability or enthusiasm for radical causes. He was, essentially, a loner. The difficulty lay in the fact that while he had the integrity and toughness to stick to his real opinions, he could not persuade others that his opinions were superior to theirs, nor could he conceal sufficiently his own good opinion of himself. Morley and Rendel, in conversation, may well have diagnosed his major weaknesses very accurately: 'An anxiety and concentration about his career has spoilt Lefevre's chances as much as the bad manners and utter want of sympathy which that sort of egoism produces.'[15]

Though George was a loner, he was anything but a revolutionary – and he loved office. That combination made him an uneasy colleague in a radical context, and explains his actions and attitudes in 1885–6. The notion that he was, in 1885, a firm, unquestioning follower of Chamberlain and Dilke, will not stand close examination. The problem for Chamberlain was that he could not bind together the small group of sympathetic leading radicals, more than momentarily. He had invited George, late in January, to meet periodically with him, Dilke, Trevelyan and 'perhaps John Morley . . . to talk over the situation and our policy.'[16] But when Shaw Lefevre and Rosebery entered the Cabinet in mid-February, Dilke told Chamberlain that the two new ministers would 'greatly help and strengthen the Cabinet to the public at this moment. But, it will weaken *us*.'[17] Clearly, George was not considered a reliable ally, and his equivocal relationship was well illustrated later in the year, when Chamberlain complained that Shaw Lefevre was 'weak as usual at a critical moment.'[18]

Disagreements between radicals, however, was only one facet of the uncertainty and weariness of the whole Cabinet. They were beset by the disaster in the Sudan, by the apparently intractable difficulties of the Irish situation, and by the tortuous progress of a further reform of the franchise, with its attendant controversies over a redistribution of seats. The Government had been in office for five years, a general election could not be long postponed, and the Liberals were uncomfortably aware of the tenuousness of their hold in the House of Commons. The atmosphere was made even more oppressive by the possibility of Gladstone's retirement, which meant that anxieties and rivalries about the succession were never further than just below the surface of the subject matter of any discussion of pending decisions or longer-term policy.

George had been a member for a mere twelve days when the Cabinet decided, only on the casting vote of the Prime Minister, not to resign. George was on Gladstone's side, in large part because of his unwillingness to see his main patron and inspirational leader step down, but also because of a consistent objection to giving up office which would have been particularly strong after so short a spell in the Cabinet. Though the issue was 'not one of political appraisal'[19] the four radicals – Chamberlain, Dilke, Shaw Lefevre and Trevelyan – were all in favour of holding on. After this close decision the following two months were largely dominated by the continuing problems of Egypt, though there was an awkward controversy about proposals for the next budget, in April. At the end of that month there began a complex argument about Ireland – whether and how the Crimes Act should be extended, and what kind of local government and land purchase bills should be introduced. Shaw Lefevre became a member of the Irish Committee, and as the debates over its business became increasingly contentious, he was to find himself driven to threaten resignation.

Chamberlain sent to Trevelyan, Shaw Lefevre and Campbell-Bannerman, the Chief Secretary for Ireland, his proposal for a central board – 'a municipal version of Home Rule', on 30 April. Campbell-Bannerman immediately rejected the scheme, as did the Lord Lieutenant, Spencer.[20] There then followed three weeks of intense manoeuvrings, confrontations, misunderstandings, and rumours which demonstrated the hopelessness of finding a generally agreed way forward. There was another discussion of the advisability of resigning, on 7 May; a virtual decision against the central board two days later; and subsequent bargaining about the nature of amendments to the Crimes Act, about the extension of the act for only one or two years, and about the introduction of a land purchase bill. But the most dramatic development was the news, given to Dilke by Randolph Churchill on 17 May, that the Conservative leaders had decided that they would not, if they took over the government, renew coercion in Ireland. Three days later, Gladstone, believing that he had an agreement with Chamberlain that the Crimes Act should be extended, but only for one year, announced that a land purchase bill would also be introduced. On the same day, as a result, Dilke and Chamberlain submitted their resignations, and on the next day Shaw Lefevre followed suit.[21]

Dilke and Chamberlain based their objections on the proposal to introduce a land purchase bill. George had some reservations about the land purchase scheme envisaged in the bill, but was not opposed to it in principle. He was, however, as always, hostile to any continuance of coercion. Nonetheless, after consulting Dilke,[22] he assured Gladstone that despite his disagreement with Chamberlain and Dilke over land purchase, he would would still feel obliged to resign with them:

> I cannot . . . but feel that the resignation of Chamberlain and Dilke will place me in a position of the greatest difficulty as regards the Coercion Bill. As you are aware from my action in November last when you offered me the post of Irish Secretary, I have always entertained the strongest objection to a renewal of the coercion Act, unless it is proved by experience that the ordinary law is insufficient. When the subject was recently discussed in the Cabinet I stated my objection. If any other member or members of the Cabinet had resigned upon this question I should certainly have joined them in so doing, but I scarcely felt justified in acting alone on this question, when Chamberlain and Dilke were prepared to give way. . . . Their resignation now, however, is connected indirectly with the Coercion Bill, and the discussions which will arise upon it, and upon the scheme for Local Government for Ireland, which I presume will be raised, will make it I fear impossible for me to support the Coercion Bill.[23]

It has been suggested that George was concerned about 'his standing in his own mind as an austere administrator sworn to Cobdenite principles, not to connivance with the manoeuvres of Dilke and Chamberlain'; that he argued his position *ex silentio*; and that probably 'he was not on close personal or political terms with any other member of the cabinet.'[24] While it is true that there is not much correspondence to or from George over this episode, the fact that he consulted Dilke before sending the letter quoted above, and that in the next few days he was very active in trying to find a *modus vivendi*, beginning with a proposal to Dilke (which Dilke recommended be passed on to Chamberlain), implies that he was in close touch with him, most likely with Chamberlain, and certainly with Gladstone. It is as well to recall that despite the furore over Irish affairs, George and Dilke had been much involved in the inter- and intra-party struggles over the reform of the franchise and the redistribution of seats, which were at least as important, if not more important, to most MPs than were the affairs of Ireland. But though George must have been on reasonably close terms with Dilke, he was no slavish follower and, as in the late 1870s, he was critical of Chamberlain, perhaps more on the grounds of the latter's tactics than over matters of policy.[25]

On 23 May, George put to Dilke two possible alternative courses on coercion. One was to restrict the extension of the act to one year. But it was the other which was to become the subject of serious cabinet discussion. George proposed that an extension of the act should 'only come into effect upon proved necessity after proclamation.' He argued that:

> on constitutional grounds coercion is only to be justified on the clearly proved failure of the ordinary law, and . . . when a coercion Act has been passed for a definite period, another trial should be made of the ordinary law before renewing it. On the whole I think [this] second alternative is the best, as it would put the Nationalists on their good behaviour – and it would show that there is an earnest desire on the part of the Government to revert to constitutional law and to dispense with coercion.[26]

This was followed up by a protest to Dilke about Chamberlain's leak of cabinet discussions to the press, which George saw as likely to increase the difficulty of getting further concessions on coercion.[27]

With the resignations of the three radicals still ineffective, there was intense bargaining between Spencer and his colleagues over how much ground he, as Lord Lieutenant, would give on the possibility of coercion only by proclamation. George's plan, which was also 'associated variously with Heneage . . . and O'Shea', was known within the Cabinet as 'Lefevre's proposal'. It was discussed at length and without resolution at meetings of 5 and 8 June, in an atmosphere heavy with the likelihood and desirability, for many, of defeat in the House and subsequent resignation. Insofar as that was 'a consummation devoutly to be wished', it came about almost immediately, when the poorly-whipped Liberals were defeated in a snap division on a proposed tax on drink, in the early hours of 9 June. The Cabinet, without serious argument, escaped from their dilemmas by resigning.[28]

The events of the thirteen months which followed the resignation are now seen, from all the evidence which has become available subsequently, as constituting one of the most confused and melodramatic periods of modern British political history. While the causes and the pressures and the incidents were complex and numerous, it was the development of the affairs of Ireland which made the most significant impact by producing a major split in the Liberal Party. Those who followed Gladstone tried to introduce a measure of Home Rule; those opposed called themselves Liberal Unionists, and threw their weight, on this issue, on the same side as the Conservatives. The initial quarrel raged for months, through two general elections and two changes of government. In July 1886, after six months in office again, the Gladstonian Liberals were soundly defeated, and were to be out of power for all but three of the next nineteen years. Politicians who saw themselves as major actors in this continuous drama had to be on centre stage throughout. Most of George Shaw Lefevre's colleagues in the Liberal cabinet which resigned in June 1885, were back in Parliament after the general election of November, and back in office early in the New Year. But George would not rejoin them in the House of Commons until April 1886; and he would not be a cabinet minister again until 1892.

To see how George Shaw Lefevre lost his way in the winter of 1885–6, we must now turn back some twenty months, to the celebration of his score of years as member for Reading. The triumphal banquet and public meeting, on 14 and 15 November 1883, with major speeches from Lord Selborne, Henry Fawcett and John Morley, as well as from George himself, was carried off with enormous confidence and without any hint that the prolonged unity and success of the Reading Liberals, just two years afterwards, would be a thing of rags and tatters.[29] In the main, that disaster was the result of the decision of Parnell to order Irish voters in England to vote for the Conservatives, which had its strongest impact on the urban constituencies; and of the worries of Anglican voters about the possibility of disestablishment. But it also reflected an unfortunate and embarrassing problem over Shaw Lefevre's candidature.

At the same time that George was celebrating at Reading, the Government, following a conference at Leeds of the National Liberal Federation, was beginning the highly-argumentative process which was to lead to the third Reform Act and to a major redistribution of seats. In the course of that long inter- and intra-party debate, Shaw Lefevre pressed for the simultaneous consideration of franchise and redistribution, against Gladstone's wishes, and was a member of the cabinet committee which dealt with the redistribution and was chaired by Dilke – who played his hand very strongly and boasted of having rid himself of his colleagues' irritating concerns.[30] George received some praise for his part in the tortuous negotiation of the whole package of reforms, and at one late stage he was apparently willing to be spokesman for his uncle, Viscount Eversley who, at 90, joined with a few others to suggest that the redistribution controversy be referred to a small group of wise men from both parties – a suggestion which came to nothing.[31] But it was George's own situation at Reading which made the matter so crucial for his future.

As the proposals for redistribution progressed it became clear that a major change would have to take place in boroughs which had hitherto returned two members. The *Standard* got hold of some leaked redistribution proposals on the very day that George was agonizing over Gladstone's offer of the chief secretaryship. Those proposals included the idea of reducing the population cut-off point for double member constituencies, and Fowler joked to Morley that 'the scheme was unmistakably "the child of Lefevre – down to 40,000 limit for 2 which saves Reading!!!'[32] But whether or not George had tried to protect his own constituency, in the last resort Reading was reduced to having only one seat. George found himself faced with a difficult local problem of his candidature, and the solution, after embarrassing negotiations, was damaging to his prospects.

The result at Reading in 1880, while safe for Shaw Lefevre, had not been too reassuring, in part because his new partner had overtaken him at the polls. Moreover, that partner, though much junior to George in national political standing and experience, was a powerful local figure. George Palmer was thirteen years older than Shaw Lefevre. He was born into a Quaker family and had joined and then succeeded the original owner of the big, expanding biscuit firm of Huntley and Palmer, among Reading's largest employers of labour. Palmer had long been closely involved in local politics and had been mayor and alderman before becoming MP in 1878. Which of these two – Shaw Lefevre or Palmer – should stand down? The resolution of that question was to leave some scars.

Palmer had all the sense of pride and proprietorship of the traditional local worthy. Undoubtedly he had strong claims as a very successful and benevolent townsman. 'He was quite ready to stand again at Reading, and his family are most anxious that he should do so', wrote George. Nor did Palmer want to stand for any other constituency, and at first 'distinctly refused' the chance of contesting a county seat. But, claimed George, 'he . . . fully recognizes my claim . . . and is quite willing to retire . . . in my favour, if I desire it.'[33] Apparently the two men had met and discussed the situation on 1 December, for Palmer wrote a letter six weeks later to the chairman of the Liberal Association in Reading, stating that he had informed Shaw Lefevre, on that date, that 'he should not be a candidate for the seat . . . in the new Parliament if he [Shaw Lefevre] would continue to sit for Reading.'[34] During December, however, George Shaw Lefevre was not entirely comfortable with the situation, and he had good reason for his discomfort.

Among prominent Reading Liberal supporters of George was one H.M. Wallis. As an old man he reminisced to Shaw Lefevre:

we, old Liberals, have never forgotten you nor pardoned Dilke and Chamberlain who instigated Palmer to cling to the seat and oust you – *Palmer told me this himself* in one of those queer bursts of self-revelation so characteristic of the man. The scene was the Tea-Room of the House of Commons – the night after the Redistribution Bill . . . was read for the first time. [i.e. 2 December 1884] Palmer had *just told you* that he resigned the seat, and Chamberlain and Dilke, your colleagues in the Cabinet, sat at Palmer's tea-table and *urged him not to do as he had promised.* 'Reading is *your* borough Palmer: Lefevre can get a seat anywhere' were Chamberlain's words (*pace* Palmer to me) – 'Joe' was a traitor in grain.[35]

George may have had no knowledge of such an episode, at the time, but he was sufficiently troubled by the possibility of a conflict to unburden himself, at some length, five days before Christmas, to Gladstone. He asked whether he should press his claims to stay on at Reading or whether he should relinquish the seat and look elsewhere, particularly to the London constituency of Marylebone, where he lived, where he had been 'strongly pressed to stand', and which in 'many respects would suit my personal convenience better.' He rehearsed various anxieties about Reading – the existence of a minority 'strongly in favour of my colleague', as opposed to a majority 'most anxious that I should continue as their member'; his fear that if he stood there was a chance that 'Mr Palmer's friends should hold aloof'; but his concern that if he resigned, 'a section of the Constituency would feel very much hurt at my retirement, would attribute it to my colleague and would show their resentment to him.' George asked not merely for advice, but for help in the shape of a letter from Gladstone, which could be made public, 'to the effect that you think it important that I should go to London and on the other hand that it would be a pity that so good a Liberal as my colleague should be forced to retire from public life.' The drift of the letter suggests that George really wanted to leave Reading, especially as he feared that, even if he stayed and won in the next contest, he would not be able to hold the seat in the long term.[36]

The Prime Minister passed the letter for comment to the Chief Whip, Lord Richard Grosvenor, who had no great respect for Shaw Lefevre. Grosvenor believed Marylebone would be 'glad to welcome' George but, unmoved by Christian charity, even on Christmas Day, he advised Gladstone to write no letter, and to 'Make Lefevre decide for himself.'[37] Gladstone's private reply to George simply pointed out the desirability of seeking pastures new:

After consulting R. Grosvenor I do not see anything in this case which would relax this prudential rule [of non-interference in particular constituency affairs] but R. Grosvenor thinks and as a private person I agree that you might very properly quit Reading inviting all your friends to support Palmer, and sail yourself, with every prosperous omen, on the other tack.[38]

But for the second time in less than three months, Shaw Lefevre was to turn down Gladstone's advice on a major aspect of his future. In retrospect, it might have been better for him to have thrown in his hand at Reading immediately. As it was, he waited long enough for some extenuating circumstances to develop, and allowed himself to be seduced by them.

The executive committee of the Reading Liberal Association, a deal troubled by these developments, had heard from both members that it would be distasteful to them to have the matter put before the general council, and that the members should be left to settle the question between themselves. Nothing was done, officially, therefore, until Palmer wrote to the chairman, Charles Smith, on 10 January, and said, distinctly, that he would not be a candidate. Palmer wrote, simultaneously to George, that:

> I am not and have not been, and have no intention of being a candidate. . . . Since the evening of December 1st, that has been my position, except that until the last fortnight I have not seen so clearly as I do now the great improbability of my yielding to pressure in the event of your leaving Reading.

This was language sufficiently equivocal as to make George's hesitations in December very justifiable.

In the knowledge that the chairman, Charles Smith, had received Palmer's letter of 10 January, Shaw Lefevre wrote to Smith on 16 January to express his willingness to be the candidate. But he still wanted the chairman to make quite sure that Palmer did not wish to reconsider the question, before Shaw Lefevre's willingness to stand was made known to the general council:

> Under the belief that I could find some other constituency willing to return me, I have been prepared to withdraw . . . if . . . Mr Palmer, whose claims on the borough are so deservedly great, should desire again to offer himself for re-election. . . . If they [the Liberal Association] should be of opinion that the interests of the party would be promoted by their endeavouring to persuade my colleague to depart from his present resolve, I shall willingly acquiesce, and will do my utmost on his behalf.

The chairman accordingly saw Palmer, who insisted that his decision was final. The situation was then put before the general council where, despite Palmer's statement of intent, there was a discussion of 'the possibility of inducing [him] to reconsider his firmly expressed determination to resign his candidature.' In the end the general council resolved, on 22 January, to accept Shaw Lefevre.[39]

But all these careful and courteous public formalities and restrained reportage concealed a bitter struggle, some of which may have been partly hidden from George. Wallis recalled that of the Palmer sons, Alfred took no part against Shaw Lefevre, but that:

> George William and Sir Walter Palmer never looked my way again if they could help themselves. 'G.W' was bitterly ashamed of himself for not resisting his father and could never pardon me who stood up to the old man – *and saw him weep* in that little 'studio' at the 'Acacias', when I wetted a pen and insisted upon his signing his 'abdication' of the one seat left to us! Lord! how he wriggled and Chas Smith coming in – *got the signature* – But he tried to repudiate it next day – But we got it into a special edition of the *Reading Observer*, and there could be no denying his own handwriting.

Whether Palmer gave up with a bad grace, or was ruthlessly pushed out, he and his supporters did not forgive, forget, and act loyally in the party's interests. Wallis considered that George was:

> *abominably* treated by one whom you had long believed your friend and colleague. What we – your supporters, suffered – the threats of legal action levelled at us in public and private; the scenes almost incredible . . . promises made – and broken: subscriptions promised and then withdrawn: spies upon our committees, and poor men insulted by the Big Rich men of the borough – *All* the family carriages sent out of Reading the night before your last polling-day, and the Factory Foremen *told-off to influence their underlings to vote against you.* Your meetings interrupted: your statements from the platform contradicted *on the platform*!!

Even though Wallis was a strong partisan who may have exaggerated somewhat in his old age, his accusations cannot be discounted and there is certainly a record of Palmer having publicly challenged George's version of the selection process, at a big Liberal rally in April 1885.[40]

Needless to say, the disagreement about who should stand for Reading went beyond the clash of personalities and simple personal interests, but it is significant that only one public reference to this aspect of the selection controversy was made at the time. At the Liberal Association meeting in February, one speaker was 'outspokenly against Lefevre because he was not in favour of disestablishment.'[41] As we shall see, that subject was the one on which the election probably turned. As for Palmer, who was obviously very resentful of losing the Reading candidacy, he was persuaded, despite his initial reluctance to consider any other constituency, to stand for the Newbury division of Berkshire

We can never know how many votes were lost to Shaw Lefevre because of the quarrel with Palmer, but as the election went against him by only 129, that quarrel cannot have been an insignificant factor in his defeat. Indeed, the local Conservatives were to claim that by choosing Shaw Lefevre over Palmer the Liberals gave them the seat.[42] Be that as it may, George would have been less than human if he had not appreciated Wallis' account of how Palmer 'intrigued against you in the factory, and in the Borough, and lost his election for the Newbury Division in consequence (Reading freeholders voting Tory to *'pay Palmer out'* – O, Lord, what times! – what times!)'

George would have saved himself some embarrassment if he had moved to Marylebone, but he would not necessarily have saved his seat in Parliament. The old Marylebone, comfortably won by two Liberals in 1880, was divided into two single-seat constituencies by the redistribution scheme. Both were won by Conservatives, and by far bigger majorities than George's opponent won Reading. George might have done better, or he might have found a more amenable constituency than Marylebone. As it was, the tide was running against him, and he had the sheer bad luck to be removed from the high political stage at just the moment when he needed desperately to be on it.

The first Salisbury Government took office in mid-June 1885. Parliament was dissolved in mid-November and the election began towards the end of that month. The dramatic – nay, the melodramatic – story of the pre-electoral manoeuvrings and their outcome, dominated by the switch of Irish support from one party to the other, and the remarkable result of a House of Commons where eighty-six Irish members exactly equalled the numerical difference between the majority Liberals and the minority Conservatives, has been told and interpreted repeatedly; as has the flying of Gladstone's Hawarden kite, the resignation of the Salisbury Government in February 1886, the subsequent attempt of Gladstone to carry Home rule, the splitting of the Liberals, and their heavy defeat in the following summer. Against that explosive background we must set the frustrating disappointment and subsequent revival of the fortunes of George Shaw Lefevre.

Inevitably, political energy in the summer and autumn of 1885 was focused on electoral possibilities, and in that context George's most obvious potential allies were his radical colleagues. Shaw Lefevre and Trevelyan were invited by Chamberlain to meet regularly with himself, Dilke and John Morley, and this was seen for long as a significant 'Cabal' or 'Junta' giving a strong lead to the radical interest. But internal disagreements and suspicions prevented any real progress towards the production of a cohesive policy, and a modern scholarly treatment of the period remarks that 'For some inexplicable reason the possibility of formulating a co-ordinated electoral strategy was not raised; consequently members of the transitory "Cabal" trod divergent paths as the general election approached.'[43]

There is no evidence in Shaw Lefevre correspondence which would modify that judgement. The five radicals did not fall out, though we have seen that Chamberlain thought George unreliable. George, for his part, viewed the possibility that Chamberlain would become the leader of the Liberals with only moderate concern:

> I had a long talk with Lefevre to-day [wrote Morley on 4 September] . . . He is all right; he only hopes that 'Chamberlain won't forget that he may now almost any day find himself leader of the whole Party, Whigs and all.' No harm in that.[44]

And Chamberlain felt able to assure Gladstone, as late as 26 October, that Shaw Lefevre would probably stand with him, Dilke and Morley in refusing to join a government which was 'not committed to backing the compulsory purchase of land by local authorities' in Ireland.[45] Meanwhile George preserved his public party position by refusing Iddesleigh's invitation to join a royal commission on the depressed state of trade. And within the party hierarchy he kept up his basic radicalism by talking of the desirability of excluding almost all peers from the next Liberal cabinet – a view which moved Hamilton to record with some asperity that 'it is rather a want of gratitude . . . considering that he owes his own promotion (to the Cabinet) to the accession of another Peer (Rosebery).'[46]

By the time Parliament was dissolved and the last campaigns began, George had to deal with a worsening situation at Reading in which the issue of the disestablishment of the Church of England, intensified for him by his unhappy relations with Palmer, was almost certainly more important to most electors than the Irish problem. He had probably not been helped by the earlier announcement in the Reading press of the commencement of payment of his £1,200 pension.[47] In mid-September, the Record listed Palmer as being in favour of disestablishment but reported that Shaw Lefevre had 'refused information' on where he stood.[48] When his election address was published, it contained no mention of disestablishment, and on 24 October he declared that as no practical measure on disestablishment would come up in the new parliament, he held himself free to take such action as he might think fit whenever, after the next session, it did arise. Thereafter he emphasized that he would not be a party to any proposal to disestablish in the coming parliament. But his protestations were all in vain.[49]

By 5 November George was seriously worried about both the disestablishment and Irish issues. He wrote to Chamberlain:

I have rather a stiff fight here. The Church party is thoroughly alarmed and though with the full assent of the Non-Cons I have promised *not* to vote for Disestablishment in the coming Parliament they are doing their utmost against me. I shall get about 100 of the moderate Churchmen to go with me. Last election I won with only 226 votes – so you see I have not a great margin.

There are about 80 Irish Catholics in the town. They are waiting orders from Parnell. Their priest tells me they are still sore about a speech I made 3 years ago. Do you think there is any way of securing their votes through the Irish Leaders? They owe me something, I think, for as you know, I was more opposed to a renewal of Coercion than any other member of the late Cabinet. When I made the speech complained of I had advised Forster and Mr Gladstone that Parnell and his friends should be released from prison and that an Arrears Bill should be passed. This I was unable to say at the time – What I believe gave offence was that I denounced the no-Rent circular. I find it impossible to get at these 80 voters personally.

The Nonconformists have lost ground here of late years chiefly owing to the absence of any men of mark and ability among them. We used to have excellent speakers among their ministers – now there is not one.[50]

But Chamberlain was in no position to help:

Unfortunately I have no hold on the Irish just now. My usual channel of communication is closed – as there is a quarrel between O'Shea and Parnell. I suggest that you should write to Labouchere who is the only man I know on our side with the least influence. If you asked him I think he would not be displeased to show that he possesses it. You can say I suggested your application if you like.[51]

We do not know whether George consulted Labouchere, but when he wrote an account of the election in 1912 he claimed that the Irish voters, whom he had so recently found it 'impossible to get at', had come to him with tears in their eyes and full of regrets, after their priest and leaders had passed on to them Parnell's instructions to abandon the Liberals.[52]

Reading polled early, on 25 November, and the Conservative won, 3,518 to 3,389. The *Reading Mercury* declared unhesitatingly that 'The Disestablishment of the Church was, undoubtedly, the rock upon which Mr Lefevre suffered shipwreck.'[53] George himself wrote a considered analysis of the voting:

My defeat was due to the defection of 70 to 80 Irish Catholics who had promised to vote for me as on previous occasions and . . . the very undue pressure of the Church party through their district visitors on the poorer class of voters, threatening them with withdrawal of Charities.

There was also a certain defection of the voters in Messrs Palmers' biscuit factory who thought that my late colleague had been unfairly treated – the Palmer family themselves gave me a loyal support. My majorities at the last 2 General Elections were only 140 and 220 so that I had little to spare.[54]

The *Reading Observer* added only a slight gloss, suggesting that fifty of the Irish Liberals either voted Conservative in response to Parnell's call, or abstained.[55]

It was a crushing disappointment for Shaw Lefevre, softened marginally by the similar loss of many urban Liberal seats, and by the fact that Dilke had only scraped home with a very small majority. Almost before the hard fact of his defeat had sunk in, he attended what was the last meeting of the 'Cabal' – though Trevelyan was not there – and helped Dilke to insist that Chamberlain drop disestablishment.[56] But while he was given sympathy by his nearest colleagues and assurances that he would soon find another seat, he can have been under no illusion as to the damage his absence from the House of Commons would do to him. In the circumstances, and no doubt pressed by his family, he took the public position that he was not immediately seeking another constituency, and went off to Mentone to nurse his wounds, to rest, and to search for a seat privately.

The first opportunity for George to return to the House of Commons came from South Edinburgh, where the member, Sir George Harrison, had just died. Shaw Lefevre had no knowledge of the local scene, but remembering that Harrison had been returned only after a contest with another Liberal, he wrote to Rosebery for advice, from Mentone, as early as 24 December. He put to Rosebery the concern he had about Ireland:

> I am personally in favour of going a long way in the direction of Federation with a local and subordinate Legislature for Ireland, very much as sketched out by Childers – would such views be favourably received at Edinburgh at this moment. Would there not be . . . opposition from the party who have returned Goschen? My candidature with these views might tend to widen the split between the two sections of the party.[57]

Rosebery's response is unknown, but it turned out that Childers who, like George, had lost his seat in the general election, had been chosen by Harrison's backers to contest South Edinburgh, to the dismay of the more radically inclined. George involved Chamberlain, and what transpired is best told in a letter to Chamberlain early in the New Year:

I ought sooner to have written to you to thank you for your intervention on my behalf in South Edinburgh. I had many communications by telegraph on the subject from the advanced Liberals of that division who appeared to be very dissatisfied with the selection of Childers by the supporters of Sir George Harrison. I feel little doubt that I should have been selected as the candidate in preference to him if the whole party had been consulted. When however I heard that he had already been announced publicly as a candidate I did not feel justified in accepting the offer of the advanced party to stand against him however good the chances might be. I telegraphed therefore that I could not allow my name to be brought forward.

And in the same letter he distanced himself a little from both Chamberlain and Gladstone over Ireland by insisting that:

it is of no use to attempt any measure which has not the hearty support of the Irish party. I should not be unprepared to go further in the direction of Federation if I could be certain of giving full satisfaction and of affecting a final settlement; but in default of this it would I think be better to attempt nothing.[58]

Though George was desperate to return to the Commons and to be a member of the next Liberal administration, his integrity would not allow him to pander to Gladstone. He sent his leader a proposal on land purchase which contained uncompromising views about the safeguarding of the property of Irish landlords and the need to give the land question priority over any transfer of authority for law and order. This was unwelcome to Gladstone, who wanted 'to avoid anything ostensible' at that stage, though he was glad to acknowledge that George had always been liberal on Ireland and that his 'spirit is with that of conciliation.' But while Gladstone denied that he had suggested calling a meeting of members of the late Cabinet, George was excluded from informal consultations on 11 and 12 January, perhaps as much because he was not in London as for any more sinister reason. No doubt it was because he was not in Parliament that he was not invited to a meeting of former ministers on 21 January, when Parliament reassembled. And when the Salisbury Government resigned within a few days and Gladstone considered his new Cabinet, Shaw Lefevre was passed over. Probably the different emphasis which he accorded some aspects of Irish policy was a cause of his being ignored. But so, too, could have been the fact that Gladstone had been very upset by George's lack of discretion in the previous months. Nor should the practical difficulties of either finding Shaw Lefevre an immediate seat in the Commons or of putting him in the Lords (if, indeed, George would have been willing to go), be dismissed lightly.[59]

George's sense of frustration must have have been particularly intense. He was reported by Reginald Brett as 'burning to be in the new Government' and expecting to succeed to Harcourt's seat at Derby, on the assumption that Harcourt would be moved to the upper house. He lobbied Richard Grosvenor and claimed that if the member for Carnarvon Boroughs, T.L.D. Jones-Parry, was given a baronetcy, he would resign and the seat would be available. He offered himself to Gladstone as 'a working Lord Lieutenant' of Ireland, 'an useful, not ornamental one' who 'should not take his wife or do any receiving . . . but do well in the administrative business' – an interesting shift from the domestic circumstances of October 1884! But the offer was refused, gracefully by the Prime Minister, according to Hamilton, but scathingly in the Harcourt camp. And several weeks later, Harcourt was recorded as likening Shaw Lefevre to 'a shark following the ship and waiting for the first man who fell overboard.'[60]

It was the beginning of April before George's luck turned. By then, Gladstone was on the point of introducing the Home Rule Bill, and it was a little ironic that George's return to the fray as a committed Home Ruler was the result of the death of the man who thought in 1882 that George might succeed him as Irish Secretary. W.E. Forster had been member for Bradford Central for over twenty years and had been 'vehemently opposed' to the bill's principle. Since his famous pilotage of the Education Act in 1870, Forster had become increasingly estranged from the radical wing of hard nonconformist and passionately dissenting Liberal activists in Bradford, the major manufacturing city of the West Riding of Yorkshire. Within a few days of his death, that wing of the local Liberals, dominating the party organization, invited George to be their candidate at a meeting on 12 April, and with remarkable speed and in the apparent absence of any rival, he was adopted. The invitation, the acceptance and the by-election followed in quick succession. George made his pitch on a single topic:

> It fell to my lot . . . to fight the first great battle for Home Rule before the electors, in one of the most influential constituencies of England. . . . I announced myself as strongly in favour of Home Rule for Ireland, and fought the battle on that issue only.[61]

The price George had to pay was the abandonment of support for the Land Bill which Gladstone had included in the package of proposed Irish legislation. It had aroused great opposition and led to Chamberlain's resignation from the Government. Despite George's promise not to support the Land Bill, local opposition to Home Rule was strong enough to reduce his majority on 21 April to 780, roughly half of Forster's majority at the end of 1885. He was back in the House of Commons, but only six weeks later the Home Rule Bill was thrown out on its second reading, and Gladstone dissolved. George faced his third election in eight months. He fought this one, as he had the previous contest, on Home Rule. He won again, but his majority slipped to 459, and he rejoined a Liberal Party at Westminster split, irredeemably, and doomed to opposition for nearly six years. George was to stay at Bradford until 1895, and had his second spell of cabinet office still before him. But in the long perspective of his parliamentary fortunes he was to find that he had escaped from the frying pan of religious politics in Reading only to fall into the slow burning fires of labour discontent in West Yorkshire. They would put an end to his career in the House of Commons.

CHAPTER XVIII

The Governor's Lady

The Hamilton Gordons served successively in Trinidad, Mauritius, Fiji, New Zealand and Ceylon, over a period of twenty-two years until Rachael's death in January 1889; and Arthur continued as Governor of Ceylon until his retirement in 1890. There were, of course, leaves spent in England and breaks on their appointments to new places, but Rachael had a few longer spells at home, including over a year of the last two of Arthur's governorship of Trinidad, most of the last two years of his Mauritius posting, and two-and-a-half years of his time in Fiji. Some parts of these lengthy stays coincided with Arthur's leaves or his necessary official presences in England, but he and Rachael were in fact separated by many thousands of miles for more than a fifth of their married life. These separations were due to a combination of care for children, for Rachael's own health, and the unacceptability of the sheer physical harshness of living conditions in the colonies.

Of the last of these, one can cite the makeshift accommodation available in Fiji when Rachael arrived only months after the initial take-over of responsibility by the British Government – 'no-one seemed to have believed Lady Gordon was really coming, and her new house is still a mere skeleton', – and the condition of the official residence in Mauritius:

> The whole house is infested with rats – my room which has a smart blue watered paper nearly new, is covered all over with holes, out of which they come at night and scamper about. I often have to get up and light a candle to get rid of their noise.[1]

Even a sceptical reading of the continuous horror stories of housing, snakes and insects, innumerable health hazards and perpetual servant problems, cannot fail to bring home the extent of the challenge faced by a woman of genteel, sheltered and, by the standards of the time, a comfortably pampered upbringing, who insisted on having two small children with her, in places where the most robust Europeans believed their chances of survival to be distinctly poor.

Rachael's only direct contacts with her own family during her time abroad were the visits of her brother George with her sister Madeleine to New

Brunswick in 1866; Madeleine's voyage to and stay with her in Trinidad from September 1866 until May 1867; and her visit to Ceylon for six months in 1886. The first of those visits was financed by Lord Overstone.[2] Rachael was alone with her husband in the colonies for about thirteen years in all, and both her children were with them until the boy was left in England to be educated while they went to Ceylon at the end of 1883. And as Arthur was frequently away from base, often on expeditions ranging from routine inspections to wars, and not infrequently involving sea journeys of considerable danger, Rachael's life in those then strangely remote territories was often lonely and desperately anxious.

Rachael's third miscarriage, according to her doctor, did her more injury than a normal confinement. The third and fourth both happened in Trinidad, the latter despite her being confined to bed for several weeks, and it is possible that she suffered one more before the successful completion of a pregnancy and the birth of her daughter, Nevil, on 12 July 1869.[3] Undeterred by her previous hardships and by being in her 43rd year, Rachael had a son eighteen months later, on the eve of Arthur's departure for Mauritius. The boy was christened George Arthur Maurice, the last name celebrating his father's new posting. But in a typical fit of pique on Arthur's part, brought on by his disgust with Mauritius, Maurice was dropped and the son was known in the family thereafter as Jack. The boy was born on 3 January 1871, in England. His sister had been born there, too, because Rachael had been advised not to return to Trinidad at the end of a period of leave in 1868; most of the second pregnancy fell in the interval at home between leaving Trinidad and sailing for Mauritius.

The last months of their time in Trinidad were clearly happy ones for Arthur and Rachael, and the baby girl seemed to thrive. Arthur enjoyed his work, but much of the early part of 1870 was obviously spent in persistent manoeuvring about his next posting – he had turned down Guiana, he wanted Ceylon, but eventually had to accept Mauritius, which he did not think – correctly – would be very desirable.[4] After five years as a consort, Rachael was thoroughly familiar with the obligations of office and was able to take a cool and critical view of them. Among their last visitors in Trinidad were Charles Kingsley and his daughter, Rose; Kingsley was writing, as he went, his travel book on the West Indies, *At Last*, which was published in 1871. Rachael had reservations:

I like [Kingsley] . . . in many ways very much. I feel that I ought to like him more – but – between ourselves I don't think he is *quite* so nice as he used to be. He has got rather spoilt by adulation, and is slightly affected and very conceited in manner (I wish he wouldn't call me 'My Lady'!) and he likes to talk and lay down the law and doesn't much care to hear others speak. But though no doubt it *is* a great privilege to have such a man staying with us, I can't bring myself to fall down and worship him, as I fancy other people do. . . . I fancy the Governor thinks so too, tho he never says, and he likes talking to him and going out with him. The second chapter goes home this Mail; it is called 'The Cottage' [i.e. the Governor's residence]. He told me it would pay for Rose's journey. He is very careful to put nothing personal in his book. It might perhaps be more amusing if he did.[5]

This view of Kingsley, like her opinion of the Trollopes nine years before, shows Rachael as plain-spokenly contemptuous of affectation, and doubtless patronizing of those a step or two below her in the complex social hierarchy of British society. But she was also hostile to anyone who 'pulled rank'. An earlier visitor to Trinidad had been Lady Herbert of Lea, widow of one of Arthur's idols, Sidney Herbert, son of the eleventh Earl of Pembroke and a ministerial colleague of his father's, whose biography he would write many years later. The Herberts' eldest son had inherited not only his father's barony, but had subsequently succeeded his uncle as thirteenth Earl of Pembroke. Of Lady Herbert, Rachael confided to a sister that 'I should like her better if she would drop their title in speaking of them to me, and not talk of "the Earl". . . . There is just *now* and *then* something not *quite* so high bred as one expects to find in her.' This reaction is representative of a Shaw Lefevre bias against what they regarded as unwelcome aristocratic and plutocratic tendencies. We saw its early manifestations in the reputed intention of John Lefevre not to raise his family above the 'middle rank'. And in the last year of her life, when Jane's daughter was married to Arthur Elliot, Rachael wrote that 'It's everything one could wish for for Maddie, and better far than if he had been very rich, as it won't take her *out* of her own people.'[6]

Rachael had a rather precise notion of exactly which rung she occupied on the social ladder. That consciousness put her sometimes into a defensive and uncertain state in dealing with her husband and his family, while often making her appear to be particularly dismissive of anyone 'below her station'. With the elevation of Charles to a viscountcy and the knighthood conferred on John, the Shaw Lefevres had achieved an entrée to the upper levels of the Establishment. But they were 'new' money as opposed to the 'old' money and status of the Aberdeens, a clan of landed Scots of whose ancient lineage Arthur was intensely aware and proud. Rachael herself was accepted warmly and kindly, but was apparently seen only as Arthur's wife. There was almost no connection established between her people and the Aberdeens. The relationship was made no easier by the strain imposed by Arthur's watchful concern for the possibility of becoming an Aberdeenshire MP, and the jealousy of his elder brothers in this and other family matters.

Nor was the handsome but distant Aberdeen family seat, Haddo House, a place of much convenience for Rachael and a small child, fresh from the tropics – 'I have got a charming warm room . . . on the drawing room floor but an immense way off. The two nurseries are below, and I can hear Baby's voice, but it's such a long distance to get there through long cold passages, that I don't often go.' The early admiration of Rachael for Caroline, wife of Arthur's brother Alexander, does not seem to have led to any close regard, but Rachael did find Ishbel, wife of the seventh Earl, Arthur's nephew, likeable, 'considerate and attentive'.[7] She must have found it not a little irksome that Arthur's favourite relative, his sister-in-law Mary Aberdeen, widow of the fifth Earl, was held up to her by her husband as a model writer of letters whose style he obviously wished Rachael could emulate![8] At the same time, Arthur was by no means unaware of some of his family's weaknesses, understood Rachael's apparent reluctance to see too much of them, hoped she would 'Turn a deaf ear to all stories about their occasional sillinesses', and admitted that he was himself 'more disgusted than anyone else at their ignorant misuse of books and objects of art of which they do not know the value.'[9]

In comparison, Arthur was drawn much more closely into Rachael's family circle, though he came to disapprove quite strongly of some of its members. But, particularly as the children grew into adolescence, their future prospects, along with his continuous anxiety about his own advancement, kept Arthur keen to maintain and exploit his more socially exalted connections. Political considerations were also involved. It may well be that Arthur's inherited higher social status, his impatient, imperious attitudes, and his mantle of powerful governmental office, reinforced Rachael's inability to find tolerance for or consolation in the company of less prestigious mortals. There is no suggestion that she was rude or unmannerly to their faces. Indeed, she conducted herself in public with all appropriate dignity. She was described by a distant kinswoman of Arthur who had been with them in Fiji as being 'as lovable and gracious as she was pleasant to the eye – the very ideal of a comely British matron and happy wife and mother.'[10]

But her letters reveal an uninhibited contempt and dislike of almost everybody and every community different from that in which she had been raised. Almost certainly, some part at least of this hostility was exaggerated, reflecting the general unhappiness which she suffered from what might fairly be called a dislocated life. The examples which follow should be read, as it were, against the quotations illustrative of the undoubted trauma of lonely apprehension and the acute homesickness which was ever with her. Nonetheless, one can be permitted to wonder whether it was possible for her to have such sentiments as are here recorded without making them apparent, to some degree, to those of whom she had so little good to say! And if her private assessments were typical of those of her stratum of society, then the charge of arrogant insensitivity often made against the English upper classes must be further strengthened.

Rachael's interests were overwhelmingly domestic; she had no special feeling for Arthur's work, and in any case he did not care to talk about it to her.[11] She was in no sense a pioneer who threw herself into good causes, organizing schools or health services or the like. The strong religious upbringing of which her mother had been so proud did not make her tolerant of the social unfitness of churchmen or missionaries. 'It's bad enough to be Low Church, but worse to have a Bishop who is not quite a gentleman', she wrote from Trinidad, and in Fiji she described the wife of a missionary as looking like 'an over-dressed but highly respectable third house-maid', explaining in the same letter that 'the missionaries here come mostly from the grocer and shoe-maker class – their wives are generally very fond of finery – are very common persons.'[12] Nor would Rachael pretend to have enthusiasms for popular hobbies. As she wrote from Trinidad, with some acerbity:

> if only I cared for ferns, flowers, etc . . . or was something of a botanist it would be better, but I *can not* get up a real liking for that kind of thing so its no use. I never consider any particular difference between a fern worth a guinea a leaf, which people rave about, and a common one.[13]

Rachael's real concerns were with family and people of her own kind. She wrote from Mauritius, 'I shall always feel lonely in the Colonies, for I *can not* . . . take up with the people one comes across. I believe I should be much happier if I were not so fastidious.' And a little later, understandably echoing the thoughts of a thousand official hostesses, she complained that 'nearly 400 persons have dined with us in the last six months – of those there are not 10 I should ever care to see again!' In Fiji, when the wife of one senior official was leaving, she commented, despairingly, 'I really don't know *what* I shall do. She is the only lady here the only person I can ever talk to – I shall miss her dreadfully.'[14] But in Fiji, where at first she probably had the most primitive conditions of living of any place they worked, one of Arthur's senior officials was both admiring and understanding of Rachael:

> Lady Gordon is a handsome woman. I would trust anything to her perfectly good sound sense and tact. I have never seen her in the least out of temper, and she is on the best of terms with the whole household. She dresses simply but very well, but the more she is dressed the better she looks. . . . She always makes the best of things, and is luckily not nervous. Of course it is a very dull life for her here, as she is very fond of society. She has always been a very bad walker, and here she is without carriage or horses and even the paths are hardly fit to walk upon, and an afternoon row inside the reef grows monotonous. . . . The ladies of Levuka don't afford her any companions; they are certainly *not* first-class.[15]

Despite the absence of tolerable company in the tropical colonies, however, Rachael was almost certainly happier there than she was in the settlements and among the numerous emigrant British of the Antipodes. She had little good to say of Australia and reported on some large function that 'all the upper ten thousand of Sydney were there and it amused one rather to see them. They are a most uninteresting lot.'[16] And as for Auckland, her first impressions speak for themselves:

It is certainly a *most* uninteresting place very like some third rate English town, exceedingly ugly and devoid of taste, not a good building or any pretty country. . . . The population seems to consist of shopkeepers and Irish servant girls – there is *no* society at least *there is not a lady* in the place – with one exception – that I am aware of.[17]

She was consistent to the end. After less than a year in Ceylon she wrote to Madeleine:

Oh dear *how* I long to be back – I shudder sometimes at the thought of five years here! To *me* it is banishment from everybody and everything I care for, and I don't, so far, feel much interest in this place. . . . The society is horrid. There is hardly a creature I *ever* care to see again.[18]

This is Rachael's story, not Arthur's, but her life cannot be appreciated without taking account of his character, attitudes and behaviour. Hamilton Gordon's reputation as one of the three great colonial governors of the third British Empire – flanked, chronologically, by Grey and Lugard – rests on the enlightened views he held of how native, subject peoples ought to be treated, on his rejection of any notion that they should be unprotected against the exploitative entrepreneurship of white settlers and traders, and on his success, particularly in Fiji, in carrying out his policies. He was, in fact, in the eyes of twentieth-century commentators, an agreeably non-racist and, in his historical context, an efficient, liberal, colonial administrator. But his humane, forward-looking, professional persona overseas was far less apparent in his limited dealings in domestic British politics; in home contexts he was a complicatedly awkward customer to deal with as a governor and as a politician.

It is notoriously difficult to balance the qualities which people bring to their professional and their private lives. Uninhibited comment in letters between husband and wife and between relatives and friends have to be put through an even more scrupulous sieve than the public record, and the dross of immediate reaction and shallow irritation discarded. But the inevitable effect of dealing only with a person's public achievement is either to leave out altogether any mention of private life, or to treat it as

SIR ARTHUR GORDON, GOVERNOR OF FIJI.

Sir Arthur Hamilton Gordon, later Baron Stanmore, *ILN*, 10 Apr 1875.

of relatively minor interest. And the exclusive treatment of private affairs could be extremely distortive of the full character of the intimate relationships between a married couple over a lifetime. Arthur Hamilton Gordon had over twenty years of widowerhood, in which he edited his papers and, to his great credit, published a great deal of correspondence about his private life which does not always reveal him in the most favourable light. But in the preface to his volumes on Fiji he suggested that, because much of the description of their life there was taken from Rachael's letters, too much prominence may have been given to its drawbacks. In the same spirit it should be said that the portrayal of Arthur's character and behaviour in these pages should be seen as part of an attempt to sketch, from the viewpoint of a man writing in the late twentieth century, the experience of a Victorian woman. It would be arrogant in the extreme to claim that full justice has been done either to the wife – or to the husband.

As a husband and a father Arthur mixed genuine affection and some sentimentality – expressed rarely on paper and then with the maximum reticence of the stiff upper lip – with heavy-handedness, a lack of sensitivity, and more than a trace of authoritarianism, adding up on many occasions to a considerable degree of charmlessness. But he and Rachael were never seriously estranged and very rarely on bad terms with each other. Her complaints were overwhelmingly related to the simple fact that she did not really want to be away from England. One observer felt that she had 'the most implicit faith in the Governor', while being 'perfectly conscious of his little weak points' and being 'very good natured and good-humoured about them.'[19] Even to her sisters she was only on a very few occasions, in her most intimate letters, openly critical of Arthur's lack of inclination to keep her informed and his propensity to take decisions without consulting her. But however loyal she was, she must have blanched and sighed over Arthur's frequent frustrations and his somewhat priggish introspection. At the same time, she may well herself have been conditioned by her parents and by their generation to be supportive, not merely understanding, of Arthur's views on femininity which, interestingly enough, he described to Mary Gladstone (Mrs Drew) nearly a year after Rachael's death:

> I have lived almost wholly out of England for the last thirty years, and even when I was, before that time, a member of English society, I lived, to a great extent, in a circle in which the manners and ideas of yet another thirty years earlier, chiefly prevailed. That a lady's voice should be low, soft and quiet; that she should be calm and serene, under every possible condition of things; that repose was an essential indication of good breeding, and its absence a fault, for which nothing could atone, were instincts deeply ingrained in me.[20]

Not too many people, men or women, Rachael presumably aside, met Arthur's standards of breeding or of conduct, and it cannot be said that he was a man whose own demeanour evoked friendliness or liking in those with whom he was not intimate. He was short, dark, short-sighted,

> not good looking, careless of his appearance. . . . Nowhere has he been popular, since he has a very bad manner with strangers, and he is perfectly aware of it and regrets it much. He is very determined, and puts aside all opposition when his mind is made up. . . . He professes to be a thorough liberal, but his aristocratic leanings come out insensibly.[21]

There are many references to Arthur's 'not over-cordial manner'[22] and it is very true that he was, himself, painfully aware 'that I am *always* awkward and clumsy. It is the consciousness of this that makes me so stiff and shy, and too often, so disagreeable.'[23] Such self-awareness has to be respected, as has the undoubted fact that Arthur was liked by his personal staff, with whom his relations were always easy.[24] But what might Rachael have felt on receiving these messages of intense piety and self-absorption during the early weeks of her first successful pregnancy?

I hope dear that you have been reading and thinking seriously to-day. The world passeth away and the fashion thereof perisheth but the word of the Lord abideth for ever. I think you do now perceive the unreal and hollow character of everything that has not its root beyond this world. Do not I pray you let my absence from your side in any manner dull or stifle this dawning perception in your heart.

I am thirty nine to-day! It is rather an awful thought that even if one lives to an extreme old age one has now lived more than half and that the best half of one's life whilst of course the chances are that the end is much nearer. May God forgive the many years misspent on which I have to look back and enable me to make a better use of such – if there are any such – as are still to come.[25]

Rachael's 'good sound sense and tact' must have seen the couple through many of Arthur's private storms of anger, disappointment and disapproval at the world around and how it treated him; but she could only have had a less effective influence on his official contacts, which were, seemingly, carried on in an atmosphere of intrigue, resentment and over-expectation. Arthur was disliked by the Colonial Office officials in London; he quarrelled at ministerial level about postings and salaries; he plagued Gladstone about his future at home or abroad; he threatened to resign; he was furious at not being given governorships he coveted, particularly in India; he refused a knighthood in 1868 because it was to be a KCMG rather than a GCMG, and had to take the lower order three years later; and for almost a decade before he achieved it, he talked with undiplomatic confidence of his right to a peerage.[26]

Some of this explosive discontent was probably justified on orthodox political or employment grounds; and no small part of it reflected the fact that, despite his enjoyment of and remarkable success as a colonial administrator, Arthur never stopped regretting that he had not become prominent in home politics. But some of it may surely have been due to the strain of a late marriage and family, which he must have known was not productive of full happiness for Rachael and the children, because of the peripatetic nature and distant settings of his career. And through all these manifestations of his partly-thwarted ambition there ran a streak of egomania. What else could explain the slightly off-centre theatricality of Arthur's arrival back in Fiji in 1878, some weeks after the University of Oxford had conferred a doctorate upon him? His successor as governor recorded, a little stonily, that Arthur 'landed from a man-of-war . . . in full uniform, covered with the scarlet silk gown of DCL . . . thus causing considerable sensation among the whites as well as natives.'[27]

Like so many of the thousands of Britons who served in the colonies, it was

Arthur's and Rachael's parental concern for the future of the children which caused them the greatest heartsearchings, uncertainties and misery. The very existence of small children dictated the places where they should or should not serve, and their doubts about the advisability of ever taking on Mauritius, for instance, were confirmed by their early experience there. 'I hate this place as much as it is possible to hate any place where grass grows, and the sun shines, and . . . on no account will I allow my wife and children to be exposed to its dangers and discomforts', declared Arthur to Gladstone.[28] But in fact neither in Mauritius nor in Fiji was the family troubled by serious illness; it was the general discomfort and lack of facilities, together with the threat of disease, which sent Rachael home for long periods from Mauritius and Fiji while Nevil and Jack were less than 11-years-old.

It is fair to remember that such services as were available to make life tolerable in those distant outposts would be provided for the governor and his family – there was no lack of servants, however much their efficiency was questionable, and throughout their time in the tropics Arthur and Rachael had the loyal and capable help of their steward and his wife, Mr and Mrs Abbey. There was also, from New Brunswick until the end of their time in Fiji, a family member in their household in the person of another Arthur – A.J.L. Gordon, a distant cousin of the Hamilton Gordons, who was taken under their wing as a boy of 16 and grew to serve as private secretary to the Governor.[29] And for their first spell in Fiji they invited a more distant kinswoman, C.F. Gordon Cumming – known intimately as Eka – to be with them. Eka had already established a reputation as a traveller and writer of travel books; she was not a very constant resident in Fiji, as she took every opportunity to move around the Pacific, not least in a French man-of-war! But she must have added colour to the lives of the family, and her subsequent books gave them some publicity.[30] Madeleine's visits were another bonus.

The concern about the children was much discussed after the whole family went home on leave from Fiji and arrived in London in September 1878. Rachael never returned to Fiji, though Arthur hoped she would rejoin him after he went back in the summer of the following year. He had always been fiercely protective of his wife and children's interests hitherto, and as we have seen, refused to go to certain places on their account. But now, when he felt very strongly the desirability of having the children grow up in English surroundings, he found Rachael very unwilling to be separated from them. There seems to have been something of a deadlock, and Rachael stayed at home with Nevil and Jack for almost two-and-a-half years.[31] During their leave from Fiji, in 1879, the Hamilton Gordons bought the Red House at Ascot; its grounds almost adjoined the property of Rachael's parents and were quite near the Ryans' home. Those months of leave were dominated by anxious argument about the future. The pull of making a settled life and thus providing a stable base for their children, which would have been possible, given Arthur's assured private income, was indeed strong, but was not to be strong enough to deter him from going back to Fiji. As he told Gladstone:

> I quit my wife, my children, my comfortable house, my good library, my nice garden – to go and live among natives who don't know anything of one's work for them, and would not be grateful if they did, and among whites who hate one for interfering with their 'British liberty' to do as they like – with the 'blacks.' Nevertheless I have not the smallest doubt that I should do wrong not to return.[32]

Arthur left London in July 1879, speeded on his way by a special service in Westminster Abbey, and had only just re-established himself in Fiji when he learned of the death of Rachael's father. This, naturally, had upset Rachael greatly, and made worse the strain of having to live apart from her husband. Arthur, who had liked and respected his father-in-law, was genuinely sympathetic. As the months passed and his own loneliness grew more intense, he seized on the possibility of being put forward for a parliamentary seat, and wanted Rachael to get legal advice as to whether he could stand whilst holding his gubernatorial office. When Rachael told him Gladstone was thinking that the time had come for him to come home, he responded, 'If only they would settle the point by electing me to the House of Commons, in my absence, it would greatly simplify matters. I should accept that as an indication where my place lay.'[33] Almost at the end of 1879, he wrote to Rachael that she would

> be amused, and by no means ill-pleased, to hear that I am at last beginning to have some wish to live in England. You see, having a house of one's own makes a great difference, and it is manifestly better for the children. If only I were able to afford it, and if the climate of England were less thoroughly detestable.[34]

And at about the same time he declared that 'if we can live in tolerable comfort at Ascot, I will get home as soon as I can – say in the course of next year.'[35] But it was not to be. Nothing came of the parliamentary seat, and the next move was to be antipodean.

How much of the official changes in Arthur's life in 1880–2 reflected purely political and administrative manoeuvring, and how much they were the result, in part, of Arthur's attempts to cope with the unsatisfactory separation from his family, is difficult to assess. In addition to being the first Governor of Fiji, he had been made High Commissioner 'in and over' the Western Pacific, in September 1877. He was utterly devoted to Fiji and to the desirability of embedding his administrative ideas there so firmly that they could not be reversed, that he wanted to go on beyond a normal term of service. But no doubt because he genuinely yearned to have his family with him, he began to put forward the notion of being appointed governor of one of the Australian self-governing colonies and combining it with the governorship of Fiji. This was not accepted by Lord Kimberley, the Colonial Secretary, but towards the end of 1880, Arthur was appointed Governor of New Zealand while retaining an uncertain degree of authority over native affairs in Fiji. It was an extremely clumsy and equivocal arrangement which assumed that Arthur, from what would be his normal base at Wellington, would make occasional visits to Fiji. But the distance alone made it impossible for Arthur to wield personal authority in Fiji, and relations with the new governor there were inescapably embarrassing. Thus the outcome was the worst of all possible worlds for Arthur – he had an authority he could not exercise effectively in the place he wanted to be, and his substantive job, as constitutional figure-head of self-governing New Zealand, was one which he hated and despised.[36]

But at least he could be reunited with his family. When the New Zealand appointment was definite, Rachael was able to go and was able and willing to take the children with her. But if Arthur had indeed used his influence to bring about this arrangement, he was at his most ungracious and unkind in discussing it with his wife. And the anger, bitterness, self-pity and reproach which she suffered from him evoked some justifiably sharp responses. It was a miserable time for them both. Rachael began to prepare to leave England late in November 1880, but did not sail until nearly the end of the following February. She wrote to Arthur:

> I have no pleasure in thinking of what will be so very distasteful to you. . . . I know *well* that you will hate New Zealand. I don't think that as far as *you* are concerned, there is any redeeming point in it, excepting *perhaps* being able to have your children with you – and you cannot suppose that I shall like it, if you are always unhappy. In fact the more I look at it the less I like the idea of the whole thing. . . . I am quite sick of being told by everyone else I see, *how* fortunate we are and what a very delightful life it will be. I know you must have felt *very* sorry when you left Fiji. I cannot of course feel the same as you do about it . . . you cannot expect me to be very fond of a place which has been the cause of this dreadful long separation from you. If I had gone back next Spring, I believe I must have left Jack, at least, behind if not both – tho' I don't know *how* I could have made up my mind to do it, or to live there without them.[37]

Arthur was by then installed in Wellington and already passionate about escaping from what he regarded as a near hopeless situation:

> I give you fair warning that I think our stay here *very precarious*. So long as I can manage to keep the control of Fiji we may get on, and for your sake and the childrens' I shall be well content to endure my life here but should

that prove unworkable, which is very likely, I have already seen enough of the government here to convince me that it would be quite *impossible* for me to continue for any time to fill the office of 'Governor' (Heaven save the mark!) of such a Colony. My one great desire then would be to get home but I should *try* to finish my time for pension qualification first. My first object is to prevent my work in Fiji being undone, my next is to be at home in my own house and with leisure to write my father's life. Here there is nothing of any real consequence to *do*, but at the same time there is no *leisure*, the Governor's time being taken up by petty and profitless routine duties and 'social' functions.[38]

This was followed by more, in the same vein, at shorter length. Poor Rachael! It is hardly surprising that she found that the letters were so 'unsatisfactory and always make me feel so miserable – that I feel more cut off from you than ever. I think it is horrid to have our lives so completely separated.' And not long before she sailed she confessed how unhappy she was about his being 'hampered by her and children' and because he was giving up Fiji for their sakes.[39]

Arthur kept up his self-pitying rage all through Rachael's long journey to join him. In Sydney she was greeted by a warning – 'you must not expect the sadness caused [by] the bitter disappointment of my wasted work – I may say my wasted life – to be hastily if ever effaced. It will be long before I take any interest, in anything whatever, again.' To which Rachael responded, '*Remember* that my hair is *quite* grey now – I think this anxious six weeks has finished it off!!!' But Arthur was never one to concede the last word to anybody else: 'You say you have grown grey. You must be prepared to find a great change in me in that respect also, and not in that respect alone. The last six months have aged me very much.'[40]

The family was together in New Zealand, save for Arthur's extended visits to Fiji, only from May 1881 for about fifteen months. Arthur had lost no time in complaining to London about his situation, and even before Rachael had arrived in Wellington he had been offered Jamaica by the Secretary of State, Lord Kimberley; that was an offer apparently kept open, but even when leaving the antipodes in August 1882, Arthur admitted to Rachael that he had no inclination to accept. They returned to England, apparently, without any certainty of another appointment. But their sojourn in New Zealand repaired at least some of the emotional ravages which the long separation had inflicted. Arthur's prose about the place was always purple – 'I hate it all most cordially – the Brummagen state on the one hand, the insolent familiarity on the other',[41] and Rachael was not enamoured of the society. But they were able to live for part of the time in Christchurch, of which they both became fond, Jack was able to attend a normal school, and the climate was, for Rachael and the children, not a problem.

Rachael packed up and went to Sydney to await Arthur, who was making a last trip to Fiji, in August 1882. When Arthur arrived, there was a suspected outbreak of infectious disease on his ship, and he had to stay aboard for some weeks in Sydney Harbour in quarantine, having occasional, shouted conversations with Rachael, who was able only to come out to see him at a safe distance from a small boat. It was an irritatingly comic interlude and perhaps not an altogether inappropriate comment on the professional and marital traumas of the two previous years. They were back in England for December, and there began again the search for a future acceptable to both of them. The outcome was one more tropical colonial governorship – Ceylon. Arthur's appointment was gazetted in July 1883, but it was not taken up until December. Rachael spent most of the year's leave at Ascot, and did not accompany Arthur on a cruise with Gladstone round the west coast of Scotland, Norway and Denmark, in the autumn. That was a trip memorable mainly for the Danish visit which brought them into contact with numerous members of the European monarchies, but also for some of the entertainment offered to the guests who came on board. Tennyson, who was a member of the party, while reading his poems when sitting wedged between the Princess of Wales and the Tsarina, so far forgot himself as to beat time on the latter and to mistake her for a maid of honour. Arthur presented his Fijian servant, dressed in native costume, who 'showed us how to kindle a fire by rubbing two pieces of wood together.' Tennyson's afterthoughts are not recorded, but Arthur's enjoyment of this voyage was spoiled by the 'constant thought of my own habitual *gaucherie*.'[42]

Only Arthur, Rachael and Nevil embarked for Colombo at the end of 1883. Jack, then 12, was to stay in England. It was a common enough experience in the colonial context, this division of parents and children, and the Hamilton Gordons had kept both their offspring with them longer than was usual. For every family it was a cruel experience, but Rachael never came to terms with it. Her anguished departure for Ceylon began the last phase of her life.

In Colombo, Arthur immediately regained his composure. 'I cannot tell you', he wrote to Mary Gladstone, 'what luxury my work here is to me after New Zealand! It is work of great interest, and it is real. One has not that humiliating feeling of being essentially a sham, which it was impossible ever to escape in New Zealand.'[43] And just as Arthur adapted as easily as he always had done in the colonies he governed so strongly, Rachael found it hard to cope with climate, unfamiliarity and loneliness. This time they and Nevil shared the loss of Jack's presence. The boy was being tutored for entrance to Winchester, and living at Ascot, where Jane Ryan was doing her best to take Rachael's place in his life. But she was too protective for Arthur, who was keen that Jack should be kept in close touch with his Aberdeen relatives. When Jack was not permitted to accept an invitation to Haddo, Arthur showed himself to be as explosive over family as over professional matters. On tour in Ceylon he wrote to Rachael:

> I know *exactly* what will happen. Ishbel has 'done her duty,' and most kindly asked Jack to Haddo. He does not go. *He will never be asked there again!* It is very natural and very kind that Jane should think *first* of his health, and that she thinks is best ensured by keeping him at her elbow, but it is really *folly* not to let him go alone if he is put into the train at one end and met at the other. Jack is 13 ½ and not a fool.'[44]

It was a first sign of tensions to come.

Rachael's attitudes in this, her seventh colony as the Governor's Lady, were repetitious but frank to the point of being self-denigratory. Before 1884 was out she wrote to her sister, Madeleine:

> How *very* full your life seems to be – it makes me long to live among people again. I don't find beautiful scenery very satisfying – I know I am of a frivolous turn and care *very* much more for people, provided they are nice. The people here are *so* disappointing – so very inferior to what I was led to expect. Arthur is quite satisfied with his work, his books, and his staff, and wishes for nothing more – (except Jack). I am always looking forward to my own house next year.[45]

And to another sister she confessed to seeing 'few people, often nobody all day. There is no one I *wish* to see. It is a great draw-back, for I don't think it is good to be so much alone. I still have a reception every Saturday from 4 till 5, and the people I would rather *not* see, always care to come! There are some eight to ten people I *rather* like and rather don't dislike.'[46]

But unlike their experience of previous postings, during the years in Ceylon the Hamilton Gordons' personal lives were heavily involved in and influenced by what was happening in England. Concern for Jack's progress became entangled with the dramatic political events of 1885–6 and their aftermath, which led to so many family disputes across the length and breadth of the land. The Shaw Lefevres and the Hamilton Gordons found themselves, if not wholly on different sides, certainly at odds with one another. With Gladstone out of office, Arthur's chance of any early return to effective political life in England was simply lost. Even more intimately, the deaths of Lady Shaw Lefevre, Rachael's mother, in February 1885, and of Jane Ryan's only son two years later, were particularly hard and poignant losses for Rachael to bear, so far away. She and Arthur, separately and together, made short visits to England, but those visits did not necessarily yield the kind of assurance and harmony for which both yearned. They travelled separately in 1885, but were in England together for the months of July to October.

Rachael's sister Madeleine, then Principal of Somerville Hall, took leave, travelled back with them and spent six months in Ceylon from November 1885 until May 1886.Rachel and Nevil were back again in England from July to November 1887, and Arthur paid a visit from April to July 1888.

When Rachael left for Ceylon late in 1883 her mother was in her 84th year, and the apprehension that they might not see each other again was strong, natural and concealed. But Emily Shaw Lefevre's quite sudden death gave Rachael, her eldest daughter, some of the unhappiest months of her life. Her feelings are perhaps best summed up in a couple of sentences from a letter to Jane a month after the funeral, detailed description of which may have been cathartic, but which made miserable initial reading:

> I have so longed for a sister or someone who knows me. The staff are most kind and thoughtful . . . I know they always remember it, but I cannot speak of it to them and I have to try and talk of other things at meals. . . . I do *so* wish I could be with you. I want someone to talk to. Arthur is *very* kind, but he never knew much of our lives before – and he has so little time.'[47]

And while their leave in the latter half of 1885 gave plenty of opportunity to talk, Rachael's emotional reserves must have been sadly depleted, not only by her anxieties about her own children and about her and Arthur's future, but also by the domestic upheaval at Ascot, as her three unmarried sisters were faced with the need to move out of the big house which John Shaw Lefevre had built only twenty years before.

Arthur may have been gratified at being back in a strong, executive position in Ceylon, but he had not stopped his feverish searchings for what he saw as better things. He had grumbled – with some attempt at heavy good humour – to Mrs Gladstone at the end of 1884 because he had not been sent to Bombay:

> an old fellow like me, who has for many many years looked to an Indian Presidency as the crown of his career, cannot repress one sigh as he sees himself passed by one ten years his junior, and who has *not* served the country in banishment for five and twenty years.

But he went on to ask whether 'one of the new Scotch constituencies would have me?' and wrote again three months later to pursue the idea further, as an early dissolution seemed likely. 'I see Aberdeen is to have two Members. I wonder if they would take me as one?'[48]

Gladstone responded to these pleas by asking the Chief Whip, Lord Richard Grosvenor, to find a seat for Arthur. Grosvenor was not hopeful. Arthur, he wrote, 'is a difficult man to get a seat for, as he is one of those unfortunately tactless men who is always "treading upon the toes" of those with whom he comes in contact in any way.'[49] It was a judgement remarkably like that which Grosvenor and others were making of Arthur's brother-in-law, George Shaw Lefevre. But nothing was coming Arthur's way by the time Rachael sailed, ahead of him, to England, and he sent her instructions, in June 1885, as to how she should respond to any questions or any opportunities which touched on his future:

> remember 1. That I should *prefer* something to do at home 2. That even without employment a peerage would keep me at home and enable me to take some part in political affairs 3. That if I must still stay out of England, I should *like* to succeed Grant Duff at Madras and have some pretentions to do so.[50]

It was all to no avail: there was no new opening for Arthur. He and Rachael had to be content with seeing Jack installed, none too happily, at Winchester. They had been increasingly aware that both the children were disadvantaged, educationally and socially, by their upbringing in remote places. Nevil, now 16, was asthmatic, and had led a peculiarly restricted life, mostly without access to girls of her own age or class and further restricted by her parents' position at the very top of the official and social hierarchies of small, inward-looking, colonial bureaucracies. She had been entirely home-educated, only recently with a governess, and it is unsurprising that she was withdrawn and unconfident. Jack and Nevil had always been very close and dependent on each other's company, so that the short reunion was all too short for them both. All in all, these months in England in 1885 were neither easy nor successful in any context, and when Arthur left to return ahead of Rachael and Nevil, he admitted that 'This has been a most unsatisfactory visit home.'[51]

Arthur could not break back into home politics, but it was from this point in time that those politics began to have a divisive influence within his and his wife's family circles. The Hamilton Gordons had arrived in England just as the Liberal cabinet, led by Gladstone, and including George Shaw Lefevre, had resigned after a long spell of internal strain, and was replaced by a minority Conservative administration led by Lord Salisbury. The subsequent crises over Irish Home Rule brought a degree of ill feeling into Hamilton Gordon and Shaw Lefevre relations, and reflected particularly the temperamental differences between the two brothers-in-law.

Both George and Arthur revered Gladstone. But Arthur, despite his more intimate connections with the Gladstone family and his sharing of religious enthusiasms with Gladstone himself, was a Peelite who tended to the Whig side of the Liberal Party. George, in contrast, had insisted from the beginning of his career that he was a radical. The argument over Ireland brought out

Arthur's more conservative inclinations, though they were modified and made equivocal by his personal devotion to Gladstone and by a sense of self-interest. George, on the other hand, despite some differences in emphasis, remained throughout a loyal Gladstonian. While their political attitudes were noticeably different, the two men were in any case not very compatible creatures, perhaps because they were a little too alike in temperament. Both were strong, outspoken exponents of their viewpoints, both were rather over serious and heavy-handed; neither was the soul of tact.

Arthur had not approved of George on first acquaintance, but admitted that he found him much improved when they met in Canada and New York in 1866, attributing the improvement to the fact that George had by then had some experience of government – 'It is curious how even a short spell of office tames down a radical.'[52] Since then there had been relatively little contact between them, though what there was seems to have been cordial. When the issue of Ireland came to the fore, however, Jack Hamilton Gordon – making his home with the Ryans during his years at Winchester – was inevitably drawn into the Shaw Lefevre community. There he saw and heard a good deal of George and his sisters. The result was to arouse Arthur's indignation and hostility.

Arthur was 'greatly disappointed' by the failure of the Whigs and Conservatives to merge after the collapse of the Liberal Government in the summer of 1886. He was not, at bottom, opposed to the idea of Home Rule, but he became increasingly critical of Gladstone's plans. He veered, therefore, though not whole-heartedly, towards the Liberal Unionist camp, and for both political and personal reasons drew closer to the Selbornes, who were by marriage connected not only to the Shaw Lefevres but also to the Cecils, and thus had direct access to the Conservative leadership. The Earl of Selborne, who had been Lord Chancellor in Gladstone's cabinets but could not stomach the idea of Home Rule, was, like Arthur, a man of high Anglican sympathies. His daughter, the Hon. Sophia Palmer, was one of the most politically aware and intellectually capable women of her time. She was 23 years younger than Arthur, but during the late 1880s they kept up a considerable correspondence on political and religious matters. Those letters are an important part of the archive of the period.[53] They include some commentary, on Arthur's part, on his anxiety about Jack, and some outspoken remarks about Rachael's brother and sisters.

By the time that Rachael and Nevil sailed for England in June 1887, to spend the long school holidays with Jack, leaving Arthur in Ceylon, the stage was set for a rather difficult year. Arthur was still concerned about what he saw as the Ryans treating Jack as a child, and he insisted to Rachael that she must pay no attention to Jack's persistent wish to leave Winchester and return with her to Ceylon. The fact was that Jack suffered greatly from not being as far advanced, academically, as the boys of his own age, and was, as a result, kept at school among those younger than himself. This situation was not to improve, and though Arthur had doubts about Selborne's judgement of people, he eventually took the earl's advice to remove Jack from Winchester and put him with private tutors to prepare him for Cambridge. This did not happen until the following year, but Rachael must have carried the problem around with her all the time she was in England.[54]

Arthur's understandable anxiety as a parent over the progress of his son's education was exacerbated by his anger over what he saw as Jack's political seduction by George Shaw Lefevre and his sisters. This anger boiled over in a remarkably frank letter to Sophia Palmer, written while Rachael was on her way to England:

Jack seems to have seen comparatively little of you these last holidays, and to have spent his time almost exclusively with home rulers. I am really vexed with his radical enthusiasm: not that a boy's politics, at his age, signify one straw, but because it does a boy harm to have his vanity flattered and his self consciousness excited by being made much of on account of any singularity about him. As 'the only boy at Winchester who is a home ruler,' (as he himself tells me proudly that he is) he is made much of by Lady Frederick [Cavendish] and the Gladstones – to say nothing of his Uncle George and those *unpleasantly* violent political ladies, my sisters-in-law. Lady Frederick sends him books and pamphlets, and I doubt if he ever sees anything on the other side. George introduces him to people I had much rather he did not know, who praise his 'independence,' and thereby tend to push him into an unreal persistence of opinion in every way injurious to him. In another way, too, I regret the results of his being so prematurely political. (Not that I have any right to find fault on that ground.) It makes him neglect society he ought to frequent, and brings him into association with folk, associating with whom is by no means desirable. He has never even called on the Abercorns, who were most unexpectedly and unnecessarily kind to him last year, and I am not sure that he has given as much time to you and Lord Selborne as he ought, while at his aunts (and his uncle's) he is thrown (when they 'entertain') into a semi infidel, semi rebel, and wholly vulgar set, who are my special abhorrence – and I am most anxious about the 'milieu' in which he grows up. It not only forms for life the manners and tone, but has many lasting effects also, to say nothing of the association with others that it leads to. Do you think you could get him introduced to the Cecils through Wolmer? An occasional visit to Hatfield would be of immense use to him. I have a great mind to write to Lady Salisbury and for the sake of old times ask her to help in licking my cub into shape.

I am dreadfully envious of Rachael and Nevil who will soon see him. I would give a good deal to do the same. My Private Secretary, Murray (who is not a little man) tells me that he has so grown that he (Murray) has to look up to him, and adds that 'he is very nice – in every way - except as to his politics, which are shocking.' . . . Please tell your father what I say about Jack, and ask him to tell me what he thinks.[55]

One hopes, for her sake, that Rachael did not know the terms on which her husband was writing to other people about her family. But Arthur did not mince his words to Rachael about George. When there seemed a possibility that George might visit India and come on to Ceylon he wrote:

I confess I am rather dismayed at the thought of George coming and hope he will not. To say nothing of political differences likely enough with a man so utterly wanting in tact, to lead to serious misunderstanding, I know very well that before he has been here half an hour, he will be teaching me my business, and I may find it rather difficult to stand that. He tried that line when we were last in England.

But he sent George an invitation, which he told Rachael was an 'act of great virtue' on his part. Perhaps he was a little mollified by receiving a copy of George's recent book on Irish history, which he found more readable and moderate than he expected. But George's visit never took place, mainly because, in Rachael's view, his wife would not allow it.[56] Arthur had other worries which touched him more deeply. He did not receive a peerage at the time of the Queen's Jubilee, despite Selborne's plea to Salisbury, and this may well have sparked one of his most self-pitying missives, inflicted on Rachael in the midst of her visit home: 'The feeling that one's active life is over – that one has got to the end of one's tether – and that with powers for a much bigger position one will never rise beyond what one is, I find decidedly disagreeable.'[57]

Rachael left home, for the last time, at the beginning of November 1887. She was particularly miserable at leaving Jack, himself unsettled and discontented; and she was worried about her spinster sisters, trying to come to terms with the loss of their mother and their Ascot home, and to face life in less affluent circumstances in London. While she was on her way back to Ceylon, Jane's son William died, and Rachael wrote to her sister Mary how she had 'felt very sad and unhappy when I went away this time, especially that last dinner . . . .I could hardly speak. Was it a sort of foreshadowing of some coming misfortunes?'[58]

She had hardly slipped back into the routine of her colonial life before Arthur, who had been brooding over Jack, decided that the boy should leave Winchester. From a letter to Jane it would seem as though Rachael was exhausted over the whole issue and despondent about her life with Arthur, who took two days himself to think about it and weigh the matter carefully. Arthur is so different to Charlie [Ryan] (and most men) – I feel that he takes matters out of my hands. I had little or nothing to say. When he really gives his attention and decides, he decides once for all – he has no doubts about it – I can only abide by his decision and *hope* it is right. It makes me feel very anxious.[59]

Arthur not only made the decision, but also took himself to England to see the necessary arrangements made. He left Ceylon on 15 March, and returned at the end of July, having seen and written with sensitivity and compassion about the state of mind of the bereaved Ryans. He had dutifully visited George, his wife Constance, and two of Rachael's sisters, all of whom were entertaining 'a cad who is standing as a Radical candidate for Poplar.' It was, for Arthur, an occasion which 'would have been pleasant if your brother and sisters could have been induced to talk for more than five minutes at [a] time on any other subject than Irish politics.'[60]

There is absolutely nothing to indicate that Rachael was in anything but sound health in the last months of 1888. Her 60th birthday had fallen while Arthur was away in England, in June. Both of them, despite Arthur's insatiable appetite for other governorships, must have been well aware that their long service abroad would come to an end in a year or two. If Rachael was weary of hearing her husband's tales of being ignored, she would have been legitimately confident that he would receive a peerage, that they would live out their lives in England with their children in easy reach, and that even by their own demanding standards, they would enjoy a very adequate level of material comfort. But, given what was to happen so soon and so unexpectedly, there is a special poignancy in a letter which Rachael sent to Jane late in September 1888, in which she admits that Jack's 'letters make me rather unhappy in one way, for I feel that his boyhood is now over, and he will be a man when I see him, and he must be changed. Seven years is a long time to be away.'[61]

Rachael's near escape from death as an infant; her adolescent illness; four or five miscarriages after a late marriage; two pregnancies in her early 40s; twenty-five years of a life marked by much inter-continental travelling; long spells in tropical climates and rough conditions; and the growing strain and anxiety about her own children, her husband's career and her family at home, must have taken their toll of her. There are many references to her difficulty in walking, to her inability to ride, and to the fact that she had put on a great deal of weight. But whether she had for any time had symptoms of basic weakness or extreme exhaustion is doubtful. There is no hint of trouble until, of a sudden, she suffered a partial stroke in mid-December. Thereafter she was increasingly paralysed, but continued to write letters until the end of the year, when the doctors insisted that she should be taken to England.

Arthur and Nevil sailed with Rachael from Colombo on 2 January 1889 and reached Malta on 19th: but by then Rachael was too ill to be moved any further. Jack, and Rachael's sisters, Emily and Madeleine, arrived from England, and a specialist was rushed to Malta; but Rachael was beyond help. She died at five o'clock on the morning of 26 January. The specialist later told Sir Henry Acland that the case was hopeless – 'Right hemiplegia with Aphasia, depending upon thrombosis of first a branch and then the whole of the left middle cerebral artery.' The lay explanation was that Rachael suffered a creeping paralysis. The doctor felt it was merciful that Rachael's life had not been prolonged, as medical science could have done ittle beyond treating symptoms; and he wanted Acland to assure Madeleine that Rachael's death had been absolutely free from pain.[62]

CHAPTER XIX

Madeleine and Somerville Hall

While two of John and Emily Shaw Lefevre's six daughters married, and three of the others became notably 'political ladies' within their own family and social circles, only Madeleine Septimia took on something of the mantle of the emergent professional woman. She was, in fact, the sole Shaw Lefevre wife or daughter from any branch of the family to venture into employment outside her home, though her elder sister, Rachael, might fairly be thought to have carried near professional responsibility as the consort of a colonial governor. Madeleine arrived on the scene in 1835 – the last of seven children born to her mother in eight years. As there was then a gap of almost seven more years before the birth of the last of the family, Emily Octavia, it is possible that for quite a while Madeleine enjoyed a special status as the likely youngest of the brood. If, in this short spell, she received any particularly favourable attention from her parents, or developed signs of having outstanding abilities or qualities of exceptional forcefulness, there is no sign in the exiguous records. Indeed, we know less of Madeleine's upbringing than of Rachael's, and apart from the fact that Madeleine was the sister chosen to be with Rachael in New Brunswick and Trinidad in 1866, we can only begin to consider her experience as a woman from the time when she was at least 35.

It has long been recognized that many Victorian women of good education, whose modern counterparts think naturally of making careers for themselves in many walks of life, were able only to fulfil any similar ambitions by involving themselves in charity and philanthropy, much of which had religious overtones. Many thousands of middle- and upper-class women took part in the numerous voluntary associations which flourished, especially from the mid-century onwards, and thereby gained an experience of what we now call social work. It is unsurprising, therefore, that there are a few pointers to the likelihood that all the unmarried daughters of John and Emily Shaw Lefevre dabbled in at least one benevolent activity – Octavia Hill's concern for improved housing. But only Madeleine seems to be a serious candidate for inclusion in the ranks of those well-to-do ladies who were prepared to invest considerable effort and to take some leadership role in one or more charitable concerns. It was through this interest that she came to the attention of those seeking a head for a new venture in the higher education of women.

None of Madeleine's sisters or cousins, any more than herself, seem to have embraced the intense piety of their mothers. Their letters, even on subjects of great emotional impact, are remarkably secular in tone. They were aware of religious questions of the day but tended to comment only on their political implications; there is nothing of the theological earnestness which runs through the correspondence between Arthur Hamilton Gordon and Sophia Palmer; and even Helen Mason, married to a clergyman, wrote without any apparent enthusiasm for or even particular consciousness of religious matters. None was disrespectful of religious faith or religious observance, and all seemed to have been orthodox attenders at church, but all show a benign indifference to or unawareness of genuinely spiritual feeling, which may have reflected the strong if untidy combination of mercantile acumen, Whiggish superiority and utilitarian philosophy so marked in the male Shaw Lefevres. Madeleine was no exception to this feminine trait in the family. Nor was she an intellectual in her father's class. But she had some academic and scholarly curiosity which was revealed in her efforts to research the origins and history of her family, and she had the same cool head for leadership and diplomacy, though perhaps not the same sheer force of personality, as her uncle Eversley. At the same time, it is highly likely that the greatest influence on her character, on her developing interests, and on the opportunities put in her way, was exercised in the first instance by her shy but extremely clever father, and to an important but lesser extent by her far more extrovert brother, George.

Despite her own relative lukewarmness towards religion, it is clear that Madeleine's involvement in charitable work came at least in part through a woman of extremely strong Anglican conviction – the Countess of Ducie, wife of the third earl. What is not clear is whether Madeleine's introduction to charitable work began before or after her brother, George, married the only daughter of the Ducies – Lady Constance Moreton – in 1874. Certainly, if Madeleine had been involved before then, it must have been in a very quiet, unobtrusive capacity. Only after 1874 was there any written evidence of her participation. Lord Ducie was a Liberal who had been MP for only a single year before he inherited the earldom in 1853, and could have been known to George at least since the latter's entry to the House of Commons. From the letters which passed between Shaw Lefevre sisters at the time of George's engagement, however, it seems unlikely that they had met any of the Ducies, previously.[1]

Lady Ducie, who was only eight years older than Madeleine, had edited a volume on *Sunday Services at Home for Young Children*, in 1851, and seven years afterwards had become, amongst many other activities, a founding member of the newly-formed Workhouse Visiting Society. Workhouse-visiting was by then 'something of a rage, not unconnected with the effects of the New Poor Law and the work of the National Association

for the Promotion of Social Science, in which women played an active part.'[2]
Here, then, additional to Lady Ducie, was another possible channel through
which Madeleine may have been introduced to charitable effort. John Shaw
Lefevre's long experience of building the workhouse system while he was
a Poor Law commissioner is bound to have left him with some continuing
interest in what he had set up, while his early membership of the Political
Economy Club and his work at the Board of Trade had stimulated his concern
for social and economic policies. We have come across his sympathy for
the idea of accepting women as university students, even though he was
unwilling to push the cause along in the late 1850s. He and George were both
involved in the affairs of the National Association for the Promotion of Social
Science, and George was one of the strong and active parliamentary sponsors
of the reform of the law relating to the property of married women.

With the two male members of the family so much engaged and well-
informed in these areas of public concern, and so generally sympathetic to
female aspirations, it would not be surprising if a daughter who showed any
real capacity and keenness for related matters was helped to become active in
them. But whether or not Madeleine had already been recruited to social work
before 1874, the new marital connection brought her to the notice of Lady
Ducie, who was to be a powerful sponsor. It may also have been significant
that in the mid-1870s Octavia Hill, who had been engaged by Lady Ducie
as a teacher of drawing for Constance, persuaded the countess to become
involved in her housing experiments, while at the same time she and George
Shaw Lefevre were working closely together in the movement to preserve the
nation's commons.[3] This inter-linkage of family and charitable concern must
have brought Madeleine into a situation where she was well-poised to take a
major part in yet another new organization.

In the spring of 1875, Mrs Nassau Senior, the daughter-in-law of the economist, took the lead in setting up the Metropolitan Association for Befriending
Young Servants, whose objective was 'to befriend young girls in domestic
service and to endeavour to improve their general condition.' This was in
some respects a separate, specialized development from the Workhouse
Visiting Society, which had undertaken, as one of its tasks, the training
of workhouse girls. The new organization was to grow rapidly, and by the
mid-1880s 'was placing over 5000 pauper girls in domestic employment each
year, about 25% of them coming out of the London Poor-Law schools.' From
its first year of operation, the Countess of Ducie and John Shaw Lefevre were
vice-presidents; in 1877 Madeleine was a member of its central committee,
and in 1878 she was listed as a visitor 'in connection with the Central Office.'
When a Local Government Board report was published in 1875, referring to
the problems of workhouse girls, Madeleine wrote to *The Times*, pointing out
the existence of the new 'voluntary association of ladies' and appealing for
additional helpers.[4] These were the surface manifestations of activity which

must have been entrusted to her on the basis of her demonstrated talent and on the attractiveness of her personality. But if she was conscious of the good impression she had created, it is unlikely that she had any real inkling of the speed with which she was to be put into a much more challenging situation.

Of the two ancient English universities, Cambridge had taken the lead in making some provision for women to enrol as students: Girton and Newnham Colleges had been set up in 1869. Progress was slower in Oxford, and it was not until ten years later that Lady Margaret Hall and Somerville Hall were established. Lectures for ladies began in the Taylor Building in 1873–4 and an Association for Promoting the Higher Education of Women in Oxford was set up in 1877. Differences over religious matters were resolved by the decision to have two halls.[5] Thereafter the association made quick progress, for both the new Halls were opened on 13 October 1879. Madeleine was appointed Principal of Somerville in the previous May, and the Council of the Hall, which chose her, was virtually the same body during most of her tenure. The chairman was the President of Trinity College, Revd John Percival. He was joined by, among others, the Provost of Queen's; G.W. Kitchin, who was the first censor of non-collegiate students in the university; the philosopher T.H. Green; George Rolleston, Professor of Anatomy and Physiology; and James Legge, Professor of Chinese. A.H.D. Acland, who was to be a notable Liberal MP and cabinet colleague of George Shaw Lefevre, was treasurer, and two ladies were joint secretaries – The Hon. Mrs Augustus Vernon Harcourt and Mrs Humphrey Ward, the latter having been prominent in the early efforts to establish the halls, and the person who first promoted the idea of giving Somerville its name.[6]

The choice of heads for such important and such controversial institutions as Lady Margaret and Somerville Halls was crucial to their chances of acceptance and success. There was no lack of scepticism and a good deal of outright hostility to the introduction of women students, and the governing bodies must have realized fully the strategic necessity of finding leaders who would be persuasive and diplomatic as well as strong and dedicated. Lady Margaret Hall was heavily Anglican in emphasis, and chose Elizabeth Wordsworth, daughter of the Bishop of Lincoln and a great-niece of the poet. It would provide for 'the liberty of members of other religious bodies', but the 'principles of the Church of England' were to be paramount. Somerville was concerned that prayers would be read daily and that its members would be encouraged to attend church on Sundays, but they intended from the outset that in the conduct of the hall members of different denominations should be placed 'on the same footing', and were content to claim that 'The life of the students will be modelled on that of an English family.'[7] These distinctions in the treatment of non-Anglicans aroused profoundly-felt anxieties among the strongly orthodox. The redoubtable Dr Liddon told the Warden of Keble that Somerville 'will probably become quite godless after a short interval.'[8] Somerville were looking, therefore, for a principal who would have at least somewhat more flexible, liberal and secular attitudes than had been demanded for Lady Margaret Hall, though they needed, equally, a woman of impeccable social and moral standing.

What neither of the councils of the new halls could have expected, or would have been seeking, was what would now be regarded as an orthodox academic woman, for the simple reason that there was, at the time, no such species. Moreover, it is doubtful if they would even have been looking for anyone who could do more than give some mild academic tutoring to the new women students. Their principal concern would have been to appoint a person who could be entrusted with the pastoral care of their charges and who would have sufficient personal poise and strength of character to hold their own in an Oxford dominated by men, and still, largely, by churchmen. There could only have been a small field of potential appointees, perhaps one or two from the earlier established Cambridge institutions, and more likely, some who had experience in the secondary schools for girls which had been founded in the last few decades. But educational qualification and experience would not be very common, and one can well imagine the relief which would have accompanied the receiving of any names from responsible sponsors, and the willingness of most of the council to take the risk of appointing a person whose background, in later years, would have been thought marginal in academic terms.

A search committee for Somerville, composed of the chairman, Professor Green, and the two secretaries, began work early in March, 1879. Letters were solicited, and the council met three times to consider them. On 23 April it was agreed to meet three of the nine ladies for whom letters of recommendation had been received, but Madeleine was not among the nine. When the three candidates were interviewed on 28 April, none was acceptable, and it was agreed that the chairman should communicate to a Miss Elliot 'the unanimous wish of the Committee that she would allow herself to be proposed for the Principalship.' Miss Elliot was not among the original nine nor, apparently, did she respond favourably to Somerville's invitation. Instead, at a meeting on 3 May, Madeleine – whose name then appears in the hall's records for the first time – was interviewed and her election recommended by 'an absolute majority of the votes of those present.' As there were twelve present, this could have meant a single opponent, or a few such, or even a totally divided committee, assuming the chairman had to use his casting vote. The decencies were then observed with a unanimous election by council.[9]

To anyone familiar with the Byzantine nature of the procedures by which university and college decisions are made, this operation will sound not unfamiliar, save in the speed with which it was carried through – particularly if one has been conditioned to a belief in the more serene pace of academic life which supposedly prevailed in Victorian Oxford. But the council, having committed themselves to open in the autumn, were obviously under great pressure to appoint a principal – Lady Margaret Hall had made their choice in the previous November.[10]

Madeleine Shaw Lefevre was neither a teacher, nor a proven scholar, and was not then or ever afterwards deeply interested in the content of education. It is highly probable, therefore, that those who suggested her must have been convinced that, despite her lack of academic qualifications, she had the kind of personality and the sorts of talents which would make a good 'head of house'. There is no unequivocal evidence as to who first put her name forward, but from a knowledge of her family position, and from the scraps of comment which she left behind, we can see the combination of people within the university world and in the social work *milieu*, who were most likely to have been involved. Her father had been for twenty years vice-chancellor of the new University of London, and would be known widely in the senior ranks of the academic community. Oxford had conferred a DCL on him as long ago as 1858, and subsequently he had been a friend and fellow-worker on Civil Service commission matters with Benjamin Jowett, Master of Balliol. Jowett already knew Madeleine well and was 'invariably kind' to her, personally, though in the earliest of Somerville days he was not particularly helpful. Several other 'leading people' in Oxford were listed by Madeleine as family friends of many years standing, including the long-serving Dean of Christ Church and Mrs Liddell, the first Warden of Keble College, E.S. Talbot and his wife, and the Aclands.[11] The wife of her brother George's partner for Reading in the House of Commons, Lady Goldsmid, was much interested in Girton College; and one could speculate, reasonably, about many other personal links. But there is little doubt that it was the social work connections which brought Madeleine to the formal attention of the council.

Madeleine's own account of the whole episode, addressed to her sister, Jane, makes clear that she was first approached about the possibility of becoming a candidate for Somerville, by Lady Ducie. She then:

spent 3 or 4 days in a state of very uncomfortable indecision. Finally however, hearing that a number of candidates were coming forward at the committee and one among them who I felt quite certain would get it, I decided to do nothing – and I heard nothing more and had quite given up thinking of it.[12]

It is highly probable that the candidate who Madeleine was confident would be given the job was the Miss Elliot to whom the council had sent so pressing an invitation. This lady was much involved in the workhouse visiting movement, and had published a pamphlet on the subject some while before.[13] It is quite likely that the Countess of Ducie may have suggested Miss Elliot first, and that on that lady's refusal John Percival, a man of considerable drive and determination, may well have exercised a chairman's prerogative and turned immediately to Madeleine.

Percival had been Headmaster of Clifton, was to become Headmaster of Rugby and, subsequently, Bishop of Hereford. A thrustful man, he was looked on with some suspicion in Oxford because of his headmasterly temperament, and was 'never quite happy during his sojourn' at Trinity.[14] He had been a major force in the creation of Somerville, and doubtless bore down on the Shaw Lefevre household with the firm intention of capturing Madeleine. He came away partially successful, but may well have brooded, on his way back to Oxford, over having found a candidate who had some very firm notions of what she would and would not do. Madeleine's own account gives some good insights into her character:

> Suddenly on Friday the president of the Committee, Dr Percival, was announced while we were at luncheon and I had an interview and agreed to come down if the Committee wished to see me – but I declined to bring any testimonials or put myself forward in any way. You can imagine what a horribly nervous and uncomfortable time I had yesterday – going before the Committee was a horrid ordeal tho' it only lasted a few minutes. I had no idea they were going to settle it so soon and it quite took my breath away when Dr Percival came up afterwards and told me I had been elected on my own terms, namely – to reside during the terms and to be free to go home during the vacations. This gives me half the year at home – and tho' it seems very horrid to me to have to be away so much still I think, and I think Papa and Mamma and all think also that when a thing comes to you quite unsought, and *possible* one ought to try and do it – I think it is a useful work tho' full of small cares and difficulties and I hate the idea of living alone – I mean without any of my own people and with no one to consult. . . . I have only taken it for a year at first.

And Madeleine acknowledged her debts: 'Of course Lady Ducie's influence has been at work and she saw him [Percival] in London and gave me a benefit. Miss Elliot has also been most kind.'[15]

Madeleine was to receive board and lodging during her time in hall, and was to be paid £100 a year. Her father remarked to his brother, Henry, that the job's 'pecuniary value is of no importance, but it will give her an interesting and creditable employment for somewhat more than six months of the year.'[16]

It is unlikely that the opening of Lady Margaret and Somerville Halls will be seen as anything but very significant in the history of the University of Oxford. But at the time, though it was, indeed, a controversial innovation, it was a development on a very small scale. Women students were not yet eligible to take degrees, and though examinations for them were instituted in the mid-1880s, they were not compulsory for those who came to live in the halls. Though the women could attend university lectures, their education was organized by a committee independent of the university and of the halls. LMH had ten members and Somerville twelve, of whom two lived out, in the first year: there were only forty-three at Somerville a decade later. The halls were unendowed and had few facilities. Their administrative costs were kept to a minimum by the unpaid work done by Oxford residents and because the principals accepted very low salaries.

Annie Rogers, who taught and lived through much of the early life of the halls, left a cool account of their character and of their clients:

> The women's colleges were not founded and endowed to support poor scholars who were undertaking a course of study with a view to service in Church and State. They were opened as hostels or halls of residence, to provide, in return for adequate payment, board and lodging for women who after a few years of residence and study would probably return to the ordinary domestic life of the time, unless they entered one of the few professions open to them. . . . Their students were not all poor, but the standard of living for women of the class to which most of them belonged was simple. . . . There were able women among the early students, but very few of conspicuous talent.

The life of the two infant halls was 'simple and happy'. But though they were 'small and insignificant . . . they had connected themselves, however precariously, with a University which had a name to conjure with, even against the spell of Cambridge.' And in no small part because of their principals, they 'were not aggressive, but they were not timid.'[17]

Madeleine was Principal of Somerville for ten years. It may have been fortunate for her that she was occupied, away from home, for a large part of a period marked by family losses. But, equally, those losses must have made her particularly vulnerable to the strains of her unfamiliar and unorthodox situation. Between the date of accepting the post, and just before taking it up, her father died. As, probably, the daughter nearest to him in cast of mind, she was deeply upset. As, clearly, the most capable of the four unmarried sisters she must have been conscious of the problems of domestic management at home, her mother being in poor health and 78-years-old. The house which John had built at Ascot was too large to maintain, and they had to reduce the number of servants considerably, John's pension having died with him. It was necessary, therefore, to re-establish themselves as a family in 41 Seymour Street.

In the middle of her term as principal, her mother died at the age of 83. It was almost certainly her concern for the future of her sisters, seemingly incompatible with continuing her responsibilities at Somerville, which led her to offer her resignation immediately after her mother's death in February 1885. She was persuaded to withdraw the resignation in return for a promised leave of absence, originally suggested as running from June 1885 until Easter 1886. In fact she delayed this leave until the autumn of 1885 and then went to Ceylon with the Hamilton Gordons for six months. After her return she worked at Somerville for three more sessions, but she must have let it be known, by the beginning of 1879 at the latest, that she intended to leave in the following summer.

It was asserted after her death, by one who had been a student at Somerville and subsequently spent a little while as the principal's secretary, that it was Madeleine's humility and high standard of duty which made her send in her resignation 'while still well and strong, in the belief that a Principal with new ideas and a fresh outlook would be good for the place she loved.'[18] There is no good reason to doubt this, but there could well have been an additional family concern and a strong sense of obligation to settle into companionable retirement with her sisters. Madeleine was 54 in May 1889. Two of her spinster sisters were older and one younger. There is no indication that the sudden, grave illness and expected return home of her eldest sister, Rachael, from Ceylon at the end of 1888 was a factor in Madeleine's decision, but it may well have strengthened her resolve. As it happened, the Somerville Council appointed a committee to report on the steps to be taken to find a replacement for her only three days before Rachael died in Malta.[19] Whatever conflicting pressures there may have been, there is no sign that Madeleine ever reconsidered her intention to retire.

But if these personal losses and domestic worries made Madeleine's life less serene than she might have wished it to be, they are not needed as a defence of any apparent weaknesses in her performance as principal. While the assessments and memorials of her are not numerous, and their dutiful encomiums have to be treated with a proper reserve, the overall verdict, both of those who wrote of her during and immediately after her tenure of office and those who have looked back from a greater distance at the progress of the women's colleges in Oxford, is remarkably favourable. What William Temple described as John Percival's 'characteristically bold and unconventional appointment' of Madeleine, had rendered Somerville 'an incalculable service.'[20]

The creation of a new institution, a new community, produces an infectious enthusiasm. Even major difficulties are viewed optimistically, and at the outset a camaraderie develops which only becomes diluted with time and growth. Madeleine had to grapple with all the nagging problems resulting from a perpetual shortage of money, uncertain possession of property, and the repetitive irritations of the minutiae of domestic management. More rewarding, though often far more worrying, was the care and the guidance of her students, for the demands of Victorian propriety on young women resident in the male-dominated society of Oxford were formidable. Above all, however, what mattered most in the longer run was the business of getting the hall accepted, and that turned on her ability to foster and maintain good relations with the university's establishment. Many women could have done equally well, no doubt, as domestic manager and student counsellor; few could have achieved Madeleine's diplomatic success.

Vera Brittain, writing of Somerville seventy years after Madeleine gave up the principalship, characterized the progress of the college in a shrewd comparison of its first three heads, Madeleine and her successors, Miss Maitland and Miss Penrose, as involving two transitions – from 'lady into woman' and from 'woman into scholar'.[21] Madeleine was, indeed, a 'lady' in that peculiarly Victorian, English sense which is still familiar, if less frequently voiced. Moreover, she was not only the child of an upper-class family, but the child of a family which had moved for two generations in high political circles. From her father, her uncle and her brother she must have imbibed from an early age the atmosphere, the language and the essential nuances of that confident but brittle world, and have long moved in it with practised ease. She 'immensely enjoyed the keen intellectual wide-awakeness of those she met' in Oxford,[22] but even if she was a little intimidated by the mental agility of the hierarchy, its members and their consorts were, in her social terms, simply provincial, though she was never guilty of making that distinction obvious.

Madeleine's natural diplomacy was enhanced by her appearance and her carriage. She was a tall, graceful woman, poised and charming in manner, who wore her grey hair á la Pompadour.[23] She tended to follow the fashionable taste for

> green serge gowns and Morris papers, depicting miniature orange trees and pomegrantes, daises and sunflowers. Every lady of true culture had an amber necklace, sleeves tight below the elbow and puffed above it; any scraps of yellowish old lace she could lay her hands upon to trim her dress, mittens in the evening, and in fact attired herself as like one of Du Maurier's aesthetic women as she could.[24]

When gardening, which she loved to do, Madeleine was remembered by one of her students as

> wearing a purple dress of some very soft material with an unbelievably long skirt, a long (three-quarters length) black jacket velvety and lacey

(I always see her in black and purple very soft garments, which seem to suit her gentle voice and manner) and a black straw hat trimmed with black lace and purple flowers and tilted to one side with a slightly rakish air. . . . She carried her head beautifully. . . . Her skin . . . was covered with a net-work of fine lines, her skin was very soft and slightly tanned and reminded me of a rose petal in a bowl of pot-pourri.[25]

The beautiful manners, the serene charm and dignity, and the reputation which she gained for having been the only early head of a women's college who could ever have laid claim to 'being something of the *grande dame*'[26] was the public side of a very shy and rather diffident person who confessed to feeling 'quite unsuited' to her new position.[27] While there is much testimony to her kindness to her charges, at least one of them recorded, after meeting Elizabeth Wordsworth, that the principal of LMH 'seemed a very genial lady, much more get-at-able than Miss Lefevre.'[28] And in the privacy of her family correspondence it is clear that Madeleine had biases and dislikes and doubts which make her a more believably human figure than might be drawn from the published memoirs. She was acutely conscious of the difficulties of dealing with students, who 'are old enough to be independent and yet requiring some restraint', and she was frank about wanting to have students from her own social stratum – 'I hope I shall have some ladies as well as the professional class.'[29]

By the beginning of Somerville's second session Rachael reported to her husband that

Madeleine is gone back to Oxford, and is getting on very well there, but she is not altogether satisfied with her new life. She has a great deal too much to do and doesn't think she will be able to stand it long, and they are sending now an inferior and younger class of girls, who give her a great deal of trouble, as they can't take care of themselves, and require incessant watching and chaperoning, and are so second rate in their ways and ideas, and make sets and cliques which are a perpetual annoyance and she feels she can't influence them or improve their tone. She says that if they go on sending such young girls she will resign. I myself disapprove of the whole thing. If it has to be at all it ought to be in London. Oxford is the very worst place, with all the undergraduates to be guarded against. The anxiety is almost unendurable and Madeleine is by nature excessively anxious and almost over conscientious. She doesn't much like Oxford, and is very much bored by the Society there, which I am not surprised at from the little I saw of it.[30]

And by 1884 it is clear from the sisters' letters that Madeleine was 'getting rather worn out' by Oxford. The idea of taking a long leave in Ceylon was being considered well before the death of their mother apparently forced the issue.[31]

That Madeleine was from time to time discontented with or disapproving of some aspects of her life as principal is unsurprising and certainly not serious enough to detract from her obvious achievements, nor should it imply that she did not enjoy and benefit from a great deal of her experience. She proved to be a calm, deliberate administrator, always with a clear policy. She was a firm but discreet disciplinarian who took immense care to know all her charges closely – and to keep in touch with them after they left.[32] And any protagonist of the importance of the small, residential hall must surely find it heart-warming to read about Madeleine's general approach, as remembered by one of her students:

> she thought our daily intercourse in College should be something like that of a country house party – many independent hours, much co-operative occupation, all the deference to 'the College' which we should accord to a hostess and all the care to contribute to the common life which would be given by fellow guests.[33]

Madeleine combined very effectively her personal social qualities with her instinctive political judgement and wide acquaintance with the great world outside Oxford. She took advice from the well-established women's colleges in Cambridge. She made a good friend of Elizabeth Wordsworth and together they defused the threat of any conflict between Lady Margaret Hall and Somerville. She recruited her brother to raise nearly £2,000 from a group of political friends, though he warned her that they were not interested in education and could not be approached a second time.[34] She helped to persuade Lord Aberdare, who had two daughters at Somerville, to organize a meeting in his home to find ways of raising money to buy the freehold of the property on which Somerville stood. Within a month of the hall opening she had to weave a difficult diplomatic course through a controversy with the Oxford Union Society over the use of its library, and recorded, dryly, how the future Lord Curzon had been 'neither courteous nor respectful to us' in a debate 'described by one who was present as discreditable and vulgar' – and how she recalled the event with some drollery on a day many years later when Curzon had just announced 'his intention to propose that Oxford University shall be opened to women on the same terms as it is open to men.' Half-way through her period of service she was careful to keep away when Convocation debated, and agreed, that women should be admitted to men's examinations, lest her presence would be taken amiss.[35]

Above all, Madeleine made herself popular and well liked by heads of colleges and senior dons, and brought many of them into helpful and friendly contact with the hall and its students. She knew the importance of initial contact, and let nothing stand in her way:

> The first time I dined out in Oxford it was at a dinner given by the Vice Chancellor, Dr. Evans of Pembroke College. A fly which I had ordered failed to appear in time. It was pouring with rain. I felt it would never do to be late at a formal dinner when caps and gowns are always worn when the the Vice Chancellor is present. There was nothing for it but to tuck myself up with a waterproof and umbrella and to run at full speed all the way down the town to Pembroke. I arrived breathless but in time to be taken in first by the Vice Chancellor – a graceful compliment on his part to mark the first appearance of the Principal of Somerville – which I was so near losing.[36]

Among her closest friends and supporters were Mark Pattison and his wife. She pulled off something of a coup by winning over Ruskin, who was lured to Somerville, met and was charmed by the students, and subsequently presented the hall with a variety of gifts. She relied greatly on Walter Pater's sister Clara, who was her second in command and took over from her during the trip to Ceylon. And she brought a steady stream of important people from outside, introducing her students to them with the deliberate intention of widening the horizons of both visitors and residents.

When Madeleine's impending departure was made known, the *Oxford Magazine*, which hitherto had reported very little about the presence of women students and the two halls, waxed eloquent in its appreciation of her:

> Somerville Hall, under her philosophic and tranquil rule, has achieved solid and genuine success. The numbers and buildings have grown; the Honours even have been more than could have been expected in so short a time; the foundations have been well and firmly laid of an institution which will, as the years roll, do more and more of lasting good. There has been from the first till now no hitch, no drawback. Its history has been altogether happy, or beyond that, it has been happy in having none. How much of all this is due to the first Lady Principal, to her self-effacing devotion, her large-minded wisdom and graceful tact, we are aware in proportion as we know Somerville and Miss Lefevre herself. When she came, everything depended on her. That . . . the task of choosing a Head a second time, will not be so difficult as momentous, is her own achievement, and a great one.[37]

No doubt such public praise must have given Madeleine great satisfaction. But being a sensitive and contemplative person, it is very likely that, had she ever known of it, she would have been as much or more gratified by the opinion of her brother-in-law, Arthur Hamilton Gordon. Arthur told Rachael, in 1888, how he was 'more than ever struck with the superiority which real work and responsibility have given to Madeleine' and how he was impressed on visiting Somerville: 'She is doing really good and useful work there and is I think happy in doing it. I liked the look of such of her young ladies as I saw there.'[38]

During her last year at Somerville, Madeleine had been much exercised over the effort to bring to Oxford the young Indian student Cornelia Sorabji who was to become, in later life, an important figure in Indian political and social affairs. The problem was mainly one of raising money, and Madeleine was out of office before Cornelia arrived to take up residence at Somerville. Late in September 1889, however, Cornelia was invited to lunch at 41 Seymour Street, when Madeleine gave her advice on what course of study to pursue and, later, helped her to choose warm clothing to withstand the cold in 'the drafty lecture rooms' of Oxford. Cornelia, then 22, wrote back to her family that Miss Shaw Lefevre was 'a very old lady and lives in a beautiful house in the West End, with two old sisters.'[39] Madeleine, let alone her sisters, might have felt that to attribute old age to ladies in their mid and late 50s, was rather premature; but there is a sense in which the young Indian woman was quite perceptive, for it is hard to avoid feeling that Madeleine dropped out of a very active professional life rather early, but had been aged by her experience.

CHAPTER XX

The Bradford Years

George Shaw Lefevre was 55 when he became the member for Bradford Central. He was a senior Gladstonian Liberal, an experienced minister, an 'old parliamentary hand', and now represented a city whose loyalty to the Liberal cause was still solid. A man so well placed, especially in the top ranks of a party severely thinned by the desertion of the Unionists, might reasonably have been expected to have been a major force and a potential contender for leadership. But for reasons already discussed, George never progressed much beyond the status he had achieved by 1885. There is nothing to show that he carried any real weight in the futile negotiations to reunite the Liberals. Gladstone recommended him to Harcourt as a possible member of the team to attend the Round Table Conference with the Unionists in 1887, but Harcourt's edited version of Gladstone's letter, forwarded to Chamberlain, cut out the reference to Shaw Lefevre.[1]

And while George published books and articles, and was a widely reported speaker, his output was that of a busy, able, practically-minded politician, intent on pursuing particular topics while not formulating or expressing any original or constructive thoughts about overall themes. But if he did not enhance his status, neither did he permit the status he had achieved to slip away from him. He kept himself in the public eye, and pressed his range of special concerns with unabated vigour. Despite the lack of enthusiasm for him among several traditional, senior Liberals, and the hostility of the new breed of collectivist thinkers in the party, he was regarded by Gladstone as too useful to be ignored, and perhaps by the weaker Rosebery as too valuable to drop. From 1892 to 1895 he found a modest place in each of their cabinets.

While an MP in opposition must earn and enhance respect among his colleagues and his constituents by being hard-working, loyal and energetic, such standard virtues in themselves hardly guarantee any special degree of popularity or notoriety. George was not popular, but he was abrasive and persistent. What ensured his newsworthiness was his utter devotion to Home Rule and his unwearying and courageous campaign against the Salisbury Government's renewal and rigorous pursuit of coercion in Ireland. His honourable and passionate rejection of coercion up to 1885 was intensified in the following seven years. It has been suggested that his attitude to Irish problems was on a higher ethical plane than that of Gladstone himself,[2] and in 1889 he declared that Parliament would never be able 'to devote . . . time and attention to those measures of reform on which the democracy of the country had set its heart', until it was free from the 'incubus of the Irish question.'[3]

Certainly he became almost obsessively involved in the battle to stop and reverse the Government's support of, or indifference to, the eviction of tenants by the most recalcitrant absentee landlords. He was a relentless critic and challenger of Balfour as Chief Secretary, though he failed to dint that minister's supreme self-confidence. He fought especially hard for several years over the troubles on the Clanricarde and other estates, and in that context he defended his distant relative, Wilfrid Scawen Blunt, who was imprisoned for his defiance of government policies. George made extensive speaking visits to the most affected parts of the country, practically inviting the authorities to arrest him. If the corpus of his writings is not impressive in the wider context of overall Liberal policies, that considerable part of it devoted to Ireland was hard-hitting and effective pamphleteering, recognized and appreciated by his colleagues.[4]

Shaw Lefevre was assiduous in his attendance at the House of Commons. There is scarcely a volume of Hansard for his years in opposition which does not record speeches and questions and interventions on his range of interests. While Ireland took first place, he was also a frequent debater on matters of defence, land law, local government, the postal service, railway legislation, public works, buildings and parks. He had always been intrigued by argument about the electoral system, and after his efforts in 1884 over the reform of the franchise and the redistribution of seats, he developed a further enthusiasm for the abolition of plural voting, which was paralleled by a passionate dislike of the idea of proportional representation. The latter became the subject of much contentious correspondence and published articles, and was to be a subject on which he was to campaign until the 1920s.[5] Outside Parliament he was busy, among other things, with a Royal Commission on Loss of Life at Sea, of which he was chairman through most of 1886 and 1887.[6]

It was the dogged persistence of Shaw Lefevre's denunciation of Balfour's Irish policy which probably provoked, on the Conservative and Unionist back-benches, a retaliatory and unscrupulous campaign against his possession of a pension for political services. After the objections raised during the elections of 1885 and 1886, recorded earlier, there was throughout the balance of 1886 and the whole of 1887 no public questioning of the award. George had taken the pension under the orthodox conditions that his private income other then his ministerial salary was inadequate to maintain his station in life, and that he would give it up 'in the event of an accession of fortune such as would carry my case outside the true scope of the Pensions Act.'[7] What transpired in 1888–9 was a campaign against George based on the assertion that his financial position had improved and that he was, as a result, taking the pension under false pretences. He also suffered from the development of that shift of opinion against the payment of perpetual pensions which Gladstone had referred to in 1885, and which was led in Parliament by the irrepressible Charles Bradlaugh.

It was put about that Shaw Lefevre had inherited a fortune. He denied it. Insofar as the assertion was not a complete fabrication, it was probably based on rumour concerning his wife's inheritance. As early as July, 1883, Hamilton recorded a problem of finding a new Lord Lieutenant for Oxfordshire, where there were Ducie estates additional to those in Gloucestershire: 'Lord Ducie might be transferred . . . from Gloucestershire . . . but the Ducie property in Oxfordshire comes from Lady Ducie and is believed to be going to descend to S. Lefevre through his wife. So a transfer is not likely.'[8] This gossip reflected a distorted view of George's marriage settlement, which apparently provided for income for George from the Oxfordshire estate in the event of his wife's death. But Constance's mother was very much alive in 1883, and lived until 1895. It is not impossible that there was a transfer of property to her daughter at the time of Constance's marriage in 1874, but less likely that such a transfer would take place, suddenly, ten or twelve years later.[9] George's financial position would have been very modestly improved after the death of *his* mother, in 1885, though certainly not by enough to justify describing the improvement as a fortune.

But whether either his mother's death or the Ducie connection had produced a measurable increase in George's income, the assertion that he was wrongly in possession of a pension was a stick with which he was beaten hard from the beginning of 1888. In the intense heat of the turmoil over Ireland there were those who attacked George either on the grounds that he had done nothing to deserve a pension, or on the grounds that support of Home Rule was in itself enough to disqualify him from receiving it![10] A short debate in the Commons in April 1888, formally concerned with the future of all ministerial pensions, was in reality aimed at George. The Government's supporters found it worthwhile to keep up the attack, irrespective of whether or not George could be proved to be at fault. As the *Bradford Observer* admitted, sadly,

> The Conservatives do not mean to let the matter drop. It is a matter of fact, and even of notoriety, that allegations about Mr Shaw Lefevre's pension have been used with great effect in election contests, to the disadvantage, not only of the Rt. Hon. gentleman, but of the party to which he belongs.[11]

There is a lack of unequivocal evidence about this episode in George's career. He never made any statement about his personal finances, and partly as a result of that silence, perhaps, there were those who continued to claim that he was receiving the pension long after he had relinquished it, and those who recalled their belief that he did indeed come into a fortune and was slow, though honest, in admitting it.[12] His wife may have come into the control of property after George had applied for his pension – one may recall Rachael's observation, in 1881, that Constance was getting more and more prosperous, and that process may have continued after 1884. And there is nothing to indicate any diminution in their standard of living, despite George's disappointment when Overstone failed to leave him anything. But even if his wife was rich, George was a proud man, almost certainly unhappy about the likelihood of not being able to make what he felt to be an acceptable financial contribution to his own household. And though he was criticized mightily by friend and foe for some of his shortcomings, he was never accused of dishonesty. There was, certainly, no detailed evidence offered by his critics – only the bare assertion that he had come into a fortune. He may have made an error of political judgement in asking for the pension; and if there was an increase in his wife's income, he might have been guilty of regarding it, technically, as not touching him. But on balance, it is probable that in the public arena he was, in this context, more sinned against than sinning.

But Shaw Lefevre was obstinate; there are a few signs that he was in no hurry to give in to his attackers, and he may have hoped that he could outride the storm. And perhaps he would have done, had his opponents only been the partisan Conservatives. As it turned out, it was almost certainly the likelihood that Bradlaugh would introduce legislative proposals about political pensions which would have been embarrassing to George, which finally drove him to capitulate. He had turned to John Morley for help. Morley acted as a go-between with Bradlaugh, but advised George that he should resign the pension before the 1889 session began. When George prevaricated, Morley wrote:

> If I were you and had made up my mind to give it up, I should do so at once and be done with it. My own notion would certainly be to send a short bare paragraph to the papers, stating simply that you have given it up – and there let it end. If any of us is asked we can say that circumstances have changed, and you no longer want it. I am sure that the less fuss, the better for you. Least said, soonest mended.[13]

George resigned the pension in February 1889.[14] For the rest of his life there were no further suggestions, in any documents, of worries on his part about money. Given the modest amount which he left on his death, it seems probable that he and his wife were mainly supported by income from her property. Indeed, George was so well satisfied with the terms of his marriage settlement that, as his wife recorded in her will, he did not wish her to make any additional provision for him in the event that he survived her. But if he did not suffer financially, his holding of the pension from 1885 to 1889 cannot but have done him harm, politically. Not only did his stance infuriate the Conservatives; it did not enhance his popularity in the House of Commons generally. And while Liberal friends were sorry that he was 'not well off', the acceptance of a pension to relieve apparent personal impecuniosity was not well thought of by at least one colleague who enjoyed real wealth. When the news that George was going to relinquish the pension reached Rosebery's dinner table, the future Prime Minister 'inveighed strongly against political pensions' and declared that 'a man embarked on politics as he embarked on any other profession with his eyes wide open, and therefore must take the consequences.'[15]

In the run-up to the general election of 1892 and the unconvincing victory of the Liberals, George hoped that he would become either Chief Secretary for Ireland or First Lord of the Admiralty – not unreasonable hopes, given his seniority, his administrative capacity, his expert knowledge and efforts in the Irish context, and his previous work on naval matters.[16] Some who did not want to see him in ministerial office, but recognized that he could not go unrewarded, suggested that he should become Chairman of Ways and Means, but George let it be known that he was not fitted for or interested in the job – surely a correct reading of his own temperament, so drastically different, in that context, from his uncle's.[17] But he was simply not a big enough political gun, among his party contemporaries, to demand so prestigious a post as the Admiralty, which went to Spencer, his old antagonist over coercion ten years earlier. Nor were his expert knowledge of Ireland, and his long battles over Home Rule and against coercion, deemed enough to override his unpopularity in the House of Commons. According to Morley, who himself became Chief Secretary, Shaw Lefevre was, 'contrary to his own belief, of no account in Ireland.'[18] Morley, however, it was recorded by Loulou Harcourt, 'had a good battle with Mr G for Lefevre and secured his retention' of a cabinet place. As a result, Gladstone considered making George Chancellor of the Duchy of Lancaster, with the intention of using him on Irish problems.[19] In the end, though, George went back to the Office of Works under Gladstone, and moved to the Local Government Board under Rosebery. In those posts he did, as he had done before, a sound departmental stint which rarely drew any excited or significant public response.

In Cabinet, George maintained his individualist, radical views, opposed Rosebery's imperialist ambitions in Africa, and espoused more full-bloodedly than ever the Gladstonian frugality towards public expenditure. Indeed, his main claim to notice in the Grand Old Man's last cabinet was that he was the only member to support the Prime Minister in the final division of opinion, over the size of the naval estimates, which was the real – though at the time, carefully concealed – reason for Gladstone's resignation in March 1894. And George's support of Gladstone raised the question of his own continuance in office.

Because it was agreed that Gladstone's resignation should be publicly attributed to poor health, the fact that Shaw Lefevre had supported him to the end, was not known outside cabinet circles. That George was sensitive on the issue of staying in office, is clear. Two days after Gladstone's resignation he was reported to be

> in a terrible state of mind not knowing whether to resign or not and saying that he cannot face his constituents at Bradford on our great Naval Expenditure after speeches he has made to them. He has tried once or twice to see Mr G but has not been allowed to do so.[20]

Three days later, immediately after he had accepted Rosebery's offer of the Local Government Board, he wrote to Gladstone explaining that he had decided to stay in the Cabinet in order to avoid the great trouble which would follow if he (George) was to resign and reveal the real grounds for Gladstone's own departure.[21] He had also been persuaded by the argument that if he retired it would leave Morley as the only 'real believer in Home Rule in the Cabinet – or perhaps I should use the word "enthusiast."'[22]

That Shaw Lefevre felt the loss of Gladstone sincerely, and no doubt anxiously, is not in question: he told his patron, after the last Gladstone cabinet meeting,

> how deeply pained I have been at the parting scene in to-day's Cabinet, and at the thought that you will to-morrow cease to be its head. I have experienced for so many years such kindness from you, and I have so thoroughly agreed with you in every phase of your policy, during the last twenty years, that more perhaps than any of your colleagues I shall feel your loss as a leader and adviser.[23]

George's arguments for staying in office were respectable but not inordinately strong in personal terms, though more defensible in the context of party interests. As with the chief secretaryship in 1884 and with the Reading seat in 1885, he chose to follow a route which, while not quite assailable in moral terms, certainly revealed the strength of his commitment to his own immediate security and status.

During Rosebery's short-lived administration, George was much exercised with proposals to eradicate plural voting; with the possibility of assisting the agricultural community through a heavily subsidised scheme of loans (he had been chairman of a Royal Commission on Agricultural Depression since 1893);[24] with the local government arrangements for London; and with legislation about parochial and district councils. Rosebery came to appreciate his abilities, and supported him wholeheartedly over his agricultural loans scheme; but they were voted down by the rest of the Cabinet, who followed Harcourt's lead.[25]

Like many of his contemporaries, George had found himself at odds with the irascible Harcourt over the years, and had not been in favour of his succeeding Gladstone. When Rosebery took over, George told a friend that, 'If only Harcourt had been more conciliatory to his colleagues the last eighteen months, he would certainly have achieved the object of his ambition. As it is he has lost it forever.'[26] But once the succession issue was settled and the disappointed Harcourt became leader in the Commons, his combative attitudes were much softened. Well after the last Liberal government of the nineteenth century had dragged itself unhappily through its final months in office, Shaw Lefevre, soured by subsequent events, came to regret that Rosebery had been preferred as premier. He wrote to Harcourt when the latter gave up as leader at the end of 1898:

> I did not sufficiently appreciate at the time, how great a wrong was done in 1894 when on the retirement of Mr Gladstone, you were not placed at the head of the Government. Much that has since taken place might have been avoided if the traditions of Parliamentary Government had then been acted on.[27]

And in his 92nd year, George unburdened himself to Harcourt's biographer, commenting – very consistently with his opinion of nearly thirty years before – on Gardiner's version of Rosebery's nomination as Prime Minister:

> I hope you will not mind my saying that I think you have attributed too much of this result to the action of John Morley. I will not deny that he took a very active part against Harcourt's claim; but I very much doubt, so far as my recollection goes, whether he would have acted in this way if he had not been supported by the majority, if not the whole of Mr Gladstone's late Cabinet. You point out yourself with great fairness how Harcourt had estranged nearly all his colleagues during the years of Mr Gladstone's last ministry. It seemed to me that a demon possessed him during this period and brought him into antagonism with nearly everyone of his colleagues. I was a subject of it myself and found it almost impossible to do business with him and I know it was the same with almost every one of his colleagues. I doubt whether any one of them was in favour of Harcourt's succession. I can speak more freely on the subject as later I fully recognized what a mistake all of us made. . . .

Strange to say also Harcourt's manners and methods completely altered when he became the actual Leader of the House of Commons instead of the occasional substitute for Mr Gladstone. He became conciliatory and good tempered to his colleagues instead of the very reverse and he showed himself eminently fit for the position and to my mind proved conclusively he ought to have been selected for the higher post.[28]

If George Shaw Lefevre contributed to the establishment of a Rosebery government, he also had a part in bringing it to an end: he was one of several ministers who were absent, unpaired, when a snap division was forced in the House – the famous 'Cordite Vote' – on 21 June 1895, and the Government was defeated. He was among the large majority of the Cabinet who subsequently thought that dissolution would be preferable to resignation, but who were overridden by Rosebery.[29] When the new Conservative administration was formed and almost immediately asked for and received a dissolution of Parliament, George was too experienced a politician to have been unduly optimistic about his party's chances. But certainly he was not over-anxious about his own situation, and went north to fight his seat, confident that he could look forward to several more years near the top of the parliamentary and party lists, even if in opposition rather than in power. As it happened, the electorate as a whole confirmed, unequivocally, any doubts George may have had about the acceptability of the Liberals. But to his immense chagrin, the voters of Bradford Central rudely and unexpectedly removed him from the Commons and, effectively, ruined any last chance he may have had of being counted among the very top leaders of the Liberal Party.

Bradford in 1886, though still a fast-growing city, had already passed the peak of its prosperity and industrial expansion as a leading centre of textile manufacture. Such a judgement would have been ill-received there by a proud community at that time. But the depression of the 1880s had reduced profits and increased costs. Wage levels had dropped and labour relations deteriorated. Nonetheless, Bradford was still loyal to the Liberals, reflecting the devotion of the merchant class to the economics of the Manchester School, and the strength of nonconformism, with its demands for the full freedom of the individual to exercise his rights in the spheres of religion and education. But despite the apparent strength of the Liberal Party, there were signs that the long-term trend was towards conservatism. In the light of increasing foreign competition and the worsening relations between capital and labour, there was a dawning recognition among the employing and middle classes of their common economic interest; while among the wealthier descendants of the earlier entrepreneurial generation, whose stern, unbending nonconformity had kept them apart from the more leisured class of long-established and predominantly Anglican country gentry, the appeal of a less rugged, more self-indulgent and more elitist social milieu was not to be denied.

The population of Bradford increased from about 200,000 to a quarter of a million during George Shaw Lefevre's ten year representation of the Central constituency. His was one of three single member constituencies introduced by the redistribution of seats in 1884. Together with the immediately adjacent town and constituency of Shipley, they covered a cohesive sector of the industrial West Riding of Yorkshire. The populace was less indigenous than might have been imagined. Industrial development had attracted as immigrants a considerable group of entrepreneurial Germans, who brought with them much cultural enthusiasm, particularly for music, as well as business acumen, and who by 1880 were well-accepted members of Bradford's mercantile establishment. At the other end of the economic and social scale was a sizeable contingent of Irish Catholic labouring men and their families. In Central Bradford these Irish voters numbered about 1,100, or over 10 per cent of the electorate. George's constituents were mainly men of modest means, but there was also on the register a significant number of business votes, many of them in respect of freehold properties owned within Central Bradford by more well-to-do voters resident in neighbouring areas.

As we have seen, the most famous of Bradford's Gladstonian politicians, W.E. Forster, had moved steadily to the right. His famous Education Bill of 1870 had involved compromises which had alienated his more fervent nonconformist supporters, while more recently his seemingly repressive attitudes as Irish Secretary had antagonized not only his Irish constituents but also many of the more radical elements in his party. Well before he died, at the beginning of 1886, therefore, the still dominant Liberals were divided. There was a moderate wing in which many of the most successful merchants, including the German immigrants, and most of the lawyers and businessmen with Anglican or mild nonconformist affiliations, found a congenial home. And there was a radical wing of hard dissenters and passionate economic individualists, still focused on the concerns of the nonconformists for the completion of the movement to eradicate all remnants of bias in religious and educational matters – a concern carrying with it a basic sympathy towards the Irish for the disabilities which they suffered.

But among the working-class men who were, or were about to be, enfranchised and unionized, and who hitherto had turned naturally to the Liberal Party, there was a growing consciousness of the problem of getting satisfaction from Liberals, whose extreme economic individualism denied the claims of those who suffered the most severe impact of market forces, for any collectivist approach which would relieve the miseries of unemployment and poverty. This dilemma was well recognized within the radical wing of the party, but was partly masked by the loyalty of a high proportion of workers, who were suspicious of the more extreme brand of trade union leaders. Ultimately, the party's failure to come to terms with the more militant labour people was the main factor in the disaster of 1895. But a decade earlier it had not seemed important by comparison with other issues.[30]

Before the redistribution of seats in 1884, the two member constituency of Bradford had been represented by distinctly opposed Liberals – Forster and the radical Alfred Illingworth, a wealthy manufacturer and large employer of local labour. When Forster died, Illingworth's faction quickly gained control of the party. Born and bred and entrepreneurially successful in the city, Illingworth was an unyielding nonconformist, a strong fighter for religious and educational equality, a supporter of Gladstone's policies for Ireland, but a totally committed free-marketeer who was strongly opposed to any further limitations of the conditions of employment. There is a strong hint that it was Illingworth who managed the ready acceptance of George Shaw Lefevre as successor to Forster.[31]

Though the more radical Liberals had not had much love for Forster, they were used to having a senior member of the Liberal government as their representative. George had achieved cabinet rank in 1885, he had strong Cobdenite beliefs, he had served at the Board of Trade, and he was a prominent radical of Illingworth's general persuasion. His stance against coercion and in favour of Home Rule was impeccably radical and strongly attractive for a constituency with many Irish voters. George, desperate to return to the House of Commons, and Central Bradford Liberals, wanting a prestigious party figure and a return to radical respectability after a long, bruising encounter with Forster, were seemingly made for each other.

And indeed, for several years there was mutual harmony and confidence between the Liberal hierarchy in Bradford and their new member. It is true that many of the moderate wing of the party, already leaning to the right, had embraced the Unionist position over Ireland, and that in the elections of 1886 Shaw Lefevre lost half the majority which Forster had enjoyed. Nonetheless, he was comfortably ensconced, and the local party hung together well, once it had digested the loss of some seven hundred previous supporters. George himself, almost certainly wisely from a constituency standpoint, concentrated on the Irish controversy and avoided involving himself heavily in other than safe party topics, during most of the Liberals' spell in opposition, though interest in Ireland flagged suddenly in 1890. It should not be implied, however, that George had become a tired and cautious politician. Late in 1889, Lord Selborne, admitting that, while 'The political atmosphere is certainly languid. . . . Gladstone is almost the only man who keeps at fever-heat – perhaps George Lefevre comes next to him.'[32]

When George entered the Cabinet again, in 1892, his ministerial duties kept him at a useful distance from the affairs of a city which was then becoming a much less comfortable place, politically, for the Liberals. The cause of that increasing discomfort was a widening gap between those in the party who wanted to accommodate the demands of labour, and those who were absolutely opposed to any interference with the free working of the market.

The incident which is seen, in retrospect, as bringing the underlying tendencies into sharp focus, was a great strike at the Manningham Mills in Bradford in 1891. So harsh were the conditions which the employers wanted to force on their workers that the strongly Liberal *Bradford Observer*, owned and edited by William Pollard Byles, gave space to those who urged that concessions be made by the employers. This not only exacerbated the feeling of all employers, Liberal and Conservative, but raised bitter quarrels within the Liberal Party, between those following Byles in urging the party to adopt policies which would ensure the retention of working-class support, and those in the ultra-free-enterprise camp, led by Illingworth, who opposed statutory increase in the age at which children could be employed, and the establishment of the eight hour working day for all employees.

The strike and the mixed Liberal response gave a boost to those in the trade union and labour movement who wanted to throw off what they saw as the restraining and contradictory influence of any capitalist-dominated organization, and establish a new party which would be wholeheartedly devoted to the direct interests and representation of the working class. Less than two years after the strike at Manningham Mills, a conference in Bradford saw the creation of the Independent Labour Party, while in the general election of 1892 a Labour candidate – Ben Tillett, leader of the London dockers – stood for Bradford West against Illingworth and a Conservative. Tillett was partly attracted to stand by his 'personal animosity' towards Illingworth, whom he regarded as the worst kind of capitalist; and he was incensed when the West Bradford Liberals tried to bribe him not to stand by offering to give him '£100 towards expenses plus a free fight against the Conservative' in Bradford East.[33] Illingworth won, but Tillett took 30 per cent of the vote and the Conservative 33 ½ per cent, reducing the Liberal majority to 253. Three years later Tillett stood again, and lost again by a larger margin – to a Conservative. But on that occasion the Independent Labour Party's decision to recommend that their supporters should abstain where no ILP candidate was standing, was the main cause of George Shaw Lefevre's defeat in the neighbouring constituency, as well as of some Liberal losses elsewhere.

This major shift of political allegiance was probably inevitable, given the ideological convictions on both sides, and the social and economic conditions of the period; and the part played in it by personal differences was a relatively minor one, though striking enough for those most immediately involved. Shaw Lefevre found himself in a delicately balanced situation. He had been heavily supported by Byles, and he became and remained for the rest of his life a friend and correspondent of Mrs (later Lady) Byles, who was the most prominent woman in Bradford Liberal politics. Byles and Shaw Lefevre both argued strongly against the creation of a Labour Party, insisting that the best interests of the working class could be protected and advanced by a Liberal Party which was flexible enough to take proper account of the legitimate grievances and aspirations of labour.

George's strong Cobdenite notions never left him, and he had no socialist sympathies; but he recognized the reality of the problems of labour and the necessity of some remedial action, which Illingworth was unwilling to contemplate. Until 1895, George was – or ensured that he was – less embroiled in the local conflict which raged over many years between Byles and the Illingworth faction, and which flared up when Byles was preferred to Illingworth's nominee for the Shipley seat, in 1892. Byles won in a straight fight with the Conservative by only 282 votes, and claimed this as a triumph of Liberal-Labour co-operation.[34] He sat until defeated in 1895, but subsequently his relations with the local party became so difficult that he left Bradford some years later and sat as a Liberal for North Salford from 1906 until his death in 1917.

There were, doubtless, great incompatibilities of temperament involved, and Shaw Lefevre had his own, if less acute, problems of the same kind. Though he could claim some Yorkshire blood, and though he was apt to be tactless and abrasive, he was a southern aristocrat by upbringing and experience, a moderate Anglican, and a sort of political animal very different from Alfred Illingworth and his hard, uncompromising, nonconformist colleagues. Even in the palmy days of their acquaintance, the *Bradford Observer* remarked that Illingworth was:

a townsman, with the characteristics of downrightness, independence and a spice of pugnacity, which are dear to the Bradford mind . . . [whereas Shaw Lefevre was] . . . genial in his manner and thorough in his liberalism [but] belongs to the official or administrative class of politicians, and is thus a quite different type from Mr Illingworth.[35]

And by 1894 George could warn Rosebery, privately, that Alfred was an awkward customer.[36]

But despite disagreement over their basic attitudes to labour, and signs of increasing strains in their relationship, George was able – in part, no doubt, because of his status as a member of the Government and in part because of his own good sense – to avoid any public dispute with the Illingworth forces. And if he could not devise an effective strategy to meet the threat which was poised by the Independent Labourites, his political instincts, honed by years of hard electoral, parliamentary and constituency experience, told him in his last years at Bradford of danger from quite another direction.

Although Shaw Lefevre's majority in 1892 had held up reasonably well, as the last Gladstone administration struggled along unsatisfactorily, checked in its Irish and reformist policies by the increasingly hostile House of Lords, George realized that he and his fellow Bradford MPs were becoming the target of extremely strong Conservative canvassing. Among other moves, Lord Randolph Churchill considered the possibility of standing against George in Central Bradford, but his last illness and death, in 1894, prevented it. There was a rumour that Edward Carson might be George's opponent, and Alfred Lyttelton was invited to be, but declined.[37] George pressed Rosebery hard, and eventually succeeded in getting the Prime Minister to make a major speech in Bradford, in October, 1894, in order to counteract Conservative pressure, which was built up by visits from Balfour, Chamberlain, Churchill and Devonshire. He spelt out the situation to Rosebery in letters which show clearly that he understood the gravity of that pressure, and which underline, in retrospect, the complacency which apparently gripped the Bradford Liberals. In one such letter he wrote:

> I doubt whether there has ever been a more determined and organized attack on a constituency by the leaders of a Party. They are well advised in doing so. There are three seats at Bradford and another at Shipley . . . which were won by Liberals at the last General Election by very narrow majorities. It is the only great town in England where all the seats are held by Liberals. There can be little doubt that the loss of Central Bradford will entail with it the loss of the other three seats and will have a very disastrous effect upon the many surrounding County seats now held by Liberals, of which Bradford is the political citadel. We also have at Bradford very serious difficulties with the Labour Party, and we are threatened with Labour candidates in all four seats.[38]

George's eventual opponent in 1895 was no Randolph Churchill or Edward Carson, but a London businessman and Liberal Unionist, J.L. Wanklyn, for whom Shaw Lefevre and his party workers expressed a more than partisan contempt, and with whom George descended into a silly and futile argument over the new candidate's commercial integrity.[39] And while the threat of Wanklyn's candidature was derided, the Liberal Party's managers in Bradford weakened Shaw Lefevre's position by a complicated manipulation of voting power. As was noted earlier, the franchise allowed voters who owned freehold property outside the constituency in which they lived and cast votes as residents, to cast votes in respect of such freehold property in other constituencies. This block of additional votes was of considerable size in Bradford – in 1885 about a thousand men had more than one vote[40] – and their registration and usage was a matter of tactical importance.

For some considerable time previous to the 1895 election, it had been the practice of the party managers to move blocks of such votes between the constituencies in order to ensure that voting strength was available where it was most needed. In one such exercise, some three-hundred property votes had been moved from West to Central Bradford in 1892, 'with Mr Illingworth's assent.'[41] In 1895, unbeknown to Shaw Lefevre, at least a hundred such votes had been moved out of Central Bradford, back to the West Bradford constituency. In the event, so small was the margin – only 41 votes – by which George lost the election, that the transfer could have cost him the result. In the ensuing post-mortem this was an issue which left bitterness between George and the Illingworth faction who controlled the party apparatus.[42]

The Conservatives won all three Bradford seats, and the Shipley seat, in July 1895. It was a great victory within the general swing away from the Liberals which led to a decade of Conservative government. The overwhelmingly important factor in Bradford was the decision of the ILP to instruct working men not to vote where there was no ILP candidate. This robbed Shaw Lefevre of three to four hundred votes. He told Rosebery that there was some element of personal animus on the part of Tillett, but he had certainly not been singled out in the overall directive of the ILP leaders:

> At the last moment 400 Independent Labour men abstained from voting at the instance of Ben Tillett who boasted after the election that he had punished me for the refusal of the Liberals to support him in the Western Division.[43]

But with so small a difference between winner and loser as 41 votes, it was possible to find several other groups whose change of heart could have swung the seat away from George. There were the Irish Catholics, who were generally loyal to the Liberals, but some of whom may have voted against George because of his party's opposition to state subsidies for parochial schools; and there were some members of the business community who disliked Shaw Lefevre's strong objections to bi-metallism, a subject of considerable discussion at the time.[44] But these and the loss of property votes were not of the same magnitude as the loss of labour support. Even so, the seat might well have been saved, despite the ILP directive, if the local Liberal organization had been less complacent and had undertaken a more careful canvass.

George was disappointed and upset, but his personal defeat was softened for him by the much greater rejection of the Liberal Party. He could write soon afterwards, more in sorrow than in anger, that:

> The seat ought to have [been] easily retained and it is most annoying to think that it was lost through over confidence. What a 'debacle' for our Party. In the boroughs it has been due to the Independent Labour Party

and Beer. In the counties to Beer and to our neglect of the Agricultural interest.[45]

Byles's *Bradford Observer*, just after the Liberal defeat, wrote confidently that if Shaw Lefevre wanted to come back at a by-election or later, Central Bradford Liberals would 'ask for no other candidate . . . and be content with none less.'[46] Alas for George, he was to receive no invitation to return.

CHAPTER XXI

Kingsworthy and Eversley

It is a normal expectation that, relatively soon after a great electoral defeat, the dust will settle and previous personal and political relationships will be re-established at a civilized and constructive level, consonant with the new situation. Such an expectation was not fulfilled after George Shaw Lefevre's loss of Central Bradford. The decencies were observed to the point where a banquet was held early in 1896, at which the four defeated Liberal candidates for Bradford and Shipley were feted. On that occasion, George made only a tactful reference to electoral problems, and Byles remarked that everyone knew the result in Central Bradford had been a fluke.[1]

But the schisms within the Bradford Liberals were too deep, and the resentments against the still-dominant Illingworth faction too bitter, to allow earlier harmonies to be restored. George was firmly in the Byles camp, and Byles was increasingly at loggerheads with the party establishment. Shaw Lefevre felt himself frozen out, as his correspondence with Mrs Byles during the next four years reveals; and there were from time to time reports in the Bradford press of Liberal Party meetings in which the confusion and embarrassment of his experience in 1895, and of his later situation *vis-á-vis* the party hierarchy, could be read clearly between the lines. The broader disagreements on policy were subordinated to petty misunderstandings over contributions to party funds, and even to support for a proposed portrait of Alfred Illingworth. George was not adopted as a candidate when Bradford East fell vacant at the end of 1896, but he did not regard himself as having made any claim, and resented the suggestion that he had been rejected.

The flavour of this unhappy aftermath to 1895 is best conveyed in some of George's own words, written during 1897 and 1898:

As time goes on I feel more than I did the breach with Bradford. It seems to me that my nine years there and my four contests are entirely wiped out of all recollection and that I might as well have never been there – I don't suppose that there will ever be a change so long as the Illingworth section has control over headquarters, though what I did to alienate them I do not know. . . .

I have never been afforded the opportunity of meeting the electors as a body since the election; . . . Illingworth and his friends have shewn no appreciation of the great wrong they did me not merely in respect of the transfer of votes – in his interest – but in their neglect to give me effective support at the last election, their want of consideration for me and my wife after the defeat, and in their shabby application to me for a contribution to the funds of the Association which had been used to effect my defeat. This last must have been made with the certainty that it would be refused by me and that they would then be free to say that I had virtually declined to stand again.

I have . . . felt far more what has happened since the defeat than the defeat itself. It has seemed to me that there was a determination in certain quarters that the cause should be ignored and that no opportunity should be given for a popular expression of regret or appreciation of what I have done during the ten years I represented Bradford. In the rough and tumble of politics one must expect a defeat, but I should have liked to part with old friends in a manner which would have left nothing but pleasant recollections.

But it was not until the autumn of 1900 that the chapter was closed. 'I met AI at the Reform Club . . . he cut me dead showing clearly the most determined hostility – I really did not care to face animosities of which this was the index – so I suppose I shall never see Bradford again, which rather saddens me.'[2]

Thus did George Shaw Lefevre write off his second unhappy departure from a long-held urban seat. In 1897 he admitted to Mrs Byles that 'whether I shall stand again for any Parliamentary seat is very doubtful.'[3] In fact he never did, but he was both tempted and pressed to try his hand again, and his decisions not to do so were as much reflections of the difficulties which assailed the Liberal Party as a whole, as they were due to more personal factors. The unlikelihood of his reappearance in Bradford Liberal politics was certainly a result of local antagonisms; but the prospects of George, despite his vintage and commitment, standing as a candidate for the Liberals anywhere, were made more doubtful by the division over the leadership of the party and the connected controversies about Liberal imperialism. George was disillusioned with Rosebery, welcomed the rise to leadership of Campbell-Bannerman (with whom he maintained a warm acquaintance) and utterly deplored the jingoistic fervour of the Boer War. It was his disapproval of the imperial ethic which led him to think seriously about trying to re-enter the parliamentary fray. But at the same time he was unwilling to take on unfamiliar, difficult constituencies or to fight what promised to be particularly angry and stressful elections. He had basically sound health and apparently boundless energy, but he was 70-years-old in April 1901, two months after Queen Victoria died.

In the summer of 1897, on the death of A.J. Mundella, one of 'the gradually diminishing circle in political life of my old colleagues', George wrote:

> I am glad that I am not likely to be asked to stand for Sheffield in place of Mundella. It would be a most disagreeable contest and in the present condition of politics it would be very difficult to frame a programme or to make a platform speech. The one topic I feel most about at the present moment, the ever growing military and naval expenditure, would not be popular at Sheffield which gains so much by expenditure on armour plate and other munitions of war, and I doubt whether, after the jingo celebrations of the Jubilee, it would be popular anywhere.[4]

But by the turn of the century, reacting gloomily to the Boer War and deploring 'the false spirit of Imperialism which is the cause of all present disasters',[5] he wrote rather ambiguously to Campbell-Bannerman:

> I begin to feel that I may have to come forward again at the General Election. Though I have never determined not to do so I have been anxious not again to tempt the fates as I do not feel equal at my age to House of Commons work – but the issues are becoming so serious that it may be the duty of everyone to do his best; and if the Liberal Party is fairly united under such a policy as you represent I suppose I must try my hand.[6]

The first constituency which offered an opportunity for George to return to the hustings was Liverpool Exchange. At the end of April 1900 John Morley thought that while Shaw Lefevre would not have 'much to gain by it', the prospect of having 'a sound and honest candidate' would be 'a distinct and very real and considerable gain for the wing of Harcourt and myself.'[7] But George was not to be drawn, and explained his reluctance in a letter to Herbert Gladstone, summarizing the response he had made to the Liberals of Liverpool Exchange:

> I could give no definite answer until immediately before the General Election and till I knew what the issues would be – that I had no desire to go again into the House of Commons on account of advancing years – but that as a matter of public duty I would stand again, provided the issue raised broadly the question of militarism, which is the main policy of the present government, and which infects not a few Liberals.
>
> I said, however, that I doubted whether I should, in any case, be a good candidate for the Exchange Division, where I heard there was a good [deal] of Liberal Imperialism, with which I have no sympathy whatsoever. I added that I was a member of the South African Conciliation Committee and was strongly opposed to the war, and to the annexation of the two Republics.
>
> I repeated this later to a gentleman who saw me on behalf of the

Committee of the Exchange Division. Since then I have heard nothing more from them and I conclude that they agree in thinking that I should not be a good candidate for the division. I feel very certain that I could not win it with my views, and I don't see any good reason for fighting a hopeless battle there.

He did not close the door on other possibilities, however, and went on:

If there should be some constituency like the Montgomery Boroughs, the Liberals of which I see have chosen J. Albert Bright, who holds views about the war very much the same as I do, I would agree to be a candidate if there were a fair prospect of success, but I certainly would not fight a country constituency involving speeches in thirty or forty places, for which I do not feel equal – my own inclination would be, and has always been for a London constituency where I could speak on London questions, in which I am much interested, and where I think I have some claim from what I have done in the past, but I suppose there is no candidature vacant there with any chance of success.

I shall be in no way disappointed at not being again in the field. I could only come forward where I could speak out my full views against militarism and expansionism in all their ways, and against the war.[8]

George told Morley of his decision. Morley, resigned to an extended Conservative regime, sent him a sympathetic reply:

I should for my part have thought your presence in the new parliament of great value, because for now and two or three years to come the real operation of importance will not be a struggle between Liberal and Tory, but between one kind of Liberal and another. In this tussle, you would have played a part. But I take it that you won't win the seat, and that being so, unless you are overflowing with energy, spare time, and spare cash, what's the good? . . . The House of Commons will not be an interesting place to us for some time to come.[9]

Campbell-Bannerman was sorry, too, but understanding, and took the opportunity to inveigh about the influence of the imperialistic wing of the party:

Except by changing the men . . . I know not how this could be counteracted, and I have not been in a position to do that in the short time I have had any authority: it ought to have been done by Harcourt long ago, although even in his time there were difficulties. A good deal of what we see is due to the simple fact that among men with money that class of views prevails: and to a constituency the money is more necessary than exact correctness of opinion.[10]

One more chance of re-entering the House of Commons came George's way, but only after he had accepted that increased deafness was a major barrier to his taking it. Almost at the end of 1901, in a gossipy letter to Mrs Byles about Irish affairs, he wished that he felt young enough 'to go over there again – but alas my infirmity is growing upon me.'[11] Six months later Herbert Gladstone asked George if he would consider 'a safe country seat.' George regretted that he could not 'return at this juncture to the House of Commons', guessing that the vacancy was in 'a great County constituency in the west – involving as has always been my lot in the past a heavy contest.' It is probable – though not absolutely definite – that the seat was Clitheroe in Lancashire, for a month later Campbell-Bannerman wrote, admitting that Clitheroe 'would be rather a heavy constituency . . . and has some special troubles with regard to labour, which one is better to avoid.' C-B still hoped that 'a pleasant seat' could be found for George, and it is possible – though the correspondence is incomplete – that he tried again, in September, 1903, but found George convinced that his deafness made him 'unfit for the House of Commons.'[12]

Thus ended a quest for a seat which had begun at Winchester, in 1859, succeeded at Reading from 1863 to 1885, and at Bradford from 1886 to 1895. But Shaw Lefevre had elective ambition in his blood; he could not resist its appeal. And if Westminster was out of reach in 1895, he would seek his electoral fortune elsewhere.

When George was ousted from Central Bradford and the House of Commons, being then untroubled by deafness, he lost little time in pursuing another representative place, this time as a Progressive member of the London County Council, which had been established in 1889. In February 1897 one of the two sitting councillors for the Haggerston division of Shoreditch resigned, and George entered the lists against a Moderate, Lord Wolverton. By this point in its short history the LCC, which had originally been expected to operate quite outside the area of national political-party strife, was deeply divided between the Progressives and the Moderates, whose titles could not conceal their respective broad alliances with the Liberals and Conservatives of Westminster.

Shaw Lefevre was right to stress that he had a long experience of heavy electoral contests. Quite apart from policy controversies, his personality seems always to have aroused some elemental opposition. Certainly, the by-election at Haggerston excited much interest, and both candidates were energetic campaigners. The appearance of an ex-cabinet minister raised suspicions that George was planning either to become the candidate for the parliamentary seat of Haggerston, or to reach the chair of the LCC – both suggestions, whether or not they contained any truth, being strongly denied. Much mud was slung in the weeks before the votes were cast, and a local journal declared that the election was 'as severe a battle as has ever been fought in connection with a London County Council vacancy.'[13]

And as in many of his contests, George won, but by no sweeping majority. He received 2,226 votes to Wolverton's 1,925 – a majority of only 301. When the regular election for the whole council came up eleven months later, George and his fellow Progressive, Lord Monkswell, carried the day in Haggerston far more easily, in a much smaller turnout, each polling a little over 2,000 votes against the 800 plus for each of the Moderate candidates.

It was quite appropriate for George to turn his attention to the LCC. He had been deeply involved in the affairs of the metropolis throughout his career. In large measure this reflected his environmental interests, initially focused on the preservation of commons, but broadening when he was at the Office of Works, to cover access to the royal parks, the introduction of tramways, important replanning of roads in Westminster and Hyde Park, and ministerial oversight of the construction of such Victorian landmarks as the Royal Courts of Justice, the Tate Gallery, and government office blocks in Whitehall. He had some business connections in the City, and partly as a result of his sister Madeleine's concerns, he took some part in charitable activities. In the wider political context he had tried hard to bring about the merging of the City into the LCC – an effort increasingly resisted by Conservatives and firmly removed from the agenda by the victory of Lord Salisbury in 1895.

It is no surprise, therefore, in the light of his bouncy enthusiasm, to find a house guest writing in July 1897 that, being 'shut out of Parliament', George 'has thrown himself with his usual energy into the work of the County Council, and talked much of tramways, water schemes, cemetries and the like dreary subjects, but which he treated with great intelligence and good sense.'[14] But the same streak of independent thinking which had never allowed Shaw Lefevre to accept, readily, dominant notions even within his own party, had not been diminished by his parliamentary misfortune, and resurfaced in his relations with the Progressive Party. Towards the end of the three year term which would be followed by another election, in March 1901, George decided that he could no longer give his full support to the Progressives, and would not stand again for membership of the council. There were, indeed, sizeable differences on policy, but in addition George, who had moved his home from Kent to Hampshire, was finding it difficult to attend to so much business in London.[15] Moreover, it is not impossible that he had in mind the desirability of leaving himself free to accept any chance which came along of returning to the House of Commons – for he did not fully abandon that idea until two years later. But it could also be that he was disillusioned about extending national party warfare into local government, for at the beginning of 1903 he considered standing for the Hampshire County Council, only to withdraw when it became clear that it would involve fighting an election on party lines.[16]

Behind all these uncertainties and withdrawals was the growing threat of deafness. By the end of 1905 Shaw Lefevre admitted to Mrs Byles that 'I cannot now hear a word at petty sessions, and have been obliged to give up that work.'[17] And there had been at least one earlier sign of some loss of robustness. When Gladstone was buried, in May 1898, the funeral service had 'an extraordinary and overpowering effect' on George. He went back to his office at the County Council and, as Lady Monkswell described it, 'was probably what we would call "took bad" . . . and thought he was *going to die.*' Brandy revived him and he was sent home in a cab. It was an incident which could be seen as a first intimation of the infirmities of age, which would reduce his ability to contemplate taking any further part in the brawling quarrels of popular politics. But as Lady Monkswell remarked, rather tartly, though George at the age of 67 felt he had suffered 'a most alarming experience', he was to live to be well over 90![18]

And, indeed, while he relinquished electoral ambition, George would soon continue his parliamentary saga 'in another place'. Campbell-Bannerman led the Liberals to a landslide victory in December 1905, and, in the following summer, he recommended George Shaw Lefevre, who just eleven years before had stumped the country calling for the abolition of the House of Lords, for a peerage. And George, being the practical politician, and no laggard in the pursuit of status, accepted. He took his uncle's old title – Eversley – but he did not have Charles' bargaining powers, and had to be content with a barony.

The Countess of Ducie died in February 1895. Whether her daughter Constance's personal fortune was immediately affected or not, the Shaw Lefevres decided a year afterwards to move their country home from Ightham in Kent to Hampshire. The main reason for this was Constance's health. At the end of 1892 she had suffered from a fall, and that may have been the beginning of the development of the rheumatism and arthritis which would trouble her for the rest of her life. She found it too cold at Ightham, and by the summer of 1896 she and George had acquired Abbotsworthy House, a small mansion in the village of Kingsworthy, a couple of miles outside Winchester. The house, originally built as a rectory for a nephew of Sir Thomas Baring in the 1830s, had been altered very substantially by the time George and Constance took possession of it. In addition to the house, they also bought some twenty-six acres of land, stretching down gently and charmingly to the River Itchen, which provided their guests with excellent fishing.

The whole property cost them a little less than £10,000. Here they were to live for over thirty years – a full generation of partial though gradually extending, remarkably active, retirement. For despite the five or six years of the LCC and the explorations of new parliamentary possibilities, the move to the quietude of Kingsworthy seems, in retrospect, a symbolic acceptance that George's hectic, thrusting, argumentative manoeuvres at the highest levels of power and influence, were over. They had to give place to still lively but more detached roles as political commentator, historian, pamphleteer and protagonist of causes dear to his heart. Somehow the title of 'elder statesman' does not quite fit so self-absorbed and unrepentant a partisan, though the respect implied by it would be entirely appropriate for so independently-minded a character.

Part of that metamorphosis involved a degree of involvement in the affairs of George and Constance's adopted village. By the end of 1902 George was chairman of the Kingsworthy Parish Council, and by about the same time had become one of the three managers of the village school. He took only a limited part in the formal work of the council – he served on it for seven years and his name appears only four times in the council's minutes – but he was benevolently inclined and helped, with both political initiatives and money, to enhance some of the leisure facilities of the village. His combative liberal instincts were much more apparent in school matters; he was particularly protective of the rights of nonconformists not to be overridden by Anglican orthodoxies, and was also concerned with the material aspects of the school – its water supply and possible dangers to the health of pupils. A more onerous responsibility for social welfare, however, was accepted by Constance who, no doubt reflecting in her action the strong charitable and religious attitudes of her mother, established a small orphanage for six girls in a cottage on the estate. The girls came from the East End of London, through the Church of England Adoption Society. Constance employed a matron, who reported to her daily. The girls were enrolled in the village school, and wore grey uniforms. They were helped with their further education, and at least a few of them were launched on successful careers.[19]

George gave up the Parish Council chairmanship in 1909, pleading great difficulty in walking as one reason for so doing; but he continued as a school manager for three more years, retiring – at 81 – in 1912. It was at that time that the Eversleys gave up their London house, and thereafter left Kingsworthy only rarely. The orphanage must have become too much for Constance, who was very ill in 1912–14,[20] and it was closed some two years after the end of the First World War, when she was crippled with arthritis. The care which George and Constance showed for the school and the orphans may well have been some compensation for their own childless state.

Abbotsworthy House, in its peaceful rural setting, may well have provided just the atmosphere needed to turn George's mind increasingly to writing. When he had complained to Mrs Byles in December 1901 that his deafness was becoming worse, he had remarked, 'I shall soon have nothing left but my pen.' And though he was still able to make his voice heard in public for many years, he was less and less able to take part in debate, or to attend lectures, meetings and the like.[21] He simply became less mobile, and at Kingsworthy after 1912 he would have had time on his hands. He had always been prepared to put pen to paper, whether to address long letters to *The Times*, or to produce pamphlets and books. Whether he earned much money thereby is unknown, but he may have become keen enough to augment his income, having by now lost both his ministerial salary and his political pension. In any event, after Bradford, George was to put much of his remarkable remaining energy into literary composition – ultimately with sad results, for if deafness had made writing more attractive, concentrated study and writing was to ruin his sight.

It is a popular notion that every person has one novel within him or her. George Shaw Lefevre was one of the multitude who must have tried to prove that notion correct, and failed. In a spell of brooding resentment after his Bradford experience, he sketched a couple of garish chapters of a novel he thought of calling 'Gutter to Gutter'. Ben Tillett and Alfred Illingworth cannot have been far from his mind. In discussing the characters of his 'hero and his foster brother the socialist', he explained that:

> As I am not a socialist I don't mean to give the latter all the best of the argument. What I desire specially to bring out is the false ideal of the manufacturing magnate, which necessarily leads to the decay of his family and final ruin.[22]

If there was more, the manuscript has never surfaced, and what exists gives no confidence that George would have found a publisher for a completed novel. He was happier when making no pretence to imaginative construction.

One other work which apparently was almost finished but was never published was a study of the settlement made with the Boers after the Majuba incident in 1881. Of the manuscript of this, too, there is no trace – a matter of some regret, as George regarded it as controversial. He consulted Leonard Courtney on details, and he asked John Morley, Wilfrid Scawen Blunt and Lord Rendel for advice as to whether the work should be published. That was in 1901-2, and George went so far as to have the first part of the text printed. But he then deferred to Morley's view that the criticism in it of Sir George Colley, the commander of the British forces, who had been killed at Majuba, 'would arouse angry passions and might even lead to violence.' He abandoned publication.[23] Seven years later, though, he asked Arthur Elliot, then Editor of the *Edinburgh Review*, for his opinion of the advisability of publication of the study, to which he had by then added a final chapter. There is no trace of Elliot's reply.[24]

Jingoism and protection were George's *betes noir* after the turn of the century, and he attacked them steadily in several pamphlets either written by him or prepared under his chairmanship for the Cobden Club and in articles in major journals. His antipathy to Chamberlain, long fed by his disgust with Joe's opposition to Home Rule and with his blatant imperialism, was specially keen. Here, for instance, is his unbridled and near uncontrollably angry view of a speech by Chamberlain on protection, in a letter to Arthur Elliot in January 1904:

> there is not a single historical reference which is not untrue . . . all his quotations from Cobden, Adam Smith and others are garbled and convey the exact opposite of the views of those men . . . all his statistics are corked and are worthless in support of his arguments . . . all his illustrations for particular trades either false or are greatly exaggerated and . . . his bundle of schemes is unworkable inconsistent one part with the other.

These sentiments were openly expressed in *Fact versus Fiction*, prepared under George's chairmanship, which has been claimed as 'Perhaps the most effective and successful of all the Cobden Club's publications.'[25]

As for the arms race, George sailed into controversy with a Cobden Club pamphlet on *The Burden of Armaments*, in 1905, calling for retrenchment.[26] He fought naval expenditure, just as he had done as Gladstone's sole supporter in cabinet in 1894, and equally without success. And just as he had been accused several times in his career of having too loose a tongue, he fell foul of Admiral Fisher on that score in 1908. In an article in the *Nation*, called 'Useless Naval Expenditure', he revealed the gist of Admiral Tirpitz's confidential report to the German Emperor on comparative naval strengths. The explosive Fisher told Viscount Esher that:

> Lord Eversley behaved most disgracefully to me! . . . Eversley stopped me in the Park and I mentioned to him *'hysteria navalis'* and that we were four times stronger than the Germans on any basis you liked to take! I'm d—d if he didn't go and tell Massingham, the Editor of the *Nation*, and he [Eversley] also wrote an article quoting my private conversation.

But George went on protesting about naval expenditure, writing two sizeable articles for the *Financial Reform Almanac* in 1910 and 1911, and writing to the Chancellor of the Exchequer, Lloyd George, enclosing his own financial memoranda, in 1911 and early in 1914.[27]

In his early 80s, Eversley produced three sizeable books. The first, *Gladstone and Ireland*, the sequel to his *Peel and O'Connell*, has already been much quoted in these pages. It was published in 1912, and was reprinted in the United States as recently as 1971. It is easy to understand George's urge to write about Ireland; but it would be difficult to guess how he came to put together a study, published in 1915, on the *Partitions of Poland*, if we did not have his prefatory explanation. He had read, 'many years ago', histories of the French Revolution by van Sybel and Albert Sorrel, and had been intrigued by 'the close connection between the tragic events in Poland and the fortunes of France in . . . 1792–5.' In late 1914, Eversley felt that, in view of the intentions expressed by the combatants to reunite the Polish provinces 'under some form of autonomous government . . . a succinct and popular account of the three partitions would be useful.'

The success of the study of Poland encouraged George to write his last book, *The Turkish Empire*, in part the outcome of his long-established interest in the eastern Mediterranean and the Balkans, which began with his view of Sebastopol and his ride from Vienna to Athens in the 1850s. The Polish book ran to two editions and was reprinted in the United States in 1973. *The Turkish Empire*, first published in 1917, was republished, with additional contributions by Valentine Chirol, in 1923 and 1924; an edition was published in Lahore in 1967, and the original was reprinted in the United States in 1969.[28] For these popular and readable contributions to the history of modern Europe, George paid a heavy price. By the time *The Turkish Empire* was finished, he was almost blind. At the end of 1917 he could not read at all. He told a friend that he could 'just manage to write but I cannot read what I have written.'[29]

Deafness discouraged but did not dissuade Eversley from attending and speaking in the Lords. He spoke in almost every session of Parliament until his 85th year, pursuing topics on which he had always had strong feelings and some special knowledge or experience – Irish tenants, the Navy, municipal representation, licensing, fisheries, agriculture, fiscal policy, commons, water supplies, ancient monuments and so on – and he had his say on the Parliament Bill of 1911. Age never took the edge off his fervent adherence to the doctrines of his old chief and idol, but he was acutely and sadly aware of the poor prospects for the survival of those doctrines. In October 1914, deeply depressed by public events, by his wife's illness and by the recent deaths of two of his sisters, he remarked to Lord Farrer that the war would lead to 'a new era in this country in which the Gladstonian tradition will be broken and forgotten.'[30] He praised John Burns for resigning in protest against the decision to go to war – 'I wish I were twenty years younger and able to enter the lists again . . . I can do no more than approve the conduct of those who like yourself dissociate themselves from a policy which is certain I fear to end in disaster to the country.'[31] And his constitutional orthodoxy caused him to regret Haldane's removal to make way for Kitchener, a professional soldier, at the War Office – 'I have an old Whig prescription in favour of the supremacy of the civil government over its experts.'[32]

Kitchener was lost at sea, and the memorial service for him was held in St Paul's Cathedral on 14 June 1916. That was just two days after George's 85th birthday, and the event stayed in his amused and gratified memory because of a compliment paid him after it ended. George, when he was 21-years-old, had carried the coronet at the funeral of the Duke of Wellington, in 1852. When he came out of the Kitchener service, he mentioned this experience to a friend, on their way to the underground station:

> No doubt, being deaf, I spoke louder than I should have done. That night one of my relatives was dining out, and during dinner a man said to him across the table: 'Who was the astonishing old peer who was saying to-day that he hadn't been at a great ceremony in St Paul's since the funeral of the Duke of Wellington?' My relative didn't know – he had never heard I was at that funeral – and asked for a description of the astonishing old peer. All the other man could tell him was that he followed me to the Underground, and I 'went down the steps like a lamplighter.'[33]

It was very fitting that Eversley should make his last major political effort in a context which had absorbed so much of his energy and had brought out so much of his resilience, his courage and his persistence - election and representation. In 1917, when he was 86, and until 1924, he devoted himself to defeating the proposal of the Speaker's Conference that proportional representation be introduced for parliamentary elections. He had been steadily opposed to the idea since 1867, had published a pamphlet on the subject in 1884, and when, thirty-three years afterwards, there seemed to be a serious possibility of its acceptance, he compiled a twenty page history and denunciation of the past experience and the current proposals.[34]

While age and infirmity prevented him from taking much part in the public debate, Eversley corresponded with a wide range of influential people, extracted relevant data from some of them, and made numerous suggestions as to how the defence of the *status quo* should best be planned and carried out. Among those people were Viscount Harcourt, Bourdett-Coutts, Austen Chamberlain, Sir Charles Oman, Lord Fitzmaurice, Sir George Young, Henry L. James, Lord Sheffield, W.G. Russell, C.P. Ilbert and W. Dickinson.[35] Nothing can better demonstrate the dogged, terrier-like fighting qualities of this remarkable 92-year-old man than his response to Violet Markham, who had told him, in 1924, that she could not find any anti-PR literature:

> I believe I am the only person who has written on the subject, and that was not for the general public. But in the general election of 1917 [sic] I wrote at the suggestion of the late Mr Bourdett Coutts a memorandum against PR which he circulated amongst Members of the House of Commmons . . . It was stated by Mr Asquith in the recent debate on PR in the House of

Commons that two days before the debate, the Liberal Party had decided to make PR a principal plank in its political programme. What I want to know is, how this decision was arrived at, whether by a general meeting of the party or by some of its principal leaders, and whether any general discussion took place. . . . Asquith is going to open a campaign in Scotland on 20th of this month, and he may very likely refer to the subject. I will lie in wait for him, in case he should again insist upon PR being a main plank of Liberal policy.[36]

Whatever else of George's political and constitutional ideas may have been ravaged by the rest of the twentieth century, his spirit can take comfort in the refusal of the British political establishment, so far, to give any but marginal houseroom to proportional representation.

To within a week of his death, Lord Eversley had *Hansard* and *The Times* read to him daily, and he kept up a sharp, informed correspondence with old colleagues and friends during his final years. He relied on the local headmaster as an amanuensis and reader. The headmaster's son, Mr Alfred Beacham, lived until January 1990, and the writer talked with him only a few months earlier. He recalled his youth and early manhood within a stone's throw of Abbotsworthy House. They were not easy years for him, but his memories of the Eversleys conveyed a vision of serene but alert old age. He told how, as a boy, he would hold open the gates for the visitors who came down for long weekends – family, friends and colleagues – among them Lloyd George, full of suspicion lest any of his conversations with Eversley might be overheard; how he would accompany the increasingly frail old man around the garden, listening to Eversley's very slow but careful speech; how Lady Eversley could go out only in her wheelchair, and how she struck him as the dominant partner. And he recalled, with obvious emotion, that his father would take no payment for his services as reader and confidant, but that Eversley insisted on providing the funds which enabled the young Alfred to be set up as a farmer in Monmouth.

On 19 April 1928, in his 97th year, George Shaw Lefevre, Baron Eversley, died. He had lived beyond his political and social times. Far differently from his uncle Charles, who had died three years younger, he must have suffered, in his last decade, from a sense of existing in a world which had moved away brutally from the assumptions, the pre-occupations, and even the apprehensions, of the mid- and late-Victorian era in which he was so active and controversial a politician. He might very well have bridled at any notion that he had mellowed, even in his nineties, for he always revelled in contentious debate. On the day of his funeral, a villager was recorded as saying that 'Kingsworthy has lost its backbone.'[37] He could have added that, at last, not the most important, or the most brilliant, but certainly the most faithful of the great William Ewart Gladstone's protégés had gone, to take his place with his mentor on the fading tapestry of Victorian Liberalism – and, perhaps, to meet again the thirteen prime ministers, seventeen lord chancellors, and seven archbishops of Canterbury whom he had known personally.

Constance, Lady Eversley, survived her husband by only ten months.

CHAPTER XXII

Requiescant

Nearly three hundred years after Peter Lefevre sought refuge in England, and over two hundred years since his great-granddaughter married Charles Shaw in Tichmarsh Church, there are numerous buildings and open spaces which bring them and their successors to mind, and more specific memorials to record their presence and their achievements. All of George Shaw's churches in Yorkshire and Rutland are in use and in good repair. John Lefevre's Three Mills still stand, in the patchy, industrial quarters of West Ham. Some of the family's London houses – in Bedford Square, in Battersea, in Eaton Place and Square, in Hyde Park Gardens, and in Bryanston Square – appear, at least in their external aspects, as they were originally built, while the sites of others are not hard to find. Further afield, at Ascot and on Wimbledon Common, the houses of the John Shaw Lefevres, the Hamilton Gordons and the Ryans are substantially unchanged architecturally, though the Red House at Ascot is now part of a business complex. Parkland at Burley in the New Forest, and country houses in Hampshire, Kent and Surrey, bear witness to their sometime occupation by Shaw Lefevres.

Heckfield Place, which three generations accepted as the focal point of family history and pride, is now admirably preserved and tastefully extended, and is used as a residential training college by Racal Electronics, plc. for their clients. There is a Lefevre Walk in Old Ford, now lined with multi-story flats built in the 1960s; and in Adelaide, South Australia, there is a Lefevre Terrace, recalling the official responsibilities of a Shaw Lefevre who never set foot there. Those who would wish to do honour to George Shaw Lefevre, Baron Eversley, can be conscious of his contributions to the public weal whenever they tread footpaths and commons, or enjoy the freedom to take their leisure in the royal parks, or contemplate the properties of the National Trust. The fellows of Somerville walk and confer in the garden which Madeleine Shaw Lefevre created for the college.

The mortal remains of many of the early Lefevres lie in a vault below Hawksmoor's Christchurch, Spitalfields. The John Shaw Lefevres are buried in the churchyard of the small, red church of All Souls, Ascot, not far from Rachael's husband and two children at South Ascot. Viscount Eversley and Henry Shaw Lefevre and several members of their families were laid to rest in the huge, unkempt yet compellingly peaceful cemetery at

Kensal Green where, alas, the inscribed stone at the grave of the Speaker has seemingly disintegrated, though those of the others are still clearly discernible. Memorials are thick on the walls of Heckfield Church; Viscount Eversley's coat-of-arms is reproduced in the stained glass of Trinity College, Cambridge; there is a plaque in the church at Bourne, near Farnham; and a graceful Grecian urn, mounted on a pedestal, marks the graves of George and Constance in Kingsworthy churchyard.

After the death of his uncle, Viscount Eversley, at the end of 1888, George Shaw Lefevre was the last remaining male of the family; and he was without an heir. If it is perhaps a little fanciful, it is surely excusable, to imagine that, in addition to enjoying and exploiting his inherited strength, vigour and tenacity, he may have felt his solitariness – the last man who would carry the name of Shaw Lefevre – as a challenge to live longer than any of his predecessors or his masculine contemporaries. At any rate, that was what he did, and most of the family story after 1888 had to be George's story. He lost his eldest sister, Rachael Hamilton Gordon, only a month after Viscount Eversley; his five remaining sisters lived into the new century, but three of his four female cousins died in the 1890s. His wife and his cousin, Sophia Wickham, survived him only by months, but his youngest sister, Emily, outlived him by eight years. All had gone by 1936. The later lives of these family members, and the experience of their few successors, round out the record.

Rachael Hamilton Gordon was buried in Malta. Arthur did not return to England at once. He took Jack and Nevil back to Ceylon with him, but Jack could only stay for a few weeks. Nevil remained while Arthur tried to persuade Madeleine to come out to be with them, but this Madeleine was unwilling to do. Some months later, Arthur sent Nevil to Scotland, to live with his sister-in-law, the widowed Mary Aberdeen. He himself retired from the governorship of Ceylon in 1890 and took up residence with both children in the Red House at Ascot. He had a chapel built to the memory of Rachael, in the Ta Braxia cemetery in Malta, and arranged for it to 'remain available for the last services of all denominations of Christians by whom this Cemetery may be used, as long as the British Empire shall endure.' The chapel survived the air bombardment of Malta, and despite the demise of Empire, services are still held in it.[1]

At an uncertain date in the first few years after Rachael's death, Arthur proposed marriage to Sophia Palmer, but she refused him, being too well aware of his shortcomings, which she thought were 'a total lack of sense of humour or personal tact.'[2] He remained a widower and lived at Ascot until his death. There he wrote biographies of his father and of Sidney Herbert, and edited the correspondence on which most of the account of his and Rachael's life in Mauritius and Fiji is based. He was raised to the peerage as Baron

Stanmore, by Gladstone, in 1893. Against his basic political instincts but out of a sense of obligation to the Prime Minister, who made his expectations very plain, Arthur voted in favour of Home Rule within days of taking his seat in the Lords. That episode led to a coolness between them for most of the last few years of Gladstone's life.[3] Although he continued to call himself a Conservative Liberal, Arthur's lack of sympathy for democracy moved him steadily rightwards in domestic terms; he voted against Lloyd George's budget in 1909 and took a hard line against the Parliament Bill which reduced the power of the House of Lords in 1911, the year before his death.

Jack Hamilton Gordon retained the more Liberal brand of loyalties which he had developed at Winchester and under the tutelage of his uncle and aunts. He served as George Shaw Lefevre's private secretary from 1892–5, and was obviously close to George. Uncle and nephew went cycling together on the Continent in 1898, and George helped in Jack's unsuccessful candidature for the North Dorset seat in the 1900 general election.[4] Years later, after he had succeeded as the second Baron Stanmore, Jack became Chief Liberal Whip in the House of Lords and served in that role from 1923 to 1944. Neither he nor Nevil married. She died in 1947 and he ten years afterwards. Their remains, like their father's, are interred in a tomb outside the redbrick church of All Souls, South Ascot, the building of which Arthur had largely financed.

Perhaps it is symbolically appropriate that their mother's grave should be so far away, for it emphasizes the sense of deprivation and dislocation from which she suffered. Rachael cannot be remembered as a powerful and bustling colonial pioneer, or as the founding spirit of philanthropic, feminine enterprises in what were then wild and remote places. Neither was she an intellectual, nor a political figure in her own right. She was a dutiful daughter; the loyal wife of an affectionate, high-minded but edgy and unfulfilled husband; a fond and, perhaps, an understandably over-caring mother; and a woman born into and bound by the habits and prejudices of her class. In all these respects she is likely to have been far more representative of the consorts of Victorian colonial governors than any of that group who may have achieved, retrospectively, fame, glamour or notoriety. Where it is unlikely that she could be outmatched is in the length of her service and in the courage that took her and her children to such primitive conditions as they endured in Mauritius and Fiji. And if, as a governor's lady, she was lonely and miserable for much of her time in the outposts of empire, that loneliness and misery was very likely reflective of the fellow feeling of all the women whose experience it was to accompany their husbands from one strange, dangerous and unfamiliar setting to another. Rachael, like all of them, could never be wholly free from the pain of separation and the fear – so sadly justified in her own case – that she, her husband and their children, might not survive their exile and live again at home among their own people.

CHILDREN OF THE DAUGHTERS OF
HENRY FRANCIS AND HELEN SHAW LEFEVRE

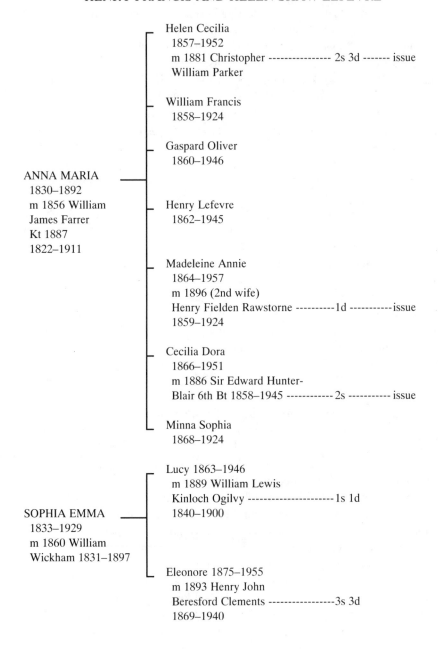

ANNA MARIA
1830–1892
m 1856 William
James Farrer
Kt 1887
1822–1911

Helen Cecilia
1857–1952
m 1881 Christopher --------------- 2s 3d ------- issue
William Parker

William Francis
1858–1924

Gaspard Oliver
1860–1946

Henry Lefevre
1862–1945

Madeleine Annie
1864–1957
m 1896 (2nd wife)
Henry Fielden Rawstorne ----------1d -----------issue
1859–1924

Cecilia Dora
1866–1951
m 1886 Sir Edward Hunter-
Blair 6th Bt 1858–1945 ------------ 2s ----------- issue

Minna Sophia
1868–1924

SOPHIA EMMA
1833–1929
m 1860 William
Wickham 1831–1897

Lucy 1863–1946
m 1889 William Lewis
Kinloch Ogilvy ---------------------1s 1d
1840–1900

Eleonore 1875–1955
m 1893 Henry John
Beresford Clements -----------------3s 3d
1869–1940

Two of Henry Francis Shaw Lefevre's daughters died in the early 1890s. The eldest, Helen Mason, widowed in 1867, outlived her much older husband by twenty-six years. There were no children of the marriage, and after Mason's death Helen settled in Brighton, regularly played host to her uncle, Viscount Eversley, made and remade her will, and died in 1893, leaving her worldly wealth divided equally between the families of her two younger sisters. The middle daughter, Anna Maria, the wife of Sir William James Farrer, was the mother of seven children, and she died a year before Helen. None of her three sons married, but one of them, Gaspard, became a successful merchant banker with Barings, as well as being a partner, with the Le Marchants, in H.S. Lefevre & Co., which stayed in business, without any Lefevres, until closed down by Duncan Stirling in 1949–50.[5] Three of the four Farrer daughters married, and in consequence, Shaw Lefevre blood still runs in the veins of some members of the Bruce, Hunter-Blair, and Oxley Parker families. The third of Henry Francis's daughters, Sophia Wickham, was to live much longer than her sisters.

Of the three daughters of Charles Shaw Lefevre and Emma Whitbread, only two survived into the 1890s. The youngest, Elizabeth, who had married Hervey George St John Mildmay, had died, aged 40, in 1867, leaving one daughter, Florence. Florence became the wife of the Revd Carleton Rashleigh and had three daughters, all of whom died unmarried. Charles's eldest daughter, Emma, the mistress of Heckfield after her mother's death, was 68 when her father died in 1888. She kept Heckfield Place going for a few years, but the estate was sold in 1896 and Emma retired to a house in Bina Gardens, Kensington, where she died in 1899, in her 80th year.

The union of Helena, Charles's second daughter, and Sir Henry Paulet St John Mildmay, Bt., began a more complicated story. Helena had seven children. Two girls died before they reached their teens. Her eldest son, who became the sixth Baronet, did not marry. The other two sons and two daughters all married, but only one son and one daughter had children. The title passed to the second son, Gerald Anthony Mildmay, in 1916. He had inherited the bulk of Viscount Eversley's fortune, but Charles had made it a condition that his grandson should add Shaw Lefevre to the family name. As a result, when Gerald Anthony became the seventh Baronet, he was known as Sir Gerald Anthony Shaw Lefevre St John Mildmay, Bt. But in 1921, perhaps because it was clear that there would be no further financial advantage in retaining the Shaw Lefevre connection, the surviving son and heir to the baronetcy, Anthony, dropped the additional names. He succeeded to the title in 1929, married twice, had only one child, a son, and died in 1947. In turn that son, the ninth Baronet, died unmarried, at the age of 23, only two years later. The title then passed to a distant kinsman who died in 1955, since when the title has remained unclaimed.

Lady Helena St John Mildmay (Nina) died in 1897. The only remaining

CHILDREN OF THE DAUGHTERS OF CHARLES AND EMMA SHAW LEFEVRE, VISCOUNT AND VISCOUNTESS EVERSLEY

HELENA (Nina)
1823–1897
  m 1851 Sir Henry
Bouverie Paulet
St John MILDMAY
5th Bt 1810–1902

Jane Emma
1851–1928
m (2nd wife) 1889
John Martin
Carr-Lloyd 1849–1919

Henry Paulet 6th Bt
1853–1916

Helena Charlotte
1854–1867

Laura Catherine
1856–1866

Constance Mary
1859–1930
m (1) 1888 John Arthur
Beach Wallington ------------------3s 3d------- issue
1853–1901
m(2) 1912 Algernon
Forbes Randolph
1865–1953

Gerald Anthony 7th Bt
1860–1929 m 1892
Isabel Emily St John
Mildmay 1861–1950 -------------- 2s 1d

Carew Hervey
1863–1937 m 1912
Elizabeth Catherine Roper
1857–1942

ELIZABETH
1827–1867
m 1859 Hervey George
St John Mildmay

Florence Wyndham 1861–1906
m 1886 Carleton Rashleigh ------- 3d
1851–1938

descendant of the Charles Shaw Lefevres is traceable through the marriage of Helena's daughter, Constance Mary, to John Arthur Beach Wallington, in 1888. There were six Wallington children: three daughters died unmarried, one son was killed in the First World War, and from the marriages of the other two sons there was only one child, the great-great-grandson of Viscount Eversley, now his only living blood relative. Apart from Gerald Anthony's financial interest, and the Wallington connection, the only other sign of close concern with the Shaw Lefevres on the part of the younger Mildmays was shown by Helena's youngest son, Carew, a convert to Roman Catholicism, whose passion was genealogy, and whose papers have helped in the compilation of this history. Carew married late in life, and died, childless, in 1937.

George Shaw Lefevre's surviving married sister, Jane Ryan, had suffered tragic blows in the loss of twin boys in infancy and her other son when he was but 22. Of all her six children, only her eldest daughter, Madeleine, married, and she did so only weeks after the burial of her brother, William – the family's trauma can be imagined. Madeleine's husband was Arthur Elliot, a younger brother of the fourth Earl of Minto. He was Liberal MP for Roxborough from 1880, but embraced the Liberal Unionist cause very strongly in 1886 and founded the Liberal Unionist Club. He lost his seat in 1892, but returned to Parliament for Durham in 1898 and was appointed Financial Secretary to the Treasury in 1903, only to find himself, as a strong free trader, so much at odds with the protectionist policy of Joseph Chamberlain that he resigned within months. Subsequently he had considerable political and literary influence as editor of the *Edinburgh Review*. Arthur Elliot, caught in the two great schisms of the Liberals, was equipped with attitudes and a personality striking enough for him to be known as 'the last of the Whigs'.

But though he had an aristocratic demeanour, Arthur did not have what Charles Ryan thought was an adequate income when he proposed to Madeleine, and the match was only made when the Wantages, through whom they had met, and who – or certainly Harriet – were extremely fond of Madeleine, settled £400 a year on her for life, and the same for her husband's life if he survived her. Thus the Wantages carried on the benevolent family interest shown by Harriet's parents, the Overstones. Arthur and Madeleine Elliot lost a firstborn son in childhood, but their second son survived and his successors are the only living direct blood relations of the John Shaw Lefevres.

Alas, for Lady Ryan herself there was to be yet another tragedy, for Madeleine Elliot succumbed to typhoid fever at her home, Dimbola on the Isle of Wight, in 1906, when she was 42. But, despite all her losses, Jane lived to be 80. She died in 1914, leaving her husband, two surviving daughters,

CHILDREN OF THE DAUGHTERS OF
JOHN AND EMILY SHAW LEFEVRE

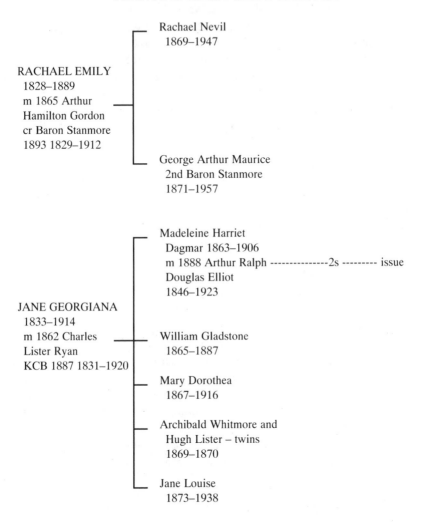

RACHAEL EMILY
1828–1889
m 1865 Arthur
Hamilton Gordon
cr Baron Stanmore
1893 1829–1912

Rachael Nevil
1869–1947

George Arthur Maurice
2nd Baron Stanmore
1871–1957

JANE GEORGIANA
1833–1914
m 1862 Charles
Lister Ryan
KCB 1887 1831–1920

Madeleine Harriet
Dagmar 1863–1906
m 1888 Arthur Ralph ---------------2s --------- issue
Douglas Elliot
1846–1923

William Gladstone
1865–1887

Mary Dorothea
1867–1916

Archibald Whitmore and
Hugh Lister – twins
1869–1870

Jane Louise
1873–1938

both unmarried, and a grandson. One of the daughters, Mary Dorothea, died in 1916. Sir Charles Ryan, much honoured for his long and distinguished career, which had culminated in his appointment as Comptroller and Auditor General, spent his last years at Ascot, in the house which had been the family home since the 1860s, and died in 1920, in his 89th year. The Ascot properties of the Shaw Lefevres, the Ryans and the Stanmores were all sold at about that time. Jane Ryan, the last of the family and one of the longer lived of her generation of Shaw Lefevres, died in 1938.

Arthur Elliot had characterized the mature John Shaw Lefevre spinsters, to his future wife, as 'very political ladies', after being introduced to them in the late 1880s. Certainly they seemed to thrive in the political society of the capital, and apparently kept the house at 41 Seymour Street until the end of the First World War, though whether and to what extent they used it themselves, is not clear. After Rachael's death and Madeleine's retirement from Somerville, Maria – whether for health or other reasons – spent her remaining years at Worthing on the Sussex coast, and died there in 1908. But Mary, Madeleine and Emily moved in 1890 to Greenhill Farm, a country house in the parish of Bourne, near Farnham in Surrey, where they lived together for twenty-five years. Madeleine died just after the beginning of the First World War, and Mary died just over a year later, in November 1915.

It seems that, after 1889, Madeleine was approached or allowed herself to be approached, with a view to drawing on her proven abilities only to a very limited degree. Though she resigned from Somerville Council on her retirement, she was re-elected to it almost immediately, remained a member for the rest of her life and took a real if quiet interest in the college's affairs. She also retained her place as a manager of the residence at Bedford College, London, which she had filled first in 1885. That was an appointment in which she would have had to exercise her diplomatic talent, for there were problems between the managers, or trustees, and the college authorities which were not resolved for several years.[6] And in or about 1891 she joined her successor at Somerville and the heads of the other Oxford and Cambridge women's colleges, to advise the Agent General of New South Wales on choosing a principal for a students' hostel in Sydney.[7]

But in the main Madeleine seems to have accepted gladly the pleasures and the limitations of a quiet, rural life and to have given her services to local interests. She became a manager of the Bourne Council Schools and was a member of the Farnham Council Schools Committee. She was in an area where many established family friends had country homes, and she made additional friends in the immediate vicinity.[8] There are indications that some of the documents on the history of her family which are in the collections at Haddo House and in the Winchester Record Office were written during these last years, and certainly she responded with a few memories to requests from Somerville. But there is nothing in the nature of finished work, and there is little to show that her earlier keenness to sketch and paint was much sustained after her visit to Ceylon. Perhaps, like her brother, she had to struggle against failing sight; perhaps Somerville tired her much more than she had expected. Whatever the experience of those last quiet years, Madeleine must have savoured the realization that she had made a reputation for herself as a woman which could stand proudly alongside the contributions her brother, father, uncles and grandfather had made to public life. What received most notice in her lifetime and at the time of her death was her grace and serenity; but in a longer perspective what seems particularly impressive was her integrity.

By the middle of the First World War, therefore, only three Shaw Lefevres were still living – George, Baron Eversley; his sister Emily; and his cousin, Sophia Wickham, the youngest daughter of Henry Francis. Sophia's husband, unlike his forbears and his wife's people, chose to stand as a Conservative in 1892 for Petersfield, and held the seat until his death in 1897. His Liberal opponent was John Bonham Carter, his near neighbour. Thus was demonstrated the continuity of the political hegemony of the landed gentry in rural England. But the political antagonism of the 1890s did not prevent one of the Wickhams' granddaughters, Charlotte Ogilvy, from becoming the wife of Sir Edgar Bonham Carter in 1926. Lady Charlotte died as recently as December 1989, aged 96. She had been the guardian of many of the portraits and memorabilia of the earlier Shaw Lefevres. One of her cousins, a member of the Irish family of Clements, is now the last representative of these descendants of Henry Francis Shaw Lefevre. Sophia Wickham lived until June 1929, when she was 96, thus surviving a few months longer than Baron Eversley.

Emily Octavia Shaw Lefevre, John and Emily's youngest daughter, born in 1842, abandoned Greenhill Farm after the deaths of her two elder sisters, and came to live in the West End of London, at 24 Connaught Square. There she died, aged 94, on 29 April 1936. She was buried in the family grave at Ascot. Charlotte Bonham Carter, when almost the same age that Emily achieved, remembered her, very distinctly, as 'one of the last of the great Victorian spinster ladies.'

It was fitting that the last of the Shaw Lefevres should have died in London. For despite their country homes and the undoubted enthusiasm which a few of them had for rural life, it was the metropolis which excited their ambition. There John Lefevre had made his fortune; there George Shaw settled, launched his son into the law and, more meaningfully, into so successful a marriage. It was in Westminster and in the City that the five Shaw Lefevre males made their political, administrative and financial reputations; and it was in London society that their families established themselves on the upper rungs of the nineteenth-century social ladder. It is unlikely that they would have taken kindly to being thought of in theatrical terms, though one or two of them had a strong sense of theatre. But if they rarely achieved what the world of the stage would regard as star billing, they belonged to that stratum of highly-competent, occasionally brilliant and always dependable players, without whom no show can go on, let alone have a long run.

APPENDIX I

A North Sea Voyage in 1862

From the Elliot Mss.

Voyage to Scotland and Visits to Ancrum, Abingdon (Sir E. Cole-brooke's), Castle Fraser, Dunecht, Penecuik, Malvin

On the . . . August 1862, Rachael and Emily with Clayton (maid) left London Bridge for Grantown. After steaming for two or three hours down the river, they were caught up by another steamer which they were told was the Leith steamer running in competition with the Grantown steamer 'City of Hamburg'. It soon became apparent that this steamer was racing them and suddenly a collision took place. Emily who was standing up was thrown down on her face by the shock. The other steamer went on its way without enquiring what damage had been done. A large hole had been made in the Leith boat which was in the middle of the river. It had to be run aground to prevent sinking. This happened somewhere near Sheerness but no town or village was in sight. Another steamer was sent for and R. and E. were promised the same accommodation on it as they were told it would be exactly like the one they were on. After eight hours, the promised steamer came looming up in the dark. R. and E. collected all their things, hurried on board to claim their cabins and then found that it was a much smaller boat with no private cabins.

Copy of a letter from Rachael to Mary, probably 1862
Ancrum Jedburgh N.B. Aug. 10th

Dear Mary,

Emily and I are going to write a sort of joint letter to tell you our adventure. I suppose you will have understood from the telegram (which I hope you got) that the voyage was most horrid, you can have no idea how disgusting. It was quite late that night when we got on board the City of Hamburg. They persuaded us into believing that she was a fine ship just like the other with every accommodation exactly the same. So E. and I climbed down to secure our state room, E, but to our disgust we found there was nothing of the kind, only two miserable general cabins quite full of berths, about ten in each to accommodate twenty-six women and children, besides one was immediately filled by the Rose children and servants. They had just been newly painted and varnished, the stench to begin with was enough to make one sick, and what it became afterwards you may imagine. Those who went down were never known to come up again!

We and Mrs Napier decided that nothing would induce us to stop below. It was then a fine night and a young snob who was to be devoted to us went to the old ship and procured three mattresses while we stole all the blankets we could lay hold of, about ten and two or three pillows and with these we made a kind of bed on a raised place over the saloon and the snob tucked us in and there we passed the night. It soon began to pour with rain and the sailors covered us all over, heads and all with tarpaulin which kept us warm but nearly stifled us. Before retiring for the night Mrs Napier produced a parcel of sandwiches and hard boiled eggs and the snob with some difficulty procured a bottle of sherry, for in the confusion the ship was in it was just impossible to get anything, everything having been thrown on board in a muddle. We passed a most wretched night and scarcely slept, the sailors were always coming to tuck us up and put on the tarpaulin which would tumble off. 'Poor dear creatures they'll get their death of cold.'

Towards morning the wind got up and it became very rough and the ship having no cargo, tossed about like a cork and she was so light, the paddles could not take hold of the water and she hardly seemed to make any progress. In the morning poor Mrs Napier succumbed and was taken down to the cabin and never came back, she was dreadfully ill. Of course it was necessary for us to make occasional expeditions down to that beastly hole from which we never expected to come up alive. Emily and Clayton were generally upset by it. I alone contrived to hold out the whole voyage. The scene below was awful, all the steerage passengers were messed up, and the floor and tables even were covered with unfortunate creatures each with a basin, the stewardess said they had never known such a time, and then the noise – the retching and screaming of babies, one lady fainted away several times and could hardly be kept alive. And the Roses' poor nurse was almost delirious.

In the morning we ordered some coffee on deck, but it all blew away before we could drink it. We stayed under our tarpaulin till 12 o'clock and then could bear it no longer and said they must land us somewhere – anywhere – but the Captain wouldn't hear of that, so the sailors set to work and knocked up a kind of shed out of a horse-box with canvas nailed round three sides situated between the funnel, the steerage kitchen, and the three horses, and just over the engine room, and here we moved our ten blankets and three mattresses and took up our quarters there for the rest of the time. About this time we discovered another lady and gentleman, Mr. and Mrs. Cholmondeley, and we invited her into the horse-box where we all three lay with Clayton at our feet. It was about the size of a four post bed; one side was open but had a high railing in front, which was most difficult to get over and one generally fell into the arms of a sailor.

We were very wretched all that day, but contrived to sleep well during the night which was extremely rough. Poor Clayton found she couldn't possibly stay in it and spent all the rest of the time sitting on deck with an umbrella over her till she was quite stiff and is still stiff but not otherwise the worse. We had our meals, such as they were, brought by a steward, but many things such as butter, fruit, and milk, had been forgotten or lost. Mrs. Cholmondeley turned out to be a very pretty nice little person and he is a son of Miss Stewart's Lord Henry Cholmondeley, and by the end we got quite intimate. She was so dowdily dressed we overlooked them at first. Towards evening we crawled out for a little and then I was nearly upset and had to rush back and lie down again. When it got dark the sailors and some of the steerage passengers came and sat round our railing and entertained us with choruses and smoked remarkably bad tobacco into us.

The third night the ship tossed about worse than ever as we got near the Forth and we seemed to be always two hours from Berwick, and at last we settled down for a third night on board, Clayton a solitary figure sitting alone on deck as usual. But about 2 o'clock we were awoke by the sound of 'Harbour! Harbour!' and found we were steaming quietly into Grantown, so we rushed up and collected our things and as soon as we anchored, procured a porter and took possession of all our luggage, delighted to escape from our misery. We then walked to the hotel where we found a waiter up, and immediately ordered hot brandy and water and biscuits (for which we had to pay 4/-) and two large cans of hot water to be taken at once to our rooms as all this time we had only once been able to wash our hands, and our clothes were in a most dreadfully dirty condition.

Mrs Cholmondeley having to hunt up her husband from the depth of the cabin, did not arrive till an hour after us. The rest of the passengers we never saw again. Our horse-box, disgusting as it was, turned out to be the greatest comfort and we were the envy of the whole ship. The next morning, Saturday, we went down to breakfast in the public room at 10 o'clock and joined the Cholmondeleys at a little table, after which we all wrote accounts of the accident to our friends and advised each other what to say. Emily and I were not a bit the worse for it and felt extremely hungry and jolly. We all went by train to Edinburgh, deposited our luggage and Clayton at the station, and went with the Cholmondeleys to the Company's office to try to get back what we had paid for the state cabins that we never had, but unfortunately the agent had gone off to the ship. Then we proceeded to the Royal Academy where we parted with the Cholmondeleys. We never met them again.

Then we did a little shopping, Clayton having to buy a bonnet, hers being quite done for by the voyage. At 4 we started for Jedburgh where we arrived at 8 and found the Ancrum servant looking out for us. We had to wait three quarters of an hour for the omnibus which had been sent three times already to meet us. We found all the family waiting dinner for us. They are most kind and we are enjoying ourselves extremely.

If it had been a fine passage it would have been most enjoyable, for the first steamer was very comfortable. We had planned to go by sea to Scotland thinking it would be much less tiring!

Note   Many weeks afterwards we got back £1.0.0 for our State rooms, much less than we paid.

Published Work of
George John Shaw Lefevre, Baron Eversley

Until he was raised to the peerage, George's articles and books were usually published under the name G. Shaw Lefevre or Rt. Hon G. Shaw Lefevre MP. He rarely used his second initial. His writings for the Cobden Club were published under the Club's title. Because of the range of his writings and of the papers and journals in which they appeared, it is impossible to claim that the following list is comprehensive, though it certainly covers the major periodicals. No attempt is made here to list the numerous letters, short contributions and reviews which George Shaw Lefevre wrote for the press. Some of the letters were of great length; many were unsigned or written under pseudonyms. A few of the letters and some of his speeches in the House of Commons were published in pamphlet form. The many draft reports and transcripts of evidence by him to the select committees and royal commissions of which he was a member, or before which he appeared, are not included here, but may be readily found in the relevant parliamentary papers.

Photographic Views of Sebastopol, taken immediately after the Retreat of the Russians, September 8 1855, London, 1856.
'Account of the Strike and Lock-out in the Building Trades in London in 1859–60' (By GJSL and T.R. Bennet); and 'Report on Trades' Societies Rules', in *Trades' Societies and Strikes*. Report of Committee on Trades' Societies appointed by the National Association for the Promotion of Social Science, London, 1860, 52–70, 114–46.
'The Conscience Clause', *Fortnightly Review*, 3, No. 14, 165–180 Dec 1865.
Preface to *Six Essays on Commons Preservation*, written in competition for prizes offered by Henry W. Peek, Esq., of Wimbledon House, London, 1867.
The Personal Payment of Rates and the Reform Act of 1867, London, 1868.
The Game Laws, London, 1874.
'Economy and Trade', Trans. of the National Association for the Promotion of Social Science, Oct 1876, London, 1877, 103–23.

'Economic Law and English Land Ownership', *Fortnightly Review*, 27, No. 121, 32–53, Jan 1877.

'British and Foreign Ships of War', *Macmillan's Magazine*, 35, 257–65, Feb 1877.

'Inaugural Address [as] President of the Statistical Society, delivered on Tuesday 20th November, 1877', *Journal of the Statistical Society*, 40, 509–30, Dec 1877.

'Greece at the Congress of Berlin', *Fortnightly Review*, New Series 24, Old Series 30, No. 140, 271–83, Aug 1878.

'The Depression of Trade, A Speech delivered at the Anniversary Dinner of the Statistical Society, on 25th June, 1878', *Journal of the Statistical Society*, 41, 427–32, Sep 1878.

'A Decade of Inflation and Depression. The Opening Address of the President of the Statistical Society, delivered on 19th November, 1878', *Journal of the Statistical Society*, 41, 573–96, Dec 1878.

'The Rescue of Epping Forest', *Contemporary Review*, 34, 45–59, Dec 1878.

'The Channel Islands', *Fortnightly Review*, NS 26, OS 32, No. 154, 474–91, Oct 1879.

Freedom of Land, National Liberal Federation, Practical Politics Series No. 3, London, 1880.

English and Irish Land Questions: Collected Essays, London, 1881.

'The Duke of Argyll and the Irish Land Bill', *Nineteenth Century*, 9, 1044–65, Jun 1881.

'Public Works in London', *Nineteenth Century*, 12, 667–86, Nov 1882.

The Purchase Clauses of the Irish Land Act, speech made in the House of Commons on 2 May 1879, and Papers written on the same subject, London, 1882.

'Principles of Fisheries Legislation', in *Papers of the Conferences held in connection with the Great International Fisheries Exhibition*, London, 1883.

'The Agricultural Holdings Act, 1883', *Nineteenth Century*, 14, 674–94, Oct 1883.

'Statues and Monuments of London', *Nineteenth Century*, 15, 28–48, Jan 1884.

'The Representation of Minorities', *Contemporary Review*, 45, 714–33, May 1884.

'Proportional Representation', National Liberal Federation, 1884. [This paper is referred to by GJSL in his 1917 pamphlet on the same subject – see below. I have been unable to find it.]

'Representation and Misrepresentation 1 – The Crusade for Proportional Representation', *Fortnightly Review*, NS 37, OS 43, No. 218, Feb 1885.

'The Question of the Land', *Nineteenth Century*, 18, 513–31, Oct 1885.

'Home Rule: Precedents', *Nineteenth Century*, 19, 424–42, Mar 1886.

'The Two Unions', *Contemporary Review*, 49, 560–78, Apr 1886.

'The Liberal Split', *Nineteenth Century*, 20, 592–608, Oct 1886.

Peel and O'Connell: a review of the Irish policy of Parliament from the Act of Union to the death of Sir Robert Peel, London, 1887.

Incidents of Coercion. A Journal of Visits to Ireland in 1882 and 1888, London, 1888.

'Public Buildings in London', *Nineteenth Century*, 24, 703–18, Nov 1888.

Irish Members and English Gaolers. The Treatment of Political Offenders, London, 1889.

'Communication from the Rt. Hon. G.J. Shaw Lefevre in The New Round Table, on the Irish question', *Westminster Review*, 132, 624–8, Dec 1889.

Combination and Coercion, London, 1890.

'Constantinople Revisited', *Nineteenth Century*, 28, 927–44, Dec 1890.

'Athens Revisited', *Contemporary Review*, 59, 290–305, Feb 1891.

'Sofia Revisited', *Contemporary Review*, 59, 546–57, Apr 1891.

'The Naval Policy of France, Past and Future', *Nineteenth Century*, 30, 606–27, Oct 1891.

'The Memoirs of General Marbot', *Contemporary Review*, 60, 853–75, Dec 1891.

Agrarian Tenures: A Survey of the Laws and Customs relating to the Holding of Land in England, Ireland and Scotland, and of the Reforms therein during recent years, London, 1893.

English Commons and Forests, London, 1894. Revised edition, titled *Commons Forests and Footpaths*, London, 1910.

Memorandum on the Stonehenge Case, London, Jun 1895.

Bi-metallism and Agricultural Depression, London, 1896.

Introduction to Papers of the Greek Committee, No. 1, NS, 1897.

'A Vindication of the Claims of Greece: an Address delivered at the Assembly Rooms, Kennington, Dec 9, 1897', *Papers of the Greek Committee*, No.7.

'The London Water Supply', *Nineteenth Century*, 44, 980–90, Dec 1898.

'London Street Improvements', *Contemporary Review*, 75, 203–17, Feb 1899.

The Treatment of the Aged Poor in Workhouses, Paper read at Hampshire Poor Law Conference, 1899.

'Trawlers and Undersized Fish', *Fortnightly Review*, NS 67, OS 73, No. 402, 1004–22, Jun 1900.

'A Visit to the Argentine Republic', *Nineteenth Century*, 50, 830–43, Nov 1901.

The Licensing Question in Hampshire. Two speeches delivered at the Hampshire Quarter Sessions in April and July, 1902, Winchester, 1902.

'Pauperism, Crime, and Drink', *The Speaker*, 20 Dec 1902.

'The Hare Family: A Reminiscence', *The Speaker*, 14 Feb 1903.

'The Navy Estimates', *The Speaker*, 21 Mar 1903.
'Gladstone in the Abbey', *The Speaker*, 25 April, 1903.
'The Naval Annual: An Extravagant Expenditure', *The Speaker*, 20 Jun 1903.
Cobden Club, *The Balance of Trade: An Explanation of the Growing Difference Between the Values of Imports and Exports*, London, 1903.
'Mr Balfour and Retaliation', *Fortnightly Review*, NS 74, OS 80, No. 444, 941–55, Dec 1903.
'The Navy Estimates', *The Speaker*, 12 Mar 1904.
Cobden Club, *Fact versus Fiction: The Cobden Club's Reply to Mr Chamberlain*, London, 1904.
Cobden Club, *The Burden of Armaments: A Plea for Retrenchment*, London, 1905.
'Rival Navies', *Contemporary Review*, 89, 153–65, Feb 1906.

The following were attributed to Lord Eversley:

'Naval Scares', *Contemporary Review*, 90, 624–38, Nov 1906.
'The House of Lords and the Education Bill', *Nineteenth Century*, 60, 1017–26, Dec 1906.
'The Decline in the Number of Agricultural Labourers in Great Britain', *Journal of the Statistical Society*, 70, 267–306, Jun 1907.
'Teutophobia', *Nineteenth Century*, 62, 187–97, Aug 1907.
'The Evicted Tenants, Ireland Act', *Fortnightly Review*, NS 82, OS 88, No. 492, 976–90, Dec 1907.
'The Anglo-German War of Armaments', *The Nation*, 25 Jan 1908.
'Campbell-Bannerman in the Abbey', *The Nation*, 23 May 1908.
'Naval Expenditure in 1909', *The Nation*, 1 Aug 1908.
'Useless Naval Expenditure', *The Nation*, 5 Sep 1908.
Cobden Club, *Tariff Makers: Their Aims and Methods*, London, 1909.
Cobden Club, *Budget and Tariff Compared*, London, 1909.
'Naval Expenditure', *Financial Reform Almanac and Year Book*, Liverpool, 1909. Also issued as a pamphlet, Dec 1910.
'The Latest Scare', *Financial Reform Almanac and Year Book*, Liverpool, 19ll, 17–39.
Gladstone and Ireland: the Irish Policy of Parliament from 1850 – 1894, London, 1912; reprinted Westport, Connecticut, 1971.
Cobden Club, *A Decade of Tariff Fooling: A Retrospect*, London, 1913.
'Marie Antoinette and Barnave', *Nineteenth Century*, 76, 350–72, Aug 1914.
The Partitions of Poland, London, 1915.
Proportional Representation, 1867–1917, privately printed, 1917.
The Turkish Empire: Its Growth and Decay, London, 1917. 2nd ed., 1923.

3rd ed., 1924, published as *The Turkish Empire from 1288 to 1914 by Lord Eversley and From 1914 to 1924 by Sir Valentine Chirol*; 3rd ed. reprinted Lahore, 1967, and New York, 1969.
'Some Reminiscences', *Cornhill Magazine*:

I.   'Lord Byron and Dr Millingen', NS 15, 471–82, Nov 1918.
II.   'Sea Fisheries', NS 15, 607–13, Dec 1918.
III.   'The Hares of Hurstmonceux', NS 16, 90–5, Jan 1919.
IV.   'My First Election to Parliament', NS 16, 150–9, Feb 1919.
V.   'At the Board of Trade', NS 16, 306–16, Mar 1919.
VI.   'At the Admiralty, 1871', NS 16, 372–82, Apr 1919.

Sources

Specific references in the notes to each chapter comprise a guide to relevant secondary literature. The collections of manuscript material consulted are listed below, together with an explanation of the use made of some of the family documents and genealogical data.

The largest concentrations of Shaw Lefevre family papers are to be found in the Aberdeen Mss at Haddo House; in the Bonham Carter, Mildmay, and Wickham Mss at the Hampshire Record Office, Winchester; in the Shaw Lefevre Mss in the House of Lords Record Office; and in the Stanmore Mss at the British Library. Papers privately held by the late Lady Bonham Carter, by Lt. Col. C.M.L. Clements, by Mr and Mrs J.W.O. Elliot, by Sir Matthew Farrer, and by Mr D.C. Holland were also used. In addition, selected portions of the following collections were examined:

Windsor: *Royal Archives*
Baring Bros: *Northbrook Mss*
Bedfordshire RO: *Whitbread Mss*
Bodleian Library, Oxford: *Harcourt Mss*
British Library: *Althorp, Bexley, Broughton, Burns, Campbell-Bannerman, Dilke, Escott, Gladstone, E. Hamilton, Layard, Murchison, Peel* and *Pentland Mss*
British Library of Political and Economic Science: *Courtney, Gardiner,* and *Markham Mss*
Chatsworth: *Devonshire Mss*
Devon RO: *Sidmouth Mss*
Essex RO: *Round Mss*
Greater London RO: *J.W. Nicholson & Co. Mss*
Guildhall Library: *Sun Life Office Mss*
House of Lords RO: *Erskine May* and *Lloyd George Mss* and *HL papers.*
India Office Library: *Sorabji Mss*
Lambeth Palace Library: *Selborne Mss*
National Library of Scotland: *Haldane, Minto* and *Rosebery Mss*
National Library of Wales: *Rendel Mss*
Nottinghamshire RO: *Wright Diaries*
Public RO: *Cardwell, Granville* and *Russell Mss*

Rose Lipman Library: *J.W. Nicholson & Co. Mss*
Royal Bank of Scotland: *Lefevre Mss*
Royal Society: *Lubbock Mss* and *Royal Society records*
Scottish RO: *Dalhousie Mss*
Somerville College, Oxford: *Shaw Lefevre Mss* and *College records*
Surrey RO: *Farrer* and *Goulburn Mss*
Trinity College, Cambridge: *College records*
University College London: *Brougham* and *Chadwick Mss*
University of Birmingham: *Joseph Chamberlain Mss*
University of Durham: *Grey Mss*
University of London: *Overstone Mss* and *University records*
University of New Brunswick: *Hamilton Gordon Mss*
University of North Carolina: *Chesson Mss*
University of Reading: *Heckfield/Eversley farm records.*
University of Southampton: *Melbourne (Broadlands)* and *Wellington Mss*
Whitbread & Company: *Company archives*
Wiltshire RO: *Radnor Mss*

There are at Haddo House and in the Bonham Carter and Mildmay Mss at the Hampshire Record Office several short, typewritten accounts of various periods in the history of the Lefevre and Shaw Lefevre families. They were almost certainly put together by Madeleine Shaw Lefevre between 1880 and 1910, and were the result, partly, of conversations with Viscount Eversley and with Madeleine's mother, Lady Emily Shaw Lefevre, when both were very elderly. While most valuable, they have to be used carefully. The discovery of some errors in them, and many useful findings and corrections of early genealogical mistakes, was due to the efforts of Carew Mildmay (1863–1937) whose papers are among the Mildmay Mss at Winchester. In addition, there is extant a most useful private memoir of Sophia Wickham by her daughter, Lucy Ogilvie, parts of which were made available by Lt. Col. Clements and by the late Lady Bonham Carter. That memoir adds substantially to the material otherwise available. Where possible, references to all these sources have been given in the notes, but where there is no attribution it should be assumed that the information came from one or more of these family documents.

Formal genealogical data and some ecclesiastical records were sought in the College of Arms; in the County Record Offices of Buckinghamshire, Essex, Hampshire, Hertfordshire, Leicestershire, Northamptonshire, North Yorkshire, West Sussex and West Yorkshire; in the Guildhall Library, and in the Greater London Record Office; in the Libraries of the London Boroughs of Newham, Tower Hamlets, and Waltham Forest, and of the Wakefield Metropolitan District Council; in the Passmore Edwards Museum; in the Peterborough Diocesan Registry; in the Huguenot Library at University

College London; in the Library of the Society of Genealogists; and in the Borthwick Institute of Historical Research at York. The Probate Registry at Somerset House was an important source. A number of local histories and manuscripts, etc., were used, though with caution, for some of them were compiled before more accurate records became available. Wherever possible, available genealogical information has been checked against original registers.

Notes

ABBREVIATIONS

BL British Library
BLPES British Library of Political and Economic Science
Bod Bodleian Library, Oxford
DNB Dictionary of National Biography
HH Haddo House
NLS National Library of Scotland
NLW National Library of Wales
PRO Public Record Office, Kew
RA Royal Archives
RO Record Office
SRO Scottish Record Office
UCL University College London
UL University of London

AHG Arthur Hamilton Gordon, Baron Stanmore (1829-1912)
CSLI Charles Shaw Lefevre (1758-1823)
CSLII Charles Shaw Lefevre, Viscount Eversley (1794-1888)
GJSL George John Shaw Lefevre, Baron Eversley (1831-1928)
HFSL Henry Francis Shaw Lefevre (1802-1880)
JGSL John George Shaw Lefevre (1797-1879)

CHAPTER I

1 M.H. Peacock, *History of the Free Grammar School of Queen Elizabeth at Wakefield*, (Wakefield, 1892), 189, 209.
2 D.A. Winstanley, *Unreformed Cambridge* (Cambridge, 1935), 200–3.
3 Pedigree of Shepley [Shipley], *Northern Genealogist*, 2 (1896).
4 The details of these appointments are contained in the Institution Act Books of the Diocese of York, preserved in the Borthwick Institute of Historical Research, York.
5 F. Wrangham, *Brief History of the Free Grammar School at Leeds* (Leeds, 1822), 24–8.
6 E.B. Chancellor, *Wanderings in Marylebone* (London, 1926), 53, 56.
7 Information provided by the Leicestershire RO. Parish records other than the registers either do not begin until after 1811, or are irrelevant.
8 D.H. Monckton, *Genealogical History of the Monckton Family* (London, 1887); Revd H.I. Longden, *Northants and Rutland Clergy*, 14 (Northampton, 1938–52.)

9   *Historical Record of the Sixty First, or the South Gloucestershire Regiment of Foot* (London, 1844).
10 Senior Bursar's Audit Books, Trinity College, Cambridge.
11 *Memoirs of the Life of Sir Samuel Romilly*, 1 (London, 1840), 72, 91.

CHAPTER II

1   Hants RO, 38M49/D23. Wickham's note of conversation with CSLII, Dec 1863.
2   'Lefevre' documents in the Huguenot Library, UCL. See, also, the records of J.W. Nicholson & Co., at the Rose Lipman Library, Hackney, D/B/NIC/1/8/10/5, Hardy to Nicholson, 8 Apr 1909. 'John' is credited with this military experience in some local histories, e.g. G.F. Bosworth, *More Walthamstow Houses* (Walthamstow Antiquarian Society Publication, No. 20, 1928).
3   R. Wailes, *Tide Mills*, 1 (1956) and E.M. Gardner, *Tide Mills, 3, The Three Mills, Bromley-by-Bow* (1957); J.W. Nicholson & Co. records at the Rose Lipman Library, Hackney, and at the Greater London RO.
4   *Morant's History and Antiquity of the County of Essex* (1768) x; S.J. Barns, *Calendar and Documents relating to Walthamstow, 1541–1862* (Walthamstow Antiquarian Society Publication, No. 21, 1929); G.E. Roebuck, *The Story of Walthamstow* (1952); Newham RO, Index to West Ham Vestry Minutes.
5   *Victoria History of Essex* 6 (London, 1973), 77.
6   Isaac's Will, Royal Bank of Scotland, CU/49/12B.
7   P. Matthias, *The Brewing Industry in England, 1700–1830* (Cambridge, 1959), 325.
8   'Currie & Co. The Early Years', *Three Banks Review* 61 (March, 1964); R. Fulford, *Glyn's 1753–1953, Six Generations in Lombard Street* (London, 1953), 186–7.
9   Guildhall Library, Ms 121019, Sun Fire Office Share Ledgers; P.G.M. Dickson, *The Sun Insurance Office, 1710–1960* (London, 1960), 280.
10 Bertram Wodehouse Currie, 1827–1896, *Recollections, Letters and Journals* 1 (Roehampton, 1901), 3–4.
11 C. Smith, *Short Essay on the Corn Trade and the Corn Laws* (1758); *Consideration of the Laws relating to the Importation and Exportation of Corn* (1759); *A Collection of Papers relating to the Price, Exportation and Importation of Corn, with a Supplement*: republished 1766 as *Three Tracts on Corn*.
12 David Hardcastle, Jun., *Banks and Bankers*, 2nd ed. (London, 1843), 12-13; *Three Banks Review*, 61, 41.
13 In addition to family records, see also the works and records cited in note 3.
14 Anthony Trollope, *Ralph the Heir* (London, 1871) Ch. XI.
15 P.W.R. Kennedy & C. Davy (eds), *The History of a Hampshire Parish: Heckfield and Mattingley: A brief, historical sketch based on the researches of the late W.J. James* (Winchester, nd).
16 H.L.L. Denney, *Memorials of an Ancient House: A History of the Family of Lister or Lyster* (Edinburgh, 1913).
17 *Victoria History of Buckinghamshire* 3 (London, 1925), 184–198.
18 Hants RO, 38M49/D23, Wm Wickham's note of conversation with CSLII, Christmas, 1863.
19 *Three Banks Review*, 61, 41.
20 Essex RO, D/DRh Z12.

bbbCHAPTER IIIcc

21 Essex RO, D/DRc F82.

CHAPTER III

1 All quotations hitherto from Kennedy & Davy (eds.), *The History of a Hampshire Parish*.
2 42 Geo. III, liv.
3 HLRO, SL Mss.
4 Hants RO, 38M49/D19, CSLII to Helen Mason, 4 Aug 1883.
5 *Survey of London*, 20 (London, 1940). Bedford Square was then on the edge of open fields and was apparently chosen on account of Helena's health, it being advisable that she should not live 'in London'. Hants RO, 38M49/ D23, Wickham's memo of conversation with CSLII, Dec 1863.
6 C.E. Mingay, *The Gentry: The Rise and Fall of a Ruling Class* (London, 1976) 13–14.
7 *The Times*, 29 Dec 1888.
8 L. Namier and J. Brooke, *The Commons, 1754–1790* 1 (London, 1964), 296; 2, 54–5, 320–22: R.G. Thorne, *The Commons, 1790–1820* 2 (London, 1986), 13–14, 42–5, 186; 3, 146–7; 4, 878–9; 5, 135–7.
9 HH 1/3, Typewritten extract from 'Memoirs of John Hodgkin', c. 1861. I can find no trace of this in Hodgkin's published work.
10 Thorne, *House of Commons* 4, 878–9.
11 The original letters are among the Sidmouth Mss, Devon RO, 152/M; a few are included in G. Pellew, *Life and Correspondence of Henry Addington, 1st Viscount Sidmouth* 1 (London, 1847), 327; 2, 220, 340–41.
12 Thorne, *House of Commons* 3, 435.
13 A.Aspinall and others, *Parliament through Seven Centuries: Reading and its M.Ps.* (London, 1962), 87.
14 Thorne, *House of Commons* 2, 42–5. CSLI's connection with de Dunstanville was quite close. When Sidmouth and his followers were excluded from government in March 1807, Charles suggested that they should buy a newspaper to represent their views and 'to counteract that evil speaking and writing which issues with such rapidity and rancour from the *canine* tribe' [i.e. the Canning group]. Charles claimed that de Dunstanville had been anxious to establish a paper for some time; see Shaw Lefevre to Sidmouth, 1 Apr 1807, quoted in A. Aspinall, *Politics and the Press, 1780–1850* (London, 1949), 85. In view of the more recent biographical references to Shaw Lefevre as an Independent Whig, it is interesting that Aspinall here refers to the Sidmouth camp as 'the only Tory group to be excluded from the . . . Portland Ministry.'
15 R.C. Baily, The Parliamentary History of Reading between 1750 and 1850 (M.A. Thesis, Reading University, 1944), 24: Aspinall, *Parliament through Seven Centuries*, 91.
16 Baily, The Parliamentary History of Reading, 15, 16.
17 Baily, 93.
18 Baily, 36.
19 Aspinall, *Parliament through Seven Centuries*, 87.
20 *Reading Mercury*, 5 May 1823.
21 Baily, The Parliamentary History of Reading, 57. Baily calculated the average cost per candidate between 1750 and 1850 as £2,000 for each election. For the 'golden key' see *Reading Mercury*, 3 Apr 1880.

22 J. Wilson, *A Biographical Index to the Present House of Commons* (London, 1808).

23 *Reading Mercury*, 5 May 1823.

24 Baily, The Parliamentary History of Reading, 128–33; Thorne, *House of Commons* 2, 14.

25 Thorne, *House of Commons* 2, 13.

26 W.S. Darter, *Reminiscences of Reading by an Octogenarian* (1889), 15.

27 P.H. Ditchfield, *Reading 70 Years Ago: A Record of Events from 1813 to 1819* (Reading, 1877), 76–7, 79.

28 Aspinall, *Parliament through Seven Centuries*, 88.

29 A.G. L'Estrange, *Life of Mary Russell Mitford* 1 (London, 1870), 64–5.

30 Compare Harriet Martineau's opinion of Mary Russell Mitford, in her *Autobiography*, ed. Maria Weston, (Boston, 1877): 'I must say that personally I did not like her so well as I liked her works. The charming *bonhommie* of her writings appeared at first in her conversation and manners; but there were other things which sadly impaired its charm. . . . What concerned me was her habit of flattery, and the twin habit of disparagement of others. I never knew her to respond to any act or course of conduct which was morally lofty. She could not believe in it, nor, of course, enjoy it: and she seldom failed to 'see through' it, and to delight in her superiority to admiration.'

31 BL Add. Mss. 31250, H. Beecke to Vansittart, 1 Jan 1806.

32 Thorne, *House of Commons* 2, 14; 5, 136–7.

33 The second Lady Sidmouth was Marianne, widow of Thomas Townsend. She was the only surviving child of Lord Stowell, and had lived a few miles from the Shaw Lefevres, at Erleigh Court, Reading. She died in 1842, Sidmouth in 1844.

34 Thorne, *House of Commons* 5, 136–7. CSLI did not sign the requisition to Tierney in 1818, and he never joined Brooks's Club.

35 E.M.G. Belfield, *Annals of the Addington Family* (Winchester, 1959), 122.

36 Royal Society, Council Minutes, 1807–8.

37 R.H. O'Byrne, *The Representative History of Great Britain and Ireland, Pt. II – Berkshire* (London, 1848), 164.

38 *Reading Mercury*, 5 May 1823.

CHAPTER IV

1 *Reading Mercury*, 5 May 1823.

2 Hants RO, 38M49/7.

3 HH 1/3, 'Memoirs of John Hodgkin'.

4 HH 1/3.

5 At least one of the violins was made by William Forster and sold to Charles Lefevre in 1791: W. Sandys and S.A. Forster, *The History of the Violin* (London, 1864), 321. After his death the violins were given to Lord Seymour.

6 Mrs Mitford to Mary Russell Mitford, 14 Nov 1802, in A.G. L'Estrange, *The Friendships of Mary Russell Mitford* 1 (London, 1882), 7, 8. Fanny Milton, daughter of the vicar of Heckfield, was to be the mother of Anthony Trollope.

7 Mrs Mitford to Mary Russell Mitford, 27 Sep 1806, in *The Friendships of Mary Russell Mitford* 1, 10, 11.

8 HH 1/3.

9 V. Martineau, *John Martineau the Pupil of Kingsley* (London, 1921), 121.

10 HH 1/47, Extract from the Diary of William Wickham, 1879.

11 HH 1/3.

12 *Victoria History of Hampshire* 2 (London, 1903), 354.

13 *The Times*, 29 Dec 1888. Charles claimed that at Cambridge he was a great tennis player, only beaten by one Scrope Davis of King's, Hants RO 38M49, Wickham's Diary, 31 Dec 1886.

14 HH 1/3.

15 Hants RO, 15M50/1341.

16 Bedfordshire RO, W3394, W3540.

17 Hants RO, 38M49/7.

18 *The Times*, 29 Dec 1888. Dickson, *Sun Insurance Office*, 280.

19 HH 1/3, 'Memoirs of John Hodgkin'.

20 HH 1/3, D. Le Marchant to T. Paynter, 24 Jan 1818.

21 HH 1/3, 22, 23, 24 Jan 1818.

22 HH 1/3, Allen to Helena Lefevre, quoting George Hammond, ?Jan 1818.

23 J.M.F. Wright, *Alma Mater or Seven Years at the University of Cambridge* 2 (Cambridge, 1827), 27.

24 HH 1/3, 'Memoirs of John Hodgkin'.

25 Mrs Burney (Madame D'Arblay), *Diary and Letters* 7 (London, 1846), 282–301: T.B. Macaulay, *Essay on Frances Burney*, 1843: HH 1/47, Madeleine Shaw Lefevre to Laverton Harris, 30 June 1912.

26 Senior Bursar's Audit Books; Exit and Redit Book 1799–1844, Trinity College, Cambridge.

27 HH 1/3, 'Memoirs of John Hodgkin'.

28 HH 1/3.

29 Hants RO, 15M50/1341.

30 HH 1/3, JGSL to Emily Wright, 26 Nov 1824.

31 HH 1/3.

CHAPTER V

1 R.E. Foster, 'Leadership, Politics and Government in the County of Hampshire during the Lord Lieutenancy of the First Duke of Wellington, 1820–1852' (Ph.D Thesis, Southampton University, 1986); and 'The Duke of Wellington at Home', *The Historian* 7, Summer 1985, 8–9.

2 Wellington Mss, 4/1/1–20, 4/2/6–12, *passim*.

3 HH 1/3.

4 Burley Manor remained in JGSL's hands until 1839–40, when he sold it. The old mansion was burned down c. 1850, and the house which replaced it has since become an hotel.

5 Bedfordshire RO, WI/6001/13, Lady Elizabeth Whitbread to Maria Edgeworth, 5 Jul 1829; WI/6001/17, Julia Grant to Maria Edgeworth, nd 1837: Hants RO 15M50/1341.

6 HH 1/3. This account is drawn entirely from this group of documents, which includes several pages of recollections of Emily Shaw Lefevre, dictated to or compiled by one of her daughters – most probably Madeleine.

7 *Thornton's History of Nottinghamshire* 2 (republished with large additions by John Thursby, London 1797), 231. The house is now the headquarters of Severn Trent Water, plc.

8 A considerable proportion of the Shaw Lefevre archive in the HLRO consists of material concerned with the Spencer estates, including letters from the Earls Spencer to JGSL. There are also over a hundred letters which passed between JGSL and the second Earl, from 1826 to 1833, in the Althorp Mss in the BL – G144, 149, 155,

158, 166.

9   Nottinghamshire RO, M5586, Diaries of Ichabod Wright 1, 7 Sep 1808: Augustus Hare, *Story of My Life* 4 (London, 1896–1900), 371–3: HH, 1/3.

10 HLRO, SL Mss, Aug–Dec 1843. The lease of Terrace House must have been extended well beyond the forty-five years which JGSL negotiated in 1828, for it remained in the family until 1895, when the freehold passed to the Society for the Promotion of Christian Knowledge. The house was acquired by the Battersea Council in 1928, and they wanted to demolish it to make way for a housing estate. There then began an agitation to save the building, and in the process claims were put forward that it had been built for the St. John family and had been designed by Wren in 1699. The agitation was successful, the building was saved and renamed Old Battersea House, and in more recent times has been restored and handsomely refurbished. It is now leased to the Forbes Foundation, which makes its lower floor available to the De Morgan Foundation for the display of the De Morgan Art Collection. This happy outcome was due more to the historical and environmental enthusiasm of those who fought for the preservation of the house than to the accuracy of their suggestions as to its origins. More recent research has shown that there is no proof that any of the St. John family ever lived there, or that Sir Christopher Wren designed it. There are good grounds for believing only that it was built in the later part of the seventeenth century, and replaced a Tudor building of the same dimensions. See especially F.T. Smallwood, 'The Story of Terrace House Battersea', in *Surrey Archives Collections*, lxiv, 1967. I am indebted to the Solicitor's Department of the London Borough of Wandsworth for access to the deeds of Terrace House which they hold.

11 HH/ 1/3.

12 Brougham Mss, UCL, 15959, Lavinia, Countess Spencer, to Brougham, 8 Dec 1830.

13 P.W. Matthews and A.W. Tuke, *History of Barclays Bank* (London, 1926), 70–71.

14 H. Price, *A Handbook of London Bankers* (London, 1890–91), 20.

15 Sidmouth Mss, 152M, CSLI to Sidmouth, 27 Jul 1809. Though he does not cite any evidence in support of the connection, the biographer of the third earl describes CSLII as 'an old family friend'. Ronald K. Huch, *The Radical Lord Radnor: The Public Life of Viscount Folkestone, Third Earl of Radnor (1779–1869)* (Minneapolis, 1977), 112.

16 Hants RO, 38M49/8/279.

17 Hants RO, 38M49/D19, CSLII to HFSL, 20 Feb 1833.

18 Hants RO, 38M49/7/166/1–9.

19 A memento of Thomas and of Bowerbank, Monkhouse, which passed into HFSL's hands, and remained in the office of H.S. Lefevre & Co. until its closure in 1949–50, is a large pair of scissors used by Thomas to cut cloth in his early years as a draper. I am obliged to the late Mr Duncan Stirling for this information.

20 Hants RO 38M49/7/113/1–10, 23 Jun and 12 Jul 1834.

21 HH 1/3.

22 Hants RO 38M49/7/113/1–10, H.D. Douglas to JGSL, 15 Aug 1834.

23 Hants RO 38M49/7/113/1–10, JGSL to CSLII, Aug 1834.

24 HH 1/3: Nottinghamshire RO, M5586, Wright Diaries, Aug 1834.

CHAPTER VI

1   BL Add. Mss 36461, 36464, 36466.

2   HC Deb 3rd series, vii, 1394, quoted in E. Porritt, *The Unreformed House of Commons* 1 (Cambridge, 1903), 36.

3 R. Southey, *Life and Correspondence* 5 (London, 1849, 50), 261: Porritt, *The Unreformed House of Commons* 1, 175–6. The DNB states, wrongly, that the third Earl Radnor offered Downton to Robert Southey in 1826 and stipulated that he should vote for the disfranchisement of the borough. But in 1826 the second Earl was still alive, and he nominated Southey because he believed he would be a guardian of the existing constitution.

4 Brougham Mss, 24644, Radnor to Brougham, 19 Jul 1831.

5 Wilts RO 490/1374, for all three letters. The account given here of this episode draws on both the original letters and on Huch, *The Radical Lord Radnor*, 111–17.

6 Wilts RO 490/1374. This and the following extract are from a Memo of Radnor's dated 9 Jul 1830.

7 HH 1/3.

8 Wilts RO 490/1374, CSLII to Radnor, 6 Aug 1830.

9 HLRO, SL Mss, Letter Book V.

10 Wellington Mss, 4/1/3/4/17.

11 J. Gore (ed.), *Creevey's Life and Times 1768–1838* (London, 1934), 342; Wilts RO, 490/1375.

12 HLRO, SL Mss, JGSL to Spencer, 14 Sep 1832.

13 HLRO, SL Mss, Letter Book vii, JGS to Spencer, 28 Jan 1832.

14 HLRO, SL Mss, Letter Book 1828–1832, JGSL to Spencer, 9 Jun 1832; Hants RO, 94M72/F12, John Bonham Carter to F.T. Baring, 28 Oct 1832.

15 HLRO, SL Mss, Letter Book vii, nd but early Jun 1832.

16 Wellington Mss, 4/1/4/1/15, Wellington to Fleming, 7 Sep 1832.

17 *Hampshire Chronicle*, 24 Sep 1832, letter dated 14 Sep; Foster, Leadership, Politics and Government, 363.

18 Wellington Mss, 4/1/4/3/27, Geo. Hollis to Wellington, 14 Oct 1832; 4/1/4/3/29, ? to Wellington, 28 Oct 1832.

19 A. Aspinall (ed.), *Three Early Nineteenth Century Diaries*, (London, 1952), 287.

20 House of Commons Journals, 7, and 26 Feb, 5 Mar 1833.

21 HLRO, SL Mss, Stanley to JGSL, 4 Feb 1834; Aspinall, *Three Early Nineteenth Century Diaries*, 378.

22 Brougham Mss, J593, Le Marchant to Wm. Brougham, Dec 1832; 16662, Le Marchant to [H] Brougham, 1834.

23 HLRO, SL Mss, Letter Book vii, JGSL to Spencer, 14 Sep 1832.

24 HLRO, SL Mss, Letter Book 1828–1832, and Letter Book Burley 1829–33.

25 Aspinall, *Three Early Nineteenth Century Diaries*, 316.

26 Aspinall, 317.

27 HH 1/3, Stanley to JGSL, 29 Mar 1833.

28 Thorne, *The House of Commons* 3, 411.

29 Aspinall, 317.

30 BL, Althorp Mss, G304, Althorp to Spencer, 30 Mar 1833. If one is fascinated by, but familiar with, the long interconnections of established families, it will be unsurprising that William, the son of Henry Lewis Wickham, born in 1831, and Sophia Emma, the youngest daughter of HFSL by his first wife, Helen Le Marchant, sister of Denis Le Marchant, were married in 1860. See ch XI.

31 HH 1/3, Emily Shaw Lefevre, 29 Mar 1833.

32 Aspinall, 317.

33 D.J. Murray, *The West Indies and the Development of Colonial Government*

1801–1834 (Oxford, 1965), 210–227.

34 HLRO, SL Mss, letters between JGSL and Stephen, May 1833 to Aug 1834.
35 Murray, 214.
36 HH 1/3, Annex to a memo by JGSL to Palmerston, 24 Jul 1856.
37 HH 1/3.
38 BL, Althorp Mss, G304, Althorp to Spencer, 4 Aug 1834.
39 S. & B. Webb, *English Poor Law History* 2 i (London, 1929), 106.

CHAPTER VII

1 Wellington Mss, 4/1/6/3/21, Dec 1834.
2 On this highly technical side of CSLII's parliamentary work, see O.C. Williams, *History of Private Bill Procedure* 1 (HMSO, 1948), 77–81, 90, 130, 173; and D. Holland and D. Menhennet (eds), *Erskine May's Private Journal 1857–1882* (London, 1957), *passim*.
3 For the committee's three brief reports and the minutes of evidence, see PP 1836, viii.
4 *Remarks on the Present State of Agriculture, in a letter addressed to his Constituents by C.S.Lefevre, Esq., M.P., Chairman of the Select Committee appointed to enquire into the State of Agriculture, Session 1836* (London, 1836).
5 W. Blacker, *Review of C.S. Lefevre Esq's Letter to his Constituents* (London, 1837); E.S. Cayley, MP *Letter to H. Handley Esq., M.P., on the Proceedings of the Agriculture Committee of 1836 and in Answer to Mr. Shaw Lefevre's Pamphlet* (London, 1836).
6 H.L. Wickham, *Letter to C.S. Lefevre on the Corn Laws* (London, 1839). For comments on CSLII's attitudes to agriculture, and his closeness to Sir Robert Peel in that context, see D.C. Moore, *The Politics of Deference: A Study of the mid-Nineteenth Century English Political System* (Hassocks, 1976), 339–41, 350, 353.
7 For the Commissioners' Report, published in 1839, see PP 1839, xix.
8 PRO 30/22/2C/89–90, CSLII to Russell, 11 Sep 1836.
9 UCL, Chadwick Mss, 18 Sep 1836.
10 PRO 30/22/2C/154–56, 22 Sep 1836. The County Rate Report had been produced by a select committee in 1834, of which CSLII was a member, see PP 1834, xiv.
11 Chadwick Mss, CSLII to Chadwick, 20 Oct 1836.
12 Chadwick Mss, nd [Sep 1836].
13 Chadwick Mss, 20 Oct and 18 Dec 1836.
14 Chadwick Mss, 28 Jan 1838.
15 Chadwick Mss, CSLII to Chadwick, 2 Mar 1839. On CSLII's role in the Commission, see A. Brundage, 'Ministers Magistrates and Reformers: the Genesis of the Rural Constabulary Act of 1839', in *Parliamentary History*, v, 1986; and his later volume, *England's Prussian Minister: Edwin Chadwick and the Politics of Government Growth, 1832–1854* (University Park and London, 1988), ch 4. See also S.E. Finer, *The Life and Times of Sir Edwin Chadwick* (London, 1952).
16 PRO 30/22/2B/311–12, CSLII to Russell, 21 Aug 1836.
17 Report of Select Committee on Survey of Parishes (Tithe Commutation Act), PP 1837, vi; Bill to declare the effect of the Act of 6 & 7 Will IV c 71 to regulate Parochial Assessments, PP 1837–38, v; Revd R. Jones, *Remarks on the Manner in which Tithes should be assessed to the Poor's Rate, under the existing law, with a Protest against the change which will be produced in that law by a Bill introduced into the House of Commons by Mr. Shaw Lefevre* (London, 1838).

18 Charles Abbot, second Baron Colchester, *Memoranda of My Life* (London, 1869), 78.

19 James Grant, *Random Recollections of the Lords and Commons*, 2nd series, 2 (London, 1838), 177–81.

20 The Committee actually spread its labours over three sessions, and CSLII was replaced on it after becoming Speaker in 1839. He was also chairman of a select committee on Standing Orders Revision in 1837–38: see PP 1837, xiii; PP 1837–38, xxiii; PP 1839 xiii. W.M. Torrens, *Memoirs of Viscount Melbourne* 2 (London, 1878), 295–9.

21 S. Walpole, *The Life of Lord John Russell* 1 (London, 1889), 322; I. Newbould, *Whiggery and Reform 1830–1841* (London, 1990) 244.

22 Torrens, *Memoirs of Viscount Melbourne* 2, 296.

23 *The Times*, 29 Dec 1888.

24 N. Gash, *Sir Robert Peel, The Life of Sir Robert Peel after 1830* (London, 1972), 221.

25 *The Times*, 29 Dec 1888.

26 Parl. Deb. 3s, 47, cols 1034–1050, 27 May 1839. Royal Archives, Queen Victoria's Journal, 21 Jun 1839.

27 Wellington Mss, 4/1/12/23, 26 Jul 1841.

28 A.H. Johnson (ed.), *Letters of Charles Greville and Henry Reeve 1836–65* (London, 1924), Greville to Reeve, 19 Jul 1841.

29 BL Add Mss 40476, Fremantle to Peel, 20 Jul 1841; Add Mss 40485, Bonham to Peel, 22 Jul 1841.

30 Gash, *Sir Robert Peel*, 267.

31 BL Add Mss 40486, Bonham to Peel, Aug [2–4?] 1841.

32 C.S. Parker, *Sir Robert Peel from his Private Papers* 2 (London, 1899), 478–9.

33 G. Kitson Clark, *Peel and the Conservative Party, 1832–41* (London, 1929), 487.

34 BL Add Mss 40476, Fremantle to Peel, 23 Jul 1841.

35 BL Add Mss 40485, Bonham to Peel, 28 Jul 1841.

36 PRO 30/22/4B, Russell to Melbourne, 4 Aug 1841.

37 The fullest statement of Peel's attitude was contained in a letter to Wellington on 1 Aug 1841 – see C.S. Parker, *Sir Robert Peel* 2, 476–77.

38 Gash, *Sir Robert Peel*, 267.

39 PRO 30/22/4B, Lady Holland to Russell, 22 Jul 1841.

40 BL Add Mss 40484, Arbuthnot to Peel, 6 Aug 1841.

41 BL Add Mss 40476, Fremantle to Peel, 23 Jul 1841.

42 BL Add Mss 40486, Peel to Stanley, nd.

43 BL Add Mss 40486, Peel to CSLII, 1 Aug 1841.

44 BL Add Mss 40486, CSLII to Peel, 4 Aug 1841. RA QVJ 4 Aug 1841.

45 PRO 30/22/4B/94–5, CSLII to Russell, 4 Aug 1841.

46 BL Add Mss 40485, Bonham to Peel, 29 Jul 1841. 'They' were 'Blackstone, Tyrell & Co.' On 3 Aug Peel told Goulburn that Lowther was 'strongly opposed' to Lefevre, and listed Sugden, Jackson, Burdett, Tyrell, D'Israeli, Nield and Blackstone as wanting to put up a Conservative candidate. Goulburn Mss II, 18.

47 BL Add Mss 40486, Bonham to Peel, 13 Aug 1841.

CHAPTER VIII

1 HLRO, SL Mss, Letter from 'Publicola', 11 Oct 1836.

2 There are scores of letters from local people in JGSL's papers in the House of

Lords. Anthony Brundage has made use of them in his study, *The Making of the New Poor Law: The politics of inquiry, enactment and implementation, 1832–39* (London, 1978).

3 HLRO, SL Mss, Stanley to JGSL, 16 Jun 1841.

4 UL, Overstone Mss, 804/1966, Ichabod Wright to Harriet Loyd, 22 Aug 1829.

5 M.C. Grobel, The Society for the Diffusion of Useful Knowledge Ph.D Thesis, UL, 1932; *Proceedings of the Political Economy Club* 6, London, 1921. John had been a fellow guest, with James Mill, of George Grote and his wife, as early as 1822 – Mrs Grote, *The Personal Life of George Grote* (London, 1873), 49.

6 HH 1/3. Official Autobiography of JGSL, c. 1875.

7 D. Pike, *Paradise of Dissent, South Australia 1829–1857* (London, 1957); E. Hodder (ed.), *The Founding of South Australia: As recorded in the Journals of Mr. Robert Gouger* (London, 1898); E. Hodder, *James Fife Angus* (London, 1891); F.H. Hitchins, *The Colonial Land and Emigration Commission* (Philadelphia, 1931); 4 & 5 Will IV c 95.

8 HH 1/3. A slightly edited version was published in *The South Australian Register Observer and Journal* on 8 Aug 1898, as a result of a casual meeting between Madeleine Shaw Lefevre and the editor, J. Harvey Finlayson, at a reception at the National History Museum in June of that year. I am very grateful to Dr. Decie Denholm of the University of Adelaide who searched herself and through colleagues for confirmation of the story. It would seem, however, that it can neither be confirmed nor denied.

9 Hitchins, *Colonial Land and Emigration Commission*, 69.

10 BL, Althorp Mss H13. For more work on the sale of the Battersea and Wandsworth estates in 1837–39, see H15.

11 HLRO, SL Mss, Letter Book X, Hutchings to Pickering, 10 Sep 1835.

12 Rowland Hill & G.B. Hill, *The Life of Sir Rowland Hill and the History of Penny Postage* (London, 1880), 1, 209–10; Frederic Hill (ed. Constance Hill), *An Autobiography of Fifty Years in Times of Reform* (London, 1894), 297. Frederic Hill recalls that the group called themselves, 'with the approval of Mr [later Sir Arthur] Helps', 'Friends in Council', but there is nothing to connect Helps with them or with the subject matter of the essays which he published under that title.

13 The 150th anniversary of the Founding of the University was marked by the publication of an illustrated history – Negley Harte, *The University of London 1836–1986* (London, 1986).

14 UL, Minutes of the Senate.

15 HLRO, SL Mss.

16 HLRO, SL Mss, Revd G. Peacock to JGSL, 19 and 22 Oct 1837.

17 UL, Minutes of the Committee of the Faculty of Laws.

18 HLRO, SL Mss.

19 HH 1/3, JGSL to Emily, Sep/Oct 1840.

20 Finer, *Life and Times of Sir Edwin Chadwick*, 148. The opinion expressed there is that John was not only at the end of his tether, but also 'timid, legalistic, without social vision.'

21 HH 1/3, JGSL to Emily, 17 Sep 1836.

22 Melbourne (Broadlands) Mss, MEL/RU/150, Melbourne to Russell, 19 Apr 1835; Brougham Mss, 16664, Le Marchant to Brougham, Oct 1835.

23 J.C. Sainty, *Office Holders. Boards of Trade 1660–1870* (London, 1974).

24 Melbourne (Broadlands) Mss, MEL/RU/82/1, 23 Apr 1839.

25 J.C.Sainty, *Office Holders. Treasury Officials 1660–1870* (London, 1972).

26 PRO 30/22/4B, Le Marchant to Russell, 9 & 26 Jul 1841; CSLII to Russell, 4 Aug 1841.

27 PRO 30/22/4B, Russell to Melbourne, 23 Jul 1841.

28 HH 1/3, Stanley to JGSL, 16 Jun 1841.

CHAPTER IX

1 W.F. Monypenny and G.E. Buckle, *The Life of Benjamin Disraeli, Earl of Beaconsfield* 1 (London, 1929), 1196, 1204–5.

2 *The Times*, 29 Dec 1888. See also Spencer Walpole, *The History of 25 Years, 1856–1865* 1 (London, 1904), 90–91.

3 Review of Hon. Robert Bourke, *Parliamentary Precedents. Being Decisions of the Rt. Hon. C.S.Lefevre, Speaker of the House of Commons on Points of Order, Rules of Debate, and the General Practice of the House* (London, 1857), in the *Athenaeum*, 21 Feb 1857; Sir John Mowbray, *70 Years at Westminster* (London, 1900), 115–6.

4 *The Times*, 29 Dec. 1888.

5 Philip Laundy, *The Office of Speaker* (London, 1964), 87–8.

6 Laundy, *The Office of Speaker*, 32.

7 HH 1/3, AHG's recollection, recorded by Madeleine Shaw Lefevre.

8 Hants RO, 15M50/1204/6, Montagu Butler to GJSL, 25 June 1901. For another example of CSLII's concern with orderly behaviour, see W. White, *Inner Life of the House of Commons* 1 (London, 1897), 130.

9 The *Times*, 29 Dec 1888.

10 Mowbray, *70 Years at Westminster*, 115–6.

11 HH 1/3, Memo of Madeleine Shaw Lefevre. CSLII recalled that, at the outset of his career as Speaker, he had discussed with Admiral Dennis Dundas how to discipline the House, and had decided 'never to overlook the slightest breach of order.' Hants RO, 38M49, Wickham Diary, 26 Dec 1883.

12 Laundy, *The Office of Speaker*, 305.

13 CSLII gave evidence to the Select Committees on Public Business, and on Private Bills, PP 1847/48, xvi; the Select Committee on Private Business, PP 1851, x; the Select Committee on the Office of Speaker, PP 1852/53, xxxiv; and the Select Committee on the Business of the House, PP 1854, vii.

14 The great work, Erskine May, *Treatise on the Law, Privileges, Proceedings and Usages of Parliament*, is now in its 21st edition (London, 1989), edited by Clifford Boulton.

15 Laundy, *The Office of Speaker*, 304–5.

16 BL Add Mss 46127, CSLII to Murchison, nd but probably 1851.

17 See e.g., PRO 30/22/8E/265–6, 273, CSLII to Russell, 27 Aug and 3 Sept, 1850.

18 BL Add Mss 40484, 40577, 40589.

19 *Britannia*, 7 Aug 1841, article by Lorgnette, reproduced in *The Museum of Foreign Literature, Science and Art*, (Philadelphia), New Series XIV, Jan–Apr 1842.

20 HH 1/3; Hants RO 15M50/1341.

21 Roundell Palmer, Earl of Selborne, *Memorials*, Part 2, 1 (London, 1896), 18; A.I. Dasent, *John Delane, 1817–1879* 2 (London, 1908), 123, Delane to Dasent, 6 Sep 1864. In fairness to Delane, when asked by Palmerston for his advice on who should succeed Shaw Lefevre, he listed as 'indispensable qualities' all those which could be said to have been possessed exactly by the retiring Speaker – see Dasent, 1, 251. And,

interestingly enough, in the context of the Irish post, Palmerston himself remarked to Grey that Eversley 'would look the part well.' Northbrook Mss, Palmerston to Grey, 6 Sep 1864.

22 V. Martineau, *John Martineau*, 124–5.

23 See two articles by Maurice F. Bond, 'Clerks of the Parliaments, 1509–1953', in *English Historical Review*, 73, 1958, 78–85, and 'The Office of Clerk of the Parliaments', in *Parliamentary Affairs*, 12, 1959, 297–310.

24 *DNB*.

25 *DNB*.

26 HH 1/2, William Brougham to JGSL, 7 Apr 1848.

27 Brougham Mss, 16684, Le Marchant to Brougham, nd (1848).

28 Select Committee on Miscellaneous Expenditure, PP 1847–48, xviii. Powys was a junior committee clerk. George Waldegrave was a committee clerk from 1845 to 1847 and then became assistant librarian. He was official secretary to Speaker Shaw Lefevre and his successor, Speaker Dennison, before himself becoming an MP in 1864.

29 According to CSLII, Ley, who kept race horses, was responsible for establishing the tradition whereby the House of Commons adjourned on Derby Day. He managed to keep the day free of motions and notices, so that the House found itself with no business, and the members (and Ley) were free to attend the race. Hants RO, 38M49, Wickham Diaries, 26 Dec 1883.

30 PRO 30/22/8E, Labouchere to Russell, 25 Aug 1850; Le Marchant to Russell, 26 Aug & 24 Sep 1850.

31 HLRO, Erskine May Mss, CSLII to May, 31 Aug 1871; PRO 30/22/8E/265–6, CSLII to Russell, 27 Aug 1850; D. Holland and D. Menhennet, *Erskine May's Private Journal, 1857–1882* (London, 1972), xi.

32 *Vanity Fair*, 1 Jul 1871.

33 *Morning Chronicle*, 21 Aug 1855.

34 HLRO, Erskine May Mss, Lefevre to May, 21 Sep 1855.

35 Holland and Menhennet, *Erskine May's Private Journals*, 1.

36 *Illustrated London News*, 7 Feb 1857. This was probably quite an accurate statement, as an official report shows that up to 1853 CSLII had been Speaker during sittings of 1826 days – over 13,439 hours, 1,245 of them after midnight – see Appendix 8 to the Report of the Select Committee on the Office of Speaker, PP 1852/53, xxxiv.

37 RA QVJ 31 Mar 1857.

38 Hants RO, 15M50/1341.

39 HLRO, Erskine May Mss, CSLII to May, nd but March 1857; Holland and Menhennet, *Erskine May's Private Journal*, ix–x.

40 A.I. Dasent, *The Speakers of the House of Commons* (London, 1911), 324, which gives no authority for the story about the rejected pension.

41 *Letters of Queen Victoria, 1837–1861* 3, ed. A.C. Benson and Viscount Esher (New York, 1907), 292; Laundy, *The Office of Speaker*, 116–7.

42 Hants RO, 38M49/7/117/1, Palmerston to CSLII, 19 Mar 1857.

43 Hants RO, 15M50/1341.

44 Hants RO, 38M49/7/117/8, Ward to CSLII, 11 May 1857.

CHAPTER X

1 H. Parris, *Constitutional Bureaucracy* (London, 1969), ch 5.

2 Amongst the considerable relevant literature, see Lucy Brown, *The Board of Trade and the Free Trade Movement, 1830–1842* (Oxford, 1958); F.E. Hyde, *Mr. Gladstone*

at the Board of Trade (London, 1934); H.L. Smith, *The Board of Trade* (London, 1928); R. Prouty, *The Transformation of the Board of Trade* (London, 1957).

3 BL Add Mss 44724, JGSL to Gladstone, 28 May 1835.

4 *The Prime Ministers' Papers: W.E. Gladstone I. Autobiographica* (London, 1971), 44.

5 Georgina Battiscombe, *Mrs Gladstone, The Portrait of a Marriage* (London, 1956), 57.

6 G.E. Marindin, *Letters of Frederic Lord Blachford* (London, 1896), 117, 124.

7 Report of Commissioners appointed to consider the steps to be taken for Restoration of the Standards of Weight and Measure, PP 1842, xxv; Report of Commissioners appointed to Supervise the Construction of New Parliamentary Standards of Length and Weight, PP 1854, xix.

8 Report to Treasury by Commissioners appointed to Inquire and Ascertain in what manner Exchequer Bills have been made out and issued, PP 1842, xviii; Report of Royal Commission on Forged Exchequer Bills, PP 1842, xviii.

9 SRO, GD45/7/52/1–45, JGSL to Dalhousie, 23 Sep 1845, Dalhousie to JGSL, 24 Sep 1845.

10 Augustus Hare, *The Story of My Life* 4, 157; Sir Henry Cole, *Fifty Years of Public Work* 1 (London, 1884), 109, 121, 172.

11 Quentin Bell, *The Schools of Design* (London, 1963), 62 – and *passim* for the whole story.

12 *Journal of Design and Manufactures* 1, 1849, quoted in Prouty, *Transformation of the Board of Trade*, 28 fn. 15.

13 HH/1/10/5, Gladstone to JGSL, 26 May 1845.

14 Hare, *Story of My Life 4*, 371–3; HH 1/2, Grey to JGSL, 21 Jan 1847; HH 1/3, Ichabod Wright to Emily Lefevre, 28 Jan 1847.

15 Brougham Mss 16676, Le Marchant to Brougham, 21 Sep 1847.

16 PRO 30/22/6C, CSLII to Russell, May 1847.

17 Brougham Mss 16676, Le Marchant to Brougham, 21 Sep 1847.

18 Henry Gunning, *Reminiscences of the University, Town and County of Cambridge from the year 1780* (London, 1854), xvi; Sir Frederick Pollock, *Personal Remembrances* 1 (London, 1887), 250–2.

19 *Daily News*, 11 Jun 1847.

20 Papers and letters concerning the election are mainly in the HH Mss and in HLRO, SL Mss, with a few in the archives of the Royal Society (Lubbock Mss L235, L236) and of Trinity College, Cambridge (Add Mss a.66, 57 & 58). The election address was published in *The Times*, 11 Jun 1847.

21 This letter, dated 13 Jul 1847, and sent from 55 Charing Cross, the headquarters of the London Committee, was printed and must have had some considerable circulation. A copy of it is at Haddo House.

22 Pollock, *Personal Remembrances*, 250–2.

23 H.S. Smith (ed. F.W.S. Craig), *The Parliaments of England* (Chichester, 1973).

24 Elliot Mss, JGSL to Sir Edward Ryan, 2 Aug 1847. It is an interesting comment on the volatility of contemporary religious allegiance that Viscount Fielding, not long after the election, and to 'the great dismay of his supporters, went over to the Church of Rome.' See Pollock, *Personal Remembrances*, 252. Clarendon could not understand 'how or why Lord Fielding occupied the place he did or what possible interest, present or future, of Church or State that raw unknown

youth was intended to advance' by his candidacy – HH Clarendon to JGSL, 5 Aug 1847. PRO 30/22/6D, Duke of Bedford and Le Marchant to Russell, July 1847: the election was followed closely by Russell, Bedford and Le Marchant. The last of these insisted in July that 'Lefevre is gaining ground decidedly', while Bedford regretted the failure of a senior figure to support John, and reported that 'Peel will be . . . angry if Goulburn is beaten. . . . He may well feel annoyed and disappointed, but ought not to be angry, as the intention was to turn out Law, not Goulburn.'

25 HH 1/2, Clarendon to JGSL, 5 Aug 1847.

26 HH 1/2, Russell to JGSL, 12 Nov 1847.

27 Notts RO, M5587, Wright Diaries, 8 Apr 1848.

28 HH 1/2, Lady Cottenham to Emily Shaw Lefevre, May [1848].

29 HH 1/10/5, Gladstone to JGSL, 1 Apr 1848.

30 BL Add Mss 44367, JGSL to Gladstone, 3 [?] May 1848.

31 PP 1850, xxxiv, Copies of Reports from J.G.S. Lefevre to the Treasury respecting the Erection of Galleries of Art at Edinburgh.

32 BL Add Mss 44368, JGSL to Gladstone, 18 Apr 1849.

33 For the official coverage of this episode, see PP 1849, xlvi, Report on the Annuity Tax in the City of Edinburgh, and Cannongate, to Sir George Grey, Bt., by J.G.S. Lefevre, 27 April 1849 [The date at the head of the text of the Report is given as 27 April 1848, but this is clearly a mis-print.]; PP 1850, xlix, Letter from J.G.S. Lefevre to Sir George Grey, Bt., respecting the Annuity Tax in Edinburgh; PP 1851, vii, Report of Select Committee on the Annuity Tax (Edinburgh).

34 See Select Committee on Abolition Act, 1860, PP 1866, viii.

35 PP 1856, lix, Copy of the Reports addressed to the Treasury in or since the year 1848 by J.G.S.Lefevre on the subject of the Fishery Board in Scotland.

36 Papers relating to the Surrender of their Charter by the New Zealand Company, PP 1851, xxxv.

37 Royal Commission to inquire into the Constitution and Government of the British Museum, PP 1850, xxiv.

38 Royal Commission on Episcopal and Capitular Estates, PP 1850, xx.

39 See, *inter alia*, Brougham Mss, 5903, JGSL to Brougham, 17 Aug 1852; 5906, JGSL to Brougham, 8 Jan 1855; 5907, JGSL to Brougham, 16 Jan 1855; BL Add Mss 44388, JGSL to Gladstone, 27 Oct 1857; 44415, JGSL to Gladstone, 24 Jun 1868; Hare, *Story of My Life*, 2 & 4, *passim*; HH 1/47, Extract from diary of William Wickham, 1879.

40 Bond, *Parliamentary Affairs*, xii, 309. For average attendance figures of peers, see a Return of 11 July, 1873, in HLRO/PO/79/9.

41 PRO 30/22/13A, Grey to Russell, 17 Jan 1856.

42 Royal Commission to inquire into Arrangements in Inns of Court and Chancery for promoting Study of Law and Jurisprudence, PP 1854–55, xviii.

43 India Act, 16 & 17 Vic. c 95 (1853).

44 G.O. Trevelyan, *Life and Letters of Lord Macaulay* (London, 1876; edition used, 1959), 609. The frequent confusion between the identities of the two Shaw Lefevres is illustrated by the list of names on the cover of the Macaulay Report, where the fifth member of the group is described as 'The Hon. the Speaker of the House of Commons', while the signatories at the end of the text include 'J.G.S.Lefevre'! – *Indian Civil Service. Report to the Rt. Hon. Sir Charles Wood, Bart., M.P.* (London, 1855).

45 HH 1/2, E. Cowper to JGSL, 29 Mar 1857.

46 HH 1/2, Dalhousie to JGSL, 12 Mar 1855.

47 HH 1/2, CSLII to JGSL, 3 Apr 1856.

48 There are printed copies at HH, in the HLRO, and in the Elliott papers, and a handwritten version addressed to Palmerston at HH.

49 Second Earl Fitzmaurice, *Life of Granville, 1815–1891* (London, 1905), Granville to Lord Canning, 30 Apr 1856.

50 Elliott Mss, ? to [?] Byrne, 12 May 1856.

51 RA A25/116, F20/51, A26/4, Palmerston to the Queen, 8 & 10 Jul 1856, 18 Jan 1857, PP Vic 12622 (1857), Woods to Grey, 23 Jan 1857.

52 Brougham Mss, 5910, JGSL to Brougham, 2 Dec 1856.

53 Fitzmaurice, *Life of Granville*, 222.

CHAPTER XI

1 Roger Fulford's very readable biography of *Samuel Whitbread, 1764–1815* (London, 1967) has little to say of Whitbread's children. Emma Laura had her 17th birthday less than three weeks before her father committed suicide.

2 Sir Denis Le Marchant, Bt., *Memoir of John Charles, Viscount Althorp, Third Earl Spencer* (London, 1876), 174.

3 Bedfordshire RO, WI/3097. The Whitbreads may have been unlucky or difficult employers of governesses. Another letter (WI/3099) in the collection is from a former governess to Emma Laura's elder sister, Elizabeth, dated 8 September 1810, when Elizabeth was 18. The ex-governess, Belinda Grant, complained that Elizabeth had been denigrating her conduct as a governess, and asked her to desist from criticizing her to friends and acquaintances, because of the damage it would do to her future welfare. 'Yours is the only family', she wrote, 'under whose roof I can remember to have lived any considerable time without gaining a good report.'

4 Hants RO, 15M50/1341; 38M49/7/D23.

5 V. Martineau, *John Martineau*, 122.

6 Estimates: Laundy, *The Office of Speaker* (London, 1964), 305.

7 Whitbread & Co., Partners' Ledgers, Articles of Partnership, Statement of capital and interest due to Eversley's executors.

8 Whitbread & Co., *Whitbread's Brewery* (London, 1947), 36. Laundy, *Office of Speaker*, 9.

9 Hants RO, 15M50/1341, 38M49/A/XIa/5/5.

10 Bedfordshire RO, WI/6001/8, Lady Elizabeth Whitbread to Maria Edgeworth, 2 Aug 1824; Erskine May Mss, CSLII to May nd 1857.

11 Selborne, *Memorials*, Part I, 2, 208–10.

12 For the relations betwen the Chewtons and Frances, Countess Waldegrave, see O.W. Hewett, *Strawberry Fair, A Biography of Frances, Countess Waldegrave, 1821–1879* (London, 1956), 53–4, 92, 109–10, 113, 147.

13 Hants RO 38M49/7/117/8, Waldegrave to CSLII, 11 March 1857. Roundell Palmer, First Earl of Selborne, who married Chewton's sister Laura in 1848, devoted a chapter of his *Memorials*, (Part I, 2) to the life of Chewton. It is almost entirely confined to a flattering account of the latter's naval and military exploits. I am most grateful to the Countess Waldegrave for information culled from the family archives about the relations which developed between the eighth Earl, Viscount Chewton, and the Charles Shaw Lefevres. Viscount Chewton's two sons each became Earl Waldegrave – the ninth and eleventh. His brothers, who are mentioned in the last paragraph of

the eighth Earl's letter to CSLII, were Samuel (1817–69), who became Bishop of Carlisle, and George (1825–1904) who took the additional family name Leslie on his marriage.

14 Hants RO, 15M50/1341.

15 For the Loyd family history, see the Overstone Mss in the UL, and D.P. O'Brien, *Correspondence of Lord Overstone*, 3 vols (London, 1971) – for the Cambridge election donation see 1, 39 fn. 1.

16 HLRO, SL Mss, JGSL to I.C. Wright, 19 Feb 1838.

17 HLRO, SL Mss, Spencer to JGSL, 23 Jul 1837.

18 HLRO, SL Mss, JGSL to Spencer, nd [c. 1842].

19 Notts RO, M5586–7, Wright Diaries, 27 Dec 1832, 6 Jul 1843.

20 BL Add Mss 44360, JGSL to Gladstone, 23 Jan 1843.

21 Notts RO, M5586, Wright Diaries, 31 Dec 1845.

22 Currie, *Recollections* 1, 35.

23 Notts RO, M5587, Wright Diaries, Jun 1849.

24 Burley Manor and ninety acres were sold to George Rooke Farnall; for Terrace House, Battersea, see Ch. V, fn. 10; 5 Hyde Park Gardens remained in the family until the 1870s – see Westminster Rate Books, Marylebone Library; West Side House, Wimbledon, is now owned by the London Borough of Merton.

25 Much of the information on which this section is based comes from a family document and from S. Chapman, *The Rise of Merchant Banking* (London, 1984). The quotation and other data is from pp. 144–6 of that volume.

26 *The Times*, 5 and 20 Oct 1847. Hants RO, 38M49/D19, HFSL's Diary, 15 Feb 1843. Dickson, *Sun Insurance Office*, 180.

27 HLRO, SL Mss, HFSL to JGSL, 20 Oct 1847.

28 BL Add Mss 44366, JGSL to Gladstone, 10 Nov 1847.

29 *The Times*, 30 Dec 1848.

30 *Complete Peerage*.

31 Hants RO, 38M49/D19, HFSL to Catherine Fanshawe (née Le Marchant) 15 Apr 1835.

32 O'Brien, *Correspondence of Lord Overstone* 1 (London, 1971), 324, fn. 6.

33 Family document, dated December 1841, four months before Elizabeth died. It must be a record of the last meeting between her and her step-daughter.

34 Hants RO, 15M50/1341.

35 Hants RO, 15M50/1341.

36 V. Martineau, *John Martineau*, 122.

37 H.J. St.John Mildmay, *A Brief Memoir of the Mildmay Family* (1913), 217–8, quoting from *Athenaeum*, 1 Dec 1808.

38 The Bouveries and the Mildmays became allied through four marriages which took place between 1809 and 1815. The second Earl Radnor had a brother, Hon. Bartholomew Bouverie (1753–1835) who, with three sons, also had three daughters. The eldest of the three, Charlotte, married Sir Henry St John Carew St John-Mildmay, fourth Bt., (1787–1848) in 1809. Charlotte did not survive giving birth to a son a year later, but the boy – baptized Henry Bouverie Paulet St John Mildmay – grew up to succeed his father and to marry Helena Shaw Lefevre. The fourth Baronet, so soon a widower, six years later – in 1815 – married his deceased wife's sister, Harriet, by special permission of the King of Wurttenberg. Harriet died in 1834. The third daughter of Bartholomew Bouverie, Anna Maria Wyndham, had meanwhile,

in 1813, married another Mildmay – the brother of the fourth Baronet – Paulet St John Mildmay (1791–1845) – and their second son, Hervey George, born in 1817, was to marry Helena Shaw Lefevre's younger sister Elizabeth, in 1859. The third Earl Radnor attached himself to the Mildmays in 1814 by marrying, as his second wife, Anne Judith, the third daughter of the third Mildmay Baronet, and the sister of the two Mildmay men who married Shaw Lefevres. Thus the third Earl Radnor, who lived until 1869, was by marriage the uncle of Helena and Elizabeth Mildmay (née Shaw Lefevre).

39 Charlotte Bonham Carter Mss, Helen Mason to Sophia Shaw Lefevre, 9 March 1859. In a comment on CSLII after his death, William Wickham remarked that 'It certainly was curious how inferior to him intellectually were his daughters and grandchildren, and how little interest they took in those topics that were most interesting to him.' Hants RO 38M49, Wickham Diary, 30 Dec 1888.

40 HH 1/46/2, Rachael Hamilton Gordon to Madeleine Shaw Lefevre, 16–23 Jan 1868.

41 Charlotte Bonham Carter Mss, H.P. Hamilton to HFSL, 6/7 May 1857. The Masons' wealth came from the Bowling iron works near Bradford. Hants RO, 38M49/D23, Wickham Diary, 22 Jun 1867.

42 Charlotte Bonham Carter Mss, Helen Mason to her father and sisters, 1860–1.

43 HH 1/3, 27 Nov. 1860.

44 Charlotte Bonham Carter Mss, letters of Helen Mason to Sophia Shaw Lefevre in 1858.

45 HH 1/3, Overstone to Emily Shaw Lefevre, 13 Dec 1858; O'Brien, *Correspondence of Lord Overstone*, 3, 1276 fn. 1. The Overstones gave over £21,000 to the Howards, Mrs. Howard being another sister of Lady Overstone and Emily Shaw Lefevre.

46 As will be recounted in chapter XV, John and Emily's daughter, Jane Georgiana, married Charles Lister Ryan. The eldest child of that union, Madeleine, married Arthur Elliot. In the Elliot Mss there is a draft, by Arthur Elliot, on 'Our Married Life to 1891'. In it he describes how his wife, Madeleine, had stayed from time to time with Harriet Wantage, 'who was throughout life almost a second mother to her and rejoiced to have her as often as she could in London or Lockinge.' This reflected an affectionate relationship between the two cousins, Jane Shaw Lefevre and Harriet Loyd, from childhood, and almost certainly explains the Wantages' later generosity to the Elliots, which is mentioned in chapter XXII. Lord Overstone died in 1883, and Harriet was the sole heir to his huge fortune. She died in 1920.

CHAPTER XII

1 George's letters to his parents from these journeys are at HH, 1/47/2. See also his DNB entry, written from 'private information and personal knowledge', by F.W. Hirst. For twelve of his pictures, see G. Shaw Lefevre, *Photographic Views of Sebastopol, taken immediately after the Retreat of the Russians, September 8, 1855* (London, 1856).

2 *Hampshire Chronicle*, 16 and 30 Apr 1859.

3 *The Times*, 13 and 30 Apr, 2 May 1859. The votes were reported elsewhere as East 402, Bonham Carter 349, Fleming 341, Shaw Lefevre 231.

4 *Berkshire Chronicle*, 7 Jan 1860; *The Times*, 11 Jan and 17 Oct 1860.

5 *Berkshire Chronicle*, 14 Jan 1860.

6 HH 1/47/2, CSLII to JGSL, 10 Oct 1860.

7 *The Times*, 9 Oct and 19 Nov 1860.

8 HH 1/47/2, CSLII to JGSL, 10 Oct 1860.

9 HH 1/47/2, GJSL to JGSL, nd but c. 8 Oct 1860.

10 *The Times*, 17 Oct 1860.

11 *Berkshire Chronicle*, 6, 13 and 20 Oct 1860.

12 *The Times*, 22 and 27 Oct 1860.

13 *The Times*, 18 Oct and 22 Nov 1860.

14 HH 1/47/2, GJSL to Maria, 15 Aug 1862.

15 *Reading Observer*, 17 Nov 1883.

16 *The Times*, 28 Sep 1863.

17 Lord Eversley, 'Some Reminiscences IV. My First Election to Parliament', *Cornhill Magazine*, New Series, 46, 150–9, Feb 1919.

18 *The Times*, 28 Sep 1863.

19 Lord Eversley, *Cornhill Magazine*, 46, 151; HH 1/2, GJSL to Maria, 30 Oct 1863; HH 1/10/5, CSLII to JGSL, 5 Mar 1864.

20 C. Kent, *Brains and Numbers: Elitism, Comtism and Democracy in Mid-Victorian England*, (Toronto, 1978), 46; D. Southgate, *The Passing of the Whigs, 1832–66* (London, 1962), 339; W. Jeans, *Parliamentary Reminiscences*, (London, 1912), 2–3.

21 Lord Eversley, *Cornhill Magazine*, 46, 151, 158; Parl. Deb., 3rd Series, clxxiii, 1475–84.

22 W. White, *The Inner Life of the House of Commons* 2 (London, 1897), 15.

23 HH 1/10/5, CSLII to JGSL, 5 Mar 1864.

24 HH 1/11/1, G.O. Trevelyan to GJSL, 23 Oct 1908.

25 Lord Eversley, 'Some Reminiscences V. At the Board of Trade', *Cornhill Magazine*, 46, 306–16, Mar 1919.

26 Royal Commission on Sea Fisheries of the United Kingdom, PP 1866, xvii, xviii; Lord Eversley, 'Some Reminiscences II. Sea Fisheries, 1863–65', *Cornhill Magazine*, 45, 607–13, Dec 1918.

27 HH 1/47/2, GJSL to Maria, 21 Oct 1862 and 19 Nov 1863.

28 HLRO, PO 248, Draft letter, JGSL to GJSL, nd but 1864.

29 G. Shaw Lefevre, *English Commons and Forests* (London, 1894; revised ed. titled *Commons Forests and Footpaths*, 1910), see esp. chs II and III for the establishment of the CPS.

30 Select Committee on Open Spaces (Metropolis), PP 1865, viii.

31 Joy Lynn Oden Wood, 'George John Shaw Lefevre, Lord Eversley: A Liberal Reformer and founder of the Conservation Movement in England', Ph.D. Thesis, Texas Christian University, 1977, chs. 3 and 4. W.H. Williams, *The Commons Open Spaces and Footpaths Preservation Society 1865–1965: A Short History of the Society and its Work*, (London, 1965). For GJSL's connections with environmental societies, see John Ranlett, 'Checking Nature's Desecration: Late Victorian Environmental Organization', *Victorian Studies*, 26, 3 (1983). For his rather uncertain part in the creation of the National Trust, see Gillian Darley, *Octavia Hill, A Life* (London, 1990), ch. 20.

32 Special Report from Select Committee on Married Women's Property Bill, PP 1867–68, vii: Select Committee on Married Women's Property Bill, PP 1868–69, viii: Married Women's Property Act, 1870, 33 and 34 Vic c. 93. For a nice comment on George, 'lucidly and logically unfolding his subject to some fifty members' on a day when matters of greater political moment were dominant, see White, *Inner Life of the House of Commons*, 2, 96–7. *A History of the Cobden Club*, by Members of the Club (London, 1939).

33 Lord Eversley, *Cornhill Magazine*, 46, 159.

34 PRO/30/22/16B/363–4, GJSL to Russell, 30 Apr 1866.

35 Spencer Childers, *Life of the Rt. Hon. Hugh C.E. Childers, 1827–1896* 1 (London, 1901), 144.

36 G. Shaw Lefevre, *The Personal Payment of Rates and the Reform Act of 1867* (London, 1868).

37 HH/1/8/4, CSLII to JGSL, nd but 7 Mar 1868; Parl Deb 3rd Series, cxl, 1150–67; *The Times*, 7 Mar 1868.

38 A detailed account of George's American concerns is given in chap II of Joy Lynn Oden Wood, 'George Shaw Lefevre'. George's House of Commons speech in 1868 was 'the first to be transmitted verbatim' via the recently completed Transatlantic Cable.

39 A.I. Dasent, *John Thadeus Delane*, (London, 1908), ii, 231–2: *The Times*, 10 Dec 1868; BL Add Mss 44417, JGSL to Gladstone, 10 Dec 1868.

40 HH 1/10/5 Gladstone to JGSL, 11 Dec 1868; BL Add Mss 44416, JGSL to Gladstone, 11 Dec 1868.

41 *Daily News*, 21 May 1898.

42 HH 1/8/4, GJSL to HFSL, 22 Nov 1868.

43 HH 1/8/4, HFSL to GJSL, 23 Nov 1868. Viscount Eversley was moving his London home from Eaton Place to Eaton Square.

44 Hants RO, 38M49/D19, JGSL to HFSL, 22 Nov 1868.

45 HH 1/47/2, GJSL to Maria, 30 Oct 1863.

46 HH 1/8/4, GJSL to HFSL, 22 Nov 1868.

47 HH 1/3, Notes from Lady Lefevre's Journal, 1872; Overstone Mss 1464, JGSL to Overstone, 18 Apr 1874; 1559, GJSL to Overstone, 20 Aug 1879.

48 HH 1/8/4, GJSL to HFSL, 22 Nov 1868.

CHAPTER XIII

1 On the struggle, see PRO 30/22/19/83, Gladstone to Russell, 25 Apr and 11 May 1860; and PRO 30/29/19/5/22, JGSL to Granville, 28 Apr 1860.

2 HH 1/3, Notes from Lady Lefevre's Journal.

3 HH 1/47/2, CSLII to JGSL, 21 Oct 1862.

4 O'Brien, *Overstone*, 3, 1064, Overstone to G.W. Norman, 18 Jan 1865.

5 Elliot Mss, JGSL to Ryan, 24 Dec 1850.

6 Elliot Mss, R. Austen Legh to Jane Ryan, 6 Feb 1929.

7 M.R.D. Foot (ed.), *The Gladstone Diaries* (Oxford, 1968), 16 Jul 1862. BL Add Mss 49227, 4 and 25 May 1888, AHG to Rachael.

8 HH 1/46; Elliot Mss, typescript copy of draft by Jane Ryan, 'A Nineteenth Century Dinner Party'.

9 BL Add Mss 46228, AHG to Mrs Gladstone, 18 Mar 1885.

10 Hare, *Story of My Life*, 2 and 4, *passim*; Hants RO, 38M49/8/194/3; HH 1/46, Correspondence between Shaw Lefevre sisters, nephews and nieces, early 1860s, 1879–80.

11 The major work of biography is J.K. Chapman, *The Career of Arthur Hamilton Gordon, First Lord Stanmore, 1829–1912* (Toronto, 1964). See also two extensive collections of correspondence in the *Transactions of the American Philosophical Society*, New Series [hereinafter *TAPS*], 51, pt 4, 1961, Paul Knaplund (ed.) 'Gladstone-Gordon Correspondence, 1851–1896', and 61, pt 2, 1971, J.K. Chapman (ed.) 'A Political Correspondence of the Gladstone Era: the letters of Lady Sophia

Palmer and Sir Arthur Gordon, 1884–1889'. Stanmore published, privately, six
volumes of letters and papers: Sir Arthur Hamilton Gordon, 1st Baron Stanmore
[hereinafter AHG], *Mauritius, Records of Private and of Public Life, 1871–74*, 2
vols, (1894), and *Fiji: Records of Private and of Public Life, 1875–80*, 4 vols,
(Edinburgh, 1897–1912). The originals and numerous other papers, mostly weeded
rather carefully by AHG, are in the Stanmore Mss at the BL: much correspondence of
his wife, and some of his own, is among the Aberdeen Mss at Haddo House: material
concerning his spell in New Brunswick from 1861 to 1866 is lodged in the library of
the University of New Brunswick as Hamilton Gordon Mss.

12 *The Times*, 18 Jan, 2 and 15 Feb 1861. The votes cast were 851 for the Conservative,
   Leslie, and 665 for AHG.
13 HG Mss, AHG to Wilberforce, 5 Oct 1861.
14 BL Add Mss 44319, Mrs Gladstone to AHG, 28 Oct 1861, printed in *TAPS*,
   51, pt 4, 38.
15 See, e.g., HG Mss, AHG to Gladstone, Jan 1864. Agnes Gladstone married the Revd
   E.C. Wickham in 1873.
16 HG Mss, Diary, 26 Nov 1861; AHG to Alfred Barry, 29 Jun 1862.
17 HG Mss, Diary, 12 May 1862.
18 HG Mss, AHG to Wilberforce, 15 Jan 1863.
19 HG Mss, Wilberforce to AHG, 22 Feb 1863.
20 HG Mss, AHG to Wilberforce, Whitsunday, 1863.
21 Selborne Mss, 1872, Roundell Palmer to AHG, 9 Oct 1863.
22 HG Mss, AHG to Wilberforce, 23 Nov 1863; Wilberforce to AHG, 10 Dec 1863.
23 HG Mss, AHG to Manners Sutton, 9 May 1864.
24 HH 1/3, Rachael to Mary, 6 Jun 1864.
25 HH 1/3, Madeleine to Mary, 15 Jun 1864.
26 HG Mss, Diary, June 1864; HH 1/3, Mary to Rachael, 11 Jun ?1864/5.
27 BL Add Mss 39114, AHG to Layard, 25 Mar 1865; HG Mss, AHG to Wilberforce,
   22 May 1865. For Arthur's edgy and devious exchanges with Cardwell over Hong
   Kong, see PRO 30/48/39.
28 HG Mss, Cardwell to AHG, 9 Jun 1865.
29 HG Mss, Caroline Gordon to Rachael, 19 Jul 1865.
30 HG Mss, AHG to Wilberforce, 31 Jul 1865.
31 Selborne Mss, 1872, Roundell Palmer to AHG, nd (1865).
32 *Morning Post and Morning Herald*, 21 Sep 1865; BL Add Mss 44320, AHG to
   Gladstone, 23 Sep 1865.
33 HG Mss, Caroline Gordon to Rachael, 19 Jul 1865.
34 HH 1/3 Bessie Wauchope to Annie Shaw Lefevre, 18 Oct 1849.
35 BL Add Mss 49230, Rachael to Madeleine, 4 Mar 1861; Rachael to her mother, 15
   Mar, 1861.
36 BL Add Mss 49230, Rachael to her mother, 12 Jun 1861; Rachael to Mary, 20 Jun
   and 2 Jul 1861; Add Mss 49228, Rachael to Jane, 27 Jul 1861.
37 BL Add Mss 49228, Rachael to Jane, 27 Sep 1861.
38 BL Add Mss 49230, Rachael to her mother, Oct 1861.
39 *TAPS*, 51, pt 4, 39.
40 *TAPS*, 51, pt 4, 85, quoting AHG to Gladstone, 21 Jan 1882.
41 BL Add Mss 49230, Rachael to Madeleine, 10 Sep 1881.
42 BL Add Mss 49271, AHG Journal, 1 Oct 1866.

43 BL Add Mss 49228, Rachael to Jane, 21 Nov 1866.

44 HG Mss, JGSL to AHG, 14 Apr 1866.

45 HH 1/12, GJSL to JGSL, 7 Nov 1866; BL Add Mss 49271, Rachael to Jane, 22 Oct and 8 Nov 1866.

CHAPTER XIV

1 R.A.J. Walling (ed.), *The Diaries of John Bright* (London, 1930), 339: Barry O'Brien, *John Bright* (London, 1910), 216–18; Lord Eversley, *Cornhill Magazine*, 46, 306–7.

2 Lord Eversley, *Cornhill Magazine*, 46, 307.

3 Kingston RO, 2572/83/2; Lord Eversley, *Cornhill Magazine*, 46, 308, 314.

4 George's sisters remembered the dinner which he gave for de Lesseps at Spring Gardens, where eighteen or twenty sat down, including the Granvilles, the Salisburys and Sir Charles Dilke, HH 1/46, ? Madeleine to George, nd; Lord Eversley, *Cornhill Magazine*, 46, 309, 312–14.

5 Lord Eversley, *Cornhill Magazine*, 46, 311–12; PP 1872, xii.

6 *Daily News*, 20 Dec 1870.

7 HH 1/13/4, Bright to GJSL, 21 Dec 1870.

8 Lord Eversley, *Cornhill Magazine*, 46, 316.

9 BL Add Mss 44153, GJSL to Gladstone, 4 Jan 1871.

10 HH 1/13/4, Fortescue to GJSL, 6 Jan 1871.

11 HH 1/13/4, Gladstone to GJSL, 5 Jan 1871.

12 BL Add Mss 44153, GJSL to Gladstone, 6 Jan 1871.

13 HH 1/13/4, GJSL to JGSL, 6 Jan 1871.

14 BL Add Mss 49225, Rachael to AHG, 16 Mar 1871; 44153, GJSL to Gladstone, 14 Mar 1871.

15 BL Add Mss 44153, GJSL to Gladstone, 30 Jan 1871; 44320, Gladstone to AHG, 30 Jan 1871.

16 Lord Eversley, 'Some Reminiscences VI. At the Admiralty, 1871', *Cornhill Magazine*, 46, 374.

17 BL Add Mss 44153, GJSL to Gladstone, 24 Mar 1873; 44442, JGSL to Gladstone, 14 Feb 1874; HH 1/10/5, Gladstone to JGSL, 17 Feb 1874.

18 Peter Gordon (ed.), *The Red Earl: the Papers of the 5th Earl Spencer*, Northampton Record Society, 1981, 115–16. The note on the election result at Reading is mistaken in giving Attenborough the votes actually cast for Goldsmid. *Reading Mercury*, 31 Jan, 7 Feb 1874.

19 AHG, *Mauritius*, 2, 406, AHG to Rachael, Dec 1873/Jan 1874; HH 1/8/6, G.W.E. Russell to GJSL, 24 Mar 1917.

20 AHG, *Mauritius*, 2, 399, 402–3, 435, Rachael to AHG, 13 and 18 Dec 1873, 2 Jan 1874. Sophia Wickham, typically, was less restrained: 'Mr Wickham tells me Lady Ducie has £19,000 a year!! what a find for George – but I can only feel astonished that the marriage is allowed. . . . I think Lady Constance must be a nice person, as Mary says she has undertaken the entire charge of eight orphan cousins. This you would think would make her unselfish, generous, very kind and judicious beyond her years which is as well with a husband so much older than herself.' Hants RO, 38M49/D23, Sophia Wickham to HFSL, nd.

21 *Gloucestershire Chronicle*, 28 Mar 1874.

22 BL Add Mss 49229, Rachael to Jane, 7 Jun 1881, 27–30 Mar 1885; 49227, Rachael to AHG, 16 Jul, 9–13 Oct 1887; AHG to Rachael, 1 Jun 1888.

23 G. Shaw Lefevre, MP, *The Game Laws* (London, 1874).

24 G. Shaw Lefevre, MP, *Freedom of Land*, National Liberal Federation, Practical Politics Series No. 3 (London, 1880). Though written in 1877, publication was deferred 'on account of the exclusive public interest then and since excited by Foreign and Indian questions.' G. Shaw Lefevre, 'Economic Law and English Land Ownership', *Fortnightly Review*, 27, 32–53, Jan 1877.

25 Select Committee on Land Titles and Transfer, PP 1878, xv; 1878–9, xi.

26 Chamberlain Mss, JC5/52/5, GJSL to Chamberlain, 8 Nov 1877.

27 S. Gwynn and G.M. Tuckwell, *The Life of the Rt. Hon. Sir Charles W. Dilke, Bart., M.P.*, 1 (London 1917), 241, 278. BL Add Mss 43910, GJSL to Dilke, 9 and 10 May 1879. Introduction to Papers of the Greek Committee, No. 1 (New Series, 1897). G. Shaw Lefevre, MP, *A Vindication of the Claims of Greece: an Address delivered at the Assembly Rooms, Kennington, Dec 9 1897*, Papers of the Greek Committee, No. 7. Chesson Mss, GJSL to Chesson, 1 and 10 Nov 1878.

28 Lord Eversley, *Gladstone and Ireland: the Irish Policy of Parliament from 1850–1894* (London, 1912; reprinted Westport, Connecticut, 1971), 79.

29 Select Committee on Irish Land Act, 1870, PP 1877, v; 1878, xv. Rt. Hon. G. Shaw Lefevre, MP, *The Purchase Clauses of the Irish Land Act, speech made in the the House of Commons on 2 May 1879, and Papers written on the same subject* (London, 1882).

30 G. Shaw Lefevre, MP, *Peel and O'Connell: a review of the Irish policy of Parliament from the Act of Union to the death of Sir Robert Peel* (London, 1887); Lord Eversley, *Gladstone and Ireland*. In H.J. Hanham, *Bibliography of British History, 1851–1914* (Oxford, 1976), J.L. Hammond's book, *Gladstone and the Irish Nation* (London, 1938, 2nd ed. 1964) is listed as 'Still the fullest account of Gladstone's Irish policy, but still needs to be supplemented by' Eversley's volume.

31 Chamberlain Mss, JC5/52/1–4, Jan–Feb 1876.

32 Devonshire Mss, A340, 872. GJSL to Hartington, 9 Jan 1880. T.A. Jenkins, *Gladstone, Whiggery and the Liberal Party, 1874–1886* (Oxford, 1988), 96–7, 133, 192–4. For an example of GJSL's extreme loyalty to Gladstone in 1877, see Spencer Childers, *Life of Rt. Hon. Hugh C.E.Childers*, 1, 245.

33 T.W. Heyck and William Klecka, 'British Radical MPs 1874–1895: New Evidence from Discriminant Analysis', *Journal of Interdisciplinary History*, 4, 161–84.

34 H.W. Lucy, *A Diary of Two Parliaments: The Disraeli Parliament 1874–1880* (London, 1885), 146.

35 BL Add Mss, 44153, Gladstone to GJSL, 26 Apr 1880.

36 The figures were: Palmer 2,513, Shaw Lefevre 2,286, Sandeman 2,067; which was broken down thus – Lefevre and Palmer 2,235, Lefevre and Sandeman 31, Palmer and Sandeman 246, Lefevre 20, Palmer 32, Sandeman 1,790; *Reading Mercury*, 3 Apr 1880.

37 *Reading Mercury*, 20 Mar 1880.

38 HH 1/47/2, CSLII to Emily Shaw Lefevre, 13 Sep 1880.

39 BL Add Mss 44153, GJSL to Gladstone, 21 Sep 1880.

40 HH 1/10, Gladstone to GJSL, 23 Sep 1880.

41 HH 1/10, Gladstone to GJSL, 27 Nov 1880.

42 BL Add Mss 44153, GJSL to Gladstone, 27 Nov 1880.

43 BL Add Mss 44153, GJSL to Godley, 30 Nov 1880.

44 HH 1/13, CSLII to GJSL, 5 Dec 1880.

45 BL Add Mss 49225, Rachael to AHG, 28 Nov 1880; AHG to Rachael, 4 Dec 1880.

CHAPTER XV

1 Lady Wantage, *Lord Wantage* (London, 1907), 286.
2 HH 1/47/2, Extract from diary of William Wickham, 1879.
3 PRO 30/22/13A, Grey to Russell, 17 Jan 1856.
4 HLRO, SL Mss, CSLII to JGSL, 24 Jan 1856.
5 BL Add Mss 44333, JGSL to Trevelyan, 20 Jan 1854.
6 Palmerston (Broadlands) Mss, HA/I/2, JGSL to Palmerston, 22 Jul 1857.
7 Brougham Mss, 5908, JGSL to Brougham, 5 Feb 1856; see also 4018, 4019, 4020, 5909, 24176, 24177, JGSL to Brougham, 1856–58.
8 PRO 30/29/23/10/389–398, Emily Shaw Lefevre to Ryan, 20 Aug 1857.
9 PRO 30/29/23/10/389–398, Ryan to Granville, 21 Aug 1857.
10 PRO 30/29/23/10/415–19, Grey to Granville, 25 Aug 1857. Grey Mss, 84 15, JGSL to Lord Grey, 20 Dec 1857
11 P. Dunsheath and M. Miller, *Convocation in the University of London: the first hundred years*, (London, 1958).
12 PRO 30/29/23/14/143, Memo by JGSL, nd but 1856–7.
13 PRO 30/29/19/4/25, JGSL to Granville, 9 May 1862. See also JGSL to Sir George Grey, 30 Jun 1856, in Northbrook Mss, N4.13.
14 Harte, *The University of London*, 114.
15 BL Add Mss 44398, JGSL to Gladstone, 8, 14, 15 Jan 1862.
16 PP 1867, xix; PP 1870, xviii.
17 Bond, *Parliamentary Affairs*, 12, 309. There are some seventy letters and other documents in the Parliamentary Office Papers of the HLRO, either to or from JGSL. They show the variety of matters which came across his desk, but are all directed to very specific tasks or enquiries arising out of normal business.
18 Royal Commission to inquire into the Condition of the Exchequer Standards, Weights and Measures, etc., PP 1867–68, xxvii.
19 The Special Commissioners were appointed under the Public Schools Act, 1868, 31 and 32 Vic c. 118.
20 Holland Mss, JGSL to Walpole, 16 Mar 1868.
21 Parl. Deb. 3s, ccxxii, 1370.
22 E.C.F. Collier (ed.), *Victorian Diarist, Extracts from the Journals of Mary Lady Monkswell, 1873–95* (London, 1944), 12.
23 Hare, *Story of My Life*, 4, 373.
24 Personal memories of William Wickham and Augustus Hare; obituaries expressing similar sentiments appeared in the proceedings of several professional societies, etc.
25 *The Times*, 29 Aug 1879.
26 Chapman, *The Rise of Merchant Banking*, 145: on the following page a chart lists 'H.S.Lefevre and Co., London (1795)'; that date must refer to the founding of the firm of John Thomas.
27 Hants RO, 38M49/7/168. Dickson, *Sun Insurance Office*, 280.
28 Hants RO, 38M49, Wickham Diary, 22 June 1867.
29 Wm. Wickham (ed.), *The Correspondence of the Rt. Hon. William Wickham from the year 1794* (London, 1870). A rich source of Sophia's attitudes is a set of letters written to her husband when he was on a trip abroad in 1879, at the time of JGSL's death – Hants RO 38M49/8/194/3.
30 BL Add Mss 49225, Rachael to AHG, 7 and 17 Dec 1880.

31 *Hampshire Chronicle*, 14 Feb 1925, article by Carew Mildmay.

32 BL Add Mss 44388, JGSL to Gladstone, 27 Oct 1857.

33 Hants RO, 15M50/1341.

34 BL Add Mss 44423, CSLII to Gladstone, 10 Nov 1869.

35 Martineau, *John Martineau*, ch. ix; Marjorie Nisbett, 'John Martineau and his Cottages', *Huguenot Society's Procs.*, 21, 1965–70, 82–5; Hants RO 15M50/1341.

36 See for instance his severe and rather punitive attitude as revealed in Hants RO, Office papers and misc. docs. Q.S., 5 letters between Chairman of Quarter Sessions and Chief Constable 1873 (formerly in filing box 25).

37 Martineau, *John Martineau*, 129.

38 Information supplied by the late Harry Foster of Racal Electronics plc; HH 1/47, CSLII to Emily Shaw Lefevre, 13 Sep 1880. There were no less than fourteen 'shrubbery men' just to keep the paths trimmed and the rhododendrons under control – James, *History of a Hampshire Parish*, 45. There is a small collection of documents at the University of Reading – HAN 7 – relating to the Eversley farms and other properties.

39 Martineau, *John Martineau*, 126: Susan Chitty, *The Beast and the Monk*, (London, 1974), 240, 251, 259; Brenda Colloms, *Charles Kingsley: the Lion of Eversley*, (London, 1975), 351.

40 Martineau, *John Martineau*, 127.

41 Hants RO, 38M49, Sermon preached by Revd Charles A. Fox in Eaton Chapel, 6 Jan 1889.

42 R.A.J. Walling (ed.), *Diaries of John Bright* (London, 1930), 499.

43 BL Add Mss 48650, Hamilton Diaries, 6 June, 1889.

44 HLRO, SL Mss, CSLII to JGSL, 24 Jan 1856; HH 1/47, CSLII to JGSL, 21 Oct 1862; Holland Mss, CSLII to Walpole, 4 April 1867.

45 HLRO, Erskine May Mss, CSLII to May, 31 Oct [1868]. The unwelcome Liberal candidate must have withdrawn, for Sclater Booth and W.W.B. Beach, both Conservatives, were returned unopposed.

46 RA QVJ 31 Mar 1857.

47 RA QVJ 6 Apr 1859.

48 RA C30/18, CSLII to Gen. Grey, 13 Jun 1859. Charles's distrust of Russell's judgement was further illustrated in 1866, when, as Prime Minister, Lord John was trying – as it turned out, unsuccessfully – to get his latest franchise reform proposal through. Lady Russell wrote to her two sons at Harrow on 15 March, 'I hear that Lord Eversley (the late Speaker) says he would take a good big bet that it won't pass. Your Papa says he is ready to bet against him that it will.' D. McCarthy and A. Russell (eds), *Lady John Russell, A Memoir* (London, 1910).

49 RA C58/114, 122, Lord Clarendon to Prince Albert 27 Mar, 25 Jun 1857.

50 RA A26/123, Palmerston to the Queen, 15 Sep 1857; E11/43, Sidney Herbert to Prince Albert, 23 Nov 1859.

51 RA D22/8, the Queen to Palmerston, 12 Sep 1864. Northbrook Mss, N4.12, Palmerston to Grey, 28 Aug and 6 Sep 1864; Grey to Palmerston, 30 Aug 1864. See also ch. IX.

52 RA Add S113, 114; Sir T. Biddulph and CSLII, 29 Mar and 1 Apr 1866.

53 RA F15/114, Disraeli to the Queen, 9 Jun 1867. Royal Commission on Volunteer Force, PP xxvii, 1862; Royal Commission on Recruitment for the Army, PP 1867 xv. For the final Report of the Commissioners on the Fine Arts, see PP 1863, xvi. Report

of Boundary Commmissioners for England and Wales, PP xx, 1867–8. M. Cowling, *1867. Disraeli, Gladstone and Revolution. The Passing of the Second Reform Bill* (Cambridge, 1967), 231, 298; F.B. Smith, *The Making of the Second Reform Bill* (Cambridge, 1966), 108, 219.

54 *The Times*, 29 Dec 1888. CSLII served on a Lords Committee on the Despatch of Public Business, PP xi, 1861.

55 Bedfordshire RO W1/6439, CSLII to S.C. Whitbread, nd, but probably May 1856.

56 Whitbread and Co., Correspondence, Jan to Mar 1885, between CSLII, S. Whitbread and R. Worsley.

57 Whitbread and Co., 19 Jan 1885, CSLII to S. Whitbread.

58 BL Add Mss 44491, 11 Jun 1885, CSLII to Gladstone.

59 H.W. Lucy, *Diary of the Salisbury Parliament, 1886–1892*, (London, 1892), 128–9.

60 Hants RO, 38M49/?7 Unattributable news clipping.

61 *The Times*, 3 Jan 1889.

CHAPTER XVI

1 RA A52/113; Add A12/581, 583, B32/8; 25–27 Nov 1880.

2 D.W.R. Bahlman (ed.), *The Diary of Sir Edward Walter Hamilton, 1880–1885* (Oxford, 1972), ii, 518–19.

3 RA A77/56, Gladstone to the Queen, 8 Dec 1883.

4 BL Add Mss 44153, GJSL to Gladstone, 10 Nov 1885.

5 HH 1/10, Gladstone to GJSL, 11 Nov 1885.

6 *Bradford Observer*, 6 Jul 1886.

7 BL Add Mss 48642, Hamilton's Diary, 27 Nov 1885; R. Rhodes James, *Rosebery* (London, 1963), 500–1; Bod. dep 384, L.V. Harcourt's Diary, 1 and 9 Aug 1892; A.L. Thorold, *Life of Henry Labouchere* (London, 1913), 182 – quoting an article in *Truth*, 5 Oct 1882; D. Brooks (ed.) *The Destruction of Lord Rosebery: from the Diary of Sir Edward Hamilton, 1894–95* (London, 1986), 130, 4 Apr 1895.

8 Lord Redesdale, *Memoirs* (London, 1916), 2, 687–8, 694–6.

9 The story is told in Hesketh Pearson, *Labby: The Life of Henry Labouchere* (London, 1936), 230–1, and in Sir George Leveson Gower, *Mixed Grill* (London, 1947), 179–80.

10 Eversley reported to his niece in 1884 that George was finding the Post Office 'dull and laborious' – Hants RO, 38M49/D19, CSLII to Helen Mason, 29 Nov 1884. GJSL was chairman of a select committee on Charitable Trusts in 1884, see 21 below; David Owen, *English Philanthropy*, (Cambridge, Mass., 1964), 295, 307, 492.

11 *Morning Post*, 9 Dec 1880.

12 BL Add Mss 44626, Memo circulated to Cabinet, 3 Jan 1881.

13 Eversley, *Gladstone and Ireland*, 183.

14 Hammond, *Gladstone and the Irish Nation*, 280–1; H. Paul (ed.), *Letters of Lord Acton to Mary Gladstone* (London, 1904), 153: Roy Jenkins, *Sir Charles Dilke, A Victorian Tragedy* (London, 1958), ch. 7.

15 BL Add Mss, 44315, Grosvenor to Gladstone, 3 May 1882.

16 Eversley, *Gladstone and Ireland*, 214.

17 Jenkins, *Dilke*, ch. 7.

18 A. Ramm (ed.), *Political Correspondence of Mr Gladstone and Lord Granville, 1876–86* (Oxford, 1962), 2, 99, Gladstone to Granville, 13 Oct 1883. Grant Duff thought at the time that George 'would not have got on with Irish MPs', while Rendel

believed George was passed over because he was 'too committed' – Rendel Mss 358, 360, 24 Jun and 21 Jul 1882.

19 W.S. Blunt, *Gordon at Khartoum* (London, 1911), 252 – from his diary for 4 June 1882.

20 BL Add Mss, 48656, Hamilton's Diary, 18 Oct 1891.

21 For a selection of GJSL's activities, see BL Add Mss 44629, Memo for Cabinet on Tenants' Compensation, 1 Feb 1883; Ramm, *Correspondence*, 2, 23; BL Add Mss 58792, correspondence with Escott on a prospective article on the Agrarian Movement in Ireland, Nov–Dec 1882; Gordon, *Red Earl*, 213n; Eversley, *Gladstone and Ireland*, chs 21–23; *Reading Observer*, 17 Nov 1883; Select Committee on Charitable Trusts and Allotments Extension Acts, PP 1884, ix, 1884–5, viii.

22 Bahlman, *Diary of Hamilton*, 2, 658, 25 July 1884; A.B. Cooke and J.R. Vincent (eds), *Lord Carlingford's Journal: Reflections of a Cabinet Minister, 1885* (Oxford, 1971), 20–1.

23 Gordon, *Red Earl*, 274, Granville to Spencer, 16 Sep 1884; BL Add Mss 44311, Spencer to Gladstone, 20 Sep 1884 – copy in BL Althorp Mss K7/354.

24 BL Add Mss 44315, Grosvenor to Gladstone, 3 Oct 1884.

25 Bahlman, *Diary of Hamilton*, 2, 700, 7 Oct 1884.

26 BL Add Mss 44311, Spencer to Gladstone, 20 Sep 1884; Gordon, *Red Earl*, 1, 30.

27 BL Althorp Mss K7/360, Gladstone to Spencer, 9 Oct 1884.

28 Eversley, *Gladstone and Ireland*, 256–7.

29 BL Add Mss 44153, GJSL to Gladstone, 10 Oct 1884.

30 Gladstone to GJSL, 10 Oct 1884, printed in H.C.G. Matthew (ed.), *The Gladstone Diaries* xi (Oxford, 1990), 222–3.

31 BL Althorp Mss K7/361, Hamilton to Spencer, 10 Oct 1884: Bahlman, *Diary of Hamilton*, 2, 702–4, 9 and 10 Oct 1884.

32 BL Althorp Mss K33/909, Spencer to Trevelyan, 9 Oct 1884.

33 NLW, Rendel Mss 681, 23 Dec 1894.

34 BL Add Mss 49232, Rachael to Emily, nd 1887.

35 BL Add Mss 44153, GJSL to Gladstone, 11 Oct 1884.

36 BL Althorp Mss K263, GJSL to Spencer, 10 Oct 1884; K33/909 Trevelyan to Spencer, 12 Oct 1884. The latter has a note scribbled on it – 'Sheets burnt at end of this letter 15.10.84.'

37 Eversley, *Gladstone and Ireland*, 256.

38 HH 1/8/5, GJSL to Lady Frederick Cavendish, 6 Aug 1912.

39 BL Althorp Mss K33, Trevelyan to Spencer, 12 Oct 1884.

40 Bahlman, *Diary of Hamilton*, 2, 705, 12 Oct 1884.

41 Ramm, *Correspondence*, 2, 278, Gladstone to Granville, 13 Oct 1884.

42 HH 1/10. This is from an undated letter, sent from Downing Street and definitely written in the mid-1880s; but it does not contain unequivocal references to the situation in October 1884, though it fits that situation more closely than any other of George's crises, and it echoes both Gladstone's comment to Granville, and Hamilton's reactions. Even in the unlikely event that it was written on another occasion, the sentiments expressed are a fair indication of Gladstone's consistently kind and patient attitude to GJSL.

43 Bahlman, *Diary of Hamilton*, 2, 728, 8 Nov 1884.

44 BL Add Mss 44153, GJSL to Gladstone, 8 Nov 1884; Bahlman, *Diary of Hamilton*, 2, 728, 9 Nov 1884; RA A78/31, Gladstone to the Queen, 10 Nov 1884.

45 BL Add Mss 44153, GJSL to Gladstone, 11 and 12 Nov 1884.

46 F.W. Hirst, *Early Life and Letters of John Morley* 2 (London, 1927), 213.

47 Selborne Mss, 1869, GJSL to Selborne, 11 Feb 1885.

CHAPTER XVII

1 See especially A.B. Cooke and John Vincent, *The Governing Passion, Cabinet Government and Party Politics in Britain, 1885–86* (Brighton, 1974); Andrew Jones, *The Politics of Reform 1884* (Cambridge, 1972); M. Barker, *Gladstone and Radicalism, The Reconstruction of Liberal Policy in Britain, 1885–1894* (Brighton, 1975); T.A. Jenkins, *Gladstone, Whiggery and The Liberal Party, 1874–1886* (Oxford, 1988); D.A. Hamer, *Liberal Politics in the Age of Gladstone and Rosebery* (Oxford, 1972); P. Stansky, *Ambitions and Strategies: The struggle for the Leadership of the Liberal Party in the 1890s* (Oxford, 1964).

2 BL Add Mss 48642, Diary of Hamilton, 27 Nov 1885.

3 Barker, *Gladstone and Radicalism*, 9–10; R.R. James, *Rosebery*, 166–7.

4 Brooks, *Destruction of Lord Rosebery*, Diary of Hamilton, 25 Aug 1894.

5 Lucy, *More Peeps at Parliament*, 501.

6 A. Birrell, *Things Past Redress* (London, 1937), 160; T.P. O'Connor, 'Men, Women and Memories', in the *Sunday Times*, 22 Apr 1928; *Punch*, 24 May 1890 and 17 Jan 1891. Tennyson's line runs – 'O the dreary dreary moorland! O the barren, barren shore!'

7 BL Add Mss 48642, Diary of Hamilton, 27 Nov 1885.

8 J.N. Figgis and R.V. Laurence (eds), *Lord Acton's Correspondence* (London, 1917), Acton to Gladstone, 18 Jan 1890.

9 A.S.T. Griffith-Boscawen, *14 Years in Parliament* (London, 1907), 48.

10 Bod dep 384, 404, L.V. Harcourt's Journal, 1 Aug 1892, 1 Mar 1894.

11 *Bradford Observer*, 13 Oct 1887

12 Collier, *Victorian Diarist, 1873–1895*, 160; and *Later Extracts from the Journals of Lady Monkswell, 1895–1909* (London, 1946), 51–2.

13 Bod dep 384, L.V. Harcourt's Journal, 5 and 8 Aug 1892; Beatrice Webb, *Our Partnership* (London, 1948), 111–12, 115.

14 Collier, *Victorian Diarist, 1895–1909*, 51–2.

15 Rendel Mss 681, Rendel Diary, 23 Dec 1894.

16 HH 1/2/3, Chamberlain to GJSL, 26 Jan 1885.

17 BL Add Mss 43887, Dilke to Chamberlain, 10 Feb 1885.

18 Chamberlain Mss JC5/24/432, Chamberlain to Dilke, 28 Sep 1885.

19 Cooke and Vincent, *Governing Passion*, 204.

20 John Wilson, *CB, A Life of Campbell-Bannerman* (London, 1973), 85–7.

21 Cooke and Vincent, *Governing Passion*, 225–44.

22 BL Add Mss 43887, Note by Dilke, 1 a.m., 21 May 1885.

23 BL Add Mss 43913, GJSL to Gladstone, 21 May 1885.

24 Cooke and Vincent, *Governing Passion*, 242.

25 On the franchise and redistribution, see Jones, *Politics of Reform*.

26 BL Add Mss 43913, GJSL to Dilke, 23 May 1885.

27 BL Add Mss 43913, GJSL to Dilke, 25 May 1885.

28 Cooke and Vincent, *Governing Passion*, 239–54.

29 For a full account of the celebrations, see *Reading Observer*, 17 Nov 1883.

30 Jones, *Politics of Reform, passim*, esp. 181; HH 1/10, Gladstone to GJSL, 12 Nov 1883; BL Add Mss 44153, GJSL to Gladstone, 7 and 11 Nov 1883;

43887, Dilke to GJSL and Trevelyan, 11 Apr 1885; Gwynn and Tuckwell, *Life of Dilke*, 2, 65–6.

31 W. Heaton, *The Three Reforms of Parliament, A History 1830–85* (London, 1885), 245, 255; Jones, *Politics of Reform*, 178.

32 Fowler to Morley, Oct 1884, quoted in Jones, *Politics of Reform*, 179.

33 BL Add Mss 44153, GJSL to Gladstone, 20 Dec 1884.

34 *Reading Observer*, 24 Jan 1885.

35 HH 1/8/3. H.M. Wallis to GJSL, 28 Mar 1924.

36 BL Add Mss 44153, GJSL to Gladstone, 20 Dec 1884.

37 BL Add Mss 44153, Grosvenor to Gladstone, 25 Dec 1884.

38 HH 1/10, Gladstone to GJSL, 27 Dec 1884.

39 *Reading Mercury* and *Reading Observer*, 24 Jan and 7 Feb 1885.

40 HH 1/8/3, H.M. Wallis to GJSL, 26 and 28 Mar 1924; *Reading Mercury*, 4 Apr 1885.

41 *Reading Observer*, 7 Feb 1885.

42 *Reading Observer*, 28 Nov 1885.

43 Barker, *Gladstone and Radicalism*, 10. For Chamberlain's invitation, see J.L. Garvin, *Life of Joseph Chamberlain*, 2 (London, 1933), 6–7.

44 Garvin, *Chamberlain*, 2, 96.

45 Denis Judd, *Radical Joe, A Life of Joseph Chamberlain* (London, 1977), 129–130.

46 BL Add Mss 48641, Diary of Hamilton, 15 Aug and 30 Sep 1885. One letter at HH 1/9/3, from Morley to GJSL, on 12 Sep 1885, deals with rumour about Irish affairs: 'It seems to me very doubtful whether there can have been any dealings at all direct between Parnell and Sexton, and Balfour. But I have reason to believe that the Archp of Dublin (RC) has been pressing his wishes on the Government, and I daresay Sexton knew what was going on. I have been in correspondence with the Archp, and feel sure that all his influence with the Nationalists will be in favour of taking whatever they can get out of the Government. Parnell, I suspect, will feel no compunction as to throwing Balfour over, when he has drawn him on far enough.

Mr Gladstone regards Balfour's move as 'very insidious', but is in no uneasiness about it: is confident that we shall be able to circumvent it; thinks that our line now is to press Balfour, and press him to say what he means. I don't see why we need go beyond that at present.'

47 *Reading Mercury*, 27 Jun 1885.

48 *The Record*, 19 Sep 1885.

49 *Reading Mercury*, 17, 24 Oct, 7 Nov 1885.

50 Chamberlain Mss JC5/52/6, GJSL to Chamberlain, 5 Nov 1885. See also Alan Simon, 'Church Disestablishment as a Factor in the General Election of 1885', *Historical Journal*, 18, No. 4 (1975), 791–820.

51 HH 1/13/2, Chamberlain to GJSL, 6 Nov 1885.

52 Eversley, *Gladstone and Ireland*, 284.

53 *Reading Mercury*, 28 Nov 1885.

54 Chamberlain Mss, JC5/52/7, JGSL to Chamberlain, 28 Nov 1885.

55 *Reading Observer*, 28 Nov 1885.

56 Simon, 'Church Disestablishment', 816.

57 Rosebery Mss, 10084 fol 290–1, GJSL to Rosebery, 24 Dec 1885.

58 Chamberlain Mss, JC5/52/9, GJSL to Chamberlain, 6 Jan 1886, quoted in part in Cooke and Vincent, *Governing Passion*, 142.

59 BL Add Mss 44153, GJSL to Gladstone, 10 Jan 1886; Cooke and Vincent, *Governing Passion*, 142–3, 323–4, 341; Gordon, *Red Earl*, 2, 12; HH 1/10, Gladstone to GJSL, 13 Jan 1886.

60 Bod dep 377, 378, L.V. Harcourt's Journal, 29 Jan, 3 and 4 Feb, 20 Mar 1886; BL Add Mss 48642, Diary of Hamilton, 6 Feb 1886. Jones-Parry got his baronetcy, but only after losing his seat in August 1886, by 136 votes.

61 Eversley, *Gladstone and Ireland*, 305.

CHAPTER XVIII

1 BL Add Mss 49228, Rachael to Jane, 23 Apr–3 May 1872; C.F. Gordon Cumming, *At Home in Fiji* (5th ed., Edinburgh, 1886) 27.

2 HH 1/3, Madeleine to Rachael, ?May–Jul 1867.

3 BL Add Mss 49228, Rachael to Jane, 6 Jan 1867, 6–8 May 1867, 9 Oct 1867.

4 BL Add Mss 49225, AHG to Rachael, 21 Aug, 17 Nov 1868, 17 Aug 1869; 49230, Rachael to her mother, 24–25 Jun 1870; 49231, Rachael to Maria, Aug 1870.

5 BL Add Mss 49228, Rachael to Jane, 7–8 Jan 1870.

6 BL Add Mss 49231, Rachael to Mary, 6 Nov 1867: see ch. II, 27; HH 1/46, Rachael to Emily, 13 Feb 1888.

7 HH 1/46, Rachael to Mary, nd 1870 and nd ?1876.

8 AHG, *Fiji*, 4, 313, AHG to Rachael, 22 May 1880.

9 AHG, *Fiji*, 4, 161, AHG to Rachael, 7 Jan 1880.

10 C.F. Gordon Cumming, *Memories*, (Edinburgh, 1904) 216.

11 There are several references to Arthur's reluctance to talk – e.g. BL Add Mss 49228, Rachael to Jane, 17 Nov 1867; 49231, Rachael to Maria, 26 Feb–8 Mar 1870.

12 BL Add Mss, 49228, Rachael to Jane, 17–24 Jan 1870; HH 1/46/2, Rachael to ? nd ?1877.

13 BL Add Mss 49228, Rachael to Jane, 7 Jul 1867.

14 BL Add Mss 49228, Rachael to Jane, 28 Oct – 16 Nov 1871; 1 Aug 1872; 49230, Rachael to Madeleine, 10 May 1876.

15 Alfred P. Maudslay, *Life in the Pacific Fifty Years Ago*, (London, 1930), 83–4.

16 BL Add Mss 49228, Rachael to Jane, 18 June 1875.

17 BL Add Mss 49232, Rachael to Emily, 9 Jan 1877.

18 BL Add Mss 49230, Rachael to Madeleine, 8 Nov 1884.

19 Maudslay, *Life in the Pacific*, 84.

20 BL Add Mss 46243, AHG to Mary Gladstone, 12 Dec 1889.

21 Maudslay, *Life in the Pacific*, 82–3.

22 Lord Ronald Gower, *My Reminiscences*, 2 (London, 1883), 210–11.

23 BL Add Mss 46243, AHG to Mary Gladstone, 25 Sep 1884.

24 Maudslay, *Life in the Pacific*, 83; Gower, *My Reminiscences*, 2, 210–11.

25 BL Add Mss 49225, AHG to Rachael, 22 and 26 Nov 1868.

26 See e.g., BL Add Mss 44321, AHG to Mrs Gladstone, 29 Dec 1884; 46228, AHG to Mrs Gladstone, 18 Mar 1885; 49225, AHG to Rachael, Dec 1879, 4 Dec 1880, 20 Apr 1881; 49226, AHG to Rachael, 7 Jun 1885; 49227, AHG to Rachael, 14 Jul 1879, 2 Apr 1888; 49230, Rachael to Madeleine, 10 May 1876, Oct 1876; 49231, Rachael to Maria, Aug 1870; Chapman, *Career of AHG*, 152–3; *TAPS*, 51, pt 4, 7, 83; AHG, *Mauritius*, 1, 41–3, 88–90; AHG, *Fiji*, 4, 278ff.

27 Sir William Des Voeux, *My Colonial Service*, 1 (London, 1903), 406–7.

28 AHG, *Mauritius*, 1, 74, AHG to Gladstone, 3 May 1871.

29 A.J.L. Gordon (1847–1918) married Caroline, daughter of AHG's elder brother, Alexander in 1885. He served AHG's nephew, the seventh Earl and first Marquess of Aberdeen, as private secretary when Aberdeen was Governor General of Canada.

30 See fns 5, 17, and C.F. Gordon Cumming, *A Lady's Cruise in a French Man-of-War*, (London, 1882). Eka (1837–1924) was a prolific writer, who made good use of her numerous family connections. See her obituary in *The Times*, 8 Sep 1924.

31 AHG, *Fiji*, iv, 214.

32 AHG to Gladstone, 11 Jul 1879, quoted in *TAPS*, 51, pt 4, 81.

33 BL Add Mss 49225, AHG to Rachael, nd Dec 1879; AHG, *Fiji*, 4, 161.

34 AHG to Rachael, 28 Dec 1879, quoted in AHG, *Fiji*, 4, 154.

35 BL Add Mss 49225, AHG to Rachael, nd Dec 1879.

36 For the complicated negotiations over Fiji and New Zealand, see Chapman, *Career of AHG*, and Des Voeux, *My Colonial Service*.

37 BL Add Mss 49225, Rachael to AHG, 23 Nov 1880.

38 BL Add Mss 49225, AHG to Rachael, 4 Dec 1880.

39 BL Add Mss 49225, Rachael to AHG, 17 Dec 1880 and 25 Jan 1881.

40 BL Add Mss 49225, AHG to Rachael, 16 Mar and 20 Apr 1881; Rachael to AHG, 4 Apr 1881.

41 BL Add Mss 49225, AHG to Rachael, 16 Mar 1881, 5 Aug 1882.

42 Sir Algernon West, *Recollections, 1832 to 1886*, 2 (London, 1899), 159–65; R.B. Martin, *Tennyson: The Unquiet Heart* (Oxford, 1980), 540–41; BL Add Mss 46243, AHG to Mary Gladstone, 25 Sep 1884.

43 BL Add Mss 46243, AHG to Mary Gladstone, Christmas Day, 1883

44 BL Add Mss 49226, AHG to Rachael, 14 Jul 1884.

45 BL Add Mss 49230, Rachael to Madeleine, 8 Nov 1884.

46 HH 1/46, Rachael to Mary, 1 Aug 1884.

47 BL Add Mss 49229, Rachael to Jane, 8 and 13 Mar 1885.

48 BL Add Mss 44321, AHG to Mrs Gladstone, 29 Dec 1884; 46228, 18 Mar 1885.

49 BL Add Mss 44316, Grosvenor to Gladstone, 4 Feb 1885.

50 BL Add Mss 49226, AHG to Rachael, 7 Jun 1885.

51 BL Add Mss 49226, AHG to Rachael, 14 Oct 1885.

52 HG Mss, AHG to Rachael, nd ?Sep 1866.

53 See ch. XIII, fn. 11.

54 BL Add Mss 49227, AHG to Rachael, 13 Feb, 15 and 30 Jun, 26 Aug 1887; 49229, Rachael to Jane, 15 Jan 1888, including extract from Selborne to AHG, 22 Dec 1887.

55 AHG to Sophia Palmer, 3 Jun 1887, printed in *TAPS*, 61, pt 2.

56 BL Add Mss 49227, AHG to Rachael, 26 Aug and 7 Sep 1887; Rachael to AHG, 9–13 Oct 1887.

57 BL Add Mss 49227, AHG to Rachael, 30 Jun, 14 and 24 Jul 1887.

58 BL Add Mss 49231, Rachael to Mary, 10 Dec 1887.

59 BL Add Mss 49229, Rachael to Jane, 15 Jan 1888.

60 BL Add Mss 49227, AHG to Rachael, 4 May and 1 Jun 1888.

61 BL Add Mss 49229, Rachael to Jane, 24 Sep 1888.

62 HH 1/46, W.R. Kynsey to Sir Henry Acland, 9 Feb 1889.

CHAPTER XIX

1 AHG, *Mauritius*, 2, 399, 402–3, 435; BL Add Mss 49225, Rachael to AHG, 26 Aug 1874.

2 F.K. Prochaska, *Women and Philanthropy in 19th Century England* (Oxford, 1980), 37.

3 E. Moberly Bell, *Octavia Hill* (London, 1942), 116–7, 143; Gillian Darley, *Octavia Hill, A Life* (London, 1990), 112; also C.E. Maurice (ed.), *Life of Octavia Hill as told in her letters* (London, 1913), *passim*.

4 Prochaska, *Women and Philanthropy*, 150; Reports of the Metropolitan Association for Befriending Young Servants, 1877–1886; *The Times*, 11 Nov 1875.

5 Elizabeth Wordsworth, *Glimpses of the Past* (London, 1913), 152–3.

6 Mrs Humphrey Ward, *A Writer's Recollections* (London, 1918), 152.

7 *The Times*, 21 Mar 1879.

8 Gwendolen Stephenson, *Edward Stewart Talbot, 1844–1934* (London, 1936).

9 Somerville College, Minutes of Council.

10 Wordsworth, *Glimpses*, 145.

11 Shaw Lefevre Mss, Somerville, Original draft of MSL's Memories of Somerville.

12 Elliot Mss, Madeleine to Jane, ?5 May 1879.

13 Margaret Elliot, *Workhouse Girls, Notes on An Attempt to Help Them*, 2nd ed. (London, 1875).

14 Wm Temple, *Life of Bishop Percival* (London, 1921), 76.

15 Elliot Mss, Madeleine to Jane, ?5 May 1879.

16 Hants RO, 38M49/D19, JGSL to HFSL, 5 May 1879.

17 A.M.A.H. Rogers, *Degrees by Degrees* (Oxford, 1938), 151–3.

18 Lilian M. Faithfull, in the *Journal of Education*, Nov 1914, 794. Miss Faithfull later became Headmistress of Cheltenham Ladies' College.

19 Somerville, Minutes of Council.

20 Temple, *Percival*, 76.

21 Vera Brittain, *The Women at Oxford* (London, 1960), 120.

22 Elliot Mss, A.H.D.Elliot's draft on 'Our Married Lives to 1891'.

23 Janet E. Courtney, *An Oxford Portrait Gallery* (London, 1931), 226; Brittain, *Women at Oxford*, 58.

24 Wordsworth, *Glimpses*, 149.

25 SL Mss, Somerville, M.T. Skues to Helen Darbishire, 26 Mar 1941.

26 *Journal of Education*, Nov 1914, 794.

27 Stella Margetson, *Leisure and Pleasure in the Nineteenth Century* (New York, 1969), 207–8.

28 SL Mss, Somerville, Frances Sheldon writing home, 13 Mar 1881.

29 Elliot Mss, Madeleine to Charles Ryan, ?5 May 1879.

30 BL Add Mss 49225, Rachael to AHG, 23 Nov 1880.

31 BL Add Mss 49230, Rachael to Madeleine, 11–18 Jul 1884; 49232, Rachael to ?Mary, 3–4 Jul 1884.

32 Lilian M. Faithfull, *In the House of My Pilgrimage* (London, 1924), ch. iv, and in *Jnl of Education*, Nov 1914, 794.

33 SL Mss, Somerville, Extract from a memoir written for Madeleine's sister, Emily, in 1914, probably by Ethel Hurlbatt.

34 George extracted a promise to contribute from Rosebery, but only on condition that it be anonymous; Rosebery Mss 10076, GJSL to Rosebery, 8 and 21 Nov 1880.

35 SL Mss, Somerville; B.A. Clough, *A Memoir of Anne Jemima Clough, First Principal of Newnham College, Cambridge* (London, 1905), 326.

36 SL Mss, Somerville, Original draft of MSL's Memories.

37 *Oxford Magazine*, 7, No. 16, 13 Mar 1889.

38 Add Mss 49227, AHG to Rachael, 22 Apr and 15 Jun 1888.

39 India Office Library, Mss Eur F165/1.

CHAPTER XX

1 Michael Hurst, *Joseph Chamberlain and Liberal Reunion: The Round Table Conference of 1887* (London, 1967), 156, 167.

2 Cooke and Vincent, *Governing Passion*, 141–3.

3 D.A. Hamer, *Liberal Politics in the Age of Gladstone and Rosebery, 128.*

4 Blunt was the great-grandson of John Lefevre's sister Magdalen, who married William Currie in 1753. One of the Currie daughters married Revd John Flutter Chandler, and a daughter of that union – Mary Chandler – married Francis Scawen Blunt in 1838. Wilfrid Scawen Blunt was nine years younger than GJSL. For the latter's accounts of his own Irish experiences, see especially his *Incidents of Coercion* (1888), *Combination and Coercion* (1890), and *Gladstone and Ireland* (1912). See also HH 1/13/2, Trevelyan to GJSL, 13 Nov 1888; and 1/9/3, Morley to GJSL, 18 Jan 1887, 30 Jan 1888, 22 May 1888. Among correspondence with Gladstone about his Irish writings, see BL Add Mss 44153, GJSL to Gladstone, 10 Jul 1887, 30 Nov 1888, 17 and 24 Aug, 21 Oct 1889; 8 Feb 1890.

5 On proportional representation, see GJSL's correspondence with fourth Earl Grey in April, 1884 – Grey Mss 212/4; and see also ch. XXI.

6 PP 1887, xliii.

7 BL Add Mss 44153, GJSL to Gladstone, 5 and 7 Dec 1883.

8 Bahlman, *Hamilton Diary*, 2, 457, 6 Jul 1883.

9 It has not been possible to see the marriage settlement; this account is an interpretation of Constance's will, made in 1923.

10 *Morning Post*, 27 Jan 1888, Letter to editor from 'Libra'; *Bradford Observer*, 30 Apr 1888.

11 Parl. Deb. 3s, 325, cols. 606–8; *Bradford Observer*, 27 Apr 1888.

12 *St. Stephen's Review*, 7 Feb 1891; H.W. Lucy, *More Peeps at Parliament*, (London, 1905), 261–3.

13 HH 1/9/3, Morley to GJSL, 31 Jan and 9 Feb 1889.

14 Return of Names of Pensioners under the Political Offices Pensions Act, 1869, PP 1893–94, L.

15 Rendel Mss 387, M.E. Grant Duff to Rendel, 20 Jan 1886; BL Add Mss 48650, Hamilton Diary, 11 Jan 1889.

16 Rendel Mss, Paper 7, 9 Jun 1891: Bod dep 384, Harcourt Jnl, 1 and 8 Aug 1892.

17 Bod dep 383, Harcourt Jnl, 28 Jul 1892: BL Add Mss 48657, Hamilton Diary, 12 Feb 1892.

18 Rendel Mss, Paper 7, 9 Jun 1891.

19 Bod dep 384, Harcourt Jnl, 13 and 14 Aug 1892.

20 Bod dep 404, Harcourt Jnl, 3 Mar 1894.

21 BL Add Mss 44153, GJSL to Gladstone, 6 Mar 1894.

22 HH 1/13, GJSL to Mrs Byles, 3 Mar 1894.

23 BL Add Mss 44153, GJSL to Gladstone, 1 Mar 1894.

24 The Commission was deeply divided, and though GJSL remained in the chair for nine months after losing office, he resigned on 20 Apr 1896. For the three reports, see PP 1894 xiv, 1896 xvi, 1897 xv.

25 Bod dep 413 and 414, Harcourt Jnl, 9 and 29 Jan 1895.

26 HH 1/13, GJSL to Mrs Byles, 3 Mar 1894.

27 GJSL to Harcourt, 15 Dec 1898, quoted in Peter Stansky, *Ambitions and Strategies*, 268–9.

28 BLPES, A.G.Gardiner Colln. 1/11, GJSL to Gardiner, 4 Oct 1923. Lord Edmund Fitzmaurice shared GJSL's views: 'I agree with you about Harcourt: I loved the man and hated the colleague. His conduct in 1883–4 during the Egyptian difficulties was odious and I had to bear the brunt of it as U/Sec for Foreign Affairs.' HH 1/8 Fitzmaurice to GJSL, 19 Mar 1923.

29 Bod dep 419, Harcourt Jnl, 21 Jun 1895.

30 I am indebted to Dr Keith Laybourn for advice on the West Yorkshire scene. This account draws heavily on a Ph.D thesis by W.D. Ross, submitted to the University of Leeds in 1977, entitled 'Bradford Politics, 1880–1906'. For the development of labour politics in Bradford in 1886–1895, and for the establishment of the ILP, see *inter alia*, Fenner Brockway, *Socialism over Sixty Years, the Life of Jowett of Bradford* (London, 1946); Jonathan Schneer, *Ben Tillett, Portrait of a Labour Leader* (Beckenham, 1982), esp. chs. 4 and 6; Ben Tillett, *Memories and Reflections* (London, 1931), 1991–2.

31 *Bradford Observer*, 22 Apr 1886.

32 Selborne Mss, 1875, Selborne to AHG, 2 Oct 1889.

33 Schneer, *Ben Tillett*, 68.

34 *Bradford Observer*, 18 Jul 1892. GJSL's blandly diplomatic stance is illustrated by the report of one of his speeches to Bradford constituents, in *The Times*, 6 Nov 1891: 'With regard to the eight hours question he was certain that they all sympathized with the agitation for shorter hours. He could not, for his part, but think that the movement in that direction, proceeded with gradually, would effect good; it would, however, not be possible for Parliament to enact any general rule upon the subject. However, for the present he would leave himself free on the subject till the report of the Royal Commission on Labour had been issued. As to labour candidates he would be glad to see more of them returned to the House of Commons, and he knew that that was the opinion of the leaders of the Liberal Party.'
For the eight-hour movement, see A.E.P. Duffy, 'The Eight Hours Day Movement in Britain, 1886–1893,' Parts I and II, in *The Manchester School of Economic and Social Studies*, 36, nos. 3 and 4, Sep and Dec 1968; Jose Harris, *Unemployment and Politics, A Study in English Social Policy 1886–1914* (Oxford, 1972), ch. 2. For the difficulties within the Liberal Party on this matter in 1889, see M. Barker, *Gladstone and Radicalism.*

35 *Bradford Observer*, 8 Jul 1886.

36 Rosebery Mss 10098, GJSL to Rosebery, 14 Oct 1894.

37 Rosebery Mss 10091, GJSL to Rosebery, 13 Sep 1893; Bradford Observer, 18 Feb, 12 and 21 Mar 1895.

38 Rosebery Mss 10092, GJSL to Rosebery, 25 Mar 1894.

39 For the arguments, see the Bradford papers during the first two weeks of July, 1895.

40 *Bradford Observer*, 28 Nov 1885.

41 *Bradford Observer*, 5 Jul 1892.

42 *Bradford Daily Argus*, 24 Jul 1895; *Bradford Observer*, 9, 24, 25 Jul 1895; *Daily Chronicle*, 24 Jul 1895.

43 Rosebery Mss 10105, GJSL to Rosebery, 24 Jul 1895.

44 *Bradford Observer*, 26 Jul 1895.

45 Rosebery Mss 10105, GJSL to Rosebery, 24 Jul 1895.

46 *Bradford Observer*, 19 Jul 1895.

CHAPTER XXI

1 *Bradford Observer*, 16 Jan 1896.

2 HH 1/13, GJSL to Mrs Byles, 24 and 28 Jul 1897, 18 Sep 1898, 12 Sep 1900.

3 HH 1/13, GJSL to Mrs Byles, 28 Jul 1897.

4 HH 1/13, GJSL to Mrs Byles, 24 Jul 1897.

5 HH 1/13, GJSL to Mrs Byles, 30 Dec 1899.

6 BL Add Mss 41227, GJSL to Campbell-Bannerman, 3 Jan 1900.

7 HH 1/11/1, Morley to GJSL, 28 Apr 1900.

8 HH 1/11/1, GJSL to Herbert Gladstone, 12 Sep 1900.

9 HH 1/11/1, Morley to GJSL, 15 Sep 1900.

10 HH 1/11/1, Campbell-Bannerman to GJSL, 30 Sep 1900.

11 HH 1/13, GJSL to Mrs Byles, 29 Dec 1901.

12 HH 1/11/1, H. Gladstone to GJSL, 17 Jun 1902; Campbell-Bannerman to GJSL, 3 Jul 1902: BL Add Mss 46059, GJSL to Viscount Gladstone, 18 Jun 1902; 41227, GJSL to Campbell-Bannerman, 7 Jul, 8 and 13 Sep 1903.

13 *The Times*, 11 Feb 1897: *London*, 11 and 18 Feb, 1897.

14 M.E. Grant Duff, *Notes from a Diary, 1896–1901* 1 (London, 1905), 250.

15 HH 1/11/1, GJSL to Collins, 1 Aug 1901; Collins to GJSL, 9 Aug 1901; 1/13, GJSL to Mrs Byles, 7 Feb 1901.

16 HH 1/13, GJSL to Mrs Byles, 5 Jan 1903.

17 HH 1/13, GJSL to Mrs Byles, 20 Nov 1905.

18 Collier, *Victorian Diarist*, 1895–1909, 48.

19 HH 1/13, GJSL to Mrs Byles, 31 Dec 1892, 15 Jul 1896. Information from the Kingsworthy Parish Council Minutes and the Old Kingsworthy School Log Books. I am particularly indebted to Albert Cooper and Barry Shurlock of the Kingsworthy Historical Society for bringing these to my attention.

20 Farrer Mss 2572, 1/62, 64, 67, GJSL to T.C. (second Baron) Farrer, 27 Dec 1912, 10 Jul 1913, 6 Oct 1914.

21 HH 1/13, GJSL to Mrs Byles, 29 Dec 1901; Farrer Mss 2572/1/70, GJSL to Farrer, 18 Jan 1916.

22 HH 1/13, GJSL to Mrs Byles, 17 and 25 Jan 1896.

23 BLEPS, Courtney Mss, viii, 78, GJSL to Courtney, 16 Jul 1901: HH 1/13, GJSL to Mrs Byles, 29 Dec 1901; 1/11/1, W.S. Blunt to GJSL, 6 Aug 1902, Rendel to GJSL, 6 Sep 1902.

24 Minto Mss, 19497, GJSL to A.R.D. Elliot, 16 Sep 1909.

25 Minto Mss, 19493, GJSL to Elliot, 13 Jan 1904. *History of the Cobden Club*, 52. GJSL wrote continuations of *Fact versus Fiction* in 1909, entitled *Tariff Makers* and *Budget and Tariff Compared*, and in 1913, *A Decade of Tariff Fooling*.

26 GJSL chaired two committees for the drafting of *Fact versus Fiction* and *The Burden of Armaments*. There was considerable overlap of membership, which included Lord Welby, Sir Algernon West, Sir Spencer Walpole, Fletcher Moulton, F.W. Hirst, J.A. Murray Macdonald, G.H. Perris, H.M. Williams, and T. Fisher Unwin. *History of the Cobden Club*, 57–8.

27 *The Nation*, 25 Jan, 1 Aug, 5 Sep 1908. A.J. Marder (ed.), *Fear God and Dread*

Nought. The Correspondence of Admiral of the Fleet Lord Fisher of Kilverstone 2 (London, 1956), 193–4. A.F. Havighurst, *Radical Journalist. H.W. Massingham (1860–1924)* (Cambridge, 1974), 187. Lord Eversley, 'Naval Expenditure' and 'The Latest Scare' in *The Financial Reform Almanac and Year Books*, 1909 and 1911. HLRO, Lloyd George Mss, C/4/10/1–4.

28 For the details of these books, see Appendix II.

29 BL Add Mss 41252, GJSL to Pentland, 17 Sep 1919; Courtney Mss, xii, 91, GJSL to Courtney, 26 Nov 1917.

30 Farrer Mss, 2572/1/67, GJSL to Farrer, 6 Oct 1914.

31 BL Add Mss 46303, GJSL to Burns, 5 Aug 1914.

32 NLS, Haldane Mss 5911, GJSL to Haldane, 29 May 1915.

33 *The Times*, 20 Apr 1928.

34 Lord Eversley, *Proportional Representation, 1867–1917*, with an Introductory Note by W. Burdett-Coutts. Privately printed, 1917.

35 Bod dep 448, Letters from GJSL to Harcourt, Jul 1917 and Jan 1918, and letters at HH 1/8/3 and 6.

36 BLPES, Violet Markham Colln., 25/50, GJSL to Markham, 10 Jun 1924.

37 'George John Shaw Lefevre (Lord Eversley) An Appreciation', in *Contemporary Review*, 133, Jun 1928.

CHAPTER XXII

1 *Malta Standard*, 30 May 1893. I am indebted to the Malta High Commission in London, and to the Department of Health in Malta, for information about the present status of the chapel.

2 *TAPS*, 61, pt 4, 15, fn. 109. Sophia Palmer married the Comte de Franqueville in 1903; Arthur was a guest at the wedding. See Lady Laura Riding, *Sophia Matilda Palmer, Comtesse de Franqueville, 1852–1915* (London, 1919).

3 Chapman, *Career of AHG*, ch. 9; *TAPS*, 61, pt 4; and Selborne Mss, 1875, a batch of letters of 1893 on AHG's position re the Irish Home Rule Bill.

4 HH 1/11/1, AHG to GJSL, 7 Oct 1900.

5 Philip Ziegler, *The Sixth Great Power: Barings 1762–1929* (London, 1988), chs 15–18; S. Chapman, *Rise of Merchant Banking*, 33, 67.

6 M.J. Tuke, *A History of Bedford College for Women, 1849–1937* (London, 1939), 136–43, 153–4, 307.

7 Clough, *Anne Jemima Clough*, 337.

8 *Farnham, Haslemere and Hindhead Herald, The Alton Mail*, 26 Sep 1914.

Index